ADMINISTRATION REPORT
OF
TRIPURA STATE
SINCE 1902

In 4 Volumes

ADMINISTRATION REPORT OF TRIPURA STATE Since 1902

IN 4 VOLUMES

VOLUME THREE
1332 T.E. to 1341 T.E.
(1923-24 A.D. to 1931-32 A.D.)

Edited by
Mahadev Chakravarti

GYAN PUBLISHING HOUSE
NEW DELHI-110002

ADMINISTRATION REPORT OF TRIPURA STATE
SINCE 1902
IN 4 VOLUMES
(History, Polity, Sociology, Anthropology)

ISBN : 81-212-0468-2 (Set)
ISBN 81-212-0471-2 VOL. 3

Published 1994 in India by
Gyan Publishing House
5, Ansari Road
New Delhi 110 002

Printed at Goyal Offset Works, Delhi.

CONTENTS

Book Seventeen

Report on the General Administration of the Tripura State for the year 1334 T.E. (1924-25 A.D.)

Book Eighteen

Report on the General Administration of the Tripura State for the year 1335 T.E. (1925-26 A.D.)

Book Nineteen

Report on the General Administration of the Tripura State for the year 1336 T.E. (1926-27 A.D.)

Book Twenty

Report on the General Administration of the Tripura State for the year 1337 T.E. (1927-28 A.D.)

Book Twenty-one

Report on the General Administration of the Tripura State for the year 1338 T.E. (1928-29 A.D.)

Book Twenty-two

Report on the General Administration of the Tripura State for the year 1339 T.E. (1929-30 A.D.)

Book Twenty-three

Report on the General Administration of the Tripura State for the year 1341 T.E. (1931-32 A.D.)

ADDENDUM

EDITOR'S NOTE

Birendrakishore Manikya was installed on the throne of Tripura on 25 November 1909 by Sir Lancelot Hare, the Lieutenant Governor of Eastern Bengal and Assam, on behalf of Lord Minto, the Viceroy and Governor-General of India. But later on J. Bartley, the Political Agent, not simply addressed the king of Tripura as 'Raja' (instead of 'Maharaja') but even asked Birendrakishore not to use the distinctive title 'Manikya' in future. But in spite of that prohibitive directive, Birendrakishore used both the titles 'Maharaja' and 'Manikya' freely. The second volume contains the *Tripura Administration Reports (TARs)* of the reign of Maharaja Birendrakishore Manikya. On 13 August 1923 Birendrakishore passed away when he was barely 40 years of age. On his death, the succession of the State and the attached zemindaries at Chakla Roshnabad (now in Bangladesh) devolved upon his son Bir Bikramkishore Dev Barman. The recognition by the Paramount Power was intimated in the Viceroy's *Kharita*, dated 5 September 1923, which was read by the Political Agent at a Durbar held at Ujjayanta Palace, Agartala. The present volume contains eight *TAR*s of the reign of Bir Bikramkishore Manikya since his accession to the throne in 1923.

As Bir Bikramkishore Manikya was only 16 years of age in 1923, the administration of Tripura was entrusted, under the direction of the Government of India, to a 'Council of Administration' under the chairmanship of Maharajkumar Navadwip Chandra Dev Barmam. Bir Bikramkishore Mánikya assumed the direct administration of the State on his twentieth birthday on 19 August 1927.

It is seen in the first two volumes how the incomes from the Chakla Roshnabad Estates helped to lay the financial foundation of the Tripura Raj upto 1331 T.E. (1921-22 A.D.). A cursory glance at Table No. I would show the situation since 1333 T.E. :-

Table No. 1

Year	*Income from the State*	*Income from the zemindaries*	*Total Income*
1333 T.E.(1923-24)	Rs. 15,82,035	Rs. 11,00,400	Rs. 26,82,435
1334 T.E.(1924-25)	Rs. 15,42,710	Rs. 10,70,937,	Rs. 26,13,647
1335 T.E.(1925-26)	Rs. 17,59,321	Rs. 12,11,339	Rs. 29,70,660
1336 T.E.(1926-27)	Rs. 18,58,281	Rs. 11,12,526	Rs. 29,70,807
1337 T.E.(1927-28)	Rs. 18,77,136	Rs. 11,46,097	Rs. 30,23,233
1338 T.E.(1928-29)	Rs. 19,46,421	Rs. 10,99,010	Rs. 30,45,431
1339 T.E.(1929-30)	Rs. 18,78,321	Rs. 10,21,483	Rs. 28,99,804
1340 T.E.(1930-31)	Rs. 13,92,709	Rs. 7,90,161	Rs. 21,82,870
1341 T.E.(1931-32)	Rs. 12,37,252	Rs. 7,88,230	Rs. 20,25,482

Regarding the total figure of revenue collection from the State in 1335 T.E. and 1336 T.E., a discrepancy is noticeable between the 'Revenue' and 'Finances' columns of the respective *TARs*. Although the income of the Durbar came down since 1339 T.E., i.e. in the last three years of the present volume, still, the above table shows beyond doubt how the zemindaries provided a solid financial foundation of the Tripura Raj. Staggering in the wealth of materials that the *TARs* contain, the tabular statements and statistical returns in each *TAR* would provide ample official information to prepare a complete history of the erstwhile princely State from various angles.

If the tables under the head 'Revenue' - as found in each *TAR* - are closely examined, it is to be seen that the toll on forest-produce was nearly equal to the total amount of land revenue. Excepting the last two years i.e. 1340 T.E. and 1341 T.E., the land revenue steadily increased and in 1339 T.E. it reached the peak point. Similarly, the receipts from forest-produce and *ghar-chuktikar* (family tax from the hill people) had reached the highest point in 1338 T.E. These are all interesting details and the fluctuations of figures under different heads of revenue in different years were closely related to the contemporary situation.

The principal export and import items remained more or less same in the twenties of the present century. Among the exports, mention should be made of timber, forest-produce of various kinds, cotton, oil-seeds (*til*, i.e. sesame, and *sarisha*, i.e. mustard seed), paddy, jute, rice and *gur*, i.e. molasses. A small quantity of tea and homespun cotton fabrics, manufactured by the hill people and specially by the Manipuris, were also exported. The principal imports were cloths and yarns, salt, *kerosine* and mustard oil, pulses, chillies, tobacco, sugar, flour, spices, areca-nuts, book and stationery. The small cottage industries worth mention were : manufacture of cotton fabrics by the hill people and the Manipuris; cane and bamboo baskets, mats, and sieves by the Tripuris; dug-outs, bowls and plates of wood by the Reangs and the Chakmas; and finally molasses by both the hill people and the Bengalees.

In between 1332 T.E. and 1341 T.E. the highest number of immigration and emigration, as evident from records, took place in 1340 T.E. (1930-31) when 1,869 families immigrated into and 1,270 families emigrated out of princely Tripura. But the *TAR* for the year 1340 T.E. could not be traced and hence, not included in the present volume. Of the eight *TARs* in the present volume, the highest immigration took place in 1332 T.E. (1,676 families immigrated into) and the largest emigration in 1341 T.E. (1,239 families emigrated out of the State). In the *TAR* for the year 1341

T.E. (1931-32) it is found that a new road extending over 32 miles was constructed in the immigration area in Kulaihaor to facilitate the transport etc. in the interior, although some portion of the road was badly damaged immediately after construction due to heavy flood. (See para 139).

In the first *TAR* of the present volume, i.e. for the year 1333 T.E. (1923-24), the total recorded population of Tripura was 3,04,437 (according to 1921 census) and in the last *TAR*, i.e. for the year 1341 T.E. (1931-32), it was only 3,82,450 (according to 1931 census). Hence, the growth of population in that decade was proper. But the rate of growth of jail population was rather heavy. From 708 in 1337 T.E. (1927-28) the jail population of princely Tripura recorded a steady growth and reached a height of 1,332 in 1341 T.E. (1931-32).

In all the *TARs* of the present volume it is mentioned that Tripura's relations with the police administration of the adjoining British districts of Bengal continued to be satisfactory and sometimes cooperation meetings were held in which the Tripura police joined and discussed matters relating to border crime and criminals with the police in British India. In spite of the claim of such 'satisfactory' relations between the Tripura Durbar and the British Raj by the *TAR*, there was also the other side of the picture. The experience of the British rulers in Bengal since the days of Bengal anti-partition agitation in 1905 and terrorism that followed in its wake and also during the political turmoil of the non-cooperation movement and particularly the developments in the Chittagong Division afforded ample causes of anxiety to them. As Tripura was bordered by British districts, such state of things, as evident from various contemporary records, sometimes became a source of grave misunderstanding during this period between the Tripura Durbar and the British Raj. It is not for nothing that the Paramount Power showed unusual interest on the reorganisation of Tripura State Troops. The five appendices (as included in the last portion of the volume) would make it clear that the main aim of the Paramount Power was to make Tripura fully dependent on them by appointing a British Military Adviser for Tripura and Manipur. The Tripura Durbar surrendered to the wishes of the British Raj. The British administrators sometimes issued letters to the Tripura Durbar for externment order of undesirable persons and from the figures of extradition (Table No. II) in the *TARs*, the gravity of the situation can easily by realized.

Table No. II

Criminal cases in which British Subjects were concerned

Year	*Cases instituted during the year*	*Total No. of cases against British Subjects*	*No. of persons against whom extradition warrants were applied*
1333 T.E.	411	554	55
1334 T.E.	375	501	120
1335 T.E.	516	619	147
1336 T.E.	385	507	77
1337 T.E.	490	577	105
1338 T.E.	342	474	45
1339 T.E.	375	490	35
1341 T.E.	378	448	96

It becomes evident from Table No. II that in 1335 T.E. (1925-26) the highest number of cases were instituted in Tripura against British subjects and the highest number of persons against whom extradition warrants were issued.

Let us now point out some other important aspects of the *TARs* as included in the present volume.

The lowest number of defaulting *taluks* brought under the operation of the Sunset Law (including the pending number of the previous year) was 75 in 1334 T.E.(1924-25) and the highest number of such defaulting *taluks* (including the pending *taluks* of the previous year) was 175 in 1341 T.E.(1931-32).

With the exception of a few *Mahals* which were let out in *ijara*, all the forests were under *khas* management in between 1333 and 1341 T.E. There were more than fifty forest stations during these years for collection of duty and prevention of forest offences.

The low rates of wages of the labourers remained more or less static in between 1333 and 1340 T.E. and in 1341 T.E. (1931-32) it showed a further downward trend.

Escapes from the jails and unnatural deaths were common items in all the *TARs*.

There were altogether 5 (five only) H.E.School in the State during the period; although one more Branch H.E.School was opened at Udaipur in 1340 T.E. (1930-31) on condition that the public would agree to bear the additional cost of maintaining extra staff for the opening of Class IX and X. There were 3 Sanskrit Tols, 6 Madarssas and Moktabs and 1 Artisan School.

From the total annual expenditure on education, as found in the *TAR*, we can have an idea about the entire education-scenario of princely Tripura in the twenties of the present century. As figures and tables can sometimes speak more than long essay and literature, it is better to have a look at Table Nos. III & IV : -

Table No. III
Some important details of expenditure on education in Tripura

Year	*Total expenditure on education*	*Primary education*	*Secondary education*	*Education for kumars & kumaris*	*Scholarships & stipends*	*Library*
1333 T.E. (1923-24)	Rs.1,23,863	Rs.29,605	Rs.39,414	Rs.31,029	Rs.5,599	Rs.2,355
1334 T.E. (1924-25)	Rs.1,00,544	Rs.16,068	Rs.39,108	Rs.6,310	Rs.7,302	Rs.2,399
1335 T.E. (1925-26)	Rs.1,08,370	Rs.21,470	Rs.37,814	Rs.11,182	Rs.6,556	Rs.2,394
1336 T.E. (1926-27)	Rs.1,16,474	Rs.21,595	Rs.41,146	Rs.16,658	Rs.8,284	Rs.1,814

Table No. IV
Bir Chandra Library (Agartala)

Year	No. of English books	No. of Bengali books	Newspapers Daily	Newspapers Weekly	Newspapers Quarterly	Newspapers Monthly	Avercge daily attendance of readers (%)	Total No. of books issued to the public
1333 T.E. (1923-24)	4,846	1,679	7	6	1	1C	8.38	1,186
1334 T.E. (1924-25)	4,853	1,747	7	-	1	8	13.02	5,309
1335 T.E (1925-26)	4,859	1,786	5	-	1	5	13.25	6,575
1336 T.E (1926-27)	4,881	1,849	5	1	1	5	13.17	3,116
1337 T.E (1927-28)	4,886	1,909	5	1	1	6	13.19	2,683
1338 T.E. (1928-29)	4,974	1,981	4	3	1	9	14.05	2,707
1339 T.E (1929-30)	5,025	2,008	5	3	-	9	14.02	3,925
1341 T.E. (1331-32)	5,025	2,207	4	1	-	4	13	3,765

1337 T.E. (1927-28)	Rs.1,26,208	Rs.21,756	Rs.41,709	Rs.22,228	Rs.9,237	Rs.1,558
1338 T.E. (1928-29)	Rs.1,33,106	Rs.23,261	Rs.42,991	Rs.24,702	Rs.10,563	Rs.2,340
1339 T.E. (1929-30)	Rs.1,41,110	Rs.25,331	Rs.50,458	Rs.26,481	Rs.9,382	Rs.2,894
1341 T.E. (1931-32)	Rs.1,27,620	Rs.27,391	Rs.50,164	Rs.24,123	Rs.7,415	Rs.1,683

A lot of conclusions can be drawn from the above two tables, but one aspect at least should be mentioned here. In spite of very low budget on 'Library' head, the average daily attendance of readers in the single library at the capital town was impressive and it was an index of the growing urge for knowledge.

Let us now have a look at some interesting points of each *TAR* separately since 1333 T.E. (1923-24).

TAR for the year 1333 T.E. (1923-24 A.D.)

During the reign of Birendrakishore Manikya (1909-23), the annual income of the State rose from eight lakhs to fourteen lakhs and that of the zemindaries from nine to eleven lakhs. The introduction of tea industry in Tripura, the improvement of communication, judiciary and forest management were his lasting achievements. The *TAR* claims that the substantial war contributions during the entire First World War period by Birendrakishore Manikya would ever remain to Tripura a source of legitimate pride.

As Bir Bikramkishore Manikya was only 16 years of age in 1923, a Council form of Government was introduced in Tripura, under the direction of the Paramount Power, when he succeeded his father. The Council of Administration adopted the portfolio system and divided the control of various Departments among the four members.

Prasanna Kumar Dasgupta, the architect of Tripura's modernization during the reign of Birendrakishore Manikya, took retirement on 6 September 1923 from the posts of both Minister of the State and Manager of the Chakla Roshnabad zemindaries. He was succeeded by Jyotish Chandra Sen who was also Vice-President of the Council of Administration. Dewan Bijoy Kumar Sen, the Chief Secretary under Birendrakishore, remained in his position and also performed the duties of the Secretary of the Council. J.D.V.Hodge continued to be the Political Agent of the State till 26 October 1923, when he was relieved by A.J. Dash. The Maharaja's education continued as before under O.C.Pulley, the guardian tutor.

There was no fresh settlement for tea cultivation during the year. In fact, tea industry had not yet recovered from the effects of the depression in the tea market during the previous few years. A total area of 356 *drones* of waste-land was settled. No permanent or *Taskhichi* settlement or *Niskar* grant was sanctioned during the year. No fresh legislation was undertaken.

The local doctor M.M. Mazumdar remained both as the Chairman of the Agartala Municipality and as the Chief Medical Officer. The general health of Agartala town was not good, owing to the prevalence of Malaria and Kala-azar (Black Fever) during the year. Small-pox and Cholera broke out in the Bisalgarh Division.

A noticeable source of income was opened in Tripura by the leasing out of tracts containing "Agar" trees. Kheda operations were successful at all places except Kamalpur. The revenue from the Feni River Mahal steadily increased since 1919-20 A.D. when the management had been handed over to the State Forest Department. The movement among a section of the people in Noakhali to collect forest-produce of Tripura free of duty subsided as a result of timely intervention by the British authorities in Bengal.

Somendra Chandra Dev Barman was in charge of the Department of Public Instruction. Other than the four existing H.E. Schools, the feeder School at Sonamura was allowed to open the Matriculation Class. The increased interest in primary education among the hill people, perhaps due to reward examination, is noticeable.

TAR for the year 1334 T.E. (1924-25 A.D.)

Under the supervision of the guardian tutor, Lt. Col. O.C.Pulley and with the active cooperation of A.J.Dash, the Political Agent, the administrative training of the 17 years' old Bir Bikramkishore Manikya commenced during the year with the headquarters at Comilla during the winter and at Shillong during the summer. The Maharaja accompanied the Political Agent in a tour of inspection both in the border of the Tippera district of Bengal and also in the interior of the State. In this connection it is to be noted that upto Book Thirteen (see Vol.II) for the year 1329 T.E. (1919-20) the *Administration Reports* were of the Tippera State and from Book Fourteen onwards, i.e. from 1330 T.E. (1920-21) onwards, the *Reports* were of the Tripura State.

The stone-metalling of the State portion of the Akhaura-Agartala road was completed during 1334 T.E. Regarding the other part of the road, which was within the jurisdiction of the British territory, an agreement was arrived at.

The work of cadastral survey in Kailashahar was continued. Timber posts had been fixed at many village borders for future reference. During the year an area of 346 *drones* of wasteland was settled. Although a Legislative Committee had been formed with sixteen members, there was no fresh legislation during the year.

Owing to the prevailing high prices of staple food crops and of imported necessaries of life, people suffered badly. At Agartala the price of rice once rose so very high that cheap Burma rice had to be imported by way of relief.

Although some propaganda works and circuit lectures were arranged in the centres of Division and Circle on the advantages of plough cultivation and field crops, no *Taccavi* advances etc. were issued to replace the existing *jhum* system.

The year is marked by an increase under the head "Land Revenue" and also by a noticeable fall of revenue in the river mahals. The reasons were underlined in different paras of the *TAR*. Among the heads of revenue, a new head of income, namely, 'Education' was for the first time introduced. But the expenditure on education head was markedly decreased during the year. This decrease was due to the transfer of the Maharaja's educational expenses to the *Nijtahabil* or privy purse which shot up from Rs. 2,60,371 in the previous year to Rs. 4,07,410 during the year. In view of the heavy cut in the educational budget, strict care was taken to extend State aid to many educational institution: hence, the decrease in the number of primary schools during the year. The decrease in the number of Non-Bengalee students is another noticeable feature. The amount under 'Charity and Donation' head also remarkably decreased from one lakh in the previous year to twenty thousand during 1334 T.E.

One more interesting feature of the financial administration of Tripura was the reorganisation of the audit arrangements and the first publication of the statement of audited activities. (See Appendix No. XXVII of the *TAR*).

In order to settle disputes between the Assam Government and the Tripura Durbar about the working of the Langai forest, a conference was held at Langai in June 1925 at the initiative of the Political Agent. The *TAR* notes with regret "recrudescence of the trouble with the people in the neighbouring district of Noakhali." (See para 142).

Small-pox broke out at Kalyanpur. There were also outbreaks of Cholera in many parts of the State, specially in Kamalpur, Bisalgarh, Kailashahar, and Udaipur Divisions. Malaria and Kala-azar raged in all growing intensity in and around Agartala. In a word, the general health of the people was not at all good.

The English section of Bir Chandra Library was at the Ujjayanta Palace and the Vernacular Section, which was open to public, was placed at a new building originally intended for the Woodburn Artisan School.

TAR for the year 1335 T.E. (1925-26 A.D.)

The *TAR* for the year 1335 T.E. begins with the following observation :

> "With unfavourable weather conditions, chronic high prices, and virulent epidemics of cattle disease raging all round, the year under report proved more or less unpropitious to the people of the State, while prolonged outbreaks of Cholera, Small-pox and Kala-azar added to the pinch of the situation."

But in the financial administration of the State, there was an increased revenue collection, compared to the previous year, particularly under the following heads : Land Revenue, Tax on cotton and oil-seeds, Toll on forest-produce, Nazars, Stamps and Court-fees, River Mahal etc. The *TAR* admits that there was an "abnormal expenditure" on account of the marriage ceremonies of two sisters of the Maharaja.

In December 1925 Bir Bikramkishore Manikya, accompanied by O.C. Pulley, the guardian tutor, met both the Viceroy and the Governor of Bengal in Calcutta and in January 1926 visited Kailashahar and the tea gardens of the area and the Unakoti tock carvings. In February 1926 the Maharaja proceeded upto Dhumachhara in the interior of the State through the Manipuri and Reang settlements and met a number of hill chiefs, conspicuous among whom was a Reang chief.

The condition of the new tea industry was not satisfactory. During the year, an area of 679 *drones* of waste-land was settled. The work of cadastral survey could not be undertaken. Bills defining the term 'Minister', amending certain sections of the Municipal Act, the Hackney Carriage etc. were passed by the Legislative Committee and received the assent of the Council of Administration.

A new Municipal Committee was formed with 9 members for the Agartala Municipality. Brojendra Kumar Chatterjee and Nagendra Nath Ray were the Chairman and Vice-Chairman of the Municipality respectively. The want of good drinking water and arrangement for proper drainage system in Agartala were keenly felt.

On the charge of illicit export of forest-produce without permit and without payment of duty, 148 cases against 310 persons were instituted during the year.

The infant classes were amalgamated with the existing 5 H.E. Schools. with the approval of the Calcutta University.

One sensational case of the year was the stamp forgery case in which the Treasurer of the Sadar General Treasury, a local influential pleader and two stamp vendors were involved. The examination of nearly one hundred witnesses and the marking of nearly five thousand documents took place. The accused pleader died in course of the trial. One of the vendors was acquitted. The other two persons were sentenced to three years' rigorous imprisonment.

The tea industry made some progress during the year and as many as 27 gardens showed marked improvement.

TAR for the year 1336 T.E. (1926-27 A.D.)

Due to inadequate rainfall in the upland areas, although it was rather excessive in the plains of the State, there was acute scarcity of food-stuff in the hill tracts. The flowering of bamboos and the consequent "rat pest" proved very detrimental to *jhum* crops. The pinch was severely felt in the Kailashahar Division, Moreover, outbreaks of Cholera and Small-pox assumed serious proportions affecting all sections of people in the upland areas. The State Medical Department invited a band of workers from Comilla Abhoy Ashram to render medical aid particularly to the panic-striken people in the interior of the Kailashahar Division where the outbreak of Cholera had assumed an epidemic form. Interestingly enough, even in such a situation, there was a marked increase in respect of 16 heads of revenue and the gross income of the State exceeded all previous records.

It was decided that the rule of the Council of Administration since December 1923 would now come to an end and that Bir Bikramkishore Manikya would be vested with the full ruling powers on completion of his 19 years on 19 August 1927. The first chapter of the *TAR* reviewed the main achievements of the Council of Administration, particularly the strong financial administration.

W.H. Nelson was appointed the Political Agent of the State after the transfer of A.J. Dash.

Other than the Hackney Carriage Bill which received the assent of the Council of Administration in the previous year, a Bill amending Act No. I of 1327 about tea gardens, a Bill amending the survey and settlement regulation and a Bill for the prevention of gambling were ultimately passed into law.

During the year, 35 tea gardens showed remarkable progress and Tripura tea fetched good prices.

An area of 1,182 *drones* of waste-land was settled and a big amount of *nazrana* was obtained by the Durbar from such settlement of waste-land.

There was a decided fall during the year in the number of Malaria and Kala-azar cases within the Agartala Municipality areas. In para 100, it is recorded :

> "The entire town was divided into 5 blocks and a gang of coolies worked in each block under a member of the Committee and undertook clearance of drains, jungles and tanks. The work produced very excellent result but the question of supplying good drinking water to the town population was not taken up by the Committee."

The Agriculture Department of the State was invited to participate in the Bengal Presidency Agricultural Exhibition at Dhaka, held on 4 January 1927, in connection with the visit of the Royal Commission of Agriculture at that place. Lord Linglithgow, the President of the above Commission, displayed keen interest in the exhibits of Tripura in that Exhibition.

One interesting item in the *TAR* should also be mentioned. A local school teacher, with some financial aid from the State, carried on research on the methods of rearing *Apis Indica*, the only domesticable race of bees in India.

TAR for the year 1337 T.E. (1927-28 A.D.)

Although it was announced in the previous year that Bir Bikramkishore Manikya would assume the direct administration of the State on his twentieth birthday on 19 August 1927, it was ultimately decided that the political function would come off on that day, but the *Shastric* ceremony of *Rajyabhisek* or Installation would follow on 29 January 1928.

The Investiture Durbar was marked by pomp and grandeur where the Governor of Bengal presented the *khilat* to the Maharaja. The entire Installation ceremony was a very huge affair and the arrangements were entrusted to a committee under the chairmanship of the Maharaja himself. The *Nazar* Durbar was also attended by a huge number of people to pay homage to the king of Tripura.

After assuming direct administration of the State, Bir Bikramkishore Manikya appointed Jyotis Chandra Sen as the Minister of the State and Manager of the Chalka zemindaries, Bijoy Kumar Sen as his Chief Secretary and Rana Bodhjung as his Private Secretary. The *Nijtahabil* or privy purse was separated from the Administration and placed in charge of Anukul Mukherjee who was lately tutor to the king.

On W.H. Nelson's transfer, H.W. Lyne was appointed Political Agent of the State in February 1928. Although a Legislative Council was consisting of 19 nominated members, there was no sitting of the Legislative Council.

An area of 867 *drones* of waste-land was settled during the year. After a lapse of several unfavourable years, *kheda* operation in the Deo Doal in the Kailashahar Division and in the Belonia-Sabrum Doal met with considerable success during the year. An impressive rise is also noticeable in the revenue from forest and river *Mahals*.

In pursuance of the policy adopted in 1334 T.E. (1924-25), a big amount was realised from school students. A slight increase of expenditure in the 'Education' head was mainly attributable to the construction of the Kumar Boarding at Comilla, extra payments made for the two Maharajkumars who continued their studies in the Rajkumar College at Raipur in the-then Central Provinces, establishment of a Tripura Boarding at Sadar etc.

As in previous years, Cholera and Small-pox appeared with virulence in some parts of the Sadar and Kailashahar Divisions. But owing to the sanitary measures taken during the year for the Installation ceremony, the health of Agartala town was generally good.

TAR for the year 1338 T.E. (1928-29 A.D.)

On 18 August 1928, Bir Bikramkishore Manikya paid his official visit to Comilla-the headquarters of the Chakla Roshnabad zemindaries as well as of British Tippera District. The king received warm welcome and presided over the *Punyaha* ceremony which fetched a record collection. However, due to a sudden attack of influenza, Bir Bikramkishore Manikya had to cut short his Comilla visit and announced a donation of Rs. 63,000 to various organisations.

During the year, the map of Tripura is included in the *TAR* for the first time. H.W. Lyne continued as Political Agent of the State upto 4 November 1928, when he was succeeded by F.W. Robertson.

The marriage of Bir Bikramkishore Manikya with the Mahrajkumari of Balrampur, a premier Rajput family of Oudh, was celebrated at Balrampur on 16 January 1929 with pomp and grandeur.The royal bridal party,which numbered about one thousand, left Agartala on 12 January 1929 and followed the railway route from Akhaura (now in Bangadesh). The total expenditure on account of the king's marriage and other counts was Rs. 3,41,258.

As the jute market in the adjoining British territory was dull, it had its effects of reducing the export of Tripura jute. The trade in rice in the upper Gumti valley was not as brisk as usual. The *TAR* admits that due to diminished production and reduction of export of jute. cotton, oil-seeds etc., and the consequent decline in the influx of traders from outside, the people suffered from scarcity of resources and money. But as the financial administration of the Tripura Raj was strong, the year is signalised by unprecedented high collection. The total forest revenue of the year particularly showed a noticeable increase. Even the *ghar-chukti kar* of the hill people showed an increase.

Among the administrative reforms initiated during the year, the following are notable:

First, the Departments of Immigration and Reclamation and also Commerce and Industry were created. A stall designated "The Calcutta State Stall" was opened in the Calcutta Congress Exhibition under the management of the Superintendent of Agriculture and specimens of many agricultural and industrial products of Tripura were exhibited.

Secondly, the First Tripura Bir Company was speedily reorganised and a modern cantonment was planned and laid out.

Thirdly, the setting apart of a fixed allotment of the Public Works budget exclusively for measures of improvement began from this year.

The cadastral survey of Agartala and its outskirts was undertaken during the year.

The following laws were enacted during the year: Motor Vehicles Act I, Act II for prevention of smuggling of elephant tusks, Stamp Act III.

Brojendra Kumar Chatterjee was renominated as Chairman of the new Municipal Committee and Sankari Mohan Chatterjee as the Vice-Chairman.

The tea industry showed good progress. The circuit lectures against *jhuming* and in favour of plough cultivation went on as usual without any concrete result. All the elephants caught through *kheda* operations from different parts of the State could not be sold during the year as there was no sufficient demand for elephants.

TAR for the year 1339 T.E.(1929-30 A.D.)

The abnormal weather conditions and torrential rains caused destructive floods during the year in Kailashahar, Dharmanagar, Sonamura, Udaipur, Amarpur Divisions and the contiguous parts of the Chakla Roshnabad zemindaries. Bir Bikramkishore Manikya granted rupees one lakh for flood relief and Stanley Jackson, the Governor of Bengal, at the time of his visit to Comilla on 22 July 1929, appreciated the steps taken in connection with flood relief.

On J.C. Sen's retirement from the post of the Minister of the State, B.K.Sen was appointed by the king as "Dewan-Shashan and Manager, Chakla", Rana Bodhjung as the Chief Secretary and Kamala Prasad Dutt as the Private Secretary. An Executive Council was formed with N.C. Dev Barman as President and B.K. Dev Barman as Vice-President. the existing Advisory Council, under the denomination "State Council", was vested with full power of administration in view of the European tour programme of Bir Bikramkishore Manikya which commenced on 20 January 1930.

C.G.B. Stevens assumed the charge of the Political Agent after the departure of F.W.Robertson. The State Bank Act, Succession Certificate Act, Census Act and Road Cess Act were implemented during the year. the First Tripura Bir company was recognised by the Government of India as an "A"class unit of the "Indian States Forces". Deputed by the Military Adviser, Captain Blaxland of the Indian Army inspected the State forces at Agartala.

Over and above religious and moral instructions imparted by *pandit* and *moulavi* once in a week in the Central Jail, the introduction of lower primary training to the willing illiterate prisoners in that jail with the help of literate prisoners is another interesting feature of the year.

To popularise adult education, a night school was opened at Agartala by local students, at the patronage of the Public Instruction Department, where traders and labouring classes received education.

Cholera and Small-pox visited some parts of the State in a rather virulent form. But, compared to previous year, the total expenditure for the Medical Department decreased. Brajendra Kumar Chatterjee, the Chairman of the Agartala Municipality, died of Small-pox and Brojendra Chandra Dutt was appointed as the Chairman.

Cattle diseases like anthrax broke out in epidemic form in the Udaipur Division and rinderpest in Sonamura and Kailashahar Divisions.

Although the total amount of export duty from tea fell off owing to low prices, five new tea gardens were settled during the year. During the year, the Assam Government accepted the recommendations of the Assam Forest Enquiry Committee and exempted the forest-produce of Tripura from examination at Rajapur and Loirpoa revenue stations in the Sylhet Forest Division. In spite of that, the all-round economic depression led to a paralysing slump in the market both for indigenous products such as cotton, jute and oil-seeds and also in timber trade.

Compared to the previous year, the State income under the heads 'Land Revenue', 'Stamps and Court-fees', '*Nazars*' and even 'Education' showed a remarkable increase during the year. The year is also marked by a change of policy of collection under the head 'Education' by including the income from school- fees in the general receipts of the year and by abolishing the 'School Fund' system under which the Fund was used to be controlled by the school authorities separately.

For drinking purposes, a number of tanks were excavated and some tube-wells were sunk in various parts of the State during the year. For the proper administration of the Chakla Roshnabad zemindaries, a new post of Deputy Manager was created at Comilla.

TAR for the year 1341 T.E. (1931-32 A.D.)

It is already seen how Tripura in the twenties could not keep herself free from the extremely gloomy trade situations due to economic depression throughout the world. The economic scenario deteriorated further with the beginning of the thirties.Tripura jute was no more a paying crop and in spite of an increased outturn, the slump in the tea market had become worse during 1341 T.E.

The deteriorating economic situation was further aggravated by the appearance of a flood which badly affected some of the Divisions of the State and the adjoining zemindaries. The number of defaulting *taluks* was never so high as it was during the year. The *kheda* operations could not be undertaken for want of bidders. No operations were undertaken in many *sal* forests for want of purchasers of timber. The already low rates of wages of labours showed a further downward trend. Cholera appeared with virulence in Khowai and Dharmanagar Divisions.

The demise of Navadwip Chandra Dev Barman, son of the late Maharaja Ishan Chandra Manikya, at his Calcutta residence and some other deaths and calamities in the palace overtook even the Raj family.

The marriage ceremony of Bir Bikramkishore Manikya with the daughter of the Maharaja of Panna was solemnized on 28 May 1931 with pomp and eclat.

C.G.B. Stevens, the Political Agent, was shot dead in his bungalow on 14 December 1931. The Durbar was deeply grieved at the incidence and expressed its strong abhorrence of the dastardly and cowardly crime committed. Offices and institutions of the State remained closed for three days as a mark of showing respect to the Political Agent.

Bir Bikramkishore Manikya attended all the sessions of the Chamber of Princes (Narendra Mandal) from 24 March to 2 April 1932 in Delhi and had important discussion with J.C.C. Davidson, the Chairman of the Indian States Enquiry Committee, in connection with the State's Memorandum to the Committee.

The total area of Agartala town, as surveyed, was found to be 218 *drones* (2.15 sq. miles) of land. The military was called upon to patrol Agartala town at night after the committal of an armed dacoity in the night of 5 April 1932. To prevent crime, military force was also sent to patrol Bisalgarh Road. A new Municipal Committee with nine members was formed with Thakur Hriday Ranjan Dev Barman as Chairman and Haridas Bhattacharjee as Vice Chairman.

One of the important achievements of the year was the reservation for the hill people 11,000 *drones* of land in the Khowai Division.

During the year, a factory for the manufacture of matches was started near Agartala.

There was neither any new legislation nor any sitting of the Legislative Council during the year. The First Tripura Bir Company was supplied during the year with H.V. Rifles (303 bore) replacing the E.Y. Rifles which was transferred to the Second Tripura Bikram Company in anticipation of that company being recognised as Indian States Forces.

Department of History
Tripura University
Agartala

Mahadev Chakravarti

Book Sixteen
Report on the General Administration of the Tripura State for the year 1333 T. E. (1923-1924 A.D.)

REPORT ON THE ADMINISTRATION OF THE TRIPURA STATE. FOR 1333 T. E. (1923-24.)

CHAPTER I—GENERAL AND POLITICAL.

Area of the State—4,116 sq. miles.

Population—3,04,437.

Gross Revenue (based on the average of the previous five years) :—

(*a*) State ... ... Rs. 13,10,000.

(*b*) Zemindaries ... ... Rs. 11,09,829.

Tribute—Nil

Ruler of the State—His Highness The Bisama-Samara-Bijayee Mahamahodaya Pancha-Srijukta Maharaja Manikya Bir Bikramkishore Dev Barman Bahadur. *Age*—16 years. (Born—19th August, 1908). *Caste*—Kshatriya (of the Lunar race).

Maharaja Birendra Kishore Manikya's death.

1. The most fateful event of the year in the State was the death of His Highness Maharaja Birendra Kishore Manikya Bahadur, which took place at 1 P. M. on the 28th *Sravan*, corresponding to the 13th August 1923.

2. Born on the 3rd November 1883, the Maharaja was barely 40 years of age when he passed away, and was in the 15th year of his Rule counting from his accession on the 13th March 1909.

Public Sympathy.

3. Never was the late Ruler's immense popularity so apparent as at the hour of his death. Pathetic manifestations of popular grief characterized the last scene and the funeral, and all business was suspended throughout the State and in the adjoining British territory, as the sad news spread. As time went on, numerous messages of condolence poured in from far and near, and from high and low alike, while offices and institutions were closed, in and outside the State, in honour of the departed. The grateful thanks of the Council are due to all who so kindly came forward with offers of sympathy and support in the State's great bereavement.

The Maharaja as a man.

4. An accomplished painter and musician, and a keen all round sportsman, Maharaja Birendra Kishore Manikya possessed in him the rare combination of the instincts of an artist and a military man. Nowhere did his attractive personality make itself felt so widely, however, as in the domain of peace-making, and in His Highness's favourite role of a peace-maker. As for his generosity, it simply knew no bounds.

The European war and the Maharaja.

5. The European war brought forth the Maharaja's martial spirit into prominent relief, as it did his attachment to the person of the King Emperor and the great cause His Majesty had so nobly espoused. Maharaja Birendra Kishore unreservedly placed the entire resources of the State

at the disposal of the Government, as soon as hostilities broke out, and did everything to ensure the active participation of his family and subjects in the cause of the Empire. The substantial war contributions made by His Highness throughout the progress of the war will ever be to the State a source of legitimate pride.

His Administration.

6. It would be premature to judge Maharaja Birendra Kishore Manikya's policy of administration, but it can be said at once that his comparatively brief Rule was not without its earnest efforts to guide the State on in the path of advancement. The income of the State rose from eight lacs to fourteen lacs during this period, and that of the zemindaries from nine to eleven. A steady progress was maintained in all directions, and among special measures adopted are noticeable (1) the improvement of communications and buildings; (2) the introduction of the Tea Industry in the State; (3) the improvement of the Judiciary and the Legislative machinery; and (4) the initiation of a sound system of Forest management.

Relations with the Paramount Power.

7. An ardent advocate of the Policy of "Identity of interests", the Maharaja succeeded in coming to a perfect understanding with the Paramount Power, and the relations between his Durbar and the Government were all that could be desired.

The *Sradh*.

8. The late Maharaja's *sradh*, was performed with due *eclat* on the 8th *Bhadra*, corresponding to the 23rd September 1923, and formed in every respect a fitting sequel to a series of stirring events.

The Succession—The incoming Ruler.

9. On the death of Maharaja Birendrakishore Manikya Bahadur, the succession of the State and the attached Zemindaries devolved upon his son, His Highness Maharaja Manikya Bir Bikramkishore Dev Barman Bahadur, who announced it under his *Rubakari*, of the 32nd *Sravan*, *i.e.* 17th August, 1923. The recognition by His Majesty the King Emperor was intimated in His Excellency the Viceroy's *Kharita*, Dated the 5th September, 1923, which was read by the Political Agent at a Durbar held at the Ujjayanta Palace on the 22nd idem.

The Council of Administration.

10. His Highness achieved legal majority during the year, under the law governing the Ruling family, but as he was only 16 years of age, the administration of the State was entrusted, under the direction of the Government of India, to a Council composed of the following members, and styled "The Council of Administration"—

1. Maharajkumar Navadwip Chandra Dev Barman Bahadur, *President.*
2. Rai Jyotish Chandra Sen Bahadur, B. A., B. C. S., *Vice-President.*
3. Maharajkumar Brajendrakishore Dev Barman Bahadur, } *Members.*
4. Thakur Pratap Chandra Roy, } *Members.*

11. The Council was formally inaugurated on the 9th December, 1923, by Mr. A. J. Dash, I. C. S., Political Agent of the State, who concluded the function with the following speech :—

Inauguration.

Gentlemen,

The Administration of the State has now been entrusted to you. Your charge will not be a light one, but as loyal subjects of His Highness the Maharaja, you will be strengthened in facing the responsibilities of your office when you keep before you this guiding principle that you administer the State in trust for His Highness.

Being assured of your loyalty in this, the Government of India have reposed confidence in you that you will so conduct the administration of the State during the term of your office, that at its close you will hand over to His Highness a State of which the subjects are peaceful and contented, and an administration wisely functioning for their benefit.

12. The President thanked the Political Agent and the Government in suitable terms for the confidence placed in him and the members of the Council.

13. On the introduction of the Council form of Government, Rai P. K. Das Gupta Bahadur, Minister of the State and Manager of His Highness's Zemindaries, retired on the 6th September 1923, after a continued service of 17 years; and he was succeeded by Rai J. C. Sen Bahadur (Vice-President of the Council) as Manager of the Chakla Roshnabad Estates. The Council adopted the portfolio system of administration and divided the control of the Departments among the members, as detailed in appendix XXVI. Dewan Bijoykumar Sen, Chief Secretary to the late Maharaja, remained in charge of the Departments under the President's portfolio, as Chief Secretary, and was also appointed Secretary to the Council.

Administrative changes.

14. Early steps were taken by the Council, on assumption of charge, to place the finances of the State on a sound basis. With this end in view, the budgets of the State and the Zemindaries were revised, and an up-to-date inventory of liabilities drawn up. Schemes were also formulated for the gradual payment of debts and adjustment of old advances. A committee composed of Maharajkumar Brajendrakishore Dev Barman Bahadur, Rai Jyotish Chandra Sen Bahadur and Dewan Bijoykumar Sen, was appointed, with Babu Jatindra Chandra Maulik as Secretary, to scrutinize all outstanding claims against the late Maharaja. Since the close of the year, Babu Kamalaprasad Dutt's name has been added to the personnel.

The Council and the finances.

15. His Highness the Maharaja's education went on as before under Lt. Colonel O. C. Pulley, guardian tutor, and His Highness generally resided for the purpose at Comilla during the winter, and at Shillong during the summer.

His Highness's Education.

16. Mr. J. D. V. Hodge, I. C. S. continued to be the Political Agent of the State till the 26th October 1923, when he was relieved by Mr. A. J. Dash, I. C. S. The Council would gratefully place on record its high appreciation of the active help that it has always received from the latter, since its inauguration.

Political Agent.

CHAPTER II—LAND ADMINISTRATION.

Charge.

17. Dewan Asita Chandra Chaudhuri, B. A. continued to be in charge of the Revenue Department of the State.

Area under Settlement.

18. As shewn in the subjoined statement, the total area under settlement and borne on the *Taujis* at the close of the year, was 589 sq. miles as against 576 sq. miles in the previous year.

Kinds of settlement.	Area in square miles.		Increase.	Decrease.	REMARKS.
	1333 T.E	1332 T.E.			
Jotes ...	250	242	12	—	
Taluks ...	339	334	5	—	
Total ...	589	576	17	—	

Tea Settlement.

19. There was no fresh settlement for tea cultivation during the year under review. This new industry in the State has not yet recovered from the effects of the depression in the tea market during the previous few years.

Rates of *Jama*.

20. The average *Jama* per *kani* of *jote* lands in *Khas Mehals* (exclusive of cesses) stood at 15 annas and 1 pie against 15 annas 4 pies in the previous year, and that in the *taluks*, at 4 annas 11 pies per *kani* against 4 annas and 5 pies. The maximum rate for *jotes* was Rs. 5 per *kani* while the minimum was 4 annas. The rates for *taluki* land were Re. 1 and annas 3 respectively.

Sources of land Revenue.

21. The different sources of land revenue demand with collection under each head are detailed below :—

Sources.	Current demand.		Arrear demand up to the end of		Realization up to the end of		REMARKS.
	1333 T.E.	1332 T.E.	1332 T.E.	1331 T.E.	1333 T.E.	1332 T.E.	
Taluks ...	1,66,033	1,46,527	1,01,355	62,068	1,16,433	93,324	
Khas Mehal jotes	3,78,404	3,72,019	7,08,887	6,76,522	3,37,278	3,41,152	
Bazars ...	4,388	4,618	1,065	1,150	4,503	4,484	
Cesses ...	34,581	32,810	52,710	47,640	28,102	27,174	
Total ...	5,83,406	5,55,974	8,64,017	7,87,380	4,86,316	4,66,134	

Demand.

22. The above statement will show that the aggregate current demand was Rs. 5,83,406. With the arrear demand of Rs. 8,64,017, the total demand of the year was Rs. 14,47,423 against Rs. 13,43,354 of the previous year. There was an increase in the current demand both in respect of *Taluk* and *jote* lands, due as usual to assessment on the expiry of the rent-free period and re-settlement after the previous term.

Collection.

23. The collections during the year amounted to Rs. 4,86,316, against Rs. 4,66,134 of the previous year. Out of the total, Rs. 2,60,864 was under current, and Rs. 2,25,452 under arrears. The percentage of current collection was 44·71 against 44·95, and that of arrears, 26·09 against 27·46. The fall in the latter case is mainly due to the non-realisation of revenue from the tea estates, the current demand for which amounted to Rs. 73,268. In the *Khas Mehal* the percentage of current collection stood at 36·71 against 38·76, and in *taluks* 62·41 against 59·79—a result that can by no means be considered satisfactory. Both the current and arrear demands however include large amounts unrealisable. During the year, Rs. 8,956 of the demand was written off after enquiry. The special officer deputed to examine the *taujis* worked for about 7 months. His work has, not however, made any appreciable progress yet.

Coercive measures—certificates.

24. Altogether 2,951 certificate cases, covering a demand of Rs. 2,40,706, were instituted during the year. With 1,202 cases, valued at Rs. 78,451, pending from the previous year, the total number of cases, awaiting final orders on disposal of preliminary notices issued on debtors, was 4,153, covering a total demand of Rs. 3,19,157. Of these, 67 cases with a demand of Rs. 12,204 were rejected or struck off, while 1270 cases carrying an aggregate value of Rs. 1,62,966 remained pending.

25. Orders under the provision of the State Certificate Act were passed during the year, in 2,816 cases with a total value of Rs. 1,43,987, making the demands absolute. With 5,320 cases pending in execution from the previous year, the total number of cases dealt with was 8,136 covering a demand of Rs. 4,35,096. Out of the total demand, Rs. 26,186 was remitted or written off, and of the remainder, Rs. 82,283 was actually realised, leaving a balance of Rs. 3,26,627. Of the total amount realised, Rs. 69,176 represents land revenue and the rest miscellaneous demands.

26. Two certificate debtors in the Udaypur Division were arrested but were released on agreeing to pay the dues by instalments. In the Kailashahar Division warrants of arrest were issued against 2 debtors who absconded and could not be arrested.

The sun-set law.

27. The number of defaulting *taluks* brought under the operation of the sun-set law (including 21 pending from the previous year) was 100. Of these, 53 were released on payment of dues with penalty, and 23 were sold off in auction, while 24 remained undisposed of at the close of the year.

Survey.

28. The results of the survey and re-survey operations are given in the statement below. It will be seen that a total area of 2,865 *drones* of land, comprising 416 *drones* of *taluk* and 2,449 *drones* of *Khas Mehal*, was surveyed, as against a toal of 4,975 *drones* in the previous year. The sanctioned programme for survey for the season was for 611 *drones* in *Khas Mehal* and 1,328 *drones* in *taluks*. Including the work pending from the previous year, the total amount of survey work to be done was 2,545 *drones* of *Khas Mehal* land and 1,513 *drones of taluk*. The failure to complete the

programme was due in the case of *Taluki Mehals* to the default of the *Talukdars,* in some instances, to pay the estimated cost of survey, while in *Khas Mehal* survey, the shortage is only nominal. The total cost incurred in the survey operations in *Khas Mehals,* was Rs. 3,804.

Names of Divisions.	Quantity of land in *drones* surveyed in 1333 T. E.			Quantity of land in *drones* surveyed in 1332 T. E.			REMARKS.
	Taluqi land.	Khas mehal land.	Total.	Taluqi land.	Khas mehal land.	Total.	
1. Sadar Division ...	272	1,128	1,400	1,412	1,400	2,812	
2. Kailashahar " ...	—	—	—	—	—	—	
3. Sonamura " ...	—	62	62	—	—	—	
4. Belonia " ...	—	—	—	91	—	91	
5. Khowai " ...	2	742	744	41	383	424	
6. Dharmanagar " ..	—	163	163	291	762	1,053	
7. Udaipur " ...	129	—	129	—	64	64	
8. Sabroom " ...	—	—	—	—	—	—	
9. Kalyanpur Sub " ...	13	80	93	—	154	154	
10. Amarpur " " ...	—	—	—	—	—	—	
11. Bisalgarh " " ...	—	—	—	—	—	—	
12. Kamalpur " " ...	—	274	274	132	245	377	
TOTAL ...	416	2,449	2,865	1,967	3,008	4,975	

29. The work of Cadastral survey in Kailashahar was continued. The staff was engaged in *Kittawar* and *Khanapuri* work. *Kittawar* in 11 villages and *khanapuri* of 10 villages were completed. The area enclosed within the *kittawar* was about 1,600 acres and *khanapuri* consisted of 12,890 *dags.* Owing to the frequent change in the staff and the missing of the traverse pegs from the field, the *kittawar* work could not be carried on regularly. The number of maps prepared was 21.

Cadastral survey.

30. The result of the Settlement work is given in the statement below. It will be seen that settlement operations were completed in respect of 3037 *drones* of *jote* land, as against 1813 in the previous year.

Settlement.

Nature of Settlement.	1333 T. E.		1332 T. E.		REMARKS.
	Area in *drones.*	*Jama* in whole rupees.	Area in *drones.*	*Jama* in whole rupees.	
1. Permanent *taluqi* settlement of cultivated land ...	—	—	563	623	
2. Permanent *taluqi* settlement of waste land	—	—	—	—	
3. *Taskhichi taluqi* settlement of cultivated land ...	—	—	—	—	
4. *Taskhichi taluqi* settlement of waste land ...	—	—	16	128	
5. *Jotedari* re-settlement of cultivated land	2,681	34,782	1,342	17,110	
6. *Jotedari* settlement of waste land.	356*	2,811	471	4,045	
TOTAL ...	3,037	37,593	2,392	21,906	

31. No permanent or *Taskhichi* settlement or *Niskar* grant was sanctioned during the year.

Permanent settlement.

32. A net increase of Rs. 12,074 in *jama* was secured by resettlement of cultivable *jote* lands, the *nazarana* secured being Rs. 24,908. The average rate of *jama* obtained per *kani* was 13 annas, against 12 annas 9 pies in the previous year.

Re-settlement of *jote* lands.

33. During the year, a total area of 356 *drones* of waste land was settled for a prospective rental of Rs. 2,811. The average *jama* per *kani* secured was 7 annas and 11 pies, against 8 annas and 7 pies in the previous year, the maximum and minimum rates being Rs. 2–8 annas and 2 annas respectively. The *Nazarana* obtained was Rs. 3,637. The rent-free period allowed varied from 1 to 5 years.

Jotedari Settlement of waste land.

34. There was a whole-time settlement officer in the Sadar Division where the work was heavy. In other places the Divisional Officers were entrusted with settlement work within their respective Divisions. The total expenditure incurred in the settlement operations of the year amounted to Rs. 3,079.

Settlement Work.

35. It will be seen that the *nazarana* obtained and obtainable by resettlement of cultivable *jote* lands and settlement of waste lands as *jotes* (Rs. 24,908 + Rs. 3,637 = Rs. 28,545) was four times the amount spent for the survey and settlement operations, while the net increase of revenue obtained was Rs. 14,885 (Rs. 12,074 + Rs. 2,811).

36. The work entrusted to the map section was the rehabilitation of old maps and preparation of traces from them for use in work outside the office. During the year 172 copies of maps were traced at a cost of Rs. 399.

The work of the map section.

CHAPTER III—PROTECTION.

I. Legislation.

37. No fresh legislation was undertaken during the year under report. In consequence of the change in the administration, the Minister and the private Secretary ceased to be members of the Legislative Council, which has been reconstituted since the close of the year.

Legislative Council.

II. Military.

38. Kumar Dinamohan Deb Barman continued to be in charge of the Military Office and the Force.

Charge.

39. At the close of the year under review, the actual strength of the Force consisted of 188 sepoys, and 51 officers of all ranks, including the Commanding officer, 2 Subedar Majors, and 2 Subedars. There were besides, a Band Master and 16 men constituting the State Band.

Strength.

40 The men were chiefly employed as before on escort duty and in furnishing guards-of-honour on ceremonial occasions

Duty.

Expenditure.

41. The total expenditure of the year amounted to Rs. 42,625 against Rs. 37,742 in the previous year. The increase is due to payment of arrear bills, purchase of uniforms, and normal grade increments allowed during the year.

Re-organization.

42. Owing to financial reasons, no steps could be taken during the year towards giving effect to the scheme of Re-organization.

III. Police.

Charge

43. Babu Jogesh Chandra Dutta B. A. continued as Superintendent of Police throughout the year.

Strength.

44. The total strength of the Police Force was 477 as in the previous year, including a staff of 10 constables maintained exclusevely for the town section. Of these 202 were able to read and write.

Training.

45. Thakur Jogendra Chandra Deb Barman a young member of the Thakur community was sent during the year to the Police Training College at Sardah to qualify himself for admission to the superior Police staff of the State.

Inspecting Staff.

46. There were altogether 4 Inspectors working under the Superintendent of Police for inspection and supervision work. Owing to various difficulties, the movement of the inspectors could not be as free and regular, during the year, as might be expected, and it is regrettable that much of the work of supervision was left undone.

Crime.

47. The total number of cases reported to the Police was 1,222 against 1,290 in the previous year. The result of the cases investigated will be seen from the subjoined table :—

Number of cases reported
1222

Enquiry refused	Number investigated	Number pending
14	1155	53

Number investigated 1155:

Maliciously false	True	Doubtful etc.
70	735	350

True 735:

Charge-sheet	Finally reported
396	339

Results of prosecution.

48. Altogether 787 persons were arrested for various offences, and 754 sent up for trial by the Police, against 736 and 661 respectively, in the previous year. Of the number sent up, 195 were convicted, 128 acquitted on compromise and 39 on withdrawl of cases, while 1 died, 8 escaped and 261 were awaiting trial at the end of the year.

49. The percentage of conviction was 60·1 against 61·48 of the previous year.

50. Of 235 persons awaiting trial at the end of the previous year, 85 were convicted, 102 acquitted or discharged, and 48 remained pending at the close of the year under review.

B. L. cases.

51. One bad livelihood case was instituted in the year under report, and it ended in conviction.

Arms Act cases.

52. There were 7 cases under the Arms Act reported during the year, in 6 of which charge sheets were submitted by the police. The other case was entered on investigation as due to mistake of fact. Of the charge sheet cases 3 ended in conviction and 3 were pending Judgment at the close of the year.

Recovery of stolen property.

53. The aggregate value of property stolen was estimated at Rs. 16,558-11-3 (against Rs. 27,980-5-0 of the last year) out of which Rs. 3,722-4-9 was recovered, the percentage of recovery being thus 22·4 against 31·65 of the previous year.

Dacoities.

54. Nine cases of dacoity were reported during the year under report against 5 of the previous year. Most of the cases were of a technical character. Of these 4 were sent up, 2 declared false, and 1 doubtful; while 2 were finally reported true. Steps were also taken during the year to guard the border by arranging patrol work in co-operation with the British Police. The results was satisfactory.

Special Staff.

55. The C. I. D. and the Information Bureau continued to do good work and proved useful.

Unnatural death and steps taken.

56. Altogether 62 cases of unnatural death were reported during the year. Regular enquiries were held by the police in every case. No suspicious case was detected.

Rewards and punishments.

57. One Sub-Inspector, 1 Naib Daroga, 2 Jamadars, 1 Writer constable, and 30 constables were fined and suspended departmentally, while 1 constable was dismissed. 4 constables were fined judicially. 6 Sub-Inspectors and 2 constables received money rewards for good service during the year, while 1 Sub-Inspector and 1 Assistant Sub-Inspector of the British Police received good service marks in consideration of valuable services rendered to the State.

Tour.

58. The Superintendent was out on tour for 38 days in all during the year under report on inspection and supervision work, against 69 days in the previous year.

Co-operation meeting.

59. The relations with the adjoining British Police continued satisfactory. 4 co-operation meetings were held in which State officers joined the British Police and discussed matters relating to border crime and criminals in general, also worked out plans for checking the movements of notorious pick-pockets and gangs of swindlers.

Expenditure.

60. The total expenditure amounted to Rs. 67,566 against Rs. 69,673 in the previous year.

61. The dfference is apparent only, being due to the exclusion of D. P. allowances paid to the establishment from the current year's figure.

IV. Justice.

62. There were 17 courts of Justice in the State during the year under report, exercising both civil and criminal jurisdiction viz.—the Khas Adalat or the Chief Court with its original and appellate sides, and 16 Courts of Magistrate-Munsiffs exercising original jurisdiction only. Babu Bhupal Chandra Ganguli B. L., continued to be the Chief Judge, Dewan Bijoy Kumar Sen, M. A., B. L., F. R. S. A., as the Sessions Judge, and Kumar Surendra Chandra Deb Barman and Uzir Brojo Krishna Deb Barman, as puisne Judges of the Khas Adalat.

Courts.

63. Owing to the retirement of two Members, as the result of the administrative changes in the State consequent on the death of the late Ruler, there was no sitting of the Privy Council during the year. 6 cases were pending before the Council, at the close of the year.

Privy Council.

64. Altogether 1,739 original criminal cases were instituted during the year under report against 1,605 of the previous year. With the balance of 588 pending from the last year, the total number of cases for disposal before the several subordinate original courts was thus 2,327 as against 2,315 of the previous year, as detailed below. Out of these 2,327 cases, 1,848 were disposed of as against 1,721 of the last year, leaving 467 cases pending at the close of the year. Thus in the year under report, the number of cases for disposal exceeded that of the previous year by 12, and there was also an increase in the disposals by 127.

Number of original criminal cases.

DESCRIPTION OF OFFENCES.	1332 T. E.	1333 T. E.
Offences against the State and public tranquillity	104	84
Offences against person	570	559
Offences against property	1,230	1,239
Other offences	411	445
TOTAL	2,315	2,327

65. The total number of pesons awaiting trial in the year under report, inclusive of the number pending from the previous year, was 2,769. The number actually brought to trial was 1,937 against 2,024 of the previous year. Of these 642 were arrested by the police, 343 were produced on warrants, 650 appeared on summons, 281 appeared voluntarily, and 17 were arrested in the presence of Magistrates.

Persons brought to trial.

66. Out of the persons brought to trial, 879 were discharged without trial, 730 were acquitted, and 477 convicted, while 14 died, 12 were transferred, 1 escaped and 656 remained under trial at the close of the year. Of the persons convicted, 172 were sentenced to various terms of imprisonment extending from below 1 month to 6 years, 302 to fine only, and 2 persons were warned for the future, while 1 person was imprisoned for life. The number of persons actually tried was 1,207 as against 969 of the previous year and the percentage of conviction was thus 39·51 as against 36·94 of last year.

Results of cases.

67. Of the 2,327 cases for disposal, the number in which British subjects were concerned was 554 against 483 of the last year. Out of these 554 cases, 401 were cognizable and 153 non-cognizable. In 71 cases British subjects were complainants, in 483 they were the accused. In 167 cases both the parties were British Subjects. In these cases 568 persons were actually under trial during the year under report against 479 of the previous year. Of them 161 were convicted, 259 acquitted or discharged, 2 died, and 146 remained under trial at the close of the year.

Cases concerning British subjects.

68 The Statement below compares the number of original criminal cases during the last 2 years.

Comparative Statement.

DESCRIPTION OF OFFENCES.	1332 T.E.	1333 T.E.	Increase.	Decrease.
Offences against the State and public tranquillity ...	62	57	0	5
Offences against person	426	443	17	0
Offences against property	828	901	73	0
Other offences	289	338	49	0
TOTAL	1,605	1,739	139	5

Increased by 134.

69. Extradition warrants were applied for against 55 persons, of whom 17 were arrested and surrendered, 20 appeared voluntarily and 18 were at large at the close of the year. Of 37 persons under trial, 10 were convicted, 8 acquitted or discharged and 19 awaited trial at the end of the year.

Extradition.

70. 19 cases, including 2 cases with 4 persons pending from previous year, came up for trial before the Sessions Court during the year under report. Out of these 19 cases, 14 were disposed of as detailed in the following table. The number of accused persons involved in these cases was 43, of whom 11 were convicted, 19 acquitted, and 13 remained under trial at the close of the year.

Sessions cases.

Description of cases.	Number of cases.	Disposed of.	Pending.	REMARKS.
Murder	1	0	1	
Culpable homicide not amounting to murder	4	3	1	
Grievous hurt	2	1	1	
Dacoity	6	5	1	
Attempt to murder	1	1	0	
False complaint	1	1	0	
Obstructing public servant in the discharge of his duty	1	0	1	
Abducting a woman to compel her marriage	1	1	0	
Abduction of a woman to seduce her to illicit intercourse	1	1	0	
Causing death by rash and neglignt act	1	1	0	
Total ...	19	14	5	

71. There were altogether 222 criminal appeals as against 210 of the previous year. They were disposed of as shown below :—

Criminal appeals.

Rejected	14
Judgment affirmed	120
Modified	18
Reversed	48
Further enquiry &c. ordered	9
	209
Pending	13
Total	222

72. The percentage of judgments affirmed and modified was 62·16 against 60·84 of the previous year.

73. The number of original civil suits instituted during the year under report was 1,863 as against 2,023 of the last year. With the preceding year's balance of 987 suits, the total number for disposal was 2,850 as against 3,097 of the previous year. They were disposed of as follows :—

Original civil suits.

Exparte	522
Admitted and compromised	355
Dismissed for want of prosecution	450
Disposed of on contest	577
	1,904
Pending	946
Total	2,850

74. The average duration of suits before the civil courts was 4 months and 16 days against 4 months 10 days in 1332 T. E.

Duration of suits.

75. The total value of suits instituted during the year was Rs. 1,53,729-4-3 as against Rs. 1,79,453-6-9 which gives an average of Rs. 82-3-1 as the value per case. Of the 1,863 suits instituted during the year under report, 630 related to lands, 917 to money transactions and 316 to other transactions. There were 1,255 suits of the value of Rs. 100 and under ; 306 suits of over Rs. 100 and below Rs. 500 ; 17 suits of over Rs. 500 and below Rs. 1,000 ; 11 suits of over Rs. 1,000 and below Rs. 5,000 ; and 1 suit of above Rs. 5000 ; while 273 suits were not estimable in money value.

Nature and value of suits.

76. The number of applications for the execution of decrees filed during the year under report was 688 and with 538 pending cases, the total number was 1,226 against 1,142 of the previous year. The aggregate value of the new applications was Rs. 1,02,617-9-0, and with the opening value of Rs. 99,300-12-3, being the value of the pending cases, the total amounted to Rs. 2,01,918-5-3. The number of applications disposed of was 767, the value of which was Rs. 88,826-13-9. The number of execution cases pending at the close of the year was 456 with the value of Rs. 1,12,697-6-3.

Execution of decrees.

Civil appeals.

77. There were 156 civil appeals filed during the year under report against 148 of the last year. With the past year's balance of 41, the total for disposal was 197 as against 173 of 1332 T. E. Out of these 165 were disposed of during the year under report against 132 of the previous year, leaving a balance of 32 cases at the close of the year.

Results of appeals.

78. The following figures indicate the results of appeals.

Decisions confirmed	... ...	93
" reversed	... ...	49
" modified	... ...	6
" remanded	... ...	4
Compromised or otherwise disposed of	...	13
		165

Percentage.

79. The percentage of judgments wholly or partly upheld, excluding the cases compromised, was 65·13 against 66·33 of the previous year.

Value and duration of appeals.

80. The total value of appeals filed during the year under report was Rs. 8,684-13-9, and the average duration of each appeal was 2 months and 5 days, as against 2 months and 10 days of the previous year.

Original side cases.

81. Altogether 19 civil suits were instituted in the Khas Adalat Original Side against 91 suits of the previous year. With the balance of 67 suits from 1332 T. E., the total number for disposal was thus 86 against 107 of the last year; of these, 31 suits were disposed of against 40 of the previous year, and 55 suits remained pending at the close of the year. There were 31 execution cases including 19 cases pending from 1332 T. E., of which 10 were disposed of and 21 remained pending at the end of the year. There were also 27 applications filed for the grant of succession and other certificates during the year; with the previous year's balance of 18, the total number of cases was 45; out of them 24 were disposed of as shown below, leaving 21 cases pending at the close of the year.

Description of cases.	Total.	Disposed of.	Pending.
Probate case	3	2	1
Succession certificate	22	13	9
Guardianship	20	9	11
Total	45	24	21

Total number of appeals.

82. It will appear from the sub-joined table that the total number of civil and criminal appeals inclusive of the number pending from last year was 419, as against 383 of the last year, and out of these, 374 were disposed of against 321 of the previous year. So in comparison with the last year, the total number of appeals increased by 36 in the present year, and

there was a corresponding increase in the disposals in the year under report by 53.

Description of appeals.	Number of appeals.		Disposed of.	
	Past year.	Present year.	Past year.	Present year.
Civil	173	197	132	165
Criminal	210	222	189	209
Total	383	419	321	374

V. Prisons.

83. There were, as before, 12 jails in the State during the year under report, one at each of the Divisions and Sub-Divisions, including the central jail at the capital.

Number of Jails.

84. The total jail population in the year under review was 749 as against 764 in the previous year—the daily average being 92·12 against 98·72 of the year before. Of the total, 323 were convicts, 407 under trials, 15 civil-side prisoners, and 4 lunatics.

Jail population.

85. The following statement shows details regarding 40 prisoners sentenced to over 2 years, as against 52 in the preceding year.

Long term Prisoners.

Class of offence.	Number of prisoners.	Occupation.	REMARKS.
Murder	12	They were employed, mainly in the central jail, in country oilmills, wheat grinding, brick manufacture, soorki-pounding, khoa-breaking, bamboo and cane manufacture, earth works, gardening, weaving and tailoring.	22 had sentences of 2 to 5 years, 12 of 5 to 10 years, 6 for life i.e. 20 years.
Culpable homicide not amounting to murder	10		
Grievous hurt	2		
Dacoity	7		
Escape from lawful custody...	2		
Robbery	1		
Rape	3		
Kidnapping	1		
Forgery	1		
Arson	1		
Total	40		

86. The jail health was generally good. Only one convict died of chronic dysentery in the central jail against 1 in the year before.

Jail health.

87. One convict escaped from the Kailashahar jail.

Escape.

88. The total income from jails amounted to Rs. 2,048-12-3 against Rs. 1,814-3-9 in the preceding year.

Jail income.

89. The expenditure for the maintenance of all the jails amounted to Rs. 13,305 as against Rs. 12,438 of the year previous.

Expenditure.

90. The new jail Dormitory could not be finished for want of provision.

Jail Building.

VI. Registration.

Registration Offices.

91. The number of Registration offices continued to be 12, *i. e.* one for each Division or Sub-Division, except at Sadar. The Divisional Collectors and Assistant Collectors acted as ex-officio Registrars. At Agartala there was a special Registrar.

Presentation and disposal.

92. The number of documents presented for Registration during the year was 9.040, as against 8,665 of the previous year. During the year under review, 128 deeds were refused registration on various grounds, while 58 remained pending at the close of the year.

Value of deeds presented and registered.

93. The total value covered by the documents presented amounted to Rs. 12,01,919, as compared with Rs. 12,89,970 of the previous year. The total value of the documents actually registered was Rs. 11,62,103 against Rs. 12,64,364. The falling off in the total value is due to the smaller number of mortgage deeds during the year and the comparatively low average value of the sale deeds.

Suits and appeals.

94. The numbers of suits and appeals filed with the officer-in-charge Registration Department, in respect of documents, the Registration of which had been refused, were 26 and 1, against 18 and 4 respectively of the previous year. 38 suits and 3 appeals (including those from the previous year) were dealt with during the year under review, with the result that all the appeals and 19 suits were disposed of, leaving 19 suits pending at the close of the year

Income and expenditue.

95. The total income from fees, and the expenditure during the year, amounted to Rs. 10,244 and Rs. 3,445 respectively, as against Rs. 9,615 and Rs. 3.318 of the previous year. The net income, therefore, was Rs. 6,799, during the year, against Rs. 6,297

VII. Municipality.

Municipality.

96. The Capital Town of Agartala, continued to have the only Municipality in the State.

Municipal Committee.

97. As in the previous year, the affairs of the Municipality were managed by a Committee of nine nominated commissioners, including an official Chairman and a non-official Vice-Chairman. The Committee held twelve sittings, the average number of attendance being 5·1. Dr. M. M. Majumdar, L.M.S., remained Chairman.

Income.

98. The total demand including realisable arrears on account of Municipal and Latrine taxes, amounted to Rs. 6,588, of which, Rs. 3,879 was actually collected. In the previous year, the collection under the above counts had come up to Rs. 3,001. The income under the Miscellaneous head, including deposits and advances recovered, amounted to Rs. 7,635, of which Rs. 5,892 was from the local Bazar. The total demand from the Bazar was Rs. 6,550.

State Grant. 99. As in the previous year, the State grant was Rs. 9,000.

Expenditure 100. The total expenditure, including the expenses for the improvement of the Bazar, during the year under report, amounted to Rs. 16,195, as against Rs. 14,949 of the preceding year.

Public health. 101. The general health of the town during the year was not good, owing to the prevalance of Malaria and Kala-azar (Black Fever).

Ishanganj Bazar. 102. The administration of the Town Bazar continued to be carried on by the Committee. Two small passages in the market were made pucca and some other minor works were undertaken and completed. The expenditure for the Bazar amounted to Rs. 1,090 and was paid out of the income of the market, ear marked for its improvement. The Bazar improvement fund accummulated to Rs. 10,562 at tho close of the year under review.

CHAPTER IV—PRODUCTION AND DISTRIBUTION.

I. Weather and Crops—Agriculture.

Rainfall. 103. The average rainfall of the year was 81·58 inches against 87·83 inches in the previous year. The quinquennial average was 89·95 inches. Dharmanagar Division had the maximum fall of 115·88 inches and Amarpur the minimum of 68·63 inches. The rainfall was adequate and seasonable.

Crops. 104. The principal crops were paddy, cotton, til, mustard, jute and sugar-cane. The weather conditions were favourable to the crops and the outturn was fair. The infant Tea Industry of the State was unable to make appreciable progress owing to economic difficulties, but a few concerns succeeded in exporting some tea.

Cattle. 105. The health of the cattle was generally good. There were however some suspicious cases in the Sadar Division, and the Veterinary Assistant was sent out to visit the affected localities and render help. As the result of the satisfactory condition of cattle, the agricultural classes are shaking off the depressing effects of the loss of cattle in the previous year.

Condition of the people. 106. The people are mostly agricultural. The main crops—paddy, mustard, jute, til, cotton and sugar-cane grew well. Cotton sold at high prices and the prevailing prices of other crops were also good ; so the condition of the people was generally satisfactory inspite of the high prices of imported articles.

Prices. 107. The prices of food grains were normal as compared with the prevailing prices in the neighbouring British Districts, the price of rice ranging from Rs. 4 to Rs. 6-8 and that of paddy from Rs. 2 to Rs. 3-12 per maund.

108. There was no appreciable change in the rates of wages. Male labourers earned from 8 annas to Re. 1 and female labourers from 5 annas to 8 annas a day. *Ghoramis* earned from 8 annas to Re. 1, and carpenters and masons from 12 annas to Re. 1-4. Most of the labourers were outsiders from the neighbouring British Districts, as well as upcountry coolies.

Wages.

109. No Taccavi advances were issued during the year.

Taccavi.

110. The Kashipur Farm continued its experiments in long-staple cotton of different varieties. The results obtained with the "Dharwar" variety were satisfactory. This variety was tried in the jhooms also, and the results were equally good. The jhoom products were sent to the Government Economic Botanist at Dacca, the Central Cotton Committee Bombay, the Banga Laksmi Cotton Mills, Messrs. Kettlewell Bullen and Co., and the Dhakeswari Mills. The reports received were encouraging. The Central Cotton Committee report stated that the jhoom products fetched Rs. 5 per maund less than the price obtained by the Bombay growers, the difference being due to unclean picking. The Economic Botanist remarked that with careful and clean picking and packing, the problem of long-staple cotton for Bengal would be satisfactorily solved, if it could be grown in the jhooms. Encouraged by the above remarks the field of experiment has been extended, and during the current season, seeds for the long-stapled variety (Dharwar) have been distributed to 2,000 jhooms and higher altitudes ranging from 15 to 600 ft. The State now has about 19,000 acres under cotton. The defects referred to above have been noted for action.

Model Farm.

II. Immigration Emigration.

111. During the year, 1,228 families immigrated into and 781 families emigrated out of the State, as against 1,676 and 1,230 respectively in the previous year.

III. Forests.

112. Dewan Asita Chandra Chaudhuri, B. A. continued to be in charge of the Department and Babu Jatindra Nath Mittra worked as Forest Officer. As in the previous year, all the State Forests were under *Khas* management.

Charge and management

113. The Department employed a staff of 19 Foresters, 17 Assistant Foresters, 10 Moharers and Clerks, 10 Rangers, 16 Head Guards, and 198 Guards and Literate Guards. Besides, there were 157 commission-agents for the sale of permits for shoulder-borne export, and there were 57 stations and offices for the collection and supervision of forest duty.

Staff.

114. There was no change in the mode of working the forests. The open unclassed forests were worked under the State Rules of 1323 T. E., the Reserved Sal Forests of the Sonamura Division under the system of Coppice with

Working.

standards, and those of the Udaipur Division under the Selection method. For the Feni river mehal the rules of the Bengal Forest Department were followed.

Sources of forest Revenue.

115. The different sources of forest revenue with collections under each head are given below :—

Heads of Revenue.	1333 T.E.	1332 T.E.	Increase.	Decrease.	REMARKS.
I. Unclassed open forests :—					
(*a*) Toll on forest produce exported by the river mehals	*3,76,876	3,25,977	50,899	—	*Rs. 1731-being income under "Agar" has been shewn against the Revenue general head in the Accounts Department.
(*b*) Toll on forest produce exported by land route under permit	83,429	77,439	5,990	—	
(*c*) Tollcollection (share) of the Feni river mehal ...	*30,116	27,219	2,897	—	
(*d*) Grazing mehal ...	7,348	6,991	357	—	*Total collection being Rs. 48,185 up to End of Chait.
(*e*) Thatching grass mehal	10,692	11,897	—	1,205	
II. Reserved Forests :— Sale of *Sal* and *Garjan* trees ...	27,201	21,957	5,244	—	
III. Elephant Kheddas	31,336	18,350	12,986	—	
TOTAL ...	5,66,998	4,89,830	78,373	1,205	

Receipts

116. The total forest revenue for the year, including the income from elephant khedas, was Rs. 5,66,998 against Rs. 4,89,830, showing an increase of Rs. 77,168. It broke the record of the year 1331 with its total of Rs. 5,04,728.

117. It will be seen that there was, a satisfactory increase under each head except in the Thatching Grass Mehal, where the shortage was due to the non-payment of the Jama by some Ijaradars. A noticeable source of income was opened and a new industry started, by the leasing out of tracts containing "Agar" trees.

Elephant Khedas.

118. Kheda operations were undertaken in the Kailashahar, Kamalpur, Bilonia, and Sabroom Divisions and were successful at all places except Kamalpur.

Feni River Mehal.

119. The mehal was under the management of the State Forest Department. This was the last year of the 5 years' term for which the management had been handed over to this State. The revenue of the year was Rs. 48,482 against Rs. 43,124 of the year before.

120. It may not be out of place to mention that during the last 5 years of management by the State, the total revenue of this station amounted to Rs. 2,31,392, against Rs. 62,226, the total of the previous 5 years, when the management was in the hands of the Government

gency, thus showing a satisfactory increase of Rs. 1,69,166 during the 5 years of State management:—

1919-20.	Rs. 38,524	1914-15.	Rs. 10,981
1920-21.	Rs. 47,238	1915-16.	Rs. 10,943
1921-22.	Rs. 54,024	1916-17.	Rs. 12,326
1922-23.	Rs. 43,124	1917-18.	Rs. 14,152
1923-24.	Rs. 48,482	1918-19.	Rs. 13,324
	Rs. 2,31,392		Rs. 62,226

121. The question of the future management of the Station had been before the Government since the latter part of the financial year, and it is a matter of satisfaction to the Department that inspite of strong opinion to the contrary, the Government have been pleased to leave the management of the Station with this State. A conference will shortly be held at which measures likely to further improve the management will be considered. The trouble with the owners of the "fee simple" lots, mentioned in the last year's report necessitated a local enquiry by the Collector of Chittagong. The enquiry, in which the State was represented by its Forest Officer, resulted in an arrangement which is likely to minimise future disputes.

Forest offences

122. During the year, there were 123 forest cases against 254 persons, of which 97 cases against 167 persons were instituted during the year and 26 cases against 87 were pending from the year before. The offences were mainly for export of forest produce without payment of duty or without permits.

Results.

123. Altogether 98 persons were convicted, 95 with fine only, and 3 with fine and imprisonment, while 26 were acquitted, 2 died before trial, and 6 were absconding. 11 cases against 27 persons were compounded, and 43 cases against 95 persons remained pending at the close of the year.

Rewards and Punishments.

124. There were two cases of reward (obtained by a guard at Kailasahar) and 7 cases of departmental punishment.

Health of the Staff.

125. The year was unfortunately very unhealthy for the Forest staff. The Station Officer at Amlighat suffered very badly from fever and attendant complications, and three officers had to be posted at Amlighat as Station Officer, one after another. The Clerk and the Ranger also suffered badly, while 2 guards died. The Assistant Forester at Sinai died of cholera at his station. The Foresters at Mohuri and Kamthana and the Marking Ranger at Dhalai suffered badly from fever, and one guard at Chhinaihani also died.

Difficulties.

126. The troubles with regard to the working of the State forests in the Langai Valley are not yet over. Correspondence with the Assam Government is going on and it is hoped that a satisfactory solution will be arrived at early.

127. The movement among a section of people in Noakhali to collect forest produce free of duty, subsided as the result of timely steps taken by the Magistrate of Noakhali at the instance of the Political Agent.

IV. Trade and Manufacture.

128. The principal exports were timber, forest produce of various kinds, cotton, oilseeds, (*til* and mustard seed) paddy, jute, rice and

molasses. A small quantity of tea, and some homespun and homewoven cotton fabrics manufactured by the hill people, specially the Manipuris, were also exported. The principal exports for the year under review and of the previous year are shown below :—

		1332 T.E.	1333 T.E.
Cotton	...	34,688 maunds.	76,590 maunds.
Til	...	28,960 ,,	52,256 ,,
Mustard Seeds		18,271 ,,	26,734 ,,
Jute	...	35,916 ,,	54,942 ,,

129. The principal imports were cloths and yarns, salt, oils (kerosine and mustard), pulses, chillies, tobacco, sugar, flour, spices, arecanuts, books and stationery. The industries worth mention were manufacture of cotton fabrics by the hill people and the Manipuris ; cane and bamboo baskets, mats and sieves by Tripuras ; and dug-outs, bowls and plates of wood by the Reangs and Chakmas ; also *Gur* (molasses) by both hill people and Bengalees.

V. Public Works.

130. Mr. Jogendra Nath Bhaduri B. A., B. E., continued as State Engineer during the year. Rai P. K. Das Gupta Bahadur, Late Minister was in charge of the Department for about 8 months, and Prince B. K. Dev Barman Bahadur, Member of the Council of Administration, for the remaining part of the year.

Expenditure.

131. The total amount of expenditure came to Rs 2,79,519 against Rs. 1,66,417 in the previous year. Of this Rs. 2,724 was spent on water supply, Rs. 49,146 on Roads and Bridges, Rs. 2,01,078 on Buildings and Rs. 2,915 on Miscellaneous works. In addition to this, Rs. 34,992 was disbursed on account of arrear Public Works bills including Rs. 10,000 paid to the Tippera District Board as contribution for repairs of the Akhaura Road. The above total excludes grain allowances paid, but includes payments from local funds.

132. The following important major woks were completed during the year under report :—

(1) Guest house building. (2) Extension of the Studio building. (3) Temple of Mahadev at Kunjabon. (4) Beer Chandra Library. (5) Substantial improvement of Bisalgarh and Birendranagar roads, with bridges and armco Culverts. (6) Bisalgarh Divisional Office and Dak Bungalow. (7) Earth work of half portion of Bisalgarh-Udaipur road—a project of 20 miles length. (8) Lung-thung to Sabroom road. (9) Pucca quarters for the lady teachers of theGirl's School. (10) Extension of His Highness's Andar.

CHAPTER V—REVENUE AND FINANCES.

I. Revenue.

133. The total collection in the year was Rs. 15,82,035 against Rs. 13,33,357 in the previous year. The average of the past five years

was Rs. 13,10,000. There was a total increase of Rs. 2,48,678 as compared with the previous year and of Rs. 2,03,755 as compared with the record year of 1331 T. E.

134. The details of income under the different heads with their variations are given in the statement below :—

Serial number.	Heads of Revenue.	1333 T. E.	1332 T. E.	As compared with 1331 T. E.		Remarks.
				Increase	Decrease.	
1	Land Revenue	4,95,508	4,74,612	20,896	—	
2	Rents of markets	4,569	4,195	374	—	
3	Family Tax in the hills	63,279	59,047	4,232	—	
4	Toll on forest produce	4,66,404	4,03,416	62,988	—	
5	Do. Do. on the Feni River	30,116	27,219	2,897	—	
6	Elephant & buffalo grazing Mehal	7,348	6,991	357	—	
7	Thatching grass Mehal	10,692	11,897	—	1,205	
8	Reserved *Sal* trees	19,371	21,957	—	2,586	
9	Tax on cotton and oil-seeds ...	2,03,606	1,02,837	1,00,769	—	
10	Royalty on elephants caught ...	31,336	7,003	24,333	—	
11	Adda Mehal	20,692	21,226	—	534	
12	Excise	47,652	36,673	10,979	—	
13	Stamps and Court-fees	58,082	59,358	—	1,276	
14	Law and Justice (Fines)... ...	3,368	1,874	1,494	—	
15	Process fees	12,132	10,077	2,055	—	
16	Registration	10,251	9,615	636	—	
17	Jail	2,442	1,692	750	—	
18	Cattle pounds	5,685	5,244	441	—	
19	Nazars	25,127	25,474	—	347	
20	Agriculture	314	323	—	9	
21	Miscellaneous	64,061	42,627	21,434	—	
	Total	15,82,035	13,33,357	2,54,635	5,957	Net increase—Rs. 2,48,678.

N. B. The above figures slightly differ from the tauji figures. They include deposits, while the tauji excludes deposits and includes adjustments of suspense accounts.

135. From the above statement it will be seen that there was increase under 15 heads and decrease under 6 heads. The increase under the head Land Revenue is noticeable as it relates mainly to *Khas Mehal*. The increase under head Forest Revenue is very satisfactory, as is that under Duty on cotton and oil seeds. The income from Elephant *Khedas* establishes a record under this head of revenue. The increase under head Excise is due to the higher *Jama* obtained by settlement.

Increase.

136. No item of decrease in the above statement calls for any comment except the figure under head Stamps and Court fees. The revenue under this head is an expanding one and ordinarily has a tendency to increase. The cause for the unexpected decrease has been found in this instance to be due to the misdeeds of some designing people, who successfully managed for some time past to tamper with State stamps. The matter is at present sub judice.

Decrease.

II. Finances.

137. The subjoined comparative statement shows the receipts and expenditure of the year in the State and the Zemindaries.

Receipts.	1332 T.R.	1333 T.R.
1. Opening balance :-		
(1) State	8,62,521	10,09,469
(2) Zemindaries ...	3,34,927	3,81,582
Total ...	11,97,448	13,91,051
2. Income :—		
(1) State	13,33,357	15,82,035
(2) Zemindaries ...	10,67,432	11,00,400
Total ...	24,00,789	26,82,435
3. Law charges recovered :—		
(1) State	—	—
(2) Zemindaries ...	57,836	48,522
Refunds and compensation for lands acquired :—		
(1) State ...	—	—
(2) Zemindaries ...	11,266	2,417
5. Deposits :—		
(1) State	1,23,857	87,865
(2) Zemindaries ...	3,980	24,323
Total ...	1,27,837	1,12,188
6. Loans :—		
(1) State	—	50,000
(2) Zemindaries ...	75,000	80,000
		1,30,000
GRAND TOTAL ...	38,70,176	43,66,613 ~~[illegible]~~

Expenditure.	1332 T.R.	1333 T.R.
1. General Administration charges :—		
(a) State	4,39,640	4,62,020
(b) Zemindaries :—		
1. Cost of management	1,49,462	1,46,216
2. Cost of litigation	1,16,221	1.22,198
Total ...	7,05,323	7,30,434
2. Revenue and Taxes on account of the Zemindaries	2,56,897	2,57,160
3. Public Works :—		
(a) State	1,79,112	3,13,316
(b) Zemindaries	64,655	1,00,105
Total ...	2,43,767	4,13,421
4. Municipality :—		
(a) State	8,725	8,988
5. Education :—		
(a) State	1,19,771	1,23,863
(b) Zemindaries	11,107	11,685
Total ...	1,30,878	1,35,548
6. Medical :—		
(a) State	64,415	1,31,931
(b) Zemindaries	9,496	10,219
Total ...	73,911	1,42,150
7. Survey and Settlement :—		
(a) State	14,368	16,159
(b) Zemindaries	2,116	1,147
Total ...	16,484	17,306
8. Agriculture :—	1,241	1,814
9. Religious Expenses :—		
(a) State	45,725	85,055
(b) Zemindaries	5,984	5,842
Total ...	51,709	90,897
10. Sultanat :—		
(a) State	78,316	1,24,651
11. Purchase of Landed Tenures :—		
(a) State	3,019	2,614
(b) Zemindaries	257	22,091
Total ...	3,276	24,705
12. Pension and Gratuity :—		
(a) State	22,800	18,085
(b) Zemindaries	2,902	3,703
Total ...	25,702	21,848
13. Ordinary *Sansar* charges :—		
(a) Ordinary expenses on account of His Highness and family including Jubraj Bahadur, princes & princesses	1,10,901	1,07,574
(b) Other branches of the Raj family ...	1,46,227	1,56,111
(c) Thakurs	34,994	28,509
(d) *Sansar* office establishment ...	10,154	10,733
(e) Electric Light	40,888	36,751
(f) Miscellaneous	58,942	53,439
Total ...	4,02,106	3,93,117
14. Charity and Donation :—		
(a) State	38,065	73,360
(b) Zemindaries	27,216	27,065
Total ...	65,281	1,00,425
15. His Highness's Nij Tahabil (Privy purse) including expenses on journeys	1,33,304	2,60,371
16. Liabilities liquidated including payment of interest on loans and repayment of deposits :—		
(a) State	88,123	1,07,514
(b) Zemindaries	1,82,717	1,68,322
Total ...	2,70,840	2,75,836
17. Miscellaneous :—		
(a) State	668	3,556
(b) Zemindaries	10,697	20,970
Total ...	11,365	24,526
18. Census	—	37,148
19. Closing Balance :—		
(a) State		
In cash	1,03,286	3,18,757
In bonds and advances	9,06,183	6,86,225
Total ...	10,09,469	10,04,982
(b) Zemindaries :—		
In cash	1,34,334	65,393
In bonds and advances	2,47,248	2,35,893
Total ...	3,81,582	3,01,286
GRAND TOTAL ...	38,70,176	43,66,613

138. It will be seen that the total receipts derived from all sources, including deposits and loans, amounted to Rs. 29,75,562 against Rs. 26,72,728 of the previous year. With the opening balance of Rs. 13,91,051, the total sum available for expenditure was Rs. 43,66,613 against Rs. 38,70,176 of the previous year.

Receipts.

139. The aggregate expenditure during the year amounted to Rs. 30,60,345 against Rs. 24,79,125 of the previous year. The increase is mainly due to (1) the adjustment of old advances (2) payment of outstanding bills of the previous year (3) abnormal expenditure necessitated by the late Maharaja's illness and Sradh, as well as the marriage of one of his daughters, and (4) purchase of Motor Cars and Palace furniture. The closing balance at the end of the year was Rs. 13,06,268 of which Rs. 3,84,150 was in cash and Rs. 9,22,118 in loans and advances. Special attention was paid by the Council of Administration to the adjustment of advances which had accummulated to Rs. 11,53,431 at the commencement of the year. This amount was reduced by Rs. 2,31,313, mostly during the last four months of the year.

Eexpenditure.

140. Important variations are explained below :—

i. ADMINISTRATION CHARGES :—

STATE—The increase is due to the usual grade increments allowed, besides payment of outstanding bills and adjustment of advances.

ZEMINDARIES—The increase is chiefly in respect of the cost of litigation due to the payment of some arrear bills.

ii. PUBLIC WORKS :—

STATE—The increase is due to adjustment of advances, payment of old bills for building materials, and to the contribution paid to the District Board of Tippera for repair of the Akhaura-Agartala Road.

ZEMINDARIES—The increase is mainly due to the thorough repair of the Dharmasagar Houses at Comilla and the electric installation therein.

iii. EDUCATION—

STATE—Increase is due to the grade increments of the teaching staff and purchase of a Motor Bus for the Tulshibati Girl School.

iv MEDICAL :—

STATE—Increase is due to grade increments, expenses incurred for the treatment of His late Highness, and the adjustment of old advances.

v. SURVEY AND SETTLEMENT :—

STATE The increase is due to payment of old outstanding bills.

vi. RELIGIOUS EXPENSES :—

STATE—The increase is due to the expenditure for the Sradha Ceremony of His late Highness and for some special Pujas in connection with his illness, besides some old advances on the latter count adjusted during the year.

vii. SULTANAT :—

STATE—Increase is due to the purchase of extra furniture for the Palace and of Motor Cars and Motor Cycles. A large sum advanced for the purchase of Elephants during the previous year was also adjusted.

viii. PURCHASE OF LANDED PROPERTY :—

ZEMINDARIES—The increase is due to the payment of the price of a house at Brindaban and of an under-tenure in Mogra, purchased some years ago.

ix. ORDINARY SANSAR CHARGES :—

OTHER BRANCHES OF RAJ FAMILY—Incerease is mainly due to adjustment of advances made to the Bara Thakur on account of his allowance.

x. CHARITY AND DONATION :—

STATE—The increase is mainly due to adjustment of advances made previously on this account.

xi. HIS HIGHNESS'S NIJTAHABIL (INCLUDING TOUR EXPENSES) :—

The increase is mainly due to the adjustment of advances made for the touring expenses of His late Highness in 1332 T. E.

xii. LIABILITIES LIQUIDATED :—

STATE—The increase is due to the large amount of deposits repaid and to payment of interest on loans.

xiii. MISCELLANEOUS :—

STATE—The increase is mainly due to the inclusion in the current year's figure certain expenditure incurred in the previous year.

ZEMINDARIES :—The increase is due to purchase of furniture for Calcutta and Comilla Houses and also for incidental expenses on the occasion of His Excellency the Governor's visit to Comilla.

xiv. Marriage :—

STATE—The expenditure is due to the marriage of a Maharaj Kumari.

CHAPTER VI—VITAL STATISTICS.

141. The State maintained 19 Dispensaries in all during the year under review.

142. The comparative statement below shows the total number of new patients treated in the dispensaries as well as their daily average:—

New patients.

PATIENTS.	1332 T.E.			1333 T.E.		
	Outdoor.	Indoor.	Total.	Outdoor.	Indoor.	Total.
	93,100	497	93,597	92,385	429	92·814
Daily average	255·06	1·36	256·42	252·41	1·17	253·58

143. Out-patients treated during the year totalled 1,49,226 as against 1,51,962 in the previous year—the daily average being 408·57 against 416·33.

Outdoor attendance.

144. Inclusive of the last year's balance of 8, indoor patients numbered 429, as against 497 in the preceding year. Of them 285 were discharged cured, 108 were relieved, 26 died, and 10 remained under treatment at the close of the year.

Indoor attendance.

145. Altogether 1,043 operations, with 26 major cases, were performed during the year, as against 792 with 20, in the year before.

Surgical operation.

146. The total number of new out-patients in the V. M. Hospital during the year was 11,310, as against 13,660 in the year before—the average daily attendance (new + old) being 54·6 against 64·50. The in-patients numbered 396 against 461; of them 258 were discharged cured, 106 were relieved, 23 died and 9 remained under treatment at the end of the year.

V. M. Hospital.

147. The total expenditure incurred during the year under report on this institution came up to Rs. 7,456-8, as against Rs. 6,955-12 of the previous year.

448. There were 116 police cases, including 10 postmortem cases, against 111 and 22 respectively of the previous year.

Police cases.

149. As before, three Kavirajes remained under the Ayurvedic Department till about the middle of the year, when the post of the senior Kaviraj was abolished. Altogether 75 patients were treated under the system, as against 85 in the previous year. The total expenditure on account of salaries and medicines in the department amounted to Rs. 6,536-0-0 against Rs. 6,055-2 of the previous year.

Ayurvedic Department.

150. Dr. Hira Lal Banerjee with one Assistant was in charge of the Homœopathic Department. The daily average of patients treated during the year under report was 51·83 aginst 55·61 in the preceding year. The total expenditure incurred on account of this Department was Rs. 5,153-5-3 against Rs. 4,532-2 in the year before.

Homœopathic Department.

151. The number of successful vaccination cases during the season was 4,472 out of 5,737, as against 5,038 out of 6,218. One small-pox Doctor and one Inspector supervised the work of vaccinators in the interior. The total expenditure incurred amounted to Rs. 1,012-1-0 as against Rs. 1,103-6-9.

Vaccination.

152. Dr. M. M. Majumdar, L. M. S., continued as the Chief Medical Officer and Dr. S. K. Dutt, L. M. S., as his Assistant.

Staff.

153. Small-pox and Cholera broke out in the Bisalgarh Division with 31 and 26 cases respectively, of which 16 and 15 proved fatal. Two Doctors including a Homœopath were deputed to the Division on the occasion.

Public health.

154. The total expenditure under the Department was Rs. 1,31,931 as against Rs. 64,415 in the preceding year. The excess is mainly due to payments (inclusive of adjustment of advances) made to different Physicians attending on His late Highness and family during the last three years.

Total Expenditure.

CHAPTER VII—PUBLIC INSTRUCTION.

Charge.

155. Thakur S. C. Dev Barman, M. A. (Harvard) was in charge of the Department.

Number of schools.

156. The number of schools in the year under review was 171 against 173 of the previous year, and the total numerical strength 5,972 against 5,570, excluding private institutions numbering 14 with 458 pupils on the rolls, as against 23 with 491 in the previous year.

H. E. Schools.

157. There were 5 High Schools—the Umakanta Academy at Agartala, the Radhakishore Institution at Kailasahar, the Brojendrakishore Institution at Bilonia, the Birbikram Institution at Dharmanagar and the Sonamura H. E. School—all affiliated to the Calcutta University. The feeder school at Sonamura was allowed to open the Matriculation Class and the Calcutta University was pleased to grant it provisional recognition for two years with effect from 1924 A. D. The teaching staff was considerably strengthened so as to suit the requirements of a fullfledged High School. The number of pupils in these High Schools was 867 against 787 in the previous year, and the average daily attendance stood at 666·90 against 561·28. There were three Boarding houses for the Hindu, Manipuri, and Mahomedan students of the Radhakishore Institution. There were also two similar boarding houses for the Brojendrakishore Institution and the same number for the Birbikram Institution. There was one private Boarding house for Kuki boys at Kailasahar supervised by the authorities of the Radhakishore Institution.

Matriculation Centre.

158. Agartala, the State capital, was as before fixed by the Calcutta University as a Centre for the Matriculation Examination for the year 1924. Only four State H. E. Schools were allowed to send up candidates to this Centre. 48 candidates sat for the examination in the year under report, as against 51 in the previous year, including one female candidate, Kumari Pulina Devi, grand-daughter of Prince Navadwip Chandra Dev Barman, Bahadur, President Council of Administration. The Department looked after the convenience of the candidates coming from Mofussil. The examination was conducted under the direct control and supervision of the Vice-President of the Council.

Results of the Matriculation Examination.

159. Altogether 48 candinates were sent up for the last Matriculation Examination from the four State H. E. Schools against 51 in the previous year. The details of the results are given below.

		No. sent ub.	passed.	1st Division.	2nd Division.	3rd Division.
1.	U. K. Accademy	19	14	10	3	1
2.	R. K. Institution	12	12	9	3	0
3.	B. K. Institution	12	12	7	5	0
4.	B. B. Institution	5	5	2	1	2

It is note-worthy that all the institutions excepting the U. K. Academy have secured cent per cent success. The results achieved by the U. K. Academy also are very fair.

160. There were 35 boarders in the Thakur Boarding House as against 31 in the previous year. Under the orders of the Council of Administration, arrangements were made for the admission of four new boarders, a fact that led to the increase in the numerical strength. All the boarders were successful at the Annual Examination and were promoted to higher classes. This is a hopeful sign. The Staff consisted of one Guardian Superintendent, one Superintending tutor, one Assistant Teacher, and one Manager and teacher.

Thakur Boarding House.

161. The comparative statement below will show the number of Non-Bengalee students receiving education in the several schools of the State :—

Non-Bengalee students.

Serial number.	Nationality.	Number of students.		Remarks.
		Past year.	Present year.	
1.	Thakurs...	138	181	After a marked increase in the previous year the falling off among the number of Tripura boys in the year under review is to be regretted. But the increase in the numerical strength of the Thakur boys is a satisfactory feature.
2.	Manipuris	782	793	
3.	Tripuras...	577	533	
4.	Reangs	21	48	
5.	Kukis	24	26	
6.	Others	87	143	
	Total	1,629	1,724	

162. Owing to various reasons, the examination for the training of teachers could not be arranged during the year under review.

Teachers' Training Examination.

163. The policy of holding the reward examination for the hill people was continued, and 200 boys appeared at the examination against 137 in the previous year. The statement above indicates increased interest in primary education among the hill people.

Reward Examination.

164. The Inspecting staff consisted of one Inspector of Schools and two Sub-Inspectors. The Inspector of Schools and Offices, Thakur S. C. Deb Barman M. A. (Harvard), visited the Kailasahar and the Sonamura Divisions and several Schools at Sadar. The Sub-Inspector of Schools of the Southern Division inspected all the Schools under his jurisdiction. The inspection work of the Sub-Inspector of Schools of the Northern Division was not satisfactory. In the year under review the Political Agent of the State visited the Umakanta Academy and the Thakur Boarding House. Maharajkumar Brojendra kishore Deb Barman Bahadur, Member-in-charge of Education, also paid a visit to the Thakur Boarding House and in company with Rai Lalit Mohan Chatterjee Bahadur M. A. President, Intermediate Board of Education, Dacca, visited the Umakanta Academy. The Inspector of Schools of the Chittagong Division also visited the Umakanta Academy, the Radhakishore Institution and the Sonamura H. E. School, and the Assistant Inspector of Schools of the Chittagong Division visited the Brojendrakishore Institution.

Inspection Work.

165. In the year under review there were 5 M. E. Schools for boys with 541 students on the rolls, as against 453 in the previous year. The average daily attendance was 377·75 against 312·99.

M. E. Schools.

166. There was only one Higher Vernacular School with 45 boys on the rolls, as against 30 in the previons year and an average daily attendance of 32·45 against 22·57.

H. V. Schools.

167. The number of Lower Vernacular Schools for boys was 23 against 22 in the previous year. In some of these schools boys and girls read together. The total numerical strength was 1146 against 1047, and the average daily attendance 849·74 against 772·73 in the previous year.

L. V. Schools.

168. There were 115 pathshalas for boys in the year under report, as against 118 in the previous year. The numerical strength was 2741 against 2624 and the average daily attendance 2000·38 against 1892·40 in the previous year. The number of Pathshalas fell off slightly, but that of students attending remained steady.

Pathshalas.

169. There was one Middle English Schools for girls, namely the Maharani Tulsibati Girls' School. The numerical strength of the school was 93 against 106, and the average daily attendance 67·40 against 75·70 in the previous year. A Motor Bus was used for the girls.

M. E Schools for Girls.

170. There were 11 Pathshalas for girls against the same number in the previous year. The numerical strength was 202 against 190 and the average daily attendance 141·09 against 123·95 in the previous year. Besides these, in some of the Pathshalas for boys, both boys and girls were taught together.

Pathshalas for Girls.

171. Altogether 330 candidates appeared at the local Scholarship Examinations against 331 in the previous year. Of these 279, including 23 girls came out successful. 23 students including one girl passed the Middle English Examination, 2 including one girl passed the Higher Vernacular Examination, 58 including 5 girls passed the Lower Vernacular Examination, and 196 including 16 girls passed the Pathshala Examination. On the result of the examinations, 16 boys and 3 girls received scholarships varying from Rs. 2 to Rs. 5 per month tenable for two to four years.

Scholarship Examination.

172. In the year under review there were 10 Schools for special training consisting of 3 Sanskrit Tols, 6 Madrassas and Moktabs and one Artisan School, against the same number in the previous year. Weaving Classes were attached to the Woodburn Atisan School and to all the Mofussil H. E. Schools. The boys of the U. K. Academy were allowed to attend the Weaving class attached to the Woodburn Artisan School. The Sanskrit Tols had 41 students on the rolls against 35 in the previous year, and the average daily attendance was 29·51 against 29·16. The *Rajakiya Sanskrit Bidyalaya* Agartala sent up 2 candidates to the Government Sanskrit Examination and 3 candidates to the examination held by the Saraswat Samaj. All the candidates came out successful.

Schools for special Training.

The Moktabs and Madrassas had 271 students on the rolls, against 280 in the previous year. The average daily attendance was 216·40 against 221·19. The Woodburn Artisan School had 25 boys on the rolls against 18, and the average daily attendance was 7·55 against 9·03 in the previous year.

Education of Princes and Princesses.

173. The Maharaj Kumars and Kumaris were placed in-charge of two teachers one of whom was a graduate. The Princesses received instruction under a graduate lady teacher and a Pandit.

Education of other Kumars.

174. Kumar Bhupendra Chandra Deb Barman continued his B. A. course in the Comilla Victoria College.

The Palace Day School for the young Kumars.

175. In the day School for the young Kumars there were 7 students on the rolls belonging to the juvenile classes of whom 5 came out successful in the Annual cxamination. A scheme for the establishment of a Boarding for these Kumars is under consideration.

Education of Thakur boys.

176. Nine Thakur boys were awarded stipends from this Department and the course of studies taken up by each is noted below :—

1. Niranjan Deb Barman—The Carmicael Medical College, Calcutta.
2. Surendra Chandra Laskar—B. L.
3. Naresh Chandra Deb Barman—Government School of Art.
4. Jogesh Chandra Deb Barman—B. Com. (Calcutta University).
5. Jaising Deb Barman—B. A.
6. Jitendra Chandra Deb Barman—B. Sc.
7. Kamal Krishna Deb Barman—B. A.
8. Nripendra Chandra Deb Barman—I. Sc.
9. Narendra Chandra Deb Barman—I. A.

177. One Thakur boy passed the I. Sc., Examination in the first division and another I. A. in the third division.

Library.

178. At Agartala the Bir Chandra Library was maintained in two separate sections, (1) The English Library being located at the Ujjayanta Palace and (2) the Vernecular section at the old Guest house Bungalow—the latter being open to the public. The number of English books was 4,846 (excluding manuscripts, against 4,890 (including manuscripts) in the previous year, and the number of Bengali books 1,679 against 1,587 in the previous year. There were 7 dailies, 6 weeklies, 1 quarterly and 10 monthlies as against 6, 8, 0 and 12 in the previous year. In the year under review the average daily attendance of readers was 8·38 against 5·45 and the total number of volumes issued to the public was 1,186 against 1,269 in the previous year.

Expenditure.

179. The total expenditure incurred in the Education Department in the year amounted to Rs. 1,23,863 against Rs. 1,19,771 of the previous year. Some important details of the expenditure are noted below :—

1.	Primary Education	Rs. 29,605
2.	Secondary Education	„ 39,414
3.	Schools for special Training	„ 3,723

4.	Boarding Institution for Thakur boys	„ 8,478
5.	Education of His Highness and other Kumars and Kumaris	„ 31,029
6.	Scholarships & Stipends	„ 5,599
7.	Library	„ 2,355
8.	Miscellaneous	„ 1,067
9.	Grain allowance	„ 2,593
	Total ...	Rs. 1,23,863

180. The annual cost of Primary Education per student was Rs. 6-4-0 while that of Secondary Education was Rs. 45-8-0. The State spends about 10 P. C. of its gross income in education.

CHAPTER VIII—ZEMINDARIES.

Chakla Roshnabad Estates.

181. The management of His Highness's Zemindaries in British India continued in the hands of Rai P. K. Das Gupta Bahadur till 22nd Agrahayan, when he was succeeded by Rai Jyotish Chandra Sen Bahadur, B. A., B. C. S. The Manager was assisted by 3 Assistant Managers and one Sub-Manager.

Management.

182. The gross revenue demand of the year was Rs. 9,59,110 against Rs. 9,54,481 in the previous year.

183. The total receipts amounted to Rs. 11,00,400 against Rs. 19,67,432 in the previous year.

184. The total expenditure in the year under review was Rs. 13,35,958 against Rs. 11,68,859 of the previous year. Of this, Rs. 2,57,160 was on account of land revenue and cesses, leaving a net income of Rs. 8,43,240. The total administration charges of the Zemindaries including public works and law charges, amounted to Rs. 3,94,399. The remainder represents special payments on account of the following items, aggregating Rs. 6,80,016.

Expenditure.

1.	His Highness's private purse ...	Rs. 2,38,371
2.	Repayment of old debts including Nij Tahabil bazar debts ...	„ 1,63,939
3.	Contribution to the State Treasury ...	„ 1,85,000
4.	Donation	„ 2,065
5.	Medical charges	„ 10,219
6.	Education charges	„ 11,685
7.	Religious ceremonies	„ 5,842
8.	Purchase of property	„ 22,091
9.	Sansar stipends	„ 15,804
10.	Contribution for Water Works at Comilla (last instalment) ...	„ 25,000
		Rs. 6,80,016

185. The result of the year's settlement operations will appear from the figures noted below :—

Settlement.

Kinds of settlement.	Addition to rental.	Nazar.
1. Railway relinquished land ...	Rs. 1	Rs. 36
2. *Taskhicki Taluk* in Town ...	„ 11	„ 2,816
3. Ordinary town settlement ...	„ 17	„ 2,262
4. *Khaspatit* settlement ...	„ 634	„ 4.785
5. Enchancement of rent ...	„ 358	„ 11,865
6. Re-settlement of auction purchased holdings ...	„ 140	„ 15,058
7. Assessment of non-rent-paying holdings	„ 25	
8. *Taskhicki Taluk* in the interior	2	„ 325
9. *Ijara*	„ 383	
	Rs. 1,571	Rs. 37,147

186. The year's operations improved the rent roll by Rs. 1,571 and brought in a *nazarana* of Rs. 37,147 against Rs. 3,200 and Rs. 46,914 in the previous year.

CHAPTER IX—MISCELLANEOUS.

187. The literary work connected with the publication of the first two parts of the Rajmala was completed during the year, and a portion of the third part taken in hand. The second part ends with the reign of Maharaja Jai Manikya and the third, with that of Maharaja Kalyan Manikya.

The Rajmala.

188. The first part is being printed in Calcutta, but as a more convenient measure, the installation of a printing press at Agartala for the work is in contemplation The total expenditure incurred during the year for the compilation amounted to Rs. 3,556.

189. Rai P. K. Das Gupta Bahadur, Minister of the State, was out on tour for 52 days during the period preceding his retirement.

Tours.

190. None of the members of the Council could make any tour of inspection during the year, the exigenices of the initial administrative measures demanding their stay at headquarters. Maharajkumar B. K. Dev Barman, however, visited the Kalyanpur and Khowai Divisions, chiefly with a view to shoot a rogue elephant that had been creating a panic in the locality by its wild depradations. The Maharajkumar succeeded in killing the animal.

191. Dewan Asita Chandra Chaudhuri, Officer-in-charge of Revenue, Forest, Agriculture and General Departments was out for 25 days.

192. The tours of the Divisional Officers and their Assistants as well as of other Officers of analogous status are noted below. The

touring of most of the Officers in the State fell short of the prescribed limit, and was, the Council regrets, generally unsatisfactory.

State.

1.	Sadar—	Divisional Officer	...	...	11 days.
		Second "	...	...	3 "
2.	Kailashahar—	Divisional "	...	...	18 "
		Second "	...	...	— "
3.	Sonamura—	Divisional "	...	...	9 "
		Second "	...	...	3 "
4.	Bilonia—	Divisional "	...	...	39 "
		Second "	...	...	16 "
5.	Khowai—	Divisional "	...	...	42 "
6,	Dharmanagar—	" "	...	...	20 "
		Additional "	...	...	10 "
7.	Udaipur—	Divisional "	...	...	24 "
8.	Sabroom—	" "	...	...	55 "
9.	Kalyanpur—	Sub-Divisional "	...	...	24 "
10.	Amarpur—	" "	...	...	6 "
11.	Bishalgarh—	" "	...	...	47 "
12.	Kamalpur—	" "	...	...	25 "
13.	The Forest Officer	... ...	...	...	92 "
14.	The Survey Superintendent	...	...	...	104 "

Zemindaries.

1.	Assistant Manager,	Central Division,	Comilla	..	37 days.
2.	"	Southern "	Feni	...	105 "
3.	"	Northern "	Mogra	...	52 "
4.	Sub-Manager	Srimangal "	...	...	101 "

DATED, AGARTALA, *The 30th September, 1924.* } By order of the Council of Administration,

B. K. Sen,
Chief Secretary.

APPENDIX.

List of the principal Laws and Regulations in force in the Tripura State during 1333 T.E.

Description.	Whether adapted from British Indian Acts.	Whether introduced during the year under report.
CRIMINAL.		
1. Regulation No. III. of 1280 T. E.		
2. Regulation No. I. of 1283 T. E.		
3. Jail Regulation, 1283 T. E.		
4. Regulation No. IV. of 1283 T. E. (Cattle trespass and pound).		
5. Regulation No. III. of 1296 T. E. (Police Regulation).		
6. Act No. IV. of 1321 T. E.–Penal Laws (an amending Act)		
CIVIL.		
1. Civil Law of 1284 T. E.		
2. Rules regarding *chit* suits (small causes) 1287 and 1300 T. E.		
3. Act No. II. of 1313 T. E.—an Act for the regulation of interest on debts.		
4. Act No. II. of 1314 T. E.—Limitation Act	Partly adapted.	
REVENUE.		
1. Act No. I. of 1286 T. E.—Stamp Act		
2. Act No. I. of 1290 T. E.—Sale Law		
3. Act No. I. of 1296 T. E.—Tenancy Act.		
4. Act No. II. of 1296 T. E.—*Abkari*		
5. Act No. II. of 1297 T. E.—Reserved forests.		
6. Act No. I. of 1304 T. E.—Duties on *til* and cotton.		
7. Act No. I. of 1306 T. E.—Registration	Do.	
8. Survey and Settlement Act, 1309 T.E.	Do.	
9. *Tuccavi* Regulation, 1310 T. E.		
10. Act No. I. of 1313 T. E.—Forests.		
11. Act No. I. of 1314 T. E.—(amending the above)		
12. A Law imposing export duty on jute and mustard-seed, 1317 T. E.		
13. Act No. II. of 1321 T.E.—Ghasuri Act		
MISCELLANEOUS.		
1. An Act promulgating certain rules as Law, 1283 T. E.		
2. Regulation for the record of judicial decisions &c., 1284 T. E. ...		
3. Municipal Regulation, 1284 T. E.		
4. Legal Practitioners' Regulation.		
5. Act No. I. of 1297 T. E.—an Act for the regulation of commissions for the examination of witnesses.		
6. Special Regulation against cow slaughter		
7. Rules of evidence		
8. Act I. of 1318 T. E.—Constitution of Courts—(an amending Act).		
9. Leave and allowance Rules	Do.	
10. Act No. I. of 1321 T. E.—Arms Act	Do.	
11. Act No. III. of 1321 T. E.—Constitution of Courts (an amending Act)		

Description.	Whether adapted from British Indian Acts.	Whether introduced during the year under report.
12. Municipal Act No. I of 1322 T. E.		
13. Revenue Sale Amendment Act—1323 T.E.		
14. An Act for the destruction of old records—1323 T.E.		
15. Act I of 1326 T. E.—Regulation regarding Privy Council Appeals.		
16. Act II of 1326 T. E.—Registration of Births and Deaths	Partly adapted.	
17. Act III of 1326 T. E.—Vaccination Act	Do.	
18. Act IV of 1326 T. E.—Public Demands Recovery Act	Do.	
19. Act V of 1326 T. E.—Excise Amendment Act		
20. Act I of 1327 T. E.—Settlement of lands for tea cultivation		
21. Regulation No. 1 of 1328 T. E.—regarding Registration of Coolies		
22. Regulation No. 2 of 1328 T. E.—regarding Export of Tea		
23. Act I of 1329 T. E.—(Absconding sepoys Act)		
24. Act II of 1329 T. E.—(Control of prices of food stuff)		
25. Act III of 1329 T. E.—(Elephants and Buffaloes grazing Act)		
26. Act IV of 1329 T. E.—(House tax on Hill tribes)		
27. Act V of 1329 T. E.—(Legal practitioners, Act)	Do	
28. Act I of 1330 T. E.—Census Act		
29. Act I of 1332 T. E.—Encumbered Estates Act.		
30. Act III of 1332 T. E.—The Opium and Intoxicating Drugs Act.		

II.

Statement showing the strength, cost, and other particulars of the Military Force in Tripura State for 1333 T. E.

Arm of service.	Number of fighting officers and men.						Details of force at the end of the current year.						Total cost on account of pay and allowances of the force, including followers.	Remarks.
	At the end of last year.	Recruited this year.	Casualties.			At the end of the current year.	Number of regiments, battalions, or Batteries.	Number of guns.	Number of men.					
			Died.	Invalided.	Discharged, deserted, &c.				European commissioned officers.	Native commissioned officers.	Non-commissioned officers.	Fighting men.		
1	2	3	4	5	6	7	8	9	10	11	12	13	14	15
Infantry ...	243	46	4	0	46	239	1	291	—	—	51	188	Rs. 42,625	

III.

Statement showing the strength, cost, discipline, and education of the Police for the year 1333 T. E.

Description of office	Number.	Pay of grade.	Total cost.	Punishments. Dismissed.	Punishments. Fined, degraded, or suspended departmentally.	Punishments. Punished judicially.	Rewards. By promotion.	Rewards. By money.	Education. Number able to read and write.	Education. Number under instruction.	Remarks.
1	2	3	4	5	6	7	8	9	10	11	12
		Rs.									
Superintendent	1	150-10-250	Rs. 67,566	—	—	—	—	—	202	—	
Probationer (A. S. P.)	1	—		—	—	—	—	—		1	At Sardah College.
Inspector	4	50 to 80		—	—	—	—	—		—	
Sub-Inspector or Daroga	25	25 to 40		—	1	—	—	6		—	
Naib Daroga	16	15 to 20		—	1	—	—	—		—	
Writer Constable	13	11		—	1	—	—	—		—	
Subadar	1	25		—	—	—	—	—		—	
Jamadar	7	15		—	2	—	—	—		—	
Constable	232	8 to 12		1	30	4	—	2		—	
Chowkidar	175	5		—	—	—	—	—		—	
Spy	3	15		—	—	—	—	—		—	
	478										

IV.

Statement showing the working of the Police in the Tripura State during the year 1333 T.E.

State.	Number of offences.		Number of accused arrested.		Number of accused sent for trial.		Number of accused convicted.		Number of accused acquitted or discharged.		Percentage convicted of accused arrested.		Percentage convicted of accused sent for trial.		REMARKS.
	Past year.	Present year.	Past year.	Present year.	Past year.	Present year.	Past year.	Present year.	Past year.	Present year.	Past year.	Present year.	Past year.	Present year.	
1	2	3	4	5	6	7	8	9	10	11	12	13	14	15	16
Tripura State	1,290	1,222	736	787	661	754	174	195	109	128	23·6	54·6*	61·48	60·1*	* Excluding 122 acquitted on compromise, 39 discharged on withdrawal, 1 dead, 8 deserted and 261 awaiting trial.

N. B.—The result of cases pending from last year has not been shown in this Statement.

V.

Statement showing the value of property stolen and amount of recoveries in the Tripura State during the year 1333 T.E.

State.	Amount stolen.		Amount recovered.		Percentage of recoveries of property stolen.		REMARKS.
	Past year.	Present year.	Past year.	Present year.	Past year.	Present year.	
1	2	3	4	5	6	7	8
Tripura State	Rs 27,980-5-0	Rs 16,958-11-3	Rs 8,854-13-0	Rs 3722-4-9	31·65	22·4	

VI.

Statement showing the number of crimes committed, number of cases disposed of, and cases awaiting trial in the Tripura State during the year 1333 T. E.

Description of offences.		Number of offences. Balance from past year.	Number of offences. Committed during the present year.	Number of offences. Total.	Number of cases disposed of during the past year.	Number of cases disposed of during the present year.	Number of cases awaiting trial.	Number of persons apprehended.	Number of persons convicted.	Number of persons sentenced. Imprisonment. Simple.	Number of persons sentenced. Imprisonment. Rigorous.	Number of persons sentenced. Imprisonment and fine. Simple.	Number of persons sentenced. Imprisonment and fine. Rigorous.	Number of persons sentenced. Fine only.	Number of persons sentenced. Whipping.	Number of persons sentenced. Capital punishment.	Number of persons sentenced. Total.	Number of persons acquitted or discharged.	Number of persons confined being insane.	Number of persons died during or before trial.	Term of imprisonment. Under one month.	Term of imprisonment. From 1 to 2 months.	Term of imprisonment. From 2 to 3 months.	Term of imprisonment. From 3 to 6 months.	Term of imprisonment. From 6 to 12 months.	Term of imprisonment. From 1 to 2 years.	Term of imprisonment. From 2 to 3 years.	Term of imprisonment. From 3 to 5 years.	Term of imprisonment. Above 5 years.	Term of imprisonment. Transportation.	Term of imprisonment. Capital punishment.	Persons awaiting trial.	Remarks.
1		2	3	4	5	6	7	8	9	10	11	12	13	14	15	16	17	18	19	20	21	22	23	24	25	26	27	28	29	30	31	32	33
Class I. Offences against the State, public tranquillity, safety and justice &c.	cognizable ...	20	28	48	39	31	17	151	18	0	7	0	0	11	0	0	18	52	0	3	1	3	0	3	0	0	0	0	0	0	0	78	
	non-cognizable	7	29	36	36	33	3	23	1	0	0	0	0	1	0	0	1	22	0	0	0	0	0	0	0	0	0	0	0	0	0	0	
Class II. Offences against person.	cognizable ...	65	171	236	176	181	55	383	a55	0	21	0	4	29	0	0	54	196	0	0	5	1	4	2	5	1	1	4	2	0	0	132	a. One person imprisoned for life.
	non-cognizable	51	272	323	275	273	50	259	32	0	0	0	1	31	0	0	32	178	0	0	0	1	0	0	0	0	0	0	0	0	0	49	b. Two cases in connection with 12 persons transferred.
Class III. Offences against property.	cognizable ...	301	722	b 1023	698	780	241	b 1336	c282	3	84	0	32	161	0	0	280	735	0	4	47	11	17	22	15	2	4	1	0	0	0	303	c. Two persons have been warned for the future.
	non-cognizable	37	179	216	193	180	36	224	39	0	5	1	0	33	0	0	30	145	0	1	2	4	0	0	0	0	0	0	0	0	0	39	
Class IV. Other offences.	cognizable ...	41	118	159	100	124	35	219	35	0	6	0	4	25	0	0	35	138	0	5	0	5	4	0	1	0	0	0	0	0	0	41	d. One person escaped.
	non-cognizable	66	220	286	204	246	40	d174	15	0	4	0	0	11	0	0	15	143	0	1	1	0	1	1	1	0	0	0	0	0	0	14	
Total cognizable ...	...	427	1039	1466	1013	1116	348	2089	390	3	118	0	40	226	0	0	387	1121	0	12	53	20	25	27	21	3	5	5	2	0	0	554	
Total non-cognizable ...	...	161	700	861	708	732	129	680	87	0	9	1	1	76	0	0	87	488	0	2	3	5	1	1	1	0	0	0	0	0	0	102	
GRAND TOTAL ...	...	588	1739	2327	1721	1848	477	2769	477	3	127	1	41	302	0	0	474	1609	0	14	56	25	26	28	22	3	5	5	2	0	0	656	

VII.

Statement showing the number of offences reported and dealt with by the various Courts in the Tripura State during the year 1333 T.E.

Name of Court.	Number of offences reported during the year.		Number of persons dealt with.								Persons disposed of.					Persons remaining at the end of the year.	Remarks.
				Brought to trial in 1331 T. E.					*Total.*								
	Last year.	Present year.	Remaining at the end of last year.	Arrested by Police.	Upon warrant.	On summons.	Voluntary.	Arrested in presence of the Magistrate.	Last year.	Present year.	Discharged without trial.	Acquitted.	Convicted.	Committed or referred.	Died, escaped, or transferred &c.		
1	2	3	4	5	6	7	8	9	10	11	12	13	14	15	16	17	18
Sadar Magistracy	379	408	140	104	122	153	7	3	621	529	229	107	101	7	3	82	
Sonamura " ...	245	217	137	67	33	77	11	0	300	325	103	85	51	2	1	83	
Bilonia " ...	143	214	89	74	18	99	95	4	215	379	103	75	76	9	4	112	
Kailashahar " ...	156	155	105	69	24	51	50	0	377	299	108	45	17	3	1	125	
Khowai " ...	87	115	3	63	15	56	1	3	103	141	37	50	36	2	3	13	
Dharmanagar " ...	168	204	140	103	36	31	71	0	279	381	78	110	72	10	3	108	
Udaipur " ...	118	127	20	29	18	76	20	0	205	163	54	42	33	0	0	34	
Sabrum " ...	33	23	4	11	7	6	0	0	53	28	9	10	7	0	0	2	
Amarpur " ...	19	21	1	10	0	5	0	5	18	21	5	5	7	0	0	4	
Kalyanpur " ...	31	35	9	15	10	11	3	2	39	50	10	20	19	0	0	1	
Kamalpur " ...	89	90	83	25	22	58	10	0	378	198	47	90	12	4	12	33	
Bisalgarh " ...	137	130	101	72	38	27	13	0	268	251	96	72	35	2	0	46	
TOTAL ...	1,605	1,739	832	642	343	650	281	17	2,855	a 2,765	879	711	466	b 39	27	643	

a Excluding 4 persons pending before the court of Sessions at the close of the previous year.

b Including 4 persons pending from last year, the total number of persons for trial before the Court of Sessions was 43; of these 11 wer econvicted, 19 acquitted and 13 remained under trial.

VIII.

Statement of Criminal cases in which British Subjects were concerned for 1333 T.E.

Description of Offences.		Cases pending since the previous year.	Cases instituted during the year.	Total number of cases.	Cases in which complainants were British subjects.	Cases in which both parties were British subjects.	Cases in which defendants were British Subjects.														Remarks.
							Cases pending since the previous year	Cases instituted during the year.	Total number of cases.	Cases disposed of. Rejected, Compromised or Dismissed without enquiry.	Cases disposed of. Tried.	Cases pending at the close of the year.	Persons under trial at the close of the previous year.	Persons brought to trial during the year.	Total number of persons under trial.	Convicted.	Acquitted or Discharged.	Died, or Escaped &c.	Under trial at the close of the year.	
Class I. Offences against the State &c.	cognizable	6	2	8	0	0	6	2	8	1	1	6	35	7	42a	0	8	1	33	Of this number 109 were discharged without trial, the cases being rejected, compromised or struck off on default. Excluding 2 dead, and 146 pending, the actual number of persons tried was 311, of whom 161 or 51·8006 were convicted as against 51·98 of the previous year.
	non-cognizable ...	0	1	1	1	0	0	0	0	0	0	0	0	0	0	0	0	0	0	
Class II. Offences against person.	cognizable	10	34	44	14	4	10	20	30	9	10	11	9	21	30	7	10	0	13	
	non-cognizable ...	9	47	56	12	27	9	35	44	30	5	9	15	17	32	3	23	0	6	
Class III. Offences against property.	cognizable	89	233	322	22	91	88	212	300	95	126	79	94	259	353	123	149	1	80	
	non-cognizable ...	9	37	46	8	21	9	29	38	23	9	6	12	48	60	19	34	0	7	
Class IV Other offences.	cognizable	5	22	27	7	4	5	15	20	8	7	5	8	17	25	7	14	0	4	
	non-cognizable ...	15	35	50	7	20	14	29	43	30	5	8	6	20	26	2	21	0	3	
Total cognizable ...		110	291	401	43	99	109	249	358	113	144	101	146	304	450	137	181	2	130	
Total non-cognizable ...		33	120	153	28	68	32	93	125	83	19	23	33	85	118	24	78	0	16	
GRAND TOTAL ...		143	411	554	71	167	141	342	483	196	163	124	179	389	568*	161	259	2	146	

IX.

Statement of Extradition Cases for 1333 T.E.

Names of Courts.	Nature of cases.	Number of persons against whom warrants were applied for.	Number of persons arrested and surrendered.	Number of persons who appeared of their own accord or were subsequently arrested within this territory.	Number at large at the close of the year.	Result.		Pending trial at the close of the year.	Remarks.
						Convicted.	Acquitted or Discharged.		
Sadar Magistracy ...	Criminal breach of trust ...	3	0	2	1	0	2	0	
	Cheating ...	1	0	1	0	0	0	1	
	Criminal breach of trust ...	1	0	1	0	0	1	0	
	Dacoity ...	2	0	2	0	0	0	2	
Sonamura „ ...	Voluntarily causing grievous hurt ...	3	0	3	0	0	0	3	
	Theft of forest produce ...	1	0	0	1	0	0	0	
Bilonia „ ...	Theft of forest produce ...	2	0	2	0	2	0	0	
	Theft of forest produce causing grievous hurt ...	6	4	0	2	4	0	0	
	Theft of forest produce ...	2	1	1	0	0	0	2	
	Theft of forest produce ...	5	0	5	0	0	0	5	
Kailashahar „ ...	Voluntarily causing grievous hurt ...	3	3	0	0	0	3	0	
	Culpable homicide not amounting to murder ...	1	0	0	1	0	0	0	
	Escape from lawful custody ...	1	0	0	1	0	0	0	
	Theft ...	1	0	0	1	0	0	0	
Dharmanagar „ ...	Theft ...	1	1	0	0	0	0	1	
	Theft ...	1	1	0	0	0	0	1	
	Theft ...	1	1	0	0	0	0	1	
	Theft ...	1	1	0	0	0	0	1	
	Theft ...	1	1	0	0	0	0	1	
	Voluntarily causing hurt by dangerous weapons or means ...	1	1	0	0	0	0	1	
	Voluntarily causing hurt by dangerous weapons or means ...	1	0	0	1	0	0	0	
	Theft and receiving stolen property ...	1	0	0	1	0	0	0	
Udaipur „ ...	Criminal breach of trust by servant... ...	2	2	0	0	2	0	0	
	Receiving stolen property ...	1	1	0	0	1	0	0	
	Theft ...	1	0	1	0	1	0	0	
	Theft ...	2	0	2	0	0	2	0	
Amarpur „ ...	Theft ...	5	0	0	5	0	0	0	
	Robbery ...	4	0	0	4	0	0	0	
	Total ...	55	17	20	18	10	8	19	

X.

Statement showing the results of appeals against decisions passed by the Criminal Courts in the Tripura State during the year 1333 T. E.

Tribunals.	Number of applications.	Number of persons and cases.																Remarks.
		Applications rejected.		Sentences.						Proceedings quashed.		Referred.		Further enquiry, &c, ordered.		Pending.		
				Confirmed.		Modified.		Reversed.										
		Persons.	Cases.	Persons.	Cases.	Persons.	Cases.	Persons.	Cases.	Persons.	Cases.	Persons.	Cases.	Persons.	Cases.	Persons.	Cases.	
Khas Adalat. ...	222	15	14	126	120	28	18	74	48	—	—	—	—	9	9	13	13	

XI.

Civil Work.—Nature and value of original suits filed and disposed of during the year 1333 T. E.

Tribunal.	Opening balance. Past year.	Opening balance. Present year.	Filed during the year, received by transfer or on remand. Past year.	Filed during the year, received by transfer or on remand. Present year.	Total. Past year.	Total. Present year.	Disposed of during the year. Past year.	Disposed of during the year. Present year.	Closing balance. Past year.	Closing balance. Present year.	Suits filed during present year. Value.	Suits re landed property.	Suits for money transaction.	Suits for other rights.	Number of suits under Rs. 100.	Number of suits above Rs. 100 and under Rs. 500.	Number of suits above Rs. 500 and under Rs. 1,000.	Number of suits above Rs. 1,000 and under Rs. 5,000.	Number of suits above Rs. 5000.	Suits disposed of during present year. Exparte.	Admitted and compromised.	Struck off the file.	Otherwise disposed of.	Value.	Average duration.	Suits not estimable in money.	Remarks.
											Rs. a. p.													Rs. a. p.	Y. m. d.		
Khas Adalat Original side	16	67	91	19	107	86	40	31	67	55	28,260-4-0	10	2	7	2	0	1	10	1	2	5	3	21	6,772-0-0	0-4-0	5	
Sadar Dewani Adalat	363	271	481	463	a844	734	523	489	271	245	38,527-15-3	171	214	73	397	70	3	0	0	155	97	147	90	32,250-10-9	0-6-17	83	
Sonamura ,,	95	106	331	252	426	358	320	245	106	113	12,916-8-6	125	99	28	171	49	3	0	0	69	20	88	68	11,965-10-3	0-8-5	29	
Bilonia ,,	38	58	129	110	167	168	109	127	58	41	4,814-7-6	64	25	21	78	10	0	0	0	60	9	28	30	5,053-10-9	0-6-27	22	
Kailashahar ,,	117	103	195	217	312	320	209	160	103	160	13,603-8-6	127	77	13	153	27	2	0	0	28	20	40	72	10,609-11-3	0-4-11	35	
Khowai ,,	20	27	98	68	118	95	91	82	27	13	4,428-13-3	10	46	12	48	7	1	0	0	20	14	7	41	5,102-4-3	0-0-14	12	
Dharmanagar ,,	78	98	153	132	231	230	133	149	98	81	6,937-2-6	10	38	84	88	20	0	1	0	23	35	26	65	8,138-7-9	0-6-8	23	
Udaipur ,,	49	40	190	227	239	267	199	237	40	30	18,035-7-3	17	207	3	163	48	2	0	0	63	93	31	50	18,796-3-6	0-3-3	14	
Sabrum ,,	2	1	14	15	16	16	15	14	1	2	1,212-12-0	0	14	1	10	5	0	0	0	6	4	3	1	872-15-0	0-1-17	0	
Amarpur ,,	4	4	9	15	13	19	9	16	4	3	2,295-0-6	2	11	2	6	9	0	0	0	5	8	0	3	2,197-6-3	0-5-0	0	
Kalyanpur ,,	4	6	26	9	30	15	24	14	6	1	596-0-0	1	5	3	4	2	0	0	0	0	0	3	11	376-0-0	0-2-17	3	
Kamalpur ,,	36	53	123	141	159	194	106	104	53	90	9181-5-0	18	88	35	99	23	2	0	0	42	21	15	26	6,682-9-6	0-5-12	17	
Bisalgarh ,,	252	153	183	195	435	348	232	236	153	112	12,870-0-0	75	91	29	126	36	3	0	0	49	29	59	99	18,258-11-6	0-4-28	30	
Total ...	1,074	987	2,023	1,863	3,097	2,850	2,060	1,904	987	946	1,53,729-4-3	630	917	316	1255	306	17	11	1	522	355	450	577	1,27,076-4-9	0-4-16	273	

a. 50 cases transferred.

XII.

Civil Work.—Results of applications for Execution of Decrees, 1333 T.E.

Tribunal.	Opening balance.		Value of opening balance for present year.	Applications brought to the Register.			Total.			Disposed of.			Closing balance.			Nature of applications pending disposal at the close of the year.			REMARKS.
	Past year.	Present year.		Past year.	Present year.	Value for present year.	Past year.	Present year.	Value for present year.	Past year.	Present year.	Value for present year.	Past year.	Present year.	Value for present year.	Below 6 months.	Below 12 months.	Above 12 months.	
			Rs. a. p.			*Rs. a. p.*			*Rs. a. p.*			*Rs. a. p.*			*Rs. a. p.*				
Khas Adalat (Original side)	13	19	35,783-0-9	7	12	29,145-0-6	20	31	64,928-1-3	1	10	13,744-3-3	19	21	51,18[illegible]-14-0	6	4	11	
Sadar Dewani Adalat ...	183	179	22,875-7-6	177	147	13,956-7-3	a. 360	b. 326	36,831-14-9	180	17	18,372-7-6	179	148	18,396-13-6	44	14	90	
Sonamura Ditto ...	44	55	3,712-13-3	88	144	8,155-12-0	132	199	11,868-9-3	77	150	7,032-14-0	55	49	4,835-11-3	38	11	0	*a.* 1 application transferred.
Bilonia Ditto ...	22	30	4,351-2-6	40	40	3,488-13-6	62	70	7,840-0-0	32	46	5,214-7-3	30	24	2,625-8-9	14	3	7	
Kailashahar Ditto ...	46	50	8,338-10-3	88	69	8,000-5-0	134	118	16,338-15-3	84	58	4,962-6-9	50	60	11,376-8-6	21	21	18	*b.* 1 application tranferred to Bishalgarh with value of Rs. 62-9-9.
Khowai Ditto ...	2	7	537-12-0	24	17	1,434-10-9	26	c. 24	1,972-6-9	19	17	1,447-12-9	7	5	193-2-6	5	0	0	
Dharmanagar Ditto ...	55	63	8,771-10-0	38	25	5,394-5-9	93	88	14,165-15-9	30	42	5,773-10-6	63	46	8,392-5-3	10	6	30	
Udaipur Ditto ...	30	39	4,930-3-0	97	99	12,666-11-9	127	138	17,596-14-9	88	115	13,138-9-3	39	23	4,458-5-6	17	1	5	*c.* 2 applications valued at Rs. 331-7-6 transferred to Kalyanpur.
Sabrum Ditto ...	0	0	0	3	5	285-7-9	3	5	285-7-9	3	4	237-11-0	0	1	47-12-9	1	0	0	
Amarpur Ditto ...	1	1	64-13-6	4	8	663-7-9	5	9	728-5-3	4	6	444-5-6	1	3	283-15-9	3	0	0	
Kalyanpur Ditto ...	0	6	700-11-9	9	12	1,082-10-9	9	18	1,783-6-6	3	14	1,251-9-3	6	4	528-13-3	4	0	0	
Kamalpur Ditto ...	26	32	5,142-10-9	44	[illegible]	3,369-9-6	70	73	8,512-4-3	38	38	4,958-5-6	32	35	3,553-14-9	26	4	5	
Bisalgarh Ditto ...	42	57	4,091-13-0	59	[illegible]	14,974-2-9	101	127	19,065-15-9	44	90	12,245-7-3	57	37	6,820-3-6	18	12	7	
Total ...	404	538	93,300-12-3	678	603	1,02,617-9-0	1,142	1,226	2,01,918-5-3	603	767	88,826-13-9	538	456	1,12,697-6-3	207	76	173	

XIII.

Civil Work.—Number and results of appeals in civil suits, 1333 T. E.

Tribunal.	Opening balance.		Filed during.		Total.		Disposed of during.		Closing balance.		Value of appeals filed during.		How disposed of.										Average duration.	
													Decisions confirmed.		Decisions reversed.		Decisions amended.		Cases remanded for retrial.		Cases compromised and otherwise disposed of.			
	Past year.	Present year.	Past year.	Present year.	Past year.	Present year.	Past year.	Present year.	Past year.	Present year.	Past year.	Present year.	Past year.	Present year.	Past year.	Present year.	Past year.	Present year.	Past year.	Present year.	Past year.	Present year.	Past year.	Present year.
											Rs. a. p.	Rs. a. p.											Y.m.d.	Y.m.d.
Khas Adalat	25	41	148	156	173	197	132	165	41	32	7,447-10-6	8,684-13-9	71	93	36	49	3	6	7	4	15	13	0-2-10	0-2-5

XIV.

Statement showing the number of persons confined in the jails and lock-ups in the Tripura State during the year 1333 T.E.

Stations.	Number of prisons.	NUMBER OF PRISONERS.				DAILY AVERAGE.		Number of prisoners remaining at the end of the year.	Cost of jail and prisoners.	Average period in days of accused under trial.	Remarks showing mortality among convicts in jail.
		Remaining from last year.	Admitted during the year.	*Total.* Past year.	*Total.* Present year.	Past year.	Present year.		Rs. a. p.		
Agartala	1	70	229	345	299	73·29	67·96	62	9,409-9-9	87	One convict died of Dysentery in the central jail.
Sonamura	1	7	39	60	41	7·17	3·53	2	479-13 9	41·13	
Bilonia	1	—	67	46	67	·09	·09	1	311-13-0	11·37	
Kailashahar	1	4	43	67	47	3·08	2·45	—	425-12-3	19·93	
Khowai	1	3	39	33	42	1·62	1·84	1	327-15-0	21·08	
Dharmanagar	1	3	108	96	111	6·97	9·64	8	1,135-1-3	40·77	
Udaipur	1	4	35	44	39	3·02	2·34	2	288-15-9	19·04	
Sabrum	1	1	14	16	15	1·33	·55	2	181-1-9	15·09	
Kalyanpur	1	—	13	2	13	·06	·20	—	152-0-0	4·08	
Amarpur	1	—	10	7	10	·01	·02	—	163-14-6	20·33	
Bishalgar	1	—	47	23	47	·82	1·21	—	127-15-0	7·38	
Kamalpore	1	2	16	25	18	1·26	2·29	—	301-8-9	61·89	
TOTAL ...	12	89	660	764	749	98·72	92·12	78	13,305-8-9	29·09	

XV.

Registration of documents in the Tripura State during the year 1333 T.E.

Name of State.	Documents presented for registration.		Nature of documents presented.										Documents registered.		Value of documents registered.		Documents of which registration has been refused.		Documents remaining unregistered at the end of the year.		Remarks.
			Mortgages.		Sale deeds.		Wills.		Money bonds.		Miscellaneous.										
	Past year.	Present year.	Past year.	Present year.	Past year.	Present year.	Past year.	Present year.	Past year.	Present year.	Past year.	Present year.	Past year.	Present year.	Past year.	Present year.	Past year.	Present year.	Past year.	Present year.	
1	2	3	4	5	6	7	8	9	10	11	12	13	14	15	16	17	18	19	20	21	22
															Rs.	*Rs.*					
Tripura State	8,665	9,040	2,494	2,320	4,178	4,388	2	6	245	207	1,746	2,119	8,571	8,907	12,64,384	11,62,103	106	128	53	58	

XVI.

Statement showing the receipts and expenditure on account of Registration during the year 1333 T.E.

Description.	Past Year.			Present Year.			Remarks.
	Number of deeds.	Value of property.	Fees realised.	Number of deeds.	Value of property.	Fees realised.	
		Rs.	Rs.		Rs.	Rs.	
Mortgages	2,494	3,03,109	2,312	2,320	2,46,731	2,134	
Sale deeds	4,178	6,64,817	4,676	4,388	6,23,981	5,115	
Will	2	—	11	6	--	41	
Money bonds	245	22,023	188	207	27,096	190	
Miscellaneous	1,746	3,00,021	2,428	2,119	3,04,111	2,764	
Total ...	8,665	12,89,970	9,615	9,040	12,01,919	10,244	
Total Expenditure ...	—	—	3,318	—	—	3,445	
Net Income ...	—	—	6,297	—	—	6,799	

XVII.

Receipts and expenditure of the Municipalities in the Tripura State during the year 1333 T.E.

NAME.	Opening balance.	RECEIPTS DURING THE YEAR.					Total in the current year.	EXPENDITURE DURING THE YEAR.		Balance at the close of the year.	REMARKS.
		Past.	Present.					Past.	Present.		
			State grant.	Tax.	Miscel-laneous.	Total.					
1	2	3	4	5	6	7	8	9	10	11	12
	Rs. A.P.	Rs. A.P.	Rs. A.P.	Rs. A.P.	Rs. A.P.	Rs. A.P.	Rs. A.P.	Rs. A.P.	Rs. A.P.	Rs. A.P.	
Agartala Municipality. ...	7,277-14-9	22,226-13-9	8,986-10-0	3,879-2-0	7,634-12-9 a	20,500-8-9	27,778-7-6	14,948-15-0	16,194-14-0 b	11,583-9-6 c	a. Including Rs. 5,891-13 as Bazar income and Rs. 611-9 as deposits and advances. b. Including Rs. 1,090-4-6 as Bazar expense and Rs. 408-9 as deposits and advances paid. c. Including Rs. 10,562-6-9 as Bazar balance.

XVIII.

Statement of rainfall in the Tripura State during the year 1333 T.E.

STATE.	Baisak.	Jaisth.	Asar.	Sravan.	Bhadra.	Asvin.	Kartik.	Agrahayan.	Pous.	Magh.	Falgoon.	Chait.	Total.	Total of past year.	Average of past 5 years.	REMARKS.
Tripura State ...	7·26	17·25	15·81	16·48	14·43	6·61	·91	·81	·11	·88	—	1·03	81·58	87·83	89·95	

XIX.

Statement as to the prices of staple food-grains for the year 1333 T.E.

Article.	During Chait (past year).			During Chait (present year).			REMARKS.
	Rs.	*a.*	*p.*	*Rs.*	*a.*	*p.*	
(1) RICE							
Maximum	8	0	0	6	8	0	
Minimum	3	5	0	4	0	0	
(2) PADDY							
Maximum	3	12	0	3	12	0	
Minimum	1	0	0	2	0	0	

XX

Expenditure on Public Works during the year 1333 T.E.

Description of work.	State Funds.			Local Funds.			Total.	Remarks.
	Original.	Repairs.	Total.	Original.	Repairs.	Total.		
	Rs.	*Rs.*	*Rs.*	*Rs.*	*Rs.*	*Rs.*	*Rs.*	
Tanks in different parts of the State	673	2,051	2,724	—	—	—	2,724	(a) See below.
Roads and bridges ...	21,416	27,730	49,146	—	—	—	49,146	
Buildings	1,43,588	55,990	1,99,578	1,500	—	1,500	2,01,078	
Miscellaneous works ...	1,589	1,326	2,915	—	—	—	2,915	
Total ...	1,67,266	87,097	2,54,363	1,500	—	1,500	2,55,863	
Minor works at the Rajbari	—	7,833	7,833	—	—	—	7,833	
Establishment charges ...	—	—	15,823	—	—	—	15,823	
Grand Total ...	1,67,266	94,930	2,78,019	1,500	—	1,500	2,79,519(a)	

(a) In addition to this, the following payments were made for works executed in the previous year.

		Rs.
Roads and Bridges	Original works	13,783
	Repair works	2,228
Buildings	Original works	7,801
	Repair works	9,943
Miscellaneous	Original works	740
	Repair works	40
Water supply	New-excavation	316
	Re-excavation	141
	Total ...	Rs. 34,992

XXI.

Statement showing the excise shops and excise revenue of the Tripura State during the year 1333 T.E.

Name of State.	Country spirit.		Country spirit, Opium and Ganja.		Ganja and Opium.		Tari.		Total.		Remarks.
	Number of shops.	Revenue.	Number of shops.	Revenue.	Number of shops.	Revenue.	Number of shops.	Revenue.	Number of shops.	Revenue.	
		Rs.		Rs.		Rs.		Rs.		Rs.	
Tripura State	—	—	25	47,547	—	—	—	—	25*	47,547†	

* Two shops in Sadar Division deal in liquor and Ganja only.

† By resettlement of shops during the year, there was an increase in revenue of Rs. 10,695 over that of the previous year.

XXII.

Statement of Medical Relief afforded in the Tripura State during the year 1333 T.E.

Dispensary.	Number of Patients Treated. (new)		Results of In-door Patients. (new)				Expenditure.	Daily Average. (old + new)			No. of Surgical Operations Performed.			No. of Persons Vaccinated During the Year.			Remarks.
	Outdoor.	Indoor.	Dis-charged.	Absented.	Died.	Remain-ing under treatment.		Outdoor.	Indoor.	Total.	Major.	Minor.	Total.	Success-fully.	Unsuc-cessfully.	Total.	
							Rs. a. p.										
1. Victoria Memorial Hospital at Agartala and the Charitable Dispensary attached to it	11,310	306	258	106	23	9	7,456-8-0	51·6	15·2	69·8	24	92	116	399	188	587	*This figure shows the actual number of outdoor patients treated, the total outdoor attendance during the year being 1,49,226 against 1,51,962 in the previous year.
2. Palace Dispensary	6,115	0	0	0	0	0	11,915-12-0	27·68	0	27·68	0	0	0	0	0	0	
3 Homoeopathic	12,333	0	0	0	0	0	5,153-5 3	51·83	0	51·83	0	0	0	0	0	0	
4. Old Agartala	6,448	0	0	0	0	0	1,501-14-6	34·54	0	34·54	0	32	32	257	122	379	
5. Bishalgar	3,063	0	0	0	0	0	980-13-9	12·71	0	12·71	0	41	41	417	24	441	
6. Sonamura	7,365	4	3	0	0	1	1,248-7-0	35·74	·17	35·91	0	86	86	252	85	337	
7. Udaipur	5,004	9	9	0	0	0	1,090-6-0	18·91	·41	19·32	1	71	72	260	62	322	
8. Amarpur	2,612	0	0	0	0	0	963-1-9	8·21	0	8·21	0	21	21	414	93	507	
9. Bilonia...	4,179	0	0	0	0	0	1,172-13-9	18·77	0	18·77	0	65	65	538	97	635	
10. Loongthung	1,882	0	0	0	0	0	868-10-3	13·45	0	13·45	0	36	36	374	35	409	
11. Sabroom	1,348	0	0	0	0	0	842-10-3	5·65	0	5·65	0	8	8	91	51	142	
12. Khowai	3,892	0	0	0	0	0	1,258-4-6	15·62	0	15·62	0	151	151	170	214	384	
13. Kalyanpur	1,265	0	0	0	0	0	927-15-6	5·63	0	5·63	0	9	9	268	32	300	
14. Kailashahar	11,740	4	2	0	0	0	1,313-11-9	38·6	·19	38·79	1	176	177	80	33	113	
15. Kamalpur	4,071	2	1	0	1	0	991-12-0	14·64	·01	14·65	0	52	52	210	43	253	
16. Dharmanagar	3,669	14	12	2	2	0	1,209-15-0	18·03	·41	18·44	0	71	71	330	140	470	
17. Fatik-roy	2,693	0	0	0	0	0	1,010-8-3	14·29	0	14·29	0	47	47	197	34	231	
18. Birendranagar	954	0	0	0	0	0	497-6-3	4,74	0	4·74	0	0	0	20	7	27	
19. Mohanpur	2,442	0	0	0	0	0	504-9-6	14·93	0	14·93	0	59	59	195	5	200	
Total	*92,385	429	285	108	26	10	40,998-9-3	408·57	16·30	424·96	26	1,017	1,043	4,472	1,265	5,737	

XXIII.

Vital statistics of the Tripura State for the year 1333 T.E.

State.	Population.	Births.		Increase.	Decrease.	Deaths.		Increase.	Decrease.	Ratio per 1,000 of population.				Remarks.
										Births.		Deaths.		
		Past year.	Present year.			Past year.	Present year.			Past year.	Present year.	Past year.	Present year.	
Tripura State ...	3,04,437	2,317	2,547	230	—	2,540	2,428	—	112	7·6	8·3	8·3	7·9	

XXIV.

Education Return (A)—Particulars as to the schools maintained during the year 1333 T.E.

Number of Schools.		Description of Schools.	Number of pupils on the rolls on the last day of Chait.		Daily average attendance.		Remarks.
Past year.	Present year.		Past year.	Present year.	Past year.	Present year.	
5	5	High English Schools	787	867	561'28	666'90	
5	5	Middle English Schools for boys ...	453	541	312'99	377'75	
1	1	Middle English School for girls ...	106	93	75'70	67'40	
1	1	Higher Vernacular School for boys	30	45	22'57	32'45	* In some of these schools boys and girls read together.
22	23	Lower Vernacular Schools for boys	1,047	1,146	772'73	849'74	
118	115	Pathsalas for boys	2,624	2,741	1,892'40	2,000'38	
11	11	Do for girls	190	202	123'95	141'09	
		Special Schools :—					
6	6	Madrassa	280	271	221'19	216'40	
3	3	Sanskrit *Tol*	35	41	29'16	29'51	
1	1	Woodburn Artisan School... ...	18	25	9'03	7'55	
TOTAL 173	171		5,570	5,972	4,021'00	4,389'17	

XXV.

Education Return (B) Race of Students, 1333 T. E.

Names of Divisions.	No. of Schools.			No. of Students.			Race.									Average daily attendance.		Remarks.
												Bengalee.						
	For boys.	For girls.	Total.	Boys.	Girls.	Total.	Thakurs.	Manipuris	Tripuras.	Reangs.	Kukis.	Hindus.	Musalmans.	Christians.	Others.	Boys.	Girls.	
1. Sadar Division ...	42	3	45	1,334	150	1,484	165	176	138	2	20	676	283	3	21	1048·93	89·24	
2. Kailashahar „	17	2	19	885	126	1,011	0	295	5	4	6	474	143	0	84	648·64	90·28	
3. Sonamura „	21	1	22	792	61	853	0	0	36	0	0	228	589	0	0	593·59	46·04	
4. Bilonia „	13	1	14	668	27	695	0	0	15	15	0	466	199	0	0	490·16	20·85	
5. Khowai „	9	1	10	189	13	202	0	20	95	0	0	58	15	0	14	123·23	10·12	
6. Dharmanagar „	14	1	15	546	37	583	0	118	0	0	0	371	92	1	1	311·04	87·94	
7. Udaipur „	5	1	6	209	12	221	0	0	0	0	0	114	107	0	0	162·52	9·43	
8. Sabrum „	8	0	8	108	8	116	0	0	41	0	0	56	19	0	0	107·00	3·00	
9. Amarpur Sub-division ...	3	0	3	49	2	51	3	0	16	27	0	4	0	0	1	35·74	1·09	
10. Kalyanpur „	4	0	4	71	0	71	0	9	62	0	0	0	0	0	0	39·18	0	
11. Kamalpur „	6	1	7	257	31	288	0	155	12	0	0	69	30	0	22	164·46	17·96	
12. Bisalghar „	17	1	18	374	23	397	13	20	113	0	0	71	180	0	0	272·24	16·49	
TOTAL ...	159	12	171	5,482	490	5,972	181	793	533	48	26	2,587	1,657	4	143	3,996·73	392·44	

XXVI.

Statement showing the distribution of Portfolios among the members of the Council of Administration, Tripura State, 1333 T. E.

Members.	Departments allotted to Portfolios.	REMARKS.
President	1. Judicial. 2. Sultanat. 3. Sansar. 4. Nij Tahabil.	
Vice-President	1. Political and Appointment. 2. Police. 3. Revenue and General. 4. Agriculture. 5. Forest. 6. Accounts and Audit. 7. Treasury and Stamps. 8. Chakla Roshnabad Estates and other Zemindaries.	
Maharajkumar B. K. Dev Barman ...	1. Jail. 2. Education and Rajmala. 3. Medical and Sanitation. 4. Military. 5. Public Works. 6. Zoo.	
Thakur P. C. Roy	1. Pilkhana and Stables. 2. Tosakhana. 3. Guest House. 4. Registration. 5. Press, Forms, Stationery, Gazette and Record Room. 6. Municipality.	

Book Seventeen
Report on the General Administration of the Tripura State for the year 1334 T. E. (1924-1925 A.D.)

REPORT ON THE ADMINISTRATION OF THE TRIPURA STATE. FOR 1334 T. E. (1924-25.)

CHAPTER I—GENERAL AND POLITICAL.

Area of the State—4,116 *sq. miles.*
Population—3,04,437.
Gross Revenue (*based on the average of the previous five years*) :—
(*a*) State ... ... Rs. 13,83,021.
(*b*) Zemindaries ... ... Rs. 11,33,017.
Tribute—Nil.
Ruler of the State—His Highness The Bisama-Samara-Bijayee Mahamahodaya Pancha-Srijukta Maharaja Manikya Bir Bikramkishore Dev Barman Bahadur. *Age*—17 years. (Born—19th August, 1908). *Caste*—Kshatriya (of the Lunar race).

The weather conditions.

1. The aggregate rainfall of the year exceeded the previous year's record, and although not abnormally off the average taking the State as a whole, was characterised by marked local variations, which seriously affected the output of the cotton crop, and hampered the export of forest produce through water routes. The result was a substantial falling off of the receipts under the connected heads, which was only partially compensated by better collections of land revenue, consequent mainly on high prices of food grains and the improved paying capacity of the tenantry.

The finances of the year.

2. The expenditure however kept pace with the income, leaving an increased cash balance, which was Rs. 1,35,489 ahead of the figure for the preceding year. The committee appointed to investigate the liabilities of the State, settled the claims scrutinised by it during the year at Rs. 14,52,607 ; and with Rs. 1,09,783 sanctioned previously, the figure accepted by the Council of Administration as representing the total liabilities at the death of the late Ruler, stood, exclusive of deposits, at Rs. 15,62,390. To expedite outside payment, the co-operation of the Dowager Maharanees was secured, and Their Highnesses, in a commendable spirit, deposited Rs. 2,03,000 in the treasury, at a low rate of interest. Altogether claims to the extent of Rs. 7,02,888 were paid up during the year ; and with Rs. 1,08,141 already paid, the total amount of liabilities liquidated up to the end of the year, came to Rs. 8,11,029 excluding deposits repaid, and to Rs. 11,28,776, including deposits.

3. The expenditure on Public Works amounted to Rs. 3,55,101, and that on Public Instruction to Rs. 1,09,931. A special expenditure

of Rs. 15,173, had to be incurred on account of the marriage ceremony referred to in para 9 below, while charitable grants were made, during the year, to the extent of Rs. 22,207. The Council also paid about Rs. 45,000 as allowance to the ministerial and menial establishment for dearness of provision.

4. Another noticeable feature of the financial administration was the rapid adjustment of old advances, which was vigorously pushed on, the previous year's balance being reduced by as much as Rs. 5,0,0574.

The Akhaura Road.

5. The question of the improvement of the Akhaura-Agartala road, a part of which is in British territory, formed the subject matter of negotiations between the Council and the District Board of Tippera, and an agreement has since been arrived at. The stone-metalling of the State portion of the road was completed during the year.

The Maharaja's Education.

6. His Highness the Maharaja's administrative training commenced during the year, under the supervision of Lt. Col. O. C. Pulley, Guardian Tutor, and with the active co-operation of Mr. A. J. Dash, I. C. S., who continued to be the Political Agent of the State. As before, His Highness's headquarters were at Comilla during the winter and at Shillong during the summer. His Highness was assisted in his studies, during the Comilla season, by Babu Brajendra Kumar Chatterjee, M. A., B. L., Assistant Manager, Chakla Zemindaries, and later on by Babu Kamala Prasad Dutt, M. A., B. L., Officer in charge of the Accounts and other Departments of the State.

His Highness's movements.

7. In pursuance of the scheme for practical training, His Highness accompanied the Political Agent on the 8th January, 1925, in a tour of inspection in the border of the Tippera district, and spent a period of about ten days, till the 17th idem, in a river trip, which proved as pleasant as it was instructive.

8. There was also a tour in the interior of the State for 10 days, in the course of which Sonamura was visited on the 25th January, and the Udaipur Division, from the 26th January to the 3rd February, 1925. His Highness, who was accompanied by Mr. A. J. Dash, I. C. S., Political Agent, Lt. Colonel O. C. Pulley, Guardian Tutor, and Dewan B. K. Sen, Chief Secretary, was accorded a most cordial reception. He met and mixed freely with all sections of the people, including hill clans under their head men, and gave suitable replies to the addresses presented, taking part at the same time in the inspection of offices and institutions, and attending a number of interesting functions arranged on the occasion. The visit to the ruins of the old capital excited special interest, and some shooting excursions proved most enjoyable. His Highness entertained the hill people at a feast, and gave some presents to the leading institutions of Udaipur as souvenirs of his first tour.

Notable events.

9. A noticeable event at the Palace was the marriage of a daughter of the late Maharaja, celebrated on the 13th February, 1925, with a son of Uzir Braja Krishana Dev Barman Bahadur of Agartala.

CHAPTER II—LAND ADMINISTRATION.

Charge.

10. Dewan Asita Chandra Chaudhuri B. A. continued to be in charge of the Revenue Department.

Area under Settlement.

11. As shewn in the subjoined statement, the total area held under settlement and borne on the *Taujis* at the close of the year under review, was 594 sq. miles as against 589 sq. miles in the previous year.

Kinds of settlement.	Area in square miles.		Increase.	Decrease.	REMARKS.
	1334 T.E	1333 T.E.			
Jotes ...	253	250	3	—	
Taluks ...	341	339	2	—	
Total ...	594	589	5	—	

Tea Settlement.

12. As in the previous year there was no fresh settlement for tea cultivation in the year under report. The present condition of this new industry is not yet quite satisfactory.

Rates of *Jama*.

13. The average of *jama* per *kani* of *jote* lands in *khas mehals* (exclusive of cesses) stood at 15 annas and 4 pies against 15 annas and 1 pie in the previous year, and the rates in the *taluks* at 5 annas and 2 pies per *kani* against 4 annas and 11 pies in the previous year. The maximum rate for *jotes* was Rs. 3/12 per *kani* while the minimum was 3 annas, and those for *taluki* land were Rs. 1/5 and annas 3 respectively.

Sources of land Revenue.

14. The different sources of land revenue demand with the collection under each head are detailed below :—

Sources.	Current demand.		Arrear demand up to the end of		Realization up to the end of		REMARKS.
	1334 T.E.	1333 T.E.	1333 T.E.	1332 T.E.	1334 T.E.	1333 T.E.	
Taluks ...	1,75,833	1,66,033	1,51,168	1,01,355	1,09,672	1,16,433	
Khas Mehal jotes	3,87,886	3,78,404	7,40,319	7,08,887	3,64,289	3,37,278	
Bazars ...	5,192	4,388	1,265	1,065	5,407	4,503	
Cesses ...	35,708	34,581	58,256	52,710	29,607	28,102	
Total ...	6,04,619	5,83,406	9,51,008	8,64,017	5,08,975	4,86,316	

Demand.

15. The above statement will show that the current demand uuder all heads was Rs. 6,04,619. With the arrear demand of Rs. 9,51,008, the total demand of the year was Rs. 15,55,627 against Rs. 14,47,423 of the previous year. There was an increase in the current demand both in respect of *taluki* and *jote* lands, due as usual to assessment on the expiry of the rent free period and resettlement after the previous term.

16. The total collections under all heads during the year amounted to Rs. 5,08975 being Rs. 2,69,572 under current and Rs. 2,39403 under arrears, against Rs. 4,86,316 in the previous year. The percentage of current collection was 44·58 against 44·71, and that of the arrears 25·17 against 26·09. The fall is mainly due to the non-realization of revenue from the tea estates, the current demand for which amounted to Rs. 83,622 and the total outstanding dues at the end of the year under review, to Rs. 1,64,026. In the *khas mehal* the percentage of current collection was 39·31 against 36·71, and in *taluki mehal*, 55·27 against 62·41. During the year Rs. 12,854 of the demand was written off after proper enquiry. The special officer deputed to examine the *taujis* worked for about eight months. The reports submitted by him after local inspections are being scrutinised in the Revenue Department.

Collection.

17. Altogether 2,668 certificate cases covering a demand of Rs. 2,11,198 were instituted during the year. With 1,270 cases, valued at Rs. 1,62,966 pending from the previous year, the total number of cases, awaiting final orders on disposal of preliminary notices issued on debtors, was 3,938, covering a total demand of Rs. 3,74,164. Of these, 350 cases with a demand of Rs. 18,478 were rejected or struck off, while 1,406 cases carrying an aggregate value of Rs. 2, 02,675 remained pending.

Coercive measures—certificates.

18. Orders under the provision of the State Certificate Act were passed during the year in 2,182 cases with a total value of Rs. 1,53,011 making the demands absolute. With 5,341 cases pending in execution from the previous year, the total number of cases dealt with was 7,523 covering a demand of Rs. 4,79,638. Out of the total demand Rs. 23,832 was remitted or written off and of the remainder, Rs. 81,176 was actually realised, leaving a balance of Rs. 3,74,630. Of the amount realised Rs. 71,242 represents land revenue and Rs. 9,934, miscellaneous demands. 5 debtors were arrested in Udaipur, 4 of whom were released, either on payment or on promise of payment by instalments. One was imprisoned for a month in the civil jail.

19. The number of defaulting *taluks* brought under the operation of the sun-set law (including 24 pending from the previous year) was 75. Of these, 51 were released on payment of dues with penalty, while 8 were sold in auction and 16 remained undisposed of at the close of the year.

Operation of the sun-set law.

20. The results of the survey including re-survey operations are given in the statement below. It will be seen that an area of 3,509 *drones* comprising 555 *drones* of *taluk* and 2,954 *drones* of *khas mehal* land was surveyed as against a total of 2,865 *drones* in the previous year. The sanctioned programme for survey for the year was 3,408 *drones* in *khas mehals* and 2,171 *drones* in *taluks*. The failure to complete the programme was, as in the previous year, due to the neglect of *talukdars* to pay up the cost promptly, and in the case of *khas mehals*, to the want of adequate staff. The total expenditure incurred in the survey operations in *khas mehals* was Rs. 4,382.

Survey.

Names of Divisions.	Quantity of land in *drones* surveyed in 1334 T. E.			Quantity of land in *drones* surveyed in 1333 T. E.			REMARKS.
	Taluqi land.	*Khas mehal* land.	Total.	*Taluqi* land.	*Khas mehal* land.	Total.	
1. Sadar Division ...	287	2,820	3,107	272	1,128	1,400	
2. Kailashahar " ...	—	—	—	—	274†	274	
3. Sonamura " ...	25	12	37	—	62	62	
4. Belonia " ...	—	—	—	—	—	—	
5. Khowai " ...	243	122	365	15*	822*	837	
6. Dharmanagar " ...	—	—	—	—	163	163	
7. Udaipur " ...	—	—	—	129	—	129	
8. Sabroom " ...	—	—	—	—	—	—	
9. Amarpur " " ...	—	—	—	—	—	—	
TOTAL ...	555	2,954	3,509	416	2,449	2,865	

* Including Kalyanpur abolished. † Including Kamalpur abolished.

Cadastral Survey.

21. The work of Cadastral Survey in Kailashahar was continued. Survey papers of some villages of Indranagar Parganah were made over for settlement. The Survey staff was engaged in *kittawar* and *khanapuri* work. *Kittawar* and *khanapuri* of 12 villages and *khanapuri* only of 11 villages were completed. The area enclosed within *kittawar* was a little over 1,400 acres, and the *khanapuri* work covered 12,627 plots. Owing to the missing of traverse pegs from the field and the out break of the cholera epedemic in some villages, the work could not be carried on regularly. The number of maps prepared was 12. Timber posts have been fixed at many village Trijunctions and in some other convenient places for future reference.

Settlement

22. The result of Settlement work is given in the statement below. It will be seen that settlement operations were completed in respect of 1,936 *drones* of *jote* land, as against 3,037 *drones* in the previous year.

Nature of Settlement.	1334 T. E.		1333 T. E.		REMARKS.
	Area in *drones*.	*Jama* in whole rupees.	Area in *drones*.	*Jama* in whole rupees.	
1. Permanent *taluqi* settlement of cultivated land ...	—	—	—	—	
2. Permanent *taluqi* settlement of waste land	—	—	—	—	
3. *Taskhichi taluqi* settlement of cultivated land ...	—	—	—	—	
4. *Taskhichi taluqi* settlement of waste land ...	—	—	—	—	
5. *Jotedari* re-settlement of cultivated land	1,590	18,484	2,681	34,782	
6. *Jotedari* settlement of waste land.	346	3,026	356	2,811	
TOTAL ...	1,936	21,510	3,037	37,593	

Taluki settlement.

23. No permanent or *Taskhichi* settlement or *Niskar* grant was sanctioned during the year.

Re-settlement of *jote* lands.

24. A net increase of Rs. 4,099 in *jama* was secured by re-settlement of *abadi jote* land, the *nazarana* secured being Rs. 13,325, the average rate of *jama* per *kani* being 11 annas 7 pies against 13 annas in the previous year.

***Jotedari* Settlement of waste land.**

25. During the year an area of 346 *drones* of waste land was settled for a prospective rental of Rs. 3,026, the average *jama* per *kani* obtained being 8 annas and 9 pies against 7 annas and 11 pies in the previous year. The maximum and minimum rates were Rs. 2-12 and 3 annas respectively. The *nazarana* realised was Rs. 4,860. The rent free period allowed was 1 to 4 years.

Settlement work.

26. There were separate settlement officers in the Sadar and Kailashahr Divisions. In other divisions the Divisional Officers were entrusted with the settlement work within their respective jurisdictions. The total expenditure incurred in the settlement operations exclusively, amounted to Rs. 1,228.

27. It will be seen that the *nazarana* obtained and obtainable by resettlement of cultivable *jote* lands and settlement of waste lands, as *jotes* (Rs. 13,325+Rs. 4,860=Rs. 18,185) was more than three times the amount spent for survey and settlement operations, while the net increase of revenue secured was Rs. 8,025 (Rs. 4,999+Rs. 3,026.)

The work of the map section.

28. A number of old maps were copied for use in the Divisional offices. During the year 132 copies of such maps were traced at a cost of Rs. 405-15-3.

Private Estates under State management.

29. As detailed below, there were altogether 7 private Estates under State management during the year under report. Orders were passed, besides, uuder the Encumbered Estates Act of 1332 T. E., placing an Estate in the Khowai Division within the purview of the Act, and possession of the property has been taken since the close of the year.

Class.	Name of Estate.	Area.	Revenue.
Encumbered	1. Kakrabon Estate	283 *drones*	1,871
	2. Jogendranagar Trust Estate	64 "	163
	3. Kamalanagar and Mohendranagar Estate	51 "	255
Unencumbered	4. Prabhu Goswami's Estate	31 "	61
	5. The Maharanee's Estate	260 "	450
	6. Late Brajakumar Thakur,s Estate	47 "	297
Endowment	7. Taranagar Estate	123 "	52

30. The subjoined table shows the demand and collection of the estates during the year. The comparatively low percentage of collection is mainly ascribable to the inclusion in the demand of a considerable amount which is fictitious, though the management also admits of room for improvement.

	DEMAND			COLLECTION			P. C. of collection
	Current	Arear	Total	Current	Arear	Total	
1.	6,337	32.399	38,736	977	5,407	6,384	16·49
2.	1,191	3,173	4,364	398	781	1,179	27·01
3.	1,273	882	2,155	649	686	1,335	61·29
4.	912	2,337	3,249	371	648	1,019	31·36
5.	5,610	8,646	14,256	1,682	3,053	4,735	33·21
6.	1,315	3,082	4,397	330	1,099	1,429	32·91
7.	2,195	5,108	7,303	1,171	1,235	2,406	32·94

CHAPTER III—PROTECTION.

I. Legislation.

31. In consequence of the change in the administration and a number of vacancies in the personnel, the old Legislative Council had to be reconstituted, and a Legislative Committee has been organised since the close of the year with sixteen members, official and non-official. There was no fresh legislation during the year, but it is hoped the work will now be pushed on vigorously.

II. Military.

Charge.

32. Kumar Dina Mohan Deb Barman continued to be in charge of the Military Office and the Force.

Strength

33. At the close of the year under review, the actual strength of the Force consisted of 155 Sepoys and 43 officers of all ranks, including the commanding Officer, 2 A. D. C.'s, 1 Subedar Major, and 2 Subedars. There were besides a Band Master and 17 men constituting the State Band.

Duty.

34. The men were chiefly employed as before on escort duty and in furnishing guards-of-honour on ceremonial occasions. 56 posts had to be kept vacant at the close of the year, as suitable candidates did not come forward.

Expenditure.

35. The total expenditure of the year, including grain allowance, amounted to Rs. 41,465 against Rs. 42,625 in the previous year. The decrease is mainly due to the vacancies.

III. Police.

Charge.

36. Babu Jogesh Chandra Dutta B. A., continued as Superintendent of Police throughout the year.

37. Probationary Assistant Superintendent of Police, Thakur Jogendra Chandra Dev Barman, who returned from the Police training College at Sardah during the year, was appointed as Assistant Supperintendent of Police. He is undergoing practical training under the supervision of the Superintendent.

Strength.

38. The total strength of the State Police was 451 including a staff of 10 constables for the Town section. The posts of 1 Inspector, 2 Darogas, 3 Naib-darogas and 22 constables were abolished in the budget for the year under report. But owing to pressure of work, the department was compelled to obtain additional sanction during the year, for the appointment of one Inspector and 6 constables out of the savings of the Police budget.

Inspecting Staff.

39. There were altogether 3 permanent Inspectors and one temporary inspecting officer as stated above, working under the Police Department. Their chief duty was to control the investigating staff and supervise their work.

Crime.

40. The total number of cases reported to the Police was 1,130 against 1,222 in the previous year.

Cases.

41. The result of cases investigated by the Police will be seen from the following table.

Number of cases reported.
1,130

Enquiry refused	Number investigated	Pending
6	1,026	98

Number investigated (1,026):

Maliciously false	True	Doubtful &c.
5	970	51

True (970):

Charge-sheet	Finally reported
360	610

Result of prosecution.

42. Altogether 743 persons were arrested for various offences and 730 sent up for trial by the Police, against 787 and 754 respectively in the previous year.

43. Of the number 730 sent up, 113 were convicted, 198 acquitted on compromise and 39 on withdrawal of cases, while 1 died, 9 escaped and 370 are awaiting trial. The percentage of conviction was 53·33 against 60·1 of the previous year. This fall appears to have to some extent been ascribable to the delay in the trial of cases, mainly due to the difficulty of securing the prompt attendance of witnesses residing in British India.

44. Of the 261 persons awaiting trial at the end of the previous year, 47 were convicted and 121 acquitted, while 93 are awaiting trial. This shows that 93 persons who were sent up by the Police in the year 1333 T. E. are still awaiting trial.

B. L. cases.

45. 3 Bad livelihood cases were instituted during the year under report all of which are still pending.

Arms Act cases.

46. Of 3 Arms Act cases, all were sent up, out of which, 1 ended in conviction, in one the accused was discharged, and the other is pending trial.

Recovery of stolen property.

47. The value of properties stolen was estimated at Rs. 20,667-11 against Rs. 16,558-11-3 of the previous year. Of this amount, Rs. 6,514-2 was recovered against Rs. 3,722-4-9 of the previous year. The percentage of recovery was thus 31·57 against 22.4 of the previous year, showing a better result in the investigation of offences against property.

Dacoities.

48. There were 8 dacoities during the year against 9 of the previous year. Most of the cases were of a petty and technical character. In two cases the accused were sent up in charge sheet, 2 were found to be false, 2 doubtful, and 2 were finally reported.

Special Staff.

49. The C. I. D. and the Information Bureau continued to work satisfactorily and proved useful in the investigation of intricate cases.

50. 60 cases of unnatural death were reported during the year. Regular enquiries were held by the police in all cases. No suspicious circumstances have been discovered in any case.

Unnatural death and steps taken.

51. 4 Sub-Inspectors, 8 Constables and 1 Chaukidar received money rewards for their good services. 34 constables were fined and suspended and 8 constables were dismissed or discharged.

Reward and punishment.

52. The Supperintendent of Police was out on tour for 84 days in all during the year against 38 days of the previous year.

Tours.

53. The relation with the police in the adjoining districts in British India continued to be satisfactory.

Co-operation.

54. Five co-operation meetings were held in whch the State Police joined and discussed matters relating to border crimes and criminals with the police in British India and worked out plans for prevention and detection of crimes.

55. A joint patrol was established at Sonamura and worked successfully.

56. The total expenditure amounted, including grain allowance, to Rs. 67,445 against Rs. 67,566 in the previous year.

Expenditure.

IV. Justice.

57. There were 13 courts of Justice in the State during the year under report, exercising both civil and criminal jurisdiction viz.—the Khas Adalat or the Chief Court with its Original and Appellate sides, and 12 Courts of Magistrate-Munsiffs exercising original jurisdiction only. Babu Bhupal Chandra Ganguli B. L., continued to be the Chief Judge, Dewan Bijoy Kumar Sen, M. A., B. L., F. R. S. A. as the Sessions Judge, and Kumar Surendra Chandra Deb Barman and Uzir Broja Krishna Deb Barman, as puisne Judges of the Khas Adalat. There were 16 Courts of Magistrate-Munsiffs, exercising original jurisdiction during the previous year, but from the beginning of the year under report, 4 Courts of Magistrate-Munsiff viz.—Courts of Bisalgarh, Kamalpur, Amarpur and Kalyanpur Divisions were abolished and were amalgamated with the Courts of Sadar, Kailasbahar, Udaipur and Khowai Divisions repectively.

Courts.

58. Altogether 1,866 original criminal cases were instituted during the year under report against 1,739 of the previous year. With the balance of 477 pending from the last year, the total number of cases for disposal before the several subordinate original courts was thus 2,343 as against 2,327 of the previous year, as detailed below. Out of these 2,343 cases, 1729 were disposed of as against 1,848 of the last year, leaving 614 cases pending at the close of the year. Thus in the year

Number of original criminal cases.

under report, the number of cases for disposal exceeded that of the previous year by 16, and there was a decrease in the disposals by 119.

DESCRIPTION OF OFFENCES.	1333 T. E.	1334 T. E.
Offences against the State and public tranquillity	84	92
Offences against person	559	531
Offences against property	1,239	1,239
Other offences	445	481
TOTAL	2,327	2,343

59. The total number of persons awaiting trial in the year under report, inclusive of the number pending from the previous year, was 2,788. The number actually brought to trial was 1,866 against 1,937 of the previous year. Of these 516 were arrested by the police, 401 were produced on warrants, 826 appeared on summons, 375 appeared voluntarily, and 14 were arrested in the presence of Magistrates.

Persons brought to trial.

60. Out of these persons brought to trial, 904 were discharged without trial, 628 were acquitted and 418 convicted, while 17 died, 14 were transferred, 1 escaped and 806 remained under trial at the close of the year. Of the persons convicted, 121 were sentenced to various terms of imprisonment extending from below 1 month to 7 years, 265 to fine only, 10 persons were warned for the future and 22 persons released on bail. The number of persons actually tried was 1,046 as against 1,207 of the previous year and the percentage of conviction was thus 39·96 against 39·51 of the previous year.

Results of cases.

61. Of the 2,343 cases for disposal, the number in which British subjects were concerned was 501 against 554 of the last year. Out of these cases, 375 were cognizable and 126 non-cognizable. In 57 cases British subjects were complainants, in 444 they were the accused. In 164 cases both the parties were British subjects. In these cases, 619 persons were actually under trial during the year under report against 568 of the previous year. Of them 200 were convicted, 289 acquitted or discharged, 3 transferred, while 127 remained under trial at the close of the year.

Cases concerning British subjects.

62. The statement below compares the number of original cases during the last 2 years.

Comparative Statement.

DESCRIPTION OF OFFENCES.	1333 T.E.	1334 T.E.	Increase.	Decrease
Offences against the State and public tranquillity ...	57	72	15	0
Offences against person	443	426	0	17
Offences against property	901	962	61	0
Other offences	338	406	68	0
TOTAL	1,739	1,866	144	17

Increased by 127.

63. Extradition warrants were applied for against 120 persons, of whom 27 were arrested and surrendered, 45 appeared voluntarily and 48 were at large at the close of the year. Of 72 persons under trial, 20 were convicted, 28 acquitted or discharged and 24 were awaiting trial at the end of the year.

Extradition.

64. 22 cases including 5 cases with 13 persons pending from last year, came up before the Sessions during the year under report. Out of these 22 cases, 17 were disposed of as detailed in the following table. The number of persons involved in these cases was 42 ; of whom 18 were convicted, 3 discharged without trial, 9 acquitted and 12 remained under trial at the close of the year.

Sessions cases.

Description of cases.	Number of cases.	Disposed of.	Pending.	REMARKS.
Murder	2	2	0	
Culpable homicide not amounting to murder	4	3	1	
Attempt to murder	1	1	0	
Grievous hurt	1	1	0	
Dacoity	2	2	0	
Robbery and hurt	1	1	0	
Kidnapping	2	2	0	
Rape	1	1	0	
Trespass	1	1	0	
Obstructing public servant in discharge of his duty	1	1	0	
Using counterfeit British currency note	3	2	1	
Using counterfeit British coin ...	1	0	1	
Forging courtfee Stamps of the Tripura State	2	0	2	
Total	22	17	5	

65. There were altogether 192 criminal appeals against 222 of the previous year. They were disposed of as shown below :—

Criminal appeals.

Rejected	12
Judgment affirmed	89
Modified	14
Reversed	49
Further enquiry &c. ordered	10
	174
Pending	18
Total	192

66. The percentage of judgments affirmed and modified was 63·58 against 62·16 of the previous year.

67. The number of original civil suits instituted during the year under report was 1,737 against 1,863 of the last year. With the preceding year's balance of 946 suits, the total number for disposal was 2,683 as against 2,850 of the previous year. They were disposed of as follows :—

Original civil suits.

Exparte...	469
Admitted and compromised	282
Dismissed for want of prosecution... ...	378
Disposed of on contest	480
	1,609
Pending	1,074
Total	2,683

Duration of suits.

68. The average duration of suits before the civil courts was 5 months and 8 days against 4 months and 16 days in 1333 T. E.

Nature and value of suits.

69. The total value of suits instituted during the year was Rs. 1,38,520-6-6 as against Rs. 1,53,729-4-3 which gives an average of Rs. 79-11-11 as the value per case. Of the 1,737 suits instituted during the year under report, 500 related to lands, 940 to money transactions and 297 to other transactions. There were 1,101 suits of the value of Rs. 100 and under; 320 suits of over Rs. 100 and below Rs. 500; 27 suits of over Rs. 500 and below Rs. 1,000; 12 suits of over Rs. 1,000 and below Rs. 5,000; while 277 suits were not estimable in money value.

Execution of decrees.

70. The number of applications for the execution of decrees filed during the year under report was 561 and with 456 pending cases, the total number was 1,017 against 1,226 of the previous year. The aggregate value of the new applications was Rs. 66,281-12-3 and with the opening value of Rs. 1,12,697-6-3, being the value of the pending cases, the total amounted to Rs. 1,78,979-2-6. The number of applications disposed of was 623, the value of which was Rs. 72,902-8-9. The number of execution cases pending at the close of the year was 394 with the value of Rs. 1,06,076-9-9.

Civil appeals.

71. There were 155 civil appeals filed during the year under report against 156 of the last year. With the past year's balance of 32, the total for disposal was 187 as against 197 of 1333 T. E. Out of these, 126 were disposed of during the year under report against 165 of the previous year, leaving a balance of 61 cases at the close of the year.

Results of civil appeals.

72. The following figures indicate the results of appeals.

Decisions confirmed	71
„ reversed	34
„ modified	6
„ remanded	4
Compromised or otherwise disposed of ...	11
	126

Percentage.

73. The percentage of judgments wholly or partly upheld, excluding the cases compromised, was 66.95 as against 65·13 of the previous year.

Value and duration of appeals.

74. The total value of appeals filed during the year under report was Rs. 19,803-15-0, and the average duration of each appeal was 2 months and 3 days against 2 months and 5 days of the previous year.

Original Side cases.

75. 22 civil suits were instituted in the Khas Adalat Original Side against 19 suits of the previous year. With the balance of 55 suits from 1333 T. E., the total number for disposal was thus 77 against 86 of the last year; of these, 28 suits were disposed of against 31 of the previous year, and 49 suits remained pending at the close of the year; and there were 32 execution

cases during the year under report including 21 cases pending from 1333 T. E.; of these, 13 were disposed of and 19 remained pending at the end of the year. There were also 25 applications filed for the grant of succession and other certificates during the year; with the balance of 21, the total number of cases was 46, out of which 33 were disposed of as shown below, leaving 13 cases pending at the close of the year.

Description of cases.	Total.	Disposed of.	Pending.
Probate case	4	2	2
Succession certificate	16	11	5
Guardianship	26	20	6
Total	46	33	13

76. Thus it will appear from the sub-joined table, that the total number of civil and criminal appeals inclusive of the number pending from the last year was 379 as against 419 of the last year, and out of these, 300 were disposed of against 374 of the previous year. So in comparison with the last year the total number of appeals decreased by 40 in the present year and there was a corresponding decrease in the disposals in the year under report by 74.

Total number of appeals.

Description of appeals.	Number of appeals.		Disposed of.	
	Past year.	Present year.	Past year.	Present year.
Civil	197	187	165	126
Criminal	222	192	209	174
Total	419	379	374	300

V. Prisons.

77. As against 12 jails in the previous year, there were in the year under review 8 jails including the Central jail at Agartala, with a population of 661 against 749, of whom 245 were convicts, 406 under-trials, 8 civil prisoners, and 2 lunatics. The daily average was 83·93 as against 92·72 in the year before.

Number of Jails.

78. With the abolition of 4 Sub-Divisions, 4 Jails were abolished during the year under report.

79. 51 prisoners were under sentence of over 2 years as against 40 in the previous year as shown in the statement below.

Long-term Prisoners.

Class of offence.	Number of prisoners.	Occupation.	REMARKS.
Murder	12	They were employed, in oilmills, brick and soorki making, bamboo work, earth work, gardening, weaving and tailoring.	21 had sentences of 2 to 5 years, 24 of 5 to 10 years, 6 for life i. e. 20 years.
Culpable homicide not amounting to murder	15		
Grievous hurt	2		
Dacoity	9		
Theft	3		
Escape from lawful custody...	1		
Robbery	4		
Rape	2		
Kidnapping	1		
Forgery	2		
Total	51		

80. The health of the jails was generally good. Only one convict died of fever and dropsy at the Central jail against 1 in the previous year. 1 under-trial died at the Kailashahar jail.

Jail health.

81. The total income from all jails was Rs. 3,147 as against Rs. 2,442 in the preceding year, and the total expenditure, excluding grain allowance, Rs. 13,188 against Rs. 13,305.

Income & expenditure.

82. One convict from the central jail and one under-trial from the Kailashahar jail escaped from the custody of the warders in charge ; but the latter was re-arrested during the year.

Escapes.

83. The construction of the new jail dormitory was taken up and has been completed since the close of the year.

Jail Building.

VI. Registration.

84. Mr. K. Dutt M. A, B. L., M. R. A. S., F. R. E. S., continued to be in charge up to Falgoon. As he was deputed to His Highness's Camp at Shillong, Mr. S. C. Deb Barman M. A. (Harvard) took up the charge of the Department.

Charge.

85. The number of the Registration Offices continued to be 9 *i. e.* one for each division or sub-division. The Divisional Collectors and Assistant Collectors acted as ex-officio Registrars. At Agartala there was a separate Registrar.

Registration office.

86. The number of documents presented for registration during the year was 9,674 as against 9,040 of the previous year. During the year under review 110 deeds were refused registration on various grounds, while 54 remained pending at the close of the year.

Presentation and disposal

87. The total value covered by the documents presented amounted to Rs. 15,29,558 as compared with Rs. 12,01,919 of the previous year. The total value of the documents actually registered was Rs. 14,96,766 as against Rs. 11,62,163.

Value of deeds presented and registered.

88. The number of suits and appeals filed before the Officer in charge, Registration Department, in respect of documents, the registration of which had been refused, was 29 and 1, against 26 and 1 respectively, of the previous year. 48 suits and 1 appeal (including those pending from the previous year) were dealt with during the year under review, with the result that 24 suits were disposed off, leaving 24 suits and 1 appeal pending at the close of the year.

The Suits and appeals.

89. The total income from fees and the expenditure during the year amounted to Rs. 11,213 and Rs. 3,639 respectively, as against Rs. 10,244 and Rs. 3,445 of the previous year. The net income during the year was therefore Rs. 7,574, which shows a normal increase.

Income and expenditure.

VII. Municipality.

90. As before the captial town Agartala had the only Municipal inistitution in the State with a population of about 8,000 according to the last Census.

Municipality.

91. The Municipality worked under a Committee of 9 members including an official Chairman and a non-official Vice-Chairman. Dr. M. M. Majunmdar L. M. S., continued to be the Chairman. The Committee had 14 sittings, the average number of attendance being 5·1.

Municipal Committee.

92. The income of the Municipality from municipal and latrine taxes was Rs. 3,943-1-6, as against Rs. 3,879 of the previous year. The demand, inclusive of the arears, was Rs. 6,755-5-3.

Income.

93. The income under the miscellaneous head, including desposits and advances recovered, amounted to Rs. 7,030-10-6. The figure also includes Rs. 4,865-11-0 realised from the local Bazar.

94. As before the State grant for the year under review was Rs. 9,000.

State Grant.

95. The total expenditure, with Rs. 1,932-2-0 incurred in the Bazar account, amounted to Rs. 16,625-6-6, as against Rs. 16,194-14-0 of the previous year.

Expenditure

96. The general health of the public within the Municpality was not good owing to the prevalance of Malaria and Kala-Azar. There was no other epidemic out-break, during the year under review.

Public health.

97. As in the previous year, the control of the Bazar remained in the hands of the Municipal committee. The total demand was Rs. 6,583-2-9 including the arear demand of Rs. 526-13-0. The total realisation came up to Rs. 4,865-11-0 against Rs. 5,891-13-0 of the previous year.

Ishanganj Bazar.

98. A road leading from the Central Road to a tank was metalled. Some other minor works of improvement were also attended to. The unfinished portion of the Bazar building was taken up at the latter part of the year and it is expected to be completed soon. The accumulated fund of Rs. 13,495-15-3 on the Bazar account, standing as balance at the end of the year, will be spent on this building.

CHAPTER IV—PRODUCTION AND DISTRIBUTION.

I. Weather and Crops—Agriculture.

Rainfall.

99. The average rainfall of the year was 106·28 inches against 81·58 in the previous year. The quinquennial average was 87·5 inches. Udaipur Division had the maximun fall of 150·61 inches and Amarpur the minimum of 73·93. The rainfall, though seasonable on the whole, was untimely in respect of, and unfavourable to, certain crops.

Crops.

100. The principal crops were paddy, Cotton, *Til*, Mustard juite and sugarcane. The weather conditions were favourable to some crops and the outturn was normal in most cases considering the aggregate yield. There were bad harvests in cotton and early paddy.

Tea Industry.

101. The Tea Industry was making some progress, though slow, and the tea produced in the State was fetching reasonable price. There were 22 gardens showing marked improvement.

Cattle.

102. The health of the cattle was not bad on the whole. There were some cases of foot and mouth disease in the Sadar Division, and the veterinary Assistant was sent out to visit the affected localities and render necessary help. On the whole 2,500 heads of cattle were treated for all sorts of diseases during the year.

Condition of the people.

103. The people are mostly agricultural. The main crops, paddy, mustard, jute, *til*, cotton and sugarcane grew fairly well. Cotton sold at Rs. 12 to 25 per maund, and the other crops also fetched good prices. The condition of the agricultural population was thus generally satisfactory inspite of the high prices of imported articles. The middle classes however suffered more or less seriously owing to the prevailing high prices of staple food crops and of imported necessaries of life. At Agartala the price of rice once rose so very high that cheap Burma rice had to be imported by way of relief.

104. The prices of food grains were similar to those in the neighbouring British districts. Rice sold from Rs. 6 to Rs. 9 and paddy from Rs. 2-12 to Rs. 4-8 per maund. The maximum price of rice in the previous year was Rs. 6/8. The marked rise was due to various complex economic causes including a larger export and an increased capacity of the agricultural classes to hold off stock in expectation of more advantageous sale. Occasionally the high rate was restricted to a particular locality, being due to the influence of the prevailing local conditions.

Prices.

105. There was no appreciable change in the rates of wages. Male labourers earned from 10 annas to Re. 1, and female labourers from 6 annas to 10 annas a day. *Ghoramis* earned from 8 annas to Re. 1, and Carpenters and Masons from 12 annas to Re. 1-4. Most of the labourers were outsiders from the neighbouring British Districts, as well as up country coolies.

Wages.

106. No Taccavi advances were issued during the year.

Taccavi.

107. The Department of Agriculture has been reorganised. One Superintendent and two wholetime demonstrators including 5 agricultural Jamadars recruited from the hill people were working during the year. There was also a part time demonstrator at Kamalpur.

Staff.

108. The Department mainly undertook during the year (1) propaganda work in general for the development of methods of agriculture and introduction of crops which could profitably be grown on the hills under the existing *joom* System ; (2) Circuit lectures in the centres of each Division or Circle, on the advantages of plough cultivation and field crops, the utility of cattle manure, the selection of seeds, and the methods of preservation of crops grown.

Propaganda work and Circuit lectures.

109. It has been proved by experiment and demonstration that Dharwar American Cotton could be grown well on the hills under plough cultivation, but high land ploughing is not yet fully understood and appreciated.

Dharwar American Cotton in *jooms*.

110. It has therefore not been found possible to introduce the exotic generally under the same method, but the hill people are attempting to grow them on a small scale under plough.

111. A serious attempt has however been made towards the cultivation of Dharwar American Cotton in the *jooms*.

112. The method of *joom* cultivation is very crude, paddy and cotton seed are mixed together and sown in the same hole. Hence the percentage of germination is not always up to the mark.

113. There is a further loss in the percentage of plants during the process of growth. It is estimated that the total loss of cotton seed and plants in the *jooms* on account of the above crude method of sowing is not less than 60 to 70 percent in some years.

114. The year under report was not very suitable for Dharwar cotton. The opening of bolls after ripening was not quite perfect. The Superintendent of Agriculture is of opinion that this

was partly due to want of loose soil in the *jooms* at the harvest time after the rains were over.

115. Through experiments it has been found that successful opening could be helped by plucking the ripe bolls and keeping them separately for a week.

116. The outturn per chattak of seed sown in jooms was found to be slightly in excess of that for Comillas and the fruiting of bolls was also 30 percent more in Dharwar than what it was with the Comillas.

117. Want of a model *joom* under the direct control of the Department is being felt ; such a farm will greatly help compilation of important statistics and enable the Department to carry on experiments with new crops.

Programme of general demonstration.

118. During the later part of the year the programe for distributing pady, potato, jute, sugarcane and Eri silk worm eggs was taken up. *Indrasail* paddy seed had a vast demand.

Kashipur Model Farm.

119. The Buri, American Dharwar and the Comillas were grown on the farm on an experimental scale. All of them were growing well and the opening of bolls was successful. Full attention could not be given to this farm as the lands have been open to flood damage lately.

120. A plot above flood level has been selected for growing seed crops and it is being run after Kishoreganj model for seed procuring through Barga System.

Nainital potato.

121. A Nainital potato crop was raised in the farm with success and the same variety of seed was distributed in the hills in several Tripura villages. There was much insect and fungus trouble during the year in those places and the crop gathered was 50 percent on the whole. The growers are however interested in the crop and intend giving a further trial next year.

Eri culture.

122. A crop of Eri silk worms was raised in the Model farm and a circuit lecture has been given on the advantages of growing Eri worms in places where there are castor plants.

Touring of Staff.

123. The Superintendent was on tour for 91 days and the demonstrators of A & B Divisions were for 102 and 115 days respectively.

General health.

124. The health of the staff was bad during the year under report on account of hill Malaria.

II. Immigration and Emigration.

125. During the year, 1,400 families immigrated into and 694 families emigrated out of the State, as against 1228 and 781 respectively in the previous year.

III. Forests.

Charge and Management.

126. Dewan Asita Chandra Chaudhuri, B. A. continued to be in charge of the Department. He was assisted by Babu Jatindranath Mitra, Forest Officer. All the forests were under Khas management, as before.

Staff.

127. The Department had a staff of 19 Foresters, 12 Rangers, 16 Assistant Foresters, 10 Mohorers, 16 Head Guards and 198 Guards and Literate Guards. Besides, there were 161 Commission-agents for the sale of permits for shoulder-borne export of forest produce. There were 58 stations for collection of duty and for prevention of forest offences.

Working.

128. The Reserved Sal Forests of the Sonamura Division were worked under the system of Coppice with standards and those of the Udaipur Division under the Selection method, while the open unclassed forests were worked under the State rules of 1323 T. E. For the Feni Mehal, the working rules of the Bengal Forest Department were followed.

Sources of revenue.

129. The collections of forest revenue from different sources are given below :—

Heads of Revenue.	1334 T.E.	1333 T.E.	Increase.	Decrease.	REMARKS.
I. Unclassed open forests :—					
(a) Toll on forest produce exported by the river mehals	3,37,881	3,76,876	—	38,995	
(b) Toll on forest produce exported by land route under permit	84,481	83,429	1,052	—	
(c) Toll collection (share) of the Feni river mehal ...	21,349	30,116	—	8,767	
(d) Grazing mehal ...	6,703	7,348		645	
(e) Thatching grass mehal	12,327	10,692	1,635	—	
II. Reserved Forests :—					
Sale of *Sal* and *Garjan* trees ...	* 32,143	27,201	4,942	—	* Including Rs. 7,946 for Garjan.
III. Elephant Kheddas	10,759	31,336	—	20,577	
TOTAL ...	5,05,643	5,66,998	7,629	68,984	

Net decrease—61,355.

Receipts.

130. The total forest revenue of the year was Rs. 5,05,643 against Rs. 5,66,998 of the previous year, showing a decrease of Rs. 61,355.

131. The fall of revenue is noticeable in the river mahals and in the Khedda operations.

132. Owing to heavy floods in the rainy season sungrass could not grow in the Feni Valley and that which grew on the hills was in many places destroyed by cattle which took shelter and grazed in those places

during the floods. Cholera also broke out in the valley in the busiest season. Several cases among the Kamlas ended fatally which not only prevented new Kamlas from coming, but many of those that were working left out of fear. The above are the main causes for the heavy fall of revenue in the Feni river mehal. In the river mehals in the northern divisions, the decrease in revenue is due to the fact that logs of timber could not be exported in large number for want of timely floods in the rivers.

Elephant Khedas.

133. Khedda operations were undertaken in the Kailashahar, Sonamura, Udaipur and Sabroom Divisions. The operations were not very successful any where except Kailashahar. Only 25 elephants were caught during the year against 53 in the previous year. This accounts for the decrease in receipts.

Feni River Mehal.

134. On the expiry of the period of five years for which the management of the joint toll station at Amlighat had been handed over to the State, a conference was held in November in 1924 under the presidency of the Commissioner of the Chittagong Division in connection with the future management of the Toll Station. On the recommendation made by the conference the Government of Bengal approved of the continuance of the existing arrangement till the 31st March, 1926, and the joint toll station continued to be under the management of the State Forest Department during the year under review.

135. The total revenue of the year was Rs. 31,170 against Rs. 48,482 in the previous year, the decrease being due to causes already mentioned.

Fee simple lots.

136. The forest produce from the Fee Simple lots was exported without much trouble between the lot-owners and the Station staff.

Forest offences.

137. During the year there were 129 forest cases against 304 persons of which 86 cases against 209 persons were instituted during the year and 43 cases against 95 persons were pending from previous year. The offences were mainly for illicit export of forest produce without permits and without payment of duty.

Results.

138. Altogether 127 persons were convicted, of whom two were sentenced to imprisonment and fine, 118 were punished with fine only, 7 were warned, 81 persons were acquitted, and 5 were absconding at the end of the year. 22 cases against 39 persons were compounded and 23 cases against 52 persons remained pending at the close of the year.

Rewards and Punishments.

139. One Ranger, one Forester, one Head Guard and three guards obtained rewards during the year. One Ranger, one Assistant Forester and two guards were degraded.

Health of the Staff.

140. The Assistant Forester of the Durgapur Checking Ghat died of cholera. One guard at Sinaibani, one at Fatikchhari and a third at Kamalasagar died of fever. The staff at Sidhai, Mohanpur, Kamthana, Kamalasagar and Amlighat suffered very badly from fever.

141. After a protracted correspondence with the Assam Forest Department authorities (through the Political Agent) regarding the troubles about the working of the Langai forests, a conference was held at Langai since the close of the year under review (in June 1925) and a joint report was drawn up and submitted by the representatives of the Assam Government and the State. It is hoped that the recommendations made will be accepted and will remove all causes of friction in the future.

Difficulties.

142. It is regrettable that there was a recrudescence of the trouble with the people in the neighbouring district of Noakhali. There were two cases of arson and some other petty cases and counter cases which are still sub judice.

IV. Trade and Manufacture.

143. The principal exports were timber, forest produce of various kinds, cotton, oilseeds, (*til* and mustard seed) paddy, jute, rice, and *Gur* (molassess). A small quantity of tea and some homespun cotton fabrics manufactured by the hill people, specially the Manipuris, were also exported. The principal exports for the year under review and of the previous year are shown below :—

	1333 T.E.	1334 T.E.
Cotton ...	76,590 maunds.	60,478 maunds.
Til ...	52,256 "	30,333 "
Mustard Seeds	26,734 "	36,185 "
Jute ...	54,942 "	51,535 "

144. The tea industry is yet quite in its infancy but it is note worthy that 2,25,533 lbs. & 3,38,272 lbs. of tea were exported in 1923 & 1924 respectively, from the gardens in this State.

145. The principal imports were cloths and yarns, salt, oils (kerosine and mustard), pulses, chillies, tobacco, sugar, flour, spices, arecanuts, books and stationery. The industries worth mention were manufacture of cotton fabrics by the hill people and the Manipuris ; cane and bamboo baskets, mats and sieves by Tripuras ; and dug-outs, bowls and plates of wood by the Reangs and Chakmas ; also *Gur* (molasses) by both hill people and Bengalees.

V. Public Works.

146. Maharajkumar B. K. Deb Barman Bahadur, Member of the Council of Administration was in charge of the Department during the year. Mr. J. N. Bhaduri, B. A., B. E., F. R. S. A., M. R. SAN. I. (London) continued as State Engineer.

147. The expenditure including disbursements from local funds came to Rs. 2,87,572 against Rs. 2,79,519 in the previous year. Of this Rs. 5,521 was spent on water supply, Rs. 77,172 on Roads and Bridges, Rs. 1,71,048 on Buildings and Rs. 15,236 on Miscellaneous works. Out of the total expenditure incurred during the year under review, the amount of Rs. 59,485 was adjusted against advances on account of. old works. A steam Road Roller costing Rs. 10,927 was purchased for improvement of the existing town roads.

Expenditure.

148. The following important major works were completed during the year under report :—

1. Stone metalling of Agartala-Akhaura Road (State portion).
2. Substantial progress of the Jail Building at Agartala.
3. Substantial progress of the Administration Building.
4. Substantial progress of the High Court Building.
5. Completion of the Dhala Road at Bilonia.
6. The Charitable dispensary at Sonamura.
7. Extension of His Highness's Andar
8. Substantial improvement of the decorations of the Palace.

CHAPTER V—REVENUE AND FINANCES.

I. Revenue.

149. The total collection in the year was Rs. 15,42,710 against Rs. 15,82,035 in the previous year. The average of the past five years was Rs. 13,83,022.

150. The details of the income under different heads with all variations are given in the statement below :—

Serial number.	Heads of Revenue.	1334 T.E.	1333 T.E.	As compared with 1333 T.E.		Remarks.
				Increase.	Decrease.	
1	Land Revenue	5,18,227	4,95,508	22,719	—	
2	Rents of markets	5,316	4,569	747	—	
3	Family Tax in the hills	64,433	63,279	1,154	—	
4	Toll on forest produce	4,30,308	4,66,404	—	36,096	
5	Do. Do. on the Feni River	21,349	30,116	—	8,767	
6	Elephant & buffalo grazing Mehal	6,703	7,348	—	645	
7	Thatching grass Mehal	12,327	10,692	1,635	—	
8	Reserved *Sal* trees	24,197	19,371	4,826	—	
9	Tax on cotton and oil-seeds ...	1,55,407	2,03,606	—	48,199	
10	Royalty on elephants caught ...	10,759	31,336	—	20,577	
11	Adda Mehal	22,419	20,692	1,727	—	
12	Excise	52,905	47,652	5,253	—	
13	Stamps and Court-fees	68,343	58,082	10,261	—	
14	Law and Justice (Fines)... ...	2,543	3,368	—	825	
15	Process fees	11,450	12,132	—	682	
16	Registration	11,213	10,251	962	—	
17	Jail	3,147	2,442	705	—	
18	Cattle pounds	5,149	5,685	—	536	
19	Nazars	29,614	25,127	4,487	—	
20	Agriculture	275	314	—	39	
21	Miscellaneous	78.719	64,061	14,658	—	
22	Education...	7,907	—	7,907	—	
	Total	15,42,710	15,82,035	77,041	1,16,366	Net decrease—Rs. 39,325

151. There was thus a total increase of Rs. 77,041 in respect of

Increase.

13 heads of revenue against a total decrease of Rs. 1,16,366 in regard to 9 heads. A new head of income, viz. Education, showing Rs. 7,907, has been for the first time introduced. Formerly all receipts under this count used to be shown as deposit and included as such in the financial statement. The increase under head "land revenue" is due to the increased capacity of the tenantry to pay the demand owing to the rise in prices of agricultural produce, added to a fair outturn. The increased sale of reserved sal trees in Udaipur and Sonamura Divisions account for the increase in this head. A detection of stamp forgery having been effected the revenue under the head "Stamps and Court fees" has appreciably increased.

152. It will be seen that the aggregate decrease is mainly contri-

Decrease.

buted by the fall off in the receipts from *toll* on forest produce, royalty on elephants caught, and tax on cotton and oil seeds. The mattter has already been noticed and explained.

II. Finances.

153. The detailed audited receipts and expenditure of the State and the Zemindaries are given separately in Appendices XXVII and XXVIII. The subjoined statement shows a consolidated abstract account as compared with that of the previous year.

154. It will be seen that the total receipts from all sources

Receipts.

including deposits and loans amounted to Rs. 29,65,939 against Rs. 29,75,562 of the previous year. With the opening balance of Rs. 13,06,268, the total sum available for expenditure was Rs. 42,72,207 against Rs. 43,66,613 of the preceding year.

155. The total expenditure during the year amounted to

Expenditure.

Rs. 33,31,024 against Rs. 30,60,345 of the previous year, the increase being due to adjustment of old advances and repayment of loans. Excluding the charges which were of abnormal character, the real ordinary expenditure of the year was Rs. 21,56,285 against Rs. 24,91,792 of the previous year. The closing balance at the end of the year was Rs. 9,41,183 of which Rs. 5,19,639 was in cash and Rs. 4,21,544 in loans and advances, against Rs. 13,06,268 in the previous year, of which 3,84,150 was in cash and 9,22,118 in loans and advances. The adjustment of numerous advances against the respective heads of charges as mentioned above contributed to the reduction of Rs. 5,00,574 in the balance of the advance accounts.

Receipts.	1333 T. E.	1334 T. E.
1. Opening balance :-		
(1) State	10,09,469	10,04,982
(2) Zemindaries ...	3,81,582	3,01,286
Total ...	13,91,051	13,06,268
2. Income :—		
(1) State	15,82,035	15,42,710
(2) Zemindaries ...	11,00,400	10,70,937
Total ...	26,82,435	26,13,647
3. Law charges recovered :—		
(1) State	—	—
(2) Zemindaries ...	48,522	67,660
4. Refunds and compensation for lands acquired :—		
(1) State ...	—	—
(2) Zemindaries ...	2,417	3,830
5. Deposits :—		
(1) State	87,865	71,284
(2) Zemindaries ...	24,323	6,518
Total ...	1,12,188	77,802
6. Loans :—		
(1) State	50,000	
(2) Zemindaries ...	80,000	2,03,000
	1,30,000	2,03,000
GRAND TOTAL ...	43,66,613	42,72,207

Expenditure.	1333 T. E.	1334 T. E.
1. General Administration charges :—		
(a) State	4,62,020	4,62,125
(b) Zemindaries :—		
1. Cost of management	1,46,216	1,36,015
2. Cost of litigation	1.22,198	95,805
Total ...	7,30,434	6,93,945
2. Revenue and Taxes on account of the Zemindaries	2,57,160	2,57,356
3. Public Works :—		
(a) State	3,13,316	2,97,487
(b) Zemindaries	1,00,105	57,614
Total ...	4,13,421	3,55,101
4. Municipality :—		
(a) State	8,988	9,250
5. Education :—		
(a) State	1,23,863	1,00,544
(b) Zemindaries	11,685	9,387
Total ...	1,35,548	1,09,931
6. Medical :—		
(a) State	1,31,931	60,313
(b) Zemindaries	10,219	10,073
Total ...	1,42,150	70,386
7. Survey and Settlement :—		
(a) State	16,159	13,617
(b) Zemindaries	1,147	1,108
Total ...	17,306	14,725
8. Agriculture :—State	1,814	4,328
9. Religious Expenses :—		
(a) State	85,055	89,691
(b) Zemindaries	5,842	6,229
Total ...	90,897	95,920
10. Sultanat :—		
(a) State	1,24,651	42,623
11. Purchase of Landed Tenures :—		
(a) State	2,614	454
(b) Zemindaries	22,091	—
Total ...	24,705	454
12. Pension and Gratuity :—		
(a) State	18,085	25,778
(b) Zemindaries	3,763	4,293
Total ...	21,848	30,071
13. Ordinary *Sansar* charges :—		
(a) Ordinary expenses on account of His Highness and family including princes & princesses	1,07,574	76,824
(b) Other branches of the Raj family...	1,56,111	1,42,763
(c) Thakurs	28,509	30,003
(d) *Sansar* office establishment ...	10,733	7,806
(e) Electric Light	36,751	22,912
(f) Miscellaneous	53,439	49,382
Total ...	3,93,117	3,29,690
14. Charity and Donation :—		
(a) State	73,360	20,230
(b) Zemindaries	27,065	1,977
Total ...	1,00,425	22,207
15. His Highness's Nij Tahabil (Privy purse) including expenses on journeys	2,60,371	4,07,410
16. Liabilities liquidated including payment of interest on loans and repayment of deposits :—		
(a) State	1,07,514	1,24,440
(b) Zemindaries	1,68,322	7,28,500
Total ...	2,75,836	8,52,940
17. Miscellaneous :—		
(a) State	3,556	3,486
(b) Zemindaries	20,970	12,505
Total ...	24,526	15,991
18. Marriage—State	37,148	15,173
19. Advances	—	3,523
20. Closing Balance :—		
(a) State		
In cash	3,18,757	3,72,122
In bonds and advances	6,86,225	2,52,472
Total ...	10,04,982	6,24,594
(b) Zemindaries :—		
In cash	65,393	1,47,517
In bonds and advances	2,35,893	1,69,072
Total ...	3,01,286	3,16,589
GRAND TOTAL ...	43,66,613	42,72,207

156. Important variations are explained below :—

i. ADMINISTRATION CHARGES :—

ZEMINDARIES—The decrease is due to the reduction of staff in the Tahasil and Divisional Offices and economy effected by minimising the institution of rent suits.

ii. PUBLIC WORKS :—

The decrease is attributable to the curtailment of expenditure to the actual requirements, and also to larger payments made during the previous year on several expensive works.

iii. EDUCATION :—

STATE—The decrease is due to the transfer of His Highness's educational expenses to Nijtahabil.

iv. MEDICAL :—

STATE—The decrease is due to the large payments of arrear medical fees in the preceding year, there being no such expenditure during the year under report.

v. SURVEY AND SETTLEMENT :—

The decrease is due to shorter programme of work undertaken during the year.

vi. AGRICULTURE :—

The increase is due to the creation of a special staff for the improvement of the cotton industry in the State.

vii. RELIGIOUS EXPENSES :—

STATE—There was no increase in reality, as the expenditure during the year included a sum of Rs. 31,105 on account of the adjustment of advances, which being excluded the real figure amounted to Rs. 58,586 only.

viii. SULTANAT :—

The decrease is attributable to extraordinary payments made in 1333 T. E. for the purchase of furniture and motor cars.

ix. PURCHASE OF LANDED PROPERTY :—

ZEMINDARIES—The difference is due to the fact that large payments had to be made during the preceding year for the price of a house at Brindaban and of an under tenure at Mogra, while no such expenditure was incurred during the year under report.

x. PENSION AND GRATUITY :—

A pretty large number of officers retired during the year and hence the increase.

xi. ORDINARY SANSAR CHARGES :—

The decrease on the whole was due to the curtailment of the Sansar expenditure during the year under review. The re-distribution of charges under sub-heads (a) & (b) contributed to the difference in those heads.

xii. CHARITY AND DONATIONS. :—

The decrease is due to restricting charitable grants in the State. The payment of Rs. 25,000 for contribution to the Comilla Water works during the year 1333 T. E. accounted for the reduction in the Zemindaries.

xiii. **Nij Tahabil.** :—

The expenditure during the year under review included Rs. 3,09,174 on account of the adjustment of advances, which being excluded, the real outlay was Rs. 98,236 only.*

xiv. **Liabilities.** :—

The total liabilities (excluding deposits) have been ascertained by a Committee appointed by the Council of Administration. The outstanding balance at the end of 1333 T. E., including an amount of Rs. 1,642 sanctioned previously by the Council but not paid, amounted to Rs. 14,54,249. Adding to this a sum of Rs. 2,03,000 subsequently borrowed at a lower rate of interest for the purpose of facilitating the early settlement of pressing debts, the total worked up to Rs. 16,57,249 of which Rs. 7,02,888 was liquidated during the year under review leaving a balance of Rs. 9,54,361 at the end of the year.

157. A noticeable feature of the financial administration is the reorganisation of the audit arrangements and the audit activities of the year.

CHAPTER VI—MEDICAL.

158. There were in all 18 dispensaries in the State during the year under report as against 19 in the previous year—the dispensary at Kalyanpur having been abolished.

New patients.

159. The total number of new patients treated in these dispensaries, as well as their daily average as compared with those of the year before, will appear from the subjoined statement.

PATIENTS.	1333 T.E.			1334 T.E.		
	Outdoor.	Indoor.	Total.	Outdoor.	Indoor.	Total.
	92,385	429	92,814	1,012,48	430	1,016,78
Daily average	252·41	1·17	253·58	277·39	1·17	278·56

Outdoor attendance.

160. The total outdoor attendance during the year under review was 1,80,482 as against 1,49,226 in the previous year—the daily average being 494·41 against 408·57.

Indoor attendance.

161. With the previous year's balance of 10, the total number of indoor patients was 430 against 429 in the preceding year. Of them 249 were discharged cured, 126 were relieved or left of their own accord, 43 died and 12 remained under treatment at the end of the year.

---

* The difference of Rs. 15,158 between the Nijtahabil figures as given in the above consolidated statement and in Appendix XXVII, is due to the adjustment during the year of an old advance which had been finally charged off previously in the financial statement of the Administration Report, without incorporation in the booked accounts.

There is a similar difference of Rs. 5,000 in respect of loans and advances.

162. There were 996 operations during the year under report against 1,043, of which 15 were major cases against 26 in the year previous.

Surgical operation.

163. New out-patients treated during the year totalled 12,504 as against 11,310 in the year before—the daily average (new+old) being 61·93 against 54·6. The number of in-patients was 394 against 396. Of them 220 were discharged cured, 125 were relieved, 40 died and 9 remained under treatment at the close of the year. The total expenditure on this institution amounted to Rs. 8,108-8-9 against Rs. 7,456-8 in the year preceding.

V. M. Hospital.

164. Altogether 118 police cases including 19 post mortem cases were admitted during the year, as against 116 and 10 respectively in the preceding year.

Police cases.

165. Two Kavirajes remained under this Department—both being posted at the capital. They treated 40 patients against 75 in the previous year. The total expenses on account of their salaries and medicines amounted to Rs. 4,268-15-6 against Rs. 6,536-0-0 of the previous year.

Ayurvedic Department.

166. As before Dr. Hira Lal Banerjee H. M. B. State Homœopath with one Assistant remained in charge of this Department. 10,111 patients were treated under this system during the year as against 12,333 in the preceding year—the daily average being 44·65 against 51·83.

Homœopathic Department.

167. The total expenses incurred in this Department was Rs. 3,187-6-9 against Rs. 5,153-5-3 in the previous year—the decrease being due to the absence of the State Homœopath on sick leave for a long period.

168. Altogether 5,120 persons out of 6,096 operated on were successfully vaccinated during the year, as against 4,472 out of 5,737 in the previous year.

Vaccination.

169. The work of vaccinators was supervised by one small-pox doctor and one Inspector. Rs. 1,095-4-3 was expended on this account against Rs. 1,012-1 in the year before.

170. Small-pox broke out in the Khowai Division near Kalyanpur. There were 22 seizures and 7 deaths.

Public health.

171. There were also outbreaks of Cholera in many parts of the State, specially in Kamalpur, Bisalgarh, Kailashahar and Udaipur Divisions.

172. Kala-Azar and Malaria raged in all their growing intensity mainly in the capital town Agartala and its vicinity, and have a tendency to spread far and wide.

Kala-Azar and Malaria.

173. One Doctor was specially appointed for the treatment of Kala-Azar cases in the capital during the year under review. Appropriate measures by way of sanitary improvements, aided by the promulgation of sanitary Laws, together with sufficient funds for adequate medical relief have become imperatively necessary to cope with these diseases and to check their spread.

174. As before Dr. M. M. Majumdar L. M. S., was the chief medical officer and Dr. S. K. Dutt, L. M. S., his assistant.

Staff.

175. Dr. M. M. Majumdar was out on tour for 15 days and Dr. S. K. Dutt for 14 days inspecting 5 and 3 dispensaries respectively.

Tour.

176. The total expenditure under the Department amounted, including grain allowance paid, to Rs. 60,313 as against Rs. 1,31,931.

Total expenditure in the Department

CHAPTER VII—PUBLIC INSTRUCTION.

177. Mr. S. C. Dev Barman, M. A. (Harvard) was in charge of the Department.

Charge.

178. The number of schools in the year under review was 138 against 171 in the previous year, and the total numerical strength 5,559 against 5,972, excluding private institutions numbering 27 with 689 pupils on the rolls, as against 14 with 458 in the previous year. In view of the retrenchment in the Budget, strict care was taken to stop State aid to those primary scools which did not come up to the standard laid down by the Department. Hence the decrease in the number of primary schools.

Number of schools.

179. In order to stimulate interest in education, school committees were appointed, mainly with powers to maintain discipline, to see to the proper attendance of boys and teachers, to foster co-operation and to keep up the school buildings in proper order. The policy involved may be said to have fairly succeeded, in so far as it evinced a growing sense of responsibility among the State subjects of the locality concerned.

180. In the year under review there were 5 High English Schools, the Umakanta Academy at Agartala, the Radhakishore Institution at Kailasahar, the Brajendrakishore Institution at Bilania, the Bir Bikram Institution at Dharmanagar and the High School at Sonamura. All the High English Schools excepting the Sonamura High School, were permanently affiliated to the Calcutta University. The Sonamura High School continued under provisional recognition for two years with effect from 1924 A. D. The building of the Sonamura High School and the Boarding houses attached thereto were under construction and the expenditure in this connection was mainly borne by the public.

H. E. Schools.

181. The number of pupils in these H. E. Schools was 899 against 867 in the previous year and the average daily attendance stood at 700·36 against 666·90. In the year under report, the Middle English School at Agartala was dissolved. The upper classes of the institution were amalgamated with the corresponding classes of the Umakanta Academy, the Infant classes only being maintained as a separate institution under the direct supervision of the Head Master of the Academy.

182. Agartala, the State Capital, was, as in the previous year, fixed by the Calcutta University as a centre for the Matriculation Examination for the year 1925. Only the five State High English Schools were allowed to send up condidates

Matriculation Centre.

to this centre. 63 condidates sat for the examination in the year under report against 48 in the previous year. The Department looked after the convenience of the candidates coming from Moffussil. The examination was conducted under the direct control and supervision of the Member of the Council of Administration in charge of Education.

Results of the Matriculation Examination.

183. Altogether 63 candidates were sent up for the last Matriculation Examination from the five State High English Schools against 48 in the previous year. The details of the results are noted below.

Name of Institution.	No. sent up.	Passed.	1st Division.	2nd Division.	3rd Division.
1. U. K. Accademy	22	20	13	7	0
2. R. K. Institution	18	16	11	5	0
3. B. K. Institution	13	11	7	3	1
4. B. B. Institution	3	3	3	0	0
5. Sonamora H. E. School	7	6	1	5	0
	63	56	35	20	1

184. The results were satisfactory. On the results of the examination seven students were awarded stipends varying from Rs. 8 to Rs. 12 P. M. tenable for two years.

Thakur Boarding House.

185. There were 35 boarders in the Thakur Boarding House against the same number in the previous year. The number of boarders successful in the last annual examination was 27 and they were promoted to higher classes. The staff consisted of one Guardian Superintendent, one Assistant tutor, one Manager and tutor, and one Private tutor.

Non-Bengalee students.

186. The comparative statement below will show the number of Non-Bengalee students receiving education in the several schools of the State :—

Serial number.	Nationality.	Number of students.		Remarks.
		Past year.	Present year.	
1.	Thakurs...	181	166	The general falling off in the numerical strength is ascribed to the withdrawal of grants from some schools which did not satisfy the required standard of the department.
2.	Manipuris	793	635	
3.	Tripuras...	533	463	
4.	Reangs	48	29	
5.	Kukis	26	66	
6.	Others	143	49	
	Total	1,724	1,408	

Reward Examination.

187. The policy of holding reward examinations for hill boys was continued and 169 boys appeared at the examination against 200 in the previous year. The fall in the numerical strength was due to outbreak of epidemic diseases in some of the centres.

Inspection Work.

188. Mr. Dev Barman, Officer in Charge of the Education Department, who is also the Inspector of Schools, visited some schools of Bilonia, Sonamura, Sadar and Bishalgarh. In the year under review, the services of the former Sub-Inspector of Schools of the Northern Division were transferred

to the teaching line and an experienced teacher was appointed towards the close of the year as Sub-Inspector in his place. The Sub-Inspector of schools of the Southern Division visited all the schools within his jurisdiction excepting those in the Sabroom Division. On average calculation his inspection work was satisfactory.

M. E. Schools.

189. In the year under review, there were 5 M. E. Schools for boys with 494 students on the rolls against the same number, with 541 pupils in the previous year. The average daily attendance was 352·18 against 377·75. In response to the demand of the local people, a new M. E. School was opened at Bishalgarh and conducted on the same lines as other M. E. Schools of the State. The new school building will be erected by the local public.

H. V. School.

190. There was only one Higher Vernacular School for boys with 43 students on the rolls as against 45 in the previous year, and an average daily attendance of 34·41 against 32·45.

L. V. Schools.

191. The number of Lower Vernacular Schools for boys was 22 against 23 in the previous year. In some of these schools boys and girls read together. The total numerical strength was 1,340 against 1,146, and the average daily attendance, 992·85 against 849·74 in the previous year.

Pathshalas.

192. There were 86 Pathshalas for boys, in the year under report, as against 115 in the previous year. The numerical strength was 2,235 against 2,741 and the average daily attendance 1705·24 against 2000·38 in the previous year. The decrease in the numerical strength was due to the withdrawal of grants from some of the Pathshalas whose conditions did not satisfy the required standard of the department.

M. E. Schools for Girls.

193. There was one Middle English School for girls, namely the Maharani Tulsibati Girls' School at Agartala, the State Capital. The numerical strength of the school was 99 aginst 93 and the average daily attendance 79·64 against 67·40 in the previous year. A Motor Bus service for the conveyance of the girls was continued during the year.

Pathshalas for Girls.

194. There were 9 Pathshalas for girls against 11 in the previous year. The numerical strength was 190 against 202 and the average daily attendance 133·32 against 141·09 in the previous year. In some of these schools, under the special order of the Education Department, girls were allowed to read the Lower Vernacular and the Upper vernacular standard. Besides these, in some of the Pathshalas for boys, both boys and girls were taught together.

Scholarship Examinations.

195. Altogether 312 candidates appeared at the local Scholarship Examinations against 330 in the previous year. Of these 259 including 22 girls came out successful. 14 students including one girl passed the Middle English Examination, 5 including one girl passed the Higher Vernacular Examination, 62 including 5 girls passed the Lower Vernacular Examination and 178 including 15 girls passed the Pathshala Examination. On the result of

the examinations, 18 boys and 5 girls received scholaships varying from Rs. 2 to Rs. 5 per month tenable for two to four years.

Schools for special Training.

196. In the year under review there were 9 schools for special training, consisting of 3 Sanskrit Tols, 5 Madrassas and Maktabs and one Artisan School, against 3, 6 and 1 respectively in the previous year. The Sanskrit Tols had 38 students on the rolls against 41 in the previous year, and the average daily attendance was 29.06 against 29·51. The Rajakiya Sanskrita Bidyalaya at Agartala sent up 5 candidates for the Government Sanskrit Examinations. The Madrassas and Maktabs had 203 students on the rolls against 271 in the previous year, and the average daily attendance was 151·41 against 216·40. The Woodburn Artisan School had 18 boys on the rolls against 25, and the average daily attendance was 6·02 against 7·55 in the previous year.

Education of Princes and Princesses.

197. The Maharaj Kumars were placed in charge of a graduate teacher. During the summer term they resided for six months with their teacher at the camp of His Highness the Maharaja Manikya Bahadur at shillong. The result of their Annual Examination was saisfactory. The Maharajkumaris received education under a graduate lady teacher and a Pandit.

Education of other Kumars.

198. Kumar Bhupendra Chandra Deb Barman who continued his B. A. course in the Comilla Victoria College during the year has since passed the B. A. Examination.

The Palace Day School for Kumars.

199. In the Day School for the young Kumars there were 7 students on the rolls belonging to the juvenile classes. 6 Kumars came out successful in the Annual Examination and were promoted to higher classes.

Education of Thakur boys.

200. Nine Thakur boys were awarded stipends from the Education Department, and the course of studies prosecuted by each is noted below :—

1. Niranjan Deb Barman—The Carmicael Medical College.
2. Surendra Chandra Laskar—B. L. (He left his college in the middle of the year.)
3. Naresh Chandra Deb Barman—Government School of Art.
4. Jogesh Chandra Deb Barman—B. Com. (Calcutta University).
5. Jaising Deb Barman—B. A.
6. Jitendra Chandra Deb Barman—B. Sc.
7. Kamal Krishna Deb Barman—B. A.
8. Nripendra Chandra Deb Barman—I. Sc.
9. Narendra Chandra Deb Barman—I. A.

201. The following students enjoyed special stipends.

Special stipends.

1. Chandrahas Sing.
2. Damanjit Rajkumar.
3. Prakash Chandra Sutradhar.
4. Asit Kumar Deb Barman.

Library.

202. At Agartala, the Bir Chandra Library was maintained in two separate sections, (1) the English Library being located at the Ujjayanta Palace and (2) the Vernacular section at the new building originally intended for the Woodburn Artisan School. The latter section was open to the public. Maharajkumar B. K. Deb Barman Bahadur, Member-in-Charge of Education,

Council of Administration, presided over the opening ceremony of the public section of the Bir Chandra Library at the new building. The number of English books (including foreign literature) was 4,853 against 4,846 in the previous year, and the number of Bengali books (including Sanskrit books) was 1,747 aginst 1,679 in the previous year In addition to these there was a moderate collection of some valuable manuscripts in the Palace Library. There were 7 Dailies, 1 quarterly, and 8 Monthlies as against 7, 1, and 10 in the previous year. In the year under review the average daily attendance of readers was 13·2 against 8·38, and the total number of volumes issued to the public was 5,309 against 1,186 in the previous year.

Expenditure.

203. The total expenditure incurred in the Education Department in the year under report amounted to Rs. 1,00,544 against Rs. 1,23,863 in the previous year. The decrease in expenditure was due to the transfer of the educational expenditure of His Highness to a separate head and the withdrawal of grants from some of the primary schools already referred to. some important details of the expenditure are noted below :—

1.	Primary Edcation	Rs.	16,068
2.	Secondary Education	,,	39,108
3.	Schools for special Training	,,	3,520
4.	Boarding Institution for Thakur boys	,,	9,014
5.	Education of Kumars and Kumaris	,,	6,310
6.	Scholarships & Stipends	,,	7,302
7.	Library	,,	2,399
8.	Miscellaneous	,,	11,948
9.	Grain allowance	,,	4,875
	Total ...	Rs.	1,00,544

Income.

204. The policy of keeping all realisations from students, including school fees, outside the finances of the State was considered open to objection. In view of the growing demand on State revenue in matters educational, Rs. 10,000 out of the accumulated fund was ordered experimentally to be incorporated in the receipts of the year, as a set off against the increased expenditure. Rs. 7,900 of the amount was paid in or adjusted within the year.

CHAPTER VIII—ZEMINDARIES.

Chakla Roshnabad Estates.

Management.

205. The management of His Highness's Zemindaries in British India continued in the hands of Rai Jyotish Chandra Sen Bahadur, B. A., B. C. S., assisted by two Assistant Managers and two Sub-managers.

206. The gross revenue demand of the year was Rs. 9,64,484 against Rs. 9,59,110 in the previous year.

207. The total receipts amounted to Rs. 11,47,065 against Rs. 11,00,400 in the preceding year. Besides this, Rs. 2,03,000 was obtained during the year from the dowager Maharanees as deposit carrying 4½ P. C. interest per annum for repayment of old debts.

Expenditure.

208. The total expenditure in the year under review was Rs. 13,36,642 including adjustment of old advances, as against Rs. 13,35,958 in the previous year. Of this Rs. 2,57,356 was on account of Land Revenue and Cesses. The total administrative charges of the Zemindaries including Public Works and Law charges amounted to Rs. 3,07,340. The remainder represents special payments on account of the following items, aggregating Rs. 7,71,946.

1.	Repayment of old debts	Rs.	7,02,888
2.	Donation	,,	1,977
3.	Medical Charges	,,	10,073
4.	Education charges	,,	9,387
5.	Religious ceremonies	,,	6,229
6.	Sansar Stipends	,,	15,780
7.	Repayment of old deposits ...	,,	25,612
		Rs.	7,71,946

Settlement.

209. The result of the year's settlement operations will appear from the figures noted below :—

	Kinds of settlement.	Addition to rental.		Nazar.	
1.	Railway relinquished land ...	Rs.	15	Rs.	58
2.	*Taskhichi Taluk* in the Town	,,		,,	2,145
3.	Ordinary town settlement ...	,,	119	,,	2,786
4.	*Khaspatit* settlement ...	,,	966	,,	7,148
5.	Enhancement of rent ...	,,	760	,,	110,75
6.	Re-settlement of auction purchased holdings ...	,,	214	,,	13,090
7.	*Taskhichi Taluk* in the interior	,,	2	,,	624
8.	*Ijara*	,,	1,282		
		Rs.	3,358	Rs.	36,926

210. The year's operations improved the rent roll by Rs. 3,358 and brought in a *nazarana* of Rs. 36,926 against Rs. 1,571 and Rs. 37,147 in the previous year.

CHAPTER IX—MISCELLANEOUS.

The Rajmala.

211. The literary work connected with the third part of the Rajmala was completed during the year, and the fourth part taken up. The printing of the first part which has been going on in Calcutta could not be finished during the year, and the work is in progress, simultaneously with the printing of the second part at the newly installed press at Agartala. The total expenditure incurred during the year, excluding the grant to the periodical *Rabi*, amounted to Rs. 2,392 against Rs. 3,556 of the year before.

212. The Vice President of the Council of Administration, Rai J. C. Sen Bahadur, was out on tour for 43 days during the year, in the course of which he inspected a number of offices and institutions.

Tours of members of the Council.

213. Dewan B. K. Sen, Chief Secretary, visited the Sonamura and Udaipur Divisions twice, mainly in connection with His Highness the Maharaja's tour, and with visits on duty to places outside the State, was altogether in camp for 31 days.

Tours of high officers.

214. Dewan Asita Chandra Chaudhuri, Officer in charge of Revenue, Forest, Agriculture and General Departments was out for 52 days.

215. The tours of other high officers have already been noticed in the connected sections.

216. The tours of the Divisional Officers and their assistants as well as of other officers of analogous status are noted below.

Divisional Officers.

State.

1.	Sadar—		
	Divisional Officer—Babu Brajendra Kumar Dutta	...	28 days.
	„ Thakur Tarini Charan Deb Barman	...	13 „
2.	Kailashahar—		
	Divisional Officer— „ Lalit Mohan Deb Barman, M. A., B. L.	...	24 „
	Second „ Babu Jyotirmoy Ghosh, M. A.	...	22 „
3.	Sonamura—		
	Divisional Officer— „ Tarit Mohan Gupta	...	43 „
	Second „ „ Prava Ranjan Das Gupta, M. A., B. L.	...	8 „
4.	Belonia—		
	Divisional Officer—Thakur Kamini Kumar Singh	...	57 „
	Second „ Babu Jogendra Lal Ganguly, B. L.	...	70 „
5.	Khowai—		
	Divisional Officer—Thakur Gokul Chandra Deb Barman	...	34 „
6.	Udaipur—		
	Divisional Officer—Babu Bisweswar Guha, B. A.	...	18 „
7.	Dharmanagar—		
	Divisional Officer— „ Ramani Mohan Goswami, M. A., B. L.	...	61 „
8.	Sabroom—		
	Divisional Officer— „ Suresh Chandra Chakravarty, B. L.	...	66 „
9.	Amarpur—		
	Sub-Divisional Officer— „ Kusum Kumar Sen, B. L.	...	23 „
10.	Touji „ „ Kunja Behari Chakravarty, M. A., B. L.	...	29 „
11.	Survey Superintendent— „ Kamini Kumar Kar ...	...	114 „
12.	Superintendent of Agriculture—Mr. J. Choudhuri ...	...	91 „
13.	Forest Officer—Babu Jatindra Nath Mitra	...	110 „

Zemindaries.

1.	Assistant Manager,	Central Division,	...	... 39	"
2.	"	Southern "	...	... 33	"
3.	Sub Manager,	Northern "	...	... 67	"
4.	"	Srimangal "	...	... 80	"

217. The Council notices with regret that the tours of the year are in some cases insufficient.

DATED, AGARTALA,
The 16th September, 1925.

By order of the Council of Administration.

B. K. Sen,
Chief Secretary.

APPENDIX.

List of the principal Laws and Regulations in force in the Tripura State during 1334 T.E.

Description.	Whether adapted from British Indian Acts.	Whether introduced during the year under report.
CRIMINAL.		
1. Regulation No. III. of 1280 T. E.		
2. Regulation No. I. of 1283 T. E.		
3. Jail Regulation, 1283 T. E.		
4. Regulation No. IV. of 1283 T. E. (Cattle trespass and pound).		
5. Regulation No. III. of 1296 T. E. (Police Regulation).		
6. Act No. IV. of 1321 T. E.–Penal Laws (an amending Act)		
CIVIL.		
1. Civil Law of 1284 T. E.		
2. Rules regarding *chit* suits (small causes) 1287 and 1300 T. E.		
3. Act No. II. of 1313 T. E.—an Act for the regulation of interest on debts.		
4. Act No. II. of 1314 T. E.—Limitation Act	Partly adapted.	
REVENUE.		
1. Act No. I. of 1286 T. E.—Stamp Act		
2. Act No. I. of 1290 T. E.—Sale Law		
3. Act No. I. of 1296 T. E.—Tenancy Act.		
4. Act No. II. of 1296 T. E.—*Abkari*		
5. Act No. II. of 1297 T. E.—Reserved forests.		
6. Act No. I. of 1304 T. E.—Duties on *til* and cotton.		
7. Act No. I. of 1306 T. E.—Registration	Do.	
8. Survey and Settlement Act, 1309 T.E.	Do.	
9. *Tuccavi* Regulation, 1310 T. E.		
10. Act No. I. of 1313 T. E.—Forests.		
11. Act No. I. of 1314 T. E.—(amending the above)		
12. A Law imposing export duty on jute and mustard-seed, 1317 T. E.		
13. Act No. II. of 1321 T.E.—Ghasuri Act		
MISCELLANEOUS.		
1. An Act promulgating certain rules as Law, 1283 T. E.		
2. Regulation for the record of judicial decisions &c., 1284 T. E. ...		
3. Municipal Regulation, 1284 T. E.		
4. Legal Practitioners' Regulation.		
5. Act No. I. of 1297 T. E.—an Act for the regulation of commissions for the examination of witnesses.		
6. Special Regulation against cow slaughter		
7. Rules of evidence		
8. Act I. of 1318 T. E.—Constitution of Courts—(an amending Act).		
9. Leave and allowance Rules	Do.	
10. Act No. I. of 1321 T. E.—Arms Act	Do.	
11. Act No. III. of 1321 T. E.—Constitution of Courts (an amending Act)		

Description.	Whether adapted from British Indian Acts.	Whether introduced during the year under report.
12. Municipal Act No. I of 1322 T. E.		
13. Revenue Sale Amendment Act—1323 T.E.		
14. An Act for the destruction of old records—1323 T.E.		
15. Act I of 1326 T. E.—Regulation regarding Privy Council Appeals.		
16. Act II of 1326 T. E.—Registration of Births and Deaths	Partly adapted.	
17. Act III of 1326 T. E.—Vaccination Act	Do.	
18. Act IV of 1326 T. E.—Public Demands Recovery Act	Do.	
19. Act V of 1326 T. E.—Excise Amendment Act		
20. Act I of 1327 T. E.—Settlement of lands for tea cultivation		
21. Regulation No. 1 of 1328 T. E.—regarding Registration of Coolies		
22. Regulation No. 2 of 1328 T. E.—regarding Export of Tea		
23. Act I of 1329 T. E.—(Absconding sepoys Act)		
24. Act II of 1329 T. E.—(Control of prices of food stuff)		
25. Act III of 1329 T. E.—(Elephants and Buffaloes grazing Act)		
26. Act IV of 1329 T. E.—(House tax on Hill tribes)		
27. Act V of 1329 T. E.—(Legal practitioners, Act)	Do	
28. Act I of 1330 T. E.—Census Act		
29. Act I of 1332 T. E.—Encumbered Estates Act.		
30. Act III of 1332 T. E.—The Opium and Intoxicating Drugs Act.		

II.

Statement showing the strength, cost, and other particulars of the Military Force in Tripura State for 1334 T. E.

Arm of service.	Number of fighting officers and men.						Details of force at the end of the current year.						Total cost on account of pay and allowances of the force, including followers.	Remarks.
	At the end of last year.	Recruited this year.	*Casualties.* Died.	*Casualties.* Invalided.	*Casualties.* Discharged, deserted, &c.	At the end of the current year.	Number of regiments, battalions, or Batteries.	Number of guns.	*Number of men.* European commissioned officers.	*Number of men.* Native commissioned officers.	*Number of men.* Non-commissioned officers.	*Number of men.* Fighting men.		
1	2	3	4	5	6	7	8	9	10	11	12	13	14	15
Infantry ...	239	33	5	0	51	216	1	291	—	—	44	172	Rs. 41,465	

III.

Statement showing the strength, cost, discipline, and education of the Police for the year 1334 T. E.

Description of office.	Number.	Pay of grade.	Total cost.	PUNISHMENTS.			REWARDS.		EDUCATION.		REMARKS.
				Dismissed.	Fined, degraded, or suspended departmentally.	Punished judicially.	By promotion.	By money.	Number able to read and write.	Number under instruction.	
1	2	3	4	5	6	7	8	9	10	11	12
		Rs.									
Superintendent of Police	1	150-10-250	67,445	—	—	—	—	—	196	—	
Asst. Superintendent „	1	75-5-100		—	—	—	—	—		—	
Inspector	3	50 to 80		—	—	—	—	—		—	
Sub-Inspector or Daroga	23	25 to 40		—	—	—	—	4		—	
Naib Daroga	15	15 to 20		—	—	—	—	—		—	
Writer Constable	13	11		—	—	—	—	—		—	
Subadar	1	25		—	—	—	—	—		—	
Jamadar	6	15		—	—	—	—	—		—	
Constable	210	8 to 12		8	34	—	—	8		—	
Chowkidar	175	5		—	—	—	—	1		—	
Spy	3	15		—	—	—	—	—		—	
	451										

IV.

Statement showing the working of the Police in the Tripura State during the year 1334 T.E.

State.	Number of offences.		Number of accused arrested.		Number of accused sent for trial.		Number of accused convicted.		Number of accused acquitted or discharged.		Percentage convicted of accused arrested.		Percentage convicted of accused sent for trial.		REMARKS.
	Past year.	Present year.	Past year.	Present year.	Past year.	Present year.	Past year.	Present year.	Past year.	Present year.	Past year.	Present year.	Past year.	Present year.	
1	2	3	4	5	6	7	8	9	10	11	12	13	14	15	16
Tripura State	1,222	1,130	787	743	754	730	195	113	128	93	54·6	47·45*	60·1	53·3*	* Excluding 101 acquitted on compromise, 39 withdrawn, 1 dead, 9 fled and 370 awaiting trial

V.

Statement showing the value of property stolen and amount of recoveries in the Tripura State during the year 1334 T.E.

State.	Amount stolen.		Amount recovered.		Percentage of recoveries of property stolen.		REMARKS.
	Past year.	Present year.	Past year.	Present year.	Past year.	Present year.	
1	2	3	4	5	6	7	8
Tripura State	Rs 16,558-11-3	Rs 20,667-11-0	Rs 3,722-4-9	Rs 6,514-2-0	22·4	31·51	

VI.

Statement showing the number of crimes committed, number of cases disposed of, and cases awaiting trial in the Tripura State during the year 1334 T. E.

Description of offences.		Number of offences.			Number of cases disposed of during the past year.	Number of cases disposed of during the present year.	Number of cases awaiting trial.	Number of persons apprehended.	Number of persons convicted.	Number of persons sentenced.								Number of persons acquitted or discharged.	Number of persons confined being insane.	Number of persons dead during or before trial.	Term of imprisonment.											Persons awaiting trial.	Remarks.
		Balance from past year.	Committed during the present year.	Total.						Imprisonment. Simple.	Imprisonment. Rigorous.	Imprisonment and fine. Simple.	Imprisonment and fine. Rigorous.	Fine only.	Whipping.	Capital punishment.	Total.				Under one month.	From 1 to 2 months.	From 2 to 3 months.	From 3 to 6 months.	From 6 to 12 months.	From 1 to 2 years.	From 2 to 3 years.	From 3 to 5 years.	Above 5 years.	Transportation.	Capital punishment.		
1		2	3	4	5	6	7	8	9	10	11	12	13	14	15	16	17	18	19	20	21	22	23	24	25	26	27	28	29	30	31	32	33
Class I. Offences against the State, public tranquillity, safety and justice &c.	cognizable ...	17	23	40	31	21	19	a183	14	0	9	0	0	5	0	0	14	75	0	2	0	0	0	5	1	2	1	0	0	0	0	91	
	non-cognizable	3	49	52	33	41	11	10	1	1	0	0	0	0	0	0	1	2	0	0	0	0	0	1	0	0	0	0	0	0	0	7	
Class II. Offences against person.	cognizable ...	55	136	191	181	137	54	b378	19	1	11	0	6	1	0	0	19	217	0	6	1	5	2	4	1	0	0	2	3	0	0	132	
	non-cognizable	50	290	340	273	289	51	250	37	0	4	0	0	33	0	0	37	187	0	1	2	0	1	·1	0	0	0	0	0	0	0	25	
Class III. Offences against property.	cognizable ...	241	796	1037	780	714	323	c1430	c280	6	52	1	24	187	0	0	270	720	0	6	24	11	15	17	5	5	1	0	5	0	0	418	
	non-cognizable	36	166	202	180	166	36	207	17	0	1	0	0	16	0	0	17	161	0	0	1	0	0	0	0	0	0	0	0	0	0	26	
Class IV. Other offences.	cognizable ...	35	96	131	124	90	41	d151	d20	2	2	0	0	15	0	0	19	61	0	1	2	0	1	0	1	0	0	0	0	0	0	68	
	non-cognizable	40	310	350	246	271	79	e179	30	0	1	0	0	8	0	0	9	106	0	1	0	0	0	0	1	0	0	0	0	0	0	39	
Total cognizable ...	...	348	1051	1399	1116	962	437	2142	333	9	74	1	30	208	0	0	322	1073	0	15	27	16	18	26	8	7	2	2	8	0	0	709	
Total non-cognizable ...	...	129	815	944	732	767	177	646	85	1	6	0	0	57	0	0	64	459	0	2	3	0	1	2	1	0	0	0	0	0	0	97	
GRAND TOTAL ...	...	477	1866	2343	1848	1729	614	2788	418	10	80	1	30	265	0	0	386	1532	0	17	30	16	19	28	9	7	2	2	8	0	0	806	

Remarks (column 33):

- a. One person escaped.
- b. Four persons transferred.
- c. Six persons transferred, 9 persons have been warned for the future and 1 person released on bail.
- d. One person transferred, and one person has been warned for the future.
- e. Three persons transferred, and 21 persons released on bail.

VII.

Statement showing the number of offences reported and dealt with by the various Courts in the Tripura State during the year 1334 T.E.

Name of Court.	Number of offences reported during the year.		Number of persons dealt with.								Persons disposed of.					Persons remaining at the end of the year.	Remarks
	Last year.	Present year.	Remaining at the end of last year.	Brought to trial in 1333 T. E.					Total.		Discharged without trial.	Acquitted.	Convicted.	Committed or referred.	Died, escaped, or transferred &c.		
				Arrested by Police.	Upon warrant.	On summons.	Voluntary.	Arrested in presence of the Magistrate.	Last year.	Present year.							
1	2	3	4	5	6	7	8	9	10	11	12	13	14	15	16	17	18
Sadar Magistracy	408	585	82	111	143	224	26	4	529	636	230	133	85	12	2	174	
Bisalgarh " ...	130	0	46	0	0	0	0	0	251	0	0	0	0	0	0	0	abolished
Sonamura " ...	217	247	83	37	44	164	65	0	325	393	176	42	43	3	7	122	
Bilonia " ...	214	227	112	134	21	83	125	5	379	480	164	120	156	2	0	38	
Kailashahar " ...	155	201	125	77	71	51	36	0	299	393	129	6	8	1	6	243	
Kamalpur " ...	99	0	33	0	0	0	0	0	198	0	0	0	0	0	0	0	"
Khowai " ...	115	129	13	38	14	12	2	0	141	189	25	106	28	2	0	28	
Kalyanpur " ...	35	0	1	0	0	0	0	0	50	0	0	0	0	0	8	0	"
Dharmanagar " ...	204	264	108	68	41	69	45	0	381	331	101	97	39	4	0	82	
Udaipur " ...	127	167	34	40	58	93	76	5	163	310	61	106	33	4	5	101	
Amarpur " ...	21	0	4	0	0	0	0	0	21	0	0	0	0	0	0	0	"
Sabrum " ...	23	46	2	11	9	21	0	0	28	43	15	9	8	1	4	6	
TOTAL ...	1,739	1,856	643	516	401	826	375	14	2,765	a 2,775	901	619	400	b 29	32	794	

a Excluding 13 persons pending before the court of Sessions at the close of the previous year.

b Including 13 persons pending from last year, the total number of persons for trial before the Court of Sessions was 42; of these, 18 were convicted. 3 discharged without trial, 9 acquitted and 12 remained under trial.

VIII.

Statement of Criminal cases in whch British Subjects were concerned for 1334 T.E.

Description of Offences.		Cases pending since the previous year.	Cases instituted during the year.	Total number of cases.	Cases in which complainants were British subjects.	Cases in which both parties were British subjects.	Cases in which defendants were British Subjects.													Remarks.
							Cases pending since the previous year	Cases instituted during the year.	Total number of cases.	Cases disposed of.		Cases pending at the close of the year.	Persons under trial at the close of the previous year.	Persons brought to trial during the year.	Total number of persons under trial.	Convicted.	Acquitted or Discharged.	Died, or Escaped &c.	Under trial at the close of the year.	
										Rejected, Compromised or Dismissed without enquiry.	Tried.									
Class I. Offences against the State &c.	cognizable	6	8	14	0	3	6	8	14	4	7	3	33	30	63	12	38	0	13	Of this number 152 were discharged without trial, the cases being dismissed, compromised or struck off on default. Excluding 3 transferred and 127 pending, the actual number of persons tried was 329, of whom 194 or 58·966 were convicted as against 51·8006 of the previous year.
	non-cognizable	1	3	4	2	0	0	2	2	1	1	0	0	1	1	1	0	0	0	
Class II. Offences against person.	cognizable	12	27	39	10	11	11	18	29	13	7	9	13	34	47	4	35	0	8	
	non-cognizable	9	37	46	10	27	9	27	36	25	4	7	6	14	20	2	16	0	2	
Class III. Offences against property.	cognizable	80	216	296	18	83	79	199	278	86	127	63	80	355	435	175	168	0	89	
	non-cognizable	6	18	24	6	11	6	12	18	10	5	3	7	4	11	1	8	0	2	
Class IV Other offences.	cognizable	4	22	26	0	5	5	21	26	12	7	7	4	19	23	4	10	0	9	
	non-cognizable	8	44	52	11	24	8	33	41	30	4	7	3	16	19	1	14	0	4	
Total cognizable		102	273	375	28	102	101	246	347	115	148	82	130	438	568	195	251	0	119	
Total non-cognizable		24	102	126	29	62	23	74	97	66	14	17	16	35	51	5	38	0	8	
Grand Total		126	375	501	57	164	124	320	444	181	162	99	146	473	619*	200	289	0	127	

IX

Statement of Extradition Cases for 1334 T.E.

Names of Courts.	Nature of cases.	Number of persons against whom warrants were applied for.	Number of persons arrested and surrendered.	Number of persons who appeared of their own accord or were subsequently arrested within this territory.	Number at large at the close of the year.	Result. Convicted.	Result. Acquitted or Discharged.	Pending trial at the close of the year.	Remarks.
Sadar Magistracy ...	Dacoity ...	1	0	1	0	0	0	1	
	Theft ...	1	1	0	0	0	1	0	
	Theft ...	1	0	1	0	1	0	0	
	Theft ...	13	0	11	2	1	10	0	
	Theft ...	3	0	3	0	0	0	3	
	Resistance to taking of property by lawful authority of public servant ...	3	0	1	2	0	0	1	
Sonamura " ...	Theft ...	6	1	5	0	0	0	6	
	Resistance or obstruction by a person to his lawful apprehension and voluntarily causing hurt to deter public servant from his duty ...	5	0	5	0	0	5	0	
	Theft ...	1	0	0	1	0	0	0	
	Resistance or obstruction by a person to his lawful apprehension and voluntarily causing hurt to deter public servant from his duty ...	7	0	0	7	0	0	0	
Bilonia " ...	Theft, rioting & rescuing offenders from lawful custody & obstructing public servant from discharge of his duty ...	6	3	3	0	1	5	0	
	Robbery* ...	1	0	1	0	1	0	0	
	Robbery ...	2	0	2	0	0	2	0	
	Theft, rescuing offenders from lawful custody & assaulting public servant with deadly weapons ...	4	3	1	0	0	4	0	
	Theft ...	1	0	1	0	1	0	0	
	Theft, obstructing a public servant from discharge of his duty, rescuing offenders from lawful custody, unlawful assembly ...	6	2	4	0	6	0	0	
	Unlawful assembly, criminal trespass, assault with deadly weapons, hurt, rioting, mischief by fire with intent to destroy a house, wrongful confinement, attempt to murder, abetment ...	30	0	1	29	0	0	1	
	Theft and escape from lawful custody ...	1	1	0	0	1	0	0	
	Theft, rioting with deadly weapon, criminal force to deter public servant from discharge of his duty, rescuing offenders and escape from lawful custody ...	7	5	2	0	7	0	0	
	Theft ...	1	0	1	0	1	0	0	
	Theft ...	9	8	1	0	0	0	9	
Kailashahar " ...	Culpable homicide not amounting to murder ...	1	0	0	1	0	0	0	
	Escape from lawful custody ...	1	0	0	1	0	0	0	
	Theft ...	1	1	0	0	0	1	0	
Dharmanagar " ...	Voluntarily causing hurt by dangerous weapons ...	1	0	1	0	0	0	1	
	Lurking house-trespass and house-breaking by night ...	2	1	0	1	0	0	1	
	Theft ...	1	0	0	1	0	0	0	
	Lurking house-trespass and house-breaking by night ...	1	0	0	1	0	0	0	
Sabroom " ...	Theft ...	3	1	0	2	0	0	1	
	Total ...	120	27	45	48	20	28	24	

C

X.

Statement showing the results of appeals against decisions passed by the Criminal Courts in the Tripura State during the year 1334 T. E.

TRIBUNALS.	Number of applications.	NUMBER OF PERSONS AND CASES.																Remarks.
		Applications rejected.		Sentences.						Proceedings quashed.		Referred.		Futher enquiry, &c, ordered.		Pending.		
				Confirmed.		Modified.		Reversed.										
		Persons.	Cases.	Persons.	Cases.	Persons.	Cases.	Persons.	Cases.	Persons.	Cases.	Persons.	Cases.	Persons.	Cases.	Persons.	Cases.	
Khas Adalat. ...	192	12	12	103	89	26	14	91	49	—	—	—	—	10	10	22	18	

XI.

Civil Work.—Nature and value of original suits filed and disposed of during the year 1334 T. E.

Tribunal.	Opening balance.		Filed during the year, received by transfer or on remand.		Total.		Disposed of during the year		Closing balance.		Suits filed during present year.									Suits disposed of during present year.						Suits not estimable in money.	Remarks.
	Past year.	Present year.	Past year.	Present year.	Past year.	Present year.	Past year.	Present year.	Past year.	Present year.	Value.	Suits *re* landed property.	Suits for money transaction.	Suits for other rights.	Number of suits under Rs. 100.	Number of suits above Rs. 100 and under Rs. 500.	Number of suits above Rs. 500 and under Rs. 1,000.	Number of suits above Rs. 1,000 and under Rs. 5,000.	Number of suits above Rs. 5000.	*Exparte.*	Admitted and compromised.	Struck off the file.	Otherwise disposed of.	Value.	Average duration.		
											Rs. a. p.													*Rs. a. p.*	*Y.m.d.*		
Khas Adalat Orginial side	67	55	19	22	86	77	31	28	55	49	22,543-14-6	7	2	13	0	0	0	12	0	2	11	11	4	36,728-14-0	0-4-0	10	
Sadar Dewani Adalat	271	245	463	631	734	983	489	499	245	489	32,492-7-3	259	283	89	387	138	13	0	0	138	81	164	116	29,382-6-3	*0-6-1	93	
Bishalgarh „	153	112	195	0	348	0	236	0	112	0	0	0	0	0	0	0	0	0	0	0	0	0	0	0	0	0	
Sonamura „	106	113	252	201	358	314	245	224	113	90	13,531-2-6	52	119	30	138	28	5	0	0	68	9	70	77	16,596-13-6	0-1-2	30	
Bilonia „	58	41	110	112	168	163	127	136	41	17	5,560-1-9	50	35	27	69	15	1	0	0	74	25	18	19	6,824-15-6	0-4-14	27	
Kailashahar „	103	160	217	280	320	530	160	221	160	309	24,318-1-6	87	151	42	210	38	5	0	0	62	44	42	73	15,352-11-6	0-4-28	27	
Kamalpur „	53	90	141	0	194	0	104	0	90	0	0	0	0	0	0	0	0	0	0	0	0	0	0	0	0	0	
Khowai „	27	13	68	113	95	127	82	101	13	26	7,223-7-0	14	82	17	69	13	0	0	0	29	11	18	43	3,506-12-0	0-1-12	31	
Kalyanpur „	6	1	9	0	15	0	14	0	1	0	0	0	0	0	0	0	0	0	0	0	0	0	0	0	0	0	
Dharmanagar	98	81	132	119	230	200	149	148	81	52	5,002-1-6	19	23	77	58	13	0	0	0	11	23	30	84	7,409-4-9	1-7-1	48	
Udaipur „	40	30	227	248	267	281	237	240	30	41	26,573-2-6	12	234	2	164	70	3	0	0	80	73	23	64	25,411-1-9	0-4-11	11	
Amarpur „	4	3	15	0	19	0	16	0	3	0	0	0	0	0	0	0	0	0	0	0	0	0	0	0	0	0	
Sabrum „	1	2	15	11	16	13	14	12	2	1	1,276-0-0	0	11	0	6	5	0	0	0	5	5	2	0	1,236-0-0	0-2-5	0	
Total ...	987	946	1,863	1,737	2,850	2,683	1,904	1,609	946	1,074	1,38,520-6-6	500	940	297	1101	320	27	12	0	469	282	378	480	1,42448-15-3	0-5-8	277	

Note :—The Courts at Bishalgarh, Kamalpur Kalyanpur and Amarpur abolished.

XII.

Civil Work.—Results of applications for Execution of Decrees, 1334 T.E.

Tribunal.	Opening balance.		Value of opening balance for present year.	Applications brought to the Register.			Total.			Disposed of.			Closing balance.			Nature of applications pending disposal at the close of the year.			REMARKS.
	Past year.	Present year.		Past year.	Present year.	Value for present year.	Past year.	Present year.	Value for present year.	Past year.	Present year.	Value for present year.	Past yaer.	Present year.	Value for present year.	Below 6 months.	Below 12 months.	Above 12 months.	
			Rs. a. p.			*Rs. a. p.*		*R.*	*Rs. a. p.*			*Rs. a. p.*			*Rs. a. p.*				
Khas Adalat (Original side)	19	21	51,183-14-0	12	11	7,417-5-9	31	32	58,601-3-9	10	13	5,712-0-6	21	19	52,889-3-3	0	7	12	
Sadar Dewani Adalat } ...	179	148	18,396-13-6	147	153	18,291-4-3	326	338	43,508-10-3	177	184	22,887-15-6	148	154	20,620-10-9	56	35	63	
Bisalgarh Ditto } ...	57	37	6,820-8-6	70	0	0	127	0	0	90	0	0	37	0	0	0	0	0	abolished
Sonamura Ditto ...	55	49	4,835-11-3	144	79	7,811-10-3	199	128	12,647-5-6	150	97	9,104-7-0	49	31	3,542-14-6	16	9	6	
Bilonia Ditto ...	30	24	2,625-8-9	40	62	4,292-12-6	70	86	6,918-5-3	46	70	5,614-5-6	24	16	1,303-15-9	12	2	2	
Kailashahar Ditto } ...	50	60	11,376-8-6	68	45	4,398-11-6	118	140	19,329-2-9	58	63	7,150-7-6	60	77	12,178-11-3	17	32	28	
Kamalpur Ditto } ...	32	35	3,553-14-9	41	0	0	73	0	0	38	0	0	35	0	0	0	0	0	”
Khowai Ditto } ...	7	5	193-2-6	17	37	4,196-12-6	24	46	4,918-12-3	17	37	2,978-7-3	5	9	1940-5-0	7	2	0	
Kalyanpur Ditto } ...	6	4	528-13-3	12	0	0	18	0	0	14	0	0	4	0	0	0	0	0	”
Dharmanagar Ditto ...	63	46	8,392-5-3	25	51	3,938-4-9	88	97	12,330-10-0	42	46	4,965-14-9	46	51	7,364-11-3	16	13	22	
Udaipur Ditto } ...	39	23	4,458-5-6	99	121	15,893-12-0	138	147	20,336-1-3	115	110	14,099-15-3	23	37	6,236-2-0	30	7	0	
Amarpur Ditto } ...	1	3	283-15-9	8	0	0	9	0	0	6	0	0	3	0	0	0	0	0	”
Sabrum Ditto ...	0	1	47-12-9	5	2	341-2-9	5	3	388-15-6	4	3	388-15-6	1	0	0	0	0	0	
Total ...	538	456	1,12,697-6-3	688	561	66,281-12-3	1,226	1,017	1,78,979-2-6	767	623	72,902-8-9	456	394	1,06,076-9-9	154	107	133	

XIII

Civil Work.—Number and results of appeals in civil suits, 1334 T. E.

Tribunal.	Opening balance.		Filed during.		Total.		Disposed of during.		Closing balance.		Value of appeals filed during.		How disposed of.										Average duration.	
													Decisions confirmed.		Decisions reversed.		Decisions amended.		Cases remanded for retrial.		Cases compromised and otherwise disposed of.			
	Past year.	Present year.	Past year.	Present year.	Past year.	Present year.	Past year.	Present year.	Past year.	Present year.	Past year.	Present year.	Past year.	Present year.	Past year.	Present year.	Past year.	Present year.	Past year.	Present year.	Past year.	Present year.	Past year.	Present year.
											Rs. a. p.	*Rs. a. p.*											*Y.m.d.*	*Y.m.d.*
Khas Adalat	41	32	156	155	197	187	165	126	32	61	8,684-13-9	19,803-15-0	93	71	49	34	6	6	4	4	13	11	0-2-5	0-2-3

XIV.

Statement showing the number of persons confined in the jails and lock-ups in the Tripura State during the year 1334 T.E.

Stations.	Number of prisons.	NUMBER OF PRISONERS. Remaining from last year.	Admitted during the year.	Total. Past year.	Total. Present year.	DAILY AVERAGE. Past year.	DAILY AVERAGE. Present year.	Number of prisoners remaining at the end of the year.	Cost of jail and prisoners.	Average period in days of accused under trial.	Remarks showing mortality among convicts in jail.
									Rs. a. p.		
Agartala	1	62	180	299	242	67·96	62·54	71	9,655	29	One convict died of fever and dropsy.
Sonamura	1	2	71	41	73	3·53	4·21	6	692	20·87	
Bilonia	1	11	108	67	119	·09	·33	1	470	11·83	
Kailashahar	1	—	63	47	63	2·45	3·78	2	551	20·28	One under trial died.
Khowai	1	1	23	42	24	1·84	1·17	3	277	16·67	
Dharmanagar	1	8	82	111	90	9·64	8·94	4	1,018	29·93	
Udaipur	1	2	36	39	38	2·34	2·61	2	370	25·51	
Sabrum	1	2	10	15	12	·55	·35	2	155	11·33	
Kalyanpur				13		·20					Abolished.
Amarpur				10		·02					
Bishalgar				47		1·21					
Kamalpur				18		2·29					
TOTAL ...	8	88	573	749	661	92·12	83·93	91	13,188	20·67	

XV.

Registration of documents in the Tripura State during the year 1334 T.E.

Name of State.	Documents presented for registration.		Nature of documents presented. Mortgages.		Sale deeds.		Wills.		Money bonds.		Miscellaneous.		Documents registered.		Value of documents registered.		Documents of which registration has been refused.		Documents remaining unregistered at the end of the year.		Remarks.
	Past year.	Present year.	Past year.	Present year.	Past year.	Present year.	Past year.	Present year.	Past year.	Present year.	Past year.	Present year.	Past year.	Present year.	Past year.	Present year.	Past year.	Present year.	Past year.	Present year.	
1	2	3	4	5	6	7	8	9	10	11	12	13	14	15	16	17	18	19	20	21	22
															Rs.	*Rs.*					
Tripura State	9,040	9,674	2,320	2,475	4,388	4,604	6	2	207	227	2,119	2,366	8,907	9,568	11,62,103	14,96,766	128	110	58	54	

XVI.

Statement showing the receipts and expenditure on account of Registration during the year 1334 T.E.

Description.	Past Year.			Present Year.			Remarks.
	Number of deeds.	Value of property.	Fees realised.	Number of deeds.	Value of property.	Fees realised.	
		Rs.	Rs.		Rs.	Rs.	
Mortgages	2,320	2,46,731	2,134	2,475	3,02,409	2,359	
Sale deeds	4,388	6,23,981	5,115	4,604	9,15,029	5,829	
Will	6	—	41	2	—	11	
Money bonds	207	27,096	190	227	22,475	206	
Miscellaneous	2,119	3,04,111	2,764	2,366	2,89,645	2,808	
Total ...	9,040	12,01,919	10,244	9,674	15,29,558	11,213	
Total Expenditure ...	—	—	3,445	—	—	3,639	
Net Income ...	—	—	6,799	—	—	7,574	

XVII.

Receipts and expenditure of the Municipalities in the Tripura State during the year 1334 T.E.

NAME.	Opening balance.	RECEIPTS DURING THE YEAR.						Total in the current year.	EXPENDITURE DURING THE YEAR.		Balance at the close of the year.	REMARKS.
		Past.	Present.						Past.	Present.		
			State grant.	Tax.	Miscel-laneous.	Total.						
1	2	3	4	5	6	7		8	9	10	11	12
	Rs. A.P.	Rs. A.P.	Rs. A.P.	Rs. A.P.	Rs. A.P.	Rs. A.P.		Rs. A.P.	Rs. A.P.	Rs. A.P.	Rs. A.P.	
Agartala Municipality. ...	11,583-9-6	27,778-7-6	9,000-0-0	3,943-1-6	7,030-10-6 a	19,973-12-0		31,557-5-6	16,194-14-0	16,625-6-6 b	14,931-15-0 c	a. Including Rs. 4,865-11 as Bazar income and Rs. 941-8 as deposits and advances recovered. b. Including Rs. 1,932-2-0 as Bazar expense and Rs. 900-0 as deposits and advances paid. c. Including Rs. 13,495-15-3 as Bazar balance.

XVIII.

Statement of rainfall in the Tripura State during the year 1334 T.E.

STATE.	Baisak.	Jaisth.	Asar.	Sravan.	Bhadra.	Asvin.	Kartik.	Agrahayan.	Pous.	Magh.	Falgoon.	Chait.	Total.	Total of past year.	Average of past 5 years.	REMARKS.
Tripura State ...	23·92	2·56	27·69	19·41	14·49	5·21	3·32	4·74	·54	1·55	1·18	1·67	106·28	81·58	87·5	

XIX.

Statement as to the prices of staple food-grains for the year 1334 T.E.

Article.	During Chait (past year).			During Chait (present year).			REMARKS.
	Rs.	*a.*	*p.*	*Rs.*	*a.*	*p.*	
(1) RICE							
Maximum	6	8	0	9	0	0	
Minimum	4	0	0	6	0	0	
(2) PADDY							
Maximum	3	12	0	4	8	0	
Minimum	2	0	0	2	12	0	

XX.

Expenditure on Public Works during the year 1334 T.E.

Description of work.	State funds.			Local funds.			Total.	Remarks.
	Original.	Repairs.	Total.	Original.	Repairs.	Total.		
	Rs.	Rs.	Rs.	Rs.	Rs.	Rs.	Rs.	
Tanks in different parts of the State	3,588	1,933	5,521	—	—	—	5,521	
Roads and bridges ...	26,751	50,421	77,172	—	—	—	77,172	
Buildings	1,10,186	59,695	1,69,881	1,167	—	1,167	1,71,048	
Miscellaneous works ...	13,939	1,297	15,236	—	—	—	15,236	
Total ...	1,54,464	1,13,346	2,67,810	1,167	—	1,167	2,68,977	
Minor works at the Rajbari	—	5,166	5,166	—	—	—	5,166	
Establishment charges ...	—	—	13,429	—	—	—	13,429	
Grand Total ...	1,54,464	1,18,512	2,86,405	1,167	—	1,167	2,87,572	

XXI.

Statement showing the excise shops and excise revenue of the Tripura State during the year 1334 T.E.

Name of State.	Country spirit.		Country spirit, Opium and Ganja.		Ganja and Opium.		Tari.		Total.		Remarks.
	Number of shops.	Revenue.	Number of shops.	Revenue.	Number of shops.	Revenue.	Number of shops.	Revenue.	Number of shops.	Revenue.	
		Rs.		Rs.		Rs.		Rs.		Rs.	
Tripura State	—	—	27	53,106	—	—	—	—	27*	53,106†	

* Two new shops opened in Dharmanagar Division.

† By new leases of shops during the year, there was an increase of revenue by Rs. 5,559 over that of the previous year.

XXII.

Statement of Medical Relief afforded in the Tripura State during the year 1334 T.E.

Dispensary.	Number of patients treated. (new)		Results of in-door patients. (new)				Expenditure.	Daily average. (old + new)			No. of surgical operations performed.			No. of persons vaccinated during the year.			Remarks.
	Outdoor.	Indoor.	Dis-charged.	Absented.	Died.	Remain-ing under treatment.		Outdoor.	Indoor.	Total.	Major.	Minor.	Total.	Success-fully.	Unsuc-cessfully.	Total.	
							Rs. a. p.										
1. Victoria Memorial Hospital at Agartala and the Charitable Dispensary attached to it	12,504	394	220	125	40	9	8,108-8-9	61·93	14·46	76·39	10	214	224	906	325	1231	*This figure shows the actual number of outdoor patients treated, the total outdoor attendance during the year being 1,80,482 against 1,49,226 in the previous year.
2. Palace Dispensary	7,660	0	0	0	0	0	10,349-5-9	56·83	0	56·83	0	0	0	0	0	0	
3. Homoeopathic	10,111	0	0	0	0	0	3,187-6 9	44.65	0	44.65	0	0	0	0	0	0	
4. Old Agartala	6,786	0	0	0	0	0	1,611-14-0	32·71	0	32·71	0	58	58	267	57	324	
5. Bishalgar	3,981	0	0	0	0	0	1,122-15-0	16·77	0	16·77	0	55	55	493	130	623	
6. Sonamura	6,137	7	7	0	0	0	1,312-13-3	27·28	·32	27·60	0	95	95	464	62	526	
7. Udaipur	4,762	6	3	0	0	3	1,110-15-3	17·48	·10	17·58	2	65	67	264	56	320	
8. Amarpur	2,621	0	0	0	0	0	932-3-9	8·40	0	8·40	0	20	20	317	14	331	
9. Bilonia...	4,614	0	0	0	0	0	1,180-0-0	20·03	0	20·03	0	69	69	146	40	186	
10. Loongthung	1,872	0	0	0	0	0	1,040-0-0	11·49	0	11·49	1	32	33	238	28	266	
11. Sabroom	1,530	0	0	0	0	0	1,083-15-0	6·62	0	6·62	0	7	7	234	6	240	
12. Khowai	3,109	0	0	0	0	0	1,467-15-9	11·67	0	11·67	1	77	78	714	114	828	
13. Kailashahar	11,827	9	7	1	1	0	1,427-13-6	71·65	·27	71·92	1	147	148	180	13	193	
14. Kamalpur	4,607	0	0	0	0	0	986-15-6	16·60	0	16·60	0	53	53	338	54	392	
15. Dharmanagar	5,071	14	12	0	2	0	1,290-6-9	21·12	·42	21·54	0	114	114	272	36	308	
16. Fatik-roy	3,279	0	0	0	0	0	1,152-11-9	12·80	0	12·80	0	38	38	287	41	328	
17. Mohanpur	3,093	0	0	0	0	0	1,102-7-0	19·65	0	19·65	0	0	0	0	0	0	
18. Dhaleswar	7,681	0	0	0	0	0	615-5-0	36·73	0	36·73	0	37	37	0	0	0	
Total	*1,01,248	430	249	136	43	12	39,083-12-9	494·41	15·57	509·98	15	981	996	5,120	976	60,96	

XXIII.

Vital statistics of the Tripura State for the year 1334 T.E.

STATE.	Population.	BIRTHS.		Increase.	Decrease.	DEATHS.		Increase.	Decrease.	RATIO PER 1,000 OF POPULATION.				REMARKS.
										BIRTHS.		DEATHS.		
		Past year.	Present year.			Past year.	Present year.			Past year.	Present year.	Past year.	Present year.	
Tripura State ...	3,04,437	2,547	2,313	—	234	2,428	2,286	—	142	8·3	7·64	7·9	7·55	

XXIV.

Education Return (A)—Particulars as to the schools maintained during the year 1334 T.E.

Number of Schools.		Description of Schools.	Number of pupils on the rolls on the last day of Chait.		Daily average attendance.		Remarks.
Past year.	Present year.		Past year.	Present year.	Past year.	Present year.	
5	5	High English Schools	867	899	666·90	700·36	
5	5	Middle English Schools for boys ...	541	494	377·75	352·18	
1	1	Middle English School for girls ...	93	99	67·40	79·64	
1	1	Higher Vernacular School for boys	45	43	32·45	34·41	
23	22	* Lower Vernacular Schools for boys	1,146	1,340	849·74	992·85	* In some of these schools boys and girls read together.
115	86	Pathsalas for boys	2,741	2,235	2,000·38	1,705·24	
11	9	Do for girls	202	190	141·09	133·32	
		Special Schools :—					
6	5	Madrassas	271	203	216·40	151·41	
3	3	Sanskrit *Tols*	41	38	29·51	29·06	
1	1	Woodburn Artisan School... ...	25	18	7·55	6·02	
Total 171	138		5,972	5,559	4,389·17	4,184·49	

XXV.

Education Return (B) Race of Students, 1334 T. E.

Names of Divisions.	No. of Schools.			No. of Students.			Race.									Average daily attendance.		Remarks.
												Bengalee.						
	For boys.	For girls.	Total.	Boys.	Girls.	Total.	Thakurs.	Manipuris	Tripuras.	Reangs.	Kukis.	Hindus.	Musalmans.	Christians.	Others.	Boys.	Girls.	
1. Sadar Division ...	41	3	44	1,522	142	1,664	162	137	229	1	13	739	351	1	31	1159·29	109·08	
2. Kailashahar „	24	2	26	982	117	1,099	0	380	0	1	53	501	164	0	0	679·39	68·88	
3. Sonamura „	21	1	22	830	70	900	1	0	34	0	0	243	622	0	0	629·11	54·65	
4. Bilonia „	10	1	11	631	23	654	0	0	17	0	0	454	183	0	0	482·02	16·92	
5. Khowai „	9	1	10	235	11	246	0	23	133	0	0	60	15	0	15	179·53	10·62	
6. Dharmanagar „	11	1	12	515	29	544	0	95	0	0	0	335	112	0	2	391·53	33·35	
7. Udaipur „	6	1	7	274	16	290	0	0	3	1	0	130	156	0	0	207·60	11·07	
8. Sabrum „	3	0	3	95	17	112	0	0	33	0	0	63	16	0	0	84·92	13·22	
9. Amarpur Sub-division ...	3	0	3	47	3	50	3	0	14	26	0	6	0	0	1	50·65	2·66	
TOTAL ...	128	10	138	5,131	428	5,559	166	635	463	29	66	2,531	1,619	1	49	3,864·04	320·45	

XXVI.

Statement showing the distribution of Portfolios among the members of the Council of Administration, Tripura State, 1334 T. E.

Members.	Departments allotted to Portfolios.	REMARKS.
President	1. Judicial. 2. Sultanat. 3. Sansar. 4. Nij Tahabil.	
Vice-President	1. Political and Appointment. 2. Police. 3. Revenue and General. 4. Agriculture. 5. Forest. 6. Accounts and Audit. 7. Treasury and Stamps. 8. Chakla Roshnabad Estates and other Zemindaries.	
Maharajkumar B. K. Dev Barman ...	1. Jail. 2. Education and Rajmala. 3. Medical and Sanitation. 4. Military. 5. Public Works. 6. Zoo.	
Thakur P. C. Roy	1. Pilkhana and Stables. 2. Tosakhana. 3. Guest House. 4. Registration. 5. Press, Forms, Stationery, Gazette and Record Room. 6. Municipality.	

APPENDIX XXVII. (A)

Statement of Audited Receipts for the year 1334 T. E.

State.

Heads of Revenue.	1333 T. E.		1334 T. E.		REMARKS.
	Revised Estimate.	Actuals.	Revised Estimate.	Actuals.	
1. Land Revenue ...	5,14,000	4,95,508	5,22,000	5,18,227	
2. Rents of markets ...	4,895	4,569	3,895	5,316	
3. Family tax in the hills	62,600	63,279	61,100	64,433	
4. Toll on Forest Produce	4,43,000	4,66,404	4,32,500	4,30,308	
5. Do on the Feni River	35,000	30,116	20,000	21,349	
6. Elephant and Buffalo grazing mehals ...	7,345	7,348	7,245	6,703	
7. Thatching grass mehals	11,000	10,692	9,000	12,327	
8. Reserved *Sal* trees ...	14,000	19,371	16,000	24,197	
9. Tax on cotton and Oil seeds ...	1,58,350	2,03,606	1,17,750	1,55,407	
10. Royalty on elephant caught ...	24,000	31,336	5,000	10,759	
11. Adda mehal ...	23,450	20,692	23,100	22,419	
12. Excise ...	44,010	47,652	49,510	52,905	
13. Stamps and Court fees	64,100	58,082	61,900	68,343	
14. Law and Justice (fines)	3,050	3,368	2,850	2,543	
15. Process Fees ...	10,490	12,132	9,740	11,450	
16. Registration ...	8,900	10,251	9,900	11,213	
17. Jail ...	2,000	2,442	2,000	3,147	
18. Cattle pounds ...	5,700	5,685	5,700	5,149	
19. *Nazars* ...	20,000	25,127	25,200	29,614	
20. Agriculture ...	500	314	500	275	
21. Miscellaneous ...	52,610	64,061	65,110	78,719	
22. School Fees ...	—	—	10,000	7,907	
Total ...	15,09,000	15,82,035	14,60,000	15,42,710	
23. Contribution from Chakla ...	1,85,000	1,85,000	—	—	
24. Deposits ...	78,685	87,865	90,000	71,284	
25. Loans ...	50,000	50,000			
	18,22,685	19,04,900	15,50,000	16,13,994	
Opening Balance :—					
Cash ...	1,03,286	1,03,286	3,18,757	3,18,757	
Advances ...	8,99,935	8,99,935	6,78,290	6,78,290	
Loans issued ...	37,627	37,627	39,314	39,314	
	10,40,848	10,40,848	10,36,361	10,36,361	
Grand Total ...	28,63,533	29,45,748	25,86,361	26,50,355	

APPENDIX XXVII. (B)

Statement of Audited Expenditure for the year 1334 T. E.

State.

Heads of Expenditure.	1333 T. E.		1334 T. E.		REMARKS.
	Revised estimate.	Actuals.	Revised Estimate.	Actuals.	
1. Controlling Charges	1,16,410	1,13,035	1,19,315	a 1,16,656	a. Includes 4,500 on account of adjustment of advances.
2. Judicial ...	28,418	27,607	33,710	b 32,895	b. Includes 1,000 on account of adjustment of advances.
3. Sansar ...	6,90,191	6,85,328	4,71,077	c 4,60,773	c. Includes 44,918 on account of adjustment of advances.
4. Sultanat ...	43,778	43,619	24,286	24,245	
5. Nijtahabil ...			4,25,928	d 4,22,568	d. Includes 3,24,332 on account of adjustment of advances.
6. Police ...	69,435	67,566	68,940	68,936	
7. Revenue ...	83,710	80,938	75,641	72,480	
8. Tahasil ...	46,175	45,278	45,700	43,379	
9. Survey & settlement	16,752	16,159	15,000	13,529	
10. Agriculture ...	2,397	1,796	5,000	4,328	
11. Forest ...	48,500	47,749	56,524	51,316	
12. Public Works ...	3,18,442	3,13,011	2,95,048	e 2,86,405	e. Includes 59,485 on account of adjustment of advances.
13. Zoo ...	19,000	18,527	11,000	10,570	
14. Medical ...	1,32,904	1,31,705	61,411	59,887	
15. Jail ...	14,465	13,700	13,200	13,188	
16. Education General ...	1,23,752	1,21,270	91,856	89,359	
17. Rajmala ...	3,560	3,556	3,500	3,486	
18. Education of Rajkumars ...	—	—	10,343	6,310	
19. Military ...	45,668	42,625	43,910	37,998	
20. Registration ...	3,113	3,445	3,762	3,639	
21. Press ...	5,205	5,118	5,398	4,806	
22. State Gazette ...	776	764	700	573	
23. Municipality ...	9,000	8,988	9,000	9,000	
24. Repayment of Deposits ...	87,776	86,712	1,38,998	f 1,35,661	f. Includes 7,443 on account of adjustment of advances.
25. Advances to employees ...	—	—	7,000	3,523	
26. Pension ...	11,523	10,910	20,000	17,380	
27. Donation ...	30	30	1,000	604	
28. Relief to distressed subjects ...	500	—	500	355	
29. Purchase of Landed Property ...	3,000	2,614	1,000	454	
30. Unforeseen charges ...	478	—	960	—	
31. Compensation for dearness of Provision ...	28,000	17,337	31,500	31,458	
Total ...	19,52,958	19,09,387	20,86,207	g 20,20,761	g. Includes 4,41,678 on account of adjustment of advances.
Closing balance :—					
Cash ...	1,55,743	3,18,757	2,31,170	3,72,122	
Advances ...	7,18,188	6,78,290	2,29,670	2,15,257	
Loans issued ...	36,644	39,314	39,314	42,215	
	9,10,575	10,36,361	5,00,154	6,29,594	
Grand Total ...	28,63,533	29,45,748	25,86,361	26,50,355	

APPENDIX XXVIII. (A)

Statement of Audited Receipts for the year 1334 T. E.

Chakla Roshnabad Estate.

Heads of Receipts.	1333 T. E.		1334 T. E.		REMARKS.
	Revised Estimate.	Actuals.	Revised Estimate.	Actuals.	
1. Rent and Cess ...	11,00,784	10,93,362	10,65,958	10,61,705	
2. Cess for Rent free holdings ...	8,216	7,038	9,000	9,232	
3. Law charges recovered	56,763	48,522	65,200	67,660	
4. Misc. receipts including deposits ...	37,089	26,740	10,292	10,348	
5. Loans Received ...	80,000	80,000	2,03,000	2,03,000	
	12,82,852	12,55,662	13,53,450	13,51,945	
Opening Balance :—					
Cash ...	1,34,334	1,34,334	65,393	65,393	
Advance ...	2,30,601	2,30,601	1,69,947	2,19,947	
Loans issued ...	16,647	16,647	15,946	15,946	
Bank deposits ...	—	—	50,000	—	
	3,81,582	3,81,582	3,01,286	3,01,286	
Grand Total ...	16,64,434	16,37,244	16,54,736	16,53,231	

APPENDIX XXVIII. (B)

Statement of Audited Expenditure for the year 1334 T. E.

Chakla Roshnabad Estate.

Heads of Expenditure.	1333 T. E. Revised Estimate.	1333 T. E. Actuals.	1334 T. E. Revised Estimate.	1334 T. E. Actuals.	Remarks.
i. 1. Revenue and Cess ...	2,58,327	2,57,160	2,59,250	2,57,356	
2. Establishment ...	1,52,850	1,45,630	1,39,200	1,35,399	
3. Settlement ...	1,403	1,147	1,200	1,108	Includes Rs. 10,000 on account of adjustment of advances.
4. Legal Expenses ...	1,22,999	1,22,198	1,10,500	95,805	
5. Education ...	12,151	11,685	9,460	9,387	Includes Rs. 5,000. on account of adjustment of advances.
6. Medical ...	10,447	10,219	10,360	10,073	
7. Public Works ...	1,07,914	1,00,105	60,000	57,614	
8. Religious Expenses	6,140	5,842	6,300	6,229	
9. Purchase of property	22,740	22,091	1,000	—	
10. Miscellaneous ...	12,066	11,481	12,000	11,046	
11. Loans and Advances	—	—	4,000	—	
12. Pension and Gratuity	2,323	3,763	6,000	4,293	
13. Forest ...	655	586	650	616	
14. Unforeseen ...	11,347	9,489	5,000	1,459	
ii. Sansar ...	15,780	15,804	15,780	15,780	
iii. Donation ...	2,050	2,065	2,000	1,977	
iv. Repayment of debts	} 1,70,000	1,63,939	7,03,000	7,02,888	
iv. (a) Repayment of deposits ...		4,383	28,740	25,612	
v. H. H's Nij-Tahabil and Tour expenses ...	2,42,820	2,38,371	—	—	
vi. Contribution to State...	1,85,000	1,85,000	—	—	
vii. Contribution for water works at Comilla ...	25,000	25,000	—	—	
	13,62,012	13,35,958	13,74,440	13,36,642	
Closing Balance :—					
Cash ...	1,07,122	65,393	1,22,946	1,47,267	
Advances ...	1,34,995	1,69,947	1,48,850	1,60,941	
Loans issued ...	10,305	15,946	8,500	8,131	
Bank deposits ...	50,000	50,000	—	—	
	3,02,422	3,01,286	2,80,296	3,16,589	
Grand-Total ...	16,64,434	16,37,244	16,54,736	16,53,231	

Book Eighteen

Report on the General Administration of the Tripura State for the year 1335 T. E. (1925-1926 A.D.)

REPORT ON THE ADMINISTRATION
OF
THE TRIPURA STATE
FOR
1335 T. E. (1925-26.)

CHAPTER I—GENERAL AND POLITICAL.

Area of the State—4,116 sq. miles.

Population—3,04,437.

Gross Revenue (based on the average of the previous five years) :—

(*a*) State ... ... Rs. 14,31,316.

(*b*) Zemindaries ... ... Rs. 11,00,144.

Tribute—Nil.

Ruler of the State—His Highness The Bisama-Samara-Bijayee Mahamahodaya Pancha-Srijukta Maharaja Manikya Bir Bikramkishore Dev Barman Bahadur. *Age*—18 years. (Born—9th August, 1908). *Caste*—Kshatriya (of the Lunar race).

The weather conditions.

1. With unfavourable weather conditions, chronic high prices, and virulent epidemics of cattle disease raging all round, the year under report proved more or less unpropitious to the people of the State, while prolonged outbreaks of Cholera, Small-pox, and Kala-azar added to the pinch of the situation. Comparatively rich harvests in rice crops and jute, as well as hill grown cotton and oil seeds, however, exerted a counteracting influence, and the high prices that prevailed kept the agricultural population fairly prosperous.

The finances of the year.

2. In the financial Administration, there was thus noticeable a markedly increased paying capacity of the tenantry, the collections of the year by far exceeding both the estimates and the previous year's figures. In spite of an abnormal expenditure of two lacs and sixteen thousand, incurred on account of the marriage ceremonies referred to below, the Council of Administration was able to pay up a further instalment of five lacs out of the liabilities of the State, making a total of over thirteen lacs, and leaving an outstanding balance of five lacs only payable almost entirely to Their Highnesses the Maharanees. Landed property was, besides, purchased to the value of eighty-six thousand, as a matter of profitable investment, while the expenditure on Public Works and Education amounted respectively to about three lacs, and one lac and twenty thousand. The Council also paid about Rupees fifty thousand to the ministerial and menial establishment as allowance for dearness of provision. It is satisfactory to note that the closing cash balance nevertheless

increased and amounted to about seven lacs, while advances aggregating Rupees eighty-seven thousand were adjusted, with the effect of reducing to that extent the fictitious portion of the balance.

His Highness's education.

3. His Highness the Maharaja's Administrative training continued under Lt. Colonel O. C. Pulley, Guardian Tutor, and a staff of Officers, as before, at Comilla and Shillong. His Highness, besides, went through a course of Military training during the year.

His Highness's movements.

4. On the 17th December, 1925, His Highness visited Calcutta accompanied by Lt. Colonel O. C. Pulley, and had the pleasure of meeting His Excellency the Viceroy and His Excellency the Governor of Bengal. The party returned to Comilla on the 5th January, 1926.

Visit to Kailashahar.

5. The most enjoyable tour of the year was in the Kailashahar Division of the State, which the Maharaja visited on the 21st January, 1926. Mr. A. J. Dash, I. C. S., Political Agent, Lt. Colonel O. C. Pulley, Guardian Tutor, Rai J. C. Sen Bahadur, Vice President of the Council, and Dewan B. K. Sen, Chief Secretary, accompanied His Highness, while Kumars P. K. Dev Barman and B. L. Dev Barman, A.D.C.'s, with Mr. K. P. Dutt and Dr. A. N. Mitra represented the regular personal staff. His Highness received a most cordial reception from the people with whom he mixed freely, joining all functions and festivities of the occasion and giving suitable replies to the addresses presented. All Offices and Institutions of the Divisional head quarters were inspected, and a special feature of the programme consisted in visits to a number of Tea Gardens of the Division. His Highness also accepted the invitation of the Manager of the Chatlapur Tea Garden in Sylhet, and availed himself of the opportunity to meet the planting community of the adjoining British District, and to examine the working of a well regulated garden in British India. A visit to the rock Carvings of the *Unakoti* hills proved very interesting.

Visit to Hill Chiefs.

6. The Political Agent and the Vice President having returned from Kailashahar Town, His Highness proceeded through the hill tracts of the Division up to Dhumachera in the interior and met a number of Hill Chiefs, conspicuous among whom was a Reang Sardar, and received from all a most hearty welcome. The journey through the Manipuri and Reang settlements of the locality proved very pleasant, and gave an idea of the state of things in the hill section. His Highness entertained all hill men and labouring classes present, as well as all hunters and beaters who took part in shooting excursions, and had the satisfaction of bagging a Royal Bengal tiger on the day of his departure for Agartala on the 4th February, 1926.

A River Trip.

7. On the 15th February following, His Highness went with the Political Agent on an instructive river trip, which lasted till the 24th idem.

Notable events.

8. The most important event of the year in the Palace was the marriage of His Highness's sister, Maharajkumari Basanta Prava Devi with Rajkumar Gajendra Pal Singh Bahadur, son of Raja Kushal Pal Singh Bahadur, M. A., L. L. B. of

Kotla, which was celebrated at Agartala with becoming *eclat* on the 9th Agrahayan *i. e.* 25th November, 1925. A number of distinguished Rajput noblemen with representatives of some Ruling Chiefs attended the function, which proved in many respects unique of its kind.

9. Another interesting ceremony at the Palace that deserves mention was the marriage of Maharajkumari Bindu Bashini Devi with Thakur Sanwant Singh Saheb of Jaipur, celebrated on the 30th Baisakh *i. e.* 13th May, 1925.

Political Agent.

10. Mr. A. J. Dash, I. C. S., continued to be the Political Agent of the State till the 12th March, 1926, when he proceeded on three months' leave, and Mr. N. L. Hindley, I. C. S., officiated during his absence.

CHAPTER II—LAND ADMINISTRATION.

Charge.

11. Dewan Asit Chandra Chaudhuri, B. A. remained in charg of the Revenue Department till Jaistha, when Babu B. K. Chatterjee, M. A., B. L., assumed the charge of the Department.

Area held under settlement.

12. As shewn in the subjoined statement, the total area held under settlement and borne on the *taujis* at the close of the year under review, was 583 sq. miles as against 594 sq. miles in the previous year.

Kinds of settlement.	Area in square miles.		Increase.	Decrease.	REMARKS.
	1335 T.E	1334 T.E.			
Jotes ...	261	253	8	—	
Taluks ...	322	341	—	19	
Total ...	583	594	8	19	

13. The decrease in the area under *taluk* settlement is due to auction purchase by the State of some *taluks* at revenue sale.

Tea Settlement.

14. As in the previous year there was no fresh settlement for tea cultivation in the year under report. The present condition of this new industry is not yet quite satisfactory.

Rates of *Jama*.

15. The average *jama* per *kani* of *jote* lands in *Khash Mehals* (exclusive of cesses) stood at 15 annas and 5 pies against 15 annas and 4 pies in the previous year, and in *taluks* at 5 annas and 2 pies as before. The maximum and the minimum rates for *jotes* were Rs. 5-13-6 and 3 annas and for *taluks* Re. 1-5 and 1-9 respectively.

16. The different sources of land revenue demand with the collection under each head are detailed below :—

Sources of land revenue.

Sources.	Current demand.		Arrear demand up to the end of		Realization up to the end of		REMARKS.
	1335 T.E.	1334 T.E.	1334 T.E.	1333 T.E.	1335 T.E.	1334 T.E.	
Taluks ...	1,67,266	1,75,833	2,14,407	1,51,168	1,42,190	1,09,672	
Khas Mehal jotes	4,01,698	3,87,886	7,41,843	7,40,319	3,94,837	3,64,289	
Bazars ...	6,975	5,192	1,229	1,265	7,002	5,407	
Cesses ...	35,682	35,708	62,330	58,256	33,074	29,607	
Total ...	6,11,621	6,04,619	10,19,809	9,51,008	5,77,103	5,08,975	

Demand.

17. The above statement will show that the aggregate current demand under all heads was Rs. 6,11,621. With the arrear demand of Rs. 10,19,809, the total demand of the year was Rs. 16,31,430 against Rs. 15,55,627 of the previous year. There was an increase in the current demand in respect of *jote* lands, due as usual to assessment on the expiry of the rent free period and resettlement after the previous term. The decrease in the current demand in respect of *taluki* lands is due to auction purchase by the State of some tea grants during the year under review, no resettlement of these lands having been allowed.

Collection.

18. The total collection under all heads during the year amounted to Rs. 5,77,103 being Rs. 2,92,686 under current and Rs. 2,84,417 under arrears, against a total of Rs. 5,08,975 in the previous year. The percentage of current collection was 47·85 against 44·58 and that of the arrears 27·89 against 25·17. In the *Khas Mehal* the percentage of current collection was 40·56 against 39·31 and in *taluki mehal*, 63·98 against 55·27 in the previous year. During the year Rs. 7,583 of the arrear demand was written off after proper enquiry.

Coercive measures—certificates.

19. Altogether 2,550 certificate cases, covering a demand of Rs. 1,73,537, were instituted during the year. With 1,406 cases, valued at Rs. 2,02,675, pending from the previous year, the total number of cases, awaiting final orders on disposal of preliminary notices issued on debtors, was 3,956, covering a total demand of Rs. 3,76,212. Of these, 365 cases with a demand of Rs. 32,320 were rejected or struck off, while 1,351 cases carrying an aggregate value of Rs. 2,20,308 remained pending.

20. Orders under the provisions of the State Certificate Act were passed during the year in 2,240 cases with a total value of Rs. 1,23,584, making the demand absolute. With 5,265 cases pending in execution from the previous year, the total number of cases dealt with was 7,505 covering a demand of Rs. 4,98,214. Out of the total demand, Rs. 17,751 was remitted or written off, and of the remainder, Rs. 1,34,329 was actually realised, leaving a balance of Rs. 3,46,134. Of the amount realised, Rs. 1,18,026 represents land revenue and Rs. 16,303 miscellaneous demands. 4 debtors were arrested in the year, of whom 3 were released on promise of payment by instalments and one unconditionally, as there was no chance of recovery of dues.

Operation of the Sun-set law.

21. The number of defaulting *taluks* brought under the operation of the Sun-set law (including 16 pending from the previous year) was 101. Of these, 67 were released on payment of dues with penalty, while 4 were sold in auction and 30 remained undisposed of at the close of the year.

Survey.

22. The results of the survey including re-survey operations are given in the statement below. It will be seen that an area of 3,712 *drones* comprising 1,006 *drones* of *taluk* and 2,706 *drones* of *Khas Mehal* was surveyed, as against a total of 3,509 *drones* in the previous year. The sanctioned programme for survey for the year was 3,584 *drones* in *Khas Mehal* and 2,662 *drones* in *taluks*. The failure to complete the programme was mainly due to the negligence of *Talukdars* to pay in costs promptly, and to the difficulty in recruitment of qualified *Ameens* and other staff for work in unhealthy stations in the interior. The total expenditure incurred in the survey operations in *Khas Mehals* was Rs. 4,873.

Names of Divisions.	Quantity of land in *drones* surveyed in 1335 T. E.			Quantity of land in *drones* surveyed in 1334 T. E.			REMARKS.
	Taluqi land.	*Khas mehal* land.	Total.	*Taluqi* land.	*Khas mehal* land.	Total.	
(Settlement Office) 1. Sadar Division ...	677	888	1,565	287	2,820	3,107	
2. Kailashahar " ...	40	504	544	—	—	—	
3. Sonamura " ...	—	—	—	25	12	37	
4. Belonia " ...	—	—	—	—	—	—	
5. Khowai " ...	21	392	413	243	122	365	
6. Dharmanagar " ...	252	72	324	—	—	—	
7. Udaipur " ...	—	—	—	—	—	—	
8. Sabroom " ...	16	401	417	—	—	—	
9. Amarpur " " ...	—	449	449	—	—	—	
TOTAL ...	1,006	2,706	3,712	555	2,954	3,509	

Cadastral Survey.

23. The work of Cadastral Survey could not be undertaken during the year. The result of settlement operations in the villages which have already been surveyed is being watched before undertaking Cadastral Survey work in more villages.

24. The result of settlement work is given in the statement below. It will be seen that settlement operations were completed in respect of 4,063 *drones* of *jote* land, as against 1,936 *drones* in the previous year.

Settlement.

Nature of Settlement.	1335 T. E.		1334 T. E.		REMARKS.
	Area in *drones.*	*Jama* in whole rupees.	Area in *drones.*	*Jama* in whole rupees.	
1. Permanent *taluqi* settlement of cultivated land ...	—	—	—	—	
2. Permanent *taluqi* settlement of waste land	—	—	—	—	
3. *Taskhichi taluqi* settlement of cultivated land ...	—	—	—	—	
4. *Taskhichi taluqi* settlement of waste land ...	—	—	—	—	
5. *Jotedari* re-settlement of cultivated land	3,384	38,290	1,590	18,484	
6. *Jotedari* settlement of waste land.	679	5,254	346	3,026	
TOTAL ...	4,063	43,544	1,936	21,510	

25. No permanent or *Taskhichi* settlement or *Niskar* grant was sanctioned during the year.

Permanent settlement.

26. A net increase of Rs. 13,225 in *jama* was secured by resettlement of *abadi jote* lands, the *nazarana* secured being Rs. 26,490. The average rate of *jama* per *kani* was 11 annas 6 pies against 11 annas 7 pies in the previous year.

Re-settlement of *jote* lands.

27. During the year, an area of 679 *drones* of waste land was settled for a prospective rental of Rs. 5,254. The average *jama* per *kani* obtained was 7 annas 9 pies against 8 annas 9 pies in the previous year. The maximum and minimum rates were Rs. 4 and 4 annas respectively. The *nazarana* realised was Rs. 8,751, the rent free period allowed ranging from 1 to 5 years.

Jotedari Settlement of waste land.

28. There were separate Settlement Officers in the Sadar and Kailashahar Divisions. In other Divisions the Divisional Officers were entrusted with the settlement work within their respective jurisdictions. The total expenditure incurred in the settlement operations exclusively, amounted to Rs. 3,239.

Settlement work.

29. It will be seen that the *nazarana* obtained and obtainable by re-settlement of cultivable *jote* lands and settlement of waste lands, as *jotes* amounted to Rs. 35,241 (Rs. 26,490+Rs. 8,751). The net increase of revenue secured was Rs. 18,479 (Rs. 13,225+Rs. 5,254).

30. As in the previous year a number of old maps were copied for use in the Divisional offices. During the year 41 copies of such maps were traced at a cost of Rs. 71.

The work of the map section.

II. Military.

35. Kumar Dina Mohan Dev Barman was in charge of the Military Office and the Forces as before.

Charge.

36. The actual strength of the Force consisted at the close of the year of 157 Sepoys and 40 Officers of all ranks, including the Officer Commanding, 2 A. D. C.'s, 1 Subedar Major and 1 Subedar. There were besides a Band Master and 20 men constituting the State Band.

Strength.

37. The men were chiefly employed as before on escort duty and in furnishing guards-of-honour on ceremonial occasions. As there were no suitable candidates, 51 posts had to be kept vacant.

Duty.

38. The total expenditure of the year, including grain allowance paid, amounted to Rs. 42,508 as against Rs. 41,465.

Expenditure.

III. Police.

39. Babu Jogesh Chandra Datta, B. A., continued as Superintendent of police throughout the year. Assistant Superintendent Sreejut Jogendra Chandra Dev Barman has been working since Fālgoon in the Police Office.

Charge.

40. The total strength of the State Police was 460 including a staff of 10 constables for the Town Section.

Strength.

41. There were 4 Inspectors working under the Superintendent. Their chief duty was to control the investigating staff and supervise their works.

Inspecting Staff.

42. The total number of cases reported to the Police was 1,282 against 1,130 in the previous year.

Crime.

43. The result of cases investigated will be seen from the following table.

Cases.

Number of cases reported.
1,282

Enquiry refused 16 | Number investigated 1,175 | Pending 91

Number investigated 1,175:

Maliciously false 5 | True 717 | Doubtful &c. 453

True 717:

Charge-sheet 372 | Finally reported 345

44. Altogether 802 persons were arrested for various offences, and 824 persons, including absconders, sent up for trial by the Police, against 743 and 730 respectively in the previous year.

Result of prosecution.

45. Of the number 824 sent up, 187 were convicted, 189 acquitted (including 10 on compromise and 70 on withdrawal of cases), while 9 escaped and 369 were awaiting trial. The percentage of conviction was 68·2 against 53·33 of the previous year.

46. Of the 370 persons awaiting trial at the end of the previous year, 78 were convicted and 239 acquitted, including 63 on compromise and 25 on withdrawal of cases, while 53 were awaiting trial.

Bad livelihood cases.

47. 2 bad livelihood cases with 14 persons were instituted during the year under report, both of which are still pending.

Arms Act cases.

48. Of 3 Arms Act cases all were sent up ; 1 person in one case was discharged, while 2 persons in 2 cases were awaiting trial at the close of the year.

Recovery of stolen property.

49. The value of property stolen was estimated at Rs. 22,696 against Rs. 20,668 of the previous year. Of this amount, Rs. 10,324 was recovered against Rs. 6,514 of the previous year. The percentage of recovery was thus 45·5 against 31·57 of the previous year, showing a better result in the investigation of offences against property.

Dacoities.

50. There were 11 cases of Dacoity reported during the year, of which 4 have been finally reported as true and 7 sent up in charge-sheet. All the cases were pending trial. One of these dacoities was accompanied with murder.

Special Staff.

51. The C. I. D. and the information Bureau continued to work satisfactorily and proved useful in the collection of information and detection of cases.

Unnatural deaths and steps taken.

52. 62 cases of unnatural death were reported during the year. Regular enquiries were held in all cases. No foul play was discovered in any of them.

Reward and punishment.

53. 2 Sub-Inspectors, 2 Naib Darogas, 1 Writer Constable, 14 Constables, 5 Choukiders and one Spy received money rewards. One Writer Constable and one Jamadar and 27 Constables were fined or suspended, while 14 Constables were dismissed or discharged.

Tours.

54. The Superintendent of Police was out on tour for 86 days in all during the year, against 84 days of the previous year.

Co-operation.

55. The relations with the Police in the adjoining districts in British India continued to be satisfactory.

56. 4 Co-operation meetings were held in which the State Police joined and discussed matters relating to border crime and criminals with the Police in British India, and worked out plans for detection and prevention of crimes.

Patrol.

57. The patrol at Sonamura co-operated satisfactorily with the Kotwali Police, Comilla, all through the year.

Expenditure.

58. The total expenditure amounted, including grain allowance paid, to Rs. 69,646 against Rs. 67,445 in the previous year.

IV. Justice.

59. There were 13 courts of Justice in the State during the year under report, exercising both civil and criminal jurisdiction, viz :—the Khash Adalat or the Chief Court with its original and appellate sides and 12 courts of Magistrate Munsiffs exercising original jurisdiction only.

Courts.

60. Babu Bhupal Chandra Ganguli, B. L. continued to be the Chief Judge, Dewan Bijoy Kumar Sen, M. A., B. L., F. R. S. A. as the Sessions Judge and Kumar Surendra Chandra Deb Barman and Uzir Broja Krishna Deb Barman, as puisne Judges of the Khas Adalat. Babu Kamala Prasad Datta, M. A., B. L., and Dewan Asit Chandra Chaudhuri, B. A., worked as additional Sessions Judges for some time, Dewan Bijoy Kumar Sen being engaged with the stamp conspiracy case referred to below, and acting as Chief Judge, in place of Babu Bhupal Chandra Ganguli during his absence on privilege leave towards the latter part of the year.

61. Altogether 2,292 original criminal cases were instituted during the year under report against 1,866 of the previous year. With the balance of 614 pending from the last year, the total number of cases for disposal before the several subordinate original courts was thus 2,906 as against 2,343 of the previous year, as detailed below ; out of these 2,906 cases, 2,253 were disposed of as against 1,729 of the last year, leaving 653 cases pending at the close of the year. Thus in the year under report, the number of cases for disposal exceeded that of the previous year by 563 and there was also an increase in the disposals by 524.

Number of original criminal cases.

DESCRIPTION OF OFFENCES.	1334 T. E.	1335 T. E.
Offences against the State and public tranquillity	92	98
Offences against person	561	649
Offences against property	1,239	16,23
Other offences	481	536
TOTAL	2,343	2,906

62. Extradition warrants were applied for against 147 persons, of whom 58 were arrested and surrendered, 38 appeared voluntarily and 51 were at large at the close of the year. Of 96 persons under trial, 16 were convicted, 50 acquitted or discharged and 30 were awaiting trial at the end of the year.

Extradition.

63. The total number of persons under trial during the year, inclusive of the number pending from the last year, was 3,608 against 2,788 of the previous year. The number actually brought to trial was 2,802. Of these686 were arrested by the Police, 552 were produced on warrants, 1,140 appeared on summons, 393 appeared voluntarily and 31 were arrested in the presence of Magistrates.

Persons brought to trial.

Results of cases.

64. Out of these 3,608 persons brought to trial, 1,174 were discharged without trial, 1,092 were acquitted and 453 convicted, while 11 died, 1 was transferred, 3 escaped and 874 remained under trial at the close of the year. Of the persons convicted, 153 were sentenced to various terms of imprisonment extending from below 1 month to 7 years, 298 to fine only and 2 persons were released on bail. The number of persons actually tried was 1,545 as against 1,046 of the previous year, and the percentage of conviction was thus 29·32 as against 39·96 of the previous year.

Cases concerning British subjects.

65. Of the 2,906 cases for disposal, the number in which British subjects were concerned was 619 as against 501 of the last year. Out of these cases 440 were cognizable and 179 non-cognizable. In 79 cases British subjects were complainants, in 540 they were the accused. In 198 cases both the parties were British subjects. In these cases 749 persons were actually under trial during the year under report as against 619 of the previous year. Of them 224 were convicted, 379 acquitted or discharged and 146 remained under trial at the close of the year.

Comparative Statement.

66. The statement below compares the number of original criminal cases during the last 2 years.

DESCRIPTION OF OFFENCES.	1334 T.E.	1335 T.E.	Increase.	Decrease.
Offences against the State and public tranquillity ...	72	68	0	4
Offences against person	426	544	118	0
Offences against property	962	1,264	302	0
Other offences	406	416	10	0
TOTAL	1,866	2,292	430	4

Net increase—426.

Sessions cases.

67. 18 cases, including 5 cases with 12 persons pending from the last year, were committed to the Sessions during the year under report. Out of these 18 cases, 15 were disposed of as detailed in the following table. The number of persons involved in these cases was 53 ; of whom 21 were convicted, 3 discharged without trial, 17 acquitted, while 1 died during trial and 11 remained under trial at the close of the year.

Description of cases.	Number of cases.	Disposed of.	Pending.	REMARKS.
Murder	2	2	0	
Culpable homicide not amounting to murder	4	2	2	
Rape	2	2	0	
Robbery	1	1	0	
Dacoity	1	1	0	
Bigamy	1	0	1	
Rioting and hurt	1	1	0	
Using counterfeit British currency notes	1	1	0	
Using counterfeit British coin ...	3	3	0	
Forging courtfee Stamps of the Tripura State	2	2	0	
Total	18	15	3	

Stamp Forgery Case.

68. The most important Sessions case of the year deserves special mention. The Treasurer of the Sadar General Treasury, a local influential pleader of extensive practice, and two Stamp Vendors were committed to the Sessions by the Sadar Magistrate under various charges including Conspiracy to forge and pass as genuine State revenue stamps. The case was hotly contested and distinguished lawyers from British India appeared on both sides. The trial which came off before Dewan B. K. Sen, Judge, Sessions Division and 4 assessors involved the examination of nearly one hundred witnesses and the marking of nearly five thousand documents. After a protracted trial the Judge in agreement with the assessors convicted the Treasurer and one of the vendors and sentenced them each to three years rigorous imprisonment on the charge of Conspiracy with additional concurrent sentences against the vendor on some other charges, while one of the vendors was acquitted. The pleader accused died in the course of the trial.

Criminal appeals.

69. There were altogether 181 criminal appeals against 192 of the previous year. They were disposed of as shown below :—

Rejected	10
Judgment affirmed	75
Modified	12
Reversed	46
Further enquiry &c. ordered	3
Proceedings quashed	2
	148
Pending	33
	181

70. The percentage of judgments affirmed and modified was 63·043 as against 63·58 of the previous year.

Original civil suits.

71. The number of original civil suits instituted during the year under report was 1,957 against 1,737 of the last year. With the preceeding year's balance of 1,074 suits the total number for disposal was 3,031 as against 2,683 of the previous year. They were disposed of as follows :—

Exparte	840
Admitted and compromised	312
Dismissed for want of prosecution... ...	255
Disposed of on contest	527
	1,934
Pending	1,097
	3,031

Duration of suits.

72. The average duration of suits before the civil courts was 3 months and 1 day against 5 months and 8 days in 1334 T. E.

73. The total value of suits instituted during the year was Rs. 1,84,783-1-6 as against Rs. 1,38,520-6-6, which gives an average of Rs. 94-6-8 as the value per case. Of the 1,957 suits instituted during the year under report, 545 related to lands, 977 to money transactions and 435 to other transactions. There were 1,270 suits of the value of Rs. 100 and under ; 346 suits of over Rs. 100 and below Rs. 500 ; 28 suits of over Rs. 500 and below Rs. 1,000 ; 14 suits of over Rs. 1,000 and below Rs. 5,000 and 3 suits over Rs. 5,000 ; while 296 suits were not estimable in money value.

Nature and value of suits.

74. The number of applications for the execution of decrees filed during the year under report was 661, and with 394 pending cases, the total number was 1,055 against 1,017 of the previous year. The aggregate value of the new applications was Rs. 77,530-1-9, and with Rs. 1,06,076-9-9, the value of the pending cases, the total amounted to Rs. 1,83,606-11-6. The number of applications disposed of, was 653, the value of which was Rs. 80,305-13-3. The number of execution cases pending at the close of the year was 402 with the value of Rs. 1,03,300-14-3.

Execution of decrees.

75. There were 163 civil appeals filed during the year under report against 155 of the last year. With the past year's balance of 61, the total for disposal was 224 as against 187 of 1334 T. E. Out of these 159 were disposed of during the year under report against 126 of the previous year, leaving a balance of 65 cases at the close of the year.

Civil appeals.

76. The following figures indicate the results of appeals.

Results of appeals.

Decisions confirmed	...	...	...	63
„ reversed	...	...	...	58
„ modified	...	...	...	9
„ remanded	...	...	...	11
Compromised or otherwise disposed of			...	18
				159

77. The percentage of judgments wholly or partly upheld, excluding the cases compromised, was 51·063 as against 66·95 of the previous year.

Percentage.

78. The total value of appeals filed during the year under report was Rs. 19,032-13-6, and the average duration of each appeal was 2 months and 2 days against 2 months and 3 days of the last year.

Value and duration of appeals.

79. 26 civil suits were instituted in the Khas Adalat Original Side against 22 suits of the previous year. With the balance of 49 suits from 1334 T. E., the total number for disposal was thus 75 against 77 of the last year ; of these, 44 suits were disposed of against 28 suits of the previous year and 31 suits remained pending at the close of the year. There were 26 execution cases during the year under report including 19 cases pending from 1334 T. E. ; of these 5 were disposed of and 21

Original side cases.

remained pending at the end of the year. There were 35 applications filed for the grant of succession and other certificates during the year; with the previous year's balance of 13, the total number of cases was 48; out of them 33 were disposed of as shown below, leaving 15 cases pending at the close of the year.

Description of cases.	Total.	Disposed of.	Pending.
Probate case	4	1	3
Succession certificate	16	13	3
Guardianship	28	19	9
Total	48	33	15

80. It will appear from the sub-joined table, that the total number of civil and criminal appeals inclusive of the number pending from the last year was 405 as against 379 of the previous year, and out of these 307 were disposed of against 300 of the previous year. So in comparison with the last year, the total number of appeals increased by 26, and there was a corresponding increase in the disposals in the year under report by 7.

Total number of appeals.

Description of appeals.	Number of appeals.		Disposed of.	
	Past year.	Present year.	Past year.	Present year.
Civil	187	224	126	159
Criminal	192	181	174	148
Total	379	405	300	307

V. Prisons.

81. Inclusive of the Central Jail at the Capital, 8 jails were maintained with a population of 612, as against 661 in the previous year. Of them 258 were convicts, 340 under-trials, 9 civil prisoners and 5 lunatics. The daily average was 87·17 against 83·93.

Number of Jails.

82. 56 prisoners were under sentence of over 2 years as against 51 of the year before, as shown in the following statement.

Long-term Prisoners.

Class of offence.	Number of prisoners.	Occupation.	REMARKS.
Murder	11	They were employed in oilmills, wheat grinding, soorki pounding, *khoa* breaking, bamboo and cane work, gardening, weaving, sewing, paddy husking, rice manufacturing &c.	32 had sentences of 2 to 5 years, 18 of 5 to 10 years, 6 for life i. e. 20 years.
Culpable homicide not amounting to murder	17		
Dacoity	9		
Robbery	3		
Theft	4		
Rape	2		
Kidnapping	1		
Escape from lawful custody ...	1		
Counterfeiting coin ...	2		
Uttering counterfeit coin and notes	4		
Forgery and Conspiracy ...	2		
Total	56		

83. Jail health was generally good throughout the year. Only one convict died of Chronic Dysentery at the Central Jail.

Jail Health.

84. One convict from the Central Jail, 4 under-trials from the Kailashahar Jail and 1 under-trial from the Khowai Jail escaped. The convict and one of the under-trial prisoners of the Kailashahar Jail were re-arrested during the year.

Escape.

85. The total income from all jails amounted to Rs. 3,350 against Rs. 3,147 of the previous year.

Jail income.

86. The total expenditure amounted to Rs. 13,633 as against Rs. 13,188.

Expenditure.

87. The new *pucca* Jail Dormitory was completed and opened by His Highness The Maharaja Manikya Bahadur on the 14th Sravan *i. e.* 30th July, 1925. It consists of two wards with an accommodation for 38 prisoners.

Jail Dormitory.

VI. Registration.

88. After the deputation of Mr. K. Dutt to His Highness's Camp at Shillong in Falgoon of the previous year the charge of the department remained temporarily with Mr. S. C. Deb Barman, M. A., (Harvard) and Babu J. C. Maulik, till Dewan A. C. Chaudhuri took over charge about the middle of the year. During the latter part of the year the charge was again for a short time with Babu B. K. Chatterjee, M. A., B. L., when Dewan A. C. Chaudhuri was on leave.

Charge.

89. The number of Registration Offices was 9, one at the Head Quarters Station of each of the Divisions or Sub-Divisions. In the moffussil the Officers in charge of the Divisions and Sub-Divisions acted as Ex-officio Registrars, while at Agartala, there was a separate Registrar for the Sadar Division.

Registration Offices.

90. Appendices XV and XVI are Registration statements and show the work of the Department.

91. The number of documents presented for registration during the year in the 9 offices was 13,265 as against 9,674 of the previous year. Of this number 136 deeds were refused registration on different grounds, while 74 remained pending at the close of the year.

Presentation and disposal.

92. The total value covered by the documents presented amounted to Rs. 22,35,371, as compared with Rs. 15,29,558 of the previous year. The total value covered by the documents actually registered was Rs. 21,12,171 as against Rs. 14,96,766 in the year before.

Value of deeds presented and registered.

93. The number of suits and appeals filed before the Officer-in-charge, Registration Department, in respect of documents the registration of which had been refused in the Registration offices, was 31 and 3 against 29 and 1 respectively in the preceding year, and there were 24 suits and 1 appeal pending from the previous year, making a total of 55 suits and 4 appeals. Out of these, 29 suits and 4 appeals were disposed of during the year leaving 26 suits pending at the end of the year.

The Suits and appeals.

95. The total income from fees and fines amounted to Rs. 15,781 against Rs. 11,213 and the expenditure to Rs. 4,336 against Rs. 3,639. The net income during the year was Rs. 11,444 against Rs. 7,574 which shows a satisfactory increase.

Income and Expenditure.

VII. Municipality.

96. The Capital Town of Agartala, continued to be the only Municipality in the State with a population of about eight thousand.

Municipality.

97. On the expiry of the term of the previous Committee a new Committee with 9 members, including an official Chairman and a non-official Vice-Chairman, was formed towards the end of the year. Care was taken to have the different interests properly represented in the Committee. Mr. B. K Chatterjee, M. A., B. L., Officer-in-charge, Revenue Department, who had experience of the working of Municipalities in a Bengal District, was nominated Chairman of the new Committee and Babu Nagendra Nath Ray, B. L., a local pleader, was elected Vice-Chairman by the unanimous vote of the Committee. There were altogether 12 sittings of the Committee (old and new) during the year, the average of attendance being 4·9. The attendance was unsatisfactory.

Municipal Committee.

98. The income of the Municipality from Municipal and Latrine Taxes was Rs. 3,399 against Rs. 3,943. The demand inclusive of arrears, was Rs. 7,293. It has been found that a large portion of the demand is irrecoverable. The new Committee made an attempt to correct the Tauji by writing off irrecoverable dues. This work should be continued. The income under the Miscellaneous Head including deposits and advances recovered was Rs. 2,053 against Rs. 2,165 in the previous year. The State grant for the year was Rs. 9,000. The total of the above receipts, excluding the income of the Bazar, amounted to Rs. 14,452.

Income.

99. The total expenditure of the Municipality including advances and refund of deposits and excluding the amount spent on the Bazar improvement, amounted to Rs. 14,117 against Rs. 14,693 in the previous year.

Expenditure.

100. The state of general health within the Municipality was on the whole worse than in the previous year, though Kala-azar cases were decidedly fewer. There were a number of sporadic cases of Cholera and Small-pox, with some fatal ones during the latter part of the year.

Public Health.

101. The want of good drinking water and proper drainage is being keenly felt. The matter is receiving attention.

102. The control of the Town Bazar remained with the Municipal Committee, which took steps to improve the food supply. The work of the Bazar Building was carried on but not finished. The total receipts from the Bazar came up to Rs. 11,026 as against Rs. 4,866 in the previous year. The increase is explained by the fact that arrears to the extent of Rs. 4,948 which was in deposit pending adjustment, was credited to the Municipality during the year. The total demand including an arrear demand of Rs. 5,624-10 was Rs. 11,766-8-6. After necessary expenditure, the Bazar improvement fund stood at Rs. 15,672-5 at the end of the year.

The Town Bazar.

103. For the last 4 years the income from the Town Bazar has been shewn as a part of the Municipal income and treated as the Municipal fund. But the Bazar income is "earmarked" for Bazar improvement, and is not to be treated as a part of the Municipal Fund, nor drawn upon for any other purpose. The income from the Bazar has therefore been shewn separately in the body of this report.

CHAPTER IV—PRODUCTION AND DISTRIBUTION.

I. Weather and Crops—Agriculture.

104. The average rainfall of the year was 108·28 inches against 106·28 in the previous year. The quinquennial average was 90·9 inches. Bilonia Division had the maximum fall of 138·97 inches and Udaipur the minimum of 70·53.

Rainfall.

The rainfall, though seasonable on the whole, was untimely in respect of and unfavourable to certain crops.

Crops. 105. The principal crops were paddy, cotton, *til*, mustard, jute and sugarcane. The weather conditions were favourable to some of these crops and the out-turn was normal in most cases considering the aggregate yield. The out-turn of cotton and *Aman* paddy was unsatisfactory in certain areas.

Tea Industry. 106. The Tea Industry made some progress during the year under review and the tea produced in the State fetched good prices. As many as 27 gardens showed marked improvement.

Cattle. 107. The health of the cattle was generally bad. There were out-breaks of foot and mouth disease in the Sadar and Khowai Divisions in particular, and the Veterinary Assistant was deputed to the affected localities to render necessary help. On the whole 3,000 heads of cattle were treated for various diseases during the year.

Condition of the people. 108. The people are mostly agricultural. The main crops, paddy, mustard, jute, potato, *til*, cotton and sugarcane grew fairly well. Cleansed cotton sold at Rs. 15 to Rs. 60 per maund and all agricultural crops fetched good prices. The condition of the agricultural population was thus more or less satisfactory in spite of high prices of imported articles. The middle classes however suffered seriously owing to the prevailing high prices of staple food crops and of imported necessaries of life.

Prices. 109. The prices of food grains were similar to those in the neighbouring British districts. Rice sold from Rs. 5-8 to Rs. 9 and paddy from Rs. 2-12 to Rs. 4 per maund. The maximum price of rice in the previous year also was Rs. 9.

Wages. 110. There was no appreciable change in the rates of wages. Male labourers earned from 10 annas to Re. 1-8 and female labourers from 4 annas to Re. 1 a day. *Gharamis* earned from 8 annas to Re. 1-4, and Carpenters and Masons from 12 annas to Re. 1-8. Most of the labourers were outsiders from the neighbouring British Districts, as well as up country coolies.

Taccavi. 111. No Taccavi advances were issued dnring the year.

Staff. 112. The staff of the Department continued to be the same as it was during the last year.

Propaganda work and Circuit lectures. 113. The Department undertook during the year, the following propaganda works :—

1. Introduction of new cotton crops in the existing *jooms* and also on the plains with plough.
2. The change of the present method of *jooming* by the introduction of single seed sowing system.
3. The giving up of *jooming* where cultivable land is available.
4. Preservation of manure and use of selected seeds.
5. Inducement to grow high land improved paddy *Kataktara* and the low land paddy *Indrasail.*
6. Eri Rearing.
7. Introduction of *Tana* sugarcane and extension of sugarcane cultivation in the *jooms.*

114. It has been found by repeated experiments that the Dharwar American Cotton does not grow well in *jooms* with the variety of seeds tried viz, *Gadak* No. 1 which gives its proper harvest as late as December, when the *jooms* are totally abandoned, while the early bolls do not open properly and are affected by rains.

Dharwar American Cotton in *jooms*.

115. The Department is on the look out for a new long stapled American variety which may suitably flower early and allow a steady harvest in the same line with the local Comilla.

116. The Department took up towards the end of the year some improved cotton varieties for experiments in *jooms*, the result of which is to be watched with interest.

Other improved varieties.

117. During the last part of the year the programme for distributing jute, as well as *Kataktara* and *Indrasail* paddy was taken up and there was a vast demand for *Indrasail* paddy which was distributed through local growers.

Seed distribution.

118. Experiments have established beyond a shadow of doubt that almost all the varieties of cotton such as the *Buri*, American Dharwar and the Comillas could be grown on the plains under plough cultivation.

Cotton growing under plough.

119. Demonstrations were also made with paddy, potato, sugarcane and jute. Seeds were distributed in different other places through local seed growers. The result was fairly satisfactory.

Other Demonstrations.

120. Potato cultivation is spreading in almost every division on river side lands, though the outturn is not quite up to the mark. This is due to the lack of irrigation system. There was less insect trouble with the potato crops during the year under report.

121. The farm land has thoroughly been reclaimed and every necessary arrangement made to utilize it as a seed farm on a small scale for the present.

Kashipur Model Farm.

122. Nainital potato, as well as American and *Matihar* tobacco were tried on a new plot of land. The results were not quite up to the mark as both sowing and planting were late.

Other crops.

123. Eri rearing went on in the farm for seed eggs and demonstration was given in some places near the farm.

Eri culture.

124. The Superintendent was out on tour for 90 days during the year.

Touring of staff.

II. Immigration and Emigration.

125. During the year 1,347 families immigrated into and 760 families emigrated out of the State, as against 1,400 and 694 respectively in the previous year.

III. Forests.

Charge and Management.

126. Dewan A. C. Chaudhuri, B. A. was in charge of the Department till 3rd Sraban when the direct charge of the Department was taken up by Rai J. C. Sen Bahadur Vice-President of the Council of Administration. He was assisted by Babu Jatindra Nath Mittra, Forest Officer. All the Forests were under *Khash* management as before.

Staff.

127. The department had a staff of 3 Forest Inspectors, 19 Foresters, 12 Rangers, 16 Assistant Foresters, 10 Moharers, 16 Head Guards and 197 Guards and Literate Guards. Besides these, there were 184 Commission Agents for the sale of permits for the shoulder-borne export of forest produce. There were 58 stations for collection of duty and prevention of forest offences.

Working.

128. The Reserved *Sal* Forests of the Sonamura Division were worked under the system of Coppice with standards and those of the Udaipur Division under the Selection Method, while the open unclassed forests were worked under the State Rules of 1323 T. E. For the Feni River *Mehal*, the working rules of the Bengal Forest Department were followed.

129. As an experimental measure, a fixed block was selected in the Langai Valley and a certain number of trees were marked therein for sale. Similarly two blocks were also selected in the Sonamura and the Udaipur Reserve Forests respectively. As the marking operations were undertaken towards the close of the year, the sale of these blocks could not be held in the year under report.

Sources of revenue.

130. The result of the collection of forest revenue is detailed below :—

Heads of Revenue.	1335 T.E.	1334 T.E.	Increase.	Decrease.	REMARKS.
I. Unclassed open forests :—					
(*a*) Toll on forest produce exported by the river mehals	3,89,487	3,37,881	51,606	—	
(*b*) Toll on forest produce exported by land route under permit	83,072	84,481	—	1,409	
(*c*) Toll collection (share) of the Feni river mehal ...	31,604	21,349	10,255	—	
(*d*) Grazing mehal ...	6,896	6,703	193	—	
(*e*) Thatching grass mehal	10.342	12,327	—	1,985	
II. Reserved Forests :— Sale of *Sal* and *Garjan* trees ...	14,199	32,143	—	17,944	
III. Elephant Kheddas	1,702	10,759	—	9,057	
TOTAL ...	5,37,302	5,05,643	62,054	30,395	

Net increase—31,659.

131. The total forest revenue of the year was Rs. 5,37,302 against Rs. 5,05,643 of the previous year, showing an increase of Rs. 31,659.

Receipts.

132. An appreciable rise of revenue is noticeable in the River Mehals and a fall in the Reserve Forests and the elephant Khedda operations. The main cause of the fall in the Reserve Forests was the regulation of the unrestricted felling of *Sal* and *Garjan* trees.

133. Khedda operations were undertaken in the Kailashahar Division only. The operations were not successful. Only one elephant was caught in the year against 25 in the previous year. This accounts for the decrease in receipts under this head.

Elephant Kheddas.

134. On the recommendations made by a conference held in November, 1924, under the presidency of the Commissioner of the Chittagong Division, the Government of Bengal approved of the continuance of the joint Toll Station at Amlighat under the management of the State Forest Department, till the 31st March, 1926. The question of the future management was not taken up in the year under review, and the joint Toll Station continued to be under the management of the State Forest Department.

Feni River Mehal.

135. The total revenue collected at the joint Toll Station in the year under review was Rs. 47,404 against Rs. 31,170 in the previous year.

136. In the year under report, the forest produce Lot No. 98 was taken in *Ijara* by the Station Officer of the Amlighat Toll Station on behaif of the Government and the State. The forest produce from the other fee simple lot also was exported without much trouble between the Station Staff and the Lot-owners.

Fee Simple Lots.

137. During the year under review there were 170 forest cases against 362 persons, of which 148 cases against 310 persons were instituted during the year, while 22 cases against 52 persons were pending from the previous year. The offences were mainly for illicit export of forest produce without permits and without payment of duty.

Forest offences.

138. Altogether 186 persons in 109 cases were convicted, of whom 15 were sentenced to imprisonment and 171 were punished with fine only. 73 persons in 22 cases were acquitted, 12 cases against 36 persons were compounded, and 27 cases against 67 persons remained pending at the close of the year.

Results.

139. No reward was awarded during the year. Three Rangers were degraded and one Literate Guard and one Guard were dismissed for misconduct.

Rewards and Punishments.

140. The health of the staff in general was normal excepting some cases of fever of a bad type.

Health of the Staff.

141. With a view to remove the troubles about the working of the Langai Forests, a conference was held at Langai in June, 1925 and a joint report was drawn up and submitted by the representatives of the Assam Government and the

General.

State, (i) recommending the abolition of the British Check Station at Damcherra, (ii) the recognition of the private property marks of traders registered in the State, (iii) the reciprocal adjustment of rights regarding free floating in certain small streams and certain other minor points. The recommendations were accepted by the Assam Government as well as by the State. It is now hoped that there will be no further trouble for the export of forest produce from the State Forests.

142. It is regrettable that there was a case of robbery in which the Forester of Kamthana Ghat was severely assaulted by some persons and robbed of State money. The case is still sub-judice.

IV. Trade and Manufacture.

143. The principal exports were timber, forest produce of various kinds, cotton, oil-seeds, (*til* and mustard seed) paddy, jute, rice and *Gur* (molassess). A small quantity of tea and some homespun cotton fabrics manufactured by the hill people, specially the Manipuris, were also exported. The principal exports for the year under review and of the previous year are shown below :—

	1334 T. E.	1335 T. E.
Cotton ...	60,478 maunds.	85,321 maunds.
Til	30,333 „	36,853 „
Mustard Seeds...	36,185 „	34,847 „
Jute	51,535 „	92,955 „

144. Altogether 5,60,568 lbs. of tea was exported in 1925 from the gardens in the State, against 3,38,272 lbs. and 2,25,533 lbs. respectively in 1924, and 1923.

145. The principal imports were cloths and yarns, salt, oils (*kerosine* and mustard), pulses, chillies, tobacco, sugar, flour, spices, arecanuts, books and stationery. The industries worth mention were manufacture of cotton fabrics by the hill people and the Manipuris ; cane and bamboo baskets, mats and sieves by Tripuras ; and dug-outs, bowls and plates of wood by the Reangs and Chakmas ; also *Gur* (molassess) by both hill people and Bengalees.

V. Public Works.

146. Maharajkumar B. K. Deb Barman Bahadur, Member of the Council of Administration was in charge of the Department during

the year. Mr. J. N. Bhaduri, B. A., B. E., F. R. S. A., M. R. SAN I. (London) continued as State Engineer.

Expenditure.

147. The expenditure including disbursements from local funds came to Rs. 2,33,711 against Rs. 2,87,572 in the previous year. Of this Rs. 4,732 was spent on water supply, Rs. 45,365 on roads and bridges, Rs. 1,60,302 on buildings and Rs. 2,792 on miscellaneous works.

148. The following important Major Works were completed during the year under report :—

1. Jail Building at Agartala.
2. Administration Building (First Portion).
3. High Court Building.
4. Decoration of the Palace.

149. Substantial progress was made in the construction of the Bishalgarh–Udaipur Road and the repairs to the Sansar Office Building.

150. The Stone metalling of the District Board portion of the Agartala–Akhaura Road could not be finished during the year under report for want of stones which the A. B. Railway had undertaken to supply but failed to do so.

151. The following buildings were completed with corrugated iron roofing during the year under report :—

1. H. H.'s Andar Extension.
2. Baithak-Khana for Maharajkumar Ranabir Kishore Dev Barman.
3. Nat-Mandir and Chandi-Mandir at Durga-Bari.
4. Kalamchora Range Office.
5. Nat-Mandir of Sib-Bari at Udaipur.
6. Jagannath-Dighi Range Office at Bilonia.
7. Radhanagar Tehsil Kutchery at Bilonia.
8. Puran Rajbari Tehsil Office at Bilonia.
9. Ghora-Kapa Tehsil Office at Sabroom.
10. Magroom Tehsil Office at Sabroom.
11. Dharmanagar Tehsil Kutchery.
12. Two Structures for maid-servants in the Palace.

CHAPTER V—REVENUE AND FINANCES.

I. Revenue.

152. The total collection in the year was Rs. 17,53,961 against Rs. 15,42,710 in the previous year. The average of the past five years was Rs. 14,31,317.

153. The details of the income under different heads with all variations are given in the statement below :—

Serial number.	Heads of Revenue.	1335 T.E.	1334 T.E.	As compared with 1334 T.E.		Remarks.
				Increase.	Decrease.	
1	Land Revenue	5,89,635	5,18,227	71,408	—	
2	Rents of markets	6,852	5,316	1,536	—	
3	Family Tax in the hills	63,118	64,433	—	1,315	
4	Toll on forest produce	4,72,559	4,30,308	42,251	—	
5	Do. Do. on the Feni River	31,604	21,349	10,255	—	
6	Elephant & buffalo grazing Mehal	6,896	6,703	193	—	
7	Thatching grass Mehal	10,342	12,327	—	1,985	
8	Reserved *Sal* trees	14,199	24,197	—	9,998	
9	Royalty on elephants caught ...	1,702	10,759	—	9,057	
10	Tax on cotton and oil-seeds ...	2,14,808	1,55,407	59,401	—	
11	Adda Mehal	21,089	22,419	—	1,330	
12	Excise	60,563	52,905	7,658	—	
13	Stamps and Court-fees	84,490	68,343	16,166	—	
14	Law and Justice (Fines)... ...	3,422	2,543	879	—	
15	Process fees	13,729	11,450	2,279	—	
16	Registration	15,781	11,213	4,568	—	
17	Jail	3,350	3,147	203	—	
18	Cattle pounds	5,869	5,149	720	—	
19	Nazars	47,489	29,614	17,875	—	
20	Agriculture	570	275	295	—	
21	Education...	7,906	7,907	—	1	
22	Miscellaneous	77,988	78,719	—	750	
	Total	17,53,961	15,42,710	2,35,687	24,436	Net increase—Rs. 2,11,251

154. There was thus a total increase of Rs. 2,35,687 in respect of 15 heads of revenue against a total decrease of Rs. 24,436 in regard to 7 heads. The increase under the head "Land revenue" is due to the realisation of arrear revenue of several Tea Estates, and to the increased capacity of the tenantry to pay the demand owing to the rise in prices of agricultural produce, mainly jute. The increase under the heads of Forest produce, and Cotton and Oil seeds was highly satisfactory.

Increase.

155. The slight decrease in Family tax and *Adda* tax requires no explanation.

Decrease.

II. Finances.

156. A consolidated abstract account showing the financial transactions of the State and Zemindaries is given below, with short explanatory notes of the striking variations :—

157. The year opened with a balance of Rs. 9,41,183 against Rs. 13,06,268 in the preceding year. During the year under review the total receipts from all sources including deposits and law charges recovered, amounted to Rs. 31,22,017 and the total sum available for expenditure was Rs. 40,63,200, as against Rs. 29,65,939 and Rs. 42,79,207 respectively in the previous year.

Receipts.

158. The total disbursement during the year came up to Rs. 30,74,930 against Rs. 33,31,024 and the closing balance Rs. 9,88,270 against Rs. 9,41,183. Of this closing balance, Rs. 5,53,275 was in cash, Rs. 1,00,000 in investment and Rs. 3,34,995 in loans and advances. As compared with the preceding year, the cash balance increased by Rs. 1,33,636. Rs. 1,00,000 of the cash was invested as fixed deposit with the Imperial Bank of India. A further reduction of Rs. 86,549 was effected under loans and advances, bringing down the figure to Rs. 3,34,995 at the close of the year.

Expenditure.

Receipts.	1334 T.E.	1335 T.E.
1. Opening balance :—		
(1) State	10,04,982	6,24,594
(2) Zemindaries ...	3,01,286	3,16,589
Total ...	13,06,268	9,41,183
2. Income :—		
(1) State	15,42,710	17,59,321
(2) Zemindaries ...	10,70,937	12,11,339
Total ...	26,13,647	29,70,660
3. Law charges recovered :—		
(1) State	—	—
(2) Zemindaries ...	67,660	57,133
4. Refunds and compensation for lands acquired :—		
(1) State ...	—	—
(2) Zemindaries ...	3,830	1,685
5. Deposits :—		
(1) State	71,284	86,764
(2) Zemindaries ...	6,518	5,775
Total ...	77,802	92,539
6. Loans :—		
(1) State	—	—
(2) Zemindaries ...	2,03,000	—
	2,03,000	—
GRAND TOTAL ...	42,72,207	40,63,200

Expenditure.	1334 T.E.	1335 T.E.
1. General Administration charges :—		
(a) State	4,62,125	4,89,890
(b) Zemindaries :—		
1. Cost of management	1,36,015	1,41,274
2. Cost of litigation	95,805	1,29,224
Total ...	6,93,945	7,60,388
2. Revenue and Taxes on account of the Zemindaries	2,57,356	2,67,026
3. Public Works :—		
(a) State	2,97,487	2,41,105
(b) Zemindaries	57,614	54,454
Total ...	3,55,101	2,95,559
4. Municipality :—		
(a) State	9,250	9,000
5. Education :—		
(a) State	1,00,544	1,08,370
(b) Zemindaries	9,387	10,228
Total ...	1,09,931	1,18,598
6. Medical :—		
(a) State	60,313	68,288
(b) Zemindaries	10,073	10,615
Total ...	70,386	78,903
7. Survey and Settlement :—		
(a) State	13,617	17,152
(b) Zemindaries	1,108	783
Total ...	14,725	17,935
8. Agriculture :—State	4,328	4,779
9. Religious Expenses :—		
(a) State	89,691	66,467
(b) Zemindaries	6,229	6,058
Total ...	95,920	72,525
10. Sultanat :—		
(a) State	42,623	40,645
11. Purchase of Landed Tenures :—		
(a) State	454	85,850
(b) Zemindaries	—	128
Total ...	454	85,978
12. Pension and Gratuity :—		
(a) State	25,778	27,488
(b) Zemindaries	4,293	4,627
Total ...	30,071	32,115
13. Ordinary *Sansar* charges :—		
(a) Ordinary expenses on account of His Highness and family including the late Maharaja's family ...	76,824	82,774
(b) Other branches of the Raj family...	1,42,768	1,39,442
(c) Thakurs	30,003	30,420
(d) *Sansar* office establishment ...	7,806	7,772
(e) Electric Light	22,912	25,032
(f) Miscellaneous	49,382	47,617
Total ...	3,29,690	3,33,057
14. Charity and Donation :—		
(a) State	20,230	21,892
(b) Zemindaries	1,977	1,659
Total ...	22,207	23,551
15. His Highness's Nij Tahabil (Privy purse) including expenses on journeys	4,07,410	1,12,509
16. Liabilities liquidated including payment of interest on loans and repayment of deposits :—		
(a) State	1,24,440	69,275
(b) Zemindaries	7,28,500	5,07,859
Total ...	8,52,940	5,77,134
17. Miscellaneous :—		
(a) State	3,486	6,162
(b) Zemindaries	12,505	15,660
Total ...	15,991	21,822
18. Marriage—State	15,173	2,16,500
19. Advances	3,523	6,906
20. Closing Balance :—		
(a) State		
In cash	3,72,122	3,96,594
In bonds and advances	2,52,472	2,14,530
Total ...	6,24,594	6,11,124
(b) Zemindaries :—		
In cash	1,47,517	1,56,681
In investment	—	1,00,000
In bonds and advances	1,69,072	1,20,465
Total ...	3,16,589	3,77,146
GRAND TOTAL ...	42,72,207	40,63,200

159. The noticeable variations in expenditure are explained below :—

i. ADMINISTRATION CHARGES :—

STATE—The main reasons for the increases were :—

(a) Payment of legal expenses to the extent of Rs. 16,000 in connection with the Stamp Forgery Case.

(b) Usual increments allowed under the time scale of pay.

(c) Increased expenditure under travelling expenses and other miscellaneous heads.

(d) Cost of Stamp papers.

(e) Payment of arrear contribution for leave and pension of Rai J. C. Sen Bahadur in excess of the amount previously drawn.

ZEMINDARIES—The increase was mainly due to the usual time scale increments of salaries, increased collection fees paid to the *Gomastas* and the institution of a larger number of rent suits.

ii. REVENUE AND TAXES :—

ZEMINDARIES—The increase was mainly due to revision of the Municipal Tax at Comilla.

iii. PUBLIC WORKS :—

STATE—The outlay under this head shows a decrease of Rs. 56,382 which is not real. Eliminating the heavy adjustment of old advances, the actual expenditure would be Rs. 2,35,615 against Rs. 2,38,002 resulting in a reduction of Rs. 2,387 only.

ZEMINDARIES—The decrease was due to the programme of work undertaken being smaller.

iv. EDUCATION :—

In the State, the increase was due to the educational expenses of two Kumars sent to the Rajkumar College at Raipur ; while in the Zemindaries the contribution granted to some institutions accounted for the increase.

v. MEDICAL :—

STATE—The increase is attributable to the adjustment of old advances to the extent of Rs. 2,780, payment of full salaries of the State Homœopath who had been on sick leave during the preceding year, and larger expenditure on travelling allowances.

vi. SURVEY AND SETTLEMENTS :—

STATE—The cost of preparation of a State map by the Surveyor General of India and the extension of Survey operations mainly accounted for the increased expenditure.

vii. RELIGIOUS EXPENSES :—

STATE—The decrease is only apparent, being mainly due to the adjustment of old advances in the accounts of the preceding year.

viii. SULTANAT :—

The post of the Palace Superintendent remained vacant during the year, and this accounts for the reduction under this head.

ix. PURCHASE OF LANDED TENURES :—

STATE—The increase was due to the purchase of Mr. Courjon's property at Comilla at a cost of Rs. 85,340.

x. PENSION AND GRATUITY :—

The increase was due to the retirement of some officers on pension, and also to payment of gratuities to the families of several deceased employees.

xi. ORDINARY SANSAR CHARGES :—

STATE—On the whole, the expenditure under this head shows an increase of Rs. 3,367 which was partly due to extra expenditure incurred for Palace guests—the number of visits to the family during the year having been much larger—and partly to the cost of electrical goods purchased on the occasion of marriage ceremonies. The total normal expenditure was however within the budget estimates of the year. The variations under sub-heads (*a*) and (*f*) are mainly due to readjustment of certain items of expenditure in the budget.

xii. NIJ TAHABIL :—

In reality there was no decrease under this head ; if the adjustment of old advances be eliminated, the real expenditure would amount to Rs. 1,02,683 against Rs. 98,236 showing an increase of Rs. 4,447 which was mainly due to increased provision made under 'H. H.'s allowance.

xiii. MISCELLANEOUS :—

The payment of a monthly contribution of Rs. 100 to a local Bengalee Magazine and the printing charges of the Rajmala account for the increase.

xiv. MARRIAGE :—

The expenditure was in connection with the cost of two marriage ceremonies in the Raj family.

xv. LIABILITIES :—

As mentioned in the previous report, a sum of Rs. 9,54,361 remained unpaid at the close of the year 1334 T. E. Adding to this figure Rs. 55,472 which represented the current interest charges and did not form part of the ascertained liabilities, the total amount payable came up to Rs. 10,09,833 of which Rs. 5,00,000 was liquidated during the year, leaving a balance of Rs. 5,09,833 at the end of the year.

160. Two separate statements comparing the receipts and expenditure of the State and the Zemindaries with the respective Revised Estimates are given in appendices XXVII and XXVIII.

161. It will be seen that in the State the actual receipts proved better than the forecast by Rs. 1,03,431, while the expenditure fell short of the Revised Estimate by Rs. 63,765. The result of these variations was to raise the anticipated surplus from Rs. 4,48,928 to Rs. 6,16,124.

162. In the Zemindaries, the increase of Rs. 86,748 under the receipts coupled with the reduction of Rs. 17,910 under expenditure resulted in an increase of Rs. 1,04,658 in the closing balance.

CHAPTER VI—MEDICAL.

163. The year under review opened with 18 dispensaries in the State as in the year before.

164. A statement of new patients as treated in all the dispensaries, as well as the daily average of new patients, in comparison with those of the previous year is given below :—

New patients.

PATIENTS.	1334 T.E.			1335 T.E.		
	Outdoor.	Indoor.	Total.	Outdoor.	Indoor.	Total.
	1,01,248	430	1,01,678	1,05,864	423	1,06,287
Daily average	277·39	1·17	278·56	290·03	1·15	291·18

165. The total outdoor attendance was 1,82,016 as against 1,80,482 in the previous year.

Outdoor attendance.

166. With the last year's balance of 12, the total number of indoor patients was 423 as against 430. Of them 279 were discharged cured, 96 were relieved or otherwise discharged, 35 died and 13 remained under treatment at the end of the year.

Indoor attendance.

167. There were 1,086 operations with 16 major cases as against 996 and 15 respectively.

Surgical operations.

168. The new out-patients treated totalled 12,068 as against 12,504 in the year before—the daily average (new+old) being 59·61 against 61·93. The number of in-patients was 382 against 394 in the preceding year. Of them 242 were cured, 95 were relieved, 34 died and 11 remained under treatment at the close of the year. The daily average was 15·15 against 14·46. The total expenditure on the institution was Rs. 8,769-7-3 against Rs. 8,108-8-9.

V. M. Hospital.

169. 165 police cases were admitted during the year under report against 118 in the year before, including 17 post mortem cases against 19.

Police cases.

170. There were two Kavirajes—both being posted at the capital town. They treated 45 patients during the year under report against 40 in the previous year. The total expenditure on account of their salaries and medicines amounted to Rs. 3,646-12-6 against Rs. 4,268-15-6 in the previous year.

Ayurvedic Department.

171. Dr. Hira Lal Banerjee, H. M. B. with one Assistant was in charge of the Department. 11,405 patients were treated against 10,111 in the preceding year. The daily average (new+old) being 68·31 against 44·65. The total expenditure was Rs. 5,458-15 as against Rs. 3,187-6-9 in the year before, the reason for the large increase being that for 6 months in the previous year, the Doctor was on leave on half pay and without pay.

Homœopathic Department.

172. 6,115 persons were successfully vaccinated out of 6,889 operations. One small-pox doctor and one vaccination Inspector inspected the work of the vaccinators in the interior. The total expenses incurred for this purpose came up to Rs. 1,168-12-9 against Rs. 1,095-4-3 in the previous year.

Vaccinations.

173. Cholera and small-pox broke out in some parts of the State specially in the Sadar Division and Udaipur Sub-Division.

Public health.

174. There were 193 deaths from Cholera and 12 deaths from Small-pox. The total number of seizures could not be definitely ascertained.

175. One doctor specially appointed for Kala-azar treatment had his headquarters at Agartala. 395 patients were treated during the year under review. Of them 243 were cured, 118 left treatment, 12 died and 22 remained under treatment. In the Muffissil Dispensaries 76 were treated in all. The total expenditure incurred on this account amounted to Rs. 823-13-9 against Rs. 613-8 in the previous year.

Kala-azar.

176. Dr. M. M. Majumdar, L. M. S., was the Chief Medical Officer and Dr. S. K. Dutt, L. M. S., his assistant. Besides there was a staff of subordinate medical men.

Staff.

177. Dr. Majumder was out on tour for 26 days and inspected 7 dispensaries.

Tour.

178. The total expenditure, including grain allowance paid, amounted to Rs. 68,288 as against Rs. 60,313 in the preceding year.

Total expenditure.

CHAPTER VII—PUBLIC INSTRUCTION.

179. Mr. S. C. Dev Barman, M. A. (Harvard) was in charge of the Department.

Charge.

180. The number of schools in the year under review was 147 against 138 in the previous year, and the total numerical strength 5,876 against 5,559 excluding private institutions numbering 15 with 390 pupils on the rolls, as against 27 with 689 in the previous year.

Number of schools.

181. In the year under review there were 5 High English Schools, the Umakanta Academy at Agartala, the Radhakishore Institution at Kailashahar, the Brojenrakishore Institution at Bilonia, the Birbikram Institution at Dharmanagar and the High School at Sonamura. All the High English Schools excepting the Sonamura High School, were permanently affiliated to the Calcutta University. The Sonamura High School has been continuing under provisional recognition with effect from 1924 A. D. The construction of the building of the Sonamura H. E. School was nearing completion and that of the Boarding Houses attached thereto was complete. The number of pupils in these H. E. Schools was 1,414 against 899 in the previous year and the average daily attendance stood at 1,014·19 against 700·36. In the year under report, the infant classes were amalgamated with the respective High English Schools, with the approval of the Calcutta University.

H. E. Schools.

182. Agartala, the State Capital, was, as in the previous year, fixed by the Calcutta University as a centre for the Matriculation Examination for the year 1926. Only the five State High English Schools were allowed to send up candidates to this centre. The Department looked after the convenience of the candidates coming from Moffussil. The Examination was conducted under the direct control and personal supervision of the Member of the Council of Administration in charge of Education.

Matriculation Centre.

183. Altogether 55 candidates were sent up for the last Matriculation Examination from the five State High English Schools against 63 in the previous year. The details of the results are noted below :—

Results of the Matriculation Examination.

	No. sent up.	Passed.	1st Division.	2nd Division.	3rd Division.
1. U. K. Academy	16	12	3	9	0
2. R. K. Institution	11	6	1	4	1
3. B. K. Institution	10	7	3	3	1
4. B. B. Institution	11	11	8	2	1
5. Sonamura School	7	1	1	0	0
Total ...	55	37	16	18	3

184. The result of the Dharmanagar B. B. Institution is creditable considering the general decline in the percentage of successes in the year's Matrculation result in the University. It is noteworthy that this Institution has secured cent per cent success this year too, and it has been doing so consecutively for some years together.

185. There were 35 Boarders in the Thakur Boarding House against the same number in the previous year. The number of boarders successful in the last Annual Examination was 23. Two boarders sat for the last Matriculation Examination, of whom one came out successful and was placed in the second division. The staff consisted of one Guardian Superintendent, one Assistant Tutor, one Private Tutor and one Manager and Tutor. Thakur Pradipta Chandra Dev Barma, Military Subedar, was appointed to train the students up inMilitary Drill.

Thakur Boarding Houuse.

186. The comparative statement below will show the number of Non-Bengalee students receiving education in the several schools of the State :—

Non-Bengalee students.

Serial number.	Nationality.	Number of students. Past year.	Present year.	Remarks.
1.	Rajkumars	0	5	
2.	Thakurs	166	179	
3.	Manipuris	635	578	
4.	Tripuras	463	500	
5.	Reangs	29	28	
6.	a. Kukis	66	12	
	b. Chakmas		9	
	c. Lushais		27	
7.	Others...	49	42	
	Total	1,408	1,380	

187. The policy of holding reward Examinations for hill boys was continued and 166 boys appeared at the Examination against 169 in the previous year.

Reward Examination.

188. Mr. S. C. Dev Barman who is also Ex-officio Inspector of schools, visited some schools of Bilonia, Sonamura, Kailashahar, Dharmanagar, Sadar, Khowai and Bishalgarh. In the year under review, one Sub-Inspector for hill schools, conversant with hill language was appointed to stimulate interest of the hill people in Primary Education and to report on the local situation and the method of teaching followed. The Sub-Inspectors of schools visited all the schools within their respective jurisdictions. On the whole, their inspection work was satisfactory.

Inspection work.

189. In the year under review, there were 6 M. E. schools for boys with 646 students on the rolls, against 5 with 494 pupils in the previous year. The average daily attendance was 474·85 against 352·18.

M. E. Schools.

190. There was only one Higher Vernacular School for boys with 48 students on the rolls as against one with 43 students in the previous year, and an average daily attendance of 38·08 against 34·41.

H. V. Schools.

191. The number of Lower Vernacular Schools for boys was 22 against the same number in the previous year. In some of these schools, boys and girls read together. The total numerical strength was 1,229 against 1,340 and the average daily attendance, 935·77 against 992·85 in the previous year.

L. V. Schools.

192. There were 93 Pathsalas for boys, in the year under report, as against 86 in the previous year. The numerical strength was 2,030 against 2,235, and the average daily attendance 1583·13 against 1705·24 in the previous year.

Pathsalas.

193. There was one Middle English School for girls, namely the Maharani Tulsibati Girls' School at Agartala, the State Capital. The numerical strength of the school was 70 against 99 and the average daily attendance 56·3 against 79·64 in the previous year. There was a Motor Bus service for the conveyance of the girls during the year.

M. E. Schools for Girls.

194. There were 9 Pathsalas for girls against the same number in the previous year. The numerical strength was 192 against 190 and the average daily attendance 138·1 against 133·32 in the previous year. In some of these schools, under the special order of the Education Department, girls were allowed to read the Lower Vernacular and the Upper Vernacular standard. Besides these, in some of the Pathsalas for boys, both boys and girls were taught together.

Pathsalas for Girls

195. Altogether 397 candidates appeared at the local Scholarship Examinations against 312 in the previous year. Of these, 328 including 24 girls came out successful. 19 students including 2 girls passed the Middle English Examination, 5 students passed the H. V. Examination, 63 including 5 girls passed

Scholarship Examination.

the L. V. Examination and 241 including 17 girls passed the Pathsala Examination. On the result of the Examinations, 15 boys and 5 girls received scholarships varying from Rs. 2 to Rs. 5 per month tenable for two to four years.

Schools for special Training.

196. In the year under review, there were 10 Schools for special training, consisting of 3 Sanskrit Tols, 6 Madrassas and Maktabs and one Artisan School, against 9, 3 and 5 respectively in the previous year. The Sanskrit Tols had 39 students on the rolls against 38 in the previous year, and the average daily attendance was 27·44 against 29·06. The Rajakiya Sanskrita Bidyalaya at Agartala sent up 5 candidates for the Government Sanskrit Examinations. The Madrassas and Maktabs had 195 students on the rolls against 203 in the previous year and the average daily attendance was 135·99 against 151·41. The Woodburn Artisan School had 13 boys on the rolls againt 18 boys and the average daily attendance was 4·71 against 6·02 in the previous year.

Education of Princes and Princesses.

197. Two Maharajkumars were admitted to the Rajkumar College at Raipur in the Central Provinces and were placed in charge of a graduate teacher. The result of their Examinations and their progress in health were satisfactory. The Maharajkumaris received education under a graduate lady teacher and a Pandit.

Education of other Kumars.

198. Kumar Bhupendra Chandra Dev Barman has been prosecuting studies in the Dacca University Law College.

The Palace Day School for the young Kumars.

199. In the Day School for the young Kumars there were 8 students on the rolls belonging to the juvenile classes.

Education of Thakur boys.

200. 8 Thakur boys were awarded stipends from the Education Department, and the course of studies prosecuted by each is noted below :—

1. Niranjan Dev Barma—Carmichæl Medical College.
2. Naresh Chandra Dev Barma—Government School of Art.
3. Jogesh Chandra Dev Barma—B. Com. (Calcutta University.)
4. Joysing Dev Barma—B. L. Class (Calcutta University).
5. Jitendra Chandra Dev Barma—B. Sc. Class.
6. Kamalkrishna Dev Barma—B. A. Class.
7. Nripendra Chandra Dev Barma—I. Sc. Class.
8. Asitkumar Dev Barma—Bengal Allen Homœopathic College.

Special Stipends.

201. The following students enjoyed special stipends.

1. Chandrahash Singha.
2. Damanjit Rajkumar.
3. Prakash Chandra Sutradhar.
4. Nitai Chand Singha.
5. Babu Chand Singha.
6. Navadwip Chandra Singha.
7. Pulin Behari Acharyya.

Library.

202. At Agartala, the Birchandra Library was maintained in two separate sections, (1) The English Library being located at the Ujjayanta Palace and (2) The Vernacular Section at the new buiding erected in the vicinity of the local

H. E. School. The latter section was open to the public. The number of English books (including foreign literature) was 4,859 against 4,853 in the previous year and the number of Bengali books (including Sanskrit books) was 1,786 against 1,747 in the previous year. In addition to these, there was a moderate collection of valuable manuscripts in the Palace Library. There were 5 Dailies, 1 Quarterly and 5 Monthlies as against 7, 1 and 8 in the previous year. In the year under review the average daily attendance of readers was 13·25 against 13·2 and the total number of volumes issued to the public was 6,575 against 5,309 in the previous year.

Expenditure.

203. The total expenditure incurred in the Education Department in the year under report, amounted to Rs. 1,08,370 against Rs. 1,00,544. Some of the more important details of the expenditure are noted below :—

1.	Primary Education	Rs. 21,470
2.	Secondary Education	,, 37,814
3.	Schools for special Training...	,, 3,818
4.	Boarding Institution for Thakur boys... ...	,, 9,212
5.	Education of Kumars and Kumaris	,, 11,182
6.	Scholarships and Stipends.	,, 6,556
7.	Library	,, 2,394

Income.

204. Rs. 7,906 was incorporated in the receipts of the year from the accumulated fund of realisations from students, known as the School Fund, in pursuance of the policy adopted in the previous year.

CHAPTER VIII—ZEMINDARIES.

Chakla Roshnabad Estates.

Management.

205. The management of His Highness's Zemindaries in British India continued in the hands of Rai Jyotish Chandra Sen Bahadur, B. A., B. C. S., assisted by three Assistant Managers and one Sub-Manager.

206. The gross revenue demand of the year was Rs. 9,88,681 against Rs. 9,64,484 in the previous year.

207. The total receipts amounted to Rs. 12,72,148 against Rs. 11,47,066 in the previous year.

Expenditure.

208. The total expenditure in the year under review was Rs. 12,15,375 including adjustment of old advances, against Rs. 13,36,642 in the previous year. Of this Rs. 2,67,026 was on account of Land Revenue and Cesses. The total administrative charges of the Zemindaries, including Public Works and

Law Charges, amounted to Rs. 3,46,150. The remainder represents special payments on account of the following items, aggregating Rs. 6,02,199.

1.	Repayment of old debts ...	...	Rs. 5,00,000
2.	Donation	...	„ 1,659
3.	Medical Charges ...	...	„ 10,615
4.	Education Charges ...	...	„ 10,228
5.	Religious Ceremonies ...	...	„ 6,058
6.	Sansar Stipends	...	„ 15,780
7.	Repayment of old deposits	...	„ 7,859
8.	Contribution to the State ...	...	„ 50,000
			Rs. 6,02,199

Settlement.

209. The result of the year's settlement operations will appear from the figures noted below :—

	KINDS OF SETTLEMENT.	ADDITION TO RENTAL.	NAZAR.
1.	*Taskhichi Taluk* in the Town	Rs. 149	Rs. 13,242
2.	Ordinary town settlement ...	„ 128	„ 5,665
3.	*Khaspatit* settlement ...	„ 1,491	„ 13,360
4.	Enhancement of rent ...	„ 1,572	„ 18,537
5.	Re-settlement of auction purchased holdings ...	„ 370	„ 20,194
6.	*Taskhichi Taluk* in the interior	„ 38	„ 863
7.	*Ijara*	„ 2,974	„ —
		Rs. 6,722	Rs. 71,861

210. This year's operations improved the rent roll by Rs. 6,722 and brought in a *nazarana* of Rs. 71,861 against Rs. 3,358 and Rs. 36,926 in the previous year.

CHAPTER IX—MISCELLANEOUS.

The Rajmala.

211. The literary work connected with the fourth part of the Rajmala was finished during the year, and an elaborate index of the first part prepared. The printing of the texts of the first and second parts, as well as of the commentaries of the first part, was completed. The total expenditure incurred during the year, excluding the grant to the periodical *Rabi*, amounted to Rs. 3,212 against Rs. 2,392 and Rs. 3,556 of the preceding two years.

Tours of the members of the Council.

212. Rai J. C. Sen Bahadur, Vice President of the Council, was out on tour of inspection for 79 days during the year, in the course of which he visited several Divisions of the State and all the Divisions of the Zemindaries.

213. Maharajkumar B. K. Dev Barman Bahadur, member of the Council, camped for 27 days in the Sabrum, Bilonia, Sadar and Udaipur Divisions. In the last two Divisions the Maharajkumar inspected the alignment of the proposed Agartala–Udaipur road. At Lungthung in Bilonia he noticed some huge idols of stone half buried in the ground.

214. Dewan B. K. Sen, Chief secretary, had to proceed on duty to Agra, Kotla, Brindaban and other places outside the State, and visited the Kailashahar Division twice, being altogether in camp for 63 days.

Tours of high Officers.

215. Dewan Asit Chandra Chaudhuri, Officer-in-charge, Revenue, Forest and other Departments was out for 5 days, and his successor Babu Brajendra Kumar Chatterjee for 13 days, while Mr. S. C. Deb Barman, Officer-in-charge, Education Department, toured for 29 days during the year.

216. Other tours have already been noticed in the connected sections.

217. The tours of the Divisional Officers and their Assistants as well as of some officers of analogous status are noted below :—

Divisional Officers.

State.

1. Sadar—
   Divisional Officer—Thakur Tarini Charan Deb Barman ... 7 days.
   Asst. Collector— Babu Prava Ranjan Das Gupta, M. A., B. L. ... 43 ,,
   ,, ,, Surendra Ch. Guha, B. A. ... 6 ,,
2. Kailashahar—
   Divisional Officer—Thakur Lalit Mohan Deb Barman, M. A., B. L. ... 74 ,,
   Second ,, Babu Jyotirmoy Ghosh, M. A. ... 21 ,,
3. Sonamura—
   Divisional Officer— ,, Bisweswar Guha, B. A. ... 35 ,,
   Second ,, Thakur Jyoti Lal Deb Barman, B. L. ... 23 ,,
4. Bilonia—
   Divisional Officer— ,, Kamini Kumar Singh ... 66 ,,
   Second ,, ,, Suresh Chandra Chakravarty, B. L. ... 62 ,,
5. Khowai—
   Divisional Officer—Thakur Gokul Chandra Deb Barman ... 34 ,,
6. Dharmanagar—
   Divisional Officer—Babu Kunja Behari Chakravarty, M. A., B. L. ... 29 ,,
7. Udaipur—
   Divisional Officer— ,, Brajendra Chandra Dutt ... 11 ,,
8. Sabroom—
   Divisional Officer— ,, Jogendra Lal Ganguly, B. L. ... 96 ,,
9. Amarpur—
   Sub-Divisional Officer— ,, Kusum Kumar Sen, B. L. ... 22 ,,
10. Survey Superintendent— ,, Kamini Kumar Kar ... 112 ,,
11. Superintendent—of Agriculture—Mr. I Choudhuri ... ... 90 ,,

Zemindaries.

1. Babu Pramada Ranjan Bhattacharjee. B. A.,
Assistant Manager, Central Division ... 44 days.

2. „ Tarit Mohan Gupta.
Assistant Manager, Southern Division ... 44 „

3. „ Surendra Nath Basu, B. L.,
Assistant Manager, Northern Division ... 79 „

4. „ Nava Kumar Chakravarty, B. L.,
Sub-Manager, Srimangal Division ... 74 „

5. „ Manada Ranjan Chaudhury, B. L., Inspector ... 242 „

DATED, AGARTALA,
The 26th September, 1926.

By order of the Council of Administration.

B. K. Sen,
Chief Secretary.

APPENDIX.

List of the principal Laws and Regulations in force in the Tripura State during 1335 T.E.

Description.	Whether adapted from British Indian Acts.	Whether introduced during the year under report.
CRIMINAL.		
1. Regulation No. III. of 1280 T. E.		
2. Regulation No. I. of 1283 T. E.		
3. Jail Regulation, 1283 T. E.		
4. Regulation No. IV. of 1283 T. E. (Cattle trespass and pound).		
5. Regulation No. III. of 1296 T. E. (Police Regulation).		
6. Act No. IV. of 1321 T. E.–Penal Laws (an amending Act)		
CIVIL.		
1. Civil Law of 1284 T. E.		
2. Rules regarding *chit* suits (small causes) 1287 and 1300 T. E.		
3. Act No. II. of 1313 T. E.—an Act for the regulation of interest on debts.		
4. Act No. II. of 1314 T. E.—Limitation Act	Partly adapted.	
REVENUE.		
1. Act No. I. of 1286 T. E.—Stamp Act		
2. Act No. I. of 1290 T. E.—Sale Law		
3. Act No. I. of 1296 T. E.—Tenancy Act.		
4. Act No. II. of 1296 T. E.—*Abkari*		
5. Act No. II. of 1297 T. E.—Reserved forests.		
6. Act No. I. of 1304 T. E.—Duties on *til* and cotton.		
7. Act No. I. of 1306 T. E.—Registration		
8. Survey and Settlement Act, 1309 T.E.	Do.	
9. *Tuccavi* Regulation, 1310 T. E.	Do.	
10. Act No. I. of 1313 T. E.—Forests.		
11. Act No. I. of 1314 T. E.—(amending the above)		
12. A Law imposing export duty on jute and mustard-seed, 1317 T. E.		
13. Act No. II. of 1321 T.E.—Ghasuri Act		
MISCELLANEOUS.		
1. An Act promulgating certain rules as Law, 1283 T. E.		
2. Regulation for the record of judicial decisions &c., 1284 T. E. ...		
3. Municipal Regulation, 1284 T. E.		
4. Legal Practitioners' Regulation.		
5. Act No. I. of 1297 T. E.—an Act for the regulation of commissions for the examination of witnesses.		
6. Special Regulation against cow slaughter		
7. Rules of evidence		
8. Act I. of 1318 T. E.—Constitution of Courts—(an amending Act).		
9. Leave and allowance Rules	Do.	
10. Act No. I. of 1321 T. E.—Arms Act	Do.	
11. Act No. III. of 1321 T. E.—Constitution of Courts (an amending Act)		

Description.	Whether adapted from British Indian Acts.	Whether introduced during the year under report.
12. Municipal Act No. I of 1322 T. E.		
13. Revenue Sale Amendment Act—1323 T.E.		
14. An Act for the destruction of old records—1323 T.E.		
15. Act I of 1326 T. E.—Regulation regarding Privy Council Appeals.		
16. Act II of 1326 T. E.—Registration of Births and Deaths	Partly adapted.	
17. Act III of 1326 T. E.—Vaccination Act	Do.	
18. Act IV of 1326 T. E.—Public Demands Recovery Act	Do.	
19. Act V of 1326 T. E.—Excise Amendment Act		
20. Act I of 1327 T. E.—Settlement of lands for tea cultivation		
21. Regulation No. 1 of 1328 T. E.—regarding Registration of Coolies		
22. Regulation No. 2 of 1328 T. E.—regarding Export of Tea		
23. Act I of 1329 T. E.—(Absconding sepoys Act)		
24. Act II of 1329 T. E.—(Control of prices of food stuff)		
25. Act III of 1329 T. E.—(Elephants and Buffaloes grazing Act)		
26. Act IV of 1329 T. E.—(House tax on Hill tribes)		
27. Act V of 1329 T. E.—(Legal practitioners, Act)	Do	
28. Act I of 1330 T. E.—Census Act		
29. Act I of 1332 T. E.—Encumbered Estates Act.		
30. Act III of 1332 T. E.—The Opium and Intoxicating Drugs Act.		
31. Amendment of Municipal Act (No. 2 of 1335 T. E.)		
32. An Act defining the term Minister (Act No 1 of 1335 T. E.)		

ii.

Statement showing the strength, cost, and other particulars of the Military Force in Tripura State for 1335 T. E.

Arm of service.	Number of fighting officers and men.						Details of force at the end of the current year.						Total cost on account of pay and allowances of the force, including followers. (Excluding grain allowance.)	Remarks.
			Casualties.						Number of men.					
	At the end of last year.	Recruited this year.	Died.	Invalided.	Discharged, deserted, &c.	At the end of the current year.	Number of regiments, battalions, or Batteries.	Number of guns.	European commissioned officers.	Native commissioned officers.	Non-commissioned officers.	Fighting men.		
1	2	3	4	5	6	7	8	9	10	11	12	13	14	15
Infantry ...	216	41	2	4	33	218	1	291 and one small cannon.	—	—	41	177	Rs. 39,219	

III.

Statement showing the strength, cost, discipline, and education of the Police for the year 1335 T. E.

Description of office.	Number.	Pay of grade.	Total cost. (Excluding grain allowance.)	Punishments.			Rewards.		Education.		Remarks.
				Dismissed.	Fined, degraded, or suspended departmentally.	Punished judicially.	By promotion.	By money.	Number able to read and write.	Number under instruction.	
1	2	3	4	5	6	7	8	9	10	11	12
		Rs.									
Superintendent of Police	1	150-10-250	66,646	—	—	—	—	—	460	—	
Asst. Superintendent „	1	75-5-100		—	—	—	—	—		—	
Inspector	4	50 to 80		—	—	—	—	—		—	
Sub-Inspector or Daroga	24	25-2-45		—	—	—	—	2		—	
Naib Daroga	13	15-1-25		—	—	—	—	2		—	
Writer Constable	13	11		—	1	—	—	1		—	
Subadar	1	25-2-45		—	—	—	—	—		—	
Jamadar	7	15-1-25		—	1	—	—	—		—	
Constable	218	8 to 12		14	27	—	—	14		—	
Chowkidar	175	5		—	—	—	—	5		—	
Spy	3	15 & 20		—	—	—	—	1		—	
	460										

IV.

Statement showing the working of the Police in the Tripura State during the year 1335 T.E.

State.	Number of offences.		Number of accused arrested.		Number of accused sent for trial.		Number of accused convicted.		Number of accused acquitted or discharged.		Percentage convicted of accused arrested.		Percentage convicted of accused sent for trial.		REMARKS.
	Past year.	Present year.	Past year.	Present year.	Past year.	Present year.	Past year.	Present year.	Past year.	Present year.	Past year.	Present year.	Past year.	Present year.	
1	2	3	4	5	6	7	8	9	10	11	12	13	14	15	16
Tripura State	1,130	1,282	743	802	730	824	113	187	93	87	47'45	68·2	53'3	34'1	

V.

Statement showing the value of property stolen and amount of recoveries in the Tripura State during the year 1335 T. E.

State.	Amount stolen.		Amount recovered.		Percentage of recoveries of property stolen.		REMARKS.
	Past year.	Present year.	Past year.	Present year.	Past year.	Present year.	
1	2	3	4	5	6	7	8
Tripura State	Rs 20,667-11-0	Rs 22,695-10-0	Rs 6,514-2-0	Rs 10,324-6-3	31'51	45'4	

VI.

Statement showing the number of crimes committed, number of cases disposed of, and cases awaiting trial in the Tripura State during the year 1335 T. E.

Description of offences.		Number of offences. Balance from past year.	Number of offences. Committed during the present year.	Number of offences. Total.	Number of cases disposed of during the past year.	Number of cases disposed of during the present year.	Number of cases awaiting trial.	Number of persons apprehended.	Number of persons convicted.	Number of persons sentenced. Imprisonment. Simple.	Number of persons sentenced. Imprisonment. Rigorous.	Number of persons sentenced. Imprisonment and fine. Simple.	Number of persons sentenced. Imprisonment and fine. Rigorous.	Number of persons sentenced. Fine only.	Number of persons sentenced. Whipping.	Number of persons sentenced. Capital punishment.	Number of persons sentenced. Total.	Number of persons acquitted or discharged.	Number of persons confined being insane.	Number of persons dead during or before trial.	Term of imprisonment. Under one month.	From 1 to 2 months.	From 2 to 3 months.	From 3 to 6 months.	From 6 to 12 months.	From 1 to 2 years.	From 2 to 3 years.	From 3 to 5 years.	Above 5 years.	Transportation.	Capital punishment.	Persons awaiting trial.	Remarks.
1		2	3	4	5	6	7	8	9	10	11	12	13	14	15	16	17	18	19	20	21	22	23	24	25	26	27	28	29	30	31	32	33
Class I. Offences against the State, public tranquillity, safety and justice &c.	cognizable ...	19	19	38	21	22	16	a164	a25	0	18	0	1	5	0	0	24	45	0	2	1	3	0	7	0	2	3	2	1	0	0	91	
	non-cognizable	11	49	60	41	47	13	9	0	0	0	0	0	0	0	0	0	7	0	0	0	0	0	0	0	0	0	0	0	0	0	2	a. One person transferred and one person released on bail.
Class II. Offences against person.	cognizable ...	54	183	237	137	187	50	432	40	0	17	0	10	13	0	0	40	271	0	1	9	5	2	6	2	0	0	3	0	0	0	120	
	non-cognizable	51	362	412	289	333	79	337	18	1	1	0	0	16	0	0	18	264	0	0	1	0	1	0	0	0	0	0	0	0	0	55	
Class III. Offences against property.	cognizable ...	323	1038	1361	714	1067	354	b1946	301	27	42	5	14	213	0	0	301	1150	0	4	40	21	6	13	1	4	0	0	0	0	0	488	b. 3 persons escaped.
	non-cognizable	36	226	262	166	207	55	279	16	0	1	0	0	15	0	0	16	214	0	0	1	0	0	0	0	0	0	0	0	0	0	49	
Class IV. Other offences.	cognizable ...	41	77	118	90	89	29	218	36	0	10	0	1	25	0	0	36	127	0	3	2	2	1	5	1	0	0	0	0	0	0	52	
	non-cognizable	79	339	418	271	361	57	223	c17	1	3	1	0	11	0	0	16	188	0	1	2	0	0	3	0	0	0	0	0	0	0	17	c. One person released on bail.
Total cognizable ...	...	437	1317	1754	962	1305	449	2760	402	27	87	5	26	256	0	0	401	1593	0	10	52	34	9	31	4	6	3	5	0	0	0	751	
Total non-cognizable ...	...	177	975	1152	767	948	204	848	51	2	5	1	0	42	0	0	50	673	0	1	4	0	1	3	0	0	0	0	0	0	0	123	
Grand Total ...	...	614	2292	2906	1729	2253	653	3608	453	29	92	6	26	298	0	0	451	2266	0	11	56	34	10	34	4	6	3	5	1	0	0	874	

VII.

Statement showing the number of offences reported and dealt with by the various Courts in the Tripura State during the year 1335 T.E.

Name of Court.	NUMBER OF OFFENCES REPORTED DURING THE YEAR.		NUMBER OF PERSONS DEALT WITH.								PERSONS DISPOSED OF.						REMARKS
				Brought to trial in 1335 T. E.					*Total.*								
	Last year.	Present year.	Remaining at the end of last year.	Arrested by Police.	Upon warrant.	On summons.	Voluntary.	Arrested in presence of the Magistrate.	Last year.	Present year.	Discharged without trial.	Acquitted.	Convicted.	Committed or referred.	Died, escaped, or transferred &c.	Persons remaining at the end of the year.	
1	2	3	4	5	6	7	8	9	10	11	12	13	14	15	16	17	18
Sadar Magistracy	585	733	174	211	256	343	13	2	636	999	381	336	101	19	2	160	
Sonamura " ...	247	341	122	126	58	179	49	2	393	536	153	173	108	2	0	100	
Bilonia " ...	227	318	38	133	35	145	223	22	480	596	252	145	95	0	0	104	
Kailashahar " ...	201	209	243	81	43	67	25	0	393	459	90	86	9	1	8	265	
Khowai " ...	129	175	28	18	55	182	7	0	189	290	69	173	20	9	0	19	
Dharmanagar " ...	264	246	82	51	37	76	49	0	331	295	86	69	35	8	1	96	
Udaipur " ...	167	213	101	43	58	97	27	0	310	326	98	74	33	2	3	116	
Sabrum " ...	46	57	6	23	10	51	0	5	43	95	42	19	31	0	0	3	
TOTAL ...	1,866	2,392	794	686	552	1,140	393	31	2,775	a 3,596	1,171	1,075	432	b 41	14	863	

a Excluding 12 persons pending before the court of Sessions at the close of the previous year.

b Including 12 persons pending from last year, the total number of persons for trial before the Court of Sessions was 53; of these, 21 were convicted, 3 discharged without trial, 17 acquitted, while 1 died during trial and 11 remained under trial.

VIII.

Statement of Criminal cases in which British Subjects were concerned for 1335 T. E.

Description of Offences.		Cases pending since the previous year.	Cases instituted during the year.	Total number of cases.	Cases in which complainants were British subjects.	Cases in which both parties were British subjects.	Cases in which defendants were British Subjects.												
							Cases pending since the previous year	Cases instituted during the year.	Total number of cases.	Cases disposed of. Rejected, Compromised or Dismissed without enquiry.	Cases disposed of. Tried.	Cases pending at the close of the year.	Persons under trial at the close of the previous year.	Persons brought to trial during the year.	Total number of persons under trial.	Convicted.	Acquitted or Discharged.	Died, or Escaped &c.	Under trial at the close of the year.
Class I. Offences against the State &c.	cognizable ...	3	5	8	0	2	3	5	8	2	4	2	13	17	30	6	16	0	8
	non-cognizable ...	0	4	4	2	1	0	2	2	1	0	1	0	0	0	0	0	0	0
Class II. Offences against person.	cognizable ...	10	24	34	5	12	9	20	29	15	9	5	8	55	63	6	40	0	17
	non-cognizable ...	7	39	46	11	25	7	28	35	29	2	4	2	13	15	1	13	0	1
Class III. Offences against property.	cognizable ...	66	301	367	40	80	63	264	327	73	175	79	89	433	522	183	237	0	102
	non-cognizable ...	3	38	41	5	21	3	33	36	23	3	10	2	33	35	6	21	0	8
Class IV. Other offences.	cognizable ...	7	24	31	0	7	7	24	31	5	13	13	9	42	51	17	25	0	9
	non-cognizable ...	7	81	88	16	50	7	65	72	50	16	6	4	29	33	5	27	0	1
Total cognizable ...		86	354	440	45	101	82	313	395	95	201	99	119	547	666	212	318	0	136
Total non-cognizable ...		17	162	179	34	97	17	128	145	103	21	21	8	75	83	12	61	0	10
GRAND TOTAL ...		103	516	619	79	198	99	441	540	198	222	120	127	622	749*	224	379	0	146

REMARKS.

* Of this number 180 were discharged without trial, the cases being dismissed, compromised or struck off on default. Excluding 146 pending, the actual number of persons tried was 423, of whom 224 or 52·955 were convicted as against 58·966 of the previous year.

IX.

Statement of Extradition Cases for the year 1335 T. E.

Names of Courts.	Nature of cases.	Number of persons against whom warrants were applied for.	Number of persons arrested and surrendered.	Number of persons who appeared of their own accord or were subsequently arrested within this territory.	Number at large at the close of the year.	Result. Convicted.	Result. Acquitted or Discharged.	Pending trial at the close of the year.	Remarks.
Sadar Magistracy ...	Theft ...	1	0	1	0	0	0	1	
	Voluntarily causing hurt and wrongful confinement ...	5	0	2	3	0	2	0	
	Theft and dishonestly receiving stolen property ...	1	0	1	0	0	1	0	
	Theft ...	2	0	1	1	0	1	0	
	Theft ...	6	0	1	5	0	1	0	
Sonamura " ...	Murder ...	2	0	0	2	0	0	0	
	Theft ...	3	0	2	1	0	1	1	
Bilonia " ...	Theft ...	1	0	1	0	0	0	1	
	Theft ...	1	1	0	0	1	0	0	
	Theft and escape from lawful custody ...	2	2	0	0	2	0	0	
	Dacoity ...	1	0	0	1	0	0	0	
	Theft ...	2	0	1	1	0	1	0	
	Theft, resistance or obstruction by a person to his lawful apprehension ...	13	13	0	0	0	13	0	
	Theft ...	7	1	6	0	0	7	0	
	Theft ...	4	3	1	0	0	4	0	
	Theft ...	10	9	1	0	0	10	0	
	Theft and escape from lawful custody ...	10	2	8	0	1	9	0	
	Theft and escape from lawful custody ...	7	0	4	3	4	0	0	
	Theft ...	2	0	2	0	2	0	0	
	Theft and escape from lawful custody ...	1	0	1	0	1	0	0	
	Unlawful assembly and voluntarily causing hurt ...	11	9	2	0	0	0	11	
	Theft and escape from lawful custody ...	10	6	2	2	0	0	8	
	Theft and escape from lawful custody ...	7	5	0	2	0	0	5	
	Theft ...	1	0	0	1	0	0	0	
	Theft ...	1	0	0	1	0	0	0	
	Theft ...	2	0	1	1	0	0	1	
	Unlawful assembly, criminal trespass and assault ...	8	0	0	8	0	0	0	
	Theft ...	3	0	0	3	0	0	0	
	Theft ...	2	0	0	2	0	0	0	
Kailashahar " ...	Escape from lawful custody ...	1	0	0	1	0	0	0	
	Escape from lawful custody ...	1	0	0	1	0	0	0	
	Escape from lawful custody ...	1	0	0	1	0	0	0	
Dharmanagar " ...	Kidnapping ...	3	1	0	2	0	0	1	
	Theft ...	1	1	0	0	0	0	1	
Sabroom " ...	Theft and dishonestly receiving stolen property ...	6	0	0	6	0	0	0	
Khowai " ...	Dacoity ...	5	5	0	0	5	0	0	
	Escape from lawful custody ...	1	0	0	1	0	0	0	
	Receiving stolen property ...	2	0	0	2	0	0	0	
	Total ...	147	58	38	51	16	50	30	

X.

Statement showing the results of appeals against decisions passed by the Criminal Courts in the Tripura State during the year 1335 T. E.

Tribunals.	Number of applications.	Number of persons and cases.																Remarks.
		Applications rejected.		*Sentences.*						Proceedings quashed.		Referred.		Futher enquiry, &c, ordered.		Pending.		
				Confirmed.		Modified.		Reversed.										
		Persons.	Cases.	Persons.	Cases.	Persons.	Cases.	Persons.	Cases.	Persons.	Cases.	Persons.	Cases.	Persons.	Cases.	Persons.	Cases.	
Khas Adalat. ...	181	15	10	97	75	20	12	73	46	2	2	—	—	7	3	58	33	

XI.

Civil Work.—Nature and value of original suits filed and disposed of during the year 1335 T. E.

Tribunal.	Opening balance. Past year.	Opening balance. Present year.	Filed during the year, received by transfer or on remand. Past year.	Filed during the year, received by transfer or on remand. Present year.	Total. Past year.	Total. Present year.	Disposed of during the year Past year.	Disposed of during the year Present year.	Closing balance. Past year.	Closing balance. Present year.
Khas Adalat Orginial side	55	49	22	26	77	75	28	44	49	31
Sadar Dewani Adalat	357	489	631	737	988	1226	499	741	489	485
Sonamura „	113	90	201	217	314	307	224	269	90	38
Bilonia „	41	17	112	123	153	140	136	119	17	21
Kailashahar „	250	309	280	274	530	583	221	253	309	330
Khowai „	14	26	113	130	127	156	101	135	26	21
Dharmanagar	81	52	119	170	200	222	148	153	52	69
Udaipur „	33	41	248	265	281	306	240	204	41	102
Sabrum „	2	1	11	15	13	16	12	16	1	0
Total...	946	1,074	1,737	1,057	2,683	3,031	1,509	1,934	1,074	1,097

Tribunal.	Suits filed during present year. Value. Rs. a. p.	Suits re landed property.	Suits for money transaction.	Suits for other rights.	Number of suits under Rs. 100.	Number of suits above Rs. 100 and under Rs. 500.	Number of suits above Rs. 500 and under Rs. 1,000.	Number of suits above Rs. 1,000 and under Rs. 5,000.	Number of suits above Rs. 5000.
Khas Adalat Orginial side	47,738-10-5	7	3	16	1	0	0	14	3
Sadar Dewani Adalat	52,834-3-9	264	273	200	414	131	12	0	0
Sonamura „	14,953-8-3	63	126	28	148	35	3	0	0
Bilonia „	5,954-8-9	54	30	39	72	22	0	0	0
Kailashahar „	24,494-11-6	94	154	26	182	56	8	0	0
Khowai „	8,791-13-3	16	113	1	106	16	0	0	0
Dharmanagar	9,794-0-3	29	46	95	104	28	1	0	0
Udaipur „	18,536-4-0	17	218	30	182	54	4	0	0
Sabrum „	1,683-5-6	1	14	0	11	4	0	0	0
Total...	1,84,783-1-6	545	977	435	1270	346	28	14	3

Tribunal.	Suits disposed of during present year. *Exparte.*	Admitted and compromised.	Struck off the file.	Otherwise disposed of.	Value. Rs. a. p.	Average duration. Y. m. d.	Suits not estimable in money.	Remarks.
Khas Adalat Orginial side	1	11	23	9	42,731-7-0	0-4-5	8	
Sadar Dewani Adalat	493	75	23	150	53,551-0-0	0-7-27	130	
Sonamura „	90	33	21	125	16,788-2-3	0-1-6	31	
Bilonia „	60	19	29	11	5,546-12-0	0-3-14	29	
Kailashahar „	65	38	69	81	19,475-5-0	0-3-25	28	
Khowai „	34	41	28	32	9,608-1-9	0-1-0	8	
Dharmanagar	32	30	33	58	8,474-5-9	0-0-27	37	
Udaipur „	59	65	25	55	13,821-7-6	0-3-8	25	
Sabrum „	6	0	4	6	1,725-5-6	0-1-24	0	
Total...	840	312	255	527	1,71721-14-9	0-3-1	296	

XII.

Civil Work.—Results of applications for Execution of Decrees, 1335 T.E.

Tribunal.	Opening balance.		Value of opening balance for present year.	Applications brought to the Register.			Total.			Disposed of.			Closing balance.			Nature of applications pending disposal at the close of the year.			Remarks.
	Past year.	Present year.		Past year.	Present year.	Value for present year.	Past year.	Present year.	Value for present year.	Past year.	Present year.	Value for present year.	Past yaer.	Present year.	Value for present year.	Below 6 months.	Below 12 months.	Above 12 months.	
			Rs. a. p.			Rs. a. p.		R.	Rs. a. p.			Rs. a. p.			Rs. a. p.				
Khas Adalat (Original side)	21	19	62,889-3-3	11	7	6,509-3-3	32	26	59,398-6-6	13	5	14,065-12-3	19	21	45,332-10-3	2	4	15	
Sadar Dewani Adalat ...	185	154	20,620-10-9	153	199	20,989-12-3	338	353	41,610-7-0	184	211	16,893-7-0	154	142	24,717-0-0	85	13	44	
Sonamura Ditto ...	49	31	3,542-14-6	79	117	14,106-1-3	128	148	17,648-15-9	97	112	13,546-9-3	31	36	4,102-6-6	26	9	1	
Bilonia Ditto ...	24	16	1,303-15-9	62	53	5,030-12-9	86	69	6,334-12-6	70	61	5,290-11-9	16	8	1,044-0-9	8	0	0	
Kailashahar Ditto ...	95	77	12,178-11-3	45	79	8,019-6-6	140	156	20,198-1-9	63	57	5,858-2-3	77	99	14,339-15-6	35	25	39	
Khowai Ditto ...	9	9	1,940-5-0	37	43	3232-13-6	46	52	5,173-2-6	37	40	4,469-12-6	9	12	703-6-0	12	0	0	
Dharmanagar Ditto ...	46	51	7,364-11-3	51	48	2,987-4-3	97	99	10,351-15-6	46	52	4,334-3-9	51	47	6017-11-9	14	9	21	
Udaipur Ditto ...	26	37	6,236-2-0	121	111	16,312-9-6	147	148	22,548-11-6	110	112	15,731-8-3	37	36	6,817-3-3	31	2	3	
Sabrum Ditto ...	1	0	0	2	4	342-2-6	3	4	342-2-6	3	3	115-10-3	0	1	226-8-3	1	0	0	
Total ...	456	394	1,06,076-9-9	561	661	77,530-1-9	1,017	1,055	1,83,606-11-6	623	653	80,305-13-3	394	402	1,03,300-14-3	214	62	126	

XIII.

Civil Work.—Number and results of appeals in civil suits, 1335 T. E.

Tribunal.	Opening balance.		Filed during.		Total.		Disposed of during.		Closing balance.		Value of appeals filed during.		How disposed of.										Average duration.	
													Decisions confirmed.		Decisions reversed.		Decisions amended.		Cases remanded for retrial.		Cases compromised and otherwise disposed of.			
	Past year.	Present year.	Past year.	Present year.	Past year.	Present year.	Past year.	Present year.	Past year.	Present year.	Past year.	Present year.	Past year.	Present year.	Past year.	Present year.	Past year.	Present year.	Past year.	Present year.	Past year.	Present year.	Past year.	Present year.
											Rs. a. p.	Rs. a. p.											Y.m.d.	Y.m.d.
Khas Adalat	32	61	155	163	187	224	126	159	61	65	19,803-15-0	19,032-13-6	71	63	34	58	6	9	4	11	11	18	0-2-3	0-2-2

XIV.

Statement showing the number of persons confined in the jails and lock-ups in the Tripura State during the year 1335 T.E.

Stations.	Number of prisons.	Number of Prisoners.				Daily Average.		Number of prisoners remaining at the end of the year.	Cost of jail and prisoners.	Average period in days of accused under trial.	Remarks showing mortality among convicts in jail.
		Remaining from last year.	Admitted during the year.	Total.							
				Past year.	Present year.	Past year.	Present year.		Rs. a. p.		
Agarlala	1	71	185	242	256	62·54	67·71	83	10,370	39	
Sonamura	1	6	93	73	99	4·21	3·91	4	662	14·94	
Bilonia	1	1	56	119	57	·33	1·23	4	348	12·36	
Kailashahar	1	2	56	63	58	3·78	4·03	3	564	25·16	One convict died of Chronic Dysentery.
Khowai	1	3	37	24	40	1·17	2·76	—	439	31·23	
Dharmanagar	1	4	49	90	53	8·94	5·47	20	792	43·10	
Udaipur	1	2	38	38	40	2·61	1·91	2	331	30·88	
Sabrum	1	2	7	12	9	·35	·15	—	127	5·25	
Total ...	8	91	521	661	612	83·93	87·17	116	13,633	25·24	

XV.

Registration of documents in the Tripura State during the year 1335 T.E.

Name of State	Documents presented for registration.		Nature of documents presented.										Documents registered.		Value of documents registered.		Documents of which registration has been refused.		Documents remaining unregistered at the end of the year.		Remarks.
			Mortgages.		Sale deeds.		Wills.		Money bonds.		Miscellaneous.										
	Past year.	Present year.	Past year.	Present year.	Past year.	Present year.	Past year.	Present year.	Past year.	Present year.	Past year.	Present year.	Past year.	Present year.	Past year.	Present year.	Past year.	Present year.	Past year.	Present year.	
1	2	3	4	5	6	7	8	9	10	11	12	13	14	15	16	17	18	19	20	21	22
															Rs.	*Rs.*					
Tripura State	9,674	13,265	2,473	3,452	4,604	5,858	2	7	227	343	2,366	3,605	9,568	13,100	14,96,766	21,12,171	110	136	54	74	

XVI.

Statement showing the receipts and expenditure on account of Registration during the year 1335 T.E.

Description.	Past Year.			Present Year.			Remarks.
	Number of deeds.	Value of property.	Fees realised.	Number of deeds.	Value of property.	Fees realised.	
		Rs.	Rs.		Rs.	Rs.	
Mortgages	2,475	3,02,409	2,359	3,452	4,91,813	3,574	
Safe deeds	4,604	9,15,029	5,829	5,858	12,76,855	7,845	
Will	2	—	11	7	--	32	
Money bonds	227	22,475	206	343	32,004	265	
Miscellaneous	2,366	2,89,645	2,808	3,605	4,34,699	4,064	
Total ...	9,674	15,29,558	11,213	13,265	22,35,371	15,780	
Total Expenditure ...	—	—	3,639	—	—	4,336	
Net Income ...	—	—	7,574	—	—	11,444	

XVII.

Receipts and expenditure of the Municipalities in the Tripura State during the year 1335 T.E.

NAME.	Opening balance.	RECEIPTS DURING THE YEAR.					Total in the current year.	EXPENDITURE DURING THE YEAR.		Balance at the close of the year.	REMARKS.
		Past.	Present.								
			State grant.	Tax.	Miscellaneous.	Total.		Past.	Present.		
1	2	3	4	5	6	7	8	9	10	11	12
	Rs. A.P.	Rs. A.P.	Rs. A.P.	Rs. A.P.	Rs. A.P.	Rs. A.P.	Rs. A.P.	Rs. A.P.	Rs. A.P.	Rs. A.P.	
Agartala Municipality. ...	14,931-15-0	31,557-5-6	9,000-0-0	3,398-9-6	13,079-4-9 a	25,477-14-3	40,409-13-3	16,625-6-6	22,966-2-3 b	17,443-11-0 c	a. Including Rs. 11,025-14-6 as income from the Bazar and Rs. 423 as deposits and advances recovered. b Including Rs. 8,849-9-3 as expenditure on Bazar improvement and Rs. 523-0 as advances and deposits paid. c. Including Rs. 15,672-5-0 of the Bazar improvement fund.

XVIII.

Statement of rainfall in the Tripura State during the year 1335 T.E.

STATE.	Baisak.	Jaisth.	Asar.	Sravan.	Bhadra.	Asvin.	Kartik.	Agrahayan.	Pous.	Magh.	Falgoon.	Chait.	Total.	Total of past year.	Average of past 5 years.	REMARKS.
Tripura State ...	12·60	19·57	16·32	13·18	18·41	10·55	1·55	·38	·44	·28	5·11	9·89	108·28	106·28	90·9	

XIX.

Statement as to the prices of staple food-grains for the year 1335 T.E.

Article.	During Chait (past year).			During Chait (present year).			REMARKS.
	Rs.	*a.*	*p.*	*Rs.*	*a.*	*p.*	
(1) RICE							
Maximum	9	0	0	9	0	0	
Minimum	6	0	0	6	0	0	
(2) PADDY							
Maximum	4	8	0	4	0	0	
Minimum	2	12	0	2	12	0	

XX.

Expenditure on Public Works during the year 1335 T.E.

Description of work.	State funds.			Local funds.			Total.	Remarks.
	Original.	Repairs.	Total.	Original.	Repairs.	Total.		
	Rs.	*Rs.*	*Rs.*	*Rs.*	*Rs.*	*Rs.*	*Rs.*	
Tanks in different parts of the State	3,943	789	47,32	—	—	—	4,732	
Roads and bridges ...	9,324	35,966	45,290	75	—	75	45,365	
Buildings	66,289	90,535	1,56,824	3,478	—	3,478	1,60,302	
Miscellaneous works ...	2,095	—	2,095	697	—	697	2,792	
Total ...	81,651	1,27,290	2,08,941	4,250	—	4,250	2,13,191	
Minor works at the Rajbari (*Karkhana*)	—	5,383	5,383	—	—	—	5,383	
Establishment charges ...	—	—	15,137	—	—	—	15,137	
Grand Total ...	81,651	1,32,673	2,29,461	4,250	—	4,250	2,33,711	

XXI.

Statement showing the excise shops and excise revenue of the Tripura State during the year 1335 T.E.

Name of State.	Country spirit.		Country spirit, Opium and Ganja.		Ganja and Opium.		Tari.		Total.		Remarks.
	Number of shops.	Revenue.	Number of shops.	Revenue demand.	Number of shops.	Revenue.	Number of shops.	Revenue.	Number of shops.	Revenue realised.	
		Rs.		*Rs.*		*Rs.*		*Rs.*		*Rs.*	
Tripura State	—	—	29	59,490	—	—	—	—	29	60,563	

XXII

Statement of Medical Relief afforded in the Tripura State during the year 1335 T.E.

Dispensary.	Number of patients treated. (new)		Results of in-door patients. (new)				Expenditure.	Daily average. (old + new)			No. of surgical operations performed.			No. of persons vaccinated during the year.			Remarks.
	Outdoor.	Indoor.	Dis-charged.	Absented.	Died.	Remain-ing under treatment.		Outdoor.	Indoor.	Total.	Major.	Minor.	Total.	Success-fully.	Unsuc-cessfully.	Total.	
1. Victoria Memorial Hospital at Agartala and the Charitable Dispensary attached to it	12,068	382	242	95	34	11	Rs. 8,274	59·61	15·15	74·76	12	157	169	1,326	265	1,531	
2. Palace Dispensary	12,326	0	0	0	0	0	10,134	74·47	0	74·47	0	0	0	0	0	0	
3. Homoeopathic	11,465	0	0	0	0	0	5,401	68·31	0	68·31	0	0	0	0	0	0	
4. Old Agartala	7,140	0	0	0	0	0	1,963	35·07	0	35·07	0	44	44	939	125	1,064	
5. Bishalgar	4,954	0	0	0	0	0	1,154	18·30	0	18·30	2	43	45	242	2	244	
6. Sonamura	6,188	6	6	0	0	0	1,376	27·53	·18	27·71	1	98	99	522	79	601	
7. Udaipur	3,820	3	3	0	0	0	1,172	13·36	·04	13·40	0	45	45	230	15	245	*This figure shows the actual number of outdoor patients treated, the total outdoor attendance during the year being 1,82,016 against 1,80,482 in the previous year.
8. Amarpur	1,601	0	0	0	0	0	854	9·53	0	9·53	0	27	27	103	1	104	
9. Bilonia...	5,361	10	10	0	0	0	1,288	25·13	·46	25·59	0	93	93	228	15	243	
10. Loongthung	2,219	0	0	0	0	0	1,217	10·99	0	10·99	1	20	21	193	6	199	
11. Sabroom	1,871	1	1	0	0	0	1,264	7·86	0	7·86	0	13	13	0	0	0	
12. Khowai	2,693	0	0	0	0	0	1,493	10·15	0	10·15	0	32	32	800	146	946	
13. Kailashahar	11,489	4	3	0	0	1	1,471	38·34	·14	38·48	0	196	196	296	36	332	
14. Kamalpur	4,161	0	0	0	0	0	1,255	16·77	0	16·77	0	40	40	395	68	463	
15. Dharmanagar	4,901	17	14	1	1	1	1,295	21·14	·37	21·51	0	73	73	463	26	489	
16. Fatik-roy	3,011	0	0	0	0	0	1,107	10·92	0	10·92	0	53	53	180	48	228	
17. Mohanpur	3,537	0	0	0	0	0	1,153	19·04	0	19·04	0	68	68	198	2	200	
18. Dhaleswar	7,040	0	0	0	0	0	1,154	30·58	0	30·58	0	74	74	0	0	0	
Total	*1,05,864	423	279	96	35	13	43,025	497·10	16·34	513·44	16	1,072	1,086	6,115	774	6,889	

XXIII.

Vital statistics of the Tripura State for the year 1335 T.E.

STATE.	Population.	BIRTHS.		Increase.	Decrease.	DEATHS.		Increase.	Decrease.	RATIO PER 1,000 OF POPULATION.				REMARKS.
										BIRTHS.		DEATHS.		
		Past year.	Present year.			Past year.	Present year.			Past year.	Present year.	Past year.	Present year.	
Tripura State ...	3,04,437	2,313	2,361	48	—	2,286	2,274	—	12	7·64	7·8	7·55	7·5	

XXIV.

Education Return (A)—Particulars as to the schools maintained during the year 1335 T.E.

Number of Schools.		Description of Schools.	Number of Pupils on the rolls on the last day of Chait.		Daily Average Attendance.		Remarks.
Past year.	Present year.		Past year.	Present year.	Past year.	Present year.	
5	5	High English Schools	899	1,414	700·36	1,014·19	
5	6	Middle English Schools for boys ...	494	646	352·18	474·85	
1	1	Middle English Schools for girls ...	99	70	79·64	56·3	
1	1	Higher Vernacular Schools for boys	43	48	34·41	38·08	
22	22	* Lower Vernacular Schools for boys	1,340	1,229	992·85	935·77	* In some of these schools boys and girls read together.
86	93	Pathsalas for boys	2,235	2,030	1,705·24	1,583·13	
9	9	Do for girls	190	192	133·32	138·1	
		Special Schools :—					
5	6	Madrassas	203	195	151·41	135·99	
3	3	Sanskrit *Tols*	38	39	29·06	27·44	
1	1	Woodburn Artisan School... ...	18	13	6·02	4·71	
TOTAL 138	147		5,559	5,876	4,184·49	4,408·56	

XXV.

Education Return (B) Race of Students, 1335 T. E.

Names of Divisions.	No. of Schools.			No. of Students.			Race.												Average daily attendance.		REMARKS.
															Bengalee.						
	For boys.	For girls.	Total.	Boys.	Girls.	Total.	Rajkumars.	Thakurs.	Manipuris	Tripuras.	Reangs.	Chakmas.	Kukis.	Lusais.	Hindus.	Musalmans.	Christians.	Others.	Boys.	Girls.	
1. Sadar Division ...	49	3	52	1,652	123	1,775	5	170	97	239	0	0	12	0	779	434	1	38	1286·47	84·64	
2 Kailashahar „	26	2	28	972	103	1,075	0	3	357	14	0	9	0	27	497	168	0	0	749·78	72·35	
3 Sonamura „	20	1	21	906	68	974	0	1	0	38	0	0	0	0	237	698	0	0	661.49	52·9	
4. Bilonia „	9	1	10	717	29	746	0	0	0	17	0	0	0	0	516	213	0	0	535·78	23·6	
5 Khowai „	9	1	10	241	16	257	0	0	14	162	0	0	0	0	64	7	10	0	188·79	11·88	
6. Dharmanagar „	10	1	11	533	18	551	0	0	110	0	0	0	0	0	363	78	0	0	321·90	27·64	
7. Udaipur „	7	1	8	293	24	317	0	2	0	1	2	0	0	0	147	165	0	0	216·09	19·28	
8. Sabrum „	3	0	3	133	14	147	0	0	0	28	0	0	0	0	92	24	0	3	112·96	9	
9. Amarpur Sub-division ...	2	0	2	33	1	34	0	3	0	1	26	0	0	0	2	1	0	1	32·3	1·71	
TOTAL ...	135	10	145	5,480	396	5,876	5	179	578	500	28	9	12	27	2,697	1,788	11	42	4,105·56	303	

XXVI.

Statement showing the distribution of Portfolios among the members of the Council of Administration, Tripura State, 1336 T. E.

Members.	Departments allotted to Portfolios.	REMARKS.
President	1. Judicial. 2. Sultanat. 3. Sansar. 4. Nij Tahabil.	
Vice-President	1. Political and Appointment. 2. Police. 3. Revenue and General. 4. Agriculture. 5. Forest. 6. Accounts and Audit. 7. Treasury and Stamps. 8. Chakla Roshnabad Estates and other Zemindaries.	
Maharajkumar B. K. Dev Barman ...	1. Jail. 2. Education and Rajmala. 3. Medical and Sanitation. 4. Military. 5. Public Works. 6. Zoo.	
Thakur P. C. Roy	1. Pilkhana and Stables. 2. Tosakhana. 3. Guest House. 4. Registration. 5. Press, Forms, Stationery, Gazette and Record Room. 6. Municipality.	

APPENDIX XXVII. (A)

Statement of Audited Receipts for the year 1335 T. E.

State.

Heads of Revenue.	1334 T. E.		1335 T. E.		Remarks.
	Revised Estimate.	Actuals.	Revised Estimate.	Actuals.	
1. Land Revenue ...	5,22,000	5,18,227	5,69,819	5,89,635	
2. Rents of markets ...	3,895	5,316	6,645	6,852	
3. Family tax in the hills	61,100	64,433	65,876	63,118	
4. Toll on Forest Produce	4,32,500	4,30,308	4,64,359	4,72,559	
5. Do on the Feni River	20,000	21,349	30,552	31,604	
6. Elephant and Buffalo grazing mehals ...	7,245	6,703	6,923	6,896	
7. Thatching grass mehals	9,000	12,327	11,662	10,342	
8. Reserved *Sal* trees ...	16,000	24,197	21,595	14,199	
9. Tax on cotton and Oil seeds ...	1,17,750	1,56,407	1,55,486	2,14,808	
10. Royalty on elephant caught ...	5,000	10,759	1,700	1,702	
11. Adda mehal ...	23,100	22,419	24,497	21,089	
12. Excise ...	49,510	52,905	56,113	60,563	
13. Stamps and Court fees	61,900	68,343	71,406	84,490	
14. Law and Justice (fines)	2,850	2,543	2,547	3,422	
15. Process Fees ...	9,740	11,450	12,999	13,729	
16. Registration ...	9,900	11,213	14,616	15,781	
17. Jail ...	2,000	3,147	3,309	3,350	
18. Cattle pounds ...	5,700	5,149	5,580	5,869	
19. *Nazars* ...	25,200	29,614	35,104	47,489	
20. Agriculture ...	500	275	446	570	
21. Miscellaneous ...	65,110	78,719	79,379	77,988	
22. School Fees ...	10,000	7,907	10,004	7,906	
(*a*) Personal Howlats recovered	—	—	5,075	5,360	
Total ...	14,60,000	15,42,710	16,55,692	17,59,321	
23. Contribution from Chakla ...	—	—	50,000	50,000	
24. Deposits ...	90,000	71,284	86,962	86,764	
25. Loans ...	—	—	—	—	
	15,50,000	16,13,994	17,92,654	18,96,085	
Opening Balance :—					
Cash ...	3,18,757	3,18,757	3,72,122	3,72,122	
Advances ...	6,78,290	6,78,290	2,15,257	2,15,257	
Loans issued ...	39,314	39,314	42,215	42,215	
	10,36,361	10,36,361	6,29,594	6 29,594	
Grand Total ...	25,86,361	26,50,355	24,22,248	25,25,679	

APPENDIX XXVII. (B)

Statement of Audited Expenditure for the year 1335 T. E.

State.

Heads of Expenditure.	1334 T. E.		1335 T. E.		REMARKS.
	Revised estimate.	Actuals.	Revised Estimate.	Actuals.	
1. Controlling Charges	1,19,316	1,16,656	1,21,225	1,20,416	
2. Judicial ...	33,710	32,895	50,500	48,401	
3. Sansar ...	4,71,077	4,60,773	6,50,130	6,46,699	
4. Sultanat ...	24,286	24,245	20,930	19,717	
5. Nijtahabil ...	4,25,928	4,22,568	1,14,330	1,12,414	
6. Police ...	63,940	63,936	68,420	66,646	
7. Revenue ...	75,641	72,480	75,000	70,640	
8. Tahasil ...	45,700	43,379	48,800	45,427	
9. Survey & settlement	15,000	13,529	18,000	16,497	
10. Agriculture ...	5,000	4,328	5,360	4,713	
11. Forest ...	56,524	51,316	56,825	52,212	
12. Public Works ...	2,95,048	2,86,405	2,43,920	2,28,461	
13. Zoo ...	11,000	10,570	10,800	10,772	
14. Medical ...	61,411	59,887	68,000	66,963	
15. Jail ...	13,200	13,188	14,250	13,633	
16. Education General ...	91,856	89,359	94,530	91,746	
17. Rajmala ...	3,500	3,486	6,000	5,949	
18. Education of Rajkumars ...	10,343	6,310	12,900	11,182	
19. Military ...	43,910	37,998	46,110	39,219	
20. Registration ...	3,762	3,639	4,380	4,336	
21. Press ...	5,398	4,503	5,210	4,427	
22. State Gazette ...	700	573	700	626	
23. Municipality ...	9,000	9,000	9,000	9,000	
24. Repayment of Deposits ...	1,38,998	1,35,661	70,000	68,859	
25. Advances to employees ...	7,000	3,523	7,000	6,996	
26. Pension ...	20,000	17,380	20,000	19,051	
27. Donation ...	1,000	601	500	250	
28. Relief to distressed subjects ...	500	355	1,000	97	
29. Purchase of Landed Property ...	1,000	454	89,500	85,850	
30. Unforeseen charges ...	960	—	3,500	957	
31. Compensation for dearness of Provision ...	31,500	31,458	36,500	36,489	
Total ...	20,86,207	20,20,761	19,73,320	19,09,555	
Closing balance :—					
Cash ...	2,31,170	3,72,122	2,29,456	3,96,594	
Advances ...	2,29,670	2,15,257	1,77,257	1,78,412	
Loans issued ...	39,314	42,215	42.215	41,118	
	5,00,154	6,29.594	4,48,928	6,16,124	
Grand Total ...	25,86,361	26,50,355	24,22,248	25,25,679	

APPENDIX XXVIII. (A)

Statement of Audited Receipts for the year 1335 T E.

Chakla Roshnabad Estate.

Heads of Receipts.	1334 T. E. Revised Estimate.	1334 T. E. Actuals.	1335 T. E. Revised Estimate.	1335 T. E. Actuals.	REMARKS.
1. Rent and Cess ...	10,65,958	10,61,705	10,99,000	12,03,813	
2. Cess for Rent free holdings ...	9,000	9,232	9,500	7,526	
3. Law charges recovered	65,200	67,660	65,200	57,133	
4. Misc. receipts including deposits ...	10,292	10,348	15,484	7,460	
5. Loans Received ...	2,03,000	2,03,000	—	—	
Total ...	13,53,450	13,51,945	11,89,184	12,75,932	
Opening Balance :—					
Cash ...	65,393	65,393	1,47,517	1,47,517	
Advance ...	1,69,947	2,19,947	1,60,941	1,60,941	
Loans issued ...	15,946	15,946	8,131	8,131	
Bank deposits ...	50,000	—	—	—	
Total ...	3,01,286	3,01,286	3,16,589	3,16,589	
Grand Total ...	16,54,736	16,53,231	15,05,773	15,92,521	

APPENDIX XXVIII. (B)

Statement of Audited Expenditure for the year 1335 T. E.

Chakla Roshnabad Estate.

Heads of Expenditure.	1334 T. E.		1335 T. E.		Remarks.
	Revised Estimate.	Actuals.	Revised Estimate.	Actuals.	
i. 1. Revenue and Cess ...	2,59,250	2,57,356	2,68,083	2,67,026	
2. Establishment ...	1,39,200	1,35,399	1,44,782	1,40,729	
3. Settlement ...	1,200	1,108	1,424	783	
4. Legal Expenses ...	1,10,500	95,805	1,33,000	1,29,224	
5. Education ...	9,460	9,387	10,576	10,228	
6. Medical ...	10,360	10,073	11,162	10,615	
7. Public Works ...	60,000	57,614	58,871	54,454	
8. Religious Expenses	6,300	6,229	6,300	6,058	
9. Purchase of property	1,000	—	157	128	
10. Miscellaneous ...	12,000	11,046	12,000	12,725	
11. Loans and Advances	4,000	—	3,000	—	
12. Pension and Gratuity	6,000	4,293	5,500	4,627	
13. Forest ...	650	616	650	545	
14. Unforeseen ...	5,000	1,459	3,000	2,935	
ii. Sansar ...	15,780	15,780	15,780	15,780	
iii. Donation ...	2,000	1,977	2,000	1,659	
iv. Repayment of debts	7,03,000	7,02,888	5,00,000	5,00,000	
iv. (a) Repayment of deposits ...	28,740	25,612	7,000	7,859	
v. Contribution to State ...	—	—	50,000	50,000	
	13,73,440	13,36,642	12,33,285	12,15,375	
Closing Balance :—					
Cash ...	1,22,946	1,47,267	1,46,416	1,56,681	
Advances ...	1,48,850	1,60,941	1,17,941	1,08,050	
Loans issued ...	8,500	8,131	8,131	12,415	
Bank deposits ...	—	—	—	1,00,000	
	2,80,296	3,16,589	2,72,488	3,77,146	
Grand Total ...	16,54,736	16,53,231	15,05,773	15,92,521	

Book Nineteen

Report on the General Administration of the Tripura State for the year 1336 T. E. (1926-1927 A.D.)

REPORT ON THE ADMINISTRATION

OF

THE TRIPURA STATE

FOR

1336 T. E. (1926-27.)

CHAPTER I—GENERAL AND POLITICAL.

Area of the State—4,116 sq. miles.

Population—3,04,437.

Gross Revenue (based on the average of the preveius five years) :—

(a) State	... ...	Rs. 16,15,141.
(b) Zemindaries	... ...	Rs. 10,49,832.

Tribute—Nil.

Ruler of the State—His Highness The Bisama-Samara-Bijayee Mahamahodaya Pancha-Srijukta Maharaja Manikya Bir Bikramkishore Dev Barman Bahadur. *Age*—18 years. (Born—19th August, 1908). *Caste*—Kshatriya (of the Lunar race).

The year.

1. While the rainfall of the year proved more or less excessive in the plains of the State, it was positively insufficient in the uplands and detrimental to *Joom* crops. Indications of scarcity of food stuff were early in evidence in the hill tracts, and to add to the trouble, the "rat pest," which had recurred in the past with unflinching regularity every twenty years, put in appearance again, following, as usual, in the wake of the curious phenomenon of the flowering of bamboos. Relief measures had soon to be started, and the distress, which was accompanied by outbreaks of Cholera and Small-pox, assumed serious proportions, affecting, since the close of the year, all sections of hill men and necessitating heavy expenditure. In spite of damage to rice crops, the agricultural population of the plains, however, fared well, owing to the high prices that generally prevailed, and so far as collection was concerned, the figures for land revenue stood far ahead of the previous year. The gross receipts, on the whole, exceeded all previous records and enabled the Council of Administration to keep to its programme of full payment of all liabilities by the end of the year, and to show, in spite of increased expenditure mostly in the improvement departments, a substantially increased cash balance.

His Highness the Maharaja.

2. His Highness the Maharaja's administrative Training was completed during the year and it was decided that His Highness would be vested with Ruling Powers on completion of his 19th year, on the 19th August, 1927.

3. This is therefore the last annual report drawn up under the authority of the Council and it will not be out of place to refer in it to the main features of its work.

The Council of Administration and its work.

4. Inaugurated on the 9th December, 1923, the Council has barely passed through three years of its existence. Its position has necessarily been peculiar—often difficult and even delicate. It must congratulate itself however on having secured the active sympathy and good will of His Highness the Maharaja and the co-operation of Their Highnesses the Dowager Maharanees—a fact that enabled it to handle smoothly many a situation that would necessarily have been trying otherwise. To His Highness it owes an everlasting debt of gratitude and to the Maharanees its grateful thanks.

The finances.

5. Early steps were taken by the Council, on assumption of charge, to place the finances of the State on a sound footing. The budgets were revised and retrenchment effected in various Departments. An up-to-date inventory of liabilities was drawn up and schemes formulated for the gradual payment of debts and adjustment of old advances. Early in 1924 a committee was appointed to scrutinize all outstanding claims and the total figure accepted as representing the liabilities at the death of the late Ruler was settled at Rs. 15,62,390. All outside claims were paid off by the end of 1925, partially with the help of a sum of Rs. 2,03,000 which Their Highnesses the Maharanees in a commendable spirit deposited in the Treasury at a low rate of interest. The income, which rose from year to year, was unprecedented during the year under report, answering best expectations and the entire liabilities, inclusive of Their Highnesses' deposit, now stand paid up with the solitary exception of one item of Rs. 13,000, the claimant for which did not turn up ; while the closing balance of the year rose to Rs. 10,59,982 against Rs. 2,37,620 in 1922-23. Another noticeable feature of the financial administration was the vigorous adjustment and substantial reduction of old advances, by far the greater portion of which represented expenditure previously incurred without budget provision. The figure for unadjusted advances stood at Rs. 1,55,106 at the end of the year, against Rs. 8,68,556 in 1922-23.

Works of improvement.

6. With regard to reforms and improvements, the Council had necessarily to adopt a policy more or less cautious. But that it was far from being inattentive to legitimate demands on the lines, would appear from the following items of expenditure sanctioned, which represent Public Works of utility, as well as educational and other measures of importance, completed during the triennium :—

1.	Khas Adalat Building	Rs.	90,227
2.	Jail Building	,,	23,786
3.	Extension of the Administration Building	,,	55,161
4.	Guest House Building	,,	46,145
5.	Stone metalling of the State portion of the Akhaura to Agartala Road	,,	32,786
6.	Stone metalling of the British portion of the Akhaura to Agartala Road	,,	44,872

7.	Bishalgarh to Udaipur Road	...	Rs. 47,114
8.	Purchase of property ...	...	" 90,000
9.	Grain allowance paid to officers	...	" 1,21,201
10.	Special educational grants	...	" 34,150

7. The Council would also offer its best thanks to Mr. A. J. Dash, I. C. S. and Mr. W. H. Nelson, I. C. S., Political Agents, for the ready and ungrudging assistance always received from them.

His Highness's Tour.

8. His Highness the Maharaja visited Calcutta on the 22nd Agrahayan, 1336 T. E. *i. e.* 8th December, 1926, accompanied by Lt. Colonel O. C. Pulley, guardian tutor, and had the pleasure of meeting His Excellency the Viceroy and His Excellency the Governor of Bengal. The party returned to head quarters on 8th Magh *i. e.* 22nd January, 1927.

Political Agent.

9. Mr. A. J. Dash, I. C. S., continued to be the Political Agent of the State till 18th March, 1927, with the exception of a period of about three months when he was on leave and Mr. N. L. Hindley officiated. On Mr. Dash's transfer, Mr. W. H. Nelson, I. C. S, was appointed Political Agent of the State.

CHAPTER II—LAND ADMINISTRATION.

Charge.

10. Babu B. K. Chatterjee, M. A., B. L., remained in charge of the Revenue Department during the year under review.

Area held under settlement.

11. As shewn in the subjoined statement, the total area held under settement and borne on the *taujis* at the close of the year was 587 sq. miles as against 583 sq. miles in the previous year.

Kinds of settlement.	Area in square miles.		Increase.	Decrease.	REMARKS.
	1336 T.E	1335 T.E.			
Jotes ...	268	261	7	—	
Taluks ...	319	322	..	3	
Total ...	587	583	7	3	

12. The decrease in the area under *taluk* settlement is due to auction purchase by the State of some *taluks* at revenue sale.

Tea Settlement.

13. As in the previous year there was no fresh settlement for tea cultivation in the year under report.

Rates of *jama*.

14. The average of *jama* per *kani* of *jote* lands in *Khash Mehals* (exclusive of cesses) stood at 15 annas and 1 pie against 15 annas and 4 pies in the previous year. The maximum rate for *jotes* was Rs. 5-13 per *kani* while the minimum was 4 annas, and for *taluks* Re. 1-8 and anas 1-9 respectively.

15. The different sources of land revenue demand with the collection under each head are detailed below :—

Sources of land revenue.

Sources.	Current demand.		Arrear demand up to the end of		Realization up to the end of		REMARKS.
	1336 T.E.	1335 T.E.	1335 T.E.	1334 T.E.	1336 T.E.	1335 T.E.	
Taluks ...	1,67,666	1,67,266	2,43,221	2,14,407	1,57,710	1,42,190	
Khas Mehal jotes	4,06,384	4,01,698	7,59,867	7,41,843	4,07,062	3,94,837	
Bazars ...	7,082	6,975	1,187	1,229	7,289	7,002	
Cesses ...	36,031	35,682	65,990	62,330	34,166	33,074	
Total ...	6,17,163	6,11,621	10,70,265	10,19,809	6,06,227	5,77,103	

Demand.

16. The above statement will show that the current demand under all heads was Rs. 6,17,163. With the arrear demand of Rs. 19,70,265, the total demand of the year was Rs. 16,87,428 against Rs. 16,31,430 of the previous year. There was an increase in the current demand in respect of *jote* lands, due as usual to assessment on the expiry of the rent free period and resettlement after the previous term. The increase in the current demand in respect of *taluki* lands is due to Survey and Settlement operations.

Collection.

17. The total collection under all heads during the year amounted to Rs. 6,06,227, being Rs. 3,01,700 under current and Rs. 3,04,527 under arrears, against Rs. 5,77,103 in the previous year. The percentage of current collection was 48·88 against 47·85 and that of the arrears 28·45 against 27·89. In the *Khas Mehal* the percentage of current collection was 40·73 against 40·56 and in *taluki mehal* the percentage was 73·26 against 63·98 in the previous year.

Coercive measures—certificates.

18. Altogether 3,090 certificate cases covering a demand of Rs. 2,21,980 were instituted during the year. With 1,351 cases valued at Rs. 2,20,308 pending from the previous year, the total number of cases awaiting final orders on disposal of preliminary notices issued on debtors, was 4,441, covering a total demand of Rs. 4,42,288. Of these 77 cases with a demand of Rs. 24,279 were rejected or struck off and Rs. 23,149 in 756 cases was realised before decree, while 1,530 cases with a total value of Rs. 2,76,590 remained pending.

19. Orders under the provisions of the State Certificate Act were passed during the year in 2,078 cases with a total value of Rs. 1,19,436 making the demands absolute. With 4,491 cases to the value of Rs. 3,46,346 pending in execution from the previous year, the total number of cases dealt with was 6,569, covering a demand of Rs. 4,65,782. Out of the total demand, Rs. 10,300 was remitted or written off, and of the remainder, Rs. 1,15,138 was actually realised leaving a balance of Rs. 3,40,344. Of the amount realised Rs. 1,00,229 represents land revenue and Rs. 14,909 miscellaneous demands. 7 debtors were ordered to be arrested in the year, of whom only one was confined in jail for 24 days and thereafter paid the whole of the dues by instalments, while partial dues were realised in 2 cases.

Operation of the Sunset law.

20. The number of defaultiug *taluks* brought under the operation of the Sunset law (including 30 pending from the previous year) was 87. Of these, 67 were released on payment of dues with penalty, while 3 were sold in auction and 17 remained undisposed of at the close of the year.

Survey.

21. The results of the survey including resurvey operations are given in the statement below. It will be seen that an area of 6,886 *drones* comprising 1,493 *drones* of *taluk* and 5,393 *drones* of *Khas Mehal* was surveyed as against a total of 3,712 *drones* in the previous year. The sanctioned programme for survey for the year was 10,490 *drones* in *Khas Mehal* and 4,098 *drones* in *taluks*. The total expenditure incurred in the survey operations in *Khas Mehals* was Rs. 8,399.

Names of Divisions.	Quantity of land in *drones* surveyed in 1336 T. E.			Quantity of land in *drones* surveyed in 1335 T. E.			REMARKS.
	Taluqi land.	*Khas mehal* land.	Total.	*Taluqi* land.	*Khas mehal* land.	Total.	
1. Sadar Division ...	314	44	358	677	888	1,565	
2. Kailashahar " ...	—	924	924	40	504	544	
3. Sonamura " ...	—	1,734	1,374	—	—	—	
4. Bilania " ...	220	790	1,010	—	—	—	
5. Khowai " ...	32	863	895	21	392	413	
6. Dharmanagar " ..	219	109	328	252	72	324	
7. Udaipur " ...	364	130	494	—	—	—	
8. Sabroom " ...	344	567	911	16	401	417	
9. Amarpur " " ...	—	232	232	—	449	449	
TOTAL ...	1,493	5,393	6,886	1,006	2,706	3,712	

22. The result of settlement work is given in the statement below. It will be seen that settlement operations were completed in respect of 3,118 *drones* of *jote* land as against 4,063 *drones* in the previous year.

Settlement.

Nature of Settlement.	1336 T. E.		1335 T. E.		REMARKS.
	Area in *drones.*	*Jama* in whole rupees.	Area in *drones.*	*Jama* in whole rupees.	
1. Permanent *taluqi* settlement of cultivated land ...	—	—	—	—	
2. Permanent *taluqi* settlement of waste land ...	—	—	—	—	
3. *Taskhichi taluqi* settlement of cultivated land ...	—	—	—	—	
4. *Taskhichi taluqi* settlement of waste land ...	—	—	—	—	
5. *Jotedari* re-settlement of cultivated land	1,936	24,451	3,384	38,290	
6. *Jotedari* settlement of waste land.	1,182	7,101	679	5,254	
TOTAL ...	3,118	31,552	4,063	43,544	

23. No permanent or *Takshichi* settlement or *Nishkar* grant was sanctioned during the year.

Taluki settlement.

24. A net increase of Rs. 12,338 in *jama* was secured by resettlement of *abadi jote* land, the *nazarana* secured being Rs. 34,707. The average rate of *jama* per *kani* being 12 annas 8 pies against 11 annas 6 pies in the previous year.

Resettlement of *jote* lands.

25. During the year an area of 1,182 *drones* of waste land was settled for a prospective rental of Rs. 7,101, the average *jama* per *kani* obtained being 6 annas against 7 annas 9 pies in the previous year. The maximum and minimum rates were Rs. 2-4 and 4 annas respectively. The *nazarana* realised was Rs. 10,897, the rent free period allowed ranging from 1 to 5 years.

Jotedari Settlement of waste land.

26. The Divisional Officers were entrusted with the settlement work within their respective jurisdictions. The total expenditure incurred in the settlement operations exclusively, amounted to Rs. 1,379.

Settlement work.

27. It will be seen that the *nazarana* obtained and obtainable by resettlement of cultivable *jote* lands and settlement of waste lands, as *jotes* amounted to Rs. 45,604 (Rs. 34,707 + Rs. 10,897). The net increase of revenue secured was Rs. 19,439 (Rs. 12,338 + Rs. 7,101).

28. As in the previous year a number of old maps were copied for use in the Divisional Offices. During the year 32 copies of such maps were traced at a cost of Rs. 67.

The work of the map section.

29. As detailed below there were altogether 9 private Estates under State Management during the year under report.

Private Estates under State Management.

Class.	Name of Estates.	Area.	Revenue.
Encumbered	1. Kakrabon Estate	283 *drones*	1,871
	2. Jogendranagar Trust Estate	64 „	163
	3. Kamalnagar and Mohendranagar Estate	51 „	255
	4. Gouranga Tripura's Estate	13 „	57
	5. Maharam Ali Chaudhuri Khanja Kha Bahadur's Estate—*Taluk*	232 „	1,352
	Jote	6 „	149
Unencumbered	6. Prabhu Goswami's Estate	31 „	61
	7. The Maharanee's Estate	260 „	450
	8. Late Brajakumar Thakur's Estate	47 „	297
Endowment	9. Taranagar Estate	123 „	52

30. The subjoined table shows the demand and collection of the estates during the year.

	Demand			Collection			P. C. of collection
	Current	Arear	Total	Current	Arear	Total	
1.	6,248	31,197	37,445	672	4,928	5,600	14·94
2.	1,189	3,701	4,890	240	869	1,109	22·68
3.	1,273	968	2,241	628	780	1,408	62·82
4.	205	195	400	40	153	193	48·25
5.	3,982	5,432	9,414	1,269	1,045	2,314	24·58
6.	913	2,494	3,407	350	678	1,028	30·14
7.	5,961	9,478	15,439	2,740	3,375	6,115	39·63
8.	1,336	2,149	3,485	416	1,188	1,604	46·02
9.	2,340	4,674	7,014	767	937	1,704	24·29

CHAPTER III—PROTECTION.

I. Legislation.

31. There were three sittings of the Legislative Committee during the year, besides a number of sittings of various select Committees dealing with draft bills.

Legislative Committee.

32. The following four bills ultimately received the assent of the Council of Administration and passed into law.

(1) The Hackney carriage bill—Act I of 1336 T. E.

(2) A bill amending Act No. I of 1327 about Tea Gardens—Act II of 1336 T. E.

(3) A bill amending the Survey and Settlement Regulation—Act III of 1336 T. E.

(4) A bill for prevention of gambling—Act IV of 1336 T. E.

33. There was no change during the year in the personnel of the Legislative Committee which consisted as before of 17 members, official and non-official, with Babu Jagadish Chandra Mazumder, M.A., B.L., as Secretary.

II. Military.

34. *Charge.* Kumar Dina Mohan Dev Barman was in charge of the Military Office and the Forces as before.

35. *Strength.* The actual strength of the Force at the close of the year under review, consisted of 183 Sepoys and 39 Officers of all ranks, including the Officer Commanding, 3 A. D. C.s, 1 Subedar Major and 1 Subedar. There were besides a Band Master and 19 men constituting the State Band.

36. *Duty.* The men were chiefly employed as before on escort duty and in furnishing Guards-of-honour on ceremonial occasions.

37. *Expenditure.* The total expenditure of the year including grain allowance paid, amounted to Rs. 43,528 as against Rs. 43,508.

III. Police.

38. *Charge.* Babu Jogesh Chandra Datta, B. A., continued as Superintendent of police throughout the year. Assistant Superintendent Sreejut Jogendra Chandra Dev Barman was on sick leave from the 24th of Aswin last.

39. *Strength.* The total strength of the State Police was 482 inncluding 10 constables for the Town Section and an additional strength of 1 Daroga and 3 constables for the re-established Jatrapur Thana, and 3 Jamadars and 15 constables for guard duties.

40. *Inspection Staff.* There were 4 Inspectors working under the Superintendent of Police. The chief duty of the Inspectors was to control the investigating staff and supervise their work. One Inspector was deputed to famine duty from the 1st of Falgoon of the year under report. As no substitute could be appointed within the year, Police work suffered to some extent specially owing to the growing importance of the Sadar Division in regard to Police work.

41. *Crime.* The total number of cases reported to the Police was 1,318 against 1,282 in the previous year.

42. *Cases.* The result of cases investigated by the Police will be seen from the following table :—

Number of cases reported.
1,318

- Enquiry refused 20
- Number investigated 1,213
  - Maliciously false 3
  - True 725
    - Charge-sheet 350
    - Finally reported 375
  - Doubtful &c. 485
- Pending 85

43. Altogether 711 persons were arrested for various offences, and 638 persons, excluding absconders sent up for trial by the Police against 802 and 824 respectively, including absconders, in the previous year.

Result of prosecution.

44. Of the number 638 sent up, 171 were convicted, 242 acquitted (including 93 on compromise and 47 on withdrawal of cases), while 1 died, 1 escaped and 223 were awaiting trial. The percentage of conviction was 62·6 against 68·2 of the previous year.

45. Of the 369 persons awaiting trial at the end of the previous year, 133 were convicted and 168 acquitted including 53 on compromise and 7 on withdrawal of cases, while 68 were awaiting trial.

Bad livelihood cases.

46. 7 bad livelihood cases with 34 persons were instituted during the year under report. Of these persons 13 were convicted and 4 discharged, while 17 persons were awaiting trial.

Arms Act Cases.

47. Of 10 Arms Act cases 2 were finally reported as true and 8 with 9 persons sent up for trial, 7 persons were convicted and 1 discharged, while 1 person in one case was awaiting trial at the close of the year.

Recovery of stolen property.

48. The value of properties stolen was estimated at Rs. 18,115-5-3 against Rs. 22,695-10 of the previous year. Of this amount Rs. 2,710-5 was recovered against Rs. 10,324-6-3 of the previous year. The percentage of recovery was thus 14·95 against 45·4 of the previous year. This is unsatisfactory.

Dacoities.

49. There were 9 cases of dacoity reported during the year of which 4 were finally reported as true and 5 sent up in charge sheets. 2 persons were convicted and 11 discharged, while 4 persons in 1 case were awaiting trial at the close of the year.

Special Staff.

50. The C. I. D. and the information Bureau continued to work satisfactorily and proved useful in the collection of informations and detecting cases.

Unnatural deaths and steps taken.

51. Altogether 56 cases of unnatural deaths were reported during the year. Regular enquiries were held by the Police in all cases. No foul play was discovered in any of them.

Rewards and Punishments.

52. 4 Darogas, 1 Naib Daroga, 1 Constable and 10 Out-siders received money rewards. 6 Darogas, 1 Jamadar, 2 Writer Constables and 36 Constables were fined, suspended &c., while 13 Constables were dismissed.

Tours.

53. The Superintendent of Police was out on tour for 84 days during the year against 86 days of the previous year.

Co-operation Meetings attended.

54. The relations with the Police in the adjoining districts in British India continued to be satisfactory. 4 Co-operation Meetings were held in which the State Police joined and discussed matters relating to border crime and criminals with the Police in British India and worked out plans for detection and prevention of crimes.

55. The patrol at Sonamura worked satisfactorily with the Kotowalli Police, Comilla, throughout the year.

Patrol.

56. The expenditure amounted, excluding grain allowance, to Rs. 68,377 against Rs. 66,288 in the previous year.

Expenditure.

IV. Justice.

57. There were 15 Courts of Justice in the State during the year under report, exercising both civil and criminal jurisdiction viz.—the Khas Adalat or the Chief Court with its original and appellate sides and 14 Courts of Magistrate-Munsiffs exercising original jurisdiction only.

Courts.

58. Babu Bhupal Chandra Ganguly, B. L., continued to be the Chief Judge, Dewan Bijoy Kumar Sen, M. A., B. L., F. R. S. A., as the Sessions Judge, and Kumar Surendra Chandra Deb Barman and Uzir Brojo Krishna Deb Barman, as puisne Judges of the Khas Adalat. Dewan Asit Chandra Chaudhury, B. A., worked as additional Sessions Judge for some time, Dewan Bijoy Kumar Sen having acted as Chief Judge in place of Babu Bhupal Chandra Ganguli during his absence on privilege leave towards the first part of the year.

59. Altogether 2,200 original criminal cases were instituted during the year under report against 2,292 of the previous year. With the balance of 653 pending from the last year, the total number of cases for disposal before the several subordinate original courts was thus 2,853 as against 2,906 of the previous year, as detailed below ; out of these 2,853 cases, 2,270 were disposed of as against 2,253 of the last year, leaving 577 cases pending at the close of the year. Thus in the year under report, the number of cases for disposal decreased from that of the previous year by 53 and there was an increase in the disposals by 23.

Number of original criminal cases.

DESCRIPTION OF OFFENCES.	1335 T.E.	1336 T.E.
Offences against the State and public tranquillity	98	98
Offences against person	649	638
Offences against property	1,623	1,565
Other offences	536	554
TOTAL	2,906	2,853

60. Extradition warrants were applied for against 77 persons of whom 30 were arrested and surrendered, 27 appeared voluntarily and 20 were at large at the close of the year. Of 57 persons under trial, 17 were convicted, 17 acquitted or discharged and 23 were awaiting trial at the end of the year.

Extradition.

61. The total number of persons awaiting trial in the year under report inclusive of the number pending from the last year was 3,617 against 3,608 of the previous year. The number actually brought to trial was 2,743. Of these 633 were

Persons brought to trial.

arrested by the Police, 493 were produced on warrants, 1,190 appeared on summons, 389 appeared voluntarily, and 38 were arrested in the presence of Magistrates.

Results of cases.

62. Out of these 3,617 persons brought to trial, 1,236 were discharged without trial, 1,018 were acquitted and 487 convicted, while 8 died, 22 were transferred and 346 remained under trial at the close of the year. Of the persons convicted, 167 were sentenced to various terms of imprisonment extending from below 1 month to 10 years, 309 to fine only, 5 persons were warned for the future and 5 persons released on bail, while 1 person was imprisoned for life. The number of persons actually tried was 1,505 as against 1,545 of the previous year, and the percentage of conviction was thus 32·35 as against 29·32 of the previous year.

Cases concerning British subjects.

63. Of the 2,853 cases for disposal, the number in which British subjects were concerned was 507 as against 619 of the previous year. Out of these cases 340 were cognizable and 167 non-cognizable. In 78 cases British subjects were complainants, in 429 they were the accused. In 179 cases both the parties were British subjects. In these cases 647 persons were actually under trial during the year under report as against 749 of the last year. Of them 151 were convicted, 375 acquitted or discharged, and 118 remained under trial at the close of the year.

64. The statement below compares the number of original criminal cases during the last 2 years.

DESCRIPTION OF OFFENCES.	1335 T. E.	133 6T. E.	Increase.	Decrease.
Offences against the State and public tranquillity ...	68	69	1	0
Offences against person	544	509	0	35
Offences against property	1,264	1,154	0	110
Other offences	416	468	52	0
TOTAL	2,292	2,200	53	145

Decreased by 92.

Sessions cases.

65. 21 cases, including 3 cases with 11 persons pending from previous year, were committed to the Sessions during the year under report. Out of these 21 cases 16 were disposed of as detailed in the following table. The number of persons involved in these cases was 68; of them 29 were convicted, 4 discharged without trial, 22 acquitted, while 1 died during trial and 12 remained under trial at the close of the year.

Description of cases.	Number of cases.	Disposed of.	Pending.	REMARKS.
Murder	3	2	1	
Culpable homicide not amounting to murder	6	5	1	
Rape	1	1	0	
Dacoity	5	5	0	
Bigamy	1	1	0	
Grievous hurt	1	1	0	
Arson	2	1	1	
Forging valuable documents of the Tripura State	2	0	0	
Total	21	16	3	

66. There were altogether 269 criminal appeals against 181 of the last year. They were disposed of as shown below :—

Criminal appeals.

Rejected	26
Judgment affirmed	124
Modified	21
Reversed	63
Further enquiry &c. ordered	10
Proceedings quashed	1
	245
Pending	24
Total	269

67. The percentage of judgments affirmed and modified was 66·21 as against 63·043 of the previous year.

68. The number of original civil suits instituted during the year under report was 2,014 against 1,957 of the previous year. With the preceding year's balance of 1,097 suits, the total number for disposal was 3,111 as against 3,031 of the last year. They were disposed of as follows :—

Original civil suits.

Exparte	836
Admitted and compromised	354
Dismissed for want of prosecution ...	316
Disposed of on contest	615
	2,121
Pending	990
Total	3,111

69. The average duration of suits before the civil courts was 3 months and 12 days against 3 months and 1 day in 1335 T. E.

Duration of suits.

70. The total value of suits instituted during the year was Rs. 2,76,546-15-3 as against Rs. 1,84,783-1-6 which gives an average of Rs. 107-8-3 as the value per case. Of the 2,014 suits instituted during the year under report, 748 related to lands, 854 to money transactions and 412 to other transactions There were 1,168 suits of the value of Rs. 100 and under ; 439 suits of over Rs. 100 and below Rs. 500 ; 24 suits of over Rs. 500 and below Rs. 1,000 ; 25 suits of over Rs. 1,000 and below Rs. 5,000 ; 4 suits of over Rs. 5,000 ; while 354 suits were not estimable in money value.

Nature and value of suits.

71. The number of applications for the execution of decrees filed during the year under report was 591 and with 402 pending cases, the total number was 993 against 1,055 of the previous year. The aggregate value of the new applications was Rs. 73,546-12-0 and with the opening value of Rs. 1,03,300-14-3, being the value of the pending cases, the total amounted to Rs. 1,76,847-10-3. The number of applications disposed of was 649, the value of which was Rs. 79,150-15-9. The number of execution cases pending at the close of the year was 344 with the value of Rs. 97,696-10-6.

Execution of decrees.

72. There were 169 civil appeals filed during the year under report against 163 of the last year. With the past year's balance of 65, the total number for disposal was 234 as against 224 of 1335 T. E. Out of these 188 were disposed of during the year under report against 150 of the previous year, leaving a balance of 46 cases at the close of the year.

Civil appeals.

73. The following figures indicate the results of appeals :—

Results of appeals.

Decisions confirmed	... ...	80
,, reversed	... ...	48
,, modified	... ...	8
,, remanded	... ...	24
Compromised or otherwise disposed of	...	28
		188

74. The percentage of judgments wholly or partly upheld excluding the cases compromised, was 55 against 51·063 of the previous year.

Percentage.

75. The total value of appeals filed during the year under report was Rs. 20,070-1-6 and the average duration of each appeal was 2 months and 1 day against 2 months and 2 days of the last year.

Value and duration of appeals.

76. 34 civil suits were instituted in the Khas Adalat Original Side against 26 of the previous year. With the balance of 31 suits from 1335 T. E., the total number for disposal was thus 65 against 75 of the last year ; of these 29 suits were disposed of against 44 suits of the previous year and 36 suits remained pending at the close of the year. And there were 26 execution cases during the year under report including 21 cases pending from 1335 T. E. ; of these 12 were disposed of and 14 remained pending at the end of the year. There were 25 applications filed for the grant of succession and other certificates during the year, with the previous year's balance of 15, the total number of cases was 40 ; out of them 33 were disposed of as shown below, leaving 7 cases pending at the close of the year.

Original side cases.

Description of cases.	Total.	Disposed of.	Pending.
Probate case	4	4	0
Succession certificate	14	8	6
Guardianship	22	21	1
Total	40	33	7

77. Thus it will appear from the subjoined table, that the total number of civil and criminal appeals inclusive of the number pending from last year was 503 as against 405 of the previous year, and out of these 433 were disposed of against

Total number of appeals.

307 of the previous year. So in comparison with the last year, the total number of appeals increased by 98 in the present year and there was a corresponding increase in the disposals in the year under report by 126.

Description of appeals.	Number of appeals.		Disposed of.	
	Past year.	Present year.	Past year.	Present year.
Civil	224	234	159	188
Criminal	181	269	148	245
Total	405	503	307	433

V. Prisons.

Number of Jails.

78. There were 8 jails in the State during the year under review, one at each of the Divisions and Sub-Divisions, including the Central Jail at the Capital.

Jail Population.

79. The total population during the year was 718 as against 612 in the year before, the daily average being 116·00 87·17, which shows a decided increase in the year under report. Of the above, 324 were convicts, 382 under trials, 7 civil prisoners and 5 lunatics.

Long-term Prisoners.

80. A statement with details about 69 prisoners sentenced to over 2 years, as against 56 in the preceding year is subjoined.

Class of offence.	Number of prisoners.	Occupation.	REMARKS.
Murder	10	They were employed in oilmills, wheat grinding, soorki pounding, *khoa* breaking, bamboo and cane work, gardening, weaving, sewing, paddy husking, rice manufacturing &c.	
Culpable homicide not amounting to murder	24		
Dacoity	16		
Robbery	3		
Theft	4		
Grievous hurt	3		
Rape	2		
Uttering counterfeit coin ...	1		
Counterfeiting coin ...	4		
Forgery and Conspiracy ...	2		
Total	69		

Jail Health.

81. The Jail health was on the whole good. One convict died of Chronic Diarrhœa and another of Meningitis. One under trial died of Chronic Malarial Fever and another of Pneumonia. In the previous year there was only one death.

With the increase in the population, rise in the rate of mortality is inevitable, though the necessity for a suitable and properly equipped hospital in connection with the Jail has to be considerd.

Escape.

82. One convict from the Central Jail, one convict from the Dharmanagar Jail, one under trial from the Sabroom Jail and one under trial from the Kailashahar Jail effected their escapes The convict of Dharmanagar Jail was re-arrested on the very day of escape.

Income and expenditure.

83. The total income and expenditure from the jails were Rs. 4,546-10-9 and Rs. 15,824 respectively as against Rs. 3,350 and Rs. 13,633 of the previous year.

Improvements.

84. The extension of the Jail enclosure, the construction of another big Dormitory for the male population and of a separate female ward, as also other necessary improvements—both sanitary and accommodative are in contemplation in view of the growing number of the population.

VI. Registration.

Charge.

85. The charge of the Department continued with Dewan A. C. Chaudhuri except during his leave, once in August and again in January-February, when Mr. S. C. Deb Barman, M. A., (Harvard), Babu B. K. Chatterjee, M.A., B.L., and Babu J. C. Maulik temporarily officiated in his place.

Registration Offices.

86. The number of Registration offices was 9 as in the previous year being one at the head-quarters Station of each of the Divisions or Sub-Divisions. In the Muffussil the Divisional and Sub-Divisional Officers and in certain divisions under the new Circular the Second officers acted as Registrars. For the Sadar Division there was a separate Registrar at Agartala.

87. Appendices XV. and XVI. are Registration Statements and shew the work of the Department.

Presentation and Disposal.

88. The number of documents presented for Registration during the year in the 9 offices mentioned above was 12,896 against 13,265 in the previous year. Of this number 156 deeds were refused registration on different grounds and 72 remained pending at the end of the year.

Value of deeds presented and registerred.

89. The total value covered by the documents presented amounted to Rs. 22,44,327 as compared with Rs. 22,35,371 in the previous year, while the total value covered by the documents actually registered was Rs. 21,63,6!3, as against Rs. 21,12,171 in the year before.

Suits and appeals.

90. The number of suits and appeals filed before the Officer-in-charge, Registration Department, in respect of documents, the registration of which had been refused in the Registration offices, was 35 and 4 against 31 and 3 respectively

in the preceding year, and there were only 26 suits pending from the previous year, making a total of 61 suits and 4 appeals. Out of these, 22 suits and 2 appeals were disposed of during the year, leaving 39 suits and 2 appeals pending at the end of the year.

Income and expenditure.

91. The total income of the Department from fees and fines amounted to Rs. 15,988 against Rs. 15,781 and the expenditure to Rs. 4,682 against Rs. 4336 in the previous year. The net income thus was Rs. 11,306 against Rs. 11,444 in the previous year.

VII. Municipality.

Municipality.

92. As before the Capital Town of Agartala was the only Municipality in the State with a population of about 8,000 according to the last Census.

Municipal Committee

93 Municipal Administration of the Capital Town of Agartala was carried on by a Committee of nine members including an Official Chairman and a Non-official Vice-Chairman. Babu Brojendra Kumar Chatterjee, M. A., B. L., Officer-in-charge, Revenue Department of the State continued to be the Chairman.

94 The Committee held 14 fourteen meetings—the average of attendance being 5·5 as against 4·9 of the previous year.

Income.

95. The total demand of Municipal and Latrine taxes including arrears amounted to Rs. 7,358 of which Rs. 709-5 was written off as unrealiseable. The total collection under the head of these taxes came up to Rs. 3,685-11-9 against Rs. 3,399 of the previous year.

96. The income under the Miscellaneous head amounted to Rs. 1,349-8-3 as against Rs. 2,053 of the previous year. This figure includes deposits and advances recovered during the year amounting to Rs. 202.

97. The State grant for the year including a special provision of Rs. 700 for epidemic diseases was Rs. 10,000,—out of which Rs. 9,706 was spent and the remainder lapsed to the State. The total income of the Municipality under all heads including the State grant actually received during the year thus amounted to Rs. 14,702-7-9 as against Rs. 14,452 of the previous year.

Expenditure.

98. The total expenditure during the year under review including Rs. 198-8 in deposits repaid and advances amounted to Rs. 15,167-15-6 against Rs. 14,117 of the previous year.

Public Health.

99. The general health of the people within the Municipality was good, though there were some cases of Cholera, Kala-azar and Small-pox. There was a decided fall in the number of Malaria and Kala-azar cases.

100. The want of good drinking water and proper drainage continues to be keenly felt. During the year under review a special Committee with Dewan B. K Sen, Chief Secretary, as President was appointed for sanitary improvement of the Town and the Chairman of the Municipality was a member of the Committee. The other members were Dr. M. M. Majumder, State Physician, Thakur H. R. Dev Barman, Sadar Collector and Babu J. N. Bhaduri, State Engineer. The entire town was divided into 5 blocks, and a gang of coolies worked in each block under a member of the Committee and undertook clearance of drains, jungles and tanks. The work produced very excellent result but the question of supplying good drinking water to the town population was not taken up by the Committee.

The Town Bazar.

101. As in the previous year the control of the Town Bazar remained in the hands of the Municipal Committee. The total demand including the arrear demand of Rs. 660-12-3 was Rs. 6,829-9-3. The total realisation came up to Rs. 5,815-11-3 and the total expenditure from the Bazar Fund amounted to Rs. 11,950.

102. The unfinished portion of the north block of the Bazar Building was completed in the year under report. The accummulated fund of Rs. 9,538-2-6 on the Bazar account standing as balance at the close of the year will be spent on the proposed central shed in the Bazar yard.

CHAPTER IV—PRODUCTION AND DISTRIBUTION.

I. Weather and Crops—Agriculture.

Rainfall.

103. The average rainfall of the year was 110·04 inches against 108·28 inches in the previous year. The quinquennial average was 93·92 inches. Dharmanagar Division had the maximum fall of 128·83 inches and Sadar the minimum of 66·05. Heavy rainfall during Poush in places injured standing crops and untimely and insufficient rainfall was unfavourable to *joom* crops.

Crops.

104. The principal crops were paddy, cotton, *til*, mustard, jute and sugar-cane. Potatoes, tobacco, chillies and pulses of various types were also grown in some parts of the State.

Rat pest in *jooms* damaged *joom* paddy to a considerable extent. The outturn of *Aus* and Poush paddy was not satisfactory.

Tea Industry.

105. The tea industry showed appreciable progress and the tea produced in the State fetched good prices. As many as 35 gardens showed marked improvement. 8,20,615 lbs. of manufactured tea was exported from the State during the year.

Cattle.

106. The health of cattle was not bad on the whole. There were rinderpest cases in Sonamura and Udaipur; foot and mouth disease prevailed to some extent in Sadar. The Veterinary Assistant toured in Mofussil for 91 days.

2,126 heads of cattle were treated for various diseases during the year.

Condition of the people.

107. The people are mostly agricultural. Unequal distribution of rainfall during the flowering time of paddy and rat pest in *jooms* made havoc to crops resulting in the scarcity of food amongst hill population. Other crops such as mustard, jute, potatoes and chillies yielded normal outturn. Cleansed cotton sold at Rs. 10 to Rs. 50 per maund. The production of jute increased but the market was more or less dull.

Prices.

108. The prices of food grains were similar to those in the neighbouring British districts. Rice sold from Rs. 6 to Rs. 10 and paddy from Rs. 2-12 to Rs. 5 per maund. The maximum price of rice in the previous year was Rs. 9.

Wages.

109. Male labourers earned from 8 annas to Re. 1-8 and female labourers from 4 annas to Re. 1 a day. *Ghoramis* earned from 12 annas to Re. 1-4 and carpenters and masons from Re. 1 to Re. 1-8. Most of the labourers were outsiders from the neighbouring British Districts as well as up country coolies.

Taccavi.

No Taccavi advances were issued during the year.

Relief operations.

110. Scarcity of food prevailed amongst hill population during the latter half of the year under review. There was partial failure of paddy crop in *jooms* owing to unfavourable rains coupled with the presence of rats in extraordinary number before harvesting. Similar damage of *joom* paddy by rats has happened previously and warned by experience the Revenue Department took prompt steps to prohibit export of rice and paddy from the affected areas and induced some local rice dealers to hold stocks of paddy and rice in the interior. The pinch was much felt in Kailashahar Division where Rangoon rice had to be sent at the end of the year to the interior for gratuitous relief and for loan distribution. In Sadar and Udaipur Divisions money loans were distributed to the needy. Two special Relief officers were employed and they were assisted by the local officers and men. The State Medical Department invited a band of workers from Comilla Abhoy Asram to render medical aid to the sufferers in the interior of the Kailasahar Division where the people were panic-striken owing to outbreak of cholera in more or less epidemic form. Rs. 13,000 was provided and spent in conducting famine relief operations during the year under review. Relief measures continued and with the exception of Sonamura the hill population of all the Divisions had to be helped by the State in the current year.

Staff.

111. The staff of the Department continued to be the same as it was during the last year.

Propaganda work and circuit lecture.

112. Propaganda work was throughout the year conducted in Sadar Division only and the following were undertaken :—

1. Introduction of better quality cotton in joom and also on the plains with plough.

2. Introduction of early superior quality paddy in *jooms* as well as an improved variety of *Aman* in the plains.

3. Extension of superior quality of jute, tobacco, sugarcane and potato crops both in highlands and plains.

4. Circuit lectures against nomadic jooming and in favour of plough cultivation.

5. Preservention of manure and use of selected seeds.

6. Introduction of Eri-rearing among the people.

Improved variety of cotton.

113. The Department took up towards the end of the year some improved cotton varieties for experiment in *jooms* the result of which is awaited with interest.

Seed distribution.

114. 5 centres in Sadar Division were opened for distribution of seeds. Stocks of improved variety of cotton seeds, *Kataktara* and *Indrasail* paddies, *Tana* sugarcane and improved jute seeds were sold out, signifying a keen anxiety on the part of the people to have departmental seeds.

Kashipur Farm.

115. The utilization of the Kashipur Farm for seed growing purpose has met with success as almost all the departmental seeds which have been distributed were grown there and this little farm was rendering every assistance towards the introduction of various crops under demonstration by the Department.

Other crops and demonstation.

116. Of the other crops it may be mentioned that roseum improved variety of cotton has been found to be very highly productive both under plough and in jooms. The *Joomiaks* are appreciating its value and the Department is also making useful attempts towards its rapid spread.

Cotton growing under plough.

117. Experiments have established beyond doubt that almost all the varieties of cotton such as the Buri, American Dharwar and the Comillas could be grown on the plains under plough cultivation.

118. Potato cultivation is spreading in almost every Division on river side lands, though the outturn in not quite up to the mark. This is due to lack of irrigation system. There was less insect trouble with the potato crops during the year under report. The average outturn is on the increase particularly in river valleys, such as the Manu, Gumti, Howrah, Dhalai and Khowai.

Eri culture.

119. Eri culture is having its demonstrations in some centres of Sadar Division.

Visit of Royal Commission of Agriculture.

120. The Department was highly honoured by an invitation to participate in the Bengal Presidency Agricultural Exhibition at Dacca, held on 4th January, 1927, in connection with the visit of the Royal Commission of Agriculture.

121. A separate stall of exhibits was assigned for the State produce and styled the Tripura State Stall. The principal agricultural products of the State were exhibited in it.

122. The President, Lord Linglithgow with all the members of the Commission honoured the stall with a visit and displayed keen interest in the exhibits.

123. The stall was also visited by the Minister of Agriculture, the Director of Agriculture, Mr. Finlow and the Divisional Commissioner.

124. An assistant teacher of the local school, an amateur Agriculturist has been going on for some time with experiments on Apis Indica, (Indian bee) the only domesticable race of bees in India. In the year under report this gentleman was allowed a lump grant of Rs. 200 from the Agriculture Department to encourage him to pursue his researches in this direction. At present very little information can be obtained about bees that may be reared with economic success in India. Apis Indica being a little different in habits and size from the successful European or American bees, the appliances and the methods of rearing, that obtain in other countries, have to be remodelled. It is hoped that the experiment in the State will be productive of good results.

Bee rearing.

125. The Superintendent was out on tour for 56 days during the year.

Touring of staff.

II. Immigration and Emigration.

126. During the year 1,052 families immigrated into and 506 families emigrated out of the State, as aginst 1,347 and 760 respectively in the previous year.

III. Forests.

127. Rai J. C. Sen Bahadur, Vice-President of the Council of Administration was in charge of the Department till the 21st of Aswin. During his absence on leave in the latter half of the year, the charge of the Department remained with Babu J. C. Maulick and also for some time with Babu Jatindra Nath Mitter, Forest Officer. With the exception of a few *Mehals* which were let out in *Ijara*, all the forests were under *Khash* management as before.

Charge and Management.

128. The Department had a staff of 4 Forest Circle Inspectors, 19 Foresters, 12 Rangers, 15 Assistant Foresters, 11 Moharers, 17 Head Guards and 197 Guards and Literate Guards. Besides these, there were 185 Commission Agents for the sale of Forest Permits, for the shoulder-borne export of minor forest produce not coming under any definite *Mehal*. There were 58 Stations for collection of duty and prevention of forest offences.

Staff.

129. The reserved *Sal* forests of the Sonamura Division were continued to be worked under the system of Coppice with standards and those of the Udaipur Division under the Improvement Method (Selection system), while the open

Working.

unclassed forests were worked under the State Rules of 1323 T. E. For the Feni River *Mehal*, the working rules of the Bengal Forest Department were followed.

130. The two coupes already selected in the Sonamura Division were marked and sold during the year under report and four more blocks in this Division were selected for work. As the marking operations were undertaken towards the close of the year, the sale of the coupes could not be held within the year under report. The two blocks selected in the Udaipur Division to be worked under Improvement Felling System were not sold as re-marking in the blocks became necessary. The block in the Langai Valley could not be worked during the year for want of purchasers as there were some difficulties in regard to the removal of timber.

131. The following table shews the result of collection of Forest

Sources of revenue. revenue :—

Heads of Revenue.	1336 T.E.	1335 T.E.	Increase.	Decrease.	REMARKS.
I. Unclassed open forests :—					
(*a*) Toll on forest produce exported by the river mehals	4,08,970	3,89,487	19,483	—	
(*b*) Toll on forest produce exported by land route under permit	84,365	83,072	1,293	—	
(*c*) Toll collection (share) of the Feni river mehal ...	29,146	31,604	—	2,458	
(*d*) Grazing mehal ...	7,339	6,896	443	—	
(*e*) Thatching grass mehal	9,029	10,342	—	1,313	
II. Reserved Forests :—					
Sale of *Sal* and *Garjan* trees ...	15,289	14,199	1,090	—	
III. Elephant Kheddas	42	1,702	—	1,660	
TOTAL ...	5,54,180	5,37,302	22,309	5,431	

Net Increase—16,878.

132. The total forest revenue of the year was Rs. 5,54,180

Receipts. against Rs. 5,37,302 in the previous year, showing an increase of Rs. 16,878.

133. An appreciable rise of revenue is noticeable in the river *Mehals* and a fall in the elephant *khedda* operations.

134. During the year under report *khedda* operations were

Khedda operations. undertaken in the Udaipur Division only, with the result that 16 elephants were caught against one in the previous year. The proceeds from the sale of the elephants caught amounted to Rs. 6,798. But owing to the State having purchased three elephants the accounts could not be adjusted for want of allotment during the year under review.

Feni River *Mehal.*

135. On the recommendations made by a Conference held in September, 1926, under the presidency of the Commissioner of Chittagong Division, the Government of Bengal approved of the continuance of the joint Toll Station at Amlighat under the management of the State Forest Department, till the 31st March, 1927. The question of the future management was under correspondence with the Government of Bengal, and the Joint Toll Station continued to be under the management of the State Forest Department. The total revenue collected at the joint Toll Station in the year under review was Rs. 43,845 against Rs. 47,404 in the previous year. This decrease is due to shortage in export during the year as compared with that of the previous year.

Fee Simple Lots.

136. In the year under report, the forest produce of the 14 as. 7⅛ p. share of the Lot No. 98 was taken in *Ijara* as in the last year, through the Station Officer of the Amlighat Toll Station on behalf of the Government and the State. Forest produce from other Fee Simple Lots was exported without trouble between the Station Staff and the Lot-owners.

Forest Offences.

137. During the year under review there were 122 Forest cases against 337 persons of which 95 cases against 270 persons were instituted during the year, while 27 cases against 67 persons were pending from the previous year. The offences were mainly for illicit export of forest produce without permits and without payment of duty. The robbery case noticed in the last year's report terminated in the conviction of the accused in the Sessions Court.

Results.

138. Altogether 138 persons in 72 cases were convicted, of whom 9 were sentenced to imprisonment and 129 were punished with fine only. 87 persons in 22 cases were acquitted, 3 cases against 8 persons were compounded and 25 cases against 104 persons remained pending at the close of the year.

Rewards and Punishments.

139. In the year no reward was awarded. One Ranger was degraded and two Guards punished with fine for irregularities and offences.

Health of the Staff.

140. The health of the Staff in general was normal. There were many cases of fever, and one of the Foresters, Birlal Deb Barman, a young and energetic subordinate fell a victim to Malaria.

General.

141. Some difficulties were still experienced in connection with the export of forest produce from the State into the Sylhet District, specially in regard to the delivery of the drift logs belonging to the State and the check exercised by the Assam Forest Department on State forest produce in transit. Correspondence on the subject was in progress between the State and the Assam Government. An early settlement of the matter is expected.

IV. Trade and Manufacture.

142. The principal exports were timber, forest produce of various kinds, cotton, oilseeds, (*til* and mustard seed) paddy, jute, rice and *Gur* (molassess). A small quantity of tea and some homespun cotton fabrics manufactured by the hill people, specially the Manipuries, were also exported. The principal exports for the year under review and of the previous year are shown below :—

	1335 T. E.	1336 T. E.
Cotton ...	85,321 maunds.	67,327 maunds.
Til	36,853 ,,	35,621 ,,
Mustard Seeds...	34,847 ,,	23,802 ,,
Jute	92,955 ,,	1,56,120 ,,

143. 3,38,272 lb., 5,60,568 lb., and 8,20,615 lb., of tea were exported in 1924, 1925, and 1926 respectively from the gardens in this State.

144. The principal imports were cloths and yarns, salt, oils (*kerosine* and mustard), pulses, chillies, tobacco, sugar, flour, spices, arecanuts, books and stationary. The industries worth mention were manufacture of cotton fabrics by the hill people and the Manipuries ; cane and bamboo baskets, mats and sieves by Tripuras ; and dug-outs, bowls and plates of wood by the Reangs and Chakmas ; also *Gur* (molassess) by both hill people and Bengalees.

V. Public Works.

145. Maharajkumar B. K. Dev Barman Bahadur, Member of the Council of Administration was in charge of the Department during the year. Mr. J. N. Bhaduri, B. A, B. E., continued as State Engineer.

Expenditure.

146. The expenditure under Public Works was Rs. 2,81,015 against Rs. 2,33,711 in the previous year. Of this Rs. 1,64,945 was spent on Buildings, Rs. 76,176 on Roads and Bridges, Rs. 9,271 on Water Supply and Rs. 5,844 on Miscellaneous Works.

147. The Bishalgarh–Udaypur Road was completed during the year under report, but the Stone metalling of the D. B. Portion of the Agartala–Akhaura Road could not be finished for want of stones which the A. B. Railway had undertaken to supply but failed to do so.

148. The following Buildings were completed with corrugated iron roofing during the year under report :—

1. Two Structures in H. H.'s Andar.
2. Godown at Sadar Jail.
3. Kumar Rajani Mohan Dev Barman's House.
4. Record Room for Sadar Collectorate.
6. Artisan School.
6. Sonamura H. E. School.
7. Jatrapur Range Office in Sonamura.
8. Beerganj Tehesil Office in Amarpur.
9. Ampi Tehesil Office in Amarpur.

10. Nalna Tehesil Office in Amarpur.
11. Bilania Tehesil Office at Bilania.
12. Forest Office at Khowai.
13. Ragna Forest Office in Dharmanagar.

CHAPTER V—REVENUE AND FINANCES.

I. Revenue.

149. The total collection in the year was Rs. 18,50,807 against Rs. 17,53,961 in the previous year.

150. The details of the income under different heads with all variations are given in the Statement below :—

Serial number.	Heads of Revenue.	1336 T.E.	1335 T.E.	As compared with 1335 T.E.		Remarks.
				Increase.	Decrease.	
1	Land Revenue	6,18,210	5,89,635	28,575	—	
2	Rents of markets	7,223	6,852	371	—	
3	Family Tax in the hills	54,595	63,118	—	8,523	
4	Toll on forest produce	4,93,335	4,72,559	20,776	—	
5	Do. Do. on the Feni River	29,146	31,604	—	2,458	
6	Elephant & buffalo grazing Mehal	7,339	6,896	443	—	
7	Thatching grass Mehal	9,029	10,342	—	1,313	
8	Reserved *Sal* trees	15,289	14,199	1,090	—	
9	Tax on cotton and oil-seeds ...	2,18,051	2,14,808	3,243	—	
10	Royalty on elephants caught ...	42	1,702	—	1,660	
11	Adda Mehal	23,063	21,089	1,974	—	
12	Excise	79,354	60,563	18,791	—	
13	Stamps and Court-fees	87,137	84,490	2,647	—	
14	Law and Justice (Fines)... ...	4,162	3,422	740	—	
15	Process fees	15,905	13,729	2,176	—	
16	Registration	15,988	15,781	207	—	
17	Jail	4,739	3,350	1,389	—	
18	Cattle pounds	6,083	5,869	214	—	
19	Nazars	52,490	47,489	5,001	—	
20	Agriculture	511	570	—	59	
21	Education...	6,810	7,906	—	1,096	
22	Miscellaneous	1,02,306	77,988	24,318	—	
	Total	18,50,807	17,53,961	1,11,955	15,109	Net increase—Rs. 96,846

151. There was thus a total increase of Rs. 1,11,955 in respect of 16 heads of revenue against a total decrease of Rs. 15,109 in regard to 6 heads. The increase under the head land revenue in due to the realisation of arrear revenue of several Tea Estates and to better collection. The increase under the head of Forest produce is satisfactory. The increase under Excise head is due to resettlement at higher jama.

Increase.

152. The decrease in Family tax is due to scarcity in the hills owing to failure of joom crops as the result of rat pest and unfavourable rainfall.

Decrease.

II. Finances.

153. A consolidated abstract account showing the financial transactions of the State and the attached Zemindaries is given below :—

Receipts.	1335 T.E.	1336 T.E.
1. Opening balance :–		
(1) State	6,24,594	6,11,124
(2) Zemindaries ...	3,16,589	3,77,146
Total ...	9,41,183	9,88,270
2. Income :—		
(1) State	17,59,321	18,58,281
(2) Zemindaries ...	12,11,339	11,12,526
Total ...	29,70,660	29,70,807
3. Law charges recovered :—		
(1) State	—	—
(2) Zemindaries ...	57,133	52,026
Refunds and compensation for lands acquired :—		
(1) State ...	—	—
(2) Zemindaries ...	1,685	1,404
5. Deposits :—		
(1) State	86,764	3,68,535
(2) Zemindaries ...	5,775	8,815
Total ...	92,539	3,77,350
6. Loans :—		
(1) State	—	—
(2) Zemindaries ...	—	—
	—	—
GRAND TOTAL ...	40,63,200	43,39,857

Expenditure.	1335 T.E.	1336 T.E.
1. General Administration charges :—		
(a) State	4,89,890	4,78,963
(b) Zemindaries :—		
1. Cost of management	1,41,274	1,44,408
2. Cost of litigation	1,29,224	1,01,347
Total ...	7,60,388	7,24,718
2. Revenue and Taxes on account of the Zemindaries	2,67,026	2,68,970
3. Public Works :—		
(a) State	2,41,105	2,90,156
(b) Zemindaries	54,454	82,616
Total ...	2,95,559	3,72,772
4. Municipality :—		
(a) State	9,000	9,706
5. Education :—		
(a) State	1,08,370	1,16,474
(b) Zemindaries	10,228	11,029
Total ...	1,18,598	1,27,503
6. Medical and Sanitation :—		
(a) State	68,288	71,740
(b) Zemindaries	10.615	11,698
Total ...	78,903	83,438
7. Survey and Settlement :—		
(a) State	17,152	15,850
(b) Zemindaries	783	809
Total ...	17,935	16,659
8. Agriculture :—State	4,779	5,479
9. Religious Expenses :—		
(a) State	66,467	65,358
(b) Zemindaries	6,058	6,122
Total ...	72,525	71,480
10. Sultanat :—		
(a) State	40,645	79,106
11. Purchase of Landed Tenures :—		
(a) State	85,850	1,896
(b) Zemindaries	128	6,805
Total ...	85,978	8,701
12. Pension and Gratuity :—		
(a) State	27,488	28,420
(b) Zemindaries	4,627	4,841
Total ...	32,115	33,261
13. Ordinary *Sansar* charges :—		
(a) Ordinary expenses on account of His Highness and family including the late Maharaja's family ...	82,774	81,029
(b) Other branches of the Raj family...	1,39,442	1,38,515
(c) Thakurs	30,420	29,240
(d) *Sansar* office establishment ...	7,772	8,471
(e) Electric Light	25,032	25,137
(f) Miscellaneous	47,617	83,082
Total ...	3,33,057	3,65,474
14. Charity and Donation :—		
(a) State	21,892	21,554
(b) Zemindaries	1,659	1,549
Total ...	23,551	23,103
15. Famine Relief—State	—	12,368
16. His Highness's Nij Tahabil (Privy purse) including expenses on journeys	1,12,509	1,26,863
17. Liabilities liquidated including payment of interest on loans and repayment of deposits :—		
(a) State	69,275	85,828
(b) Zemindaries	5,07,859	5,07,849
Total ...	5,77,134	5,93,677
18. Miscellaneous :—		
(a) State	6,162	6,122
(b) Zemindaries	15,660	15,477
Total ...	21,822	21,599
19. Marriage—State	2,16,500	18,504
20. Advances	6,906	6,840
21. Closing Balance :—		
(a) State		
In cash and Bank Deposit ...	3,96,594	8,35,130
In bonds and advances	2,14,530	2,11,889
Total ...	6,11,124	10,47,019
(b) Zemindaries :—		
In cash and Bank Deposit ...	2,56,681	2,24,852
In bonds and advances	1,20,465	1,47,765
Total ...	3,77,146	3,72,617
GRAND TOTAL ...	40,63,200	43,89,857

154. It will be seen that the total receipts from all sources including deposits and law charges recovered, amounted to Rs. 34,01,587 against Rs. 31,22,017 in the previous year. The above figure includes a deposit of Rs. 2,60,000 from Their Highnesses the Maharanees, for which an equivalent amount was subsequently held in the Central Bank as fixed deposit. With the opening balance of Rs. 9,88,270, the total sum available for expenditure excluding the deposit money of the Maharanees, was Rs. 41,29,857 as against Rs. 40,63,200 in the preceding year.

Receipts.

155. The total expenditure during the year amounted to Rs. 29,70,221 against Rs. 30,74,930 in the previous year, the decrease being mainly due to absence of certain abnormal items of expenditure, which had to be incurred in the previous year in connection with the marriages in the Raj family and the purchase of properties. The closing balance at the end of the year came up to Rs. 14,19,636 against Rs. 9,88,270. Of this balance Rs. 6,31,238 was in cash in the Treasuries, Rs. 4,28,744 in the Imperial Bank and Rs. 3,59,654 in loans and advances.

Expenditure.

156. It will be seen that even with the adjustment during the year of a sum of Rs. 29,862 on account of old advances, the balance for loans and advances increased by Rs. 24,659 which was due to certain current advances remaining unadjusted during the year and also to the investment of Rs. 20,000 in the Comilla Raj Central Bank.

157. The noticeable variations in expenditure are explained below :—

i. Administration Charges :—

State—The non-payment of leave salary as well as leave and pension contribution of the Vice-President, who was absent on leave for five months during the year, mainly contributed to the decrease under this head.

Zemindaries—The increase under cost of management was due to usual time scale increments, reward for improved collection, and creation of new posts. The institution of a smaller number of rent suits accounted for the decrease under the cost of litigation.

ii. Public Works :—

The increase was due to larger payments made on several expensive Road and Building works in the State and the Zemindaries.

iii. Municipality :—

A special grant made to the Agartala Municipality for the prevention of Epidemic diseases increased the expenditure under this head.

iv. Education :—

The increase in the State was mainly due to the establishment of a Kumar Boarding at Comilla and also to certain unusual payments made for the educational expenses two Kumars at Raipur.

v. Medical and Sanitation :—

In the State the increase was mainly due to the special provision made for the Sanitary improvement of the Agartala Town. While in the Zemindaries the time scale increment and extra cost of medicines for dispensaries accounted for the increase.

vi. SURVEY AND SETTLEMENT :—

STATE—The decrease was partly due to the post of the Settlement Officer remaining vacant for the greater part of the year, and partly to non-payment of certain bills during the year.

vii. SULTANAT :—

The expenditure incurred for the improvement of the Dais in the Durbar Hall and the purchase of certain Motor Cars accounted for the increase under this head.

viii. PURCHASE OF LANDED PROPERTY :—

The decrease in the State was attributable to the extraordinary payment made in the previous year for the purchase of Mr. Courjon's property at Comilla, while the increase in the Zemindaries was due to the price paid for an under-tenure required for the new market at Comilla.

ix. ORDINARY SANSAR CHARGES :—

The increase was mainly under the sub-head miscellaneous, which included among others the following unusual expenditure :—

(*a*) Payment of outstanding bills relating to the marriage expenses incurred in the previous year.

(*b*) Price of an elephant previously purchased.

(*c*) Heavy expenditure incurred for the treatment of His Highness's sister who was seriously ill.

(*d*) Cost of performance of certain social and religious rites.

x. FAMINE RELIEF :—

STATE—Owing to the scarcity of food stuff in the hills, a sum of Rs. 12,368 was spent for the relief of the distressed subjects.

xi. NIJ TAHABIL :—

Increased tour expenses, payment of Col. Pulley's passage money, adjustment on a more extensive scale of old advances are mainly the factors which contributed to the increase under this head.

xii. MARRIAGES : —

The expenditure of Rs. 18,504 represents liabilities incurred in the previous year but not paid for want of allotment.

xiii. LIABILITIES :—

As mentioned in the previous report, a sum of Rs. 5,09,183 remained unadjusted at the close of the year 1335 T. E. During the year under report, this amount was paid up with interest thereon except an item of Rs. 13,000 ; the claimant for which did not turn up.

158. Two separate statements comparing the receipts and expenditure of the State and the Zemindaries with the respective Revised Estimates are given in Appendices XXVII and XXVIII.

159. In the State the large difference that has occurred in actual receipts as compared with the Revised Estimate is due to the receipt of Rs. 2,60,000 as deposit from Their Highnesses the Maharanees which was not provided for, in the Estimate. Excluding this abnormal item, the actual receipts exceeded the forecast by Rs. 1,36,816, while the expenditure fell short by Rs. 71,607. These variations effected an

improvement of Rs. 2,08,423 over the estimated closing balance, bringing up the real surplus to Rs. 7,92,019.

160. In the Zemindaries the increase of Rs. 8,494 under the receipts coupled with the reduction of Rs. 52,904 under expenditure, resulted in an increase of Rs. 61,398 in the closing balance.

CHAPTER VI—MEDICAL.

161. During the year under report 18 Dispensaries in all continued to be maintained by the State—the Victoria Memorial Hospital at the Capital included.

New Patients.

162. A comparative statement of the total number of new patients treated in all Dispensaries and their daily average are shewn below.

PATIENTS.	1335 T.E.			1336 T.E.		
	Outdoor.	Indoor.	Total.	Outdoor.	Indoor.	Total.
	1,05,864	423	1,06,287	98,211	427	98,638
Daily average	290·03	1·15	291·18	269·07	1·16	270·23

Outdoor attendance.

163. The out-door attendance (new + old) totalled 1,67,383 as against 1,82,016 in the preceding year—the daily average being 458·51 against 497·10.

Indoor attendance.

164. Inclusive of the previous year's balance of 13, the total in-patients numbered 427 as against 423 of the preceding year. Of them, 272 were discharged cured, 119 were relieved or discharged otherwise, 21 died and 15 remained under treatment at the close of the year.

Surgical Operations.

165. Altogether 1,173 operations including 29 major cases were performed as against 1,086 and 16 respectively of the previous year.

V. M. Hospital.

166. The total nnmber of new out-patients treated was 11,833 as against 12,068 in the preceding year—the daily average (new + old) being 56·40 against 59·61. The number of in-patients was 400 against 382. Of them, 249 were cured, 115 were either relieved or otherwise discharged, 21 died and 15 remained under treatment at the end of the year. The daily average was 15·58 against 15·15. Rs. 9,337 was expended on this institution during the year under review against Rs. 8,769-7-3—the small increase being due to the grade increments of pay.

Police Case.

167. Altogether 172 Police cases were attended to during the year including 17 Postmortem cases as against 165 and 17 respectively in the previous year.

Ayurvedic Department.

168. As before, two Kavirajes both posted at the Capital Town, treated 70 patients amongst themselves, during the year under review as against 45 in the preceding year. The expenditure covering their salaries and medicines totalled Rs. 3,892-9-6 against Rs. 3,646-12-6 in the year before.

169. Dr. Hira Lal Banerjee, H. M. B., State Homœopath with one Assistant, treated 10,075 patients under this system as against 11,405 in the previous year—the daily average (new + old) being 59·25 against 68·31. Rs. 4,862 was spent in this Department against 5,458-15—the decrease being attributed to the absence of the State Homœopath on sick leave for some months.

Homœopathic Department.

170. 7,423 Vaccine operations were successful out of a total of 9,009 as against 6,115 and 6,889 respectively of the previous year. The permanent Small-pox Doctor assisted by two Inspectors inspected the work of the vaccinators. The total expense on this account stood at Rs. 1,236-11-3 against Rs. 1,168-12-9 in the year before.

Vaccinations.

171. Cholera broke out in a few places making a toll of about a hundred. Small-pox appeared in rather severe form in some parts in the interior, specially amongst the hill tribes who had hitherto been averse to vaccination and revaccination. So far as could be ascertained, there were 98 deaths out of 537 attacks. The epidemic had the effect of inducing the affected tribes to submit to the vaccination in blocks. The Small-pox doctors treated 346 cases of whom 272 were cured.

Public Health.

172. In addition to the permanent Doctor specially appointed for the treatment of such cases at the Capital, another Doctor had to be temporarily appointed for the neighbouring places. 233 patients were treated during the year under review against 395 in the preceding year. Of them 134 were cured, 79 left treatment, 3 died and 17 remained under treatment at the close of the year. In the Moffussil Dispensaries 118 cases were treated in all. The total expenditure on this account amounted to Rs. 1,032-14-6 as against Rs. 823-13-9 in the previous year.

Kala-azar.

173. The insanitary condition of the Capital Town necessitated the expenditure of Rs. 4,998 for clearing the jungles throughout and keeping the drains in good order. This expenditure was fully justified by the fact that both Kala-azar and Malaria went down to an appreciable extent during the year.

Sanitation.

174. Dr. M. M. Majumdar, L. M. S., was the Chief Medical Officer and Dr. S. K. Dutt, L. M. S., his Assistant. Besides, a staff of subordinate medical men, a Lady Doctor and several Mid-wives were retained on their respective duties.

Staff.

175. Dr. M. M. Majumder toured out for 14 days and inspected 5 dispensaries. Dr. S. K. Dutt was also out on tour for 4 days inspecting 2 dispensaries.

Tour.

176. The total expenditure incurred in the Medical Department in the year under review amounted to Rs. 70,278 as against Rs. 66,963 in the preceding year.

Total Expenditure.

CHAPTER VII—PUBLIC INSTRUCTION.

Charge.

177. Mr. S. C. Deb Barman, M. A. (Harvard) continued to be in charge of the Education Department.

Number of schools.

178. The total number of schools during the year was 143 against 147 in the previous year, and the total numerical strength 6,331 against 5,876, excluding private institutions numbering 10 with 180 pupils on the rolls as against 15 with 390. Some Pathshalas were raised to the status of L. V. Schools, while some were discontinued as they did not work well. The number of Primary Schools thus decreased on the whole.

H. E. Schools.

179. In the year under review there were 5 High English Schools in the State—the Umakanta Academy at Agartala, the Radhakishore Institution at Kailasahar, the Brajendrakishore Institution at Bilania, the Birbikram Institution at Dharmanagar and the High School at Sonamura. All the High English Schools were affiliated to the Calcutta University—the Sonamura School having been permanently recognised during the year. The construction of the building of the Sonamura H. E. School was complete. That of a corrugated iron structure for the Infant classes and also of a tiffin shed, likewise with corrugated iron roof, was on the verge of completion. The number of pupils in these H. E. Schools was 1,429 against 1,414 in the previous year and the average daily attendance stood at 1,033·62 against 1,014·19.

Matriculation Centre.

180. Agartala, the State Capital, was, as in the previous year, fixed by the Calcutta University as a Centre for the Matriculation Examination for the year 1927. Only the State High English Schools were allowed to send up candidates to this Centre. The Department looked after the convenience of the candidates coming from Muffussil. The examination was conducted under the direct control and supervision of the Member of the Council of Administration in charge of Education.

Results of the Matriculation Examination.

181. Altogether 55 candidates were sent up for the last Matriculation Examination from the five State High English Schools against 55 in the previous year. Besides these, a teacher from the Dharmanagar B. B. Institution also sat for the Matriculation Examination in this Centre. The details of the result are noted below :—

	No. sent up.	Passed.	1st Division.	2nd Division.	3rd Division.
1. U. K. Academy	14	11	9	2	0
2. R. K. Institution	10	7	6	1	0
3. B. K. Institution	14	9	4	5	0
4. B. B. Institution	11	9	5	4	0
5. Sonamura School	6	5	4	1	0
Total ...	55	41	28	13	0

182. The results were satisfactory considering the general low percentage of successes in the last Matriculation Examination of the Calcutta University. The newly affiliated Sonamura H. E. School deserves every credit in this respect.

183. In the year under review, there were 7 M. E. Schools for boys with 803 pupils on the rolls, against 6 with 646 students in the previous year. The average daily attendance was 608·09 against 474·85.

M. E. Schools

184. There was only one Higher Vernacular School for boys with 50 students on the rolls as against one with 48 students in the previous year, and an average daily attendance of 40·25 against 38·08.

H. V. Schools.

185. The number of Lower Vernacular Schools for boys was 22 against the same number in the previous year. The total numerical strength was 1,210 against 1,229 and the average daily attendance, 922·13 against 935·77 in the previous year. In some of these schools, boys and girls read together.

L. V. Schools.

186. There were 89 Pathshalas for boys, in the year under report, as against 93 in the previous year. The total numerical strength was 2,344 against 2,030, and the average daily attendance 1,814.02 against 1,583·13 in the previous year.

Pathshalas.

187. There was one Middle English School for girls, namely the Maharani Tulsibati Girls' School at Agartala, the State Capital. The numerical strength was 85 against 70 and the average daily attendance 70·4 against 56·3 in the previous year. There was a Motor Bus for the conveyance of the girls during the year.

M. E. Schools for girls.

188. There were 9 Pathshalas for girls against the same number in the previous year. The numerical strength of the school was 189 against 192 and the average daily attendance 137·07 against 138·1 in the previous year. In some of these institutions, under the special order of the Education Department, girls were allowed to read the Lower Vernacular and Upper Vernacular Standard. Besides these, in some of the Pathshalas for boys, both boys and girls were taught together.

Pathshalas for girls.

189. Altogether 405 candidates appeared at the local Scholarship Examinations against 397 in the previous year. Of these, 287 including 24 girls came out successful. 28 students including 1 girl passed the Middle English Examination, 1 student passed the H. V. Examination, 63 including 4 girls passed the L. V. Examination and 195 including 19 girls passed the Pathshala Examination. On the result of the Examinations 17 boys and 6 girls received scholarships varying from Rs. 2 to Rs. 5 per month tenable for two to four years.

Scholarship Examination.

190. In the year under review, there were 9 schools for special training, consisting of 3 *Sanskrit Tols*, 5 *Madrassas* and *Maktobs* and one Artizan School, against 3, 6 and 1 respectively in the previous year. The *Sanskrit Tols* had 42 students on the rolls against 39 in the previous year and the average daily attendance was 28·03 against 27·44. The *Rajakiya Sanskrit Bidyalaya* at Agartala sent up 6 candidates for the Government *Sanskrit* Examinations. The *Madrassas* and *Maktobs* had 167 students

Schools for special Training.

on the rolls against 195 in the previous year, and the average daily attendance was 113·87 against 135·99. The Woodburn Artizan School had 12 boys on the rolls against 13 boys, and the average daily attendance was 5·53 against 4·71 in the previous year.

Non-Bengalee students.

191. The comparative statement below will show the number of Non-Bengalee students receiving education in the several schools of the State :—

Serial number.	Nationality.	Number of students.		Remarks.
		Past year.	Present year.	
1.	Rajkumars	5	8	
2.	Thakurs	179	180	
3.	Manipuris	578	614	
4.	Tripuras	500	583	
5.	Reangs	28	30	
6.	a. Kukis	12	42	
	b. Chakmas	9	12	
	c. Lushais	27	21	
7.	Others...	42	47	
	Total	1,380	1,537	

Reward Examination.

192. The policy of holding Reward Examinations for hill boys was continued and 158 boys appeared at the Examination against 166 boys in the previous year.

Education of Princes and Princesses.

193. Two Maharajkumars continued their studies in the Rajkumar College at Raipur in the Central Provinces being placed in charge of a graduate teacher as in the previous year. The result of their examinations and their progress in health were satisfactory. The Maharajkumaris received education as before under a graduate lady teacher and a Pandit.

Education of other Kumars.

194. Kumar Bhupendra Chandra Deb Barman has been prosecuting studies in the University Law College.

Comilla Kumar Boarding House.

195. The Rajkumar Boarding Institution was started with 4 Maharajkumars and 4 Kumars at Comilla in June, 1926. All of them were admitted to the Zilla School. The results shown by the inmates at the Annual Examination of the School were very satisfactory. Kumar Nandalal Deb Barman stood 1st. in Class VI. and Maharajkumar Hemanta Kishore Deb Barman stood 2nd. in "all round progress" in the junior classes. A considerable improvement was noticed in the health of the boarders in course of a few months' stay at Comilla. The Kumars were placed in charge of a Graduate Superintending Tutor who in addition to his tutorial work looked after the management of the Boarding. Another private tutor coached some of the Kumars in the morning.

The Palace Day School for the Young Kumars.

196. In the Day School for the young Kumars there were 6 students on the rolls belonging to the juvenile classes.

197. 8 Thakur boys were awarded stipends from the Education Department and the course of studies prosecuted by each is noted below :—

Education of Thakur boys.

1. Niranjan Deb Barman—Carmichael Medical College.
2. Joysing Deb Barman—B. L. Class (Calcutta University).
3. Jitendra Chandra Deb Barman—B. Sc. Class.
4. Kamal Krishna Deb Barman—B. A. Class.
5. Nripendra Chandra Deb Barman—I. Sc. Class.
6. Satish Chandra Deb Barman—B. L. Class (Calcutta University).
7. Parendra Chandra Deb Barman—I. A. Class.
8. Suresh Chandra Deb Barman—Government School of Art, Calcutta.

198. There were 35 Boarders in the Thakur Boading House against the same number in the previous year. The number of Boarders successful in the last Annual Examination was 20. One Boarder sat for the last Matriculation Examination and came out successful being placed in the First Division. The staff consisted of one Guardian Superintendent, one Graduate Resident Tutor, one Assistant Tutor and one Manager and Tutor. The services of Thakur Pradipta Chandra Deb Barman, Military Subedar, who was appointed in the previous year to train the boarders up in Military Drill, were no longer required in the year under report. The daily average attendance of the boarders was 28·01, the decline being mainly due to bad health.

Thakur Boarding House.

199. In order to attract hill boys to higher education, as an experimental measure, a Boarding House (attached to the U. K. Academy) was opened at Agartala last year accommodating ten hill boys, all of whom got admitted to the School. The boys received free boarding and lodging having a Superintendent Tutor to look after their studies as well as the boarding management. This Institution received encouraging support from leading head men of Tippera villages.

Tripura Boarding House.

200. There was also another Tippera Boarding House attached to Khowai M. E. School which also received due attention of the Department. The local hill people enthusiastically collected funds to provide this Institution with a permanent house. The Department agreed to sanction all necessary recurring expenditure for this Institution, special grants being made during the year for a cook and a Private Tutor.

201. The following students enjoyed special stipends :—

Special Stipends.

1. Chandrahas Singha.
2. Prokash Chandra Sutradhar.
3. Babu Chand Singha.
4. Navadwip Chandra Singha.
5. Pulin Behari Acharjya.
6. Radharaman Pandey.
7. Mohendra Kumar Roy.
8. Monoranjan Chakravarty.

202. Mr. S. C. Deb Barman, who is also Ex-Officio Inspector of Schools, visited some Boarding Institutions and Schools of Comilla, Bilania, Sonamura, Kailasahar, Dharmanagar, Sadar and Khowai, the tour, on the whole, comprising 32 days. Dr. W. A. Jenkins, D. SC., I. E. S., Inspector of Schools, Chittagong Division, also visited all the State H. E. Schools on behalf of the Calcutta University. He was favourably impressed with the general condition of the State Institutions. The Council of Administration takes this opportunity to record its appreciation of the valuable suggestions made by him for further improvement.

Inspection Work.

203. In the year under review the inspection work of the hill schools suffered a great deal owing to the death of the Sub-Inspector of hill schools. Another Sub-Inspector of hill schools conversant with hill language was, however, appointed in the latter part of the year. The Sub-Inspectors of Schools visited all the schools within their respective jurisdictions. On the whole, their inspection work was satisfactory.

204. At Agartala, the Bir Chandra Library was maintained in two seperate sections, (1) The English Library being located at the Ujjayanta Palace and (2) The Vernacular Section at the new building erected in the vicinity of the local H. E. School. The latter Section was open to the public. The number of English books (including foreign literature) was 4,881 against 4,859 in the previous year and the number of Bengali books (including Sanskrit books) was 1,849 against 1,786 in the previous year. In addition to these, there was a moderate collection of valuable manuscripts in the Palace Library. There were 5 Dailies, 1 Quarterlies, 5 Monthlies and 1 Weekly as against 5, 1 and 5 respectively in the previous year. In the year under review the average daily attendance in the Library rooms was 13·7 against 13·25 and the total uumber of volumes issued to the public was 3,116 against 6,575 in the previous year.

Library.

205. The total expenditure incurred in the Education Department in the year under report, amounted to Rs. 1,16,474 against Rs. 1,08,370. Some of the more important details of expenditure are noted below :—

Expenditure.

Heads of Expenditure.	Amount.	REMARKS.
	Rs.	
1. Primary Education ...	21,595	
2. Secondary Education ...	41,146	The increase is due to general grade increment and the Tripura Boarding House at Sadar.
3. School for special Training	3,907	
4. Boarding Institution for Thakur boys	9,420	
5. Education of Kumars and Kumaris	16,658	The increase is due to the Kumar Boarding House being started at Comilla.
6. Scholarships and Stipends	8,284	The increase is due to some special stipends.
7. Library	1,814	The decrease is due to the death of the Librarian.

206. Rs. 6,810 was incorporated in the general receipts of the year in the State from the accummulated fund of realisations from students, known as the School Fund, in pursuance of the policy adopted in the previous year.

Income.

CHAPTER VIII—ZEMINDARIES.

Chakla Roshnabad Estates.

207. The management of His Highness's Zemindaries in British India continued in the hands of Rai Jyotish Chandra Sen Bahadur, B. A., B. C. S., except for the period 22nd Kartic to 24th Chyte during which he was on leave and Maharajkumar N. Ch. Deb Barman Bahadur was in charge. The Manager was assisted by three Assistant Managers and one Sub-Manager as before.

Management.

208. The gross Revenue demand of the year was Rs. 10,00,451 against Rs. 9,88,681 in the previous year.

209. The total receipts amounted to Rs. 11,67,712 against Rs. 12,72,148 in the previous year. The fall was mainly in the Northern Division where the price of jute was very much lower than in the preceeding year and the paddy crop was also not satisfactory and the paying capacity of the tenants was reduced in consequence.

210. The total expenditure in the year under review was Rs. 11,79,300 including adjustment of old advances against Rs. 12,15,375 in the previous year. Of this Rs. 2,68,970 was on account of Land Revenue and Cesses. The total administrative charges of the Zemindaries including Public Works and Law charges amounted to Rs. 3,56,303. The remainder represents special payments on account of the following items, aggregating Rs. 5,54,027.

Expenditure.

1.	Repayment of old debts ...	...	Rs. 4,99,999
2.	Donation	...	,, 1,549
3.	Medical charges ...	...	,, 11,698
4.	Education charges ...	...	,, 11,029
5.	Religious ceremonies ...	...	,, 6,122
6.	Sansar stipends ...	...	,, 15,780
7.	Repayment of old deposits	...	,, 7,850
			Rs. 5,54,027

211. The result of the year's Settlement operations will appear from the figures noted below :—

Settlement.

KINDS OF SETTLEMENT.	ADDITION TO RENTAL.	NAZAR.
1. Railway relinquished land ...	Rs. 7	Rs. 99
2. *Kaimi and Takshishi Taluk* in the Town ...	,, 7	,, 727
3. Ordinary Town Settlement	,, 165	,, 7,914
4. *Khaspatit* settlement ...	,, 1,126	,, 7,992

KINDS OF SETTLEMENT.	ADDITION TO RENTAL.	NAZAR.
5. Enhancement of rent ...	Rs. 1,628	Rs. 13,068
6. Re-settlement of auction purchased holding ...	" 229	" 12,407
7. *Takshishi Taluk* in the interior	" 16	" 286
8. *Ijara*	" 1,085	
	Rs. 4,263	Rs. 43,105

212. This year's operation improved the rent roll by Rs. 4,263 and brought in a *nazarana* of Rs. 43,105 against Rs. 6,722 and Rs. 71,861 in the previous year.

CHAPTER IX—MISCELLANEOUS.

The Rajmala.

213. The printing of the 1st part of the Rajmala with that of the greater portion of the text of the 2nd part was completed during the year. The literary work connected with the fourth part could not make sufficient progress owing to the time that the editor had to devote to the Introduction, indexing and preface of the first part, as well as to the printing of maps and sketches. The total expenditure incurred during the year, excluding the grant to the periodical *Rabi*, amounted to Rs. 6,098 against Rs. 3,212, Rs. 2,392 and Rs. 3,556 of the previous three years.

Tours of the members of the Council

214. Rai J. C. Sen Bahadur, Vice-President of the Council, was out on tour for 40 days during the 1st 5 months and 24 days of the year. He enjoyed the Pujah holidays and was on leave in continuation till 24th Chaitra, 1336 T. E. *i. e.* 7th April, 1927, owing to illness. Maharajkumar B. K. Dev Barman Bahadur, was out on tour for 24 days, visiting the Dharmanagar and Sonamura Divisions of the State as well as inspecting the Udaipur Road.

215. Dewan B. K. Sen, Chief secretary, was out for 13 days only during the year, as his presence at Agartala was necessary for work as a Judge of the khas Adalat.

216. Babu B. K. Chaterjee, Officer-in charge, Revenue Department, toured for 26 days. Other tours have been noticed in the connected sections.

217. The tours of the Divisional Officers and their Assistants, the Survey Superintendent and the Superintendent of Agriculture are noted below. The Council notices with regret that some tours of the year are unsatisfactory.

State.

1. Sadar—

Divisional Officer—	Thakur Hriday Ranjan Deb Barman ...	31 days.
Asst. Collector—	Babu Prabharanjan Das Gupta, M. A., B. L. ...	38 "
Probationer—	Kumar Nrasingh Chandra Deb Barman ...	24 "

2. Kailashar—
Divisional Officer—Thakur Lalit Mohan
Deb Barman, M. A., B. L. ... 8 days.
" " Babu Sasanka Bhusan Roy, M. A.... 43 "
Second " " Jyotirmoy Ghosh, M. A. ... 23 "
" " Thakur Gokul Chandra
Deb Barman ... 8 "

3. Sonamura—
Divisional Officer—Bisweswar Guha, B. A. ... ... 60 "
Second " Thakur Jyoti Lal
Deb Barman, B. L. ... ... 21 "

4. Bilania—
Divisional Officer—Babu Kamini Kumar Singh ... 55 "
In charge D. O. " Jyotirmoy Ghosh, M. A. ... 5 "
Second Officer " " " ... 7 "

5. Khowai—
Divisional Officer—Thakur Gokul Chandra
Deb Barman ... 11 "
In charge D. O.—Babu Jatindra Mohan Sen ... 6 "

6. Dharmanagar—
Divisional Officer—Babu Kunja Behari
Chakravarty, M. A. B. L. ... 40 "

7. Udaipur—
Divisional Officer—Jogandra Lal
Ganguly, B. L. ... ... 50 "

8. Sabroom—
Divisional Officer—Thakur Lalit Mohan
Deb Barman, M. A. B. L. ... 33 "

9. Amarpur—
Divisional Officer—Babu Surendra Chandra
Guha, B. A. ... ... 72 "

10. Survey
Superintendent—Babu Kamini Kumar Kar ... 28 "

11. Superintendent
of Agriculture—Mr. J. Choudhuri ... ... 56 "

Zemindaries.

1. Babu Pramada Ranjan Bhattacharjee, B. A.,
Assistant Manager, Central Division ... 17 days.
2. " Tarit Mohan Gupta,
Assistant Manager, Southern Division ... 65 "
3. " Surendra Nath Basu, B. L.,
Assistant Manager, Northern Division ... 72 "
4. " Naba Kumar Chakravarty, B. L.,
Sub Manager, Srimangal, ... 62 "
5. " Manada Ranjan Chaudhuri, B. L.,
Inspector, Chakla Roshnabad Estates, ... 141 "

DATED, AGARTALA,
The 18th August, 1927.

By order of the Council of Administration.
B. K. Sen,
Chief Secretary.

APPENDIX

List of the principal Laws and Regulations in force in the Tripura State during 1336 T. E.

Description.	Whether adapted from British Indian Acts.	Whether introduced during the year under report.
CRIMINAL.		
1. Regulation No. III. of 1280 T. E.		
2. Regulation No. I. of 1283 T. E.		
3. Jail Regulation, 1283 T. E.		
4. Regulation No. IV. of 1283 T. E. (Cattle trespass and pound).		
5. Regulation No. III. of 1296 T. E. (Police Regulation).		
6. Act No. IV. of 1321 T. E.–Penal Laws (an amending Act)		
CIVIL.		
1. Civil Law of 1284 T. E.		
2. Rules regarding *chit* suits (small causes) 1287 and 1300 T. E.		
3. Act No. II. of 1313 T. E.—an Act for the regulation of interest on debts.		
4. Act No. II. of 1314 T. E.—Limitation Act	Partly adapted.	
REVENUE.		
1. Act No. I. of 1286 T. E.—Stamp Act		
2. Act No. I. of 1290 T. E.—Sale Law		
3. Act No. I. of 1296 T. E.—Tenancy Act.		
4. Act No. II. of 1296 T. E.—*Abkari*		
5. Act No. II. of 1297 T. E.—Reserved forests.		
6. Act No. I. of 1304 T. E.—Duties on *til* and cotton.		
7. Act No. I. of 1306 T. E.—Registration	Do.	
8. Survey and Settlement Act, 1309 T. E.	Do.	
9. *Tuccavi* Regulation, 1310 T. E.		
10. Act No. I. of 1313 T. E.—Forests.		
11. Act No. I. of 1314 T. E.—(amending the above)		
12. A Law imposing export duty on jute and mustard-seed, 1317 T. E.		
13. Act No. II. of 1321 T. E.—Ghasuri Act		
MISCELLANEOUS.		
1. An Act promulgating certain rules as Law, 1283 T. E.		
2. Regulation for the record of judicial decisions &c., 1284 T. E. ...		
3. Municipal Regulation, 1284 T. E.		
4. Legal Practitioners' Regulation.		
5. Act No. I. of 1297 T. E.—an Act for the regulation of commissions for the examination of witnesses.		
6. Special Regulation against cow slaughter		
7. Rules of evidence		
8. Act I. of 1318 T. E.—Constitution of Courts—(an amending Act).		
9. Leave and allowance Rules	Do.	
10. Act No. I. of 1321 T. E.—Arms Act	Do.	
11. Act No. III. of 1321 T. E.—Constitution of Courts (an amending Act)		

Description.	Whether adapted from British Indian Acts.	Whether introduced during the year under report.
12. Municipal Act No. I of 1322 T. E.		
13. Revenue Sale Amendment Act—1323 T.E.		
14. An Act for the destruction of old records—1323 T.E.		
15. Act I of 1326 T. E.—Regulation regarding Privy Council Appeals.		
16. Act II of 1326 T. E.—Registration of Births and Deaths	Partly adapted.	
17. Act III of 1326 T. E.—Vaccination Act	Do.	
18. Act IV of 1326 T. E.—Public Demands Recovery Act	Do.	
19. Act V of 1326 T. E.—Excise Amendment Act		
20. Act I of 1327 T. E.—Settlement of lands for tea cultivation		
21. Regulation No. 1 of 1328 T. E.—regarding Registration of Coolies		
22. Regulation No. 2 of 1328 T. E.—regarding Export of Tea		
23. Act I of 1329 T. E.—(Absconding sepoys Act)		
24. Act II of 1329 T. E.—(Control of prices of food stuff)		
25. Act III of 1329 T. E.—(Elephants and Buffaloes grazing Act)		
26. Act IV of 1329 T. E.—(House tax on Hill tribes)		
27. Act V of 1329 T. E.—(Legal practitioners, Act)	Do	
28. Act I of 1330 T. E.—Census Act		
29. Act I of 1332 T. E.—Encumbered Estates Act.		
30. Act III of 1332 T. E.—The Opium and Intoxicating Drugs Act.		
31. Amendment of Municipal Act (No. 2 of 1335 T. E.)		
32. An Act defining the term Minister (Act No 1 of 1335 T. E.)		
33. Hackney Carriage Bill.		
34. A Bill amending Act (No. I of 1336 T. E.)		
35. A Bill amending Rules about Survey and Settlement.		
36. A Bill for prevention of gambling.		

ii.

Statement showing the strength, cost, and other particulars of the Military Force in Tripura State for 1336 T. E.

Arm of service.	Number of fighting officers and men.						Details of force at the end of the current year.						Total cost on account of pay and allowances of the force, including followers. (Excluding grain allowance.)	Remarks.
	At the end of last year.	Recruited this year.	Casualties.			At the end of the current year.	Number of regiments, battalions, or Batteries.	Number of guns.	Number of men.					
			Died.	Invalided.	Discharged, deserted, &c.				European commissioned officers.	Native commissioned officers.	Non-commissioned officers.	Fighting men.		
1	2	3	4	5	6	7	8	9	10	11	12	13	14	15
Infantry ...	218	52	1	1	21	247	1	291 and one small cannon.	—	—	40	207	Rs. 40,240	

III.

Statement showing the strength, cost, discipline, and education of the Police for the year 1336 T.E.

Description of office.	Number.	Pay of grade.	Total cost. (Excluding grain allowance.)	Punishments. Dismissed.	Punishments. Fined, degraded, or suspended departmentally.	Punishments. Punished judicially.	Rewards. By promotion.	Rewards. By money.	Education. Number able to read and write.	Education. Number under instruction.	Remarks.
1	2	3	4	5	6	7	8	9	10	11	12
		Rs.									
Superintendent of Police	1	150-10-250	68,377	—	—	—	—	—	1	—	
Asst, Superintendent „	1	75-5-100		—	—	—	—	—	1	—	
Inspector	4	50 to 80		—	—	—	—	—	4	—	
Daroga	25	25-2-45		—	6	—	—	4	25	—	
Naib Daroga	13	15-1-25		—	—	—	—	1	13	—	
Writer Constable	13	11		—	2	—	—	—	13	—	
Subadar	1	25-2-45		—	—	—	—	—	1	—	
Jamadar	10	15-1-25		—	1	—	—	—	9	—	
Constable	236	8 to 12		13	36	—	—	1	200	—	
Chowkidar	175	5		—	—	—	—	—	—	—	
Spy	3	15 & 20		—	—	—	—	—	—	—	
	482			13	45			6	267		

IV.

Statement showing the working of the Police in the Tripura State during the year 1336 T.E.

State.	Number of offences.		Number of accused arrested.		Number of accused sent for trial.		Number of accused convicted.		Number of accused acquitted or discharged.		Percentage convicted of accused arrested.		Percentage convicted of accused sent for trial.		REMARKS.
	Past year.	Present year.	Past year.	Present year.	Past year.	Present year.	Past year.	Present year.	Past year.	Present year.	Past year.	Present year.	Past year.	Present year.	
1	2	3	4	5	6	7	8	9	10	11	12	13	14	15	16
Tripura State	1,282	1,318	802	711	824	638	187	171	87	102	68·2	54·3	68·2	62·2	

V.

Statement showing the value of property stolen and amount of recoveries in the Tripura State during the year 1336 T. E.

State.	Amount stolen.		Amount recovered.		Percentage of recoveries of property stolen.		REMARKS.
	Past year.	Present year.	Past year.	Present year.	Past year.	Present year.	
1	2	3	4	5	6	7	8
Tripura State	Rs 22,695-10-0	Rs 18,115-4-3	Rs 10,324-6-3	Rs 2,710-5-0	45·4	14·95	

VI.

Statement showing the number of crimes committed, number of cases disposed of, and cases awaiting trial in the Tripura State during the year 1336 T. E.

Description of offences.		Number of offences: Balance from past year.	Number of offences: Committed during the present year.	Number of offences: Total.	Number of cases disposed of during the past year.	Number of cases disposed of during the present year.	Number of cases awaiting trial.	Number of persons apprehended.	Number of persons convicted.	Number of persons sentenced: Imprisonment: Simple.	Number of persons sentenced: Imprisonment: Rigorous.	Number of persons sentenced: Imprisonment and fine: Simple.	Number of persons sentenced: Imprisonment and fine: Rigorous.	Number of persons sentenced: Fine only.	Number of persons sentenced: Whipping.	Number of persons sentenced: Capital punishment.	Number of persons sentenced: Total.	Number of persons acquitted or discharged.	Number of persons confined being insane.	Number of persons dead during or before trial.	Term of imprisonment: Under one month.	Term of imprisonment: From 1 to 2 months.	Term of imprisonment: From 2 to 3 months.	Term of imprisonment: From 3 to 6 months.	Term of imprisonment: From 6 to 12 months.	Term of imprisonment: From 1 to 2 years.	Term of imprisonment: From 2 to 3 years.	Term of imprisonment: From 3 to 5 years.	Term of imprisonment: Above 5 years.	Term of imprisonment: Transportation.	Term of imprisonment: Capital punishment.	Persons awaiting trial.	Remarks.
1		2	3	4	5	6	7	8	9	10	11	12	13	14	15	16	17	18	19	20	21	22	23	24	25	26	27	28	29	30	31	32	33
Class I. Offences against the State, public tranquillity, safety and justice &c.	cognizable ...	16	22	38	22	26	12	160	43	0	10	0	8	25	0	0	43	59	0	0	0	0	0	1	8	9	0	0	0	0	0	58	*a.* Three persons transferred.
	non-cognizable	13	47	60	47	45	15	20	0	0	0	0	0	0	0	0	0	16	0	0	0	0	0	0	0	0	0	0	0	0	0	4	
Class II. Offences against person.	cognizable ...	50	207	257	187	192	65	*a*462	66	0	25	0	18	23	0	0	66	264	0	4	6	4	2	9	3	6	4	3	5	1	0	125	*b.* Nine persons transferred and two persons have been warned for the future.
	non-cognizable	79	302	381	333	321	60	307	34	3	0	2	0	29	0	0	34	229	0	0	5	0	0	0	0	0	0	0	0	0	0	44	
Class III. Offences against property.	cognizable ...	354	922	1276	1007	998	278	*b* 1940	*b*286	5	75	0	9	195	0	0	284	1209	0	4	19	18	23	16	1	3	0	3	6	0	0	432	
	non-cognizable	55	232	287	207	244	43	*c*335	21	0	2	0	0	19	0	0	21	242	0	0	1	0	0	1	0	0	0	0	0	0	0	64	*c.* Eight persons transferred.
Class IV. Other offences.	cognizable ...	29	111	140	89	109	31	231	22	1	8	0	1	12	0	0	22	130	0	0	1	3	2	1	3	0	0	0	0	0	0	79	
	non-cognizable	57	357	414	361	341	73	*d*162	*d*15	0	1	0	0	6	0	0	7	105	0	0	1	0	0	0	0	0	0	0	0	0	0	40	*d.* Two persons transferred, five persons released on bail, and three persons have been warned for the future.
Total cognizable ...	...	449	1262	1711	1305	1325	386	2793	417	6	118	0	36	255	0	0	415	1662	0	8	26	25	27	27	15	18	4	6	11	1	0	694	
Total non-cognizable ...	...	204	938	1142	948	951	191	824	70	3	3	2	0	54	0	0	62	592	0	0	7	0	0	1	0	0	0	0	0	0	0	152	
GRAND TOTAL ...	...	653	2200	2853	2253	2276	577	3617	487	9	121	2	36	309	0	0	477	2254	0	8	33	25	27	28	15	18	4	6	11	1	0	846	

VII.

Statement showing the number of offences reported and dealt with by the various Courts in the Tripura State during the year 1336 T.E.

Name of Court.	Number of offences reported during the year.		Number of persons dealt with.								Persons disposed of.					Persons remaining at the end of the year.	Remarks.
			Remaining at the end of last year.	Brought to trial in 1335 T. E.					Total.								
	Last year.	Present year.		Arrested by Police.	Upon warrant.	On summons.	Voluntary.	Arrested in presence of the Magistrate.	Last year.	Present year.	Discharged without trial.	Acquitted.	Convicted.	Committed or referred.	Died, escaped, or transferred &c.		
1	2	3	4	5	6	7	8	9	10	11	12	13	14	15	16	17	18
Sadar Magistracy	733	709	160	209	187	273	6	5	999	840	311	188	121	27	0	193	
Sonamura " ...	341	222	100	112	42	117	51	3	536	425	101	159	86	3	4	72	
Bilonia " ...	318	243	104	84	22	113	222	23	596	568	160	193	73	6	0	136	
Kailashahar " ...	209	243	265	79	70	135	34	1	459	584	206	101	48	3	1	225	
Khowai " ...	175	167	19	18	46	187	7	0	290	277	64	133	12	5	14	49	
Dharmanagar " ...	246	263	96	41	15	122	41	0	295	315	113	84	48	12	9	49	
Udaipur " ...	213	303	116	83	106	208	17	6	326	536	258	108	59	1	1	109	
Sabrum " ...	57	50	3	7	5	35	11	0	95	61	19	30	11	0	0	1	
TOTAL ...	2,292	2,200	863	633	493	1,190	389	38	3,596	a 3,606	1,232	996	458	b 57	29	834	

a Excluding 11 persons pending before the court of Sessions at the close of the previous year.

b Including 11 persons pending from last year, the total number of persons for trial before the Court of Sessions was 68; of these, 29 were convicted. 4 discharged without trial, 22 acquitted, while 1 died during trial and 12 remained under trial.

VIII.

Statement of Criminal cases in which British Subjects were concerned for 1336 T. E.

DESCRIPTION OF OFFENCES.		Cases pending since the previous year.	Cases instituted during the year.	Total number of cases.	Cases in which complainants were British subjects.	Cases in which both parties were British subjects.	CASES IN WHICH DEFENDANTS WERE BRITISH SUBJECTS. Cases pending since the previous year.	Cases instituted during the year.	Total number of cases.	Cases disposed of. Rejected, Compromised or Dismissed without enquiry.	Cases disposed of. Tried.	Cases pending at the close of the year.	Persons under trial at the close of the previous year.	Persons brought to trial during the year.	Total number of persons under trial.	Convicted.	Acquitted or Discharged.	Died, or Escaped &c.	Under trial at the close of the year.	REMARKS.
Class I. Offences against the State &c.	cognizable ...	2	4	6	0	0	2	4	6	2	3	1	8	16	24	4	10	0	10	
	non-cognizable ...	1	3	4	2	0	1	1	2	1	0	1	0	0	0	0	0	0	0	
Class II. Offences against person.	cognizable ...	5	27	32	4	18	5	23	28	15	9	4	17	42	59	10	39	2	8	* Of this number 177 were discharged without trial, the cases being dismissed, compromised or struck off on default. Excluding 3 dead and 118 pending, the actual number of persons tried was 349, of whom 151 or 43·266 were convicted as against 52·955 of the previous year.
	non-cognizable ...	4	42	46	12	26	4	30	34	20	8	6	1	44	45	4	36	0	5	
Class III. Offences against property.	cognizable ...	81	189	270	32	67	79	159	238	83	103	52	102	301	403	118	201	1	83	
	non-cognizable ...	10	60	70	10	41	10	50	60	42	9	9	8	52	60	7	49	0	4	
Class IV. Other offences.	cognizable ...	13	19	32	3	9	13	16	29	13	13	3	9	34	43	7	31	0	5	
	non-cognizable ...	6	41	47	15	18	6	26	32	24	3	5	1	12	13	1	9	0	3	
Total cognizable ...		101	239	340	39	94	99	202	301	113	128	60	136	393	529	139	281	3	106	
Total non-cognizable ...		21	146	167	39	85	21	107	128	87	20	21	10	108	118	12	94	0	12	
GRAND TOTAL ...		122	385	507	78	179	120	309	429	200	148	81	146	501	647*	151	375	3	118	

IX.

Statement of Extradition Cases for the year 1336 T. E.

Names of Courts.	Nature of cases.	Number of persons against whom warrants were applied for.	Number of persons arrested and surrendered.	Number of persons who appeared of their own accord or were subsequently arrested within this territory.	Number at large at the close of the year.	Result. Convicted.	Result. Acquitted or Discharged.	Pending trial at the close of the year.	Remarks.
Sadar Magistracy ...	Dacoity ...	5	3	2	0	0	0	5	
	Theft ...	4	0	4	0	3	1	0	
	Culpable homicide not amounting to murder ...	3	0	3	0	0	0	3	Committed to Sessions.
	Receiving stolen property ...	3	2	1	0	1	2	0	
	Escape from lawful custody ...	2	0	2	0	2	0	0	
	Wrongful confinement and rape ...	2	0	2	0	0	0	2	
Sonamura " ...	Cheating ...	1	1	0	1	1	0	0	
	Theft ...	2	2	0	0	1	0	1	
	Escape from lawful custody ...	1	1	0	0	0	1	0	
	Theft ...	1	0	0	1	0	0	0	
Bilonia " ...	Theft ...	3	3	0	0	3	0	0	
	Wrongful assembly, assault resistance to lawful apprehension, rescuing offenders from lawful custody ...	7	0	7	0	0	7	0	
	Theft ...	1	1	0	0	1	0	0	
	Theft, unlawful assembly, escape from lawful custody, resistance to lawful apprehension, rescuing offenders from lawful custody ...	3	0	3	0	3	0	0	
	Theft ...	1	0	1	0	1	0	0	
	Unlawful assembly and theft ...	7	5	2	0	0	0	7	
	Theft, resistance to lawful apprehension, rescuing offenders from lawful custody ...	3	0	0	3	0	0	0	
	Unlawful assembly, criminal trespass, theft and assault ...	3	0	0	3	0	0	0	
Kailashahar " ...	Culpable homicide not amounting to murder ...	1	0	0	1	0	0	0	
	Theft ...	1	1	0	0	0	0	1	
	Escape from lawful custody ...	1	1	0	0	0	0	1	
	Escape from lawful custody ...	1	0	0	1	0	0	0	
	Escape from lawful custody ...	1	1	0	0	1	0	0	
	Theft ...	1	0	0	1	0	0	0	
Khowai " ...	Criminal breach of trust ...	1	1	0	0	0	0	1	
	Kidnapping ...	1	1	0	0	0	0	1	
Dharmanagar " ...	Theft ...	6	0	0	6	0	0	0	
Sabroom " ...	Theft ...	4	3	0	1	0	2	1	
	Unlawful assembly and hurt ...	7	4	0	3	0	4	0	
	Total ...	77	30	27	20	17	17	23	

X.

Statement showing the results of appeals against decisions passed by the Criminal Courts in the Tripura State during the year 1336 T. E.

Tribunals.	Number of applications	Number of persons and cases.																Remarks.
		Applications rejected.		Sentences.						Proceedings quashed.		Referred.		Furher enquiry, &c, ordered.		Pending.		
				Confirmed.		Modified.		Reversed.										
		Persons.	Cases.	Persons.	Cases.	Persons.	Cases.	Persons.	Cases.	Persons.	Cases.	Persons.	Cases.	Persons.	Cases.	Persons.	Cases.	
Khas Adalat. ...	269	35	26	146	124	52	21	97	63	1	1	—	—	10	10	29	24	

XI.

Civil Work.—Nature and value of original suits filed and disposed of during the year 1336 T. E.

Tribunal.	Opening balance.		Filed during the year, received by transfer or on remand.		Total.		Disposed of during the year		Closing balance.	
	Past year.	Present year.	Past year.	Present year.	Past year.	Present year.	Past year.	Present year.	Past year.	Present year.
Khas Adalat Original Side	49	31	26	34	75	65	44	29	31	36
Sadar Dewani Adalat	489	485	737	787	1,226	1,272	741	828	485	444
Sonamura „	90	38	217	186	307	224	269	188	38	36
Bilonia „	17	21	123	141	140	162	119	127	21	35
Kailashahar „	309	330	274	308	583	638	253	428	330	210
Khowai „	26	21	130	132	156	153	135	100	21	53
Dharmanagar	52	69	170	230	222	299	153	179	69	120
Udaipur „	41	102	265	188	306	290	204	235	102	55
Sabrum „	1	0	15	8	16	8	16	7	0	1
Total...	1,074	1,097	1,957	2,014	3,031	2,111	1,934	2,121	1,097	990

Tribunal.	Suits filed during present year.									Suits disposed of during present year.						Suits not estimable in money.	Remarks.
	Value.	Suits re landed property.	Suits for money transaction.	Suits for other rights.	Number of suits under Rs. 100.	Number of suits above Rs. 100 and under Rs. 500.	Number of suits above Rs. 500 and under Rs. 1,000.	Number of suits above Rs. 1,000 and under Rs. 5,000.	Number of suits above Rs. 5000.	Exparte.	Admitted and compromised.	Struck off the file.	Otherwise disposed of.	Value.	Average duration.		
	Rs. a. p.													Rs. a. p.	Y. m. d.		
Khas Adalat Original Side	129,922-5-6	21	3	10	0	0	0	25	4	1	18	5	5	63,210-7-6	0-4-4	5	
Sadar Dewani Adalat	63,901-10-9	335	269	183	400	209	14	0	0	430	129	90	179	55,136-2-9	0-11-12	164	
Sonamura „	15,268-1-9	55	106	25	115	45	1	0	0	55	10	19	104	17,911-14-3	0-1-1	25	
Bilonia „	6,887-7-9	95	13	33	99	13	2	0	0	58	19	38	12	6,164-3-6	0-2-13	27	
Kailashahar „	18,391-11-6	146	153	9	233	42	3	0	0	151	83	69	125	36,517-12-9	0-3-12	30	
Khowai „	8,292-15-6	26	102	4	76	26	0	0	0	33	26	20	21	4,978-12-6	0-0-28	30	
Dharmanagar	18,551-14-9	56	59	115	136	52	3	0	0	30	29	43	72	8,840-11-3	0-0-24	39	
Udaipur „	14,388-1-0	12	143	33	107	48	1	0	0	77	38	26	94	9,694-13-0	0-3-16	32	
Sabrum „	942-10-9	2	6	0	2	4	0	0	0	1	2	1	3	814-10-9	0-3-2	2	
Total...	2,76,546-15-3	748	854	412	1168	439	24	25	4	836	354	316	615	2,03,269-8-3	0-3-12	354	

XII.

Civil Work.—Results of applications for Execution of Decrees, 1336 T.E.

Tribunal.	Opening balance.		Value of opening balance for present year.	Applications brought to the Register.			Total.			Disposed of.			Closing balance.			Nature of applications pending disposal at the close of the year.			REMARKS.
	Past year.	Present year.		Past year.	Present year.	Value for present year.	Past year.	Present year.	Value for present year.	Past year.	Present year.	Value for present year.	Past yaer.	Present year.	Value for present year.	Below 6 months.	Below 12 months.	Above 12 months.	
			Rs. a. p.			*Rs. a. p.*	*R.*		*Rs. a. p.*			*Rs. a. p.*			*Rs. a. p.*				
Khas Adalat (Original side)	19	21	45,332-10-3	7	5	10,957-10-6	26	26	56,290-4-9	5	12	7,343-4-0	21	14	48,947-0-9	1	3	10	
Sadar Dewani Adalat ...	154	142	24,717-0-0	199	258	23,884-9-6	353	400	48,601-9-6	211	221	22,428-5-9	142	179	26,173-3-9	108	37	34	
Sonamura Ditto ...	31	36	4,102-6-6	117	60	9,501-10-0	148	96	13,604-0-6	112	79	10,694-12-0	36	17	2,909-4-6	16	0	1	
Bilonia Ditto ...	16	8	1,044-0-9	53	38	4,934-12-3	69	46	5,978-13-0	61	36	4,993-9-3	8	10	985-3-9	10	0	0	
Kailashahar Ditto ...	77	99	14,339-15-6	79	63	6,076-0-0	156	162	20,415-15-6	57	98	10,856-11-9	99	64	9,559-8-9	17	16	31	
Khowai Ditto ...	9	12	703-6-0	43	35	4,084-1-6	52	47	4,787-7-6	40	39	3,110-0-0	12	8	1,677-7-6	8	0	0	
Dharmanagar Ditto ...	51	47	6,017-11-9	48	59	5,261-6-0	99	106	11,279-1-9	52	77	7,718-4-9	47	29	3,560-13-0	20	6	3	
Udaipur Ditto ...	37	36	6,817-3-3	111	69	8,544-15-6	148	105	15,362-2-9	112	82	11,477-13-3	36	23	3,884-5-6	22	0	1	
Sabrum Ditto ...	0	1	226-8-3	4	4	301-10-9	4	5	528-3-0	3	5	528-3-0	1	0	0	0	0	0	
Total ...	394	402	1,33,00-14-3	661	591	73,546-12-0	1,055	993	1,76,847-10-3	653	649	79,150-15-9	402	344	97,696-10-6	202	62	80	

XIII.

Civil Work.—Number and results of appeals in civil suits, 1336 T. E.

Tribunal.	Opening balance.		Filed during.		Total.		Disposed of during.		Closing balance.		Value of appeals filed during.		How disposed of.										Average duration.	
													Decisions confirmed.		Decisions reversed.		Decisions amended.		Cases remanded for retrial.		Cases compromised and otherwise disposed of.			
	Past year.	Present year.	Past year.	Present year.	Past year.	Present year.	Past year.	Present year.	Past year.	Present year.	Past year.	Present year.	Past year.	Present year.	Past year.	Present year.	Past year.	Present year.	Past year.	Present year.	Past year.	Present year.	Past year.	Present year.
											Rs. a. p.	*Rs. a. p.*											*Y.m.d.*	*Y.m.d.*
Khas Adalat	61	65	163	169	224	234	159	188	65	46	19,032-13-6	20,070-1-6	63	80	58	48	9	8	11	24	18	28	0-2-2	0-2-1

XIV.

Statement showing the number of persons confined in the jails and lock-ups in the Tripura State during the year 1336 T.E.

Stations.	Number of prisons.	Number of Prisoners. Remaining from last year.	Admitted during the year.	Total. Past year.	Total. Present year.	Daily Average. Past year.	Daily Average. Present year.	Number of prisoners remaining at the end of the year.	Cost of jail and prisoners.	Average period in days of accused under trial.	Remarks showing mortality among convicts in jail.
									Rs.		
Agartala	1	83	261	256	344	67·71	96·47	111	12,576	65·8	
Sonamura	1	4	84	99	88	3·91	4·33	19	692	16·86	
Kailashahar	1	3	77	58	80	4·03	6·20	4	830	28·96	
Bilonia	1	4	52	57	56	1·23	2·82	—	507	20·42	One convict died of Chronic Diarrhœa. One convict died of Meningitis.
Khowai	1	—	27	40	27	2·76	·49	2	222	8·04	One undertrial died of Double Pneumonia.
Dharmanagar	1	20	51	53	71	5·47	3·34	3	589	15·46	One undertrial died of Malarial Fever with enlarged Spleen.
Udaipur	1	2	41	40	43	1·91	2·21	—	296	18·30	
Sabrum	1	—	9	9	9	·15	·14	—	112	2·2	
TOTAL ...	8	116	602	612	718	87·17	116·00	139	15,824	22·00	

XV.

Registration of documents in the Tripura State during the year 1336 T.E.

Name of State	Documents presented for registration.		Nature of documents presented.										Documents registered.		Value of documents registered.		Documents of which registration has been refused.		Documents remaining unregistered at the end of the year.		Remarks.
			Mortgages.		Sale deeds.		Wills.		Money bonds.		Miscellaneous.										
	Past year.	Present year.	Past year.	Present year.	Past year.	Present year.	Past year.	Present year.	Past year.	Present year.	Past year.	Present year.	Past year.	Present year.	Past year.	Present year.	Past year.	Present year.	Past year.	Present year.	
1	2	3	4	5	6	7	8	9	10	11	12	13	14	15	16	17	18	19	20	21	22
															Rs.	*Rs.*					
Tripura State	13,285	12,896	3,452	3,456	5,858	5,634	7	6	343	385	3,605	34,15	13,100	12,742	21,12,171	21,63,613	136	156	74	72	

XVI.

Statement showing the receipts and expenditure on account of Registration during the year 1336 T.E.

Description.	Past Year.			Present Year.			Remarks.
	Number of deeds.	Value of property.	Fees realised.	Number of deeds.	Value of property.	Fees realised.	
		Rs.	Rs.		Rs.	Rs.	
Mortgages	3,452	4,91,813	3,574	3,456	5,37,078	3,517	
Sale deeds	5,858	12,76,855	7,845	5,634	11,71,329	7,951	
Will	7	—	32	6	2,155	26	
Money bonds	343	32,004	265	385	54,101	318-8	
Miscellaneous	3,605	4,34,699	4,064	3,415	4,79,664	4,175-8	
Total ...	13,265	22,35,371	15,780	12,896	22,44,327	15,988	
Total Expenditure ...	—	—	4,336	—	—	4,682	
Net Income ...	—	—	11,444	—	—	11,306	

XVII.

Receipts and expenditure of the Municipalities in the Tripura State during the year 1336 T.E.

NAME.	Opening balance.	RECEIPTS DURING THE YEAR.					Total in the current year.	EXPENDITURE DURING THE YEAR.		Balance at the close of the year.	REMARKS.
		Past.	Present.					Past.	Present.		
			State grant.	Tax.	Miscellaneous.	Total.					
1	2	3	4	5	6	7	8	9	10	11	12
	Rs. A.P.	Rs. A.P.	Rs. A.P.	Rs. A.P.	Rs. A.P.	Rs. A.P.	Rs. A.P.	Rs. A.P.	Rs. A.P.	Rs. A.P.	
Agartala Municipality. ...	17,443-11-0	40,409-13-3	9,706-0-0	3,685-11-9	7,165-3-6 *a*	20,556-15-3	37,961-14-0	22,966-2-3	27,117-13-3 *b*	10,844-0-9 *c*	*a*. Including Rs. 5,815-11-3 as income from the Bazar and Rs. 202 as deposits and advances recovered. *b*. Including Rs. 11,949-13-9 as expenditure on Bazar improvement and Rs. 198-8 as advances and deposits paid. *c*. Including Rs. 9,538-2-6 of the Bazar improvement fund.

XVIII.

Statement of rainfall in the Tripura State during the year 1336 T.E.

STATE.	Baisak.	Jaisth.	Asar.	Sravan.	Bhadra.	Asvin.	Kartik.	Agrahayan.	Pous.	Magh.	Falgoon.	Chait.	Total.	Total of past year.	Average of past 5 years.	REMARKS.
Tripura State ...	11'64	11'85	15'57	17'17	17'63	8'50	2'07	'10	2'54	1'98	2'15	8'94	110'04	108'28	93'92	

1. Maximum 128'83—Dharmanagar Division. 2. Minimum 66'05—Sadar Division.

XIX.

Statement as to the prices of staple food-grains for the year 1336 T.E.

Articles.	During Chait (past year).			During Chait (present year).			Remarks.
	Rs.	*a.*	*p.*	*Rs.*	*a.*	*p.*	
(1) Rice							
Maximum	9	0	0	10	0	0	
Minimum	6	0	0	6	0	0	
(2) Paddy							
Maximum	4	0	0	4	8	0	
Minimum	2	12	0	2	12	0	

XX.

Expenditure on Public Works during the year 1336 T.E.

Description of work.	State funds.			Local funds.			Total.	Remarks.
	Original.	Repairs.	Total.	Original.	Repairs.	Total.		
	Rs.	*Rs.*	*Rs.*	*Rs.*	*Rs.*	*Rs.*	*Rs.*	
Buildings	85,244	79,627	1,64,871	—	—	—	1,64,945	
Roads and bridges ...	45,055	31,121	76,176	—	—	—	76,176	
Tanks	63,42	2,929	9,271	—	—	—	9,271	
Miscellaneous works ...	5,768	76	5,844	—	—	—	5,844	
Total ...	1,42,409	1,13,753	2,56,162	—	—	—	2,56,236	
Minor works at the Rajbari (*Karkhana*)	—	6,172	6,172	—	—	—	6,172	
Establishment charges ...	—	—	18,681	—	—	—	18,681	
Grand Total ...	1,42,409	1,19,925	2,81,015	—	—	—	2,81,089	

XXI.

Statement showing the excise shops and excise revenue of the Tripura State during the year 1336 T.E.

Names of Divisions.	Country Spirit.		Country Spirit, Opium and Ganja.		Ganja and Opium.		Tari.		Total.		Remarks.
	Number of shops.	Revenue.	Number of shops.	Revenue demand.	Number of shops.	Revenue.	Number of shops.	Revenue.	Number of shops.	Revenue realised.	
		Rs.		Rs.						Rs.	
1. Sadar	1	5,500	7	24,198	—	—	—	—	8	29,698	
2. Kailashahar ...	1	1,590	7	14,528	—	—	—	—	8	16,118	
3. Sonamura	—	—	1	3,785	—	—	—	—	1	3,785	
4. Belonia	—	—	1	1,750	—	—	—	—	1	1,750	
5. Khowai	—	—	4	13,260	—	—	—	—	4	13,260	
6. Dharmanagar ...	—	—	4	9,141	—	—	—	—	4	9,141	
7. Udaipur	—	—	2	2,891	—	—	—	—	2	2,891	
8. Sabroom	—	—	1	830	—	—	—	—	1	830	
9. Amarpur	1	15	1	36	—	—	—	—	2	51	
	3	7,105	28	70,419	—	—	—	—	31	77,524	

F

XXII.

*Statement of Medical Relief * afforded in the Tripura State during the year 1336 T.E.*

Dispensary.	Number of Patients Treated. (new)		Results of In-door Patients. (new)				Expenditure.	Daily Average. (old + new)			No. of Surgical Operations Performed.			No. of Persons Vaccinated during the Year.			Remarks.
	Outdoor.	Indoor.	Dis-charged.	Absented.	Died.	Remain-ing under treatment.		Outdoor.	Indoor.	Total.	Major.	Minor.	Total.	Success-fully.	Unsuc-cessfully.	Total.	
1. Victoria Memorial Hospital at Agartala and the Charitable Dispensary attached to it...	11,833	400	249	115	21	15	Rs. 9,337	56·41	15·58	71·99	17	285	302	948	411	1,359	
2. Palace Dispensary ...	10,257	0	0	0	0	0	10,453	61·32	0	61·32	0	0	0	0	0	0	
3. Homoeopathic ...	10,075	0	0	0	0	0	4,862	59·25	0	59·25	0	0	0	0	0	0	* This Statement excludes figures regarding Kaviraji treatment.
4. Old Agartala ...	5,035	0	0	0	0	0	1,437	23·98	0	23·98	0	45	45	960	187	1,147	
5. Bishalgar ...	5,320	0	0	0	0	0	1,251	20·29	0	20·29	0	59	59	1,369	243	1,612	
6. Sonamura ...	6,730	6	6	0	0	0	1,531	32·00	·18	32·18	1	80	81	493	50	543	
7. Udaipur ...	3,606	0	0	0	0	0	1,221	13·32	0	13·32	0	39	39	215	30	245	
8. Amarpur ...	802	0	0	0	0	0	931	4·09	0	4·09	1	13	14	231	44	275	
9. Bilonia... ...	5,257	8	7	1	0	0	1,309	23·79	·31	24·10	0	110	110	54	6	60	
10. Loongthung ...	2,512	0	0	0	0	0	1,111	11·02	0	11·02	1	27	28	157	17	174	† This figure shows the actual number of outdoor patients treated, the total outdoor attendance during the year being 1,67,383 against 1,82,016 in the previous year.
11. Sabroom ...	2,5 3	2	2	0	0	0	1,292	9·95	·08	10·03	0	41	41	297	2	299	
12. Khowai ...	4,893	0	0	0	0	0	1,442	16·87	0	16·87	0	46	46	922	220	1,142	
13. Kailashahar ...	8,890	0	0	0	0	0	1,131	27·83	0	27·83	4	163	167	329	142	471	
14. Fatik-roy ...	2,468	0	0	0	0	0	1,062	9·64	0	9·64	0	49	49	74	12	86	
15. Kamalpur ...	3,997	0	0	0	0	0	1,106	17·46	0	17·46	0	43	43	327	66	393	
16. Dharmanagar ...	4,930	11	8	3	0	0	1,420	26·46	·31	26·77	5	88	93	913	147	1,060	
17. Mohanpur ...	2,498	0	0	0	0	0	1,042	11·23	0	11·23	0	8	8	134	9	143	
18. Dhaleswar ...	6,525	0	0	0	0	0	1,324	33·60	0	33·60	0	48	48	0	0	0	
Total ...	†98,211	427	272	119	21	15	43,262	458·51	16·46	474·49	29	1,144	1,173	7,423	1,586	9,009	

XXIII.

Vital statistics of the Tripura State for the year 1336 T.E.

State.	Population.	Births.		Increase.	Decrease.	Deaths.		Increase.	Decrease.	Ratio per 1,000 of population.				Remarks.
										Births.		Deaths.		
		Past year.	Present year.			Past year.	Present year.			Past year.	Present year.	Past year.	Present year.	
Tripura State ...	3,02,657	2,361	2,509	148	—	2,274	2,595	321	—	7·8	8·28	7·5	9·8	

XXIV.

Education Return (A)—Particulars as to the schools maintained during the year 1336 T.E.

Number of Schools.		Description of Schools.	Number of Pupils on the rolls on the last day of Chait.		Daily Average Attendance.		Remarks.
Past year.	Present year.		Past year.	Present year.	Past year.	Present year.	
5	5	High English Schools	1,414	14,29	1,014·19	1,033·62	
6	7	Middle English Schools for boys ...	646	803	474·85	608·09	
1	1	Middle English Schools for girls ...	70	85	56·3	70·40	
1	1	Higher Vernacular Schools for boys	48	50	38·08	40·25	
22	22	* Lower Vernacular Schools for boys.	1,229	1,210	935·77	922·13	* In some of these schools boys and girls read together.
93	89	* Pathsalas for boys	2,030	2,344	1,583·13	1,814·02	
9	9	Do for girls	192	189	138·1	137·07	
		Special Schools :—					
6	5	Madrassas	195	167	135·99	113·87	
3	3	Sanskrit *Tols*	39	42	27·44	28·03	
1	1	Woodburn Artisan School... ...	13	12	4·71	5·53	
TOTAL 147	143		5,876	6,331	4,408·56	4,773·01	

XXV.

Education Return (B) Race of Students, 1336 T. E.

Names of Divisions.	No. of Schools.			No. of Students.			Race.												Average daily attendance.		Remarks.
															Bengalee.						
	For boys.	For girls.	Total.	Boys.	Girls.	Total.	Rajkumars.	Thakurs.	Manipuris	Tripuras.	Reangs.	Chakmas.	Kukis.	Lusais.	Hindus.	Musalmans.	Christians.	Others.	Boys.	Girls.	
1. Sadar Division ...	48	3	51	1,830	135	1,965	8	167	150	297	0	0	42	0	740	546	3	12	1,423'01	98'86	
2. Kailashahar „	23	2	25	980	97	1,077	0	0	347	32	2	12	0	21	503	160	0	0	726'43	69'84	
3. Sonamura „	20	1	21	935	81	1,016	0	10	0	37	0	0	0	0	253	716	0	0	691.86	53'71	
4. Bilonia „	9	1	10	778	11	789	0	0	0	0	0	0	0	0	568	221	0	0	573'85	10'44	
5. Khowai „	9	1	10	238	14	252	0	0	15	156	0	0	0	0	55	5	0	21	198'41	0	
6. Dharmanagar „	11	1	12	611	41	652	0	0	102	0	0	0	0	0	407	141	0	2	422'95	33'23	
7. Udaipur „	7	1	8	324	24	348	0	1	0	26	2	0	0	0	150	169	0	0	257'92	18'91	
8. Sabrum „	4	0	4	182	15	197	0	0	c	35	0	0	0	0	105	46	0	11	152'40	8'10	
9. Amarpur Sub-division ...	2	0	3	33	2	35	0	2	0	0	26	0	0	0	5	1	0	1	31'88	1'21	
TOTAL ...	133	10	143	5,911	420	6,331	8	180	614	583	30	12	42	21	2,786	2,005	3	47	4,478'71	294'30	

XXVI.

Statement showing the distribution of Portfolios among the members of the Council of Administration, Tripura State, 1336 T. E.

Members.	Departments allotted to Portfolios.	REMARKS.
President	1. Judicial. 2. Sultanat. 3. Sansar. 4. Nij Tahabil.	
Vice-President	1. Political and Appointment. 2. Police. 3. Revenue and General. 4. Agriculture. 5. Forest. 6. Accounts and Audit. 7. Treasury and Stamps. 8. Chakla Roshnabad Estates and other Zemindaries.	
Maharajkumar B. K. Dev Barman ...	1. Jail. 2. Education and Rajmala. 3. Medical and Sanitation. 4. Military. 5. Public Works. 6. Zoo.	
Thakur P. C. Roy	1. Pilkhana and Stables. 2. Tosakhana. 3. Guest House. 4. Registration. 5. Press, Forms, Stationery, Gazette and Record Room. 6. Municipality.	

APPENDIX XXVII. (A)

Statement of Audited Receipts for the year 1336 T. E.

State.

Heads of Revenue.	1335 T. E.		1336 T. E.		Remarks.
	Revised Estimate.	Actuals.	Revised Estimate.	Actuals.	
1. Land Revenue ...	5,69,819	5,89,635	5,92,000	6,18,210	
2. Rents of markets ...	6,645	6,852	7,000	7,223	
3. Family tax in the hills	65,876	63,118	60,000	54,595	
4. Toll on Forest Produce	4,64,359	4,72,559	4,85,000	4,93,335	
5. Do on the Feni River	30,552	31,604	30,000	29,146	
6. Elephant and Buffalo grazing mehals ...	6,923	6,896	7,000	7,339	
7. Thatching grass mehals	11,662	10,342	10,000	9,029	
8. Reserved *Sal* trees ...	21,595	14,199	14,000	15,289	
9. Tax on cotton and Oil seeds ...	1,55,486	2,14,808	1,50,000	2,18,051	
10. Royalty on elephant caught ...	1,700	1,702	9,000	42	
11. Adda mehal ...	24,497	21,089	23,000	23,063	
12. Excise ...	56,113	60,563	70,000	79,354	
13. Stamps and Court fees	71,406	84,490	85,000	87,137	
14. Law and Justice (fines)	2,547	3,422	4,000	4,162	
15. Process Fees ...	12,999	13,729	14,000	15,905	
16. Registration ...	14,616	15,781	13,000	15,988	
17. Jail ...	3,309	3,350	4,000	4,739	
18. Cattle pounds ...	5,580	5,869	5,500	6,083	
19. *Nazars* ...	35,104	47,489	50,000	52,490	
20. Agriculture ...	446	570	500	511	
21. Miscellaneous ...	79,379	77,988	90,000	1,02,306	
22. School Fees ...	10,104	7,906	10,000	6,810	
23. Personal Howlats recovered	5,075	5,360	7,000	7,474	
Total ...	16,55,692	17,59,321	17,40,000	18,58,281	
24. Contribution from Chakla ...	50,000	50,000	—	—	
25. Deposits ...	86,962	86,764	90,000	3,68,535	
26. Loans ...	—	—	—	—	
	17,92,654	18,96,085	18,30,000	22,26,816	
Opening Balance :—					
Cash ...	3,72,122	3,72,122	3,96,594	3,96,594	
Advances ...	2,15,257	2,15,257	1,78,412	1,78,412	
Loans issued ...	42,215	42,215	41,118	41,118	
	6,29,594	6,29,594	6,16,124	6,16,124	
Grand Total ...	24,22,248	25,25,679	24,46,124	28,42,940	

APPENDIX XXVII. (B)

Statement of Audited Expenditure for the year 1336 T. E.

State.

Heads of Expenditure.	1335 T. E.		1336 T. E.		Remarks.
	Revised estimate.	Actuals.	Revised Estimate.	Actuals.	
1. Controlling Charges	1,21,225	1,20,416	1,13,670	1,12,159	
2. Judicial ...	50,500	48,401	36,520	35,638	
3. Sansar ...	6,50,130	6,46,699	5,19,813	5,12,916	
4. Sultanat ...	20,930	19,717	25,082	23,715	
5. Nijtahabil ...	1,14,330	1,12,414	1,30,821	1,26,775	
6. Police ...	68,420	66,646	71,010	68,377	
7. Revenue ...	75,000	70,640	77,990	74,010	
8. Tahasil ...	48,800	45,427	49,050	45,729	
9. Survey & settlement	18,000	16,497	19,000	13,898	
10. Agriculture ...	5,360	4,713	5,520	5,389	
11. Forest ...	56,825	52,212	58,660	54,173	
12. Public Works ...	2,43,920	2,29,461	2,94,000	2,81,089	
13. Zoo ...	10,800	10,772	8,500	8,270	
14. Medical & Sanitation	68,000	66,968	72,560	70,278	
15. Jail ...	14,250	13,633	17,620	15,824	
16. Education General ...	94,530	91,746	96,898	94,206	
17. Rajmala ...	6,000	5,949	6,132	6,098	
18. Education of Rajkumars ...	12,900	11,182	19,612	16,658	
19. Military ...	46,110	39,219	44,050	40,240	
20. Registration ...	4,380	4,336	4,970	4,682	
21. Press ...	5,210	4,427	4,350	4,133	
22. State Gazette ...	700	626	700	594	
23. Municipality ...	9,000	9,000	10,000	9,706	
24. Repayment of Deposits ...	70,000	68,859	86,400	85,828	
25. Advances to employees ...	7,000	6,906	7,000	6,840	
26. Pension ...	20,000	19,051	21,000	20,476	
27. Donation ...	500	250	100	60	
28. Relief to distressed subjects ...	1,000	97	16,000	12,368	
29. Purchase of Landed Property ...	89,500	85,850	5,500	1,834	
30. Unforeseen charges ...	3,500	957	4,000	3,041	
31. Compensation for dearness of Provision ...	36,500	36,489	36,000	35,917	
Total ...	19,73,320	19,09,555	18,62,528	17,90,921	
Closing balance :—					
Cash ...	2,29,456	3,96,594	3,99,066	* 8,35,130	* Includes Bank Deposit of Rs. 3,28,744.
Advances ...	1,77,257	1,78,412	1,43,412	1,55,106	
Loans issued ...	42,215	41,118	41,118	61,783	
	4,48,928	6,16,124	5,83,596	10,52,019	
Grand Total ...	24,22,248	25,25,679	24,46,124	28,42,940	

APPENDIX XXVIII. (A)

Statement of Audited Receipts for the year 1336 T. E.

Chakla Roshnabad Estate.

Heads of Receipts.	1335 T. E.		1336 T. E.		REMARKS.
	Revised Estimate.	Actuals.	Revised Estimate.	Actuals.	
1. Rent and Cess ...	10,99,000	12,03,813	11,02,000	11,04,239	
2. Cess for Rent free holdings ...	9,500	7,526	7,461	8,287	
3. Law charges recovered	65,200	57,133	52,816	52,026	
4. Misc. receipts including deposits ...	15,484	7,460	4,000	10,219	
5. Loans Received ...	—	—	—	—	
Total ...	11,89,184	12,75,932	11,66,277	11,74,771	
Opening Balance :—					
Cash ...	1,47,517	1,47,517	1,56,681	1,56,681	
Advance ...	1,60,941	1,60,941	1,08,050	1,08,050	
Loans issued ...	8,131	8,131	12,415	12,415	
Bank deposits ...	—	—	1,00,000	1,00,000	
Total ...	3,16,589	3,16,589	3,77,146	3,77,146	
Grand Total ...	15,05,773	15,92,521	15,43,423	15,51,917	

APPENDIX XXVIII. (B)

Statement of Audited Expenditure for the year 1336 T. E.

Chakla Roshnabad Estate.

Heads of Expenditure.	1335 T. E. Revised Estimate.	1335 T. E. Actuals.	1336 T. E. Revised Estimate.	1336 T. E. Actuals.	Remarks.
i. 1. Revenue and Cess ...	2,68,083	2,67,026	2,70,296	2,68,970	
2. Establishment ...	1,44,782	1,40,729	1,47,963	1,43,844	
3. Settlement ...	1,424	783	1,424	809	
4. Legal Expenses ...	1,33,000	1,29,224	1,26,086	1,01,347	
5. Education ...	10,576	10,228	12,268	11,029	
6. Medical ...	11,162	10,615	11,802	11,698	
7. Public Works ...	58,871	54,454	96,495	82,616	
8. Religious Expenses	6,300	6,058	6,381	6,122	
9. Purchase of property	157	128	8,000	6,805	
10. Miscellaneous ...	12,000	12,725	8,059	10,644	
11. Loans and Advances	3,000	—	3,000	—	
12. Pension and Gratuity	5,500	4,627	5,000	4,841	
13. Forest ...	650	545	650	564	
14. Unforeseen ...	3,000	2,935	5,000	4,833	
ii. Sansar ...	15,780	15,780	15,780	15,780	
iii. Donation ...	2,000	1,659	7,000	1,549	
iv. Repayment of debts	5,00,000	5,00,000	5,00,000	4,99,999	
iv. (a) Repayment of deposits ...	7,000	7,859	7,000	7,850	
v. Contribution to State ...	50,000	50,000	—	—	
	12,33,285	12,15,375	12,32,204	11,79,300	
Closing Balance :—					
Cash ...	1,46,416	1,56,681	1,14,222	1,24,852	
Advances ...	1,17,941	1,08,050	84,582	1,35,537	
Loans issued ...	8,131	12,415	12,415	12,228	
Bank deposits ...	—	1,00,000	1,00,000	1,00,000	
	2,72,488	3,77,146	3,11,219	3,72,617	
Grand Total ...	15,05,773	15,92,521	15,43,423	15,51,917	

Dated, Agartala, the 5th October, 1928.

MAY IT PLEASE YOUR HIGHNESS,

I have the honour to submit the accompanying Report on the General Administration of the State and the attached Zemindaries for the year 1337 T. E., extending from the 14th April 1927 to the 13th April 1928.

I have the honour to be
YOUR HIGHNESS'S
Most obedient servant,
Jyotis Chandra Sen,
Minister.

Book Twenty

Report on the General Administration of the Tripura State for the year 1337 T. E. (1927-1928 A.D.)

REPORT ON THE ADMINISTRATION

OF

THE TRIPURA STATE

FOR

1337 T. E. (1927-28.)

CHAPTER I—GENERAL AND POLITICAL.

Area of the State—4,116 sq. miles.

Population—3,04,437.

Gross Revenue (based on the average of the previous five years) :—

(*a*) State ... ... Rs. 18,63,536.

(*b*) Zemindaries ... ... Rs. 11,94,988.

Tribute—Nil.

Ruler of the State—His Highness The Bisama-Samara-Bijayee Mahamahodaya Pancha-Srijukta Maharaja Manikya Bir Bikramkishore Dev Barman Bahadur. *Age*—19 years. (Born—19th August, 1908). *Caste*—Kshatriya (of the Lunar race).

His Highness the Maharaja.

1. Early in the previous year, it had been settled that His Highness the Maharaja would assume the direct administration of the State on his twentieth birthday on the 19th August, 1927. It was at first thought desirable that the Investiture Ceremony would be coincident with the *Shastric* Ceremony of *Rajyabhishek* or Installation, but as no convenient auspicious date could be found suitable for both, it was ultimately decided that the political function would come off as previously intended, while the Installation would follow on the 29th January, 1928.

Preparation for the Investiture.

2. Only those who are acquainted with the deep-rooted feelings of veneration in which the Ruling House of Tripura is held by the people in and around the State, can form an idea of the outburst of enthusiasm evoked by the formal announcement of the date of His Highness's Investiture. The Council of Administation soon set about arranging all preliminaries, and the preparations for the historic event proceeded quietly but vigorously in charge of a strong committee headed by the President of the Council himself, at a pace of progress such as could only be expected in the case of a task so universally congenial.

Distinguished Guests.

3. The guests who were expected to grace the occasion with their presence included His Excellency the Governor of Bengal and Lady Jackson, besides a number of distinguished visitors of high rank, both European and Indian, and every possible step was taken to accord all a befitting reception.

4. The Investiture Durbar which was held on the 2nd Bhadra, 1337 T. E. corresponding to the 19th August, 1927, proved worthy of the occasion, both in respect of the unique gathering that attended it and the scenic grandeur that it presented, not only to the Durbaris themselves, but to the surging crowd outside the Hall, that crammed the spacious grounds and occupied every nook of vantage.

The Investiture Durbar.

5. In the course of the imposing and interesting ceremonials that followed, His Excellency the Governor as the leading actor in the function received, as the Representative of the Paramount Power, the *Peshkash* of 125 Gold Mohurs from His Highness, touching and remitting it, and in presenting the *khilat* from His Excellency the Viceroy, gracefully placed a pearl necklace, which formed a part thereof, round His Highness's neck.

6. As His Highness took his seat on the *Gadi*, led gently by the arm by His Excellency, amidst the firing of a salute of 13 guns, the Guard-of-honour, drawn up at the entrance, presented arms and the Military Band played the State national anthem. His Excellency rose and read, as a Royal salute of 31 guns boomed in the distance, His Excellency the Viceroy's *Kharita* which in graceful terms announced the investment of His Highness with full Ruling Powers, and offered His Highess the Viceroy's hearty congratulations and sympathy, to which His Excellency the Governor in a neat speech added his own good wishes and felicitations, declaring, in conclusion, His Highness duly invested. As the Chief Secretary to the Government of Bengal recited the full title of His Highness, a salute of 13 guns was again fired and the Guard-of-honour outside presented arms, while the Band played the State anthem. Rising slowly, as His Excellency resumed his seat, His Highness, in a clear and impressive voice, offered up a prayer to God Almighty and then thanked His Excellency and His Excellency the Viceroy, with assurance of loyalty to the throne and the Empire, for their gracious message of good will. "It will be my best endeavour," concluded His Highness, "to do my duty by the Empire and to its humble unit, my State, and I shall always bear in mind that in the loyal discharge of my individual duties would lie the general welfare and that in the health, prosperity and education of the subjects of a State lies the secret of its strength."

7. A number of interesting functions arranged for the occasion ended in a State Banquet at the Ujjayanta Palace attended by a large number of guests. His Highness proposed the toast of the King-Emperor which received due loyal response and proposed again in a very impressive speech, which was highly appreciated, the toast of the distinguished guests. His Excellency replied in suitable terms and repeated his congratulations and assurances of friendship.

State Banquet.

8. His Highness received a number of addresses from various sections of the people and gave suitable replies to all. Two other most imposing functions that followed the Investiture and the birthday festivities, were

Addresses and *Nazar* Durbar.

the Public audience and the *Nazar* Durbar, the first of which was attended by a huge gathering of people. The Nazar Durbar was the first court held by His Highness in which the pick of the State Society were presented to do homage to His Highness.

Administrative Changes.

9. The Council of Administration handed over to His Highness their trust on the day of the Investiture and its career terminated after nearly four years of useful and arduous work.

10. His Highness in a *Rubakari* appointed Rai Jyotis Chandra Sen Bahadur, the Vice-President of the retiring Council as the Minister of the State and Manager of the Zemindaries, Dewan Bijoy Kumar Sen as his Chief Secretary with charge of Sansar and other Palace Departments, and Rana Bodhjung Bahadur as his Private Secretary.

11. An Advisory Council was also appointed with His Highness as President and five members, two official and three non-official. The non-official members were Maharajkumar N. C. Dev Barman Bahadur, Vice-President, Maharajkumar B. K. Dev Barman Bahadur and Uzir Braja Krishna Dev Barman Saheb, while the Minister and the Chief Secretary were ex-officio official members.

12. A Legislative Council was also appointed with Babu Kamala Prosad Dutt, who became Assistant Private Secretary, as Secretary.

13. The Nij Tahabil or Privy Purse was separated from the Administration and placed in charge of Babu Anukul Mukherjee lately tutor to His Highness.

14. Lt. Colonel O. C. Pulley remained on His Highness's staff and Captain Kumar P. K. Dev Barman, A. D. C. was appointed Military Secretary.

15. The Military Department came under His Highness's direct control.

The Installation Ceremony.

16. The *Rajyabhishek* or Installation Ceremony in the course of which His Highness was to sit for the first time on the ancient historic *Singhasan* of his House, came off agreeably to the programme fixed up previously, on the 15th Magh, 1337 T. E., corresponding to the 29th January, 1928. It was a huge affair and the arrangements were entrusted to a committee of which His Highness personally was the President, Maharajkumar B. K. Dev Barman Bahadur the Vice-President, and Dewan B. K. Sen, General Secretary, with a number of official and non-official members, all with portfolios.

17. A commodious and picturesque amphitheatre was erected for the imposing ceremony with sitting accommodation for over two thousand and a vast open space in front where nearly a lac of people could stand and witness the great function.

18. The daily inrush of people from outside however outdid all expectations giving cause for grave anxiety as the momentous day drew nigh. Strict sanitary measures including compulsory vaccination and cholera inoculation were adopted by way of precaution, and judging from the result, proved eminently successful

19. The list of invited guests included many distinguished persons from outside, both European and Indian.

20. The following extracts from publications of the time will give some idea of the historic ceremony :—

"Unforgettable scenes of magnificence provided a setting for 29th January's *abhishek* ceremony of His Highness the Maharaja Manikya Bahadur, Ruler of Tripura, when a crowd of over a lac saw His Highness enthroned in accordance with the religious rites of countless generations of illustrious forebears. The significance of the ceremony at the Pandal struck a responsive chord in the hearts of the great multitude who cheered the young Maharaja lustily."

"The procession from the Ujjayanta palace to the Pandal defied description. Huge elephants, richly caparisoned, carrying howdahs that sparkled with gems worth a King's ransom, participated. The bejewelled *Chaturdol* borne by a score of scarlet-clad bearers in which His Highness journeyed to the Pandal glittered with thousand gems, and the dress worn by His Highness conveyed subtle suggestion of illimitable wealth. The whole epitomized the immemorial wealth and splendour of the East. Cymbals clashed incessantly during the 1500 year old ceremony. State troops presented arms as His Highness approached the ancient historic ivory *Singhasan* (throne) of the Lunar race, really used only once in the lifetime of a Maharaja, while somberly clad Brahmin priests chanted their prayers and blessings. The Maharaja bore himself superbly. After giving *anjali* to the God Laksmi Narayan, His Highness went round the *Singhasan* seven times, preceded by leading pundits and followed by his staff, and a great shout of jubilation greeted his ascension on the gleaming throne."

"The performance of *tika* by the *Suba*, or the surviving representative of the Chief of the now defunct Feudal Military system, was the signal for another outburst, while cheering Brahmins of high erudition surrounded His Highness and invoked blessings on him sprinkling at the same time holy water from various sacred places on his robes."

The elephant procession.

"A striking feature in connection with the Installation ceremony was an elephant procession through the town. It was a brilliant spectacle in which over 80 huge elephants took part. They were all gorgeously trapped with gold and silver cloth, while bright daubs of pigment on their foreheads gave the festival a picturesque aspect. His Highness rode in State in a magnificent *Chaturdol* and members of the family and high State officials wearing exquisite robes, rode in lavishly bejewelled howdahs. A special feature was an array of hill chiefs with their tribal troops, all clad in crude and ancient military costume and carrying their respective decorated banners and insignias. Indeed the wealth and beauty of the scene defy description and the route was thickly lined with a vast cheering concourse of people who stayed on for hours as the procession, which extended for miles, passed."

"On return to the Palace there was again a remarkable demonstration of affection for His Highness on the part of his subjects."

"At the State Banquet on the night of the 29th January the toast of His Highness the Maharaja was proposed in eulogistic terms by the Nawab Bahadur of Murshidabad, who alluded to His Highness's illustrious ancestry and the whole-hearted rejoicing of his subjects on his installation and expressed the wish that his rule might be happy and prosperous. Rajkumar Gajendra Pal Singh also paid a tribute to His Highness, and on behalf of the guests warmly thanked the Maharaja for his generous hospitality."

State Banquet.

His Highness responded in suitable terms.

Other Subsidiary functions & festivities.

21. Among the other subsidiary functions and festivities of the occasion may be mentioned, the feeding of the public, the distribution of alms and clothes to the poor, His Highness's visits to the temples and mosques, the Nazar Durbar, and the Investiture Durbar on the 31st January, at which the following titles were conferred : *viz.*, ***Mahamanyabar*** on Maharajkumars N. C. Dev Barman Bahadur and B. K. Dev Barman Bahadur, ***Manyabara*** on Rai J. C. Sen Bahadur and Rana Bodhjung Bahadur, "Dewan Bahadur" on Dewan B. K. Sen, "Uzir Bahadur" on Uzir Braja Krishna Dev Barman Saheb, "Dewan Saheb" on Babus Kamala Prasad Dutt and Anukul Mukherjee, and "Naib Dewan" on Thakur Golak Chandra Dev Barman.

Maharajkumari Bibhasprabha's Marriage

22. Yet another important function of the year was the marriage of Maharajkumari Bibhasprabha Devi, His Highness's second sister, with Jubaraj Subhag Singji Bahadur, Heir apparent of Baria State, which was celebrated with great *eclat* at Agartala on the 26th Falgoon corresponding to 10th March, 1928. The bridegroom's father, His Highness Captain Maharaol Shree Sir Ranjit Singji Bahadur, K. C. S. I., Ruler of Baria, with His Highness Maharaja Saheb of Santrampur and two other Ruling Princes, with many distinguished guests of high rank attended the function as His Highness's guests. The alliance between two ancient Rajput families of eastern and western India has a significance and importance of its own.

His Highness's movements.

23. His Highness left for Mussoorie on the 3rd September, 1927 for a short period of rest after which, with the exception of a flying visit to Calcutta in December, he was mainly at Agartala throughout, busy with the preliminary work connected with the organisation of the new Administration.

Political Agent.

24. Mr. W. H. Nelson, I. C. S., continued to be the Political Agent of the State till 31st January, 1928 with the exception of a period of about 3 weeks, when Mr. H. G. S. Bivar, I. C. S., was in charge of the office of the Political Agent. On Mr. Nelson's transfer, Mr. H. W. Lyne, I. C. S., was appointed Political Agent of the State.

CHAPTER II—LAND ADMINISTRATION.

Charge.

25. Babu B. K. Chatterjee, M. A., B. L., continued to be in charge of the Revenue Department during the year under review

26. As shewn in the subjoined statement, the total area held under settlement and borne on the *taujis* at the close of the year was 597 sq. miles as against 587 sq. miles in the previous year.

Area held under Settlement.

Kinds of settlement.	Area in square miles.		Increase.	Decrease.	REMARKS.
	1337 T.E.	1336 T.E.			
Jotes ...	278	268	10	—	
Taluks ...	319	319		—	
Total ...	597	587	10	—	

27. The increase in the area under *jote* settlement is due to new settlement.

28. As in the previous year there was no fresh settlement for tea cultivation in the year under report.

Tea Settlement.

29. The average of *jama* per *kani* of *jote* lands in *Khash mehals* (exclusive of cesses) stood at 14 annas and 11 pies against 15 annas and 1 pie in the previous year. The maximum rate for *jotes* was Rs. 12-13 per *kani* while the minimum was 4 annas, and for *taluks* Re. 1-8 and anna 1 pies 9 respectively.

Rates of *Jama.*

30. The different sources of land revenue demand with the collection under each head are detailed below :—

Sources of land revenue.

Sources.	Current demand.		Arrear demand up to the end of		Realization up to the end of		REMARKS.
	1337 T.E.	1336 T.E.	1336 T.E.	1335 T.E.	1337 T.E.	1336 T.E.	
Taluks ...	1,65,665	1,67,666	2,50,591	2,43,221	1,53,059	1,57,710	
Khas Mehal jotes	4,16,787	4,06,384	7,47,808	7,59,867	4,00,775	4,07,062	
Bazars ...	8,019	7,082	935	1,187	7,559	7,289	
Cesses ...	36,663	36,031	66,970	65,990	33,751	34,166	
Total ...	6,27,134	6,17,163	10,66,304	10,70,265	5,95,144	6,06,227	

31. The above statement will show that the current demand under all heads was Rs. 6,27,134. With the arrear demand of Rs 10,66,304, the total demand of the

Demand.

year was Rs. 16,93,438 against Rs. 16,87,428 in the previous year. There was an increase in the current demand in respect of *jote lands* due, as usual, to assessment on the expiry of the rent-free period and resettlement after the previous term. The decrease in the current demand in respect of *taluki* lands is due to *Khas* purchase of some tea garden *taluks* in auction sale for arrears of revenue in 1335 T. E., the demand not having been previously deducted.

Collection.

32. The total collection under all heads during the year amounted to Rs. 5,95,144, being Rs. 3,18,212 under current and Rs. 2,76,932 under arrears, against Rs. 6,06,227 in the previous year. The percentage of current collection was 50·74 against 48·88, and that of the arrears 25·97 against 28·45. The percentage of current collection was 40·32 in the *Khas Mehal* and 75·09 in the *Taluki mehal* against 40·73 and 73·26 respectively in the previous year.

Coercive measures—certificates.

33. Altogether 3,650 certificate cases, covering a demand of Rs. 1,79,812 were instituted during the year. With 1,530 cases valued at Rs. 2,76,590 pending from the previous year, the total number of cases awaiting final orders on disposal of preliminary notices issued on debtors, was 5,180, covering a total demand of Rs. 4,56,401. Of these, 75 cases with a demand of Rs. 1,291 were rejected or struck off, and Rs. 15,315 in 655 cases was realised before decree, while 2,086 cases with a total value of Rs. 3,35,453 remained pending.

34. Orders under the provisions of the State Certificate Act were passed during the year in 2,361 cases with a total value of Rs. 1,03,848, making the demands absolute. With 3,981 cases covering a demand of Rs. 3,40,344 pending in execution from the previous year, the total number of cases dealt with was 6,342 covering a demand of Rs. 4,44,192. Out of the total demand, Rs. 9,391 was remitted or written off, and of the remainder, Rs. 1,14,100 was actually realised, leaving a balance of Rs. 3,20,701. Of the amount realised Rs. 91,225 represents land revenue and Rs. 22,875 miscellaneous demands. 13 debtors were ordered to be arrested in the year, of whom only 2 were confined in jail, one for 12 and another for 16 days. Nothing could however be realised from them. Partial dues were realised from some of the debtors and instalments were allowed to others.

Operation of the Sunset law.

35. The number of defaulting *taluks* brought under the operation of the Sunset law (including 17 pending from the previous year) was 83. Of these, 64 were realised on payment of dues with penalty, while 3 were sold in auction and 16 remained undisposed of at the close of the year.

Survey.

36. The results of the survey (including resurvey) operations are given in the statement below. It will be seen that an area of 7,709 *drones* comprising 2,713 *drones* of *taluk* and 4,996 *drones* of *Khas mehal* was surveyed as against a total of 6,886 *drones* in the previous year. The sanctioned programme for survey for the year was for 6,635 *drones* in *khas mehal* and 3,891 *drones*

in *taluks.* The total expenditure incurred in the survey operations in *khas mehal* was Rs. 6,046.

Names of Divisions.	Quantity of land in *drones* surveyed in 1337 T. E.			Quantity of land in *drones* surveyed in 1336 T. E.			REMARKS.
	Taluqi land.	*Khas mehal* land.	Total.	*Taluqi* land.	*Khas mehal* land.	Total.	
1. Sadar Division ...	427	219	646	314	44	358	
2. Kailashahar " ...	228	575	803	—	924	924	
3. Sonamura " ...	117	2,508	2,625	—	1,734	1,734	
4. Bilonia " ...	678	687	1,365	220	790	1,010	
5. Khowai " ...	1,119	137	1,256	32	863	895	
6. Dharmanagar " ..	144	171	315	219	109	328	
7. Udaipur " ...	—	699	699	364	130	494	
8. Sabroom " ...	—	—	—	344	567	911	
9. Amarpur Sub " ...	—	—	—	—	232	232	
TOTAL ...	2,713	4,996	7,709	1,493	5,393	6,886	

37. The result of settlement work is given in the statement below. It will be seen that the settlement operations were completed in respect of 2,987 *drones* of *jote* land as against 3,118 *drones* in the previous year.

Settlement.

Nature of Settlement.	1337 T. E.		1336 T. E.		REMARKS.
	Area in *drones.*	*Jama* in whole rupees.	Area in *drones.*	*Jama* in whole rupees.	
1. Permanent *taluqi* settlement of cultivated land ...	—	—	—	—	
2. Permanent *taluqi* settlement of waste land ...	—	—	—	—	
3. *Taskhichi taluqi* settlement of cultivated land ...	—	—	—	—	
4. *Taskhichi taluqi* settlement of waste land ...	—	—	—	—	
5. *Jotedari* re-settlement of cultivated land	2,120	21,337	1,936	24,451	
6. *Jotedari* settlement of waste land.	867	5,950	1,182	7,101	
TOTAL ...	2,987	27,287	3,118	31,552	

38. No permanent or *Takshichi* settlement or *Niskar* grant was sanctioned during the year.

Taluki settlement.

39. A net increase of Rs. 9,257 in *jama* was secured by resettlement of *abadi jote* land, the *nazarana* secured being Rs. 27,221. The average rate of *jama* per *kani* was 10 annas 1 pie against 12 annas 8 pies in the previous year.

Resettlement of *jote* lands.

Jotedari settlement of waste land.

40. During the year an area of 867 *drones* of waste land was settled for a prospective rental of Rs. 5,950 the average *jama* per *kani* obtained being 6 annas 10 pies against 6 annas in the previous year. The maximum and minimum rates were Rs. 2-4 and 4 annas respectively. The *nazarana* realised was Rs. 17,211, the rent-free period allowed ranging from 1 to 4 years.

Settlement work.

41. The Divisional Officers were entrusted with the settlement work within their respective jurisdictions. In Sonamura, however, a separate wholetime Settlement Officer worked for 5 months in the latter half of the year under review. The total expenditure incurred in the settlement operations exclusively, amounted to Rs. 2,412.

42. It will be seen that the *nazarana* obtained and obtainable by resettlement of cultivable *jote* lands and settlement of waste lands, as *jotes*, amounted to Rs. 44,432 (Rs. 27,221 + Rs. 17,211). The net increase of revenue secured was Rs. 15,207 (Rs. 9,257 + Rs. 5,950).

Private Estates under State Management.

43. As detailed below there were altogether 10 private estates under State management during the year under report.

Class.	Name of Estates.	Area.	Revenue.
Encumbered	1. Kakrabon Estate	283 *drones*	1,871
	2. Jogendranagar Trust Estate	64 „	163
	3. Kamalnagar and Mohendranagar Estate	51 „	255
	4. Gouranga Tripura's Estate	13 „	57
	5. Maharam Ali Chaudhuri Khanja Kha Bahadur's Estate—*Taluk*	232 „	1,352
	Jote	6 „	149
	6. Thakur Nalini Mohan Deb Barma's Estate	62 „	170
Unencumbered	7. Prabhu Goswamis' Estate	31 „	61
	8. The Maharanee's Estate	260 „	450
	9. Late Brajakumar Thakur's Estate	47 „	297
Endowment	10. Taranagar Estate	123 „	52

44. The subjoined table shows the demands and collections of the estates during the year.

	Demand			Collection			P. C. of collection
	Current	Arrear	Total	Current	Arrear	Total	
1.	6,541	31,845	38,386	627	3,287	3,914	10·20
2.	1,198	3,781	4,979	286	659	945	18·97
3.	1,272	833	2,105	550	439	989	46·98
4.	204	207	411	190	203	393	95·09
5.	3,791	7,100	10,891	1,350	1,308	2,658	24·40
6.	—	—	—	—	—	—	—*
7.	923	2,379	3,302	370	629	999	30·25
8.	6,699	9,324	16,023	2,244	1,897	4,141	25·84
9.	1,591	1,881	3,472	312	520	832	26·81
10.	3,086	5,310	8,396	940	970	1,910	22·75

* No collection was made as the Estate came under State management a few days before the close of the year.

CHAPTER III—PROTECTION.

I. Legislation.

Legislative Committee.

45. There was only one sitting of the old Legislative Committee before its dissolution and the only bill which it submitted to the Council of Administration for sanction was a Bill to amend the State Tenancy Act which ultimately came up before His Highness and passed into law during the year, after assent, as Act I of 1337 T. E.

Legislative Council.

46. A Legislative Council was constituted under His Highness's orders dated the 7th Bhadra, consisting of 19 members, official and non-official, with His Highness as the President, Mahamanyabar Maharajkumar N. C. Deb Barman Bahadur and Mahamanyabar Maharajkumar B. K. Deb Barman Bahadur as the Vice-Presidents and Dewan Saheb Kamala Prasad Dutt, M. A., B. L. as the Secretary. There was no sitting of the Legislative Council during the year as most of the members were busily engaged in connection with His Highness's Installation Ceremony and the marriage ceremony of one of the sisters of His Highness mentioned above.

II. Military.

Charge.

47. Major Kumar Dina Mohan Deb Barman Bahadur was in charge of the Military Office and the Forces as before.

Strength.

48. The actual strength of the Force consisted, at the close of the year, of 242 Sepoys and 44 Officers of all ranks, including the Officer Commanding, 1 Lieutenant, 1 Subedar Major, 3 Subedars, 4 Jamaders, 1 Probationer Jamader, 1 Havildar Major, 14 Havildars and 18 Amaldars. There were, besides, a Band Master and 19 men constituting the State Band. As there were no suitable candidates, 35 posts had to be kept vacant.

Duty.

49. The men were chiefly employed, as before, on escort duty and in furnishing Guards-of-honour on ceremonial occasions.

Expenditure.

50. The total expenditure of the year, excluding grain allowance paid to the extent of Rs. 3,059, amounted to Rs. 77,911 as against Rs. 40,240. The increase in the expenditure was mainly due to the reorganisation of the No. I Tripura Company.

III. Police.

Charge.

51. Lieut. Jogesh Chandra Dutt, B. A., continued as Superintendent of Police throughout the year. Assistant Superintendent Srijut Jogendra Chandra Deb Barma continued to be on sick leave all through the year under report.

52. The total strength of the State Police was 465, that of the previous year being reduced by 2 Jamadars and 15 constables owing to the force having been relieved of the duty of guarding the Sadar Jail at Agartala which was entrusted during the year to jail-warders.

Strength.

53. There were 4 Inspectors working under the Superintendent of Police. The chief duty of the Inspectors was to control the investigating staff and supervise their work.

Inspecting Staff.

54. The total number of cases reported to the Police was 1377 against 1318 in the previous year.

Crime.

55. The result of the cases investigated by the police will be seen from the following table :—

Number of cases reported.
1,377

Enquiry refused 21 | Number investigated 1,229 | Pending 127

Maliciously false 2 | True 719 | Doubtful &c. 508

Charge-sheet 383 | Finally reported 336

56. Altogether 830 persons were arrested for various offences and 721 persons sent up for trial by the police against 711 and 638 respectively in the previous year.

Result of prosecution.

57. Of the number 721 sent up, 167 were convicted and 205 acquitted (including 70 on compromise and 33 on withdrawal of cases) while 35 escaped, and 314 were awaiting trial. The percentage of convictions was 23·1 against 26·8 of the previous year. Of the 223 persons awaiting trial at the end of the previous year, 47 were convicted and 134 acquitted (including 33 on compromise and 29 on withdrawal of cases) while 42 were awaiting trial.

58. 7 bad livelihood cases with 17 persons were instituted during the year under report. Of these persons, 11 were convicted and 2 discharged, while 4 persons were awaiting trial.

Bad livelihood cases.

59. Of 5 Arms Act cases, 1 was finally reported as true and 4 with 6 persons sent up for trial. Three persons were convicted while 3 persons in one case were awaiting trial at the close of the year.

Arms Act Cases.

60. The value of properties stolen was estimated at Rs. 24,329-15-6 against Rs. 18,115-5-3 of the previous year. Of this amount, Rs. 11,272-13-3 was recovered against Rs. 2,710-5 of the previous year. The percentage of recovery was thus 46·33 against 14·95 of the previous year. This was satisfactory.

Recovery of stolen property.

61. There were 5 cases of dacoity reported during the year of which 3 were finally reported as true and 2 sent up in charge sheets. One person was convicted and 3 discharged.

Dacoity.

62. The C. I. D. and the information Bureau continued to work satisfactorily and proved useful in the collection of information and detecting cases.

Special Staff.

63. Altogether 67 cases of unnatural deaths were reported during the year. Regular enquiries were held by the Police in all cases. No foul play was discovered in any of them.

Unnatural deaths and steps taken.

64. Two Darogas, 2 Naib Darogas, 1 Writer Constable, 4 constables, 1 Chaukidar and 8 outsiders received money reward. Three Darogas and 20 constables were fined, degraded or suspended, while 1 Daroga, 6 constables, and 6 chaukidars were dismissed or discharged.

Rewards and punishments.

65. The Superintendent of Police was out on tour for 65 days during the year against 84 days in the previous year. The Investiture Ceremony and the Installation Ceremony of His Highness the Maharaja Manikya Bahadur detained the Superintendent of Police at Sadar for a considerable period.

Tours.

66. The relations with the police in the adjoining districts in British India continued to be satisfactory.

Police co-operation.

67. The patrol at Sonamura worked satisfactorily with the Kotwali Police, Comilla, throughout the year.

Patrol.

68. The expenditure amounted, excluding grain allowance, to Rs. 80,480 against Rs. 68,377 in the previous year.

Expenditure.

IV. Justice.

69. There were 14 Courts of Justice in the State during the year under report, exercising both Civil and Criminal Jurisdiction viz. the Khas Adalat or the Chief Court with its original and appellate sides and 13 Courts of Magistrate-Munsiffs exercising original Jurisdiction only.

Courts.

70. By an order of His Highness dated the 15th Bhadra 1337 T. E., the Chief Judge, Khas Adalat, the Minister, and Babu Kamala Prosad Dutt M. A. B. L. were appointed, temporarily, as members of the Privy Council to dispose of appeals pending before the said Council. There were 19 such appeals pending, none of which could be disposed of within the year.

Privy Council.

71. Babu Bhupal Chandra Ganguly, B. L., Chief Judge, was taken seriously ill early in the year and had unfortunately to proceed on long leave preparatory to retirement. Dewan B. K. Sen Bahadur, M. A., B. L., F. R. S. A., Judge, Sessions Division was appointed to officiate as Chief Judge in which capacity he has continued since. Dewan A. C. Chaudhuri

acted as Sessions Judge in place of the latter, while Kumar S. C. Deb Barman and Uzir B. K. Deb Barman continued as Puisne Judges.

Number of original criminal cases.

72. Altogether 2,280 original criminal cases were instituted during the year under report against 2,200 of the previous year. With the balance of 577 pending from the last year, the total number of cases for disposal before the several subordinate original courts was thus 2,857 as against 2,853 of the previous year as detailed below ; out of these 2,857 cases, 2,238 were disposed of as against 2,276 of the last year, leaving 619 cases pending at the close of the year. Thus in the year under report, the number of cases for disposal increased from that of the previous year by 4 and there was a decrease in the disposals by 38.

DESCRIPTION OF OFFENCES.	1336 T. E.	1337 T. E.
Offences against the State and public tranquillity	98	141
Offences against person	638	657
Offences against property	1,563	1,475
Other offences	554	584
TOTAL	2,853	2,857

Extradition.

73. During the year under report extradition warrants were applied for against 105 presons of whom 31 were arrested and surrendered, 23 persons appeared voluntarily and 51 were at large at the close of the year. With 29 persons pending trial at the close of the previous year, 83 persons were under trial during the year of whom 19 were convicted, 43 were acquitted or discharged 21 were awaiting trial at the end of the year.

Persons brought to trial.

74. The total number of persons awaiting trial in the year under report inclusive of the number pending from the last year was 3,739 against 3,617 of the previous year. The number actually brought to trial was 2,893. Of these, 836 were arrested by the Police, 524 were produced on warrants, 1,111 appeared on summons, 384 appeared voluntarily and 38 were arrested in the presence of a Magistrate.

Results of cases.

75. Out of these 3,739 persons brought to trial, 1,396 were discharged without trial, 818 were acquitted, 573 convicted, 8 died, 3 escaped while 2 were confined being insane, and 939 remained under trial at the close of the year. Of the persons convicted 171 were sentenced to various terms of imprisonment extending from below 1 month to 15 years, 384 to fine only, 3 persons were warned for the future and 13 persons released on bail, while 2 persons were ordered to pay maintenance. The number of persons actually tried was 1,391 as against 1,505 of the previous year, and the percentage of convictions was thus 41·19 as against 32·35 of the previous year.

Cases concerning British subjects.

76. Of the 2,857 cases for disposal the number in which British subjects were concerned was 577 as against 507 of the previous year. Out of these cases 429 were cognizable and 148 non-cognizable. In 75 cases British subjects were complainants, in 502 they were the accused.

In 196 cases both the parties were British subjects. In these cases 680 persons were actually under trial during the year under report as against 647 of the last year. Of these, 243 were convicted, 290 acquitted or discharged, 1 escaped, 1 died and 145 remained under trial at the close of the year.

Comparative statement.

77. The statement below compares the number of original criminal cases during the last 2 years.

DESCRIPTION OF OFFENCES.	1336 T.E.	1337 T.E.	Increase.	Decrease.
Offences against the State and public tranquillity ...	69	114	45	0
Offences against person	509	532	23	0
Offences against property	1,154	1,154	0	0
Other offences	468	480	12	0
TOTAL	2,200	2,280	80	0

Increased by 80.

Sessions cases.

78. 17 cases, including 5 cases with 12 persons pending from the previous year were committed to the Sessions during the year under report. All of them were disposed of as detailed below in the following table. The number of persons involved in these cases was 56 ; of these, 33 were convicted, 4 discharged without trial and 19 acquitted.

Description of cases.	Number of cases.	Disposed of.	Pending.	REMARKS.
Murder	2	2	0	
Culpable homicide not amounting to murder	3	3	0	
Dacoity	6	6	0	
Bigamy	1	1	0	
Arson	1	1	0	
Forging valuable documents of the Tripura State	2	2	0	
Grievous hurt	1	1	0	
False complaint	1	1	0	
Total	17	17	0	

Criminal appeals.

79. There were altogether 199 criminal appeals against 269 of the last year. They were disposed of as shown below :—

Rejected	28
Judgment affirmed	73
Modified	15
Reversed	29
Further enquiry &c. ordered	18
Proceedings quashed	2
	165
Pending	34
	199

80. The percetage of judgments affirmed and modified was 70·3 as against 66·21 of the previous year.

Original civil suits.

81. The number of original civil suits instituted during the year under report was 2,086 against 2,014 of the previous year. With the preceding year's balance of 990 suits,

the total number for disposal was 3,076 as against 3,111 of the last year. They were disposed of as follows :—

Exparte	833
Admitted and compromised	342
Dismissed for want of prosecution ...	322
Disposed of on contest	501
	1,998
Pending	1,078
Total	3,076

Duration of suits.

82. The average duration of suits before the civil courts was 3 months and 24 days against 3 months and 12 days in 1336. T. E.

Nature and value of suits

83. The total value of suits instituted during the year was Rs. 2,37,449-9-6 as against Rs. 2,76,546-15-3 which gives an average of Rs. 113-13-3 pies the value per case. Of the 2086 suits instituted during the year under report, 576 related to lands, 1,119 to money transactions and 391 to other transaction. There were 1225 suits of the value of Rs. 100 and under ; 419 suits of over Rs. 100 and below Rs. 500 ; 35 suits of over Rs. 500 and below Rs. 1,000 ; 34 suits of over Rs. 1,000 and below Rs. 5,000 ; 5 suits of over Rs. 5,000 ; while 368 suits were not estimable in money value.

Execution of decrees.

84. The number of applications for the execution of decrees filed during this year was 686 and with 344 pending cases, the total number was 1030 as against 993 of the last year. The aggregate value of the new applications was Rs. 93,220-5-3 and with the opening value of Rs. 97,696-10-6 being the value of the pending cases, the total amounted to Rs. 1,90,916-15-9. The number of aplications disposed of was 603 the value of which was Rs. 76,671-7. The number of execution cases pending at the close of the year was 427 with the value Rs. 1,14,245-8-9.

Civil appeals.

85. There were 174 civil appeals filed during this year, against 169 of the previous year. With the last year's balance of 46, the total for disposal was 220 against 234 of 1336 T. E. Out of these, 130 were disposed of during the year under report against 188 of the last year, leaving a balance of 90 cases at the close of the year.

Results of appeals.

86. The following figures indicate the results of appeals :—

Decisions confirmed	67
,, reversed	16
,, modified	8
,, remanded	25
Compromised or otherwise disposed of ...	14
	130

Percentage.

87. The percentage of judgments wholly or partly upheld, excluding the cases compromised, was 64·65 as against 55 of the last year.

88. The total value of appeals filed during present year was Rs. 33,433 and the average duration of each appeal was 2 months and 2 days as against 2 months and 1 day of the previous year.

Value and duration of appeals.

89. 46 civil suits were instituted in the Khas Adalat Original Side against 34 of the last year. With the balance of 36 suits from 1336 T. E., the total number for disposal was thus 82 as against 65 of the previous year. Of these, 32 suits were disposed of against 29 suits of the previous year, and 50 suits remained pending at the close of the year. There were 31 execution cases during the year under report including 14 cases pending from the last year, of these 7 were disposed of and 24 remained pending at the close of the year. There were 37 applcations filed for the grant of Sucession and other certificates during the year. With the previous year's balance of 7, the total number of cases was 44, out of which 26 were disposed of as shown below, leaving 18 cases pending at the close of the year.

Original Side cases.

Description of cases.	Total.	Disposed of.	Pending.
Probate case	1	0	1
Succession certificate	20	13	7
Guardianship	23	13	10
Total	44	26	18

90. Thus it will appear from the sub-joined table, that the total number of civil and criminal appeals inclusive of the number pending from last year was 419 against 503 of the previous year, and out of these 295 were disposed of against 433 of the previous year. In comparison with the previous year, the total number of appeals decreased by 84 and there was a corresponding decrease in the disposals in the year under report by 138, which was due to (1) the serious illness of the Chief Judge, (2) considerable decrease of the number of working days in the year in consequence of the important functions of the year and (3) the long absence from head-quarters of the Officiating Chief Judge on duty.

Total number of appeals.

Description of appeals.	Number of appeals.		Disposed of.	
	Past year.	Present year.	Past year.	Present year.
Civi	234	220	188	130
Criminal	269	199	245	165
Total	503	419	433	295

V. Prisons.

91. There were 8 jails in the State during the year under report including the Central Jail at the Capital.

Number of Jails.

92. With the previous year's balance of 139, the total number of prisoners was 708 as against 718 in the preceding year. Of these, 323 were convicts, 373 undertrials,

Jail population.

7 civil prisoners and 5 lunatics. The daily average was 117·22 against 116·00 in the previous year.

93. Sixty prisoners were under sentence of 2 years and above, as against 69 in the previous year, as shown in the statement below.

Long-term prisoners.

Class of offence.	Number of prisoners.	Occupation.	REMARKS.
Murder	13	They were employed in oilmills, wheat grinding, *soorki* pounding, *khoa* breaking, bamboo and cane work, gardening, weaving, tailoring, paddy husking, rice manufacturing &c.	30 had sentences of 2 to 5 years, 23 of 5 to 10 years, 7 for life *i. e.* 20 years.
Culpable homicide not amounting to murder	15		
Dacoity	12		
Robbery	1		
Theft	3		
Grievous hurt	6		
Rape	2		
Counterfeiting coin ...	4		
Forgery and Conspiracy ...	2		
Outraging modesty of woman	2		
Total	60		

94. The health of the Jail was generally good throughout the year. Only 1 convict died of Kala-azar and 1 lunatic died of apoplexy at the Central Jail.

Jail Health.

95. One undertrial escaped from the Sabrum Jail.

Escape.

96. Twenty convicts were released on the auspicious occasion of the Installation of His Highness the Maharaja Manikya Bahadur and the periods of imprisonment of others were reduced by one-fourth to one-third of the total sentence.

Release.

97. The income from the Central Jail amounted to Rs. 4,559 as against Rs. 4,546-10-9 in the year before, the subsidiary jails not contributing any amount.

Income.

98. The total expenditure during the year was Rs. 17,834 as against Rs. 15,824 in the preceding year.

Expenditure.

VI. Registration.

99. The charge of the Department continued with Dewan Asita Chandra Chaudhuri, B. A., till his deputation to Khas Adalat as Sessions Judge in Bhadra, Babu Brajendra Kumar Chatterjee, M. A., D. L., remaining in charge during the rest of the year.

Charge.

100. The number of Registration offices was 9 as in the previous year, viz, one at the headquarters station of each of the Divisions or Sub-Division. In the Muffussil the Divisional and Sub-Divisional Officers and in certain Divisions the Second Officers acted as Registrars as before. For the Sadar Division there was a separate Registrar at Agartala as usual.

Registration Offices.

101. Appendices XV and XVI are Registration Statements and shew the work of the Department.

102. The number of documents presented for registration during the year in the 9 Offices mentioned above was 12,894 against 12,896 in the previous year. Of this number, 173 deeds were refused registration on different grounds and 496 remained pending at the end of the year.

Presentation and Disposal.

103. The total value covered by the documents presented amounted to Rs. 22,37,308 as compared with Rs. 22,44,327 in the previous year, while the total value covered by the documents actually registered was Rs. 21,45,657 as against Rs. 21,63,613 in the year before.

Value of deeds presented and registered.

104. The number of suits and appeals filed before the Officer-in-charge, Registration Department, in respect of documents, the registration of which had been refused in the Registration Offices, was 30 and 2 against 35 and 4 respectively in the preceding year. There were 39 suits and 2 appeals pending from the previous year, making a total of 69 suits and 4 appeals. Out of these, 47 suits and 2 appeals were disposed of during the year, leaving 22 suits and 2 appeals pending at the end of the year.

Suits and appeals.

105. The total income of the Department from fees and fines amounted to Rs. 15,828 against Rs. 15,988 and the expenditure to Rs. 4,573 against Rs. 4,682 in the previous year. The net income thus was Rs. 11,255 against Rs. 11,306 in the previous year.

Income and Expenditure.

VII. Municipality.

106. The Agartala Municipality is the only Municipal Institution within the State with a population of about 8,000 according to the last census.

Municipality.

107. As in the previous year, the Municipal Administration of the Capital Town of Agartala was vested in a Committee of nine nominated commissioners including an official Chairman and a non-official Vice-chairman. Babu Brajendra Kumar Chatterjee, M. A., B. L., Officer-in-charge, Revenue Department of the State continued to be the Chairman. There were altogether 11 sittings of the Committee during the year under review—the average attendance being 4·2 against 5·5 of the previous year. The attendance was unsatisfactory.

Municipal Committee.

108. The State grant for the year including the provision for epidemic disease was Rs. 9,000 out of which Rs. 8,973 was spent and the remainder lapsed to the State. The total demand of Municipal and Latrine taxes including arrears amounted to Rs. 6,933-4 of which Rs. 173-15-6 was irrecoverable. The actual collection under these heads came up to Rs. 3,727-8-6 against Rs. 3,685-11-9 in the previous year. The income under the Miscellaneous head amounted to Rs. 2,223-0-6 against Rs. 1,349-8-3 in the previous year. This figure includes deposits and advances recovered

Income.

during the year amounting to Rs. 331-4 and excludes Town Bazar income. Thus the total income of the Municipality including the State grant actually received amounted to Rs. 15,023-9 against Rs. 14,702-7-9 during the previous year.

Expenditure.

109. The total expenditure during the year under review including Rs. 128-12 in deposits repaid and advances came up to Rs. 15,885-1-3 against Rs. 15,167-15-6 during the previous year.

Town Bazar.

110. As in the previous year the control of the Town Bazar was in the hands of the Municipal Committee. The total demand including the arrear demand of Rs. 1,218-10-6 was Rs. 7,941-1-6. The total realization came up to Rs. 5,746-10-6 and the total expenditure from the Bazar fund was Rs. 4,716-7-6. The central yard of the biweekly market was filled up with earth brought from the old bed of the river. The accumulated sum of Rs. 10,567-5-6 in the Bazar account, standing as balance at the close of the year, will be spent on the improvement of the Town Bazar.

General Health.

111. The general health of the people within the Municipality was good, although there were some cases of cholera and chicken-pox. Kala-azar cases were decidedly fewer. The want of good drinking water and proper drainage is being keenly felt. The matter is receiving attention.

Miscellaneous.

112. Both the Investiture and Installation Ceremonies of His Highness The Maharaja Manikya Bahadur took place in the year under review. In connection with the former a special committee for sanitation and water supply work was appointed, and the Chairman of the Municipality was a member of the Committee. Other members were Dr. M. M. Mazumdar, L. M. S., State Physician, Babu R. M. Goswami, M. A., B. L., Sadar Magistrate, and Lieut. J. N. Bhaduri, B. A., B. E., State Engineer. The Municipality took active part in properly managing the works that were in its charge. During the Installation Ceremony the sanitation and water supply works were managed by the Sanitation Department assisted by the Municipality when necessary.

CHAPTER IV—PRODUCTION AND DISTRIBUTION.

1. Weather and Crops—Agriculture.

Rainfall.

113. The average rainfall of the year was 78·37 inches against 110·04 inches in the previous year. The quinquennial average was 98·81 inches. Dharmanagar Division had the maximum fall of 110·42 inches and Amarpur Sub-division the minimum of 51·92. Insufficient and untimely rainfall was unfavourable to crops.

Crops.

114. The principal crops were paddy, cotton, *til*, mustard, jute and sugar-cane. Potatoes, tobacco, chillies and pulses of various types were also grown in some parts of the State. The outturn of cotton and early paddy was unsatisfactory.

115. The tea industry showed appreciable progress and the tea produced in the State fetched good prices. As many as 39 gardens showed marked improvement. 9,40,062 lbs. of tea was produced in the gardens in State territory in the calendar year 1927.

Tea Industry.

116. The health of cattle was not bad on the whole. Authrax cases prevailed to some extent in Kailashahar Division and foot and mouth and rinderpest diseases in some parts of the Sadar Division. The Veterinary Assistant toured in Mofussil for 32 days. 1663 head of cattle were treated for various diseases during the year.

Cattle.

117. The people are mostly agricultural. Crops such as mustard, jute, potatoes and chillies yielded normal outturn. Cleansed cotton sold at Rs. 15 to Rs. 40 per maund. The production of jute decreased due to dullness of market. The condition of the Hill population in the northern part of the State improved after the *joom* harvest during the latter half of the year under review.

Condition of the people.

118. The prices of food grains were similar to those in the neighbouring British districts. Rice sold from Rs. 5-10 to Rs. 10 and paddy from Rs. 3 to Rs. 4-12 per maund.

Prices.

119. Male labourers earned from 12 annas to Re. 1-8 and female labourers from 8 annas to Re. 1 a day. Gharamis earned from Re. 1 to Re. 1-8 and carpenters and masons from Re. 1 to Re. 1-8. Most of the labourers were outsiders from the neighbouring British districts, as well as up-country coolies.

Wages.

120. No Taccavi advances were issued during the year.

Taccavi.

121. A sum of about Rs. 13,000 had been distributed as loan among the hill population in the year 1336 T. E. and a further sum of Rs. 36,000 was distributed as loan among them during the first half of the year under review. Rs. 7153 was realised towards capital and Rs. 230 towards interest before the close of the year. The Joomias promised to pay the balance within the current year after gathering their *Joom* harvest. Measurers were taken for prohibiting export of rice and paddy from the affected areas. Rangoon rice had to be sent to the interior of Kailashahar Division and Amarpur Sub-Division for distribution as loans and for sale at cost price. Only eleven maunds of rice was distributed as gratuitous relief in Kailashahar Division. Paddy for seeds was also distributed among the hill people.

Relief Operations.

122. The staff of the Department of Agriculture continued to be the same as it was during the last year.

Staff.

123. Propaganda work was conducted throughout the year in Sadar Division and the following were undertaken :—

Propaganda work and Circuit lecture.

1. Introduction of better quality cotton in *joom* and also in the plains with plough.

2. Introduction of early superior quality paddy in *Jooms* as well as some other improved varieties of Aman in the plains.

3. Extension of superior quality of jute, tobacco, sugarcane and potato crops both in high lands and plains.

4. Circuit lectures against nomadic jooming and in favour of plough cultivation.

5. Preservation of manure and use of selected seeds.

6. Introduction of Eri rearing among the people.

Garo cotton.

124. Some important Garo or Tura variety of cotton was introduced in the *jooms* with success and the growers being fully satisfied with the results, are adopting the seeds with earnestness. About 10 mds. of seeds were sold during the year.

Paddy seed distribution.

125. Kataktara, Indrasail, Dadkhani and Charnak have earned great popularity among the Hill and low land agricultural population and the spread of Kataktara is very remarkable. There was very great demand during the year under report for different kinds of paddy seeds, and the State Department is now almost in a position to carry out a systematic propaganda in connection with the spread of improved varieties of paddy, for both high and low lands.

Jute cultivation.

126. Improved varieties of seeds have been distributed at different centres, and the spread is both rapid and steady. The joomiahs are also growing Chinsura green and other varieties in *jooms* under jooming methods.

Improved varieties of Sugar Cane.

127. Yellow and striped Mauritius Canes are spreading in Sadar Division, and attempt is being made to spread their popularity through local growers.

Eri Rearing.

128. Eri rearing was tried at several centres and with conspicuous success.

Kashipur Farm.

129. The utilization of the Kashipur Farm for seed growing purpose has been an increasing success and it is now able to meet the local demand to a great extent. Tobacco, cotton, potato, paddy, jute, sugarcane, and radish were the principal crops grown during the year as seed crops.

Seed distribution in farming areas.

130. The Superintendent of Agriculture was deputed to Deo Valley with his staff to look after the agricultural condition of the people. Paddy seeds were distributed among the people in large quantities. Potato cultivation is spreading in the river valley areas and the progress is satisfactory.

Touring of the Staff.

131. The Superintendent was out on tour for 72 days during the year.

II. Immigration and Emigration

132. During the year 1497 families immigrated into and 879 families emigrated out of the State, as against 1,652 and 506 respectively in the previous year.

III. Forests.

Charge and Management. 133. Dewan Sahib K. Dutt Esq., M. A., B. L., M. R. A. S., F. E. S. (Lond) was in charge of the Department till the 3rd of Poush. Since that date, the charge of the Department remained with Babu Jatindra Nath Mitter. With the exception of a few ***Mehals*** which were let out in ***Ijara***, all the forests were under ***Khash*** management as before.

Staff. 134. The Department had a staff of 4 Forest Circle Inspectors, 19 Foresters, 12 Rangers, 15 Assistant Foresters, 11 Moharers, 17 Head Guards and 199 Guards and Literate Guards. Besides these there were 165 Commission Agents for the sale of forest permits for the shoulder-borne export of minor forest produce not coming under any definite ***Mehal***. There were 60 Stations for collection of duty and prevention of forest offences.

Working. 135. The Reserved *Sal* Forests of the Sonamura Division continued to be worked under the system of Coppice with standards and those of the Udaipur Division under the Improvement Method, while the open unclassed forests were worked under the State Forest Rules of 1323 T. E. For the Feni River *Mehal*, the working rules of the Bengal Forest Department were followed.

136. The marking of the four blocks selected in the Sonamura Division was finished, but the sale of the coupes could not be held within the year under report. Only one of the two blocks selected and marked in the Udaipur Division to be worked under Improvement Felling System was sold, and no work was undertaken in the other coupe.

Sources of Revenue. 137. The following table shews the result of collection of forest revenue :—

Heads of Revenue.	1337 T.E.	1336 T.E.	Increase.	Decrease.	REMARKS.
I. Unclassed open forests :—					
(*a*) Toll on forest produce exported by the river mehals	4,71,580	4,08,970	62,610	—	
(*b*) Toll on forest produce exported by land route under permit	74,417	84,365	—	9,948	
(*c*) Toll collection (share) of the Feni river mehal ...	36, 90	29,146	7,144	—	
(*d*) Grazing mehal ...	8,326	7,339	987		
(*e*) Thatching grass mehal	7,619	9,029	—	1,410	
II. Reserved Forests :— Sale of *Sal* and *Garjan* trees ...	6,784	15,289	—	8,505	
III. Elephant Kheddas	36,713	42	36,671	—	
TOTAL ...	6,41,729	5,54,180	1,07,412	19,863	

Net increase 87,549.

Receipts.

138. The total forest revenue of the year under report was Rs. 6,41,729 against Rs. 5,54,180 in the previous year, showing an increase of Rs. 87,549.

139. An appreciable rise of revenue is noticeable in the river Mehals and the Elephant *Khedda* Mehals and a slight fall in the permit Mehals. Timely floods facilitated export of timbers by the rivers, while want of a good demand for minor forest produce accounts for the decrease under the head Permit Mehal. There was a fall of revenue under *Sal* and *Garjan* as, with one exception, none of the *Sal* coupes in the Sonamura and the Udaipur Divisions, could be sold during the year under review.

Khedda Operations.

140. During the year under report *Khedda* operations were undertaken in the Manoo and Deo Doals in the Kailashahar Division, Bilonia-Sabroom Doal in the Bilonia and the Sabroom Divisions and Longai Doal in the Dharmanagar Division. The *Khedda* operations in the Deo Doal and the Bilonia-Sabroom Doal were successful, but the operations in the other Doals which were rather late in starting, failed. 26 elephants were caught in the Deo Doal and 19 in the Bilonia-Sabroom Doal making a total of 45 elephants against 16 in the previous year.

Feni River Mehal.

141. The Government of Bengal agreed to the continuance till the 31st March, 1931, of the Joint Toll Station at Amlighat under the management of the State Forest Department. The total revenue collected at the Joint Toll Station in the year under review was Rs. 52,290 against Rs. 43,845 in the previous year.

Fee Simple Lots.

142. As the major portion of the area of the 14 *as.* 7⅛ *p.* share of the Lot No. 98 under the Chittagong Collectorate was brought under tea cultivation the forest produce from this portion of the Lot was not taken in *Ijara* on behalf of the Government and the State, as in previous years. The forest produce from this Lot as well as from the other Fee Simple Lots was exported without any trouble between the Station staff and the Lot owners.

Forest offences.

143. During the year under review there were 171 forest cases against 374 persons, of which 25 cases against 104 persons were pending from the previous year. The offences were mainly for illicit export of forest produce without permits and without payment of duty.

Results.

144. Altogether 169 persons in 83 cases were convicted, of whom 15 were sentenced to imprisonment and 154 were punished with fine only. 77 persons in 22 cases were acquitted, and 8 cases against 22 persons were compounded. 58 cases against 106 persons remained pending at the close of the year.

Rewards and Punishments.

145. No rewards were sanctioned during the year under review. Two Foresters, one Ranger, one Assistant Forester and one Moharer were degraded for misconduct. Two Guards and one Boatman were dismissed and two Guards were placed under supension pending trial.

Health of the Staff.

146. Excepting the death of a Guard from Cholera, the health of the staff in general was normal.

147. There was a regrettable accident in the Matinagar Beat Office, where a Forest Guard was killed by a tiger. The father of the deceased guard was granted a bonus from the State.

Accidents.

148. Some difficulties were being still experienced in connection with the export of forest produce from the State into Sylhet District, specially in regard to the delivery of the drift logs belonging to the State, and the check exercised by the Assam Forest Department on State forest produce in transit and the fee levied thereon. Correspondence on the subject was in progress between the State and the Assam Government when the year closed.

General.

IV. Trade and Manufacture.

149. The principal exports were timber, forest produce of various kinds, cotton, oil-seeds, (*til* and mustard seed) pady, jute, rice and *Gur* (molasses). A small quantity of tea and some homespun cotton fabrics manufactured by the hill people, especially the Manipuris, were also exported. The principal exports for the year under review and of the previous year are shewn below :—

	1336 T. E.	1337 T. E.
Cotton ...	87,553 maunds.	69,093 maunds.
Til	35,621 "	30,295 "
Mustard seeds	23,802 "	18,630 "
Jute	1,56,120 "	1,24,655 "

150. 5,28,322 lbs, 7,90,771 lbs and 10,13,109 lbs of tea were exported in 1335 T. E., 1336 T. E. and 1337 T. E. respectively.

151. The principal imports were cloths and yarns, salt, oils (*kerosine* and mustard), pulses, chillies, tobacco, sugar, flour, spices, arecanuts, books and stationery. The industries worth mention were manufacture of cotton fabrics by the hill people and the Manipuris; cane and bamboo baskets, mats and sieves by Tripuras; and dug-outs, bowls and plates of wood by the Reangs and Chakmas; also *Gur* (molasses) by both hill people and Bengalees.

V. Public Works.

152. Mahamanyabar Maharajkumar B. K. Deb Barman Bahadur, Member of the Council of Admininistration, was in charge of the Department till the 2nd Bhadra, 1337 T. E. Since then Rai J. C. Sen Bahadur, Minister was in charge of the Department.

153. Lieut. J. N. Bhaduri, B. A., B. E., continued as State Engineer.

154. The expenditure including disbursements from local funds came to Rs. 3,10,097 against Rs. 2,81,015 in the previous year. Of this Rs. 2,05,620 was spent on buildings, Rs. 64,008 on roads and bridges, Rs. 4,762 on water-supply

Expenditure.

and Rs. 7,422 on miscellaneous works. Besides this expenditure Rs. 95,073 was spent for Public Works in connection with His Highness's Investiture and the Installation Ceremony.

155. The following important major works were completed during the year under report :—

1. An amphitheatre for His Highness's Installation Ceremony.
2. Stone-metalling of the District Board portion of Agartala-Akhaura Road.
3. Decorated wooden ceiling in the Ball room of the Ujjayanta Palace.
4. A new Indian gate on the Central Road on the occasion of H. E. Governor's visit.
5. Improvement of the State Physician's quarters.
6. A new Dak Bungalow at Agartala.
7. Improvement of the Kunjaban Palace for the accommodation of His Excellency the Governor of Bengal and Party.
8. Improvement of the Ujjayanta Palace.
9. Masonry railings around the two Palace lakes.
10. A spacious Godown for the Palace Sultanat.
11. Alterations and improvement of Lalmahal.
12. A new building for the Sansar Office.
13. Three Bungalows at Kunjaban.
14. Decorative pillars between the two Palace gates.
15. Durgabari Road extension.
16. Pucca drains on both sides of the newly extended roads in the Palace compound.
17. Bridges on Dhala Road at Bilonia.
18. *Sal* wood piling at Sonamura to prevent erosion of the river Goomti.
19. Additional structures for the power house with foundation for a fifty H. P. Ruston Engine.
20. Bar Library at Agartala.
21. Post-mortem house at Agartala.
22. Two Structures in His Highness's Andar.

156. The following buildings were completed with C. I. roofing during the year under report :—

i. Siddhinagar Tahasil Office in Bilonia.
ii. Motai Tahasil Office in Bilonia.
iii. Dharmanagar Post Office.
iv. Sabroom Post Office.
v. Sonamura Thana.
vi. Kalamchaura Thana.
vii. Tahasil Katchery at Kailashahar.
viii. Bisalgarh M. E. School.
ix. Sidhai Forest Office.
x. Police Court at Udaipur.

CHAPTER V—REVENUE AND FINANCES.

I. Revenue.

157. The total collection in the year was Rs. 18,77,136 against Rs. 18,50,807 in the previous year.

158. The details of income under different heads with all variations are given in the statement below :—

Serial number.	Heads of Revenue.	1337 T.E.	1336 T.E.	As compared with 1336 T.E.		Remarks.
				Increase.	Decrease.	
1	Land Revenue	6,02,891	6,18,210	—	15,319	
2	Rents of markets	7,658	7,223	435	—	
3	Family Tax in the hills	60,223	54,595	5,628	—	
4	Toll on forest produce	5,45,997	4,93,335	52,662	—	
5	Do. Do. on the Feni River	36,290	29,146	7,144	—	
6	Elephant & buffalo grazing Mehal	8,326	7,339	987	—	
7	Thatching grass Mehal	7,619	9,029	—	1,410	
8	Reserved *Sal* trees	6,784	15,289	—	8,505	
9	Tax on cotton and oil-seeds ...	1,56,486	2,18,051	—	61,565	
10	Royalty on elephants caught ...	36,713	42	36,671	—	
11	Adda Mehal	23,202	23,063	139	—	
12	Excise	85,485	79,354	6,131	—	
13	Stamps and Court-fees	89,530	87,137	2,393	—	
14	Law and Justice (Fines)... ...	4,012	4,162	—	150	
15	Process fees	15,495	15,905	—	410	
16	Registration	15,828	15,988	—	160	
17	Jail	4,559	4,739	—	180	
18	Cattle pounds	5,895	6,083	—	188	
19	Nazars	49,733	52,490	—	2,757	
20	Agriculture	611	511	100	—	
21	Education...	8,661	6,810	1,851	—	
22	Miscellaneous	1,05,138	1,02,306	2,832	—	
	Total	18,77,136	18,50,807	1,16,973	90,644	Net increase—Rs. 26, 329

Increase.

159. There was thus a total increase of Rs. 1,16,973 in respect of 12 heads of revenue and a total decrease of Rs. 90,644 in regard to 10 heads.

160. The increase as compared with the previous year under the head "Family tax in the hills" is due to better *jhoom* harvest. The increase under the head of forest produce is satisfactory. *Kheda* operation met wlth success after a lapse of several unpropitious years and fetched in a substantial revenue. The increase under excise head is due to resettlement at higher *jama*.

161. The decrease under head "Land revenue" is due to dullness of market in jute crop affecting the people of Udaypur, Sonamura and Bilonia Divisions generally. The decrease under head "Tax on cotton and oilseeds" is due to unfavourable weather conditions during the harvest season.

II. Finances.

162. A consolidated abstract account showing the financial transactions of the State and the attached Zemindaries as compared with those of the previous year is given below :—

Receipts.	1336 T.E.	1337 T.E.
1. Opening balance :–		
(1) State	6,11,124	10,47,019
(2) Zemindaries ...	3,77,146	3,72,617
Total ...	9,88,270	14,19,636
2. Income :—		
(1) State	18,58,281	18,77,136
(2) Zemindaries ...	11,12,526	11,46,097
Total ...	29,70,807	30,23,233
3. Law charges recovered :—		
(1) Zemindaries ...	52,026	43,228
4. Refunds and compensation for lands acquired :—		
(1) Zemindaries ...	1,404	2,890
5. Deposits :—		
(1) State	3,68,535	83,751
(2) Zemindaries ...	8,815	7,418
Total ...	3,77,350	91,169
GRAND TOTAL ...	43,89,857	45,80,156

Expenditure.	1336 T.E.	1337 T.E.
1. General Administration charges :—		
(a) State	4,78,963	5,51,457
(b) Zemindaries :—		
1. Cost of management	1,44,408	1,44,597
2. Cost of litigation	1,01,347	96,490
Total ...	7,24,718	7,92,544
2. Revenue and Taxes on account of the Zemindaries	2,68,970	2,69,253
3. Public Works :—		
(a) State	2,90,156	3,12,791
(b) Zemindaries	82,616	50,612
Total ...	3,72,772	3,63,403
4. Municipality—State	9,706	8,073
5. Education :—		
(a) State	1,16,474	1,26,208
(b) Zemindaries	11,029	10,884
Total ...	1,27,503	1,37,092
6. Medical and Sanitation :—		
(a) State	71,740	81,128
(b) Zemindaries	11,698	11,963
Total ...	83,438	93,091
7. Survey and Settlement :—		
(a) State	15,850	14,443
(b) Zemindaries	809	827
Total ...	16,659	15,270
8. Agriculture :—State	5,479	4,789
9. Religious Expenses :—		
(a) State	65,358	62,414
(b) Zemindaries	6,122	6,215
Total ...	71,480	68,629
10. Sultanat—State	79,106	54,283
11. Purchase of Land Tenures :—		
(a) State	1,896	240
(b) Zemindaries	6,805	27,758
Total ...	8,701	27,998
12. Pension and Gratuity :—		
(a) State	28,420	31,225
(b) Zemindaries	4,841	5,137
Total ...	33,261	36,362
13. Ordinary *Sansar* charges :—		
(a) Ordinary expenses on account of His Highness and family including the late Maharaja's family ...	81,029	84,917
(b) Other branches of the Raj family ...	1,38,515	1,36,750
(c) Thakurs	29,240	31,434
(d) *Sansar* office establishment ...	8,471	9,901
(e) Electric Light	25,137	19,020
(f) Miscellaneous	83,082	69,226
Total ...	3,65,474	3,51,248
14. Charity and Donation :—		
(a) State	21,554	23,945
(b) Zemindaries	1,549	3,073
Total ...	23,103	27,018
15. Famine Relief—State	12,368	30,373
16. His Highness's Nij Tahabil (Privy purse) including expenses on journeys	1,26,863	1,20,045
17. Liabilities liquidated including payment of interest on loans and repayment of deposits :—		
(a) State	85,828	77,016
(b) Zemindaries	5,07,849	35,568
Total	5,93,677	1,12,584
18. Miscellaneous :—		
(a) State	6,122	9,903
(b) Zemindaries	15,477	12,957
Total ...	21,599	22,860
19. Marriage—State	18,504	3,37,111
20. Advances to employees—State ...	6,840	7,768
21. Advances to employees—Zemindaries	—	2,516
22. Investiture—State	—	2,07,201
23. Installation—State	—	4,66,080
Total ...	29,70,221	35,50,401
24 Closing Balance :—		
(a) State		
In Cash	5,06,386	1,33,006
At Bank	3,28,744	2,65,742
In bonds and advances	2,11,889	2,96,037
Total ...	10,47,019	6,94,785
(b) Zemindaries :—		
In Cash	1,24,852	1,03,746
At Bank	1,00,000	1,05,052
In bonds and advances	1,47,765	1,20,082
Total ...	3,72,617	3,28,880
Total of State & Zemindaries' balances ..	14,19,636	10,23,065
GRAND TOTAL	43,89,857	45,80,156

163. The year opened with a balance of Rs. 14,19,636 against Rs. 9,88,270 in the preceding year. During the year under review, the total receipts from all sources including deposits and Law charges recovered amounted to Rs. 31,60,520 against Rs. 34,01,587 during the previous year, the decrease being mainly due to the fact that the latter figure included Rs. 2,60,000 received as deposits from Their Highnesses the Maharanis. The total sum available for expenditure including the opening balance was, therefore, Rs. 45,80,156 as against Rs. 43,89,857 in the preceding year.

Receipts.

164. The total expenditure during the year amounted to Rs. 35,56,491 against Rs. 29,70,221 in the previous year, showing an increase of Rs. 5,86,270 which was mainly due to abnormal items of expenditure incurred in connection with His Highness's Investiture and Installation ceremonies as well as a marriage in the Raj Family. The closing balance at the end of the year was Rs. 10,23,665 against Rs. 14,19,636. Of this balance, Rs. 2,36,752 was in cash in the Treasuries, Rs. 3,70,794 in the Banks and Rs. 4,16,119 in loans and advances. The abnormal expenditure referred to above, caused a corresponding reduction in the balance, while the inflation in the figures for loans and advances was due to certain current advances remaining unadjusted at the close of the year.

Expenditure.

165. The noticeable variations in expenditure are explained below :—

i. ADMINISTRATION CHARGES :—

STATE—The main reasons for the increase were—

(a) Re-organisation of the State Miltary Forces involving higher outlay.

(b) Entertainment of the Armed Police.

(c) Establishment of the Private Secretary Office.

(d) Re-placement of military guards by jail-warders in the Sadar Central Jail.

(e) Adjustment of the price of elephants purchased for the Administration.

ii. COST OF LITIGATION :—

ZEMINDARIES—The institution of a smaller number of suits accounted for the decrease under this head.

iii. PUBLIC WORKS :—

STATE—The increase was due to expensive road and building works, undertaken during the year The amount shown under this head was exclusive of the expenditure incurred for special works directly connected with the Installation Ceremony and debited against the connected head of expenditure.

ZEMINDARIES—The extra expenditure incurred in constructing a new daily market and the improvement of the Dharmasagar House in the previous year accounted for the decrease under this head.

iv. MUNICIPALITY :—

STATE—The discontinuance of the special grant for the Agartala Municipality for prevention of Epidemic diseases led to the reduction of expenditure.

v. EDUCATION :—

The increase was mainly attributable to (*a*) the Kumar Boarding at Comilla being worked for the full year, (*b*) extra payments made for Raipur College expenses, (*c*) establishment of a Tripura Boarding at Sadar and (*d*) the usual grade increments.

vi. MEDICAL AND SANITATION :—

STATE—The increase was principally due to grade increments, expenses incurred for the treatment of the late Bhramara Kumari and the purchase of Surgical apparatus for the V. M. Hospital.

vii. SURVEY AND SETTLEMENTS :—

STATE—The small variation under this head was due to non-payment of certain bills during the year.

viii. RELIGIOUS EXPENSES :—

STATE—The decrease was due to economies effected in some Pujas.

ix. SULTANAT :—

STATE—The reduction under this head was attributable to the unusual payments made in the preceding year for the purchase of motor cars and for the improvement of the *Dais* in the Durbar Hall.

x. PURCHASE OF LAND TENURES :—

ZEMINDARIES—The increase was due to the payment of the price of Khoda Noaj Khan's house at Comilla.

xi. PENSION AND GRATUITY :—

STATE—The increase was due to retirement of some officers and also payment of some arrear bills.

xii. ORDINARY SANSAR EXPENSES :—

STATE—On the whole, the expenditure under this head shows a reduction of Rs. 14,226, which was due to curtailment of expenditure specially under the Sub-heads "Electric Light" and "Miscellaneous." The absence of any additional payments such as had to be made in 1336 T. E. for cost of certain social and religious rites also contributed to the decrease.

xiii. FAMINE RELIEF :—

STATE—Owing to the scarcity of food stuffs in the hills a sum of Rs. 30,373 was spent for the relief of the distressed subjects, in addition to the amount of Rs. 12,368 disbursed in the previous year.

xiv. NIJ TAHABIL :—

The non-adjustment of certain bills in connection with H. H.'s tour contributed to the decrease under this head.

xv. LIABILITIES :—

Of the amount shewn under this head, Rs. 25,000 represents the last remnant of the old bonded debts with interest thereon which was previously sanctioned by the Council of Administration, and the balance of Rs. 87,584 was for repayment of deposits etc.

xvi. MISCELLANEOUS :—

The increase in the State was due to certain extra expenditure incurred for printing the 1st volume of Rajmala and to the payment of an outstanding bill of the India Sanitation Improvement Company, while the decrease in Zemindaries was due to savings under the head "Unforseen."

166. Two statements comparing the receipts and expenditure of the State and Zemindaries with the respective Revised Estimates are given in appendices XXVI, XXVII.

167. In the State, the actual receipts fell short of the Revised Estimate by Rs. 34,613 while there was a reduction of Rs. 1,46,598 under expenditure. The net result of these fluctuations raised the anticipated surplus from Rs. 5,87,800 to Rs. 6,99,785.

CHAPTER VI—MEDICAL.

168. The year under review opened with 18 Dispensaries in the State as in the previous year.

New patients.

169. The total number of new patients treated in all the Dispensaries as well as their daily average as compared with those of the previous year are shown in the following table.

	1336 T.E.			1337 T.E.		
	Outdoor.	Indoor.	Total.	Outdoor.	Indoor.	Total.
PATIENTS.	98,211	427	98,638	94,782	492	95,274
Daily average	269·07	1·16	270·23	258·96	1·34	260·30

Out-door attendance.

170. The total out-door attendance (new + old) was 1,68,429 as against 1,67,383 in the previous year, the daily average being 460·18 against 458·51.

In-door attendance.

171. With the last year's balance of 15, the total number of in-door patients was 492 as against 427 in the year before. Of the above, 336 were discharged cured, 111 were relived or discharged otherwise, 38 died and 7 remained under treatment at the close of the year.

Surgical Operation.

172. There were 1,196 operations performed with 24 major cases. The previous year's figures were 1,173 and 29 respectively.

V. M. Hospital.

173. New out-patients treated totalled 10,996 as against 11,833 in the previous year. The daily average of attendance including both new and old patients was 51·87 against 56·40. The total in-patients numbered 436 as against 400 in the year previous. Of these, 291 were discharged cured, 103 relieved, 37 died and 5 remained under treatment—the daily average being 14·82 against 15·58. The total expenditure on this institution amounted to Rs. 9,891 against Rs. 9,337 in the previous year.

Police case.

174. 184 Police cases were admitted during the year as against 172 in the preceding year, including 18 postmortem cases against 17.

Ayurvedic Department.

175. In the beginning of the year under report the services of two Kavirajes were continued in this Deparment. One of them died during the year. 53 patients were

treated by them against 70 in the previous year. The total expenses incurred for their salaries and for medicines amounted to Rs. 3281-14-3 against Rs. 3892-9-6.

176. Dr. Hira Lal Banerjee, H. M. B., with one Assistant treated 14,695 patients as against 10,075 in the preceding year, the daily average (new + old) being 99·47 against 59·25. The total expenditure for this Department amounted to Rs. 5,657 as against Rs. 4,862.

Homoeopathic Department.

177. 8562 persons were successfully vaccinated out of 12369, against 7423 out of 9009 in the preceding year. Two small-pox Doctors assisted by two vaccination Inspectors inspected the work of the vaccinators in the interior. There were 402 seizures from small-pox with 63 deaths so far as reported. Of the above seizures the State small-pox Doctors treated 131 persons of whom only ten died. The total expenses on this account amounted to Rs. 1,546-10-6 as against Rs. 1,236-11-3 in the previous year.

Vaccination and small-pox.

178. 164 patients were treated at the capital during the year under review as against 233 in previous year. Of these 103 were cured, 50 left treatment, 3 died and 8 remained under treatment. In the moffussil Dispensaries 64 cases were treated as against 118 in the year before. The total expenditure on this account amounted to Rs. 958-3-6 against Rs. 1032-14-6 in the previous year.

Kala-azar.

179. During the year under report cholera and small-pox appeared with virulence in some parts of the State, specially in Sadar and Kailashahar Divisions and made heavy toll amongst the inhabitants. There were 574 seizures from cholera with 146 deaths, so far as reported. Had it not been for the intensive and extensive measures for cholera inoculation and vaccination adopted both in anticipation of and during the epidemics, the toll would have been far greater.

Public Health.

180. The health of the capital town was generally good, owing to the sanitary measures taken during the year at a cost of Rs. 3,346 against Rs. 4,998 in the previous year.

Sanitation.

181. Dr. M. M. Mojumdar, L. M. S., was the Chief Medical Officer and Dr. S. K. Dutt, L. M. S., his Assistant. Besides a staff of subordinate medical men, a Lady Doctor and three midwives were retained in their respective duties.

Staff.

182. Neither the Chief Medical Officer nor his Assistant could inspect the outlying dispensaries on account of their occupation in the various important functions during the year under report.

Tour.

183. The total expenditure incurred for the Medical Department including Sanitation in the year under review amounted to Rs. 79,597, as against Rs. 70,278 for the previous year.

Total Expenditure.

CHAPTER VII—PUBLIC INSTRUCTION.

184. Mr. S. C. Deb Barman, M. A. (Harvard) continued to be in charge of the Education Department.

Charge.

185. The total number of schools during the year was 170 against 140 in the previous year, and the total numerical strength 6,848 against 6,331; excluding private institutions numbering 17 with 617 pupils on the rolls, as against 10 with 180. Some Pathshalas were raised to the status of L. V. Schools, while some new Pathshalas were sanctioned during the year under report. Thus the number of Primary Schools increased on the whole.

Number of Schools.

186. The number of H. E. Schools in the State remained as before, viz., the Umakanta Academy at Agartala, the Radhakishore Institution at Kailashahar, the Brojendrakishore Institution at Bilonia, the Birbikram Institution at Dharmanagar and the Navadwip Chandra Institution at Sonamura. The H. E. School at Sonamura was named Navadwip Chandra Institution after Maharajkumar Navadwip Chandra Deb Barman Bahadur, the President of the Council of Administration, by order of the then Member-in-Charge of Education with the approval of His Highness the Maharaja Manikya Bahadur. All the High Schools are affiliated to the Calcutta University. The number of pupils in these H. E. Schools was 1,450 against 1429 in the previous year, and the average daily attendance stood at 1,092·49 against 1,033·62.

H. E. Schools.

187. Agartala, the State Capital, was, as in the previous year, selected by the Calcutta University as a Centre for the Matriculation Examination for the year 1928. Only the State High English Schools were allowed to send up candidates to this Centre. The Examination was conducted under the direct control and supervision of the Minister, Tripura State, in charge of Education. The Department looked after the convenience of the candidates coming from Muffussil.

Matriculation Centre.

188. Altogether 51 candidates were sent up for the last Matriculation Examination from the five State High English Schools, against 55 in the previous year. Besides these, a teacher from the Dharmanagar B. B. Institution also sat for the Matriculation Examination at this Centre. The details of the result are noted below :—

Results of the Matriculation Examination.

		No. sent up.	Passed.	1st Division.	2nd Division.	3rd Division.
1.	U. K. Academy	14	12	7	5	0
2.	R. K. Institution	9	7	2	3	2
3.	B. K. Institution	17	15	5	10	0
4.	B. B. Institution	6	5	3	2	0
5.	N. Ch. Institution	5	3	0	1	2
	Total ...	51	42	17	21	4

189. Considering the general low percentage of successes in the last Matriculation Examination of the Calcutta University the results were, on the whole, satisfactory.

190. In the year under review, there were 8 M. E. Schools for boys with 986 pupils on the rolls, against 7 with 803 pupils in the previous year. The average daily attendance was 753·55 against 608·09.

M. E. Schools.

191. There was only one Higher Vernacular School for boys with 62 students on the rolls as against one with 50 students in the previous year, and the average daily attendance was 46·77 against 40·25.

H. V. Schools.

192. The number of Lower Vernacular Schools for boys was 21 against 22 in the previous year. The total numerical strength was 1,191 against 1,210 and the average daily attendance 879·55 against 922·13 in the previous year. In some of these schools, boys and girls read together.

L. V. Schools.

193. There were 115 Pathshalas for boys, in the year under report, as against 89 in the previous year. The total numerical strength was 2,643 against 2,344 and the average daily attendance 2,031·32 against 1814·02 in the previous year.

Pathshalas.

194. There was one Middle English School for girls, namely the Maharani Tulsibati Girls' School at Agartala, the State Capital. The numerical strength was 75 against 85 and the average daily attendance 53·60 against 70·40 in the previous year. There was a motor bus for the conveyance of the girls during the year. By special permission of this Department some girls were allowed to continue their higher studies in this school under the graduate Head Mistress.

M. E. Schools for girls.

195. There were 10 Pathshalas for girls against 9 Pathshalas in the previous year. The numerical strength of the schools was 236 against 189 and the average daily attendance 168·23 against 137·07 in the previous year. In some of these institutions, under the special orders of the Education Department, girls were allowed to read the Lower Vernacular and Upper Vernacular Standard. Besides these, in some of the Pathshalas for boys, both boys and girls were taught together. In some of the Girls' Schools located at the Divisional Head-quarters, the male teachers were substituted by lady teachers.

Pathshalas for girls.

196. Altogether 456 candidates appeared at the local Scholarship Examinations against 405 in the previous year. Of these, 364 including 27 girls came out successful. 24 students including 3 girls passed the Middle English Examination, 6 students passed the H. V. Examination, 93 including 4 girls passed the L. V. Examination and 241 including 20 girls passed the Pathshala Examination. On the result of the examinations 18 boys and 5 girls received scholarships varying from Rs. 2 to Rs. 5 per month tenable for two to four years.

Scholarship Examination.

197. In the year under review, there were 9 schools for special training, consisting of 3 *Sanskrit Tols*, 5 *Madrassas* and *Maktobs* and 1 Artisan School, against the same number respectively in the previous year. The *Sanskrit Tols* had 43 students on the rolls against 42 in the previous

Schools for special Training.

year and the average daily attendance was 27·24 against 28·03. The *Rajakiya Sanskrit Bidyalaya* at Agartala sent up 3 candidates for the Government *Sanskrit* Examination against 6 in the previous year. The *Madrassas* and *Maktobs* had 152 students on the rolls against 167 in the previous year and the average daily attendance was 94·11 against 113·87. The Woodburn Artisan School had 10 boys on the rolls against 12 boys, and the average daily attendance was 5·03 against 5·53 in the previous year.

Non-Bengalee Students.

198. The comparative statement below will show the number of non-Bengalee students receiving education in the several schools of the State :—

Serial number.	Nationality.	Number of students.		Remarks.
		Past year.	Present year.	
1.	Rajkumars	8	7	
2.	Thakurs	180	170	
3.	Manipuris	614	611	
4.	Tripuras	583	732	
5.	Reangs	30	22	
	a. Kukis	42	25	
6.	*b.* Chakmas	12	2	
	c. Lushais	21	0	
7.	Others...	47	84	
	Total	1,537	1,653	

Reward Examinations.

199. The policy of holding Reward Examinations for hill boys was continued and 185 boys appeared at the examination against 158 boys in the previous year.

Education of Princes and Princesses.

200. Two Maharajkumars continued their studies in the Rajkumar College at Raipur in the Central Provinces being placed in charge of a graduate teacher as in the previous year. The results of their examinations and their progress in health were satisfactory. The Maharajkumaris received education as before under a graduate lady teacher and a Pandit.

Education of other Kumars.

201. Kumar Bepin Behari Deb Barman has been prosecuting studies in the Ashutosh College, Calcutta.

Comilla Kumar Boarding House.

202. There were 6 Maharajkumars, 5 Kumars and 1 Rana Bahadur against 4 Maharajkumars and 4 Kumars in the previous year. Nine of them were admitted to the Zilla school, Comilla. The results shown by the inmates at the annual examination of the school were satisfactory. The Kumars were placed in charge of a Superintending Tutor who, in addition to his tutorial work, looked after the management of the Boarding. Another private tutor coached some of the Kumars in the morning.

The Day School for the Young Kumars.

203. In the Day School for the young Kumars there were 6 students on the rolls belonging to the juvenile classes against the same number in the previous year.

204. Nine Thakur boys were awarded stipends from the Education Department and the course of studies prosecuted by each is noted below :—

Education of Thakur Boys.

1. Niranjan Deb Barman—Carmichæl Medical College.
2. Joysing Deb Barman—B. L. Class (Calcutta University).
3. Jitendra Chandra Deb Barman—B. L. Class (Calcutta University).
4. Suresh Chandra Deb Barman—Govt. School of Art, Calcutta.
5. Parendra Chandra Deb Barman—I. A. Class (Calcutta Ashutosh College).
6. Satish Chandra Deb Barman—B. L. Class (Calcutta University).
7. Hiron Kumar Deb Barman—I. Sc. Class (Comilla Victoria College).
8. Benode Behari Deb Barman—I. A. Class (Comilla Victoria College).
9. Harendra Chandra Deb Barman—I. Sc. Class (Calcutta Ashutosh College).

Thakur Boarding House, Agartala.

205. There were 35 boarders in the Thakur Boarding House against the same number in the previous year. The number of boarders successful in the last annual examination was 28. Three boarders sat for the last Matriculation Examination and came out successful, all being placed in the Second Division. The staff consisted of one Guardian Superintendent, one Graduate Resident Tutor, one Assistant Tutor, and one Manager and Tutor. The daily average attendance of the boarders was 30·89 against 28·01 in the previous year.

Tripura Boarding House, Agartala.

206. There were 10 hill boys in the Tripura Boarding House attached to the U. K. Academy against the same number in the previous year. The boys received free boarding and lodging aud had a Superintendent Tutor to look after their studies as well as the boarding managament. This institution received encouraging support from leading head men of Tripura villages.

207. There was also another Tripura Boarding House attached to Khowai M. E. School which also received due attention of the Department. The local hill people enthusiastically collected funds to provide this institution with a permanent house. The Department agreed to sanction all necessary recurring expenditnre for this Institution, special grants being made during the year for a cook and a private tutor. Sufficient funds have been raised from hill people for the construction of a permanent Boarding House which is expected to be completed next year.

Special Stipends.

208. The following students enjoyed special stipends :—

1. Chandrahas Singha.
2. Prokash Chandra Sutradhar.
3. Navadwip Chandra Singha.
4. Pulin Behari Acharjya.

5. Radha Raman Pandey.
6. Mohendra Kumar Roy.
7. Nagendra Narayan Chaudhuri.

Inspection Work.

209. Mr. S. C. Deb Barman, M. A., who is also ex-officio Inspector of Schools, visited some Boarding Institutions and Schools at Comilla, Sonamura, Udaipur and Kailashahar, the tour, on the whole, comprising 16 days.

210. The Sub-Inspectors of Schools visited all the schools within their respective jurisdictions. On the whole, their inspection work was satisfactory.

Library.

211. At Agartala, the Bir Chandra Library was maintained in two separate sections, (1) the English Library, being located at the Ujjayanta Palace and (2) the Vernacular Section in the building erected in the vicinity of the local H. E. School. The latter Section was open to the public. The number of English books (including foreign literature) was 4,886 against 4,881 in the previous year and the number of Bengali books (including Sanskrit books) was 1,909 against 1,849 in the previous year. In addition to these, there was a moderate collection of valuable manuscripts in the Palace Library. There were 5 Dailies, 1 Quarterly, 6 Monthlies and 1 Weekly as against 5, 1, 5 and 1 respectively in the previous year. In the year under review the average daily attendance in the library rooms was 1319 against 1317, and the total number of volumes issued to the public was 2683 against 3116 in the previous year. Maharajkumar Narottam Kishore Deb Barman was appointed as State Librarian in the middle of the year.

Expenditure.

212. The total expenditure incurred in the Education Department in the year under report, amounted to Rs. 1,26,208 against Rs. 1,16,474. Some of the more important details of expenditure are noted below :—

1.	Primary Education	Rs.	21,756
2.	Secondary Education	"	41,709
3.	School for special Training	"	3,641
4.	Boarding Institution for Thakur boys ...	"	9,413
5.	Education of Kumars and Kumaris	"	22,228
6.	Scholarships and Stipends	"	9,237
7.	Library	"	1,558
8.	Tripura Boarding	"	1,184
9.	Miscellaneous	"	9,417
		Rs.	1,20,143
10.	Grain Allowance	"	6,065
		Rs.	1,26,208

Income.

213. Rs. 8661 was incorporated in the general receipts of the the State from the accumulated realisations from students, in pursuance of the policy adopted in the year 1334 T. E.

CHAPTER VIII—ZEMINDARIES.

Chakla Roshnabad Estates.

Management.

214. The management of His Highness's Zemindaries in British India continued in the hands of Rai J. C. Sen Bahadur, B. A., B. C. S. He was assisted by three Assistant Managers and one Sub-Manager as before.

215. The gross revenue demand of the year was Rs. 10,06,968 against Rs. 10,00,451 in the previous year.

Receipts.

216. The total receipts amounted to Rs. 11,99,633 (including Rs. 3,747 on account of the Tripura Raj Central Co-operative Bank and Rs. 706 on account of *Debuttar mehal*) against Rs. 11,74,771 in the previous year. The rise in collection is mainly due to the voluntary payment of arrear dues by some tenants in connection with the Installation Ceremony of His Highness.

Expenditure.

217. The total expenditure in the year under review was Rs. 12,43,370 including adjustment of old advances and contribution to the State, against Rs. 11,79,300 in the previous year. Of this, Rs. 2,69,253 was on account of Land Revenue and Cesses. The total administrative charges of the Zemindaries including Public Works and Law Charges amounted to Rs. 3,42,207. The remainder represents special payments on account of the following items, aggregating Rs. 6,31,910.

1.	Repayment of old debts	Rs.	25,000
2.	Donation	,,	1,760
3.	Medical charges	,,	11,963
4.	Education charges	,,	10,884
5.	Religious ceremonies	,,	6,215
6.	Sansar stipends	,,	15,520
7.	Repayment of old deposits ...	,,	10,568
8.	Contribution to the State	,,	5,50,000
		Rs.	6,31,910

Settlement.

218. The result of the year's settlement operations will appear from the figures noted below :—

	Kinds of settlement.	Addition to rental.		Nazar.	
1.	Railway relinquished land ...	Rs.	5	Rs.	6
2.	Settlement of Rent-free holding ...	,,	12	,,	0
3.	Ordinary Town Settlement ...	,,	195	,,	7,278
4.	*Khaspatit* ,, ...	,,	1,083	,,	8,107
5.	Enhancement of rent ...	,,	1,902	,,	23,587
6.	Resettlement of auction purchased holdings ...	,,	147	,,	10,723
7.	*Ijara*	,,	480	,,	0
		Rs.	3,824	Rs.	49,701

219. This year's operation improved the rent roll by Rs. 3,824 and brought in a *nazarana* of Rs. 49,701 against Rs. 4,263 and Rs. 43,105 respectively in the previous year.

CHAPTER IX—MISCELLANEOUS.

The Rajmala.

220. The first part of the Rajmala was published during the year under review. With the exception of the connected maps and sketches, which were under preparation, the printing of the 2nd part was completed, while the printing of the 3rd part was in progress. The total expenditure incurred during the year amounted to Rs. 8,604 against Rs. 6,098 in the previous year.

Services Enquiry Committee.

221. Under orders of His Highness, dated 26-7-37 T. E., a Committee composed of Dewan Saheb Kamala Prasad Dutt, M.A., B.L., M. R. A. S., F. R. E. S., and Thakur Kamini Kumar Singha was appointed to enquire into the condition of the services generally, and to suggest means for improving the prospects of Gazetted and Ministerial officers and others, and at the same time effecting such economies as might be possible in the different branches of the administration. The Committee had not concluded its labours when the year closed.

Tours.

222. Rai J. C. Sen Bahadur was out on tour for 13 days during the first four months of the year, as Vice-President, Council of Administration. After his appointment as Minister and Manager, he was on tour for 9 days, making a total of 22 days during the year. The successive important functions at Headquarters prevented his being out for a longer period.

223. Dewan B. K. Sen Bahadur, Chief Secretary was out for 75 days.

224. Babu Brajendra Kumar Chatterjee, M. A., B. L., Officer-in-charge, Revenue Department, toured for 27 days.

225. The tours of the Divisional Officers and their Assistants, the Survey Superintendent and the Superintendent of Agriculture are as follows :—

State.

1. Sadar—

Divisional Officer—	Thakur Hriday Ranjan Deb Barman	...	23 days.
Asst. Collector—	Babu Prava Ranjan Das Gupta, M. A., B. L.	...	8 „
Probationer—	Kumar Narsingha Chandra Deb Barman Bahadur	...	11 „

2. Kailashahar—

Divisional Officer—	Babu Sasanka Bhusan Roy, M. A.	...	84 „
Second „	Thakur Gokul Chandra Deb Barman	...	23 „

3. Sonamura—

Divisional Officer—	Thakur Rebati Mohan Deb Barman	...	65 „
Second „ „	Jyoti Lal Deb Barman, B. L	...	35 „
Settlement „ „	Babu Bisweswar Guha, B. A.	...	23 „

4. Bilonia—
Divisional Officer—Babu Kamini Kumar Singha ... 50 „
Second „ „ Jyotirmoy Ghosh, M. A. ... 42 „

5. Khowai—
Divisional Officer—Babu Sarada Charan Sarkar, M. A., B. L. ... 23 „

6. Dharmanagar—
Divisional Officer—Babu Kunja Behari Chakravarty, M. A., B. L. ... 41 „

7. Udaipur—
Divisional Officer—Babu Jogendra Lal Ganguly, B. L. ... ... 110 „

8. Sabroom—
Divisional Officer—Thakur Lalit Mohan Deb Barman, M. A., B. L. ... 35 „

9. Amarpur—
Sub-Divisional Officer—Babu Surendra Chandra Guha, B. A. ... ... 45 „

10. Survey
Superintendent—Babu Kamini Kumar Kar ... 101 „

11. Superintendent
of Agriculture—Mr. J. C. Choudhuri ... ... 72 „

Zemindaries.

1. Babu Pramada Ranjan Bhattacharjee, B. A.,
Assistant Manager, Central Division ... 52 days.

2. „ Tarit Mohan Gupta,
Assistant Manager, Southern Division ... 81 „

3. „ Surendra Nath Basu, B. L.,
Assistant Manager, Northern Division ... 130 „

4. „ Naba Kumar Chakravarty, B. L.,
Sub-Manager, Srimangal ... 68 „

5. „ Manada Ranjan Chaudhuri, B. L.,
Inspector, Chakla Roshnabad Estates ... 22 „

226. The touring done by the Divisional officers of Sadar, Khowai, Dharmanagar and Sabroom as well as by the Assistant Manager, Central Division and the Inspector during the year was inadequate.

DATED, AGARTALA,
The 5th October, 1928.

Jyotis Chandra Sen,
Minister.

APPENDIX.

List of the principal Laws and Regulations in force in the Tripura State during 1337 T.E.

Description.	Whether adapted from British Indian Acts.	Whether introduced during the year under report.
CRIMINAL.		
1. Regulation No. III. of 1280 T. E.		
2. Regulation No. I. of 1283 T. E.		
3. Jail Regulation, 1283 T. E.		
4. Regulation No. IV. of 1283 T. E. (Cattle trespass and pound).		
5. Regulation No. III. of 1296 T. E. (Police Regulation).		
6. Act No. IV. of 1321 T. E.–Penal Laws (an amending Act)		
CIVIL.		
1. Civil Law of 1284 T. E.		
2. Rules regarding *chit* suits (small causes) 1287 and 1300 T. E.		
3. Act No. II. of 1313 T. E.—an Act for the regulation of interest on debts.		
4. Act No. II. of 1314 T. E.—Limitation Act	Partly adapted.	
REVENUE.		
1. Act No. I. of 1286 T. E.—Stamp Act		
2. Act No. I. of 1290 T. E.—Sale Law		
3. Act No. I. of 1296 T. E.—Tenancy Act.		
4. Act No. II. of 1296 T. E.—*Abkari*		
5. Act No. II. of 1297 T. E.—Reserved forests.		
6. Act No. I. of 1304 T. E.—Duties on *til* and cotton.		
7. Act No. I. of 1306 T. E.—Registration	Do.	
8. Survey and Settlement Act, 1309 T.E.	Do.	
9. *Tuccavi* Regulation, 1310 T. E.		
10. Act No. I. of 1313 T. E.—Forests.		
11. Act No. I. of 1314 T. E.—(amending the above)		
12. A Law imposing export duty on jute and mustard-seed, 1317 T. E.		
13. Act No. II. of 1321 T.E.—Ghasuri Act		
MISCELLANEOUS.		
1. An Act promulgating certain rules as Law, 1283 T. E.		
2. Regulation for the record of judicial decisions &c., 1284 T. E. ...		
3. Municipal Regulation, 1284 T. E.		
4. Legal Practitioners' Regulation.		
5. Act No. I. of 1297 T. E.—an Act for the regulation of commissions for the examination of witnesses.		
6. Special Regulation against cow slaughter		
7. Rules of evidence		
8. Act I. of 1318 T. E.—Constitution of Courts—(an amending Act).	Do.	
9. Leave and allowance Rules	Do.	
10. Act No. I. of 1321 T. E.—Arms Act		
11. Act No. III. of 1321 T. E.—Constitution of Courts (an amending Act)		

Description.	Whether adapted from British Indian Acts.	Whether introduced during the year under report.
12. Municipal Act No. I of 1322 T. E.		
13. Revenue Sale Amendment Act—1323 T.E.		
14. An Act for the destruction of old records—1323 T.E.		
15. Act I of 1326 T. E.—Regulation regarding Privy Council Appeals.		
16. Act II of 1326 T. E.—Registration of Births and Deaths	Partly adapted.	
17. Act III of 1326 T. E.—Vaccination Act	Do.	
18. Act IV of 1326 T. E.—Public Demands Recovery Act	Do.	
19. Act V of 1326 T. E.—Excise Amendment Act		
20. Act I of 1327 T. E.—Settlement of lands for tea cultivation		
21. Regulation No. 1 of 1328 T. E.—regarding Registration of Coolies		
22. Regulation No. 2 of 1328 T. E.—regarding Export of Tea		
23. Act I of 1329 T. E.—(Absconding sepoys Act)		
24. Act II of 1329 T. E.—(Control of prices of food stuff)		
25. Act III of 1329 T. E.—(Elephants and Buffaloes grazing Act)		
26. Act IV of 1329 T. E.—(House tax on Hill tribes)		
27. Act V of 1329 T. E.—(Legal practitioners, Act)	Do	
28. Act I of 1330 T. E.—Census Act		
29. Act I of 1332 T. E.—Encumbered Estates Act.		
30. Act III of 1332 T. E.—The Opium and Intoxicating Drugs Act.		
31. Amendment of Municipal Act (No. 2 of 1335 T. E.)		
32. Act No. I of 1335 T. E.—(Defining the term Minister)		
33. Act I of 1336 T. E.—(Hackney Carriages)		
34. Act II of 1336 T. E.—(Amending Act I of 1327.)		
35. Act III of 1336 T. E.—(Amending the Survey & Settlement Regulation)		
36. Act IV of 1336 T. E.—(Prevention of gambling)		
37. Act I of 1337 T. E.—(Amending the State Tenancy Act 1 of 1296 T. E.)		

II.

Statement showing the strength, cost, and other particulars of the Military Force in Tripura State for 1337 T.E.

Arm of service.	Number of fighting officers and men.						Details of force at the end of the current year.						Total cost on account of pay and allowances of the force, including followers. (excluding grain allowance.)	Remarks.
	At the end of last year.	Recruited this year.	*Casualties.*			At the end of the current year.	Number of regiments, battalions, or Batteries.	Number of guns.	*Number of men.*					
			Died.	Invalided.	Discharged, deserted, &c.				European commissioned officers.	Native commissioned officers.	Non-commissioned officers.	Fighting men.		
1	2	3	4	5	6	7	8	9	10	11	12	13	14	15
Infantry ...	247	222	2	5	156	306	1	297 and one small cannon.	—	—	45	261	Rs. 77,911	

III.

Statement showing the strength, cost, discipline, and education of the Police for the year 1337 T. E.

Description of office.	Number.	Pay of grade.	Total cost. (Excluding grain allowance.)	Punishments.			Rewards.		Education.		Remarks.
				Dismissed.	Fined, degraded, or suspended departmentally.	Punished judicially.	By promotion.	By money.	Number able to read and write.	Number under instruction.	
1	2	3	4	5	6	7	8	9	10	11	12
		Rs.									
Superintendent of Police	1	150-10-250	80,480	—	—	—	—	—	1	—	
Asst. Superintendent „	1	75-5-100		—	—	—	—	—	1	—	
Inspector	4	50 to 80		—	—	—	—	—	4	—	
Daroga	25	25-2-45		—	3	—	—	2	25	—	
Naib Daroga	13	15-1-25		1	—	—	—	2	13	—	
Writer Constable	13	11		—	—	—	—	1	13	—	
Subadar	1	25-2-45		—	—	—	—	—	1	—	
Jamadar	8	15-1-25		—	—	—	—	—	8	—	
Constable	221	8 to 12		6	20	—	—	4	200	—	
Chowkidar	175	5		6	—	—	—	1	—	—	
Spy	3	15 & 20		—	—	—	—	—	—	—	
Total ...	465			13	23			10	266		

IV.

Statement showing the working of the Police in the Tripura State during the year 1337 T.E.

State.	Number of offences.		Number of accused arrested.		Number of accused sent up for trial.		Number of accused convicted.		Number of accused acquitted or discharged.		Percentage convicted of accused arrested.		Percentage convicted of accused sent up for trial.		REMARKS.
	Past year.	Present year.	Past year.	Present year.	Past year.	Present year.	Past year.	Present year.	Past year.	Present year.	Past year.	Present year.	Past year.	Present year.	
1	2	3	4	5	6	7	8	9	10	11	12	13	14	15	16
Tripura State	1,318	1,377	711	830	638	721	171	167	102	205 *	24'	20'1	26'8	23'1	* Including 70 on compromise and 33 on withdrawal of cases.

V.

Statement showing the value of property stolen and amount of recoveries in the Tripura State during the year 1337 T. E.

State.	Amount stolen.		Amount recovered.		Percentage of recoveries of property stolen.		REMARKS.
	Past year.	Present year.	Past year.	Present year.	Past year.	Present year.	
1	2	3	4	5	6	7	8
Tripura State	Rs 18,115-4-3	Rs 24,329-15-6	Rs 2,710-5-0	Rs 11,272-13-3	14'95	46'33	

VI.

Statement showing the number of crimes committed, number of cases disposed of, and cases awaiting trial in the Tripura State during the year 1337 T. E.

Description of offences.	Number of offences: Balance from past year.	Number of offences: Committed during the present year.	Number of offences: Total.	Number of cases disposed of during the past year.	Number of cases disposed of during the present year.	Number of cases awaiting trial.	Number of persons apprehended.	Number of persons convicted.	Number of persons sentenced: Imprisonment: Simple.	Number of persons sentenced: Imprisonment: Rigorous.	Number of persons sentenced: Imprisonment and fine: Simple.	Number of persons sentenced: Imprisonment and fine: Rigorous.	Number of persons sentenced: Fine only.	Number of persons sentenced: Whipping.	Number of persons sentenced: Capital punishment.	Number of persons sentenced: Total.	Number of persons acquitted or discharged.	Number of persons confined being insane.	Number of persons dead during or before trial.	Term of imprisonment: Under one month.	Term of imprisonment: From 1 to 2 months.	Term of imprisonment: From 2 to 3 months.	Term of imprisonment: From 3 to 6 months.	Term of imprisonment: From 6 to 12 months.	Term of imprisonment: From 1 to 2 years.	Term of imprisonment: From 2 to 3 years.	Term of imprisonment: From 3 to 5 years.	Term of imprisonment: Above 5 years.	Term of imprisonment: Transportation.	Term of imprisonment: Capital punishment.	Persons awaiting trial.	Remarks.
1	2	3	4	5	6	7	8	9	10	11	12	13	14	15	16	17	18	19	20	21	22	23	24	25	26	27	28	29	30	31	32	33
Class I. Offences against the State, public tranquillity, safety and justice &c. — cognizable ...	12	20	32	26	28	4	94	39	0	14	1	1	23	0	0	39	43	0	3	2	0	6	2	4	0	2	0	0	0	0	9	*a.* Two persons released on bail.
Class I. — non-cognizable	15	94	109	45	94	15	36	*a* 5	0	0	0	0	3	0	0	3	22	0	0	0	0	0	0	0	0	0	0	0	0	0	9	*b.* Two persons escaped and two persons released on bail.
Class II. Offences against person. — cognizable ...	65	274	339	192	244	95	*b* 622	*b* 46	0	29	0	1	14	0	0	44	371	0	1	4	3	0	8	7	4	0	0	4	0	0	202	*c.* Two persons released on bail and three persons have been warned for the future.
Class II. — non-cognizable	60	253	318	321	267	51	294	38	0	0	0	3	35	0	0	38	212	1	0	3	0	0	0	0	0	0	0	0	0	0	43	*d.* One person escaped.
Class III. Offences against property. — cognizable ...	278	962	1240	998	925	315	1996	*c* 374	0	94	1	9	265	0	0	369	1064	1	3	40	15	15	20	9	3	2	0	0	0	0	554	*e.* Seven persons released on bail and two persons have been ordered to pay maintenance.
Class III. — non-cognizable	43	192	235	244	202	33	251	17	1	0	0	0	16	0	0	17	187	0	1	1	0	0	0	0	0	0	0	0	0	0	46	
Class IV. Other offences. — cognizable ...	31	143	174	109	133	41	*d* 276	34	1	8	0	2	23	0	0	34	206	0	0	0	3	2	1	5	0	0	0	0	0	0	35	
Class IV. — non-cognizable	73	337	410	341	345	65	170	*e* 20	0	6	0	0	5	0	0	11	109	0	0	4	0	1	0	1	0	0	0	0	0	0	41	
Total cognizable	386	1399	1785	1325	1330	455	2988	493	1	145	2	13	325	0	0	486	1684	1	7	46	21	23	31	25	7	4	0	4	0	0	800	
Total non-cognizable	191	881	1072	951	908	164	751	80	1	6	0	3	59	0	0	69	530	1	1	8	0	1	0	1	0	0	0	0	0	0	139	
GRAND TOTAL	577	2280	2857	2276	2238	619	3739	573	2	151	2	16	384	0	0	555	2214	2	8	54	21	24	31	26	7	4	0	4	0	0	939	

VII.

Statement shewing the number of offences reported and dealt with by the various Courts in the Tripura State during the year 1337 T.E.

Name of Court.	Number of offences reported during.		Number of persons dealt with.								Persons disposed of.					Persons remaining at the end of the year.	Remarks
			Remaining at the end of last year.	Brought to trial in 1336 T. E.					Total.								
	Last year.	Present year.		Arrested by Police.	Upon warrant.	On summons.	Voluntary.	Arrested in presence of the Magistrate.	Last year.	Present year.	Discharged without trial.	Acquitted.	Convicted.	Committed or referred.	Died, escaped, or transferred &c.		
1	2	3	4	5	6	7	8	9	10	11	12	13	14	15	16	17	18
Sadar Magistracy	709	671	193	303	205	298	23	15	840	1,037	438	205	143	11	0	240	
Sonamura " ...	222	284	72	109	52	148	57	1	425	439	105	101	74	11	0	148	
Bilonia " ...	243	286	136	119	38	96	194	13	568	596	176	194	143	5	2	76	
Kailāshahar " ...	243	221	225	115	46	173	16	4	584	579	219	109	65	3	6	177	
Khowai " ...	167	148	49	34	30	34	34	0	277	181	59	55	25	4	0	38	
Dharmanagar " ...	263	353	49	49	59	147	45	0	315	349	137	49	38	8	4	113	
Udaipur " ...	303	261	109	62	78	181	12	5	536	447	219	86	47	2	1	92	
Sabrum " ...	50	56	1	45	16	34	3	0	61	99	39	0	5	0	0	55	
TOTAL ...	2,200	2,280	834	836	524	1,111	384	38	3,606	a 3,727	1,392	799	540	b 44	13	939	

a Excluding 12 persons pending before the Court of Sessions at the close of the previous year.

b Including 12 persons pending from last year, the total number of persons for trial before the Court of Sessions was 56; of these, 33 were convicted, 4 discharged without trial and 19 acquitted.

VIII.

Statement of Criminal cases in which British Subjects were concerned for 1337 T. E.

Description of Offences.		Cases pending since the previous year.	Cases instituted during the year.	Total number of cases.	Cases in which complainants were British subjects.	Cases in which both parties were British subjects.	Cases in which defendants were British Subjects.														Remarks.
							Cases pending since the previous year	Cases instituted during the year.	Total number of cases.	Cases disposed of.		Cases pending at the close of the year.	Persons under trial at the close of the previous year.	Persons brought to trial during the year.	Total number of persons under trial.	Convicted.	Acquitted or discharged.	Died or escaped &c.	Under trial at the close of the year.	
										Rejected, compromised or dismissed without enquiry.	Tried.									
Class I. Offences against the State &c.	cognizable	1	4	5	0	1	1	4	5	0	2	3	10	8	18	14	0	0	4	
	non-cognizable ...	1	9	10	2	2	1	7	8	5	2	1	0	3	3	3	0	0	0	
Class II. Offences against person.	cognizable	4	58	62	14	31	4	44	48	15	11	22	8	79	87	4	50	1	32	* Of this number 127 were discharged without trial, the cases being dismissed, compromised or struck off on default. Excluding 1 escaped, 1 died and 145 pending, the actual number of persons tried was 406, of whom 243 or 59·85 were convicted as against 43·266 of the previous year.
	non-cognizable ...	6	31	37	7	21	6	24	30	24	3	3	5	16	21	3	18	0	0	
Class III. Offences against property.	cognizable	57	278	335	29	84	52	254	306	82	142	82	83	398	481	207	171	1	102	
	non-cognizable ...	9	38	47	7	29	9	31	40	31	4	5	4	20	24	3	20	0	1	
Class IV. Other offences.	cognizable	3	24	27	4	4	3	20	23	10	10	3	5	28	33	7	25	0	1	
	non-cognizable ...	6	48	54	12	24	5	37	42	23	9	10	3	10	13	2	6	0	5	
Total cognizable ...		65	364	429	47	120	60	322	382	107	165	110	106	513	619	232	246	2	139	
Total non-cognizable ...		22	126	148	28	76	21	99	120	83	18	19	12	49	61	11	44	0	6	
Grand Total ...		87	490	577	75	196	81	421	502	190	183	129	118	562	680*	243	290	2	145	

IX.

Statement of Extradition Cases for the year 1337 T. E.

Names of Courts.	Nature of cases.	NUMBER BORNE ON THE REGISTER.				NUMBER BROUGHT TO TRIAL.			Number at large at the close of the year.	RESULT.		Number of persons awaiting trial (after arrest) at the close of the year.	REMARKS.
		Number of persons at large at the close of the previous year.	Number of persons awaiting trial at the close of the previous year.	Number of persons against whom warrants were applied for during the year.	Total.	Number of persons arrested and surrendered within the year.	Number of persons who appeared of their own accord or were subsequently arrested in the State.	Total (Number of persons pending trial at the end of last year + the number arrested this year.)		Convicted.	Acquitted or discharged.		
Sadar Magistracy	Dacoity	0	5	0	5	0	0	5	0	5	0	0	
	Culpable homicide not amounting to murder	0	3	0	3	0	0	3	0	3	0	0	
	Wrongful confinement and rape	0	2	0	2	0	0	2	0	0	0	2	
	Theft	0	0	6	6	2	1	3	3	2	0	1*	* Committed to Sessions
	Criminal breach of trust as servant	0	0	3	3	1	2	3	0	0	3	0	
	Causing grievous hurt	0	0	1	1	0	1	1	0	0	0	1	
	Criminal breach of trust and theft	0	0	1	1	1	0	1	0	1	0	0	
	Rescuing offenders from lawful custody	0	0	4	4	4	0	4	0	0	0	4	
	Criminal breach of trust	0	0	1	1	0	0	0	1	0	0	0	
	Theft and receiving stolen property	0	0	2	2	0	0	0	2	0	0	0	
Sonamura ,, ...	Theft	0	1	39	40	12	0	13	27	0	0	13	
	Unlawful assembly, resisting lawful apprehension and rescuing offenders	0	0	10	10	0	10	10	0	0	10	0	
Bilonia ,, ...	Unlawful assembly and theft	0	7	0	7	0	0	7	0	0	7	0	
	Theft, resisting lawful apprehension and escape from lawful custody	0	3	0	3	0	0	3	0	3	0	0	
	Unlawful assembly, criminal trespass, theft and assault ...	0	3	0	3	0	0	3	0	0	3	0	
	Theft and escape from lawful custody	0	0	6	6	1	2	3	3	1	2	0	
	Unlawful assembly, assault, causing hurt, outraging the modesty of a woman and kidnapping	0	0	5	5	3	2	5	0	0	5	0	
	Unlawful assembly, causing hurt and theft	0	0	5	5	3	2	5	0	0	5	0	
	Theft	0	0	3	3	1	2	3	0	0	3	0	
Kailashahar ,, ...	Theft	0	1	3	4	0	1	2	2	2	0	0	
	Escape from lawful custody	0	1	0	1	0	0	1	0	1	0	0	
Khowai ,, ...	Criminal breach of trust	0	1	0	1	0	0	1	0	1	0	0	
	Kidnapping	0	1	0	1	0	0	1	0	0	1†	0	† Compounded
	Cheating	0	0	1	1	0	0	0	1	0	0	0	
	Theft	0	0	1	1	0	0	0	1	0	0	0	
Dharmanagar ,, ...	Theft	0	0	6	6	0	0	0	6	0	0	0	
	Highway robbery	0	0	1	1	0	0	0	1	0	0	0	
Udaipur ,, ...	Theft and receiving stolen property	0	0	3	3	1	0	1	2	0	1	0	
Sabroom ,, ...	Theft	0	1	4	5	2	0	3	2	0	3	0	
	Total	0	29	105	134	31	23	83	51	19	43	21	

X.

Statement showing the results of appeals against decisions passed by the Criminal Courts in the Tripura State during the year 1337 T. E.

TRIBUNALS.	Number of applications.	NUMBER OF PERSONS AND CASES.																Remarks.
		Applications rejected.		Sentences.						Proceedings quashed.		Referred.		Furher enquiry &c, ordered.		Pending.		
				Confirmed.		Modified.		Reversed.										
		Persons.	Cases.	Persons.	Cases.	Persons.	Cases.	Persons.	Cases.	Persons.	Cases.	Persons.	Cases.	Persons.	Cases.	Persons.	Cases.	
Khas Adalat. ...	199	46	28	106	73	18	15	33	29	2	2	—	—	25	18	80	34	

XI

Civil Work.—Nature and value of original suits filed and disposed of during the year 1337 T. E.

Tribunal.	Opening balance.		Filed during the year, received by transfer or on remand.		Total.		Disposed of during the year		Closing balance.		Suits filed during present year.									Suits disposed of during present year.						Suits not estimable in money.	Remarks.
	Past year.	Present year.	Past year.	Present year.	Past year.	Present year.	Past year.	Present year.	Past year.	Present year.	Value.	Suits re landed property.	Suits for money transaction.	Suits for other rights.	Number of suits under Rs. 100.	Number of suits above Rs. 100 and under Rs. 500.	Number of suits above Rs. 500 and under Rs. 1,000.	Number of suits above Rs. 1,000 and under Rs. 5,000.	Number of suits above Rs. 5000.	*Exparte.*	Admitted and compromised.	Struck off the file.	Otherwise disposed of.	Value.	Average duration.		
											Rs. a. p.													*Rs. a. p.*	*Y. m. d.*		
Khas Adalat Original Side	31	36	34	46	65	82	29	32	36	50	90,925·5·0	31	4	11	0	0	0	34	5	4	12	5	11	72,219·14·6	0·4·3	7	
Sadar Dewani Adalat	485	444	787	676	1,272	1,120	828	718	444	402	45,043·14·3	283	245	148	319	191	13	0	0	426	102	39	151	57,671·13·3	0·11·28	153	
Sonamura "	38	36	186	202	224	238	188	165	36	73	17,424·6·9	61	104	37	101	53	4	0	0	56	17	79	13	13,990·15·3	0·1·3	44	
Bilonia "	21	35	141	132	162	167	127	137	35	30	6,065·13·3	78	24	30	75	12	1	0	0	58	21	36	22	5,164·0·3	0·4·2	44	
Kailashahar "	330	210	306	221	638	531	428	313	210	218	21,317·7·6	61	237	23	237	39	5	0	0	117	41	64	91	20,980·12·6	0·3·15	40	
Khowai "	21	53	132	120	153	173	100	115	53	58	8,673·4·0	4	116	0	102	16	2	0	0	19	39	34	23	6,749·5·3	0·1·28	0	
Dharmanagar	69	120	230	217	299	337	179	194	120	143	16,525·13·3	41	59	117	140	29	4	0	0	30	39	51	74	12,988·2·3	0·0·24	44	
Udaipur "	102	55	188	354	290	409	235	310	55	99	30,249·9·6	14	321	19	245	71	6	0	0	118	69	11	112	26,411·4·6	0·3·13	32	
Sabrum "	0	1	8	18	8	19	7	14	1	5	1,224·0·0	3	9	6	6	8	0	0	0	5	2	3	4	861·0·0	0·3·15	4	
Total...	1,097	990	2,014	2,086	3,111	3,076	2,121	1,998	990	1,078	2,37,449·9·6	576	1119	391	1225	419	35	34	5	833	342	322	501	2,17,037·3·9	0·3·24	368	

XII.

Civil Work.—Results of applications for Execution of Decrees, 1337 T.E.

Tribunal.	Opening balance.		Value of opening balance for present year.	Applications brought to the Register.			Total.			Disposed of.			Closing balance.			Nature of applications pending disposal at the close of the year.			Remarks.
	Past year.	Present year.		Past year.	Present year.	Value for present year.	Past year.	Present year.	Value for present year.	Past year.	Present year.	Value for present year.	Past year.	Present year.	Value for present year.	Below 6 months.	Below 12 months.	Above 12 months.	
			Rs. a. p.			Rs. a. p.			Rs. a. p.			Rs. a. p.			Rs. a. p				
Khas Adalat (Original side)	21	14	48,947-0-9	5	17	15,335-6-6	26	31	64,282-7-3	12	7	8,815-12-3	14	24	55,466-11-0	11	3	10	
Sadar Dewani Adalat ...	142	179	26,173-3-9	258	189	21,489-0-3	400	368	47,662-4-0	221	206	22,810-6-0	179	162	24,851-14-0	89	30	43	
Sonamura Ditto ...	36	17	2,909-4-6	60	62	7,475-11-6	96	79	10,385-0-0	79	45	6,624-13-9	17	34	3,760-2-3	28	4	2	
Bilonia Ditto ...	8	10	985-3-9	38	29	3,188-6-0	46	39	4,173-9-9	36	33	3,563-12-6	10	6	609-13-3	4	1	1	
Kailashahar Ditto ...	90	64	9,559-3-9	63	150	18,815-11-9	162	214	28,374-15-6	98	107	11,439-11-9	64	107	16,935-3-9	71	21	15	
Khowai Ditto ...	12	8	1,677-7-6	35	41	3,774-7-0	47	49	5,451-14-6	39	31	3,144-6-3	8	18	2,307-8-3	15	2	1	
Dharmanagar Ditto ...	47	29	3,560-13-0	59	65	4,390-10-3	106	94	7,951-7-3	77	65	5,366-7-6	29	29	2,584-15-9	22	6	1	
Udaipur Ditto ...	36	23	3,884-5-6	69	132	18,751-0-0	105	155	22,635-5-6	82	109	14,906-1-0	23	46	7,729-4-6	36	8	2	
Sabrum Ditto ...	1	0	0	4	1	0	5	1	0	5	0	0	0	1	0	1	0	0	
Total ...	402	344	97,696-10-6	591	686	93,220-5-3	993	1,030	1,90,916-15-9	649	603	76,671-7-0	344	427	1,14,245-8-9	277	75	75	

XIII.

Civil Work.—Number and results of appeals in civil suits, 1337 T. E.

Tribunal.	Opening balance.		Filed during.		Total.		Disposed of during.		Closing balance.		Value of appeals filed during.		How disposed of.										Average duration.	
													Decisions confirmed.		Decisions reversed.		Decisions amended.		Cases remanded for retrial.		Cases compromised and otherwise disposed of.			
	Past year.	Present year.	Past year.	Present year.	Past year.	Present year.	Past year.	Present year.	Past year.	Present year.	Past year.	Present year.	Past year.	Present year.	Past year.	Present year.	Past year.	Present year.	Past year.	Present year.	Past year.	Present year.	Past year.	Present year.
											Rs. a. p.	*Rs. a. p.*											*Y.m.d.*	*Y.m.d.*
Khas Adalat	65	46	169	174	234	220	188	130	46	90	20,070-1-6	33,433-0-0	80	67	48	16	8	8	24	25	28	14	0-2-1	0-2-2

XIV.

Statement showing the number of persons confined in the jails and lock-ups in the Tripura State during the year 1337 T.E.

Stations.	Number of prisons.	Number of Prisoners.				Daily Average.		Number of prisoners remaining at the end of the year.	Cost of jails and prisoners.	Average period in days of stay of accused under-trial.	Remarks showing mortality among convicts in jail.
		Remaining from last year.	Admitted during the year.	Total.							
				Past year.	Present year.	Past year.	Present year.				
									Rs.		
Agartala	1	111	196	344	307	96·47	93·81	69	14,009	36·8	
Sonamura	1	19	61	88	80	4·33	3·88	2	700	18·4	
Kailashahar	1	4	60	80	64	6·20	3·33	9	577	21·65	
Bilonia	1	--	49	56	49	2·82	3·21	2	492	38·47	One convict died of Kala-azar and one lunatic died of Apoplexy.
Khowai	1	2	44	27	46	·49	3·71	5	485	39·11	
Dharmanagar	1	3	51	71	54	3·34	3·38	3	714	23·05	
Udaipur	1	—	98	43	98	2·21	5·68	11	721	5·59	
Sabrum	1	—	10	9	10	·14	·22	—	136	8·4	
Total ...	8	139	569	718	708	116·00	117·22	101	17,834	23·93	

XV.

Registration of documents in the Tripura State during the year 1337 T.E.

Name of State.	Documents presented for registration.		NATURE OF DOCUMENTS PRESENTED.										Documents registered.		Value of documents registered.		Documents of which registration has been refused.		Documents remaining unregistered at the end of the year.		REMARKS.
			Mortgages.		Sale deeds.		Wills.		Money bonds.		Miscellaneous.										
	Past year.	Present year.	Past year.	Present year.	Past year.	Present year.	Past year.	Present year.	Past year.	Present year.	Past year.	Present year.	Past year.	Present year.	Past year.	Present year.	Past year.	Present year.	Past year.	Present year.	
1	2	3	4	5	6	7	8	9	10	11	12	13	14	15	16	17	18	19	20	21	22
															Rs.	*Rs.*					
Tripura State	12,896	12,894	3,456	3,746	5,634	5,525	6	9	385	389	3,415	3,225	12,7[illegible]2	12,297	21,63,613	21,45,657	156	173	72	496	

XVI

Statement showing the receipts and expenditure on account of Registration during the year 1337 T.E.

Description.	Past year.			Present year.			Remarks.
	Number of deeds.	Value of property.	Fees realised.	Number of deeds.	Value of property.	Fees realised.	
		Rs.	Rs.		Rs.	Rs.	
Mortgages	3,456	5,37,078	3,517	3,746	6,13,299	3,959	
Sale deeds	5,634	11,71,329	7,951	5,525	11,26,469	7,524	
Will	6	2,155	26	9	3,900	41	
Money bonds	385	54,101	318-8	389	35,970	314	
Miscellaneous	3,415	4,79,664	4,175-8	3,225	4,57,670	3,990	
Total ...	12,896	22,44,327	15,988	12,894	22,37,308	15,828	
Total Expenditure ...	—	—	4,682	—	—	4,573	
Net Income ...	—	—	11,306	—	—	11,255	

XVII.

Receipts and expenditure of the Municipalities in the Tripura State during the year 1337 T.E.

NAME.	Opening balance.	RECEIPTS DURING THE YEAR.					Total in the current year.	EXPENDITURE DURING THE YEAR.		Balance at the close of the year.	REMARKS.
		Past.	Present.								
			State grant.	Tax.	Miscel-laneous.	Total.		Past.	Present.		
1	2	3	4	5	6	7	8	9	10	11	12
	Rs. A. P.	Rs. A. P.	Rs. A. P.	Rs. A. P.	Rs. A. P.	Rs. A. P.	Rs. A. P.	Rs. A. P.	Rs. A. P.	Rs. A. P.	
Agartala Municipality. ...	10,896-1-3	37,961-14-0	8,973-0-0	3,727-8-6	8,069-11-0 a	20,770-3-6	31,666-4-9	27,117-13-3	20,601-8-9 b	11,064-12-0 c	a. Including Rs. 5,746-10-6 as income from the Bazar and Rs. 331-4-0 as deposits and advances recovered. b. Including Rs. 4,716-7-6 as expenditure on the Bazar improvement and Rs. 128-12 as advances and deposits paid. c. Including Rs. 10,567-5-6 of the Bazar improvement fund and Rs. 497-6-6 as income from the Municipality.

XVIII.

Statement of rainfall in the Tripura State during the year 1337 T.E.

STATE.	Baisak.	Jaisth.	Asar.	Sravan.	Bhadra.	Asvin.	Kartik.	Agrahayan.	Pous.	Magh.	Falgoon.	Chait.	Total.	Total of past year.	Average of past 5 years.	REMARKS.
Tripura State ...	15·77	10·24	12·62	14·27	12·17	8·22	1·69	—	—	·11	2·51	·77	78·37	110·04	98·81	

1. Maximum 110·42—Dharmanagar Division. 2. Minimum 51·92—Amarpur Sub-Division.

XIX

Statement as to the prices of staple food-grains for the year 1337 T.E.

Articles.	Past year during Chait.			Present year during Chait.			REMARKS.
	Rs.	*a.*	*p.*	*Rs.*	*a.*	*p.*	
(1) RICE							
Maximum	10	0	0	10	0	0	
Minimum	6	0	0	5	10	0	
(2) PADDY							
Maximum	4	8	0	4	8	0	
Minimum	2	12	0	3	0	0	

XX.

Expenditure on Public Works during the year 1337 T.E.

Description of work.	State funds.			Local funds.			Total.	Remarks.
	Original.	Repairs.	Total.	Original.	Repairs.	Total.		
	Rs.	*Rs.*	*Rs.*	*Rs.*	*Rs.*	*Rs.*	*Rs.*	
Buildings	1,02,872	98,617	2,01,489	2,331	1,800	4,131	2,05,620	
Roads and Bridges ...	25,592	37,716	63,308	700	—	700	64,008	
Tanks	3,134	1,628	4,762	—	—	—	4,762	
Miscellaneous works ...	7,284	138	7,422	—	—	—	7,422	
Total ...	1,38,882	1,38,099	2,76,981	3,031	1,800	4,831	2,81,812	
Minor works at the Rajbari (*Karkhuna*)	—	—	2,767	—	—	—	2,767	
Establishment charges ...	—	—	25,518	—	—	—	25,518	
Grand Total ...	1,38,882	1,38,099	3,05,266	3,031	1,800	4,831	3,10,097 (*a*)	

Remarks:

(*a*) Besides this expenditure Rs. 95,073 was spent on the following works :—

(1) Public Works for H. H.'s Installation Ceremony ... Rs. 70,778
(2) Do for Investiture ... „ 24,295

Rs. 95,073

XXI.

Statement showing the excise shops and excise revenue of the Tripura State during the year 1337 T.E.

Name of State.	Country spirit.		Country spirit, Opium and Ganja.		Ganja and Opium.		Tari.		Total.		Remarks.
	Number of shops.	Revenue. demand.	Number of shops.	Revenue demand.	Number of shops.	Revenue. demand.	Number of shops.	Revenue. demand.	Number of shops.	Revenue realised.	
		Rs.		Rs.						Rs.	
Tripura State	2	30	30	83,790	—	—	—	—	32	85,485	

XXII.

Statement of Medical Relief afforded in the Tripura State during the year 1337 T.E.*

Dispensary.	Number of patients treated. (new)		Results of in-door patients. (new)				Expenditure.	Daily average. (old + new)			No. of surgical operations performed.			No. of persons vaccinated during the year.			Remarks.
	Outdoor.	Indoor.	Dis-charged cured.	Relieved or dis-charged otherwise	Died.	Remain-ing under treatment.		Outdoor.	Indoor.	Total.	Major.	Minor.	Total.	Success-fully.	Unsuc-cessfully.	Total.	
							Rs.										
1. Victoria Memorial Hospital at Agartala and the Charitable Dispensary attached to it ...	10,996	436	291	103	37	5	9,891	51·87	14·82	66·69	14	218	232	847	977	1,824	
2. Palace Dispensary	8,119	0	0	0	0	0	10,562	50·45	0	50·45	0	0	0	0	0	0	
3. Homœopathic	14,693	0	0	0	0	0	5,637	99·47	0	99·47	0	0	0	0	0	0	* This Statement excludes figures regarding Kaviraji treatment.
4. Old Agartala...	4,166	0	0	0	0	0	1,586	20·35	0	20·35	0	48	48	637	89	726	
5. Bishalgar	4,450	0	0	0	0	0	1,332	16·71	0	16·71	1	75	76	1,303	332	1,635	
6. Sonamura	6,055	24	24	0	0	0	1,653	27·34	·47	27·81	0	118	118	1,109	371	1,480	
7. Udaipur	4,250	0	0	0	0	0	1,481	15·98	0	15·98	0	43	43	1,346	529	1,875	
8. Amarpur	571	0	0	0	0	0	1,173	2·67	0	2·67	0	6	6	90	123	213	
9. Bilonia	4,942	7	3	3	0	1	1,592	21·84	·24	22·08	0	88	88	142	35	177	
10. Loongthung	2,547	0	0	0	0	0	1,209	11·01	0	11·01	0	25	25	182	19	201	† This figure shows the actual number of outdoor patients treated, the total outdoor attendance during the year being 1,68,429 against 1,67,383 in the previous year.
11. Sabroom	2,658	4	4	0	0	0	1,451	10·33	·24	10·57	0	74	74	0	0	0	
12. Khowai	4,913	0	0	0	0	0	1,415	17·14	0	17·14	1	48	49	882	209	1,091	
13. Kailashahar	7,191	0	0	0	0	0	1,505	23·75	0	23·75	5	135	140	848	815	1,663	
14. Fatikroy	2,731	0	0	0	0	0	930	12·16	0	12·16	0	45	45	467	206	673	
15. Kamalpur	3,214	0	0	0	0	0	1,161	14·81	0	14·81	0	31	31	257	67	324	
16. Dharmanagar...	5,018	21	14	5	1	1	1,398	23·36	1·61	24·97	3	86	89	231	21	252	
17. Mohanpur	2,654	0	0	0	0	0	1,059	10·50	0	10·50	0	46	46	221	14	235	
18. Dhaleswar	5,612	0	0	0	0	0	1,320	30·64	0	30·64	0	86	86	0	0	0	
Total	† 94,782	492	336	111	38	7	46,375	460·38	17·38	477·76	24	1,172	1,196	8,562	3,807	12,369	

XXIII.

Vital statistics of the Tripura State for the year 1337 T.E.

State.	Population.	Births.		Increase.	Decrease.	Deaths.		Increase.	Decrease.	Ratio per 1,000 of population.				Remarks.
										Births.		Deaths.		
		Past year.	Present year.			Past year.	Present year.			Past year.	Present year.	Past year.	Present year.	
Tripura State ...	3,02,571	2,509	1,956	—	553	2,595	2,113	—	482	8·28	6·4	9·8	6·9	

XXIV.

Education Return (A)—Particulars as to the schools maintained during the year 1337 T.E.

Number of Schools.		Class of Schools.	Number of pupils on the rolls on the last day of Chait.		Average daily attendance.		Remarks.
Past year.	Present year.		Past year.	Present year.	Past year.	Present year.	
5	5	High English Schools	14,29	1,450	1,033'62	1,092'49	
7	8	Middle English Schools for boys ...	803	986	608'09	753'55	
1	1	Middle English Schools for girls ...	85	75	70'40	53'60	
1	1	Higher Vernacular Schools for boys	50	62	40'25	46'77	* In some of these schools boys and girls read together.
22	21	* Lower Vernacular Schools for boys	1,210	1,191	922'13	879'55	
89	115	* Pathsalas for boys	2,344	2,643	1,814'02	2,031'32	
9	10	Do for girls	189	236	137'07	168'23	
		Special Schools :—					
5	5	Madrassas	167	152	113'87	94'11	
3	3	Sanskrit *Tols*	42	43	28'03	27'24	
1	1	Woodburn Artisan School... ...	12	10	5'53	5'03	
TOTAL 143	170		6,331	6,848	4,773'01	5,151'89	

XXV.

Education Return (B) Race of Students, 1337 T. E.

Names of Divisions.	No. of Schools.			No. of Students.			Race.											Average daily attendance.		REMARKS.
															Bengalee.					
	For boys.	For girls.	Total.	Boys.	Girls.	Total.	Rajkumars.	Thakurs.	Manipuris	Tripuras.	Reangs.	Chakmas.	Kukis.	Lusais.	Hindus.	Musalmans.	Christians.	Others.	Boys.	Girls.	
1. Sadar Division ...	57	3	60	2,071	142	2,213	7	160	129	310	0	0	25	0	949	604	5	24	1,464·27	99·38	
2. Kailashahar "	29	3	33	970	112	1,082	0	0	365	36	0	2	0	0	468	211	0	0	698·69	71·99	
3. Sonamura "	21	1	22	1,040	78	1,118	0	8	0	51	0	0	0	0	288	771	0	0	808·40	64·28	
4. Bilonia "	11	1	12	842	17	859	0	0	0	0	18	0	0	0	594	241	0	6	680·73	12·5	
5. Khowai "	10	1	11	264	14	278	0	0	21	143	0	0	0	0	66	31	0	17	188·44	10·84	
6. Dharmanagar "	11	1	12	553	25	578	0	1	96	0	0	0	0	0	367	111	0	3	401·30	35·62	
7. Udaipur "	9	1	10	396	20	416	0	1	0	87	2	0	0	0	101	225	0	0	334·64	18·65	
8. Sabrum "	6	0	6	241	14	255	0	0	0	92	0	0	0	0	106	49	0	8	212·40	13·73	
9. Amarpur Sub-division ...	5	0	5	44	5	49	0	0	0	13	2	0	0	0	8	0	0	26	31·49	4·54	
TOTAL ...	159	11	170	6,421	427	6,848	7	170	611	732	22	2	25	0	2,947	2,243	5	84	4,820·36	331·53	

APPENDIX XXVI. (A)

Statement of Audited Receipts for the year 1337 T. E.

State.

Heads of Revenue.	1336 T. E.		1337 T. E.		REMARKS.
	Revised Estimate.	Actuals.	Revised Estimate.	Actuals.	
1. Land Revenue ...	5,92,000	6,18,210	6,20,000	6,02,891	
2. Rents of markets ...	7,000	7,223	7,000	7,658	
3. Family tax in the hills	60,000	54,595	55,000	60,223	
4. Toll on Forest Produce	4,85,000	4,93,335	5,80,000	5,45,997	
5. Do on the Feni River	30,000	29,146	35,000	36,290	
6. Elephant and Buffalo grazing mehals ...	7,000	7,339	8,000	8,326	
7. Thatching grass mehals	10,000	9,029	8,000	7,619	
8. Reserved *Sal* trees ...	14,000	15,289	8,000	6,784	
9. Tax on cotton and Oil seeds ...	150,000	2,18,051	1,60,000	1,56,486	
10. Royalty on elephants caught ...	9,000	42	25,000	36,713	
11. Adda mehal ...	23,000	23,063	23,000	23,202	
12. Excise ...	70000	79,354	80,000	85,485	
13. Stamps and Court fees	85,000	87,137	90,000	89,530	
14. Law and Justice (fines)	4,000	4,162	4,000	4,012	
15. Process Fees ...	14,000	15,905	17,000	15,495	
16. Registration ...	13,000	15,983	16,000	15,828	
17. Jail ...	4,000	4,739	4,000	4,559	
18. Cattle pounds ...	5,500	6,083	6,000	5,895	
19. *Nazars* ...	50,000	52,490	50,000	49,733	
20. Agriculture ...	500	511	500	611	
21. School Fees ...	10,000	6,810	8,000	8,661	
22. Duty on Tea ...	—	—	15,000	19,841	
23. Personal Howlats recovered	7,000	7,474	7,000	7,255	
24. Interest on Bank deposit ...	—	—	5,000	3,500	
25. Miscellaneous ...	90,000	1,02,306	90,000	74,542	
Total ...	17,40,000	18,58,281	19,21,500	18,77,136	
26. Deposits ...	90,000	3,68,535	74,000	83,751	
27. Contribution from Chakla ...	—	—	5,50,000	5,50,000	
Total ...	18,30,000	22,26,816	25,45,500	25,10,887	
Opening Balance :—					
Cash ...	3,96,594	3,96,594	8,35,130	8,35,130	
Advances ...	1,78,412	1,78,412	1,55,106	1,55,106	
Loans issued ...	41,118	41,118	61,783	61,783	
Total ...	6,16,124	6,16,124	10,52,019	10,52,019	
Grand Total ...	24,46,124	28,42,940	35,97,519	35,62,906	

APPENDIX XXVI. (B)

Statement of Audited Expenditure for the year 1337 T. E.

State.

Heads of Expenditure.	1336 T. E.		1337 T. E.		Remarks.
	Revised estimate.	Actuals.	Revised Estimate.	Actuals.	
1. Controlling Charges	1,18,720	1,16,886	1,16,441	1,14,241	
2. Revenue General ...	77,990	74,010	78,824	76,448	
3. Survey & Settlement	19,000	13,898	17,470	14,373	
4. Tahasil ...	49,050	45,729	50,141	47,176	
5. Agriculture ...	5,520	5,389	4,924	4,681	
6. Registration ...	4,970	4,682	4,806	4,573	
7. Police ...	71,010	68,377	83,396	80,460	
8. Judicial ...	36,520	35,638	35,000	34,663	
9. Jail ...	17,620	15,824	18,629	17,834	
10. Forest ...	58,660	54,173	59,207	52,822	
11. Medical ...	72,500	70,278	77,335	76,251	
12. Sanitation ...	—	—	5,000	3,346	
13. Municipality ...	10,000	9,706	9,000	8,973	
14. Education General ...	96,898	94,206	1,02,358	97,915	
15. Education of Rajkumar's ...	19,612	16,658	21,740	* 22,228	* The excess expenditure is covered by subsequent re-appropriation sanctioned under Education Department No. $\frac{3188}{5—9B}$ dated 7-12-37 T. E.
16. Public Works ...	2,94,000	2,81,089	3,11,000	3,05,266	
17. Small Donations ...	100	60	550	410	
18. Relief to distressed subjects ...	16,000	12,368	41,500	30,373	
19. Purchase of Landed Property ...	5,500	1,834	6,000	240	
20. Repayment of Deposits ...	86,400	85,828	75,000	66,751	
21. Interest on Deposits	—	—	13,000	10,265	
22. Unforeseen charges ...	4,000	3,041	5,000	4,024	
23. Compensation for dearness of Provision ...	36,000	35,917	39,000	38,971	
24. Advances to employees ...	7,000	6,840	8,000	7,768	
25. Pension ...	21,000	20,476	23,500	22,893	
26. Advisory Council ...	—	—	2,310	2,310	
27. Chief Secretary's Office & H. H.'s Tour	—	—	42,810	24.508	
28. Palace Sultanat ...	25,082	23,715	25,463	24,825	
29. Zoo ...	8,500	8,270	6,300	* 6,498	* The excess expenditure is covered by subsequent re-appropriation sanctioned by the Chief Secretary under No. 578, dated 13-12-37 T. E.
30. H. H.'s Private Secretary's Office ...	—	—	8,487	8,084	
31. Rajmala ...	6,132	6,098	9,043	8,604	
32. Military Secretary's Office ...	—	—	2,300	1,557	
33. Military ...	44,050	40,240	98,196	77,911	
34. Nijtahabil ...	1,30,821	1,26,775	1,03,035	1,03,035	
35. H. H.'s Investiture ...	—	—	2,10,000	2,07,201	
36. Marriage ...	—	—	3,50,000	3,37,111	
37. H. H.'s Installation	—	—	4,81,000	4,66,080	
38. Sansar ...	5,19,813	5,12,916	4,63,054	4,52,494	
Total ...	18,62,528	17,90,921	30,03,719	28,63,121	
Closing balance :—					
Cash ...	3,99,066	8,35,130	3,44,911	3,98,748	
Advances ...	1,43,412	1,55,106	1,51,106	2,10,816	
Loans issued ...	41,118	61,783	91,783	90,221	
	5,83,596	10,52,019	5,87,800	6,99,785	
Grand Total ...	24,46,124	28,42,940	35,97,519	35,62,906	

APPENDIX XXVII. (A)

Statement of Audited Receipts for the year 1337 T. E.

Chakla Roshnabad Estate.

Heads of Receipts.	1336 T. E.		1337 T. E.		Remarks.
	Revised Estimate.	Actuals.	Revised Estimate.	Actuals.	
1. Rent and Cess ...	11,02,000	11,04,239	11,68,800	11,37,731	
2. Cess for Rent free holdings ...	7,461	8,287	9,500	8,366	
3. Law charges recovered	52,816	52,026	65,200	43,228	
4. Misc. receipts including deposits ...	4,000	10,219	4,983	10,308	
5. Loans Received ...	—	—	—	—	
Total ...	11,66,277	11,74,771	12,48,483	11,99,633	
Opening Balance :—					
Cash ...	1,56,681	1,56,681	1,24,852	1,24,852	
Advance ...	1,08,050	1,08,050	1,35,537	1,35,537	
Loans issued ...	12,415	12,415	12,228	12,228	
Bank deposits ...	1,00,000	1,00,000	1,00,000	1,00,000	
Total ...	3,77,146	3,77,146	3,72,617	3,72,617	
Grand Total ...	15,43,423	15,51,917	16,21,100	15,72,250	

APPENDIX XXVII. (B)

Statement of Audited Expenditure for the year 1337 T. E.

Chakla Roshnabad Estate.

Heads of Expenditure.	1336 T. E.		1337 T. E.		REMARKS.
	Revised Estimate.	Actuals.	Revised Estimate.	Actuals.	
i. 1. Revenue and Cess ...	2,70,296	2,68,970	2,71,248	2,69,253	
2. Establishment ...	1,47,963	1,43,844	1,51,610	1,44,086	
3. Settlement ...	1,424	809	1,424	827	
4. Legal Expenses ...	1,26,086	1,01,347	1,10,000	96,490	
5. Education ...	12,268	11,029	11,008	10,884	
6. Medical ...	11,802	11,698	12,481	11,963	
7. Public Works ...	96,495	82,616	71,512	50,612	
8. Religious Expenses	6,381	6,122	7,140	6,215	
9. Purchase of property	8,000	6,805	34,500	27,758	
10. Miscellaneous ...	8,059	10,644	11,000	12,174	
11. Loans and Advances	3,000	—	3,000	2,516	
(a) Irrecoverable loans written off	—	—	—	1,313	
12. Pension and Gratuity	5,000	4,841	6,000	5,137	
13. Forest ...	650	564	650	511	
14. Unforeseen ...	5,000	4,833	7,500	783	
ii. Sansar ...	15,780	15,780	15,540	15,520	
iii. Donation ...	7,000	1,549	7,100	1,760	
iv. Repayment of debts	5,00,000	4,99,999	25,000	25,000	
iv. (a) Repayment of deposits ...	7,000	7,850	14,000	10,568	
v. Contribution to State ...	—	—	5,50,000	5,50,000	
	12,32,204	11,79,300	13,10,713	12,43,370	
Closing Balance :—					
Cash ...	1,14,222	1,24,852	70,850	1,03,746	
Advances ...	84,582	1,35,537	1,22,485	1,09,608	
Loans issued ...	12,415	12,228	12,000	10,474	
Bank deposits ...	1,00,000	1,00,000	1,05,052	1,05,052	
	3,11,219	3,72,617	3,10,387	3,28,880	
Grand Total ...	15,43,423	15,51,917	16,21,100	15,72,250	

To

His Highness The Bisama-Samara Bijoyee Mahamahodaya
Pancha-Srijukta Maharaja Manikya
BIR BIKRAM KISHORE DEV BARMAN BAHADUR,

Maharaja of Tripura.

Dated, Agartala, the 28th August, 1929.

MAY IT PLEASE YOUR HIGHNESS,

I have the honour to submit the accompanying Report on the General Administration of the State and the attached Zemindaries for the year 1338 T. E., corresponding to the period extending from the 14th April, 1928 to the 13th April, 1929.

2. The charge of the Administration during the year under review was in the hands of the Minister, Rai Jyotis Chandra Sen Bahadur, except for two months and a half, from the 17th May to the 30th July, 1928, when I officiated as Minister during his absence on leave.

3. Since the close of the year, the Rai Bahadur has again been obliged to go out on long sick leave, and I have been appointed by Your Highness to administer the departments in his charge under the designation "Dewan–Shashan and Manager, Chakla."

I have the honour to be,
YOUR HIGHNESS's most obedient servant,
B. K. Sen,
DEWAN–SHASHAN.

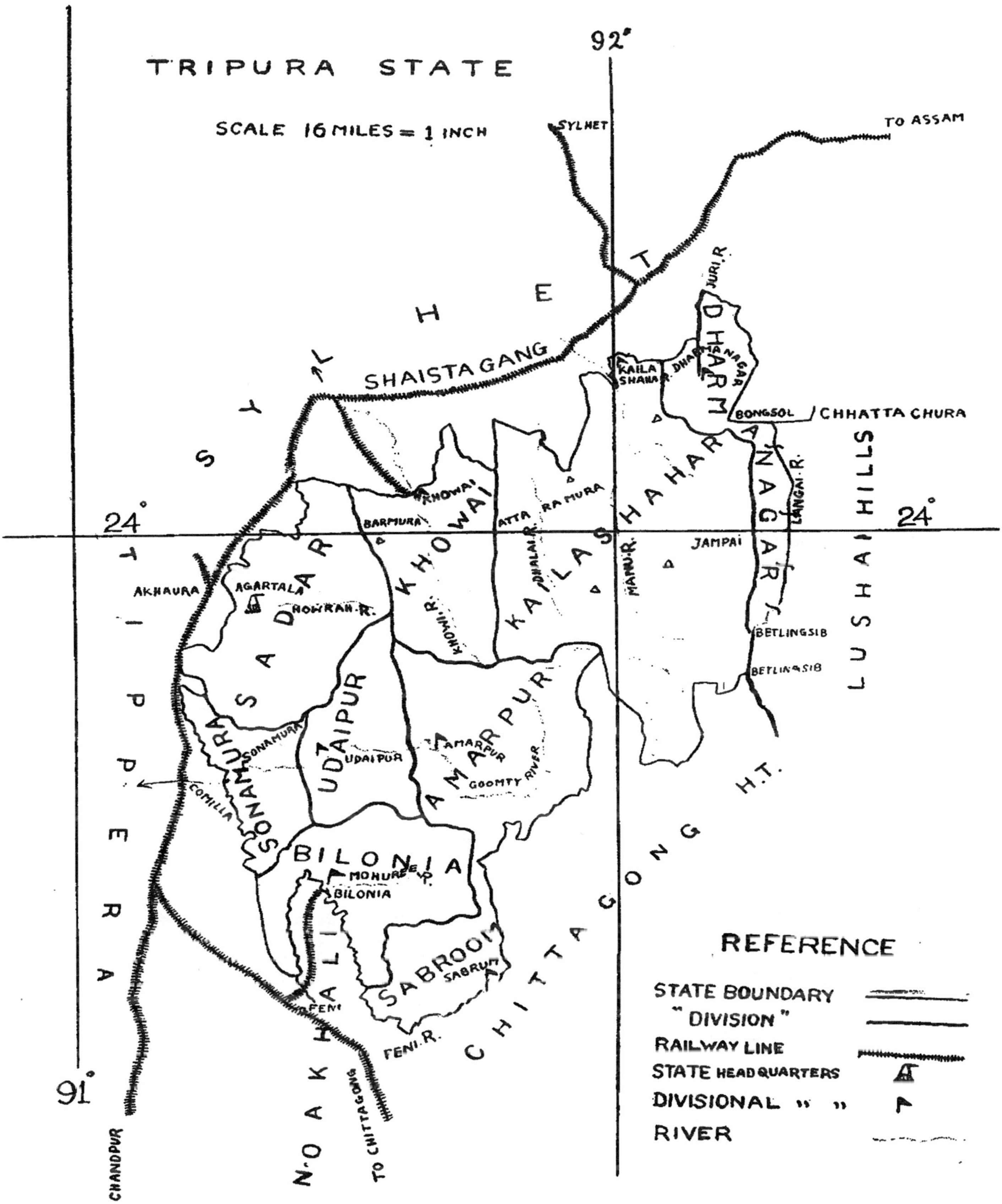
TRIPURA STATE
SCALE 16 MILES = 1 INCH
92°
24°
91°
SYLHET
TO ASSAM
SHAISTAGANG
JURI R.
DHARMANAGAR
KAILASHAHAR
BONGSOL
CHHATTA CHURA
LUSHAI HILLS
LANGAI R.
KHOWAI
BARMURA
ATTA RA MURA
DHALAI R.
MANU R.
JAMPAI
AKHAURA
AGARTALA
HOWRAH R.
SADAR
KHOWAI R.
BETLINGSIB
UDAIPUR
AMARPUR
GOOMTY RIVER
SONAMURA
COMILLA
TIPPERA
CHITTAGONG H.T.
BILONIA
MOHURI R.
SABROOM
SABRUM
FENI
FENI R.
CHITTAGONG
NOAKHALI
CHANDPUR
TO CHITTAGONG
REFERENCE
STATE BOUNDARY
" DIVISION "
RAILWAY LINE
STATE HEAD QUARTERS
DIVISIONAL " "
RIVER

Book Twenty-one
Report on the General Administration of the Tripura State for the year 1338 T. E. (1928-1929 A.D.)

REPORT ON THE ADMINISTRATION OF THE TRIPURA STATE FOR 1338 T. E. (1928-29.)

CHAPTER I—GENERAL AND POLITICAL.

Area of the State—*4.116 sq. miles.*
Population—*3,04,437*
Gross Revenue (*based on the average of the previous five years*) :—
(*a*) State ... ... Rs. 19,30,930.
(*b*) Zemindaries ... ... Rs. 11,99,637.
Tribute—Nil.
Ruler of the State—His Highness The Bisama-Samara-Bijayee Mahamahodaya Pancha-Srijukta Maharaja Manikya Bir Bikramkishore Dev Barman Bahadur. *Age*—20 years. (Born—19th August, 1908). *Caste*—*Kshatriya* (of the Lunar race).

I.

His Highness's marriage.

1. Early in the year it was announced that the marriage of His Highness the Maharaja Manikya Bahadur had been settled with the sixth Maharajkumari Saheba of Balrampur—a daughter of the late Maharaja Sir Bhagabati Prasad Sing Bahadur, K. C. I. E., K. B. E. and sister of the present Maharaja Saheb.

2. This alliance between the historic House of Tripura and the premier Rajput *Talukdar* family of Oudh caused all round satisfaction.

The *Tilak* Ceremony.

3. A deputation of *Sardars* representing the Maharaja of Balrampur soon arrived, and the *Tilak* or betrothal ceremony was performed with becoming *eclat* at the Ujjayanta Palace, Agartala, on the 20th May, 1928.

The Marriage Ceremony.

4. The marriage ceremony was celebrated at Balrampur on the 16th January, 1929, and proved in every way worthy of the alliance, both in respect of the distinguished gathering that attended it, and the spectacular grandeur that the functions of the occasion presented.

Distinguished guests.

5. His Excellency the Governor of the United Provinces graced the ceremony with his presence, while among the guests were a number of Ruling Chiefs, Maharajas, Rajas and other eminent men, both European and Indian.

The Bridal Party—enthusiastic ovations.

6. His Highness, accompanied by a bridal party, which numbered about one thousand, left Agartala on the 12th January, 1929, and received an ovation not only at Agartala and all along the route to the Railway station, but from a huge concourse of people at Akhaura, as the bridal specials left. Similar ovations followed at Chandpur as the party boarded the special steamers,

and at Goalundo, where it entrained again. It was arranged that the trains from Goalundo would proceed upto Calcutta and then start back for Balrampur *via* Naihati and Bandel. As the Bridegroom's special steamed in with its precious load, a distinguished gathering on the gaily decorated platform of the Sealdah Station accorded it an enthusiastic welcome. Floral presents were abundantly in evidence, and even the saloons and carriages of the train had their share of attention from friendly hands. Similar receptions at Benares and Lucknow followed, and at Benares in particular—the band in attendance, the sumptuous meals laid for members of the bridal party in tastefully decorated tents, and the crowd of holy priests vying with one another in their eagerness to offer blessings to His Highness, created an atmosphere of warmth and heartiness never to be forgotten.

Reception at Balrampur.

7. At Balrampur the welcome accorded to His Highness by Maharaja Pateswariprasad Sing Bahadur and his staff was all that could be desired, and the tender care and lavish hospitality meted out to each individual member of the *Barat*, and to each individual guest, answered to the best traditions of the house. The arrangements were indeed unexceptionable, and every praise is due to the worthy Special Manager of the Raj, Kunwar Saheb Jashabir Sing, and his assistants, who spared no pains to ensure their success. The Durbar records here its high and grateful appreciation.

Messages of congratulation.

8. Congratulations poured in from all quarters and included kind messages of good will from His Excellency the Governor of Bengal, His Excellency the Governor of the United Provinces, a number of Indian Princes and Chiefs, as well as many other leading men. At a State Banquet held at Balrampur on the 17th January, the Hon'ble Mr. A. W. Pim, C. S. I., C. I. E., I. C. S., Finance Member of the United Provinces, proposed in felicitous terms, the toast of the bride and the bridegroom, which was most enthusiastically responded to. His Highness gave a suitable reply.

Return to Agartala.

9. His Highness returned to Agartala on the 23rd January, 1929 with Her Highness the Maharanee Saheba, who was accorded by high and low alike a most warm reception, and the auspicious ceremony came to a close in the midst of a week of rejoicings and festivities.

First official visit to Comilla.

10. Another event unique in its character deserves special mention. This was the first official visit, on the 18th August, 1928, of His Highness, to Comilla, the headquarters station of British Tippera District as well as the Maharaja's vast Zemindaries.

11. The welcome that His Highness received on the occasion from all sections of people, official and non-official, was indeed unprecedented in the annals of the town.

His Highness's entry into Comilla town.

12. His Highness was received at the station by Mr. H. W. Lyne, I. C. S., District Magistrate (& ex-officio Political Agent of the State) as well as the members of a committee composed of the elite of the town representing all caste and creed. A guard of honour detailed under Government

orders presented arms, while a band of Boy Scouts joined. An address of welcome was read on the platform to which His Highness gave an appreciative reply. The vast gathering that attended and the enthusiasm all displayed beggar description. It was with difficulty that His Highness's carriage could pass through the monster crowd struggling to rush in with a view to garland him or touch his feet, while as the procession passed through the decorated streets and houses of the town, ladies showered rice and flowers from the terraces and blew conch shells.

Addresses by Public bodies.

13. His Highness received addresses of welcome from the District Board, the Municipality, the People's Association, the Khadimal Islam, the Anjuman-i-Islamia, the Hindu Mahasabha, the Widow Remarriage Society, the Birchandra Library and Club, the Traders' Association, the Postal Club the local Chamber of Commerce, the Abhaya Asram, the Nurnagar Talukdars' Association and other representative bodies, besides those from different sections of his tenants and officials. To all these addresses His Highness gave sympathetic replies, that were highly appreciated for the kind and often lofty sentiment pervading.

Visits to religious & educational institutions.

14. Visits to religious institutions, both Hindu and Mahomedan, as well as to colleges, schools and libraries followed, and presented further opportunities for public ovations, while His Highness made contributions for purposes of worship in the temples and mosques, and for the feeding of the children.

His Highness's sudden illness.

15. A number of other public functions forming a part of the programme, including an address by the ladies, had to be abandoned to the great disappointment of all, owing to a sudden attack of influenza with which His Highness was unfortunately laid up.

The State Banquet and garden party.

16. The visit thus came to a sudden and almost dramatic end, following a State Banquet and a Garden party at His Highness's residence at which all sections of Comilla society were widely represented.

17. Before departure the Maharaja announced donations to public Institutions aggregating Rs. 63000, as detailed in Chapter VIII following.

Visits to other places.

18. On recovery His Highness went to Mussoorie for a brief period of rest and change, and visited Simla, Delhi, and Agra before return, the tour extending from the 11th September to the 20th October, 1928.

19. He was, besides, out twice during the year staying at Shillong from 23rd May to 16th June, 1928, and at Calcutta from 17th December 1928 to 2nd January 1929, and met His Excellency the Governor of Assam at Shillong, and both His Excellency the Viceroy and His Excellency the Governor of Bengal at Calcutta.

Another wedding.

20. Another wedding in the Ruling family, which also deserves notice, came off on the 10th March 1929, when Maharajkumari Sephalika Devi, a step sister of His Highness was married to Captain Rana Jhappat Jung Bahadur of Allahabad.

21. Rai J. C. Sen Bahadur, B. A., B. C. S., went out on leave and was absent from 17th May to the 30th July 1928, when Dewan B. K. Sen Bahadur, M. A.. B. L. officiated as Minister.

Administrative changes.

22. Mr. H. W. Lyne, I. C. S. continued as Political Agent of the State upto 4th November 1928, when he was succeeded by Mr. F. W. Robertson, I. C. S., who assumed charge on the 5th idem. Mr. Robertson paid his first formal visit to His Highness at Agartala on 7th December, 1928, and His Highness returned the visit on the same day.

The Political Agent.

II.

23. The rainfall of the year was on the whole below the average and unevenly distributed. In the northern parts of the State it was more or less excessive and in the southern divisions, insufficient, Crops were affected generally, and the outturn of cotton and jute fell off considerably in comparison with the previous year. The dullness of the jute market in the adjoining British territories had the effect of reducing the export of the commodity, and in the upper Gumti valley the trade in rice was not as brisk as usual. The result was a scarcity of money from which the lower tracts in the southern portions of the State suffered for a time.

The year.

24. The economic condition however may be said to have been on the whole decidedly fair throughout the year, and, in the financial administration, the improved paying capacity of the tenantry was indicated by better collections in the State, where the income rose from Rs, 18,77,136 to Rs. 19,46,421 giving a net increase of Rs, 69,285. The gross receipts of the year in the State and the Zemindaries aggregated Rs, 33,05,772 against Rs. 31,60,520 and inspite of heavy abnormal expenditure on account of His Highness's marriage and other counts, totalling Rs, 3,41,258, and considerably increased allotments on Public Works and other heads, the closing balance stood at Rs, 9,60,673.

The finances of the year.

25 Among the reforms initiated during the year, may be mentioned the following :—

Reforms.

(*a*) The earmarking of a fixed allotment in the Public Works Budget for measures of improvement. The total amount spent on such works stood at Rs. 1,78,099.

(*b*) The Re-organization of the State Military forces and the laying out of a cantonment station with necessary buildings of upto-date pattern.

(*c*) The creation of the Departments of Immigration and Reclamation, under the control of the Chief Secretary, and of the Department of Commerce and Industry under the Officer-in-charge, Revenue Department.

CHAPTER II—LAND ADMINISTRATION.

Charge.

26. Babu B. K. Chatterjee, M. A., B. L., continued to be in charge of the Revenue Department during the year under review.

27. As shown below, the total area held under settlement at the close of the year was 616 sq. miles as against 597 sq. miles in the previous year, giving an increase of 19 sq. miles during the year.

Kinds of settlement.	Area in square miles.		Increase.	Decrease.	REMARKS.
	1338 T.E.	1337 T.E.			
Jotes ...	293	278	15	—	
Taluks ...	323	319	4		
Total ...	616	597	19		

28. The increase in the area under *jote* settlement is due to new settlements and that under *taluk* is due to resettlement of 2 auction-purchased *taluks* during the year.

Tea Settlement.

29. There was no fresh settlement for tea cultivation in the year under report but 2 gardens purchased by the State in auction sale for arrears of revenue were resettled with the highest bidders, the *Nazarana* secured being Rs. 4,518.

Rates of *Jama.*

30. The average *jama* per *kani* of *jote* lands in *khas mehals* (exclusive of cesses) stood at 14 annas and 10 pies, against 14 annas and 11 pies in the previous year. The maximum rate for *jotes* was Rs. 12 per *kani* and the minimum 3 annas; while the rates for *taluks* were Re. 1-8 and anna 1 pies 9 respectively. The maximum rate for *jotes* was however confined to specially advantageous areas about the town.

Sources of land revenue.

31. The different sources of the land revenue demand with the collections under each head are detailed below :—

Sources.	Current demand.		Arrear demand up to the end of		Realization up to the end of		REMARKS.
	1338 T.E	1337 T.E.	1337 T.E.	1336 T.E.	1338 T.E.	1337 T.E.	
Taluks ...	1,67,267	1,65,665	2,67,297	2,50,591	1,68,639	1,53,059	
Khas Mehal jotes	4,34,365	4,16,787	7,53,825	7,47,808	3,88,186	4,00,775	
Bazars ...	8,322	8,019	1,393	935	8,154	7,559	
Cesses ...	37,782	36,663	69,415	66,970	34,073	33,751	
Total ...	6,47,736	6,27,134	10,91,930	10,66,304	5,99,052	5,95,144	

32. The above statement shows that the current demand under all heads was Rs. 6,47,736. With the arrear demand of Rs. 10,91,930, the total demand of the year was Rs. 17,39,666 against Rs. 16,93,438 in the previous year. There was an increase in the current demand in respect of *jote* lands due, as usual, to assessment on the expiry of the rent-free period and resettlement after the previous term.

Demand.

33. The total collection under all heads during the year amounted to Rs. 5,99,052 ;—Rs. 3,25,435 under current and Rs. 2.73,617 under arrears, as against Rs. 5.95,144 in the previous year. The percentage of current collection was 52·42 against 50·74 and that of arrears 25·06 against 25·97. In the *Khas Mehal* the percentage of current collection was 37·47 against 40·32 and in *Taluki Mehal*, 81·81 against 75·09.

Collection.

34. Altogether 5,070 certificate cases, covering a demand of Rs. 2,08,637 were instituted during the year. With 2086 cases valued at Rs. 3,35,453 pending from the previous year, the total number of cases coming up for final orders on disposal of preliminary notices issued on debtors, was 7156 covering a total demand of Rs. 5,44,090. Of these, 45 cases with a demand of Rs. 3,522 were rejected or struck off, and Rs. 19,895 in 792 cases was realised before decree, while 3340 cases with a total value of Rs. 3,37,500 remained pending.

Coercive measures—certificates.

35. Orders under the provisions of the State Certificate Act were passed during the year in 2979 cases with a total value of Rs. 1.83,173 making the demands absolute. With 3936 cases covering a demand of Rs. 3,20,701 pending in execution from the previous year, the total number of cases dealt with, was 6915 covering a demand of Rs. 5,03,874. Out of the total demand. Rs. 4,662 was remitted or written off, and of the remainder, Rs. 1,19,588 was actually realised, leaving a balance of Rs. 3,89,624. Of the amount realised Rs. 92,475 represents land revenue and Rs. 27,113 miscellaneous demands. 9 debtors were ordered to be arrested in the year, of whom 2 were temporarily committed to jail but were released on time being allowed. Partial dues were realised from some of the debtors and instalments were allowed to others.

36. The number of defaulting *taluks* brought under the operation of the Sunset law (including 16 pending from the previous year) was 77. Of these 64 were released on realisation of dues with penalty, while 2 were sold in auction and 11 remained undisposed of at the close of the year.

Operation of the Sunset law.

37. The results of the survey (including resurvey) operations are given in the subjoined statement. It will be seen that an area of 6433 *drones*, comprising 1268 *drones* of *taluk* and 5165 *drones* of *Khas mehal* was surveyed, as against a total of 7709 *drones* in the previous year. The sanctioned programme of survey for the year was for 6740 *drones* in *Khas mehal* and 2341 *drones*

Survey.

in *taluks*. The total expenditure incurred in the survey operations in *khas mehal* was Rs. 7,942.

Names of Divisions.	Quantity of land in *drones* surveyed in 1338 T. E.			Quantity of land in *drones* surveyed in 1337 T. E.			REMARKS.
	Taluki land.	*Khas mehal* land.	Total.	*Taluki* land.	*Khas mehal* land.	Total.	
1. Sadar Division ...	917	189	1,106	427	219	646	
2. Kailashahar " ...	205	757	962	228	575	803	
3. Sonamura " ...	—	1,799	1,799	177	2,508	2,625	
4. Bilonia " ...	—	843	843	678	687	1,365	
5. Khowai " ...	—	261	261	1,119	137	1,256	
6. Dharmanagar " ...	—	266	266	144	171	315	
7. Udaipur " ...	146	690	836	—	699	699	
8. Sabroom " ...	—	358	358	—	—	—	
9. Amarpur Sub " ...	—	2	2	—	—	—	
TOTAL ...	1,268	5,165	6,433	2,713	4,996	7,709	

Cadastral Survey.

38. A survey on a big scale (32" = 1 mile) of the Agartala town and some portions of its outskirts was undertaken during the year under report. The boundary was traversed by theodolite and seven sheets prepared. *Kittawar* or interior filling of these sheets was completed during the year. *Khanapuri* work has not yet been taken up owing to the alteration effected by various proposals for improvement of the town taken in hand by the P. W Department. The expenditure incurred for the above was Rs. 1,409.

Settlement.

39. The result of settlement work is given in the statement below. It will be seen that the settlement operations were completed in respect of 407 *drones* of *Taskhichi Taluki* land and in respect of 4,340 *drones* of *jote* land, as against 2,987 *drones* of *jote* in the previous year.

Nature of Settlement.	1338 T. E.		1337 T. E.		REMARKS.
	Area in *drones*.	*Jama* in whole rupees.	Area in *drones*.	*Jama* in whole rupees.	
1. Permanent *taluki* settlement of cultivated land ...	—	—	—	—	
2. Permanent *taluki* settlement of waste land	—	—	—	—	
3. *Taskhichi taluki* settlement of cultivated land ...	—	—	—	—	
4. *Taskhichi taluki* settlement of waste land	407	3,266	—	—	
5. *Jotedari* re-settlement of cultivated land	3,793	46,147	2,120	21,337	
6. *Jotedari* settlement of waste land	547	4,358	867	5,950	
TOTAL. ...	4,747	53,771	2,987	27,287	

40. 2 *Taskhichi taluks* under tea cultivation purchased by the State in auction sale for arrears of revenue were resettled—one in Sadar Division and the other in Kailashahar Division, and Rs. 2,600 and Rs. 1,918 repectively were realised as *Nazar*.

Taluki settlement.

41. A net increase of Rs. 24,215 in *jama* was secured by resettlement of *abadi jote* lands, the *nazarana* secured being Rs. 45,295. The average *jama* per *kani* was 12 annas 2 pies against 10 annas 1 pie in the previous year.

Re-settlement of *jote* lands.

42. During the year, an area of 547 *drones* of waste land was settled for a prospective rental of Rs. 4,358, the average *jama* per *kani* obtained being 8 annas 4 pies against 6 annas 10 pies in the previous year. The maximum and minimum rates were Rs. 2-4 and 3 annas respectively. The *nazarana* realised was Rs. 13,695, the rent-free period allowed ranging from 1 to 4 years.

Jotedari settlement of waste land.

43. A separate wholetime Settlement Officer worked in Sonamura, Udaipur and Amarpur Divisions, during the latter half of the year under review. In other places Divisional Officers were entrusted with the settlement work within their respective jurisdictions. The total expenditure incurred in the settlement operations exclusively, amounted to Rs. 3,242.

Settlement Work.

44. It will be seen that the *nazarana* obtained and obtainable by *Taskhichi taluki* resettlement was Rs. 4,518 and that by resettlement of cultivable *jote* lands and settlement of waste lands as *jotes*, amounted to Rs. 63,662 (Rs. 49.967 + Rs. 13,695). The net increase of revenue secured was Rs. 31,839 (Rs. 3,266 + Rs. 24,215 + Rs. 4,358).

45. As detailed below, there were altogether 10 private estates under State management during the year.

Private Estates under State Management.

Class.	Name of Estates.	Area.	Revenue.
Encumbered	1. Kakrabon Estate	283 *drones*	1,871
	2. Jogendranagar Trust Estate	64 ,,	163
	3. Kamalnagar and Mohendranagar Estate	51 ,,	255
	4. Gouranga Tripura's Estate	13 ,,	57
	5. Maharam Ali Chaudhuri Khanje Khan Bahadur's Estate—*Taluk*	236 ,,	1,230
	Jote	6 ,,	149
	6. Thakur Nalini Mohan Deb Barma's Estate	68 ,,	170
Unencumbered	7. Prabhu Goswamis' Estate	31 ,,	61
	8. Dowager Maharanee's Estate	260 ,,	450
	9. Late Brajakumar Thakur's Estate	47 ,,	297
Endowment	10. Taranagar Estate	140 ,,	52

46. The following table shows the demands and collections of these estates during the year. The demands include a considerable portion which is irrecoverable, and this really accounts for the low percentage of

collection. The figures nevertheless display a more or less unsatisfactory state of things.

Estate No.	Demand			Collection			P. C. of collection
	Current	Arrear	Total	Current	Arrear	Total	
1.	7,321	32,032	39,353	1,300	5,457	6,757	17·17
2.	1,260	4,034	5,294	295	490	785	11·05
3.	1,272	1,115	2,387	361	610	971	40·6
4.	204	18	222	139	14	153	68·90
5.	3,925	8,233	12,158	1,391	1,200	2,591	21·31
6.	1,163	2,266	3,429	440	971	1,411	41·15
7.	913	2,303	3,216	335	867	1,202	37·37
8.	7,470	11,881	19,351	2,776	3,459	6,235	32·22
9.	1,653	2,714	4,367	634	1,244	1,878	43·00
10.	3,087	6,486	9,573	837	1,683	2,520	26·32

CHAPTER III—PROTECTION.

I. Legislation.

Change of personnel of the Legislative Council.

47. During the year under report there were certain changes in the personnel of the Legislative Council. Dewan Asita Chandra Chaudhuri, B. A. who retired from the State Civil Service ceased to be its member, while four new members—three official and one non-official, as detailed below, were taken in :

1. Lieutenant (Hon.) J. N. Bhaduri, B. E.,
   State Engineer.
2. Babu Jatindra Nath Mitra,
   Officer-in-charge, Forest Department.
3. Dewan Saheb Anukul Mukharjee, B. A.,
   Secy. His Highness's Nij Tahabil.
4. Mr. Bijoy Kumar Chatterjee, M. A., B. L.,
   Advocate—Calcutta High Court and
   M. L. C.—Bengal.

The total number of members thus came to 22.

Sittings of the Legislative Council.

48. There were 8 sittings of the Legislative Council and with the exception of one, all the sittings were held under the presidency of His Highness the Maharaja Manikya Bahadur.

Laws enacted.

49. Altogether 9 bills came up before the Council, out of which the following were passed and became law duly on receipt of His Highness's assent.

i. State Motor Vehicles Act I of 1338 T. E.

ii. An Act—being Act II of 1338 T. E.—for prevention of smuggling of elephant tusks.

iii. State Stamp Act III of 1338 T. E.

50. The following important circulars, issued during the year, may be mentioned :—

1. Circular No. 13 dated 5-8-38 T. E.—making the Revenue Department's permission a condition binding on the Managers of Court of Wards properties for appearance either as plaintiff or defendant in civil suits.

2. Circular No. 16 dated 14-10-38 T. E.—allowing exemption of export duty on tea sweepings under certain circumstances.

3. Circular No. 17 dated 7-11-38 T. E.—regarding grant of mutation to purchasers of *taluks*, not residing in the State.

II. Military.

51. Major Kumar Dina Mohan Deb Barman Bahadur was in charge of the Military forces as before.

Charge.

52. An arrangement was arrived at during the year with the Government of India, under which the Durbar agreed to organise and maintain for the present one company of Infantry as a regular unit of the Indian State Forces.

Arrangement with Government.

53. The First Tripura Bir Company which had been formed sometime ago, was speedily reorganised in pursuance of the arrangement, under the personal supervision of His Highness the Maharaja, and made very satisfactory progress in respect of training and discipline.

The First Tripura Bir Company.

54. The Company Commander, Lieutenant Kumar B. L. Dev Barman Bahadur, as well as two other Officers, Lieutenant Rana Jhappat Jung Bahadur and Lieutenant Kumar Balindra Kishore Deb Barman Bahadur, had undergone six months' training with the 1/8th Gurkha Rifles at Shillong sometime ago, and the first named Officer fully justified his selection as the Commander of the Bir Company. Several other Officers and men were also sent to Shillong for training.

The Company Commander—Training of Officers.

55. A cantonment was planned and laid out on a very convenient and attractive site, with spacious accommodation for upto-date barracks, family quarters, and Bell of-Arms as well as parade and practice grounds. The construction of all buildings has since been taken up.

Cantonment.

56. The actual strength of the Force including that of the Bir Company was 365 at the close of the year, as detailed in appendix II. The total expenditure of the year amounted to Rs. 89,661 against Rs. 77,911 of the year previous, the increase being due to the re-organization of the forces.

Strength & Expenditure.

III. Police.

57. Lieutenant (Hon) Jogesh Chandra Dutt, B. A. continued as Superintendent of Police during the year.

Charge.

58. The total strength of the Police Force in the year under report, exclusive of the armed section, was 455 against 465. There was, besides, a contingent of armed police numbering 35 against 35. In view of the growing importance of the capital, the necessity for increased strength of the town section both for preventing crime and regulating traffic has been felt. The decrease in the total strength as compared with the previous year is apparent only, being due to the transfer of the duty of guarding jails from the police to a separate staff of jail-warders.

Strength.

59. The total number of village chaukidars was 175 only which is considered inadequate, specially in view of the vast hill and jungle tracts in the interior that render the duty of watch and ward extremely difficult. As it is, the strength gives an average of 23·52 square miles per head, considering the total area of the State, and 4·57 square miles per head, in the inhabited area. The scattered distribution of the population and the generally wild nature of the country render the charge even in the inhabited area unmanageable.

Rural Police.

60. There were 4 Inspectors working under the Superintendent of Police as before—one being a temporary hand. The long absence of the Assistant Superintendent of Police on sick leave was felt, though no arrangement for the work of this officer could be made during the year.

Inspecting Staff.

61. There were altogether 23 Sub-Inspectors and 14 Naib Darogas during the year empowered to investigate cases and prosecute offenders. The staff may be said to have worked well.

Investigating and Prosecuting Staff.

62. A small staff was also retained for C. I. D. work, and the work of this branch appears to have been fairly satisfactory.

C. I. D. and Intelligence Staff.

63. The total number of cases reported to the police was 1336 against 1,377 in the previous year.

Crime.

64. The result of cases investigated will be seen from the following table :—

Number of cases reported
1,336.

Enquiry refused	Number investigated	Number pending
15	1,195	126

Number investigated 1,195:

Maliciously false	True	Doubtful etc.
92	771	332

True 771:

Charge-sheet	Finally reported
429	342

65. Altogether 964 persons were arrested for various offences, and 821 persons sent up for trial by the police, against 830 and 721 respectively in the previous year.

Result of Prosecution.

66. Of the number 821 sent up, 169 were convicted and 252 acquitted (including 108 on compromise and 61 on withdrawal of cases)

while 4 died, 1 escaped and 395 were awaiting trial. The percentage of conviction was 20·58 against 23·1 of the previous year and must be considered low.

67. Of the 314 persons awaiting trial at the end of the previous year, 74 were convicted and 147 acquitted (including 20 on compromise and 41 on withdrawal of cases) while 93 were awaiting trial.

Bad livelihood.

68. 3 bad livelihood cases with 3 persons, were instituted during the year under report. All the persons were convicted.

Arms Act cases.

69. Of 12 Arms Act cases, 3 were finally reported as true, and 9 with 14 persons sent up for trial. 7 persons were convicted and 3 acquitted, while 4 persons were awaiting trial at the end of the year.

Recovery of stolen property.

70. The value of property stolen was estimated at Rs. 16,199-3-9 against Rs. 24,329-15-6 of the previous year. Of this amount, Rs. 3,540-10-9 was recovered against Rs. 11,272-13-3 of the previous year. The percentage of the recovery was thus 21·8 against 46·33 of the previous year. The result was unsatisfactory.

Dacoities.

71. There were 11 cases of dacoity reported during the year, of which 4 were finally reported as true and 7 sent up in charge sheets. 9 persons were convicted and 5 discharged, while 13 persons were awaiting trial at the end of the year.

Unnatural deaths and steps taken.

72. Altogether 63 cases of unnatural death were reported during the year. Regular enquiries were held by the police in all cases. No crime was discovered in connection with any.

Rewards and punishment.

73. 5 Darogas, 3 Naib Darogas received money rewards, while 1 Jamadar and 2 constables were dismissed, 23 constables were fined or suspended, and 1 constable was judicially convicted.

Tours.

74. The Superintendent of Police was on tour for 147 days during the year against 65 days in the previous year.

Co-operation.

75. The relation with the police in the adjoining districts in British India continued to be satisfactory.

Patrol.

76. The patrol at Sonamura worked satisfactorily in co-operation with the Kotwali police, Comilla, throughout the year.

Expenditure.

77. The expenditure amounted to Rs. 77,145 against Rs. 80,480 in the previous year.

IV. Justice.

Courts.

78. There were 14 Courts of Justice in the State during the year under report, exercising both Civil and Criminal Jurisdiction viz :—the Khas Adalat or the Chief Court with its original and appellate sides and 13 courts of Magistrate-Munsiffs exercising original jurisdiction only.

79. Dewan B. K. Sen Bahadur, M. A., B. L., F. R. S. A. continued as Chief Judge during the year, except for a period of two months and a half, when he officiated as Minister, and Dewan Saheb K. P. Dutt, M. A., B. L. acted as Chief Judge. Dewan A. C. Chaudhuri, B. A. Sessions Judge and Uzir B. K. Deb Barman, Puisne Judge, having retired from office, Babu Ramani Mohan Goswami, M. A., B. L. of the State Civil Service was appointed Sessions Judge and Thakur Lalit Mohan Deb Barman, M. A., B. L. of the State Civil Service as Puisne Judge. Kumar S. C. Deb Barman, Puisne Judge, had retired in the month of Jaistha, 1338 T. E. but owing to pressure of work he was temporarily re-appointed in the month of Aswin and continued till the end of the year.

Khas Adalat.

80. Altogether 2,076 original criminal cases were instituted during the year under report, against 2,280 of the previous year. With the balance of 619 pending from the last year, the total number of cases for disposal before the several subordinate original courts was thus 2,695 as against 2,857 of the previous year as detailed below ; out of these 2,695 cases, 1,989 were disposed of during the year, as against 2,238 of the past year, leaving 706 cases pending at the close of the year. Thus in the year under report, the number of cases for disposal decreased from that of the past year by 162 and there was also a decrease in the disposals by 249.

Number of original criminal cases.

DESCRIPTION OF OFFENCES.	1337 T. E.	1338 T. E.
Offences against the State and public tranquillity	141	125
Offences against person	657	714
Offences against property	1,475	1,334
Other offences	584	522
TOTAL	2,857	2,695

81. Extradition was applied for against 45 persons during the year. With 51 persons pending surrender at the close of the preceding year the total number of persons involved in the requisitions was 96. Out of this number, 14 were arrested and surrendered by the British Indian Police and 16 appeared of their own accord or were arrested within the State subsequently.

Extradition.

82. The total number of persons awaiting trial in the year under report, inclusive of the number pending from the last year was 3,561 against 3,739 of the previous year. The number actually brought to trial was 2,622. Of these, 656 were arrested by the Police, 478 were produced on warrants, 1,070 appeared on summons, 382 appeared voluntarily and 36 were arrested in the presence of the Magistrates.

Persons brought to trial.

83. Out of these 3,561 persons brought to trial, 1,403 were discharged without trial, 731 were acquitted and 444 convicted, 10 died, 1 escaped, and 972 remained under trial at the close of the year. Of the persons convicted, 164 were

Results of cases.

4

sentenced to various terms of imprisonment extending from below 1 month to 7 years, 276 to fine only, 3 persons were warned for the future and 1 person was released on security. The number of persons actually tried was 1175 as against 1391 of the previous year and the percentage of convictions was thus 37·78 against 41·19 of the previous year.

84. Of the 2695 cases for disposal, the number in which British subjects were concerned was 474 as against 577 of the previous year. Out of these cases 345 were cognizable and 129 non-cognizable. In 57 cases British subjects were complainants, in 417 they were the accused. In 161 cases both the parties were British subjects. In these cases 518 persons were actually under trial during the year under report, as against 680 of the past year. Of these, 131 were convicted, 267 acquitted or discharged and 120 remained under trial at the close of the year.

Cases concerning British subjects.

85. The statement below compares the number of original criminal cases which were instituted during the last 2 years.

Comparative Statement.

DESCRIPTION OF OFFENCES.	1337 T.E.	1338 T.E.	Increase.	Decrease.
Offences against the State and public tranquillity ...	114	106	0	8
Offences against person	532	568	36	0
Offences against property	1,154	986	0	168
Other offences	480	416	0	64
TOTAL	2,280	2,076	36	240

Decreased by 204.

86. 23 cases were committed to the Sessions during the year under report against 17 cases of the previous year. Out of these 23 cases, 15 were disposed of as detailed in the following table. The number of persons involved in these cases was 74; of them 32 were convicted, 11 discharged without trial and 13 acquitted, while 18 remained under trial at the close of the year.

Sessions cases.

Description of cases.	Number of cases.	Disposed of.	Pending.	REMARKS.
Murder	3	1	2	
Culpable homicide not amounting to murder	3	2	1	
Dacoity	4	4	0	
Arson	4	2	2	
Grievous hurt	1	1	0	
Rape	1	0	1	
Kidnapping	2	2	0	
Obstructing public servant in discharge of his duty	2	1	1	
Robbery and grievous hurt	1	1	0	
Dacoity and grievous hurt	1	0	1	
Death by rash and negligent act ...	1	1	0	
Total	23	15	8	

87. There were altogether 196 criminal appeals against 199 of the previous year. They were disposed of as shown below :—

Criminal appeals.

Rejected	13
Judgment affirmed	90
Modified	16
Reversed	25
Further enquiry &c. ordered	18
	162
Pending	34
Total	196

88. The percentage of judgments affirmed and modified was 73·61 as against 70·3 of the previous year.

89. The nuber of original civil suits instituted during the year under report was 2216 against 2086 of the previous year. With the preceding year's balance of 1078 suits, the total number for disposal was 3294 as against 3076 of the last year. They were disposed of as follows :—

Original civil suits.

Exparte	964
Admitted and compromised	402
Dismissed for want of prosecution	291
Disposed of on contest	455
	2112
Pending	1182
Total	3294

90. The average duration of suits before the civil courts was 3 months and 20 days, against 3 months and 24 days in 1337 T. E.

Duration of suits.

91. The total value of suits instituted during the year was Rs. 1,98,387-14-6 against Rs. 2,37,449-9-6 in the preceding year which gives an average value of Rs. 89-8-4 pies per case. Of the 2216 suits instituted during the year under report, 537 related to lands, 1255 to money transaction and 424 to other transactions. There were 1289 suits of the value of Rs. 100 and under ; 455 suits of over Rs. 100 and up to Rs. 500 ; 118 suits of over Rs. 500 and upto Rs. 1000 ; 25 suits of over Rs. 1000 and below Rs. 5000 ; while 329 suits were not estimable in money value.

Nature and value of suits.

93. The number of applications for the execution of decrees filed during this year was 848 and with 427 pending cases, the total number was 1275 as against 1030 of the last year. The aggregate value of the new applications was Rs. 1,05,850-2-3 and with the opening value of Rs. 1,14,245-8-9 being the value of the pending cases, the total amounted to Rs. 2,20,095-11-0. The number of applications disposed of was 737, the value of which was Rs. 94,903-5.3. The number of execution cases pending at the close of the year was 538 with the value of Rs. 1,25,192-5-9.

Execution of decrees.

Civil appeals.

94. There were 179 civil appeals filed during this year, against 174 of the previous year. With the last year's balance of 90, the total for disposal was 269 against 220 of 1337 T. E. Out of these, 147 were disposed of during the year under report against 130 of the last year, leaving a balance of 122 cases at the close of the year.

Results of appeals.

95. The following figures indicate the results of appeals :—

Decisions confirmed	...	...	...	50
" reversed	...	...	...	7
" modified	...	...	...	29
" remanded	...	...	...	37
Compromised or otherwise disposed of			...	24
				147

Percentage.

96. The percentage of judgments wholly or partly upheld, excluding the cases compromised, was 64·22 as against 64·65 of the last year.

Value and duration of appeals.

97. The total value of appeals filed during present year was Rs. 37,248-9-9 p. and the average duration of each appeal was 2 months and 4 days, as against 2 months and 2 days of the previous year.

Original Side cases.

98. 25 civil suits were instituted in the Khas Adalat Original Side against 46 of the last year. With the balance of 50 suits from 1337 T. E., the total for disposal was thus 75 as against 82 of the previous year. Of these, 27 suits were disposed of against 32 suits of the previous year and 48 suits remained pending at the close of the year. There were 20 execution cases during the year under report including 24 cases pending from the last year. Of these, 11 were disposed of and 15 remained pending at the close of the year. There were 23 applications filed for the grant of succession and other certificates during the year. With the previous year's balance of 18, the total number of cases was 41, out of which 25 were disposed of as shown below, leaving 16 cases pending at the close of the year.

Description of cases.	Total.	Disposed of.	Pending.
Probate case	3	1	2
Succession certificate	13	11	2
Guardianship	25	13	12
Total	41	25	16

Total number of appeals.

99. Thus it will appear from the sub-joined table that the total number of civil and criminal appeals inclusive of the number pending from the last year was 465 against 419 of the previous year, and out of these, 309 were disposed of against 295 of the previous year. In comparison with the previous year, the

total number of appeals increased by 46 and there was a corresponding increase in the disposals in the year under report by 14.

Description of appeals.	Number of appeals.		Disposed of.	
	Past year.	Present year.	Past year.	Present year.
Civil	220	269	130	147
Criminal	199	196	165	162
Total	419	465	295	309

V. Prisons.

Number of Jails.

100. There were 8 jails in the State during the year under review, one at each of the Divisions and Sub-Divisions, including the Central jail at the capital.

Jail population.

101. The total jail population during the year was 810 as against 708 in the year before—the daily average being 101·60 against 117·22. Of the above, 322 were convicts, 481 under-trials, 5 civil prisoners and 2 lunatics.

Long-term prisoners.

102. A statement with details of 65 prisoners sentenced to over 2 years, as against 60 in the year previous is sub-joined.

Class of offence.	Number of prisoners.	Occupation.	REMARKS.
Murder	11	They were employed in oilmills, wheat grinding, *soorki* pounding, *khoa* breaking, bamboo and cane work, gardening, weaving, tailoring, paddy husking, rice manufacturing &c.	39 had sentences of 2 to 5 years, 21 of 5 to 10 years, 5 for life *i. e.* 20 years.
Culpable homicide not amounting to murder	10		
Grievous hurt	1		
Theft	2		
Dacoity	12		
Counterfeiting coin	1		
Forgery and Conspiracy. ...	2		
Outraging modesty of woman	1		
Unlawful assembly	17		
Robbery	7		
Escape from lawful custody ...	1		
Total	65		

Jail health.

103. The health of the jail was generally good. Only 3 convicts died during the year—one of cholera, one of malarial fever and one of chronic nephritis.

Escape.

104. One under-trial from the Kailashahar jail, 2 under-trials from the Udaipur jail, one convict and one under-trial from the Khowai jail, one under-trial from the Dharmanagar jail escaped during the year under report. None of them

could be rearrested, but one under-trial of the Udaipur jail surrendered himself before the Khash Adalat later on.

105. The total income from the Central jail amounted to Rs. 3,664 as against Rs. 4559 in the preceding year.

Income.

106. The total expenditure during the year was Rs. 18,536 as against Rs. 17,834 of the year before.

Expenditure.

VI. Registration.

107. The charge of the Department continued with late Babu B. K. Chatterjee, M. A., B. L.

Charge.

108. The number of Registration Offices was 9 as in the previous year, there being one at each of the Divisional or Sub-Divisional headquarters stations. In the moffussil, except for certain Divisions for which the Second officers worked as Registrars, the Divisional Officers acted as Registrars for their respective Divisions, while in the Sadar Division there was a separate Registrar at Agartala.

Registration Offices.

109. Appendices XV & XVI are Registration Statements and show the work of the Department.

110. The number of documents presented for registration during the year in the 9 offices mentioned above was 11,866 against 12,894 in the previous year. Of this number, 159 deeds were refused registration on different grounds and 1,255 remained pending at the end of the year.

Presentation and Disposal.

111. The total value covered by the documents presented amounted to Rs. 21,20,235 as against Rs. 22,37,308 in the previous year, while the total value covered by the documents actually registered was Rs. 20,48,167 as against Rs. 21,45,657 in the year before.

Value of deeds presented and registered.

112. The number of suits and appeals filed before the Officer-in-charge, Registration Department in respect of documents, the registration of which had been refused in the Registration offices, was 45 and 9 against 30 and 2 respectively, in the preceding year, and there were only 22 suits and 2 appeals pending from the previous year, making a total of 67 suits and 11 appeals. Out of these, 33 suits and 7 appeals were disposed of during the year, leaving 34 suits and 4 appeals pending at the end of the year.

Suits and appeals.

113. The total income from fees and fines amounted to Rs. 15,202 against Rs. 15,828 and the expenditure, to Rs. 5,007 against Rs. 4,573 in the previous year. The net income thus was Rs. 10,195 against Rs. 11,255 in the year before.

Income and Expenditure.

VII. Municipality.

114. As before, the Capital Town of Agartala had the only municipal institution in the State, the population within the municipal limits being about 8,000.

Municipality.

115. On the expiry of the term of the previous committee, a new committee was formed towards the end of the year. Mr. B. K. Chatterjee, M. A., B. L., Officer-in-charge, Revenue Department, was renominated Chairman and Babu Sankari Mohan Chatterjee, M. A., B. L., a local pleader, was elected Vice-Chairman by the unanimous vote of the committee. The committee had 5 five sittings with an average attendance of 5·1 against 4·2 of the previous year.

Municipal Committee.

116. The income of the municipality on account of municipal and latrine taxes was Rs. 3,860-6-3 against Rs. 3,727-8-6 of the previous year. The total demand from these sources, inclusive of arrears, was Rs. 7,511-10-6 of which Rs. 53-8 was irrecoverable.

Income.

117. The income under the Miscellaneous head amounted to Rs. 2,404-1-9 against Rs. 2,223-0 6. The figure excludes the income from the Bazar.

118. As before, the State grant for the year under review was Rs. 10,000 of which Rs. 9,998-15-3 was spent and the remainder lapsed to the State. Thus the total receipts of the municipality, including the State grant actually received, amounted to Rs. 16,263-7-3 against Rs. 15,023-9 of the previous year.

119. The total expenditure incurred during the year under review, inclusive of Rs. 145 in deposits refunded and advances issued, amounted to Rs. 16,239-15-3 against Rs, 15,885-1-3 of the previous year.

Expenditure.

120. The control of the bazar continued to be in the hands of the Municipal Committee. The total demand was Rs. 8,543-7-3 including the arrear demand of Rs. 2068-2-3. The total realization came up to Rs. 6,098-9 and the total expenditure from the bazar fund was Rs. 558-5. The accumulated balance of Rs. 16,107-9-6 on the bazar account at the close of the year, stands earmarked for the improvement of the bazar.

Ishanganja Bazar.

121. The general health of the public within the municipality was good. There was no epidemic out-break of any diseases during the year under review.

Health.

CHAPTER IV—PRODUCTION AND DISTRIBUTION.

I. Weather and Crops—Agriculture.

122. The average rainfall of the year was 87·67 inches against 78·37 inches in the previous year. The quinquennial average was 96·91 inches. Kailashahar Division had the maximum fall of 105·14 inches and Amarpur Sub-Division the

Rainfall.

minimum of 46·24. The rainfall was unevenly distributed and was on the whole unfavourable to crops.

Crops.

123. The principal crops were paddy, cotton, *til*, mustard, jute, and sugarcane. Potatoes, tobacco, chillies and pulses of various types were also grown in some parts of the State. The outturn of cotton and oil-seeds during the year was unsatisfactory.

Tea Industry.

124. The tea industry showed appreciable progress and the tea produced in the State fetched good prices. Two tea gardens purchased by the State in auction for arrears of revenue were resettled with the highest bidders on a *Nazarana* of Rs. 4,518. As many as 39 gardens showed marked improvement. The total yield of tea during the year 1928 is estimated at 10,96,045 lbs.

Cattle.

125. The health of cattle was fair during the year although "Anthrax" cases prevailed to some extent in Sadar and Udaipur Divisions, "Foot and mouth disease" in Sabrum and Amarpur Divisions, and "Rinderpest" in Khowai Division. The Veterinary Surgeon toured in mofussil for 20 days. 1,766 heads of cattle were treated for various diseases during the year.

Condition of the people.

126. The people are mostly agricultural. Outturn of crops, such as mustard, potatoes and chillies was normal. Cleansed cotton sold at Rs. 20 to Rs. 45 per maund. The production of jute decreased on account of dullness of market. Owing to diminished production and export of jute, cotton and oil-seeds, and to decreased export of paddy from the upper Gumti valley and consequent decline in the influx of traders from outside, the people, specially in the lower tracts, suffered from scarcity of money. No scarcity of food was however felt.

Prices.

127. The prices of food grains were lower than those of the previous year and were similar to those in the neighbouring British districts. Rice sold from Rs. 4 to Rs. 7-4 and paddy from Rs. 2 to Rs. 4 per maund.

Wages.

128. Male labourers earned from 12 annas to Re. 1-8 and female labourers from 4 annas to Re. 1 a day. Carpenters earned from Re. 1 to Rs. 2, Thatchers" obtained from 10 annas to Re. 1-4, and masons from Re. 1 to Rs. 2. Most of the labourers were outsiders from the neighbouring British districts. as well as upcountry coolies. The local people are taking to carpentry and other artizan works at a slow pace.

Taccavi.

129. No *Taccavi* advances proper were issued during the year.

Relief Operations.

130. Of Rs. 49,000 which had been issued as distress loan to the hillpeople in 1336 T. E. and 1337 T. E., Rs. 7,153 was realised in 1337 T. E. and Rs. 12,305 in the year under report, the outstanding balance at the close of the year being Rs. 26,179. In Kailashahar Division Rs. 15,000 was recovered out of a total loan of Rs. 24,000, in the Sadar Division only Rs. 435 out of a total of Rs. 8,000 and in Dharmanagar Division only Rs. 103 out of a total of Rs. 1,447.

131. The subjoined statement shows the recovery of distress loans in the year under report and the outstanding balance at the close of the year.

Names of Divisions.	Amount Realised.			Balance.	Remarks.
	Capital.	Interest.	Total.		
	Rs.	*Rs.*	*Rs.*	*Rs.*	
Sadar	435	135	570	7,758	
Kailashahar ...	10,266	926	11,192	10,226	
Bilonia	90	8	98	169	
Khowai	261	0	261	278	
Dharmanagar ...	25	3	28	1,319	
Udaipur	50	3	53	2,129	
Sabroom	56	8	64	0	
Amarpur	35	4	39	4,300	
Total ...	11,218	1,087	12,305	26,179	

132. *Staff.* The establishment of the Agriculture Department continued to be the same as in the previous year.

133. *Propaganda work and Circuit lectures.* The Superintendent of Agriculture visited all the Divisions of the State mainly in connection with propaganda work, which was as follows :—

(1) Introduction of better quality of cotton in *jooms*, as also in the plains with plough.

(2) Introduction of early superior quality of paddy in *jooms* as well as some other improved varieties of *Aman* in the plains.

(3) Extension of the cultivation of superior quality of jute, tobacco, sugarcane and potato crops both in highlands and river valleys.

(4) Preservation of manure and use of selected seeds.

(5) Circuit lectures against nomadic *jooming* and in favour of plough cultivation.

134. *Garo cotton.* Garo cotton is having a promising natural expansion. The cultivation of the variety is very popular.

135. *Paddy seed distribution.* The improved varieties of paddy such as Dadkhani, Dodsar, and Charnak are having prominence and popularity. The *Joom* types of paddy which are usually late in harvest bids fair to be given up by the people in the lower regions. The department is making necessary arrangements for distribution of seeds through local *Joomias* and loweland farmers.

136. *Jute Cultivation.* There are great possibilites for jute cultivation in some parts of the State but there is an all-round hesitation about growing jute on an extensive scale owing to the fluctuating nature of the market.

137. *Improved varieties of Sugarcane.* Sugarcane cultivation is thriving in certain localities, mostly in northern divisions of the State. A systematic survey has been taken up and the Department is taking steps to introduce and extend the cultivation of new improved varieties.

138. Eri rearing was tried in selected localities and the result proved promising.

Eri Rearing.

139. The farm was utilized, as in the previous year, as a seed-farm for helping propaganda work.

Kashipur Farm.

140. Seed distribution engrossed the best part of the attention of the propaganda staff and the people were found to be eager to have the co-operation of the department. There was increasing demand for improved seeds.

Seed distribution in farming areas.

141. The Superintendent of Agriculture was out on tour for 92 days both within and outside the State in connection with propaganda work, inspection duties, as also on special duty.

Touring.

II. Immigration and Emigration.

142. During the year 1,381 families immigrated into and 566 families emigrated out of the State, as against 1,497 and 179 respectively in the previous year.

III. Forests.

143. Babu Jatindra Nath Mitra was in charge of the Department. With the exception of a few Mahals which were let out in *Ijara*, all the forests were under *Khas* management as before.

Charge and Management.

144. The Department had a staff of 1 Station Officer, 3 Forest Circle Inspectors, 1 Assistant Forest Circle Inspector 17 Foresters, 22 Assistant Foresters and Rangers, 9 Moharers, 21 Head Guards and 106 Guards and Literate Guards. Besides these there were 181 Commission Agents for the sale of forest permits for the shoulder-borne export of minor forest produce not coming under any definite *Mehal*. There were 52 stations for collection of duty and prevention of forest offences.

Staff.

145. The Reserved Sal Forests of the Sonamura Division continued to be worked under the system of Coppice with standards and those of the Udaipur Division under the Improvement Method, while the open unclassed forests were worked under the State Forest Rules of 1323 T. E. For the Feni River *Mehal*, the working rules of the Bengal Forest Department were followed.

Working.

146. The sale of the four coupes selected and marked in the Sonamura Division could not be held within the year under report. Works were continued in only one of the two blocks selected and marked in the Udaipur Division, and no work was undertaken in the other coupe as this was not sold in the year under report.

147. The following table shews the result of the collection of forest revenue :—

Sources of Revenue.

Heads of Revenue.	1338 T.E.	1337 T.E.	Increase.	Decrease.	REMARKS.
I. Unclassed open forests :—					
(a) Toll on forest produce exported by the river mehals	5,17,238	4,71,580	45,658	—	
(b) Toll on forest produce exported by land route under permit	79,842	74,417	5,425	—	
(c) Toll collection (share) of the Feni river mehal ...	35,382	36,290	—	908	
(d) Grazing mehal ...	8,530	8,326	204	—	
(e) Thatching grass mehal	7,990	7,619	371	—	
II. Reserved Forests :— Sale of *Sal* and *Garjan* trees ...	4,173	6,784	—	2,611	
III. Elephant Kheddas	16,682	36,713	—	20,031	
TOTAL ...	6,69,837	6,41,729	51,658	23,550	

Net increase—28,108.

148. The total forest revenue of the year under report was Rs. 6,69,837 against Rs. 6,41,729 in the previous year, showing an increase of Rs. 28,108.

Receipts.

149. An appreciable rise of revenue is noticeable in the River *Mehals* and fall in the elephant *khedda mehals*. The revised rates of duty on forest produce were enforced in the year under report and these enhanced rates and constant inspection of the *ghats* account mainly for the increase under the head River *Mehals*. There is also a slight increase under the head Permit *Mehals*. This was due to better circuit work by the preventive staff.

150. During the year under report *Khedda* operations were undertaken in the Manoo, Deo and Dhalai Doals in the Kailashahar Division, Udaipur Amar-sagar Doal in the Udaipur Division, and Suknachhari Doal in the Sonamura Division. The *Khedda* operations in the Deo, Dhalai, Udaipur-Amarsagar and Suknachhari Doals were successful but the operations in the Manoo Doal which were rather late in starting failed. No *Khedda* operation was undertaken in the Beloniya-Sabroom Doal though it had been leased out. 7 elephants were caught in the Deo Doal, 12 in the Dhalai Doal, 4 in the Udaipur-Amarsagar Doal and 27 in the Suknachhari Doal working out a total of 50 elephants against 45 in the previous year. All the elephants caught could not be sold in the year under report and some of the elephants were sold at a low price as there was

Khedda operations.

no sufficient demand for elephants. This accounts for the decrease under this head.

Feni River *Mehal*.

151. The joint Toll Station at Amlighat continued to be under the management of the State Forest Department. The total revenue collected at the joint Toll Station in the year under review was Rs. 51,382 against Rs. 52,290 in the previous year. The Government of Bengal agreed to the proposal for medical relief to the wood-cutters at Amlighat Toll Station. Accordingly a doctor of the Sub-Assistant Surgeon class with one compounder was appointed temporarily for three months from January last and temporary quarters for the doctor and sheds for wood-cutters were erected.

Fee Simple Lots.

152. As the major portion of the area of the 14 as. 7⅛ p. share of the Lot No. 98 under the Chittagong Collectorate was brought under tea cultivation, the forest produce from this portion of the lot was not taken in *Ijara* this time on behalf of the Government and the State. As in the previous year the forest produce from this lot as well as from the other Fee Simple Lots was exported without any friction between the Station Staff and the Lot owners.

Forest Offences.

153. During the year under review there were 212 forest cases against 384 persons, including 58 cases against 106 persons pending from the previous year. The offences were mainly for illicit export of forest produce without permits and without payment of duty.

Results.

154. Altogether 164 persons in 87 cases were convicted of whom 14 were sentenced to imprisonment and 150 were punished with fine only. 96 persons in 48 cases were acquitted and 11 cases against 13 persons were compounded. 66 cases against 111 persons remained pending at the close of the year.

Rewards and Punishments.

155. No rewards were sanctioned in the year under review. One Ranger was degarded and one Head Guard, one Literate Guard and three guards were dismissed for misconduct. The two guards who were placed under suspension pending trial in the previous year were dismissed from service on the result of the trial.

Health of the Staff.

156. Excepting the death of a guard from fever and diarrhoea, the health of the staff in general was normal.

Accidents.

157. There was a regrettable accident in the year under report; Head Guard Sashi Mohan De of Kashirampur Beat Office while coming to Sadar was killed in a motor car accident.

Patrol Staff.

158. In the year under review a special staff was appointed for forest patrol work. The staff consisted of one Forester, two Head Guards and 14 guards who were given special training for their work.

General.

159. Some difficulties were being still experienced in connection with the export of forest produce from the State into Sylhet district, specially in regard to the delivery of the drift logs belonging to the State and the check exercised

by the Assam Forest Department on State forest produce in transit and the fee levied thereon. Correspondence on the subject was in progress between the State and the Assam Government when the year closed.

160. The Officer-in-charge was out on tour for 49 days.
Tour.

IV. Trade and Manufacture.

161. The Department of Commerce and Industries was created during the year under report. A stall designated "The Calcutta State Stall" was opened in the Calcutta Congress Exhibition under the management of the Superintendent of Agriculture and specimens of many of the agricultural and industrial products of the State were exhibited. The step was not without success, as numerous enquiries from various quarters have followed indicating ample room for the expansion of the trade of the State. The Department, in view of these enquiries, have diverted its attention specially to cottage weaving industries.

162. The principal exports were timber, forest produce of various kinds, cotton, oil-seeds (til and mustard seed), paddy, jute, tea, rice and *Gur* (molasses). Some homespun cotton fabrics manufactured by the hill people, especially the Manipuries, were also exported. The principal exports of the year under review and of the previous year are shewn below :—

	1337 T. E.	1338 T. E.
Cotton ...	69,093 maunds,	59,309 maunds.
Til	30,295 ,,	30,713 ,,
Mustard seeds	18,630 ,,	19,545 ,,
Jute... ...	1,24,655 ,,	80,394 ,,

163. 7,90,771 lbs. 10,13,109 lbs. and 10,96,045 lbs. of tea were exported in 1336 T. E., 1337 T. E. and 1338 T. E. respectively.

164. The principal imports were cloths and yarns, salt, oils (*kerosine* and mustard) pulses, chillies, tobacco, sugar, flour, spices, arecanuts, books and stationery. The industries worth mention were cotton fabrics manufactured by the hill people and the Manipuris; cane and bamboo baskets, mats and sieves by the Tripuras; and dug-outs, bowls and plates of wood by the Reangs and Chakmas; also *Gur* (molasses) by both hill people and Bengalees.

Public Works.

165. Lieutenant (Hony.) J. N. Bhaduri B. A, B. E. continued to be the State Engineer during the year.

Charge.

166. A special feature of the Public Works Budget of the year was the setting apart of a defined allotment exclusively for works of improvement. The actual expenditure under this head amounted to Rs. 1,78,099 against a provision of Rs. 2,00,000.

A special feature.

167. The plan of work involved—

The plan of improvement.

(1) The extension of the area of the Capital town.

(2) The improvement of the roads of the town.

(3) Erection of new public buildings in the town.

(4) Improvement of water supply and town lighting.

(5) Improvement of communication in the interior including road making and clearance of water routes.

(6) Laying out of a separate cantonment station.

168. The total expenditure on Public works amounted to Rs. 3,51,512 against Rs. 3,10,097 of the previous year. Of the total amount, Rs. 2,53,318 was spent on buildings, Rs. 52,236 on roads and bridges, Rs. 3,269 on water supply and Rs. 15,202 on miscellaneous works.

Expenditure.

169. The following major works of the year may be mentioned :—

(1) A new addition to the Palace—for residence of distinguished guests.

(2) A new garage with office rooms and godowns.

(3) A large godown at the Palace.

(4) A new Record Room in the Administration Office compound.

(5) The Chakla Office building.

(6) Widening and straightening of the roads of the town.

(7) Various works of town improvement.

(8) A Thana house in the mofussil.

(9) Improvement of His Highness's sitting room and of the *andar*.

CHAPTER V—REVENUE AND FINANCES.

I. Revenue.

170. The total collections in the year stood at Rs. 19,46,421 against Rs. 18,77,136 in the previous year.

171. The details of the receipts under different heads with all variations are given in the statement below :—

Serial number.	Heads of Revenue.	1338 T.E.	1337 T.E.	As compared with 1337 T.E.		Remarks.
				Increase.	Decrease.	
1.	Land Revenue	6,08,942	6,02,891	6,051	—	
2.	Rents of markets	7,313	7,658	155	—	
3.	Family Tax in the hills	65,221	60,223	4,998	—	
4.	Toll on forest produce	5,97,080	5,45,997	51,083	—	
5.	Do. Do. on the Feni River	35,382	36,290	—	908	
6.	Elephant & buffalo grazing Mehal	8,530	8,326	204	—	
7.	Thatching grass Mehal	7,990	7,619	371	—	
8.	Reserved *Sal* trees	4,173	6,784	—	2,611	
9.	Tax on cotton and oil-seeds ...	1,50,241	1,56,486	—	6,245	
10.	Royalty on elephants caught ...	16,682	36,713	—	20,031	
11.	Adda Mehal	24,163	23,202	961	—	
12.	Excise	92,718	85,485	7,233	—	
13.	Stamps and Court-fees	89,692	89,530	162	—	
14.	Law and Justice (Fines)... ...	4,459	4,012	447	—	
15.	Process fees	15,089	15,495	—	406	
16.	Registration	15,202	15,828	—	626	
17.	Jail	3,664	4,559	—	895	
18.	Cattle pounds	5,980	5,895	85	—	
19.	Nazars	44,064	49,733	—	5,669	
20.	Agriculture	—	611	—	611	
21.	Education...	8,518	8,661	—	143	
22.	Tea Export duty	17,107	—	17,107	—	
23.	Jute Export duty	30,857	—	30,857	—	
24.	Recovery of personal advances	6,546	—	6,546	—	
25.	Recovery of personal loans ...	2,365	—	2,365	—	
26.	Interest on bank deposits... ..	18,733	—	18,733	—	
27.	Miscellaneous	65,210	1,05,138	—	39,928	
	Total	19,46,421	18,77,136	1,47,358	78,073	Net increase— Rs. 69,285.

172. The increase under the head "Family tax in the hills" is due to better collection in Kailashahar Division. That under "excise" is due to resettlement of *mahals* at higher *jama*. "Forest" shows a satisfactory increase.

Increase.

173. There has been a small decrease under the head "Tax on cotton and oilseeds" as compared with the previous year, but as compared with 1336 T.E. the decrease is considerable, viz. Rs. 67,810. This is due to unsatisfactory outturn of cotton and oilseeds owing to unfavourable weather conditions.

Decrease.

174. On the whole there was an aggregate improvement of Rs. 1,47,358 in respect of 16 heads of income against a total decrease of Rs. 78,073 in 11, the resultant net increase being Rs. 69,285.

II. Finances.

175. A consolidated abstract account showing the financial transactions of the State and the attached Zemindaries as compared with those of the previous year is given below :—

Receipts.	1337 T.E.	1338 T.E.
1. Opening balance :-		
(1) State	10,47,019	6,94,785
(2) Zemindaries ...	3,72,617	3,28,880
Total ...	14,19,636	10,23,665
2. Income :—		
(1) State	18,77,136	19,46,421
(2) Zemindaries ...	11,46,097	10,99,010
Total ...	30,23,233	30,45,431
3. Law charges recovered :—		
(1) Zemindaries ...	43,228	47,947
4. Refunds and compensation for lands acquired :—		
(1) Zemindaries ...	2,890	9,533
5. Deposits :—		
(1) State	83,751	60,446
(2) Zemindaries ...	7,418	42,415
Total ...	91,169	1,02,861
6. Loans received :—		
(1) State	—	1,00,000
GRAND TOTAL ...	45,80,156	43,29,437

Expenditure.	1337 T.E.	1338 T.E.
1. General Administration charges :—		
(a) State	5,51,457	5,45,147
(b) Zemindaries :—		
1. Cost of management	1,44,597	1,54,961
2. Cost of litigation	96.490	1,09,287
	2,41,087	2.64.248
Total ...	7,92,544	8,09,395
2. Revenue and Taxes on account of the Zemindaries	2,69,253	2,70,852
3. Public Works :—		
(a) State	3,12,791	3,55,337
(b) Zemindaries	50.612	58,064
Total ...	3,63,403	4,13,401
4. Electric Light—State	19,020	24.727
5. Municipality—State	8,973	9,915
6. Education :—		
(a) State	1,26,208	1,33,106
(b) Zemindaries	10,884	10,992
Total ...	1,37,092	1,44,098
7. Medical and Sanitation :—		
(a) State	81,128	73,725
(b) Zemindaries	11,963	12,329
Total ...	93,091	86,054
8. Survey and Settlement :—		
(a) State	14,443	19,391
(b) Zemindaries	827	1,063
Total ...	15,270	20.454
9. Agriculture :—State	4,789	4,129
10. Religious Expenses :—		
(a) State	62,414	63,713
(b) Zemindaries	6,215	6,635
Total ...	68,629	70.348
11. Sultanat—State	54,283	55,181
12. Purchase of Land Tenures :—		
(a) State	240	3,500
(b) Zemindaries	27,758	4,270
Total ...	27,998	7,770
13. Pension and Gratuity :—		
(a) State	31,225	34,636
(b) Zemindaries	5.137	5,091
Total ...	36,362	39,727
14. Ordinary *Sansar* charges :—		
(a) His Highness's own and the late Maharaja's family	84,917	82,300
(b) Other branches of the Raj family...	1,36,750	1,35,741
(c) Thakurs	31,434	31,887
(d) *Sansar* office establishment ...	9,901	11,037
(e) Miscellaneous	69,226	86.675
Total ...	3,32,228	3,47,640
15. Charity and Donation :—		
(a) State	23,945	63,985
(b) Zemindaries	3,073	35.481
Total ...	27,018	99,466
16. Famine Relief—State	30,373	—
17. His Highness's Nij Tahabil :—		
(a) State	1,03,135	1,20,000
(b) Zemindaries	—	3,00.000
Total ...	1,03,135	4,20,000
18. His Highness's tour	16,910	54,000
19. Payment of liabilities and deposits :—		
(a) State	77,016	91,057
(b) Zemindaries	35,568	9,202
Total ...	1,12,584	1,00,259
20. Miscellaneous :—		
(a) State	9,903	6,790
(b) Zemindaries	12,957	27,352
Total ...	22,860	34,142
21. Advances to employees :—		
(a) State	7,768	13,467
(b) Zemindaries...	2,516	2,481
Total ...	10,284	15,948
22 His Highness's Marriage	—	2,13,624
23 Maharajkumari's Marriage	3,37,111	66,878
24. Investiture—State	2,07,201	9,383
25. Installation—State	4,66,080	51,373
Total ...	35,56,491	33,68,764
26. Closing Balance :—		
(a) State		
In Cash	1,33,006	1,50,161
At Bank	2,65,742	29,374
In bonds and advances	2,96,037	4.76,953
Total ...	6,94,785	6,56,488
(b) Zemindaries :—		
In Cash	1,03,746	72 066
At Bank	1,05,052	1,10,630
In bonds and advances	1,20,082	1,21,489
Total ...	3,28,880	3,04,185
Total of State & Zemindaries' balances ...	10,23,665	9,60,673
Total of State & Zemindari's expenditure ...	35,56,491	33,68,764
GRAND TOTAL ...	45,80,156	43,29,437

Receipts.

176. It will be seen that the total receipts from all sources including deposits, loans, as well as law charges and advances recovered, amounted to Rs. 33,05,772 against Rs. 31,60,520. With the opening balance of Rs. 10,23, 665, the total sum available for expenditure was Rs. 43,29,437 as against Rs. 45,80,156 in the preceding year. The actual income of the State and Zemindaries, excluding deposits and loans, was however Rs. 31,02,911 showing an improvement of Rs. 33,560 over that of the previous year.

Expenditure.

177. The total expenditure during the year amounted to Rs. 33,68,764 against Rs. 35,56,491 in the previous year, showing a reduction of 1,87,727 which was mainly due to an indirect cause, namely the heavy extraordinary payments made in 1337 T. E. in connection with His Highnes's Investiture and Installation Ceremonies and the Maharaj Kumari's marriage. The closing balance at the end of the year under review was Rs. 9,60,673 against Rs. 10,23,665. Of this balance, Rs. 2,22,227 was in cash in the treasuries, Rs. 1,40,004 in the banks and Rs. 5,98,442 in loans and advances. A sum of Rs. 2,30,000 was invested during the year as loan on mortgage of properties, and this accounts for the increase in the closing balance under the head "Bonds & Advances" and consequent reduction in the Bank balance.

178. The noticeable variations in expenditure are explained below :—

i. ADMINISTRATION CHARGES :—

STATE—The retrenchments effected on the recommendation of the Committee appointed for the purpose as also the absence of several non-recurring charges, such as had to be met in 1337 T. E., mainly contributed to the reduction under this head.

ZEMINDARIES—The increase under cost of management was due to the payment of half a month's salary to the employess as reward on the occasion of the Punyah Ceremony, which was graced for the first time by the presence of His Highness and signalised by unprecedented high collection ; and also to the regradation of pay of the Law Agents' staffs. The increase under cost of litigation was attributable to the institution of a larger number of rent suits.

iii. PUBLIC WORKS :—

STATE—The increase was due to the expenditure on certain important building and road works in the town of Agartala for which a special allotment was made in the Budget under the head "Improvement."

ZEMINDARIES—The payment of contribution towards the cost of the Goomti embankment during the year was responsible for the increase.

iv. ELECTRICT LIGHT :—

STATE—The increase was due to the payment of some outstanding bills.

v. MUNICIPALITY :—

The payment of enhanced contribution to the Municipality accounts for the increase.

vi. EDUCATION :—

STATE—The payment of an allowance to the Vice-Principal of the Raipur Raj-Kumar college, increased establishment charges for Comilla Kumar Boarding, the grant of new stipends, and increments allowed under the time scale of pay, were the main factors which contribute to the increase.

vii. MEDICAL AND SANITATION :—

STATE—The absence of any extraordinary expenditure which had to be met in the preceding year, viz, the expenditure incurred for the treatment of a fatal case of illness at the Palace and also for the purchase of surgical apparatus, acccounts for the decrease.

viii. SURVEY AND SETTLEMENT :—

STATE—The increase was due to a larger programme of the survey operations, during the year.

xii. PURCHASE OF LAND TENURES :—

The increase in the State was due to certain payments made for the acquisition of land required in connection with improvement works at Agartala, while the decrease in the Zemindaries is accountable to heavy expenditure incurred during the preceding year for purchase of a house at Comilla.

xiii. PENSION & GRATUITY :—

STATE—The increase was due to the retirement of a senior officer and also to a larger number of cases of gratuities paid to the families of deceased employees.

xiv. ORDINARY SANSAR CHARGES :—

The decrease under the Sub-head (*a*) "Expenses on account of His Highness" and Family was due to non-payment of certain allowances during the year, and the increase under (*d*) "Sansar Office Establishment" was attributable to increments allowed to the ministerial staff under the time scale of pay and also to the increase in the number of ***Binondia*** guards with an improved scale of pay. The variations under (*e*) "Miscellaneous" was due to the inclusion of Rs. 16357 on account of the Marriage expenses of Shephalika Kumari and of the charges for the medical treatment of the fifth Dowager Maharanee.

xv. CHARITY & DONATION :—

The figures for the year under report comprise, among others, the following noticeable payments.

1. Contribution of Rs. 25,000 to the Special Organisation Branch of the Chamber of Princes.

2. Part payment of various donations sanctioned by His Highness on the occasion of his first formalvisit to Comilla.

3. Contribution of Rs. 5000 towards the extension of the Comilla Hospital (1st instalment)

xviii. His Highness's TOUR :—

The adjustment of certain outstanding accounts pending from the previous year mainly contributes to the increase under this head.

xix. LIABILITIES :—

The expenditure under this head mostly represents repayment of ordinary deposits and interest charges. A sum of Rs. 1,00,000 obtained as a temporary loan from the Nijtahabil during the year could not be repaid within the year owing to the necessity for payment of certain unforeseen expenses that were not provided for in the original Budget.

xx. MISCELLANEOUS :—

The increase in the Zemindaries was due to extra expenditure in connection with His Highness's Visit to Comilla during the Punyah Ceremony.

As the accounts of the expenditure in connection with His Highness's Investiture, Installation and Maharaj-Kumari's Marriage Ceremonies could not be closed within the preceding year, many outstanding bills had to be cleared during the year under report. In addition to this, expenditure to the extent of Rs. 2,13,624 had to be incurred in connection with His Highness's marriage ceremony which took place towards the close of the year.

179. Two statements comparing the receipts and expenditure of the State and of the Zemindaries showing the respective revised estimates are given in appendices XXVII and XXVIII.

180. In the State the actual receipts fell short of the revised estimate by Rs. 3,133 while there was a saving of Rs. 59,407 under the expenditure. The result of these variations was the rise of the cash balance from Rs. 1,30,214 to Rs. 1,79,535. The saving referred to above occurred mainly under the heads—Forest, Education, Repayment of Old Deposits, Military, P. W. Improvements and Installation.

181. In the Zemindaries there was as compared with the Revised Estimates, an increase of Rs. 8705 under the Receipts and a saving of Rs. 21,175 under Expenditure. These vatriations resulted in an increase in the closing balance.

182. Babu J. C. Maulik continued to be incharge of the Accounts Department. With a view to remove the dual control over the treasuries, the Treasury Department was amalgamated with the Department of Accounts from the beginning of the year under review.

CHAPTER VI—MEDICAL.

183. As in the year before, the Victoria Memorial Hospital at the capital and 17 other dispensaries were maintained by the State during the year under report.

184. The following comparative statement for the two consecutive years shows the total number of new patients treated in the above hospital and dispensaries together with their daily average.

New patients.

PATIENTS.	1337 T. E.			1338 T. E.		
	Outdoor.	Indoor.	Total.	Outdoor.	Indoor.	Total.
	94,782	492	95,274	1,01,111	423	1,01,534
Daily average	258·96	1·34	260·30	277·01	1·15	278·16

Out-door attendance.

185. 1,78,8[illegible]3 patients (new+old) sought outdoor relief as against 1,68,429 in the preceding year. So the daily average rose from 4[illegible]0·18 in 1337 T. E. to 489·87 in 1338 T. E.

In-door attendance.

186. Inclusive of the last year's balance of 7, the total in-patients numbered 423 as against 492 in the year previous. Of them, 280 were discharged cured, 114 were relieved or otherwise discharged, 12 died and 17 remained under treatment at the end of the year.

Surgical operations.

187. Altogether 1,259 operations including 19 major cases were performed as against 1,196 and 24 respectively of the previous year.

Police Case.

188. Altogether 173 Police cases were attended to during the year including 15 postmortem cases, as against 184 and 18 respectively of the year before.

V. M. Hospital.

189. The total number of new out-door patients treated was 13,857 as against 10,996 in the preceding year—the daily average (new+old) being 68·57 against 51·87. The number of in-patients was 393 as against 436 in the year before. The daily average (new+old) was 17·11 against 14·82. Inspite of the decreased number of patients, the increase in the daily average was due to the treatment continued after discharge of some chronic cases. Of these patients, 262 were discharged cured, 102 were relieved or otherwise discharged, 12 died and 17 remained under treatment at the end of the year. The total expenditure on the V. M. Hospital amounted to Rs. 9,495 during the year under review against Rs. 9,891 of the previous year.

Ayurvedic Department.

190. One Kaviraj posted in the capital treated 38 patients during the year under report as against 53 of the previous year. The expenditure on account of his salary and the prices of medicines amounted to Rs. 2,676-10-6 against Rs. 3,281-14-3.

Homœopathic Department.

191. Dr. Hira Lal Banerjee, H. M. B., with his two assistants treated 15,096 patients, as against 14,695 in the previous year, the daily average (new+old) being 94·28 against 99·47. Rs. 5,638 was spent for this Department as against Rs. 5,657 in the year before.

Vaccination.

192. 7,551 vaccine operations were successful out of a total of 9,221 as against 8,562 and 12,369 respectively of the previous year. Inspection of the work of vaccinators in the interior was done by the two permanent small-pox doctors assisted by two inspectors. The total cost on this account was Rs. 1,414 against Rs. 1,546-10-6 of the preceding year.

Kala-azar.

193. 53 patients were treated at the capital during the year under report as against 164 in the year before. Of them 33 were cured and 20 left treatment. In moffussil dispensaries 75 cases were treated against 64. Of them 72 were cured and 2 left treatment.

Public Health.

194. Cholera broke out in a few places making a toll of about 80. Small-pox appeared in rather severe form in some parts of the State ; specially in Kailashahar and Dharmanagar Divisions. So far as could be ascertained, there were 65 deaths out of 283 seizures. The small-pox doctors treated 184 patients, of whom 163 were cured.

Sanitation.

195. Owing to the continuance of sanitary measures adopted as in the previous year, the health of the capital town was on the whole good. The expenditure on these special measures amounted during the year to Rs. 4,379 against Rs. 3,346 in the preceding year.

Staff.

196. As before Dr. M. M. Majumdar, L. M. S. was the Chief Medical Officer and Dr. S. K. Dutt, L. M S. his assistant. One bacteriologist was appointed permanently for clinical work at the V. M. Hospital laboratory. In addition, there was a staff of subordinate medical men, one lady doctor and two midwives.

Tour.

197. Dr. M. M. Majumdar was out on tour for 12 days and inspected four dispensaries, while, Dr. S. K. Dutta toured for 2 days and inspected one dispensary.

Total expenditure.

198. Inclusive of the expenses on sanitation, the total expenditure incurred in the Medical Department in the year under report was Rs. 73,725 as against Rs. 79,597 in the preceding year. The decrease is due to an indirect cause namely, the extra expenditure incurred in the previous year in connection with the Investiture and Installation Ceremonies as well as a fatal case of illness in the Ruling family.

Improvement.

199. The construction of a *pucca* out-door building, an operation theatre of an up-to date plan, a separate cholera ward and a septic ward is in contemplation towards the improvement of the Victoria Memorial Hospital.

CHAPTER VII—PUBLIC INSTRUCTION.

Charge.

200. Mr. S. C. Deb Barman, M. A. (Harvard) continued to be in charge of the Education Department.

Number of Schools.

201. The total number of schools during the year was 168 against 170 in the previous year, and the total numerical strength 7,345 against 6,848, excluding 52 pupils reading in private institutions numbering 2, as against 617

in 17. Four Pathshalas were discontinued in Kailashahar Division and one in Khowai, and three new ones were opened during the year—one in Sadar, one in Sonamura and the other in Dharmanagar Division.

H. E. Schools.

202. There were as before 5 H. E. Schools in the State, *viz.*—the Umakanta Academy at Agartala, Radhakishore Institution at Kailashahar, Brajendrakishore Institution at Bilonia, Birbikram Institution at Dharmanagar, and Navadwip Chandra Institution at Sonamura. All the H. E. Schools are affiliated to the Calcutta University. The number of pupils in these H. E. Schools was 1,589 against 1,450 in the previous year, and the average daily attendance stood at 1,182·54 against 1,092·49.

Matriculation Centre.

203. Agartala, the State Capital, continued to be a centre for the Matriculation Examination for the year 1929. Only the State H. E. Schools were allowed to send up candidates to this centre. The examination was conducted under the direct control and supervision of the Minister. The Department looked after the convenience of the candidates coming from moffussil.

Results of the Matriculation Examination.

204. Altogether 77 candidates were sent up for the Matriculation Examination from the five State H. E. Schools, against 51 in the previous year. Owing to illness, one of the candidates could not sit for the examination. A teacher from Dharmanagar B. B. Institution also appeared at the Matricutation Examination at this centre. The details of the result are noted below :—

	No. sent up.	Passed.	1st Division.	2nd Division.	3rd Division.
1. U. K. Academy	29	17	10	5	2
2. R. K. Institution	12	9	7	2	0
3. B. K. Institution	12	4	1	1	2
4. B. B. Institution	12	8	3	5	0
5. N. Ch. Institution	12	5	2	3	0
Total ...	77	43	23	16	4

205. The results, in comparison with those of previous years, were not, on the whole, satisfactory.

M. E. Schools for boys.

206. In the year under review, there were 8 M. E. Schools for boys with 990 pupils on the rolls, against 8 with 986 pupils in the previous year. The average daily attendance was 760·78 against 753·55. Representations were received from the local public of Udaipur Division for raising the status of the local M. E. School to that of an H. E. School. The Department accepted the proposal and as a preliminary step, it was decided to add one higher class every year. Accordingly Class VII was added to the Radhakishorepur M. E. School during the year and a graduate teacher was appointed from the beginning of the new session after X'mas holidays. The local public offered to contribute for the building and equipments and actually raised about Rs. 3000. It is hoped that the fund will gradually increase and meet the estimated expenditure for a suitable building and necessary equipments.

207. There was only one Higher Vernacular School for boys with 77 students on the rolls as against one with 62 students in the previous year, and the average daily attendance was 53·51 against 46·77.

H. V. School.

208. The number of Lower Vernacular Schools for boys was 22 against 21 in the previous year. The total numerical strength was 1,239 against 1,191 and the average daily attendance 893·87 against 879·55 in the previous year. In some of these schools, boys and girls read together.

L. V. Schools.

209. There were 112 Pathshalas for boys in the year under report, as against 115 in the preceding year. The total numerical strength was 2,830 against 2,643 and the average daily attendance 2,311·36 against 2,031·32. In some of these schools boys and girls were taught together.

Pathshalas for boys.

210. There was one Middle English School for girls, namely the Tulsibati Girls' School at Agartala, capital of the State. The numerical strength was 66 against 75 and the average daily attendance 48·30 against 53·60 in the previous year. A motor bus was maintaind as before by the Department for the conveyance of the girls to and from school. By special permission of this Department some girls were allowed to continue higher studies in this school under the tuition of the Head Mistress, who is a graduate of the Calcutta University.

M. E. Schools for girls.

211. There were 10 Pathshalas for girls against 10 in the previous year. The numerical strength of the schools was 319 against 236 and the average daily attendance 223·10 against 168·23 in the previous year. In some of these institutions girls were allowed, under the special orders of the Education Department, to read the Lower Vernacular standard.

Pathshalas for girls.

212. Altogether 478 candidates appeared at the different scholarship examinations of these State, against 456 in the previous year. Of these, 368 including 28 girls came out successful. 26 students including 2 girls passed the M. E. Examination, one student passed the H. V. Examination, 81 including 4 girls passed the L. V. Examination and 260 including 22 girls passed the *Pathshala* Examination. On the result of the examinations 18 boys and 4 girls received scholarships varying from Rs. 2 to Rs. 5 per month tenable for two to four years.

Scholarship Examination.

213. In the year under review, there were 9 schools for special training, consisting of 3 *Sanskrit Tols*, 5 *Madrassas* and *Moktabs* and 1 Artisan School, against the same number respectively in the previous year. The *Sanskrit Tols* had 34 students on the rolls against 43 in the previous year and the average daily attendance was 27·42 against 27·24. The Rajakiya Sanskrit Vidyalaya at Agartala sent up one candidate for the Government Sanskrit Examination against 3 in the previous year, and 2 candidates for the Sanskrit Examination of Saraswat Samaj against nil in the previous year. The *Madrassas* and *Moktabs* had 183 students on the rolls as against 152 in the previous year and the average daily attendance was 164·37 against 94·11. The Woodburn Artisan

Schools for special training.

School had 18 boys on the rolls against 10, and the average daily attendance was 6·25 against 5·03 in the previous year. Four students of this school were awarded stipends from the *Sansar* Department.

Non-Bengalee Students.

214. The comparative statement below will show the number of non-Bengalee students receiving education in the several schools of the State :—

Serial number.	Nationality.	Number of students.		Remarks.
		Past year.	Present year.	
1.	Rajkumars	7	9	
2.	Thakurs	170	176	
3.	Manipuris	611	660	
4.	Tripuras	732	753	
5.	Reangs	22	42	
6.	Kukis	25	18	
7.	Chakmas	2	0	
8.	Lushais	0	0	
9.	Others...	84	88	
	Total	1,653	1,746	

Reward Examination.

215. The policy of holding Reward Examinations for hill boys was continued and 209 boys appeared at the examination against 185 boys in the previous year.

Education of Princes & Princesses.

216. Two Maharajkumars continued their studies in the Rajkumar College at Raipur in the Central Provinces being placed in charge of a graduate teacher as in previous years. The results cf their examinations and their progress in health were satisfactory. The Maharajkumaris received their education as before under a graduate lady teacher and a Pandit.

Education of other Kumars.

217. Kumar Bepin Behari Deb Barman and Kumar Bankim Behari Deb Barman have been prosecuting their studies in the Ashutosh College, Calcutta.

Kumar Boarding House at Comilla.

218. The Kumar Boarding had 12 inmates against the same number in the previous year, of whom 11 were from the different branches of the Ruling family and one, a Rana Bahadur, the son of a Maharajkumari. The sad and premature death of Maharajkumar Barun Kishore Deb Barman, one of the inmates, in consequence of an attack of septic fever early in the year is noted with deep regret. Nine of the inmates were reading in the Zilla School, Comilla. The results shown by them at the annual examination of the school were satisfactory. The Kumars were under the charge of a Superintending Tutor, who, in addition to his tutorial work, looked after the management of the boarding. Another private tutor coached some of the Kumars in the morning.

The Day School for the young Kumars.

219. In the Day School for the young Kumars there were 3 students on the rolls against 6 in the previous year.

Education of Thakur boys.

220. Eleven Thakur boys were awarded stipends from the Education Department. The course of studies prosecuted by each is noted below :—

1. Jitendra Chandra Deb Barman—B. L. Class, Calcutta University.
2. Satish Chandra Deb Barman—B. L. Class, Calcutta University.

3. Niranjan Chandra Deb Barman—Carmichæl Medical College, Calcutta.
4. Amarendra Chandra Deb Barman—I. A. Class, Comilla Victoria College.
5. Surendra Chandra Deb Barman—I. A. Class, Comilla Victoria College.
6. Brajendra Chandra Deb Barman—I Sc. Class, Calcutta Ripon College.
7 Sushil Krishna Deb Barman—I. Sc. Class, Calcutta Ripon College.
* 8. Hiran Kumar Deb Barman—I. Sc. Class, Comilla Victoria College.
* 9. Benode Behari Deb Barman—I. A. Class, Comilla Victoria College.
10. Suresh Chandra Deb Barman—Government School of Arts, Calcutta.
11. Harendra Chandra Deb Barman—Bengal Forest School, Kurseong.

Thakur Boarding House, Agartala.

221. There were 34 boarders in the Thakur Boarding House against 35 in the previous year. The number of boarders successful in the last annual examinations was 30. Four boarders sat for the last Matriculation Examination, of whom 3 came out successful, 2 being placed in the 1st. Division and 1 in the 2nd. Division. One of them secured a State Scholarship of Rs. 8, tenable for 2 years. The staff consisted of one Guardian Superintendent, one graduate Resident Tutor, one Assistant Tutor and one Manager and Tutor. The daily average attendance of the boarders was 27·4 against 30·89 in the previous year.

Tripura Boarding House, Agartala.

222. There were 10 regular and 4 temporary boarders in the Tripura Boarding House for Tripura boys attached to the U. K. Academy against 10 in the previous year. The boys received free boarding and lodging and had a Superintending Tutor to look after their studies as well as the boarding management.

Tripura Boarding House at Khowai.

223. There was, as before, another Tripura Boarding House for Tripura boys attached to the Khowai M. E. School. The local hill-people enthusiastically collected funds to provide this institution with a permanent house. The P. W. Department agreed to bear one-third of the total expenditure involved.

Special Stipends.

224. The following students enjoyed special stipends :—

† 1. Babu Chand Singha.
2. Chandrabash Singha.
† 3. Navadwip Chandra Singha.
4. Kuleswar Singha.
† 5. Prakash Chandra Sutradhar.
6. Mahendra Kumar Roy.

---

* No. 8 and 9 appeared at the I. Sc. and I. A. Examinations of the Calcutta University and passed in the 2nd. Division.

† Nos. 1 and 3 appeared at the B. A. Examination and came out successful. No. 5 completed his course of training in Kanchrapara E. B. Loco Shop and received his final certificate. He has since been appointed a probationer in the Power House at Agartala.

10

7. Radha Raman Pandey.
8. Upendra Kumar Das.
9. Bhagabati Charan Bhattacharjya.
10. Badriprosad Deb Barman.

225. Mr. S. C. Deb Barman, M. A. (Harvard), who is also the ex-officio Inspector of Schools, inspected the Rajkumar Boarding at Comilla and the schools at Sadar, Khowai and Belonia Divisions. He visited the Raipur Rajkumar College and also attended as a representative of the State, along with Babu Bhupendra Chandra Chakravarty, M. A., Assistant Head Master, U K. Academy, the All India Teachers' Conference held in Bombay on November 3, 1928. He further visited Baroda State to enquire about the working of the compulsory Primary Education Act and its various educational activities. Altogether he was out for 48 days during the year.

Inspection Work.

226. The Sub-Inspectors of Schools visited all the schools within their respective jurisdictions. Their inspection work was satisfactory.

227. At Agartala, the Bir Chandra Library was maintained in two separate sections. (1) The English Library, located at the Ujjayanta Palace and (2) The Vernacular Section in the building in the vicinity of the local H. E. School. The latter section was open to the public. The number of English books (including foreign literature) was 4,974 against 4,886 in the previous year, and the number of Bengali and Sanskrit books was 1,981 against 1,909 in the previous year. There were 4 Dailies against 5 in the previous year, 1 Quarterly against 1, 9 Monthlies against 6, and 3 Weeklies against 1. In the year under review, the average daily attendance in the library rooms was 14·5 against 13·9 and the total number of books issued to the public was 2,707 against 2,683 in the previous year. Maharajkumar Narottam Kishore Deb Barman continued to be the Librarian.

Library.

228. The total expenditure, incurred for the Education Department in the year under report, amounted to Rs. 1,33,106 against Rs. 1,26,208. Some of the more important details of expenditure are noted below :—

Expenditure.

1.	Primary Education	Rs.	23,261
2.	Secondary Education	„	42,991
3.	School for special Training	„	3,766
4.	Boarding Institution for Thakur boys ...	„	9,301
5.	Education of Kumars and Kumaris	„	24,702
6.	Scholarships and Stipends	„	10,563
7.	Library	„	2,340
8.	Tripura Boarding	„	1,366
9.	Miscellaneous	„	10,303
		Rs.	1,28,593
10.	Grain Allowance	„	4,513
		Rs.	1,33,106

229. Rs. 8200 was incorporated in the general receipts of the State from the accumulated realisations from students, in pursuance of the policy adopted in the year 1334 T. E.

Income.

CHAPTER VIII—ZEMINDARIES.

Chakla Roshnabad Estates.

230. Except for a period of two months and a half, the management of His Highness's Zemindaries in British India continued during the year to be in the hands of Manyabara Rai J. C. Sen Bahadur, B. A., B. C. S., who was as before assisted by three Assistant Managers and one Sub-Manager. During the Rai Bahadur's absence from the 17th May to the 30th July, 1928, on leave, Dewan Bahadur B. K. Sen, M. A., B. L. officiated.

Management.

231. The memorable event of the year was His Highness the Maharaja Manikya Bahadur's first State visit to Comilla, where His Highness stayed for 11 days, from the 3rd to the 10th Bhadra, and personally presided over the *Punyaha* ceremony of the Raj which fetched a record collection.

232. On his arrival and during his stay at Comilla, His Highness was most cordially received by all sections of the people including the local Government officials. Addresses were presented by a number of public bodies, all of which were suitably replied to.

233. Before leaving Comilla His Highness announced a donation of Rs. 63,000 as detailed below :—

(1)	For the improvement of the Town Hall and extension of Tripura Club Rooms— Town Hall— Rs. 8,000 Tripura Club— „ 3,500	Rs.	11,500
(2)	Tippera District Board	„	10,000
(3)	Sadar Local Board	„	5,000
(4)	Sadar Hospital Building	„	15,000
(5)	Abhaya Asram Hospital	„	10,000
(6)	Comilla M. E. School Building improvement	„	1,000
(7)	Girls' H. E. School Building improvement	„	1,000
(8)	Shah Suja Masjid Building improvement	„	1,500
(9)	Bidhaba Bibaha Sahayak Samiti ...	„	1,500
(10)	Tatwajnan Sabha...	„	1,000
(11)	Hindu Sabha	„	1,000
(12)	Postal Club	„	500
(13)	Khadimal Islam Mahapratisthan ...	„	500
(14)	For sweets to the students	„	2,850
(15)	*Pranami* to the Devalayas and *Sinni* to Shah Suja Masjid and other small donations	„	650
		Rs.	63,000

234. The gross revenue demand of the year was Rs. 10,07,985 against Rs. 10,06,968 in the previous year.

Receipts.

235. The total receipts amounted to Rs. 11,98,905 (including Rs. 24,630 on account of the Tripura Raj Central Co-operative Bank and Rs. 6,643 on account of *Debottar Mehals*) against Rs. 11,99,633 in the previous year.

Expenditure.

236. The total expenditure in the year under review was Rs. 12,23,600 including adjustment of old advances and contributions to the State, against Rs. 12,40,854 in the previous year. Of this, Rs. 2,70,852 was on account of Land Revenue and Cesses. The total administration charges of the Zemindaries, including Public Works and Law Charges, amounted to Rs. 3,60,088. The remainder represents special payments on account of the following items, aggregating Rs. 5,92,660.

(1)	Loans and Advances	Rs.	2,481
(2)	Donations	,,	35,481
(3)	Medical charges	,,	12,329
(4)	Education charges	,,	10,992
(5)	Religious ceremonies	,,	6,635
(6)	*Sansar* stipends	,,	15,540
(7)	Repayment of old deposits ...	,,	9,202
(8)	Improvement Loans and Contributions to the State ...	,,	5,00,000
		Rs.	5,92,660

237. The result of the year's settlement operations will appear from the figures noted below :—

	KINDS OF SETTLEMENT.	ADDITION TO RENTAL.		NAZAR	
(1)	Railway relinquished land ...	Rs.	52	Rs.	60
(2)	*Kaimi* and *Takshishi Taluk* in the Comilla town ...	,,	15	,,	23
(3)	Ordinary town settlement ...	,,	216	,,	5,911
(4)	*Khaspatit*	,,	1,252	,,	10,398
(5)	Enhancement of rent ...	,,	1,243	,,	19,969
(6)	Re-settlement of auction purchased holdings ...	,,	113	,,	7,861
(7)	Settlement of rent-free holding	,,	20		
(8)	*Takshishi Taluk* in the Moffusil	,,	18	,,	1,775
			2,929		45,997

238. This year's operations improved the rent roll by Rs. 2,929 and brought in a *nazarana* of Rs. 45,997 against Rs. 3,824 and Rs. 49,701 respectively in the previous year.

CHAPTER IX—MISCELLANEOUS.

Rajmala.

239. The second part of the Rajmala (Chronicles of the State) was published in the year under report. The delay in the publication of this part is mainly due to the difficulties experienced in respect of printing. The third part is in the

press. The expenditure amounted to Rs. 6,790 against Rs. 8,604 in the previous year.

Tours of high Officers.

240. Rai Jyotis Chandra Sen Bahadur, Minister of the State toured for 51 days during the year, while Dewan B. K. Sen Bahadur, Chief Secretary to His Highness, was out for 81 days, in and outside the State, including 23 days of camping as Officiating Minister.

Departmental Heads.

241. Among the Departmental Heads, Babu Brajendra Kumar Chatterjee, Officer-in-charge, Revenue Department was in camp for 36 days, inclusive of 18 days' tour on special duty. The tours of other officers of the status have been noted in the connected sections.

Divisional Officers.

242. Among the Divisional Officers in the State, the only tour worth mention was that of Thakur Kamini Kumar Singh, Divisional Officer of Sonamura, being 84 days. No other tour of the year was upto the standard.

Assistant Managers.

243. In the Zemindaries Babu Pramadaranjan Bhattacharjee, Assistant Manager, Central Division, was out for 86 days and Babu Surendra Nath Bose, Assistant Manager Northern Division, for 93 days. The touring of the Assistant Manager, Southern Division, and the Sub-Manager Srimangal, was inadequate.

244. It is indeed a matter of regret that the officers in charge of Divisions, as well as their assistants, did not see their way to be in camp more frequently, as was their clear duty, with a view to see to the wants and needs of the people, and to give sufficient assistance in the all important work of the development of the State. It can only be hoped that coming years will witness better results.

DATED, AGARTALA,
The 28th August, 1929.

B. K. Sen
Dewan, Shashan.

APPENDIX.

List of the principal Laws and Regulations in force in the Tripura State during 1338 T.E.

Description.	Whether adapted from British Indian Acts.	Whether introduce during the year und report.
CRIMINAL.		
1. Regulation No. III. of 1280 T. E.		
2. Regulation No. I. of 1283 T. E.		
3. Jail Regulation, 1283 T. E.		
4. Regulation No. IV. of 1283 T. E. (Cattle trespass and pound).		
5. Regulation No. III. of 1296 T. E. (Police Regulation).		
6. Act No. IV. of 1321 T. E.–Penal Laws (an amending Act)		
CIVIL.		
1. Civil Law of 1284 T. E.		
2. Rules regarding *chit* suits (small causes). 1287 and 1300 T. E.		
3. Act No. II. of 1313 T. E.—an Act for the regulation of interest on debts.		
4. Act No. II. of 1314 T. E.—Limitation Act	Partly adapted.	
REVENUE.		
1. Act No. I. of 1286 T. E.—Stamp Act		
2. Act No. I. of 1290 T. E.—Sale Law		
3. Act No. I. of 1296 T. E.—Tenancy Act.		
4. Act No. II. of 1296 T. E.—*Abkari*		
5. Act No. II. of 1297 T. E.—Reserved forests.		
6. Act No. I. of 1304 T. E.—Duties on *til* and cotton.		
7. Act No. I. of 1306 T. E.—Registration	Do.	
8. Survey and Settlement Act, 1309 T.E.	Do.	
9. *Tuccavi* Regulation, 1310 T. E.		
10. Act No. I. of 1313 T. E.—Forests.		
11. Act No. I. of 1314 T. E.—(amending the above)		
12. A Law imposing export duty on jute and mustard-seed, 1317 T. E.		
13. Act No. II. of 1321 T.E.– Ghasuri Act		
MISCELLANEOUS.		
1. An Act promulgating certain rules as Law, 1283 T. E.		
2. Regulation for the record of judicial decisions &c., 1284 T. E. ...		
3. Municipal Regulation, 1284 T. E.		
4. Legal Practitioners' Regulation.		
5. Act No. I. of 1297 T. E.—an Act for the regulation of commissions for the examination of witnesses.		
6. Special Regulation against cow slaughter		
7. Rules of evidence		
8. Act I. of 1318 T. E.—Constitution of Courts—(an amending Act).		
9. Leave and allowance Rules	Do.	
10. Act No. I. of 1321 T. E.—Arms Act	Do.	
11. Act No. III. of 1321 T. E.—Constitution of Courts (an amending Act)		

Description.	Whether adapted from British Indian Acts.	Whether introduced during the year under report.
12. Municipal Act No. I of 1322 T. E.		
13. Revenue Sale Amendment Act—1323 T.E.		
14. An Act for the destruction of old records—1323 T.E.		
15. Act I of 1326 T. E.—Regulation regarding Privy Council Appeals.		
16. Act II of 1326 T. E.—Registration of Births and Deaths	Partly adapted.	
17. Act III of 1326 T. E.—Vaccination Act	Do.	
18. Act IV of 1326 T. E.—Public Demands Recovery Act	Do.	
19. Act V of 1326 T. E.—Excise Amendment Act		
20. Act I of 1327 T. E.—Settlement of lands for tea cultivation		
21. Rules of Import and Sale of Opium—1327 T. E.		
22. Regulation No. 1 of 1328 T. E.—regarding Registration of Coolies		
23. Regulation No. 2 of 1328 T. E.—regarding Export of Tea		
24. Act I of 1329 T. E.—(Absconding sepoys Act)		
25. Act II of 1329 T. E.—(Control of prices of food stuff)		
26. Act III of 1329 T. E.—(Elephants and Buffaloes grazing Act)		
27. Act IV of 1329 T. E.—(House tax on Hill tribes)	Do	
28. Act V of 1329 T. E.—(Legal practitioners, Act)		
29. Act I of 1330 T. E.—Census Act		
30. Act I of 1332 T. E.—Encumbered Estates Act.		
31. Act III of 1332 T. E.—The Opium and Intoxicating Drugs Act.		
32. Rules and Regulations under the Opium and Intoxicating Drugs Act III of 1332 T. E.		
33. Amendment of Municipal Act (No. 2 of 1335 T. E.)		
34. Act No. I of 1335 T. E.—(Defining the term Minister)		
35. Act I of 1336 T. E.—(Hackney Carriages)		
36. Act II of 1336 T. E.—(Amending Act I of 1327)		
37. Act III of 1336 T. E.—(Amending the Survey & Settlement Regulation)		
38. Act IV of 1336 T. E.—(Prevention of gambling)		
39. Act I of 1337 T. E.—(Amending the State Tenancy Act 1 of 1296 T. E.)		
40. Land Acquisition Rules under Act I of 1337 T. E.		
41. State Motor Vehicles Act I of 1338 T. E.		
42. Act II of 1338 T. E. for prevention of smuggling of elephant tusks.		
43. State Stamp Act III of 1338 T. E.		

II

Statement showing the strength, cost and other particulars of the Military Force in Tripura State for 1338 T. E.

Arm of service.	Number of fighting officers and men.						Details of force at the end of the current year.						Buglers.	Total cost on account of pay and allowances of the force, including followers.	Remarks.
	At the end of last year.	Recruited this year.	Casualties.			At the end of the current year.	Number of regiments, battalions, or Batteries.	Number of guns.	Number of men.						
			Died.	Invalided.	Discharged, deserted, &c.				Commisioned Officers. European.	Commisioned Officers. Indian.	Non-commissioned officers.	Fighting men.			
1	2	3	4	5	6	7	8	9	10	11	12	13	14	15	16
Infantry ...	286	261	3	—	200	344	1	321 and one small cannon.	—	15*	29	295	5	Rs. 89,661	* Including 4 officers of superior rank.
Band Party	20	5	—	—	4	21	—	—	—	—	1 Band master.	20 Band men.	—		
Total ...	306	266	3	—	204‡	365	1	321 and one small cannon.	—	15	30	315	5	Rs. 89,661	

‡ In view of the work of Re-organisation of the Forces as a unit of the Indian State Forces, recruits are being thoroughly tested before confirmation. Hence the increase in the number of discharges etc.

III.

Statement showing the strength, cost, discipline, and education of the Police for the year 1338 T. E.

Description of office.	Number.	Grade of pay.	Total cost. (Excluding grain allowance.)	PUNISHMENTS.			REWARDS.		EDUCATION.		REMARKS.
				Dismissed.	Fined, degraded or suspended departmentally.	Punished judicially.	By promotion.	By money.	Number able to read and write.	Number under instruction.	
1	2	3	4	5	6	7	8	9	10	11	12
		Rs.									
Superintendent of Police	1	200-10-300		—	—	—	—	—	1	—	
Asst. Superintendent „	1	75-5-100		—	—	—	—	—	1	—	
Inspector	3	55 to 90		—	—	—	—	—	3	—	
Daroga	23	25-2-45		—	—	—	—	5	23	—	
Naib Daroga	14	15-1-25		—	—	—	—	3	14	—	
Writer Constable	13	15-0-0		—	—	—	—	—	13	—	
Subadar	1	25-2-45		—	—	—	—	—	1	—	
Jamadar	6	15-1-25		1	—	—	—	—	6	—	
Constable	215	10 to 13	77,145	2	23	1	—	—	200	—	
Chowkidar	175	5-0-0		—	—	—	—	—	—	—	
Spy	3	15 & 20		—	—	—	—	—	—	—	
Armed Jamadar	1	20-1-30		—	—	—	—	—	1	—	
„ Havildar	2	19-1-25		—	—	—	—	—	2	—	
„ Writer Constable	1	15-0-0		—	—	—	—	—	1	—	
„ Amaldar (Naik)	4	15-1-20		—	—	—	—	—	4	—	
„ Lance Naik	2	14-1-15		—	—	—	—	—	2	—	
„ Constable	25	14-1-15		—	—	—	—	—	22	—	
Total ...	490			3	23	1		8	294		

IV.

Statement showing the working of the Police in the Tripura State during the year 1338 T. E.

State.	Number of offences.		Number of accused arrested.		Number of accused sent up for trial.		Number of accused convicted.		Number of accused acquitted or discharged.		Percentage convicted of accused arrested.		Percentage convicted of accused sent up for trial.		REMARKS.
	Past year.	Present year.	Past year.	Present year.	Past year.	Present year.	Past year.	Present year.	Past year.	Present year.	Past year.	Present year.	Past year.	Present year.	
1	2	3	4	5	6	7	8	9	10	11	12	13	14	15	16
Tripura State	1,377	1,336	830	964	721	821	167	169	205	252 *	20·1	17·53	23·1	20·58	* Including 108 on compromise and 61 on withdrawal of cases.

V.

Statement showing the value of property stolen and amount of recoveries in the Tripura State during the year 1338 T. E.

State.	Amount stolen.		Amount recovered.		Percentage of recoveries of property stolen.		REMARKS.
	Past year.	Present year.	Past year.	Present year.	Past year.	Present year.	
1	2	3	4	5	6	7	8
Tripura State	Rs 24,329-15-6	Rs 16,199-3-9	Rs 11,272-13-3	Rs 3,540-10-9	46·33	21·23	

VI

Statement showing the number of crimes committed, number of cases disposed of, and cases awaiting trial in the Tripura State during the year 1338 T. E.

Description of offences.	Number of offences. Balance from past year.	Number of offences. Committed during the present year.	Number of offences. Total.	Number of cases disposed of during the past year.	Number of cases disposed of during the present year.	Number of cases awaiting trial.	Number of persons apprehended.	Number of persons convicted.	Number of persons sentenced. Imprisonment. Simple.	Number of persons sentenced. Imprisonment. Rigorous.	Number of persons sentenced. Imprisonment and fine. Simple.	Number of persons sentenced. Imprisonment and fine. Rigorous.	Number of persons sentenced. Fine only.	Number of persons sentenced. Whipping.	Number of persons sentenced. Capital punishment.	Number of persons sentenced. Total.	Number of persons acquitted or discharged.	Number of persons confined being insane.	Number of persons died during or before trial.	Term of imprisonment. Under one month.	Term of imprisonment. From 1 to below 2 months.	Term of imprisonment. From 2 to below 3 months.	Term of imprisonment. From 3 to below 6 months.	Term of imprisonment. From 6 to below 12 months.	Term of imprisonment. From 1 to below 2 years.	Term of imprisonment. From 2 to below 3 years.	Term of imprisonment. From 3 to below 5 years.	Term of imprisonment. 5 years and above.	Term of imprisonment. Transportation.	Term of imprisonment. Capital punishment.	Persons awaiting trial.	Remarks.
1	2	3	4	5	6	7	8	9	10	11	12	13	14	15	16	17	18	19	20	21	22	23	24	25	26	27	28	29	30	31	32	33
Class I. Offences against the State, public tranquility, safety and justice &c. — cognizable ...	4	33	37	28	23	14	75	a18	0	14	0	0	3	0	0	17	48	0	0	0	0	0	0	0	0	0	14	0	0	0	9	a. One person released on bail.
Class I. — non-cognizable	15	73	88	94	70	18	14	2	0	2	0	0	0	0	0	2	11	0	0	0	0	0	0	2	0	0	0	0	0	0	1	b. One person escaped.
Class II. Offences against person. — cognizable ...	95	252	347	244	244	103	b673	71	2	26	0	16	27	0	0	71	349	0	2	6	12	10	9	3	1	1	2	0	0	0	250	c. Two persons have been warned for the future.
Class II. — non-cognizable	51	316	367	267	302	65	294	15	0	3	0	0	12	0	0	15	235	0	1	1	0	0	1	1	0	0	0	0	0	0	43	d. One person has been warned
Class III. Offences against property. — cognizable ...	315	803	1118	925	801	317	c1785	291	3	61	0	18	207	0	0	289	1007	0	2	34	17	6	6	6	5	2	3	3	0	0	485	
Class III. — non-cognizable	33	183	216	202	175	41	228	12	1	5	0	0	6	0	0	12	176	0	1	1	5	0	0	0	0	0	0	0	0	0	39	
Class IV. Other offences. — cognizable ...	41	158	199	133	123	76	303	25	1	9	0	0	15	0	0	25	176	0	3	1	2	2	4	1	0	0	0	0	0	0	99	
Class IV. — non-cognizable	65	258	323	345	251	72	d189	10	1	2	0	0	6	0	0	9	132	0	1	3	0	0	0	0	0	0	0	0	0	0	46	
Total cognizable	455	1246	1701	1330	1191	510	2836	405	6	110	0	34	252	0	0	402	1580	0	7	41	31	18	19	10	6	3	19	3	0	0	843	
Total non-cognizable	164	830	994	908	798	196	725	39	2	12	0	0	24	0	0	38	554	0	3	5	5	0	1	3	0	0	0	0	0	0	129	
GRAND TOTAL	619	2076	2695	2238	1989	706	3561	444	8	122	0	34	276	0	0	440	2134	0	10	46	36	18	20	13	6	3	19	3	0	0	972	

VII.

Statement showing the number of offences reported and dealt with by the various Courts in the Tripura State during the year 1338 T.E.

Name of Court.	Number of offences reported during.		Number of persons dealt with.								Persons disposed of.					Persons remaining at the end of the year.	Remarks
			Remaining at the end of last year.	Brought to trial during present year.					Total.								
	Last year.	Present year.		Arrested by Police.	Upon warrant.	On summons.	Voluntary.	Arrested in presence of the Magistrate.	Last year.	Present year.	Discharged without trial.	Acquitted.	Convicted.	Committed or referred.	Died, escaped, or transferred &c.		
1	2	3	4	5	6	7	8	9	10	11	12	13	14	15	16	17	18
Sadar Magistracy	671	584	240	201	195	297	31	21	1,037	985	328	173	71	24	0	389	
Sonamura „ ...	284	239	148	78	47	172	43	1	439	489	176	107	104	23	0	79	
Bilonia „ ...	286	234	76	73	14	74	162	3	596	402	174	72	67	3	0	86	
Kailashahar „ ...	221	218	177	116	15	65	20	3	579	396	135	111	40	1	1	108	
Khowai „ ...	148	128	38	30	23	39	34	0	181	164	66	32	10	2	1	53	
Dharmanagar „ ...	353	327	113	63	72	148	64	0	349	460	206	30	16	5	7	196	
Udaipur „ ...	261	302	92	76	103	268	18	8	447	565	286	137	92	15	1	34	
Sabrum „ ...	56	44	55	19	9	7	10	0	99	100	21	56	12	1	1	9	
TOTAL ...	2,280	2,076	939	656	478	1,070	383	36	3,727	3,561	1,392	718	412	* 74	11	954	

* All of these persons were committed to the Sessions; of these 32 were convicted, 13 acquitted, 11 discharged without trial and 18 remained under trial at the close of the year.

VIII.

Statement of Criminal cases in which British Subjects were concerned for 1338 T. E.

DESCRIPTION OF OFFENCES.		Cases pending since the previous year.	Cases instituted during the year.	Total number of cases.	Cases in which complainants were British subjects.	Cases in which both parties were British subjects.	Cases in which defendants were British Subjects: Cases pending since the previous year	Cases instituted during the year.	Total number of cases.	Cases disposed of: Rejected, compromised or dismissed without enquiry.	Cases disposed of: Tried.	Cases pending at the close of the year.	Persons under trial at the close of the previous year.	Persons brought to trial during the year.	Total number of persons under trial.	Convicted.	Acquitted or discharged.	Died or escaped &c.	Under trial at the close of the year.	REMARKS.
Class I. Offences against the State &c.	cognizable	3	5	8	0	2	3	5	8	2	4	2	4	7	11	1	9	0	1	
	non-cognizable ...	1	4	5	1	0	1	3	4	3	0	1	0	0	0	0	0	0	0	
Class II. Offences against person.	cognizable	24	17	41	6	24	22	13	35	14	13	8	32	19	51	4	40	0	7	
	non-cognizable ...	3	36	39	6	25	3	30	33	26	1	6	0	16	16	1	7	0	8	
Class III. Offences against property.	cognizable	82	188	270	22	62	82	166	248	74	106	68	102	253	355	122	158	0	75	
	non-cognizable ...	5	54	59	15	30	5	39	44	38	4	2	1	36	37	1	34	0	2	
Class IV. Other offences.	cognizable	4	22	26	3	5	3	20	23	4	5	14	1	34	35	2	9	0	24	
	non-cognizable ...	10	16	26	4	13	10	12	22	13	3	6	5	8	13	0	10	0	3	
Total cognizable ...		113	232	345	31	93	110	204	314	94	128	92	139	313	452	129	216	0	107	
Total non-cognizable ...		19	110	129	26	68	19	84	103	80	8	15	6	60	66	2	51	0	13	
GRAND TOTAL ...		132	342	474	57	161	129	288	417	174	136	107	145	373	518*	131	267	0	120	

* Of this number 161 were discharged without trial, the cases being dismissed, compromised or struck off on default. Excluding 120 pending, the actual number of persons tried was 237, of whom 131 or 55·27 were convicted as against 59·85 of the previous year

IX.

Statement of Extradition Cases for the year 1338 T.E.

Names of Courts.	Nature of cases.	Number Borne on the Register.				Number Brought to Trial.			Result.		Number at large at the close of the year.	Number of persons awaiting trial (after arrest) at the close of the year.	Remarks.
		Number of persons at large at the close of the previous year.	Number of persons awaiting trial at the close of the previous year.	Number of persons against whom warrants were applied for during the year.	Total.	Number of persons arrested and surrendered within the year.	Number of persons who appeared of their own accord or were subsequently arrested in the State within the year.	Total (Columns 4+7+8).	Convicted.	Acquitted or discharged.			
Sadar Magistracy	Theft ...	3	1	3	7	1	3	5	1	4	2	0	
	Criminal breach of trust ...	1	0	1	2	0	0	0	0	0	2	0	
	Theft and receiving stolen property ...	2	0	0	2	0	1	1	0	1	1	0	
	Causing grievous hurt ...	0	1	0	1	0	0	1	1	0	0	0	
	Rescuing offenders from lawful custody ...	0	4	0	4	0	0	4	0	0	0	4	
	Wrongful confinement and rape ...	0	2	0	2	0	0	2	0	0	0	2*	* Committed to Sessions.
	Cheating ...	0	0	1	1	1	0	1	0	1	0	0	
	Criminal breach of trust by servant ...	0	0	1	1	0	1	1	1	0	0	0	
Bilonia ,, ...	Theft and escape from lawful custody ...	3	0	0	3	2	0	2	2	0	1	0	
	Culpable homicide not amounting to murder ...	0	0	5	5	1	1	2	0	0	3	2†	† Committed to Sessions.
	Theft ...	0	0	1	1	1	0	1	1	0	0	0	
	Lurking house trespass ...	0	0	3	3	0	0	0	0	0	3	0	
Sonamura ,, ...	Theft ...	27	13	6	46	4	7	24	1	9	22	14	
Kailashahar ,, ...	Theft ...	2	0	1	3	0	0	0	0	0	3	0	
Dharmanagar ,, ...	Theft ...	6	0	0	6	0	0	0	0	0	6	0	
	Highway robbery ...	1	0	0	1	0	0	0	0	0	1	0	
	Criminal trespass and assault with deadly weapons ...	0	0	12	12	0	0	0	0	0	12	0	
	Theft and wrongful confinement ...	0	0	2	2	0	0	0	0	0	2	0	
Khowai ,, ...	Cheating ...	1	0	0	1	0	1	1	0	1	0	0	
	Theft ...	1	0	1	2	0	1	1	1	0	1	0	
Udaipur ,, ...	Theft and receiving stolen property ...	2	0	1	3	0	0	0	0	0	3	0	
	Criminal breach of trust ...	0	0	2	2	0	0	0	0	0	2	0	
	Criminal breach of trust by servant ...	0	0	1	1	0	1	1	0	0	0	1	
Sabroom ,, ...	Theft ...	2	0	3	5	3	0	3	0	1	2	2	
	Escape from lawful custody ...	0	0	1	1	1	0	1	0	0	0	1	
	Total ...	51	21	45	117	14	16	51	8	17	66	26	

C

X.

Statement showing the results of appeals against decisions passed by the Criminal Courts in the Tripura State during the year 1338 T. E.

Tribunals.	Number of applications.	Number of persons and cases.																Remarks.
		Applications rejected.		*Sentences.*						Proceedings quashed.		Referred.		Furher enquiry &c, ordered.		Pending.		
				Confirmed.		Modified.		Reversed.										
		Persons.	Cases.	Persons.	Cases.	Persons.	Cases.	Persons.	Cases.	Persons.	Cases.	Persons.	Cases.	Persons	Cases.	Persons.	Cases.	
Khas Adalat ...	196	19	13	148	90	37	16	46	25	—	—	—	—	25	18	62	34	

XI.

Civil Work—Nature and value of original suits filed and disposed of during the year 1338 T. E.

Tribunal.	Opening balance.		Filed during the year, received by transfer or on remand.		Total.		Disposed of during the year.		Closing balance.		Suits filed during present year.									Suits disposed of during present year.						Suits not estimable in money.	Remarks.
	Past year.	Present year.	Past year.	Present year.	Past year.	Present year.	Past year.	Present year.	Past year.	Present year.	Value.	Suits *re* landed property.	Suits for money transaction.	Suits for other rights.	Number of suits under Rs. 100.	Number of suits above Rs. 100 and under Rs. 500.	Number of suits above Rs. 500 and under Rs. 1,000.	Number of suits above Rs. 1,000 and under Rs. 5,000.	Number of suits above Rs. 5,000.	*Ex parte.*	Admitted and compromised.	Struck off the file.	Otherwise disposed of.	Value.	Average duration.		
											Rs. a. p.													*Rs a. p.*	*Y.m.d.*		
Khash Adalat Original side	36	50	46	25	82	75	32	27	50	48	41,702-7-6	19	4	2	0	0	0	24	0	0	16	6	5	39,793-10-0	0-4-6	1	
Sadar Dewani Adalat	444	402	676	648	1,129	1,050	718	660	402	390	37,659-3-9	243	212	193	305	126	101	0	0	488	97	4	71	40,864-13-9	0-11-29	116	
Sonamura ,,	36	73	202	208	238	281	165	201	73	80	14,319-1-9	81	100	27	123	41	4	0	0	68	17	52	64	13,562-5-9	0-1-23	35	
Bilonia ,,	35	30	132	146	167	176	137	123	30	53	7,753-5-3	62	42	42	101	24	0	0	0	44	27	39	13	7,400-5-9	0-3-9	21	
Kailashahar ,,	210	218	321	348	531	566	313	282	218	284	28,243-12-0	85	225	38	209	57	9	1	0	70	37	81	94	20,296-8-6	0-3-7	72	
Khowai ,,	53	58	120	136	173	194	115	140	58	54	8,951-4-0	6	130	0	108	27	1	0	0	44	53	16	27	7,836-8-0	0-1-9	.0	
Dharmanagar ,,	120	143	217	192	337	335	194	194	143	141	12,116-10-0	26	72	94	112	33	1	0	0	40	35	38	81	17,615-6-6	0-2-8	46	
Udaipur ,,	55	99	354	491	409	590	310	462	99	128	45,153-14-9	14	449	28	315	136	2	0	0	202	117	52	91	43,271-2-6	0-2-29	38	
Sabrum ,,	1	5	18	22	19	27	14	23	5	4	2,488-3-6	1	21	0	11	11	0	0	0	8	3	3	9	1,969-5-3	0-4-19	0	
Total ...	990	1,078	2,086	2,216	3,076	3,294	1,998	2,112	1,078	1,182	1,98,387-14-6	537	1255	424	1289	455	118	25	0	964	402	291	455	1,926,40-2-0	0-2-25	329	

XII.

Civil Work.—Results of applications for Execution of Decrees, 1338 T.E.

Tribunal.	Opening balance.		Value of opening balance for present year.	Applications brought to the Register.			Total.			Disposed of.			Closing balance.			Nature of applications pending disposal at the close of the year.			Remarks.
	Past year.	Present year.		Past year.	Present year.	Value for present year.	Past year.	Present year.	Value for present year.	Past year.	Present year.	Value for present year.	Past year.	Present year.	Value for present year.	Below 6 months.	Below 12 months.	Above 12 months.	
			Rs. a. p.			*Rs. a. p.*			*Rs. a. p.*			*Rs. a. p.*			*Rs. a. p.*				
Khas Adalat (Original side)	14	24	55,466-11-0	17	2	2,048-15-0	31	26	57,515-10-0	7	11	13,959-15-9	24	15	43,555-10-3	6	2	7	
Sadar Dewani Adalat ...	179	162	24,851-14-0	189	291	32,790-7-0	368	453	57,642-5-0	206	242	25,073-15-9	162	211	32,568-5-3	121	48	42	
Sonamura Ditto ...	17	34	3,760-2-3	62	65	9,866-12-3	79	99	13,626-14-6	45	71	8,936-11-9	34	28	4,690-2-9	23	3	2	
Bilonia Ditto ...	10	6	609-13-3	29	43	4,353-11-9	39	49	4,963-9-0	33	27	4,087-12-6	6	12	875-12-6	10	1	1	
Kailashahar Ditto ...	64	107	16,935-3-9	150	109	15,389-11-3	214	216	32,324-15-0	107	123	13,177-11-3	107	93	19,147-3-9	41	24	28	
Khowai Ditto ...	8	18	2,307-8-3	41	45	5,271-10-6	49	63	7,579-2-9	31	40	4,825-10-6	18	23	2,753-8-3	19	2	2	
Dharmanagar Ditto ...	29	29	2,584-15-9	65	55	5,907-2-9	94	84	8,492-2-6	65	48	3,856-13-6	29	36	4,635-5-0	25	9	2	
Udaipur Ditto ...	23	46	7,729-4-6	132	231	28,026-1-3	155	277	35,755-5-9	109	159	19,164-12-3	46	118	16,590-9-6	94	17	7	
Sabrum Ditto ...	0	1	0	1	7	2,195-10-6	1	8	2,195-10-6	0	6	1,819-14-0	1	2	375-12-6	1	1	0	
Total ...	344	427	1,14,245-8-9	686	848	1,05,850-2-3	1,030	1,275	2,20,095-11-0	603	737	94,903-5-3	427	538	1,25,192-5-9	340	107	91	

XIII.

Civil Work—Number and results of appeals in civil suits, 1338 T. E.

Tribunal.	Opening balance.		Filed during.		Total.		Disposed of during.		Closing balance.		Value of appeales filed during.		How disposed of. Decisions confirmed.		Decisions reversed.		Decisions amended.		Cases remanded for retrial.		Cases compromised and otherwise disposed of.		Average duration.	
	Past year.	Present year.	Past year.	Present year.	Past year.	Present year.	Past year.	Present year.	Past year.	Present year.	Past year.	Present year.	Past year.	Present year.	Past year.	Present year.	Past year.	Present year.	Past year.	Present year.	Past year.	Present year.	Past year.	Present year.
											Rs. a. p.	*Rs. a. p.*											*Y.m.d.*	*Y.m.d.*
Khas Adalat	46	90	174	179	220	269	130	147	90	122	33,433-0-0	37,248-9-9	67	50	16	7	8	29	25	37	14	24	0-2-2	0-2-4

XIV.

Statement showing the number of persons confined in the jails and lock-ups in the Tripura State during the year 1338 T. E.

Stations.	Number of prisons.	Number of Prisoners.				Daily Average.		Number of prisoners remaining at the end of the year.	Cost of jails and prisoners.	Average period in days of stay of accused under-trial.	Remarks showing mortality among convicts in jail.
		Remaining from last year.	Admitted during the year.	Total.							
				Past year.	Present year.	Past year.	Present year.				
									Rs.		
Agartala	1	69	283	307	352	93·81	77·54	100	14,530	37·2	
Sonamura	1	2	117	80	119	3·88	5·9	12	796	20·4	
Bilonia	1	2	50	49	52	3·21	·13	4	400	20·48	
Kailashahar	1	9	57	64	66	3·33	4·49	8	715	16·54	Three convicts died during the year :— one from cholera. one from malarial fever. one from chronic Nephritis.
Dharmanagar	1	3	50	54	53	3·38	2·91	2	595	21·47	
Udaipur...	1	11	80	98	91	5·68	5·87	3	752	5·87	
Sabrum	1	—	23	10	23	·22	1·16	5	265	24·13	
Khowai	1	5	49	46	54	3·71	3·60	6	483	19·77	
Total ...	8	101	709	708	810	117·22	101·60	140	18,536	20·73	

XV

Registration of documents in the Tripura State during the year 1338 T.E.

Name of State.	Documents presented for registration.		Nature of documents presented. Mortgages.		Sale deeds.		Wills.		Money bonds.		Miscellaneous.		Documents registered.		Value of documents registered.		Documents of which registration has been refused.		Documents remaining unregistered at the end of the year.		Remarks.
	Past year.	Present year.	Past year.	Present year.	Past year.	Present year.	Past year.	Present year.	Past year.	Present year.	Past year.	Present year.	Past year.	Present year.	Past year.	Present year.	Past year.	Present year.	Past year.	Present year.	
1	2	3	4	5	6	7	8	9	10	11	12	13	14	15	16	17	18	19	20	21	22
															Rs.	Rs.					
Tripura State	12,894	11,866	3,746	3,143	5,525	5,297	9	10	389	334	3,225	3,082	12,297	11,948	21,45,657	20,48,167	173	159	496	255	

XVI

Statement showing the receipts and expenditure on account of Registration during the year 1338 T.E.

Description.	Past Year.			Present Year.			Remarks.
	Number of deeds.	Value of property.	Fees realised.	Number of deeds.	Value of property.	Fees realised.	
		Rs.	Rs.		Rs.	Rs.	
Mortgages	3,746	6,13,299	3,959	3,143	4,47,374	3,286	
Sale deeds	5,525	11,26,469	7,524	5,297	11,25,971	7,696	
Will	9	3,900	41	10	1,450	57	
Money bonds	389	35,970	314	334	42,716	322	
Miscellaneous	3,225	4,57,670	3,990	3,082	5,02,724	3,841	
Total ...	12,894	22,37,308	15,828	11,866	21,20,235	15,202	
Total Expenditure ...	—	—	4,573	—	—	5,007	
Net Income ...	—	—	11,255	—	—	10,195	

XVII.

Receipts and expenditure of the Municipalities in the Tripura State during the year 1338 T.E.

NAME.	Opening balance.	RECEIPTS DURING THE YEAR.					Total in the current year.	EXPENDITURE DURING THE YEAR.		Balance at the close of the year.	REMARKS.
		Past.	Present.								
			State grant.	Tax.	Miscel-laneous.	Total.		Past.	Present.		
1	2	3	4	5	6	7	8	9	10	11	12
	Rs. A.P.	Rs. A.P.	Rs. A.P.	Rs. A.P	Rs. A.P.	Rs. A.P.	Rs. A.P.	Rs. A.P.	Rs. A.P.	Rs. A.P.	
Agartala Municipality. ...	11,064-12-0	31,666-4-9	9,998-15-3	3,860-6-3	8,502-10-9 *a*	22,362-0-3	33,426-12-3	20,601-8-9	16,798-4-3 *b*	16,628-8-0 *c*	*a.* Including Rs. 6,098-9-0 as income from the Bazar and Rs. 447 as deposits and advances recovered. *b.* Including Rs. 558-5-0 as expenditure on the Bazar improvement and Rs. 145 as advances and deposits paid. *c.* Including Rs. 16,107-9-6 of the Bazar improvement fund and Rs. 520-14-6 as income from the Municipality.

The figures exclude Rs. 83-15-3 subsequently refunded to the State. This explains the difference in the corresponding figures in Audit Statement XXVI (B).

XVIII

Statement of rainfall in the Tripura State during the year 1338 T.E.

	Baisak.	Jaisth.	Asar.	Sravan.	Bhadra.	Asvin.	Kartik.	Agrahayan.	Pous.	Magh.	Falgoon.	Chait.	Total.	Average of past 5 years.	REMARKS.
1338 T. E. ...	6·55	23·58	12·59	11·90	12·90	14·15	1·99	—	—	·48	.27	3·26	87·67	96·91	
1337 T. E. ...	15·77	10·24	12·62	14·27	12·17	8·22	1·69	—	—	·11	2·51	·77	78·37	98·81	

1. Maximum 105·14—Kailashahar Division. 2. Minimum 46·24—Amarpur Sub-Division.

XIX

Statement as to the prices of staple food-grains for the year 1338 T. E.

Articles.	Price per maund during Chait, 1337 T. E.			Price per maund during Chait, 1338 T. E.			REMARKS.
	Rs.	a.	p.	Rs.	a.	p.	
(1) RICE							
Maximum	10	0	0	7	4	0	
Minimum	5	10	0	4	0	0	
(2) PADDY							
Maximum	4	8	0	4	8	0	
Minimum	3	0	0	2	0	0	

XX.

Expenditure on Public Works during the year 1338 T.E.

Description of work.	State funds.			Local funds.			Total.	Remarks.
	Original.	Repairs.	Total.	Original.	Repairs.	Total.		
	Rs.	*Rs.*	*Rs.*	*Rs.*	*Rs.*	*Rs.*	*Rs.*	
Buildings	1,70,547	80,421	2,50,968	2,850	—	2,850	2,53,818	
Roads and Bridges ...	19,255	32,981	52,236	—	—	—	52,236	
Tanks	910	2,359	3,269	—	—	—	3,269	
Miscellaneous works ...	13,396	1,806	15,202	—	—	—	15,202	
Total ...	2,04,108	1,17,567	3,21,675	2,850	—	2,850	3,24,525	
Minor works at the Rajbari (*Karkhana*)	—	4,188	4,188	—	—	—	4,188	
Establishment charges ...	—	—	22,799	—	—	—	22,799	
Grand Total ...	22,04,108	1,21,755	3,48,662	2,850	—	2,850	3,51,512	

XXI

Statement showing the excise shops and excise revenue of the Tripura State during the year 1338 T. E.

Name of State.	Country Spirit.		Country Spirit, Opium and Ganja.		Opium and Ganja.		Tari.		Total.		Remarks.
	Number of shops.	Revenue. demand.	Number of shops.	Revenue demand.	Number of shops.	Revenue. demand.	Number of shops.	Revenue. demand.	Number of shops.	Revenue realised.	
		Rs.		Rs.						Rs.	
Tripura State	1	15	31	92,750	—		—	—	32	92,718	

XXII

Statement of Medical Relief afforded in the Tripura State during the year 1338 T.E.*

Dispensary.	Number of Patients Treated. (new) Outdoor.	Indoor.	Results of In-door Patients. (new) Discharged cured.	Relieved or discharged otherwise.	Died.	Remaining under treatment.	Expenditure.	Daily Average. (old + new) Outdoor.	Indoor.	Total.	No. of Surgical Operations Performed. Major.	Minor.	Total.	No. of Persons Vaccinated during the Year. Successfully.	Unsuccessfully.	Total.	Remarks.
1. Victoria Memorial Hospital at Agartala and the Charitable Dispensary attached to it ...	13,857	393	262	102	12	17	Rs. 9,495	63·57	17·11	85·68	11	247	258	646	260	906	
2. Palace Dispensary	8,527	0	0	0	0	0	10,274	54·27	0	54.27	0	0	0	0	0	0	
3. Homœopathic	15,096	0	0	0	0	0	5,638	9·428	0	94·28	0	0	0	0	0	0	* This Statement excludes figures regarding Kaviraji treatment.
4. Old Agartala... ...	4,599	0	0	0	0	0	1,268	28·37	0	28·67	0	43	43	624	151	775	
5. Bishalgar	5,982	0	0	0	0	0	1,319	23·77	0	23·77	1	88	89	834	38	872	
6. Sonamura	5,711	5	5	0	0	0	1,701	24·57	·17	24·74	1	128	129	164	36	200	
7. Udaipur	5,145	0	0	0	0	0	1,302	20·89	0	20·89	0	59	59	174	73	247	
8. Amarpur	604	0	0	0	0	0	903	2·73	0	2·73	0	15	15	78	4	82	
9. Bilonia	4,492	1	1	0	0	0	1,447	22·91	·03	22·94	4	84	88	347	38	385	
10. Loongthung	2,174	0	0	0	0	0	814	8·36	0	8·36	0	41	41	203	22	225	† This figure shows the actual number of outdoor patients treated, the total outdoor attendance during the year being 1,78,833 against 1,68,429 in the previous year.
11. Sabroom	2,634	1	1	0	0	0	1,155	11·10	·03	11·13	0	50	50	1,300	18	1,318	
12. Khowai	5,700	0	0	0	0	0	1,458	19·08	0	19.08	0	53	53	724	140	864	
13. Kailashahar	7,491	0	0	0	0	0	2,025	24·55	0	24·55	0	140	140	68	115	183	
14. Fatikroy	18,75	0	0	0	0	0	950	7·41	0	7·41	0	18	18	942	533	1,475	
15. Kamalpur	4,104	0	0	0	0	0	1,322	19·44	0	19·44	0	56	56	327	46	373	
16. Dharmanagar	3,973	23	11	12	0	0	1,581	17·77	·84	18·61	2	75	77	198	40	238	
17. Mohanpur	4,030	0	0	0	0	0	871	16·07	0	16·07	0	74	74	922	156	1,078	
18. Dhaleswar	5,117	0	0	0	0	0	1,358	25·43	0	25·43	0	60	60	0	0	0	
Total	†1,01,111	423	280	114	12	17	44,881	489·87	18·18	508·05	19	1,240	1,259	7,551	1,670	9,221	

XXIII.

Vital statistics of the Tripura State for the year 1338 T.E.

STATE.	Population.	BIRTHS.		Increase.	Decrease.	DEATHS.		Increase.	Decrease.	RATIO PER 1,000 OF POPULATION.				REMARKS.
										BIRTHS.		DEATHS.		
		Past year.	Present year.			Past year.	Present year.			Past year.	Present year.	Past year.	Present year.	
Tripura State ...	3,02,421	1,956	2,244	288	—	2,113	2,394	281	—	6·4	7·42	6·9	7·93	

XXIV.

Education Return (A)—Particulars as to the schools maintained during the year 1338 T.E.

Number of Schools. Past year.	Number of Schools. Present year.	Class of Schools.	Number of pupils on the rolls on the last day of Chait. Past year.	Number of pupils on the rolls on the last day of Chait. Present year.	Average daily attendance. Past year.	Average daily attendance. Present year.	Remarks.
5	5	High English Schools	1,450	1,580	1,002·49	1,182·54	
8	8	Middle English Schools for boys ...	986	990	753·55	760·78	
1	1	Middle English School for girls ...	75	66	53·60	48·30	
1	1	Higher Vernacular School for boys	62	77	46·77	53·51	* In some of these schools boys and girls read together.
21	22	* Lower Vernacular Schools for boys	1,191	1,239	879·55	893·87	
115	112	* Pathsalas for boys	2,643	2,830	2,031·32	2,311·36	
10	10	Do for girls	236	319	168·23	223·10	
		Special Schools :—					
5	5	Madrassas and Muktabs	152	183	94·11	104·37	
3	3	Sanskrit *Tols*	43	34	27·24	27·42	
1	1	Woodburn Artisan School... ...	10	18	5·03	6·25	
TOTAL 170	168		6,848	7,345	5,151·89	5,611·50	

XXV

Education Return (B) Race of Students, 1338 T. E.

Names of Divisions.	No. of Schools.			No. of Students.			Race.												Average daily attendance.		Remarks.
							Hindus.														
	For boys.	For girls.	Total.	Boys.	Girls.	Total.	Rajkumars.	Thakurs.	Manipuris.	Tripuras.	Bengalees.	Others.	Reangs.	Chakmas.	Kukis.	Lusais.	Musalmans.	Christans.	Boys.	Girls.	
1. Sadar Division ...	58	3	61	2,300	141	2,441	9	173	150	332	1,134	18	0	0	18	0	604	3	1,757·17	100·45	
2. Kailashahar „ ...	25	3	28	1,037	177	1,214	0	1	380	58	542	0	4	0	0	0	229	0	750·02	113·47	
3. Sonamura „ ...	22	1	23	1,070	82	1,152	0	1	3	51	277	0	0	0	0	0	820	0	833·75	64·83	
4. Bilonia „ ...	11	1	12	907	36	943	0	0	0	2	643	10	19	0	0	0	269	0	686·06	25·05	
5. Khowai „ ...	9	1	10	238	13	251	0	0	28	123	54	22	0	0	0	0	24	0	179·43	10·12	
6. Dharmanagar „ ...	12	1	13	573	53	626	0	0	99	4	421	1	0	0	0	0	101	0	430·88	45·50	
7. Udaipur „ ...	9	1	10	401	28	429	0	1	0	90	111	0	0	0	0	0	227	0	339·82	24·68	
8. Sabrum „ ...	6	0	6	214	13	227	0	0	0	92	97	0	0	0	0	0	38	0	182·13	80·1	
9. Amarpur Sub-division ...	5	0	5	61	1	62	0	0	0	1	5	37	19	0	0	0	0	0	59·13	1·00	
TOTAL ...	157	11	168	6,801	544	7,345	9	176	660	753	3,284	88	42	0	18	0	2,312	3	5,218·39	393·11	

APPENDIX XXVI (A)

Statement of Audited Receipts for the year 1338 T. E.

State.

Heads of Revenue.	1337 T. E.		1338 T. E.		Remarks.
	Revised Estimate.	Actuals.	Revised Estimate.	Actuals.	
1. Land Revenue ...	6,20,000	6,02,891	6,10,000	6,08,942	
2. Rents of markets ...	7,000	7,658	8,000	7,813	
3. Family tax in the hills	55,000	60,228	62,000	65,221	
4. Toll on Forest Produce	5,80,000	5,45,997	5,92,000	5,97,080	
5. Do on the Feni River	35,000	36,290	36,000	35,382	
6. Elephant and Buffalo grasing mehals ...	8,000	8,326	8,000	8,530	
7. Thatching grass mehals	8,000	7,619	8,000	7,990	
8. Reserved *Sal* trees ...	8,000	6,784	6,000	4,178	
9. Tax on cotton and Oil seeds ...	1,60,000	1,56,486	1,26,000	1,50,241	
10. Royalty on elephants caught ...	25,000	36,713	20,000	16,682	
11. Adda mehal ...	23,000	23,202	22,000	24,163	
12. Excise ...	80,000	85,485	90,000	92,718	
13. Stamps and Court fees	90,000	86,530	90,000	89,692	
14. Law and Justice (fines)	4,000	4,012	4,000	4,459	
15. Process Fees ...	17,000	15,495	15,000	15,089	
16. Registration ...	16,000	15,828	16,000	15,202	
17. Jail ...	4,000	4,559	4,000	3,661	
18. Cattle pounds ...	6,000	5,895	6,000	5,980	
19. *Nasars* ...	50,000	49,733	46,000	44,061	
20. Agriculture ...	500	611	—	—	
21. School Fees ...	8,000	8,661	8,000	8,518	
22. Duty on Tea ...	15,000	19,841	20,000	17,107	
23. Duty on jute ...	—	—	35,000	30,857	
24 Personal Howlats recovered	7,000	7,255	7,000	6,516	
25. Personal Loans recovered ...	—	—	3,000	2,305	
26. Interest on Bank deposit ...	5,000	3,500	18,000	18,733	
27. Miscellaneous ...	90,000	74,542	54,000	65,310	
Total ...	19,21,500	18,77,136	19,16,000	19,46,421	
28. Deposits ...	74,000	83,751	94,000	60,446	
29. Contribution from Chakla ...	5,50,000	5,50,000	2,00,000	2,00,000	
30. Loans ...	—	—	1,00,000	1,00,000	
Total ...	25,45,500	25,10,887	23,10,000	23,06,867	
Opening Balance :—					
Cash ...	8,35,130	8,35,130	3,98,748	3,98,748	
Advances ...	1,55,106	1,55,106	2,10,816	2,10,816	
Loans ...	61,783	61,783	90,221	90,221	
Total ...	10,52,019	10,52,019	6,99,785	6,99,785	
Grand Total ...	35,97,519	35,62,906	30,09,785	30,06,652	

APPENDIX XXVI (B)

Statement of Audited Expenditure for the year 1338 T. E.

State.

Heads of Expenditure.	1337 T. E.		1338 T. E.		Remarks.	
	Revised estimate.	Actuals.	Revised Estimate.	Actuals.		
1. Controlling Charges	1,16,441	1,14,241	91,035	89,813		
2. Revenue General ...	78,824	76,448	84,227	82,884		
3. Survey & Settlement	17,470	14,373	19,629	19,391		
4. Tahasil ...	50,141	47,176	55,803	54,397		
5. Agriculture ...	4,924	4,681	5,746	4,129		
6. Registration ...	4,803	4,573	5,245	5,007		
7. Police ...	83,896	80,480	79,720	77,145		
8. Judicial ...	35,900	34,663	31.676	31,144		
9. Jail ...	18,629	17,884	19,006	18,536		
10. Forest ...	59,207	52,822	64,682	60,251		
11. Medical ...	77,335	76,251	70,734	69,316		
12. Sanitation ...	5.000	3.346	5,000	4,379		
13. Municipality ...	9,000	8.973	10,000	9,915		
14. Education General ...	1,02,358	97,915	1,11,595	1,08,404		
15. Education of Rajkumars ...	21,740	22,228	26,235	24,702		
16. (*a*) Public Works ...	3,11,000	3,05,260	1,73,771	1,70,563		
(*b*) Improvement ...	—	—	1,85,000	1,78,099		
17. Electric Light ...	—	—	25,744	24,727		
18. Small Donations ...	550	410	1,000	1,108		
19. Relief to distressed subjects ...	41,500	30,373	700	—		
20. Purchase of Landed Property ...	6,000	240	3,500	3,500		
21. Repayment of Deposits ...	75,000	66.751	80,000	75,597		
22. Interest on Deposits	13.000	10.265	12,000	11,070		
23. Unforeseen charges ...	5,000	4,024	2,300	1,774		
24. Advances to employees ...	8,000	7,768	7,000	6,467		
25. Loans to employees ...	—	—	7,000	7,000		
26. Pension ...	23,500	22,893	26,000	25,890		
27. Compensation for dearness of Provision ...	39.000	38,971	—	—		
28. Advisory Council ...	2,310	2,310	3,900	3,900		
29. Chief Secretary's Office & H. H.'s Tour	42.810	24.508	67,318	67,204		
30. Palace Sultanat ...	25,463	24,825	27,248	26,841		
31. Zoo ...	6,300	6,496	6,700	6,675		
32. H. H.'s Private Secretary's Office ...	8,487	8 024	14,552	14,421		
33. Rajmala Office ...	9,013	8,601	6,826	6,799		
34. Military Secretary's Office ...	2,300	1,557	3,000	3,000		
35. Military ...	98,196	77,911	94,620	89,061		
36. Nijtahabil ...	1,03,035	1,03.035	1,20.000	1,20,000		
37. H. H.'s Investiture ...	2,10,000	2,07,201	10,000	9,383		
38. H. H.'s Marriage ...	—	—	2,15,000	2,13.024		
39. H. H.'s Installation	4,81,000	4,60,080	57,000	51,379		
40. Maharajkumari Srila-Srimati Bivas Prava Debi's Marriage	3.50,000	3,37,111	67,000	66,878		
Total ...	25.46.665	24,10,627	18,97,992	18,44,998		
41. Sansar ...	4,63,054	4,52,494	4,86,539	4,80,166		
Total ...	30.09,719	28,63,121	23,84,571	23,25,164		
42. Chamber of Princes ..	—	—	25,000	25,000		
Total ...	30,09,719	28,63,121	24,09,571	23,50,164		
Closing balance :—						
Cash ...	3,44,911	3,98,748	1,30,214	* 1,79,535	* Cash ...	1,50,161
Advances ...	1,51,106	2,10,816	1,80,000	1 85,542	In Bank ...	29,374
Loans issued ...	91,783	90,221	2,90,000	2,91,411		
Total ...	5,87,800	6,99,785	6,00,214	6,56,488		1,79,535
.. Grand Total ...	35,97,519	35,62,906	30,09,785	30,00,652		

APPENDIX XXVII. (A)

Statement of Audited Receipts for the year 1338 T. E.

Chakla Roshnabad Estate.

Heads of Receipts.	1337 T. E.		1338 T. E.		Remarks.
	Revised Estimate.	Actuals.	Revised Estimate.	Actuals.	
1. Rent and Cess ...	11,68,800	11,37,781	11,05,800	10,84,526	
2. Cess for Rent free holdings ...	9,500	8,366	11,200	14,484	
3. Law charges recovered	65,200	43,228	60,200	47,947	
4. Misc. receipts including deposits ...	4,983	10,308	13,000	51,948	
Total ...	12,48,483	11,99,633	11,90,200	11,98,905	
Opening Balance :—					
Cash ...	1,24,852	1,24,852	1,03,986	1,03,746	
Advance ...	1,35,537	1,35,537	1,22,537	1,09,608	
Loans issued ...	12,228	12,228	12,000	10,474	
Bank deposits ...	1,00,000	1,00,000	1,05,052	1,05,052	
Total ...	3,72,617	3,72,617	3,43,575	3,28,880	
Grand Total ...	16,21,100	15,72,250	15,33,775	15,27,785	

APPENDIX XXVII. (B)

Statement of Audited Expenditure for the year 1338 T. E.

Chakla Roshnabad Estate.

Heads of Expenditure.	1337 T. E.		1338 T. E.		Remarks.
	Revised Estimate.	Actuals.	Revised Estimate.	Actuals.	
i. 1. Revenue and Cess ...	2,71,248	2,69,253	2,72,351	2,70,852	
2. Establishment ...	1,51,610	1,44,086	1,56,554	1,54,339	
3. Settlement ...	1,421	827	1,424	1,063	
4. Legal Expenses ...	1,10,000	96,490	1,15,000	1,09,287	
5. Education ...	11,008	10,584	11,248	10,992	
6. Medical ...	12,481	11,963	12,597	12,329	
7. Public Works ...	71,512	60,612	63,060	58,064	
8. Religious Expenses	7,140	6,215	7,151	6,635	
9. Purchase of property	34,500	27,758	47,00	4,270	
10. Miscellaneous ...	11,000	12,174	28,000	26,454	
11. Loans and Advances	3,000	2,516	2,500	2,481	
(a) Irrecoverable loans written off	—	1,313	—	—	
12. Pension and Gratuity	6,000	5,137	5,500	5,091	
13. Forest ...	650	511	650	622	
14. Unforeseen ...	7,500	783	1,000	898	
ii. Sansar ...	15,540	15,520	15,540	15,540	
iii. Donation ...	7,100	1,760	35,500	35,481	
iv. Repayment of debts	25,000	25,000	—	—	
iv. (a) Repayment of deposits ...	14,000	10,568	12,000	9,202	
v. Nijtahabil Contribution ...	—	—	3,00,000	3,00,000	
vi. Marriage Contribution ...	—	—	2,00,000	2,00,000	
vii. Contribution to State ...	5,50,000	5,50,000	—	—	
Total ...	13,10,713	12,43,370	12,44,775	12,23,600	
Closing Balance :—					
Cash ...	70,850	1,03,746	57,033	72,066	
Advances ...	1,22,485	1,09,608	1,09,537	1,11,147	
Loans issued ...	12,000	10,474	11,800	10,342	
Bank deposits ...	1,05,052	1,05,052	1,10,630	1,10,630	
Total ...	3,10,387	3,28,880	2,89,000	3,04,185	
Grand Total ...	16,21,100	15,72,250	15,33,775	15,27,785	

To

His Highness The Bisama-Samara-Bijayee Mahamahodaya
Pancha-Srijukta Maharaja Manikya
BIR BIKRAM KISHORE DEV BARMAN BAHADUR,
Maharaja of Tripura.

Dated, Agartala, the 14th August, 1930.

MAY IT PLEASE YOUR HIGHNESS,

I have the honour to submit the accompanying Report on the General Administration of the State and the attached Zemindaries for the year 1339 T. E., corresponding to the period extending from the 14th April, 1929 to the 13th April, 1930.

I have the honour to be
Your Highness's most obedient servant,
B. K. Sen,
DEWAN-SHASHAN.

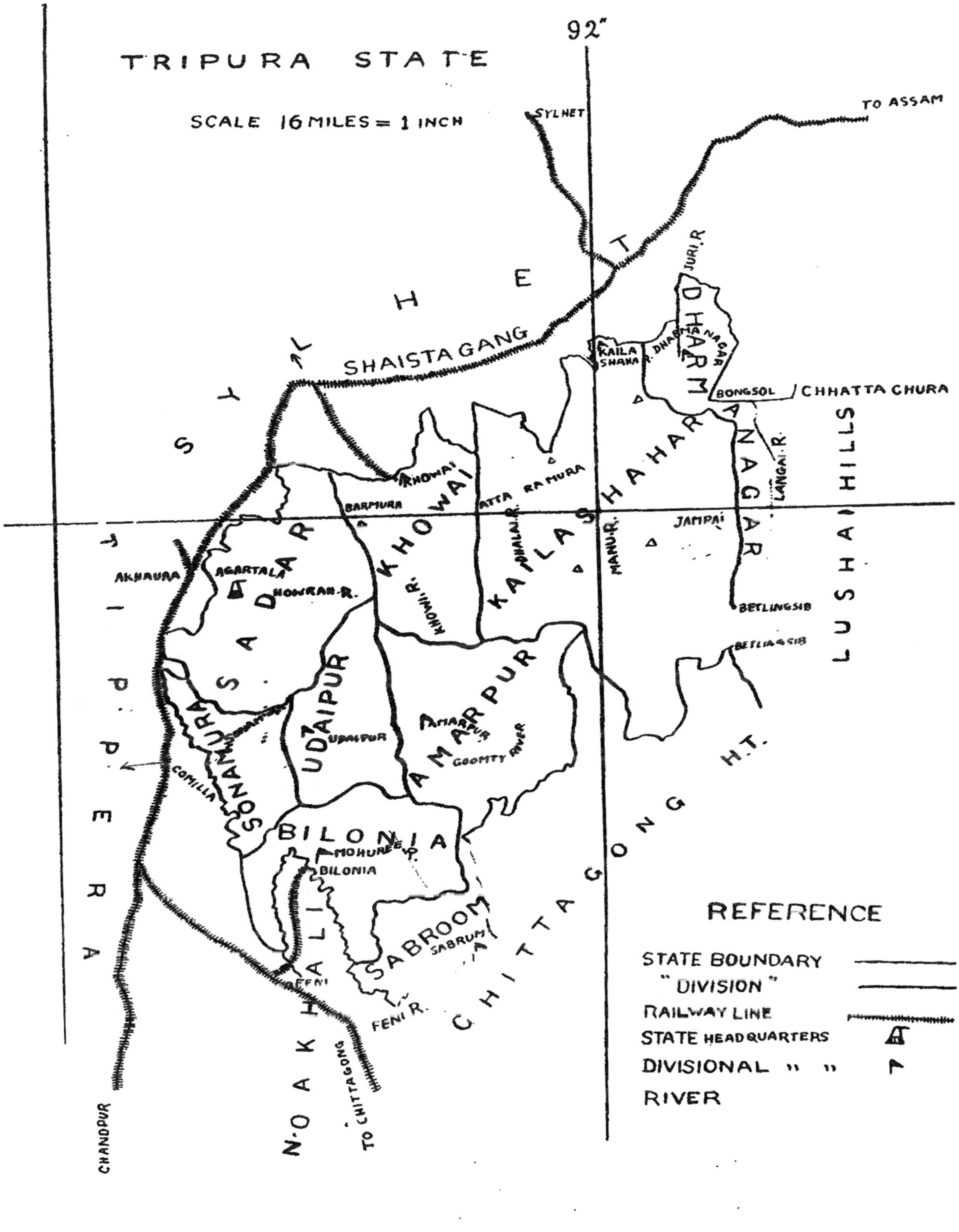

TRIPURA STATE
SCALE 16 MILES = 1 INCH
92"
SYLHET
TO ASSAM
SHAISTAGANG
JURI R.
DHARMANAGAR
KAILA SHAHAR
BONGSOL
CHHATTA CHURA
KHOWAI
BARMURA
ATTA RA MURA
LANGAI R.
LUSHAI HILLS
JAMPAI
MANU R.
AKHAURA
AGARTALA
HOWRAH R.
SADAR
KAILASHAHAR
BETLINGSIB
UDAIPUR
AMARPUR
GOOMTY RIVER
SONAMURA
COMILLA
TIPPERA
BILONIA
MOHURE R.
SABROOM
SABRUM
FENI
FENI R.
CHITTAGONG H.T.
CHITTAGONG
NOAKHALI
TO CHITTAGONG
CHANDPUR
REFERENCE
STATE BOUNDARY
" DIVISION "
RAILWAY LINE
STATE HEAD QUARTERS
DIVISIONAL " "
RIVER

Book Twenty-two
Report on the General Administration of the Tripura State for the year 1339 T. E. (1929-1930 A.D.)

REPORT ON THE ADMINISTRATION OF THE TRIPURA STATE FOR 1339 T. E. (1929-30.)

CHAPTER I—GENERAL AND POLITICAL.

Area of the State—*4,116 sq. miles.*
Population—*3,04,437.*
Gross Revenue (*based on the average of the previous five years*):—
(*a*) State ... ... Rs. 20,05,191.
(*b*) Zemindaries ... ... Rs. 12,07,728.
Tribute—Nil.
Ruler of the State—His Highness The Bisama-Samara-Bijayee Mahamahodaya Pancha-Srijukta Maharaja Manikya Bir Bikramkishore Dev Barman Bahadur. *Age*—21 years. (Born—19th August, 1908). *Caste*—*Kshatriya* (of the Lunar race).

I.

The year and the people—floods.

1. The year under report was unique in its unpropitious character throughout. With its advent came abnormal weather conditions and torrential rains, that caused destructive floods in as many as five of the administrative Divisions of the State, as well as in the contiguous parts of the attached Zemindaries, occasioning, for the time being at least, more or less severe distress. Early crops were almost entirely lost in the affected localities, while in some adjoining low areas, where the excess water accumulated, the suffering of the people proved both intense and prolonged.

Trade depression and unrest.

2. The pinch of the situation was accentuated by the world-wide trade depression, which gradually made itself felt in a more and more marked degree, in and about the State, as elsewhere, in the shape of scarcity of money, unsettled prices, and dead slumps in the market for jute, cotton and other indigenous commodities. A rapid decline in the usually brisk local trade in forest produce followed, owing to the destitute condition to which border British subjects were soon reduced, and the result, on the whole, was a growing unrest which, as the year advanced, manifested itself in phases that demanded close vigilance.

Flood relief.

3. Relief measures were speedily arranged after the floods, both in the State and the Zemindaries, and the gloomy outlook of things had, it may be noted, its silver lining in the commendable spirit of all-round co-operation that was happily in evidence in connection with the operations. Foremost came His Highness's grant of rupees one lac, though it was ultimately found possible to meet a substantial part of the demand for first aid by indirect methods, and from extraneous sources, and to divert a portion of the State grant to works of more lasting utility. Through the kind offices of the District Magistrate of Tippera, some of the affected villages in the Chakla

Roshnabad Estates shared the benefit of Government distress loans, and spontaneous assistance was received in various shapes from different other sources, to the estimated value of Rs. 25,000. Remission and suspension of rents, where necessary, and issue of free forest permits were allowed, and public works of importance promptly undertaken in the interior, to afford facilities for earning to a class of the distressed. Loans were, besides, arranged and issued from the Tippera Raj Central Bank, through the ready co-operation of the Bank authorities, to the extent of Rs. 54,000, while the total expenditure on direct State aid, in gratuitous relief and loans, as adjusted within the year, stood at Rs. 56,000. To all who collaborated with the Durbar in the difficulty are due its most grateful thanks.

The finances of the year.

4. As might be expected, the situation was not without its effects on the finances of the year, and the collections from the permanent sources of income fell off from Rs. 31,02,911 in the previous year to Rs. 30,09,502, showing a decline of Rs. 93,409; though with realisations from other sources, the receipts amounted to Rs. 34,37,701 against Rs. 33,05,772 and the gross amount available for expenditure including the opening balance, to Rs. 43,98,374, against Rs. 43,29,437. The major part of the programme for the year could thus be carried through, inspite of larger expenditure allotted to measures of improvement, and the special expenditure on relief operations. The total expenditure during the year was Rs. 34,23,952 against Rs. 33,68,764, which left a closing balance of Rs. 9,74,422 against Rs. 9,60,673.

II.

The Governor's visit to Comilla.

5. A notable event of the year was the visit of His Excellency the Governor of Bengal to Comilla, the headquarters station of the British District of Tippera and of His Highness's Chakla Roshnabad Estates. Sir Stanley and Lady Jackson were pleased to stay at His Highness's Dharmasagar residence on the occasion, and Dewan B. K. Sen Bahadur, Dewan-Shashan, received Their Excellencies on their arrival. In the Durbar held by His Excellency, in which the Dewan-Shashan represented His Highness, His Excellency was kind enough to refer in graceful terms to the steps taken by His Highness in connection with flood relief.

Administrative changes.

6. Rai J. C. Sen Bahadur, B. A., B. C. S., Minister of the State went out on six months' leave early in the year, and had unfortunately to retire from service, owing to failing health, at the end of the period. On the Rai Bahadur's departure on leave, Dewan B. K. Sen Bahadur M. A., B. L., was appointed by His Highness to administer the departments in his charge under the designation "Dewan-Shashan and Manager, Chakla", and the arrangement continued after the Minister's retirement. In the retiring Minister the State lost the services of a disinterested adviser and an able administrator, whose innate goodness, besides, rendered him immensely popular. Consequent on the above change, Manyabara Rana Bodhjung Bahadur was appointed Chief Secretary to His Highness, and Dewan Saheb Kamala Prasad Dutt, M. A., B. L., as Private Secretary with the additional charge

of the Sansar Department, which was transferred from the Chief Secretary's portfolio.

Executive Council.

7. An important administrative measure of the year was the appointment of an Executive Council by His Highness with Mahamanyabara Maharajkumar N. C. Dev Barman Bahadur and Mahamanyabara Maharajkumar B. K. Dev Barman Bahadur, as President and Vice-President respectively, and the Dewan-Shashan, the Chief Secretary to His Highness, and the Dewan Sansar Department, as members with portfolio. The Council was vested with finality of jurisdiction to a certain extent in respect of some clasess of cases coming up before His Highness for orders.

State Council.

8. In view of the European tour mentioned below, His Highness was also pleased to vest the existing Advisory Council with full powers of administration during his absence, under the denomination of "State Council", the personnel consisting of Mahamanyabara Maharajkumar N. C. Dev Barman Bahadur, President, Mahamanyabara Maharajkumar B. K. Dev Barman Bahadur, Vice-President, Dewan B. K. Sen Bahadur, Dewan–Shashan, Dewan Saheb Kamala Prasad Dutt, Offg. Chief Secretary, and Uzir B. K. Dev Barman Bahadur.

An important Conference.

9. A Conference was held in the Ujjayanta Palace at Agartala on the 21st November, 1929, and subsequent days, in which all the leading officers of the State and some retired officers participated with great enthusiasm, and discussed for a fortnight, under the presidency of His Highness, many of the important problems of the administration.

Demise of the Fifth Dowager Maharanee.

10. A very sad event of the year was the death on the 16th September, 1929, at Mussoorie, of Her Highness Maharanee Churamani Mahadevi, the Fifth Dowager Maharanee, who succumbed after a prolonged illness. The deceased Maharanee was a daughter of the late General Rana Padamjung Bahadur of Nepal, and was widely respected in the State. Under His Highness's orders all offices and institutions were closed for a week in her honour.

The Political Agent.

11. Mr. F. W. Robertson, I. C. S., continued as the Political Agent of the State till the 5th March, 1930, when on his transfer on promotion as the Commissioner of the Presidency Division, Mr. C. G. B. Stevens, I. C. S., assumed charge on the forenoon of the 6th March.

III.

His Highness's movements.

12. His Highness was pleased to visit Shillong early in the year for a short period of change and rest, staying at the station, from the 17th May to the 15th June, 1929. A tour in Western India followed, in the course of which His Highness visited Nainital, Mussoorie, Kashmere and the North Western Frontier Provinces, including the Khyber Pass, the camping extending from 15th July to 23rd September 1929. While at Uri in Kashmere, the party was overtaken by serious floods and was entirely cut off for days, the return being thus delayed. The usual Christmas

visit to Calcutta lasted from 21st December, 1929, to 7th January, 1930. At Nainital His Highness met His Excellency the Governor of the United Provinces, and at Calcutta, His Excellency the Governor of Bengal.

The European tour.

13. His Highness's long contemplated European tour commenced during the year on the 20th January, 1930, on which date His Highness left Agartala, visiting Calcutta and Bombay *en route*, and sailing from the latter place on the 1st February, 1930, by the Lloyd Triestino steamship S. S. Gange. The staff accompanying consisted of Lt.-Colonel O. C. Pulley, Chief Staff Officer, Manyabara Rana Bodhjung Bahadur, Chief Secretary, and A. D. C's, Captain Rana Nepaljung Bahadur, Captain Kumar Brajalal Dev Barman Bahadur and Captain Kumar Balindrakishore Dev Barman Bahadur.

14. His Highness received enthusiastic ovations on the eve of departure from Agartala, as well as at Calcutta and Bombay. There were a number of farewell addresses and parties, some of which evinced the genuine good will of many distinguished members of Indian society in the two metropolitan towns towards His Highness and the State. Both His Excellency the Governor of Bengal and His Excellency the Governor of Bombay were pleased to honour His Highness by invitations to dinner which His Highness thankfully accepted, while special and grateful mention may be made of the hearty send-off accorded by His Highness Captain Maharaol Shree Sir Ranjit Singhji Bahadur, K. C. S. I., Maharaja of Baria, who very kindly came all the way from his State to see His Highness off.

CHAPTER II—LAND ADMINISTRATION.

Charge.

15. Babu B. K. Chatterjee, M. A., B. L., continued to be in charge of the Revenue Department till 14th Jaistha. Mr. S. C. Deb Barman, M. A., (Harvard) Officer-in-charge, Education Department remained in charge of this Department till the 27th Kartic, over and above his own duties, owing to the former's leave of absence and death during leave. The latter and Thakur K. K. Singh worked in this Department from 28th Kartic in addition to other duties assigned to them, a distribution of the departmental work having been effected. In the untimely death of Babu Brajendra Kumar Chatterjee the Durbar lost a very able and experienced officer.

Area held under Settlement.

16. As shown in the subjoined statement, the total area held under settlement and borne on the *taujis* at the close of the year was 637 sq. miles as against 616 sq. miles in the previous year.

Kinds of settlement.	Area in square miles.		Increase.	Decrease.	REMARKS.
	1339 T.E.	1338 T.E.			
Jotes ...	313	293	20	—	
Taluks ...	324	323	1		
Total ...	637	616	21		

17. The increase in the area under *jote* settlement is due to new settlements, resettlements, and to the resumption of 541 *drones* of *taluki* land in the Sadar Division belonging to Her Late Highness the 5th Maharani owing to her death during the year under review. Against the above 541 *drones* excluded from *taluki touji*, there was however an area of 645 *drones* of *taluki* land settled during the year, with a resultant increase of 1 sq. mile.

Tea Settlement.

18. There were 5 fresh settlements of *Khas* land for tea cultivation during the year under report. 2 parties, in 60 *drones* of *taluki* land, were also allowed by the Durbar to cultivate tea. One garden purchased by the State in auction sale for arrears of revenue was besides resettled during the year. The *Nazaranas* secured for these transactions were Rs. 5378, Rs. 525 and Rs. 364 respectively.

Rates of *Jama*.

19. The average *jama* per *kani* of *jote* lands in *Khas mehals* (exclusive of cesses) stood at 14 annas and 9 pies against 14 annas and 10 pies in the previous year. The maximum and minimum rates for *jotes* were Rs. 20 and 6 annas per *kani*, and those for *taluks* Re. 1, and 8 annas 9 pies, respectively. The maximum *jote* rate was, however, a special one in respect of a small piece of bazar land of a very advantageous position.

Sources of Land Revenue.

20. The different sources of the land revenue demand with the collection under each head are detailed below :—

Sources.	Current demand.		Arrear demand up to the end of		Realization up to the end of		Remarks.
	1339 T.E	1338 T.E.	1338 T.E.	1337 T.E.	1339 T.E.	1338 T.E.	
Taluks ...	1,66,530	1,67,267	2,62,789	2,67,297	1,69,026	1,68,639	
Khas Mehal jotes	4,63,774	4,34,365	7,95,457	7,53,825	4,21,642	3,88,186	
Bazars ...	7,822	8,322	1,306	1,393	7,629	8,154	
Cesses ...	39,363	37,782	72,454	69,415	35,839	34,073	
Total ...	6,77,489	6,47,736	11,32,006	10,91,930	6,34,136	5,99,052	

Demand.

21. The above statement shows that the current demand under all heads was Rs. 6,77,489. With the arrear demand of Rs. 11,32,006, the total demand of the year was Rs. 18,09,495 against Rs. 17,39,666 in the previous year. There was an increase in the current demand in respect of *jote* lands due, as usual, to assessment on the expiry of the rent-free period and resettlement after the previous term. There was a decrease in the current demand in respect of *taluki* land owing to the transfer of the late Fifth Maharani's *taluk* to *Khas mehal*, coupled with the fact that the new *taluki* settlements had an initial rent-free period.

22. The total collection under all heads during the year amounted to Rs. 6,34,136, being Rs. 3,26,855 under current and Rs. 3,07,281 under arrear, as against Rs. 5,99,052 in the previous year. The percentage of current collection was 48·25 against 52·42 and that of arrear collection 27·15 against 25·06. In the *Khas Mehal* the percentage of current collection was 36·39 against 37·47 and in *Taluki mehal*, 80·05 against 81·81 in the previous year. The percentage is unsatisfactory.

Collection.

23. Altogether 4,635 certificate cases, covering a demand of Rs. 2,28,732, were instituted during the year. With 3,340 cases valued at Rs. 3,37,500 pending from the previous year, the total number of cases awaiting final orders on disposal of preliminary notices issued on debtors, was 7,975, covering a total demand of Rs. 5,66,232. Of these, 36cases with a demand of Rs. 5,831 were rejected or struck off and Rs. 29,399 in 1360 cases was realised before decree, while orders under the provisions of the State Certificate Act were passed during the year in 3,734 cases with a total value of Rs. 1,40,963 making the demands absolute ; 2,845 cases with a total value of Rs. 3,90,039 thus remaining pending.

Coercive measures—Certificates.

24. With 4,470 cases to the value of Rs. 3,89,624 pending in execution from the previous year, the total number of cases dealt with was 8,204, covering a demand of Rs. 5,30,587. Out of the total demand, Rs. 6,876 was remitted or written off, and of the remainder, Rs. 1,07,003 was actually realised, leaving a balance of Rs. 4,16,708. Of the amount realised, Rs. 96,633 represents land revenue and Rs. 10,370 miscellaneous demands. 2 judgment debtors in Bilonia Division were confined in jail but were subsequently released as nothing could be realised from them.

25. The result of settlement work is given in the statement below. It will be seen that the settlement operations were completed in respect of 713 *drones* of *Takshichi Taluki* land and 5543 *drones* of *jote* land, as against 407 *drones* and 4340 *drones* respectively in the previous year.

Settlement.

Nature of Settlement.	1339 T. E. Area in *drones*.	1339 T. E. *Jama* in whole rupees.	1338 T. E. Area in *drones*.	1338 T. E. *Jama* in whole rupees.	REMARKS.
1. Permanent *taluki* settlement of cultivated land ...	—	—	—	—	
2. Permanent *taluki* settlement of waste land	—	—	—	—	
3. *Taskhichi taluki* settlement of cultivated land ...	—	—	—	—	
4. *Taskhichi taluki* settlement of waste land	713	5,742	407	3,266	
5. *Jotedari* re-settlement of cultivated land	5,095	56,843	3,793	46,147	
6. *Jotedari* settlement of waste land	448	4,042	547	4,358	
TOTAL. ...	6,256	66,627	4,747	53,771	

26. 5 fresh *Takshichi* tea gardens were settled—4 in Kailashahar Division and 1 in Sadar Division. Rs. 5518 was realised as *Nazar*. A rent free period of 3 years was allowed in each case. One *Takshichi Taluk*, comprising 75 *dronss* under tea cultivation, purchased by the State in auction sale for arrears of revenue in Sadar Division, was resettled with a reduced area of 45 *drones*, and the *Nazar* secured was Rs. 364.

Garden settlement.

27. A net increase of Rs. 25,518 in *jama* was secured by resettlement of *abadi jote* land, the *nazarana* being Rs. 59,175. The average *jama* per *kani* was 11 annas 2 pies against 12 annas 2 pies in the previous year.

Resettlement of *jote* lands.

28. During the year, an area of 448 *drones* of waste land was settled for a prospective rental of Rs. 4,042, the average *jama* per *kani* obtained being 9 annas 4 pies against 8 annas 4 pies in the previous year. The maximum and minimum rates were Rs. 2-7 and 6 annas respectively. The *nazarana* realised was Rs. 5,621, while the rent free period allowed ranged from 1 to 3 years.

Jotedari settlement of waste land.

29. No wholetime Settlement officer was employed in any Division in the State. The Divisional Officers were entrusted with settlement work within their respective jurisdictions. The total expenditure incurred in the settlement operations was Rs. 2,960.

Settlement work.

30. The number of defaulting *taluks* brought under the operation of the Sunset Law (including 11 pending from the previous year) was 87. Of these, 59 were released on payment of dues with penalty, while 3 were sold in auction and 25 remained undisposed of at the close of the year.

Operation of the Sunset Law.

31. The results of the survey (including resurvey) operations are given in the statement below. It will be seen that an area of 9003 *drones*, comprising 1328 *drones* of *taluk* and 7675 *drones* of *Khas mehal* was surveyed as against a total of 6,433 *drones* in the previous year. The sanctioned programme for survey for the year was for 10,060 *drones* in *Khas mehal* and 1,439 *drones* in *taluks*. The total expenditure incurred in the survey operations in *Khas mehal* was Rs. 10,729.

Survey

Names of Divisions.	Quantity of land in *drones* surveyed in 1339 T. E.			Quantity of land in *drones* surveyed in 1338 T. E.			REMARKS.
	Taluki land.	*Khas mehal* land.	Total.	*Taluki* land.	*Khas mehal* land.	Total.	
1. Sadar Division ...	176	2,198	2,374	917	189	1,106	
2. Kailashahar „ ...	31	835	866	205	757	962	
3. Sonamura „ ...	54	1,830	1,884	—	1,799	1,799	
4. Bilonia „ ...	—	720	720	—	843	843	
5. Khowai „ ...	—	160	160	—	261	261	
6. Dharmanagar „ ...	251	718	969	—	266	266	
7. Udaipur „ ...	816	895	1,711	146	690	836	
8. Sabroom „ ...	—	319	319	—	358	358	
9. Amarpur Sub „ ...	—	—	—	—	2	2	
TOTAL ...	1,328	7,675	9,003	1,268	5,165	6,433	

32. *Khanapuri* work of seven sheets was undertaken at Agartala, but owing to the alterations made by the P. W D. for improvement of the town, *Ki awar* work of some of the sheets had to be revised, with the resu't that *k anapuri* part of 2 sheets was left unfinished at the end of the year. In a''. *khanapuri* of 6048 *Dags* was finished during the year.

Town Survey.

33. Owing to the expansion during the year of the town area at Agartala to the east and west, the extended portions were traversed and 3 new sheets were prepared. The tota' exp:nditure incurred in the work was Rs. 525.

34. Compilation of maps on a sca'e of 1 = mi e from the survey maps of Sadar, Bi'onia and Sabroom Divisions was undertaken during the year. In a' , 521 maps were reduced from various scales to 1″ = 1 mile sca'e. Tracing work was a'so simultaneously undertaken by the staff engaged in the ccmpi ation work. Almost all the maps that were compi ed had to be traced on cloth. The expenditure incurred was Rs. 438-7-6.

Map Compilation work.

35. A separate staff was maintained to trace some maps to be supplied for the use of the Divisiona' O fices and the Tahasil staff. They were paid on contract. In all 106 maps were traced and the expenditure incurred came to Rs. 193-7-3.

36. It will be seen that the *nazarana* obtained and obta'nable by *Tashkhichi taluki* settlement, resettlement of *abadi j* land, and settlement of waste land as *joies* amounted to Rs. 72.725 Rs. 5,882 + Rs. 59,175 + Rs. 7,668). The net increase of revenue secured was Rs. 35,302 (Rs. 5,742 + Rs. 25,518 + Rs. 4,042).

37. As detailed below there were a tog.ther 10 private estates under State management during the year under report.

Private Estates under State Management.

Class.	Name of Estates.	Area	Revenue.
Encumbered	1. Kakrabon Estate	83 *drones*	1,871
	2. Jogendranagar Trust Estate	0	163
	3. Kamalnagar and Mohendranagar Estate	51 „	255
	4. Gouranga Tripura's Estate	1 „	57
	5. Maharam Ali Ch...dhuri Khanje Khan Bahadur's Estate—*Taluk*	236 „	1,230
	Jote	6 „	149
	6. Thakur Nalini Mohan Deb Barma's Estate	68 „	170
Unencumbered	7. Prabhu Goswamis' Estate	31 „	61
	8. Dowager Maharanee's Estate	260 „	450
	9. Late Brajakumar Thakur's Estate	47 „	297
Endowment	10. Taranagar Estate	140 „	52

38. The subjoined table shows the demands and collections of the estates during the year. Though there is a considerable portion of the demand in most cases which appears to be fictitious, and allowances must be made for the exceptionally bad year, the collections are nevertheless

more or less unsatisfactory. A special enquiry has been directed on the point.

Estate No.	DEMAND			COLLECTION			P. C. of collection
	Current	Arrear	Total	Current	Arrear	Total	
1.	6,645	32,596	69,241	782	7,465	8,247	11·91
2.	1,272	4,509	5,781	382	716	1,098	18·99
3.	1,272	1,416	2,688	289	696	985	36·19
4.	204	69	273	143	62	205	75·09
5.	3,949	9,567	13,516	1,404	1,457	2,861	21·17
6.	1,163	2,018	3,181	470	648	1,118	35·86
7.	935	2,014	2,949	307	535	842	28·55
8.	9,020	13,116	22,136	3,872	3,842	7,714	34·84
9.	1,799	2,489	4,288	875	1,236	2,111	49·23
10.	3,653	7,053	10,706	1,479	2,461	3,940	37·73

CHAPTER III—PROTECTION.

I. Legislation.

Legislative Council.

39. There were five sittings of the Legislative Council during the year under report. His Highness the Maharaja Manikya Bahadur personally presided over the meetings.

Laws enacted.

40. The subjoined bills were passed by the Legislative Council during the year and all of them subsequently received the assent of His Highness and became law.

(1) Tripura State Bank Act (Act I of 1339 T. E.)
(2) Tripura Succession Certificate Act (Act II of 1339 T. E.)
(3) Tripura Census Act (Act III of 1339 T. E.)
(4) Tripura Public Works and Road Cess Act (Act IV of 1339 T. E.)

II. Military.

Charge.

41. Major Kumar Dina Mohan Deb Barman Bahadur continued to be in charge of the Military forces as before.

Strength.

42. The actual strength of the forces about the close of the year was 403 against 365, the corresponding figure for the previous year.

The First Tripura Bir Company.

43. The First Tripura Bir Company was recognised during the year by the Government of India as an "A" class unit of the "Indian States Forces."

44. Lieutenant Kumar B. L. Deb Barman Bahadur, Lieutenant Rana Jhappat Jung Bahadur and Lieutenant Kumar Balindra Kishore Deb Barman Bahadur were deputed to Shillong again during the year to be attached to the 1/8th Gurkha Rifles as before, for the purposes of field training. Five other Indian subordinate officers and probationers as well as 5 N. C. O's also received training during the year at Shillong. The services of a Signalling Instructor of the Indian Army were also secured for training of men locally.

Training of Officers.

45. Deputed by the Military Adviser, Captain Blaxland of the Indian Army visited Agartala and inspected the cantonment and the forces from 18th March to 25th March, 1930. His suggestions were highly appreciated by the Department.

Inspections.

46. The construction of the cantonment town and the buildings made satisfactory progress during the year, and the First Tripura Bir Company removed to the new barracks constructed for them.

Cantonment Buildings.

47. The total expenditure of the year, exclusive of the cost of construction of the cantonment buildings, which was met from the Public Works Department, amounted to Rs. 1,29,297 against Rs. 89,661, the increase being due to the measures for improvement under the scheme of reorganisation previously adopted.

Expenditure.

III. Police.

48. Lieutenant (Hony.) J. C. Datta, B. A., continued as Superintendent of Police during the year. Thakur Jogendra Chandra Dev Barman, Assistant Superintendent of Police, who was on sick leave, expired during the latter part of the year—a promising career, it is a matter of regret, being thus cut short in the prime of life. Babu Naresh Kumar Bhattacharjee, B. Sc. was thereafter selected for the post and deputed to the Police Training College at Sardah for training.

Charge.

49. The total numerical strength of the police force during the year, was 496 against 490 in the previous year.

Strength.

50. The total number of village chaukidars was 175 as in the previous year.

Rural Police.

51. There were 4 Inspectors of Police, one of whom was a temporary hand. The chief duty of the Inspectors was to supervise cases of heinous offence.

Inspecting Staff.

52. There were 22 Darogas instead of 23, and 15 Naib Darogas instead of 14 in the previous year, one post in the cadre of the Darogas having been decreased and one in the cadre of the Naib-Darogas increased.

Investigating and prosecuting staff.

53. A small staff consisting of one Daroga, one Naib Daroga and 5 constables worked in the C. I. D.

C. I. D. and Intelligence staff.

54. The total number of cases reported during the year under report was 1295 against 1336 in the previous year.

Crime.

The results of cases investigated will be seen from the following table :—

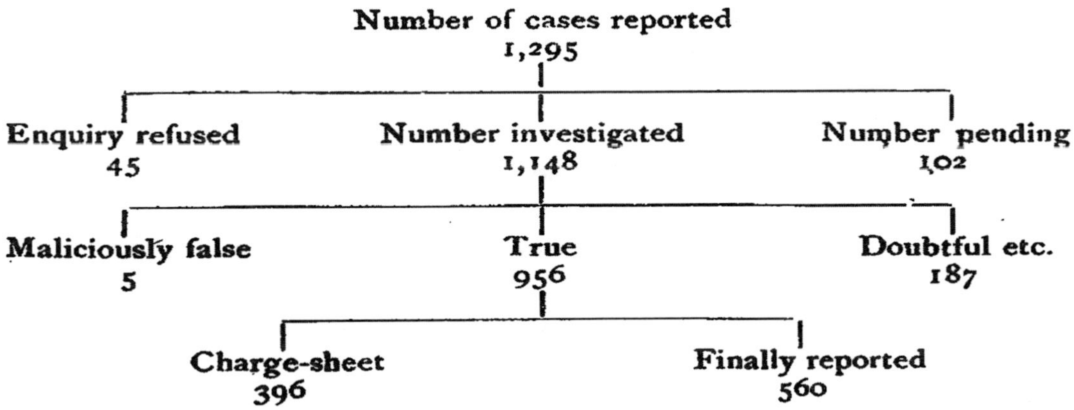

Result of prosecution.

55. Altogether 772 persons were arrested in connection with various offences and 718 persons sent up for trial by the police against 964 and 821 respectively in the previous year.

56. Of the number 718 sent up, 133 were convicted, and 221 acquitted (including 104 on compromise and 40 on withdrawal of cases), while 2 died and 362 awaited trial (excluding absconding accused). The percentage of conviction was 18·52 against 20·58 of the previous year, a result that must be considered unsatisfactory.

57. In addition to the 395 persons awaiting trial at the end of the previous year, 16 absconding accused were arrested during the year under report, making the total before the courts 411 ; of these, 79 were convicted, 214 acquitted (including 67 on compromise, 53 on withdrawal of cases) and 118 were awaiting trial.

Bad livelihood cases.

58. 2 Bad livelihood cases with 14 persons as accused were instituted during the year. Two were convicted. Of the remaining 12 persons, 6 are still awaiting trial. Two persons escaped from jail and 4 remained absconding.

Arms Act cases.

59. Of 9 Arms Act cases, one was reported as doubtful and 8 cases with 11 persons were sent up. All these cases resulted in conviction.

Recovery of stolen property.

60. The total value of property stolen during the year amounted to Rs. 15,149-14-3 against Rs. 16,199-3-9 of the previous year. Of this amount, Rs. 2,991-13-6 was recovered against Rs. 3,540-10-9 of the previous year. The percentage of recoveries was only 19·74 against 21·8 of the previous year and 46·33 in 1337 T. E., thus showing again a regrettable deterioration in this important branch of police work.

Dacoities.

61. There were 9 cases of dacoities reported during the year, of which 4 were finally reported. 18 persons were sent up in charge-sheets in connection with the 5 remaining cases, of whom 12 were acquitted and 6 were awaiting trial.

Unnatural deaths and steps taken.

62. There were altogether 82 cases of unnatural deaths. Regular enquiries were held by the police in all these cases and no foul play was detected.

Rewards & punishments.

63. 1 Daroga, 1 Naib Daroga, 1 Jamadar and 6 constables received money rewards while 3 constables were dismissed. 2 Darogas, 2 Writer Constables were fined or suspended and 3 constables were judicially punished.

Tours.

64. The Superintendent was out on tour for 85 days against 147 days in the previous year.

Co-operation.

65. The relations with the neighbouring districts in British India continued to be satisfactory.

Patrol.

66. The patrol at Sonamura worked well with the Kotwali Police, Comilla.

Expenditure.

67. The expenditure amounted to Rs. 81,399 against Rs. 77,145 in the previous year.

IV. Justice.

Courts.

68. There were 15 courts of justice in the State during the year under report exercising both civil and criminal jurisdiction viz :—the Khas Adalat or the Chief Court with its original and appellate sides and 14 Courts of Magistrate-Munsiffs exercising original jurisdiction only.

Khas Adalat.

69. Dewan B. K. Sen Bahadur M. A., B. L., F. R. S. A. continued as Chief Judge till 16th Jaistha 1339 T. E., when he was appointed Dewan-Shashan, and Kumar S. C. Deb Barman Bahadur, Puisne Judge, officiated as Chief Judge till 1st. Agrahayan, 1339 T. E. Babu Jnanendra Mohan Das B. L., retired District and Sessions Judge, was then appointed Chief Judge of the Khas Adalat. Puisne Judge Thakur Lalit Mohan Deb Barman M. A., B. L., was in charge of the original side upto the Puja vacation. On his transfer thereafter to Sonamura as Divisional Officer, Babu Ramani Mohan Goswami M. A., B. L., Sessions Judge, served in both the capacities till the end of the year.

Number of original criminal cases.

70. Altogether 2,095 original criminal cases were instituted during the year under report, as against 2,076 of the previous year. With the balance of 706 pending from the last year, the total number of cases for disposal before the several subordinate original courts was thus 2,801 against 2,695 of the previous year as detailed below ; out of these 2801 cases, 2072 were disposed of, as against 1989 of the last year, leaving 729 cases pending at the close of the year. Thus in the year under report, the number of cases for disposal increased from that of

the last year by 106 and there was also an increase in the disposals by 83.

DESCRIPTION OF OFFENCES.	1338 T.E.	1339 T.E.
Offences against the State and public tranquillity	125	111
Offences against person	714	730
Offences against property	1,334	1,465
Other offences	522	495
TOTAL	2,695	2,801

71. Extradition of 35 persons was asked for during the year. With 67 persons pending surrender at the close of the previous year, the total number of offenders involved in the requisitions was 102, of whom 26 persons were arrested and surrendered by the British Indian Police and 13 persons appeared of their own accord or were subsequently arrested within the State.

Extradition from British India.

72. The total number of persons awaiting trial in the year under report, inclusive of the number pending from the last year, was 3,552 against 3,561 of the previous year. The number brought to trial in the year under report was 2580. Of these 651 were arrested by the police, 501 were produced on warrants, 1,035 appeared on summons, 356 appeared voluntarily and 37 were arrested in the presence of the Magistrates.

Persons brought to trial.

73. Out of the 3,552 persons before the courts including sessions, 1,150 were discharged without trial, 840 were acquitted, 501 were convicted, 14 died, 1 escaped, 20 were transferred and 1026 remained under trial at the close of the year. Of the persons convicted, 151 were sentenced to various terms of imprisonment extending from below 1 month to 6 years, 336 to fine only, 1 person was released on bail, and 7 persons were warned for the future, while 5 persons were imprisoned for life and 1 was sentenced to be hanged ; though the death sentence was commuted by the Appellate Court to one of rigorous imprisonment for life. The number of persons actually tried was 1,341 as against 1,175 of the previous year, and the percentage of convictions was thus 37·36 against 37·78 of the previous year.

Results of cases.

74. Of the 2,801 cases for disposal, the number in which British subjects were concerned was 490 as against 474 of the previous year. Out of these cases, 361 were cognizable and 129 non-cognizable. In 51 cases British subjects were complainants and in 439 they were the accused. In 133 cases both the parties were British subjects. In these cases 594 persons were actually under trial during the year under report, against 518 of the previous year. Out of these, 178 were convicted, 252 acquitted or discharged, 3 died and 161 remained under trial at the close of the year.

Cases concerning British subjects.

75. The statement below compares the number of original criminal cases which were instituted during the last 2 years.

Comparative Statement.

DESCRIPTION OF OFFENCES.	1338 T. E.	1339 T.E.	Increase.	Decrease.
Offences against the State and public tranquillity ...	106	79	0	27
Offences against person	568	562	0	6
Offences against property	986	1,107	121	0
Other offences	416	347	0	69
TOTAL	2,076	2,095	121	102

Increased by 19.

76. 15 cases were committed to the Sessions during the year under report. There were also 8 cases pending from the previous year. Out of these 23 cases, 20 were disposed of as detailed in the following table. The number of persons involved in these cases was 65; of whom 20 were convicted, 34 acquitted and 11 remained under trial at the close of the year.

Sessions cases.

Description of cases.	Number of cases.	Disposed of.	Pending.	REMARKS.
Murder	5	5	0	
Culpable homicide not amounting to murder	2	1	1	
Dacoity	1	0	1	
Arson	3	3	0	
Grievous hurt	3	2	1	
Rape	1	1	0	
House breaking and abduction ...	1	1	0	
Obstructing public servant in discharge of his duty	1	1	0	
Using counterfeit British currency note...	1	1	0	
Dacoity and grievous hurt	1	1	0	
Simple hurt	1	1	0	
Robbery and grievous hurt	1	1	0	
Mischief by fire	1	1	0	
Death by rash and negligent act ...	1	1	0	
Total	23	20	3	

77. There were altogether 207 criminal appeals as against 196 of the previous year. They were disposed of as shown below :—

Criminal appeals.

Rejected	39
Judgment affirmed	45
Modified	24
Reversed	13
Further enquiry &c. ordered	15
	136
Pending	71
Total	207

78. The percentage of judgments affirmed and modified was 71·13 as against 71·14 of the previous year.

79. The number of original civil suits instituted during the year under report was 2,495 as against 2,216 of the previous year. With the preceding year's balance of 1,182 suits, the total number for disposal was 3,677. against 3,294 of the previous year. They were disposed of as follows :—

Original civil suits.

Exparte	1,178
Admitted and compromised	410
Dismissed for want of prosecution ...	325
Disposed of on contest	586
	2,499
Pending	1,178
Total	3,677

80. The average duration of suits before the civil courts was 3 months and 16 days as against 3 months and 20 days in 1338 T. E.

Duration of suits.

81. The total value of civil suits instituted during the year was Rs. 2,61,046-0-9, as against Rs. 1,98,387-14-6 which gives an average of Rs. 104-10-0 per case. Of the 2,495 suits instituted during the year under report, 568 related to lands, 1,453 to money transaction and 474 to other transactions. There were 1,472 suits of the value of Rs. 100 and under ; 560 suits of over Rs. 100 and below Rs. 500 ; 120 suits of over Rs. 500 and below Rs. 1,000 ; 33 suits of over Rs. 1,000 and below Rs. 5,000 ; 2 suits of over Rs. 5,000 ; while 308 suits were not estimable in money value.

Nature and value of suits.

82. The number of applications for the execution of decrees filed during the year was 861, and with 538 pending cases the total number was 1,399 against 1,275 of the previous year. The aggregate value of the new applications was Rs. 1,16,020-6-0, and with the pending value of Rs. 1,25,192-5-9, being the value of the pending cases, the total amounted to Rs. 2,41,212-11-9. The number of applications disposed of was 766, the value of which was Rs. 93,175-14-9. The number of execution cases pending at the close of the year was 633 with the value of Rs. 1,48,036-13-0.

Execution of decrees.

83. There were 146 civil appeals filed during the year, as against 179 of the previous year. With the last year's balance of 122, the total for disposal was 268, as against 269 of the previous year. Out of these, 130 were disposed of during the year under review, as against 147 of the last year, leaving a balance of 138 cases at the close of the year.

Civil appeals.

84. The following figures indicate the results of appeals :—

Results of appeals.

Decisions confirmed	66
„ reversed	19
„ modified	6
„ remanded	25
Compromised and otherwise disposed of ...	14
	130

Percentage. 85. The percentage of judgments wholly or partly upheld, excluding the cases compromised, was 62·06 as against 64·22 of the last year.

Value and duration of appeals. 86. The total value of appeals filed during present year was Rs. 61,737-15-0 and the average duration of each appeal was 2 months and 6 days, against 2 months and 4 days of the previous year.

Original Side cases. 87. 50 civil suits were instituted in the Khas Adalat Original Side, as against 25 of the last year. With the balance of 48 suits from 1338 T. E., the total for disposal was thus 98 against 75 of the previous year. Of these 39 suits were disposed of as against 27 suits of the previous year, and 59 suits remained pending at the close of the year. There were 26 execution cases during the year under report including 15 cases pending from the last year. Of these only 1 was disposed of and 25 remained pending at the close of the year. There were 22 applications filed for the grant of succession and other certificates during the year. With the previous year's balance of 16, the total number of cases was 38; out of which 9 were disposed of as shown below, leaving 29 cases pending at the close of the year.

Description of cases.	Total.	Disposed of.	Pending.
Probate case	3	0	3
Succession certificate	9	1	8
Guardianship	26	8	18
Total	38	9	29

Total number of appeals 88. Thus it will appear from the sub-joined table, that the total number of civil and criminal appeals, inclusive of the number pending from last year was 475 as against 465 of the previous year, and out of these 266 were disposed of as against 309 of the last year. In comparison with the previous year, the total number of appeals increased by 10 and there was a decrease in the disposals in the year under report by 43. The decrease in the disposals is due to the fact that there was no permanent Chief Judge for a long time.

Description of appeals.	Number of appeals.		Disposed of.	
	Past year.	Present year.	Past year.	Present year.
Civil	269	268	147	130
Criminal	196	207	162	136
Tota	465	475	309	266

V. Prisons.

89. In addition to the Central Jail at the Capital, there were 7 Sub-jails in the different Divisions and Sub-Divisions of the State during the year under report.

Number of Jails.

90. Inclusive of the previous year's balance of 140, the total number of prisoners was 842 as against 810 in the previous year. Of them 338 were convicts, 487 under-trials, 15 civil prisoners and 2 lunatics.

Jail population.

91. The daily average increased from 101·60 in the previous year to 114·28 in 1339 T. E. The number of prisoners remaining in the jails at the end of the year was 105. Convicts released under the Remission Rules numbered 8 against 25 in the preceding year.

The daily average.

92. The following table shows details about the offence and sentence of the 56 prisoners who were under more than 2 years' imprisonment against 65 in the previous year.

Long-term prisoners.

Class of offence.	Number of prisoners.	Occupation.	REMARKS.
Murder	12	They were employed in brick manufacture, oilmills, wheat grinding, *soorki* pounding, *khoa* breaking, bamboo and cane work, gardening, weaving, tailoring, paddy husking, rice manufacturing &c.	32 had sentences of 2 to 5 years, 13 of 5 to 10 years, 11 for life *i. e.* 20 years.
Culpable homicide not amounting to murder	9		
Grievous hurt	1		
Theft	1		
Pick-pocketing	1		
Dacoity	12		
Robbery	4		
Unlawful assembly	14		
Kidnapping	1		
Arson	1		
Total	56		

93. In the early part of the year under review, there was a serious out-break of dysentery in the Central Jail which accounted for 3 deaths out of 31 attacks. Prompt and necessary action led to the successful control of the disease within a short time. But for the above out-break, the health of the Central Jail was on the whole good. Three more deaths took place—one from apoplexy, one from enlarged spleen and anaemia, and one due to grievous hurt caused by another convict.

Sickness and mortality.

94. During the year under review there were altogether 9 escapes from the jails viz., escape of one convict from the Central Jail, of one convict and one under-trial from Sonamura Jail, of one under-trial from Dharmanagar, of one under-trial from Khowai, 2 under-trials from Belonia and 2 under-trials from Kailashahar. Of these, 4 were recaptured in the course of the year.

Escapes and recaptures.

95. A notable event of the year was the introductoin of lower primary training to the willing illiterate prisoners in the Central Jail with the help of a literate convict. A few of them eagerly interested themselves in study and prepared

Education.

for the next Lower Primary Examination. Apart from the above, religious and moral instructions were also imparted by a *pandit* and a *moulavi* once a week. It is hoped, these measures will have some reformative influence on the prisoners in the jail.

Warder guard.

96. The revised pay of the warders in the Central Jail has not been sufficiently attractive for permanent service, though it has brought in recruits from the up-country and places beyond the State.

97. The gradual introduction of an entire warder establishment in all sub-jails, thereby dispensing with the system of guarding by the military and the police, as in vogue at present, is under consideration.

Income and expenditure.

98. The net income during the year from the Central Jail only, totalled Rs. 1683, as against Rs. 3664 in the year previous. This decrease is apparent only being due to the difference in adjustment and accounting.

99. The total expenditure on account of all jails stood at Rs. 22,159 against Rs. 18,536 for the previous year.

VI. Registration.

Charge.

100. The charge of the Department continued with late Babu B. K. Chatterjee, M. A., B. L., till 14th Jaistha and with Mr. Somendra Chandra Deb Baraman, M. A. (Harvard) upto 27th Kartic, and then with Thakur K. K. Singha, Naib Dewan, till the end of the year.

Registration Offices.

101. The number of registration offices continued to be 9 as in the previous year, being one at the headquarters station of each of the Divisions or Sub-Divisions. In the mofussil the Divisional and the Sub-Divisional Officers and in certain Divisions the Second Officers acted as Registrars. For the Sadar Division there was a separate Registrar at Agartala.

Registration and Disposal.

102. The total number of documents presented for registration during the year including 255 documents pending at the end of the previous year, was 12,089 against 12,362. Of this number, 122 deeds were refused registration on different grounds and 377 remained pending at the end of the year.

Value of deeds presented and Registered.

103. The total value covered by the documents presented including those pending at the end of the last year, amounted to Rs. 20,23,206 as compared with Rs. 21,20,235, while the total value covered by the documents actually registered was Rs. 19,95,905 as against Rs. 21,45,657 in the year before.

Suits and appeals.

104. The number of suits and appeals filed in the Registration Department in respect of documents, the registration of which had been refused in the Registration Offices, was 31 and 4 against 45 and 9 respectively in the preceding year. There were 34 suits and 2 appeals pending from the previous year, making a total of 65 suits and 6 appeals. Out of these, 23 suits and

1 appeal were disposed of during the year, leaving 42 suits and 5 appeals pending at the end of the year.

Income and Expenditure.

105. The total income of the Department from fees and fines amounted to Rs. 14,865 as against Rs. 15,202, and the expenditure to Rs. 5002 against Rs. 5007 in the previous year. The net income thus amounted to Rs. 9863 against Rs. 10,195 in the previous year.

VII. Municipality and Sanitation.

Municipality.

106. As in the previous year, the State had only one municipality in the capital town of Agartala with a population of about 8,000.

Committee.

107. The municipality was administered by a committee of nine members—all nominated. On the sad death of the official Chairman Babu Brajendra Kumar Chatterjee, M. A., B. L., Officer-in-charge, Revenue Department, from small-pox in the early part of the year under report, the non-official Vice-Chairman Babu Sankari Mohan Chatterjee, M. A., B. L., pleader, had to carry on the administration till the appointment, as Chairman, in the latter part of the year, of Babu Brajendra Chandra Dutt, a retired Magistrate-Collector of the State. Altogether 13 sittings of the committee were held during the year, the average attendance of members being 6·1 as against 5·1 of the year before.

Income.

108. Out of the total demand of Rs. 8,458-8-3 on account of municipal and latrine taxes including arrears, the total collection came up to Rs. 3,920-2-9 as against Rs. 3,860-6-9 for the previous year. Of the demand Rs. 146-15-3 had to be written off as irrecoverable.

109. The miscellaneous income from all sources totalled Rs. 1,517-7-0 as against Rs. 2,404-1-9 in the preceding year. The decrease was due to the transfer of the income from motor licence to the Political Department. The Bazar income is excluded from this head.

110. The State grant for the year was Rs. 12,000 inclusive of the special provision for sanitary works within the Municipal limits. Of the grant, Rs. 766 lapsed to the State for not having been spent on the re-excavation of a tank. So the actual State grant was Rs. 11,234 and the total income from all sources, exclusive of the Bazar income, stood at Rs. 16,671-9-9 as against Rs. 16,263-7-3 of the year previous.

Expenditure.

111. The total expenditure during the year under review on all counts, including expenses on some sanitary measures, came up to Rs. 17,008-0-3 as against Rs. 16,239-15-3 in the year before.

Ishanganj Bazar.

112. As before, the control and management of the bazar were vested in the hands of the Municipal Committee. The bazar income has been exclusively set apart for the improvement of the bazar. Inclusive of the arrear demand, the total demand for the bazar amounted to Rs. 9,425-11-3, as against Rs. 8,543-7-3

of the previous year, while the total realization was Rs. 6,670-11-9 as against Rs. 6,098-9-0. The total expenditure against the bazar fund was Rs. 967-8-9.

113. The accumulated balance of the bazar fund at the end of the year under review stood at Rs. 21,810-12-6. The proposed construction of the central market shed had to be put off in view of a proposal to shift the Bazar to a more open space.

Health.

114. The general health of the Municipal Town was on the whole satisfactory. Kala-azar recrudesced to a small extent. 3 cases of small pox and 25 cases of cholera were reported.

Sanitation.

115. Dr. M. M. Majumdar, L. M. S., was entrusted with the charge of the Sanitation and Municipal Departments, during the year under review. Under his direct control and supervision some minor sanitary works were carried on in the town at a cost of Rs. 1,375-5-3. The proposed excavation of a large tank in a part of the town, decided upon during the year as a sanitary measure, could not be undertaken owing to the early outbreak of the monsoons.

CHAPTER IV—PRODUCTION AND DISTRIBUTION.

I. Weather and Crops—Agriculture.

The charge of the Department.

116. The charge of the Department of Agriculture was transferred to Manyabara Rana Bodhjung Bahadur, Chief Secretary, who was assisted by Mr. J. C. Chäudhury, Superintendent of Agriculture, during the year.

Rainfall.

117. The average rainfall of the year was 106·01 against 87·67 in the previous year. The quinquennial average was 98·13. Kailashahar Division had the maximum fall of 153·90 , and Sonamura Division the minimum of 78·33″. The distribution was uneven.

Temparature.

118. The highest rise of temperature during the year was noted as 95° on the 11th day of Asharh, and the lowest as 56° on the 8th day of Magh. The general tendency of temperature at the capital town of Agartala was that of a submontane region. Spring season lasted for 5 to 7 weeks.

Floods.

119. Five Divisions of the State, viz., Kailashahar, Sonamura, Dharmanagar, Udaipur and Amarpur had visitations of heavy flood during the early rainy months. The suffering for the time being was great and. all early crops were entirely lost in the affected areas. Prompt relief measures were arranged, the amount distributed in gratuitous relief and loans, as adjusted within the year, amounting to Rs. 20,483 and suspension of realisation of previous loans to Rs. 20,808.

120. The outturn of tea as compared with the previous year was not unsatisfactory, but the total amount of export duty fell off owing to low prices. Five fresh tea gardens, with an area of 668 *drones* were settled during the year under review, and one tea garden auction purchased by the State was partly resettled with a diminished area of 45 *drones.* Permission was also granted to two parties to cultivate tea in an area of 60 *drones* of *taluki* land.

Tea industry.

121. Field labourers such as ploughmen, weeders etc. got 8 annas to Re. 1-8 per day. Reclamation labourers, jungle breakers 8 annas to Re. 1-8 per day. Garden labourers 8 annas to 12 annas per day. Joom labourers 8 to 12 annas per day. Thatchers 12 annas to Re. 1 per day. Masons Re. 1 to Rs. 2 per day. Carpenters Re. 1 to Re. 1-8 per day. Earth workers and tank excavators Re. 1-4 to Re. 1-12 per day. There was thus no substantial falling off in the rates inspite of the prevailing distress, a phenomenon due to the comparative dearth of local labour.

Labour and wages.

122. The prices of food grains were similar to those in the neighbouring British districts. Rice sold at Rs. 4-8 to Rs. 8 per maund. Prices of oil-seeds were Rs. 4 to Rs. 11 per maund.

Prices during the year.

123. The people were generally affected by the all-round economic depression which led to a paralysing slump in the market for indigenous commodities such as cotton, jute and oilseeds. The floods of the year made the situation worse. An unprecedented scarcity of money was in evidence all round, and absolutely no loan was available except from the State.

Condition of the people.

124. Cattle diseases also put in appearance in the year under report. The total number of animals treated by the Veterinary Surgeon during the year was 1609 in all. Anthrax broke out in epidemic form in the Udaipur Division during the early part of the year and rinderpest in Sonamura and Kailashahar Divisions. The Veterinary Surgeon was out on tour for 34 days.

Cattle.

125. The activities of the Department were mainly confined to propaganda work for introduction of improved varieties of staple crops and horticultural produce, also for extension of *eri* culture. Seeds and seedlings were grown in the Kashipur farm and distributed.

The activities of the Department.

126. The Superintendent of Agriculture was engaged in departmental organization duties in the office and was only out for 32 days during the year on mofussil duties.

Touring.

II. Immigration and Emigration.

127. During the year, 1286 families immigrated into and 508 families emigrated out of the State, as against 1,381 and 566 respectively in the previous year.

III. Forests.

Charge and management. 128. Babu Jatindra Nath Mitra, Naib Dewan, was in charge of the Department. With the exception of a few *Mahals* which were let out in *Ijara*, all the forests were under *Khas* management as before.

Staff. 129. The Department had a staff of 1 Station Officer, 3 Forest Circle Inspectors, 1 Assistant Forest Circle Inspector, 17 Foresters, 22 Assistant Foresters and Rangers, 9 Mohurers, 21 Head Guards, and 196 guards and Literate guards. Besides these, there were 187 Commission Agents for the sale of forest permits for the shoulder-borne export of minor forest produce not coming under any definite *Mahal*. There were 52 stations for collection of duty and prevention of forest offences.

Working. 130. The Reserved Sal Forests of the Sonamura Division continued to be worked under the system of Coppice with standards and those of the Udaipur Division under the Improvement Method, while the open unclassed forests were worked under the State Forest Rules of 1323 T. E. For the Feni River *Mahal* the working rules of the Bengal Forest Department were followed.

131. The four coupes selected and marked in the Sonamura Division were sold in the year under report; but as the sale took place at the fag end of the year no operations were undertaken in the coupes during the year. Re-marking was done in the two blocks selected in the Udaipur Division but no work was undertaken as the coupes were not sold in the year under report.

Sources of Forest Revenue. 132. The following table shows the results of the collection of forest revenue :—

Heads of Revenue.	1339 T.E.	1338 T.E.	Increase.	Decrease.	REMARKS.
I. Unclassed open forests :—					
(*a*) Toll on forest produce exported by the river mehals	3,97,586	5,17,238	—	1,19,652	
(*b*) Toll on forest produce exported by land route under permit	86,282	79,842	6,440	—	
(*c*) Toll collection (share) of the Feni river mehal ...	38,406	35,382	3,024	—	
(*d*) Grazing mehal ...	7,427	8,530	—	1,103	
(*e*) Thatching grass mehal	7,960	7,990	—	30	
II. Reserved Forests :— Sale of *Sal* and *Garjan* trees ...	2,351	4,173	—	1,822	
III. Elephant Kheddas	17,114	16,682	432	—	
TOTAL ...	5,57,126	6,69,837	9,896	1,22,607	

Net decrease—1,12,711

133. The total forest revenue of the year under report was Rs. 5,57,126 against Rs. 6,69,837 in the previous year showing a decrease of Rs. 1,12,711.

Receipts.

134. A considerable fall of revenue is noticeable in the River *Mahals* and some increase under the head Permit *Mahals*. Unusual slump in timber trade and want of demand for forest produce in general account mainly for the fall under the head River *Mahals*. The increase under the head Permit *Mahal* was due to better circuit work by the preventive staff.

135. During the year under report *Kheda* operations were undertaken in the Bilonia Doal in Bilonia Division, Khowai Doal in the Khowai Division, Manoo, Deo and Dhalai Doals in the Kailashahar Division and Sukhnachhari Doal in the Sonamura Division. The *Kheda* operations in the Bilonia and the Khowai Doals were succesful but the operations in the Manoo, Deo, Dhalai and Sukhnachhari Doals failed. No *Kheda* operations were undertaken in the Udaipur-Amarsagar and Sabroom Doals though leased out. 30 elephants were caught in the Bilonia Doal and 20 in the Khoai Doal working out a total of 50 elephants against the same number in the previous year. All the elephants caught could not be sold in the year under report and some of the elephants were sold at a low price as there was no sufficient demand for elephants.

Kheda Operations.

136. The joint Toll Station at Amlighat continued to be under the management of the State Forest Department. The total revenue collected at the joint Toll Station in the year under review was Rs.. 56,406 against Rs. 51,382 in the previous year. As in the previous year, a doctor of the Sub-Assistant Surgeon class was appointed temporarily for four months from December last for giving medical relief to the wood-cutters at Amlighat Toll Station as well as to the station staff.

Feni River Mahal.

137. As in the previous year, the forest produce from Lot No. 98 as well as from the other Fee Simple Lots was exported under passes granted by the Collector of Chittagong, without any friction between the station staff and the lot owners.

Fee Simple Lots.

138. In the year under review there were 186 forest cases against 315 persons, including 66 cases against 111 persons pending from the previous year. The offences were mainly for illicit export of forest produce without permits and without payment of duty.

Forest Offences.

139. Altogether 108 cases against 173 persons were tried, of whom 4 were sentenced to imprisonment, 118 were punished with fine only and 51 were acquitted. 19 cases against 34 persons were compounded and 59 cases against 108 persons remained pending at the close of the year.

Results.

140. No rewards were sanctioned in the year under report. One Ranger and two Guards were dismissed, three Foresters were fined and one Ranger and one Head-Guard were degraded for misconduct.

Rewards and Punishments.

141. The health of the staff in general was normal.

142. The patrol staff consisted of one Forester, two Head Guards and 14 guards. The staff worked in the Sadar, Sonamura and Bilonia Divisions.

Patrol Staff.

143. On the recommendation of the Assam Forest Enquiry Committee, the Government of Assam was pleased to abolish the fee charged for the transit pass issued in exchange of the State *Bhatial*, and to decide that forest produce from the Tripura State need not be taken for examination to the Government revenue stations at Rajapur and Loirpoa in the Sylhet Forest Division. The Assam Government also accepted the recommendation of the Forest Enquiry Committee that axe-cut marks in drift timber exported from the State should be recognised up to 31st March, 1930, pending introduction of hammer marks by the State. The above decisions of the Assam Government minimised the difficulties that were being experienced in the previous years in connection with the export of forest produce from the State into the Sylhet District.

General.

144. The Naib Dewan was out on tour for 86 days in the year under report.

Tour.

IV. Trade and Manufacture.

145. The principal exports were timber, forest produce of various kinds, cotton, oil-seeds (*til* and mustard seed), paddy, jute, tea, rice and *Gur* (molasses). Some homespun cotton fabrics manufactured by the hillpeople, especially the Manipuris, were also exported. The principal exports for the year under review and of the previous year are shewn below :—

	1338 T. E.	1339 T. E.
Cotton ...	59,309 maunds,	69,710 maunds.
Til	30,713 „	33,006 „
Mustard seeds	19,545 „	23,080 „
Jute... ...	80,394 „	82,250 „

146. Altogether 10,13,109 lbs., 10,96,045 lbs. and 14,02,725 lbs. of tea were exported in 1337 T. E., 1338 T. E. and 1339 T. E. respectively.

147. The principal imports were clothes and yarns, salt, oils (kerosine and mustard), petrol, pulses, chillies, tobacco, sugar, flour, spices, arecanuts, books and stationery. The industries worth mention were manufacture of cotton fabrics by the hillpeople and the Manipuris; cane and bamboo baskets, mats and sieves by Tripuras; and dug-outs, bowls and plates of wood by the Reangs and Chakmas; also *Gur* (molasses) by both hillpeople and Bengalees.

V. Public Works.

148. Hony. Lieutenant J. N. Bhaduri, B. A., B. E. continued as State Engineer during the year. The Dewan-Shashan was personally in charge of the Public Works Department.

Charge.

149. An Improvement Committee with Dewan B. K. Sen Bahadur, Dewan-Shashan, as President and 7 other high officials as members, and one of them, Babu Pramada Ranjan Bhattacharjee, Deputy Manager, Chakla Roshnabad Estates, as Secretary, was appointed by His Highness during the year to draw up a scheme for works of improvement, mainly relating to Public Works. The Committee held a meeting on 28. 8. 39 T. E. in the presence of His Highness and formulated a scheme for improvement works entailing a total expenditure of 52 lacs to be carried out in 16 years with the expenditure distributed over 20 years. This scheme was kept in view so far as possible in drawing up the budget for the following year.

Improvement Committee.

150. The total expenditure on Public Works amounted to Rs. 4,67,541 against Rs. 3,51,512, out of which Rs. 2,71,692 represents original improvement works under the following heads :—

Expenditure.

(1)	Buildings ...	...	Rs. 1,83,559
(2)	Roads and Bridges	...	„ 56,334
(3)	Miscellaneous works	...	„ 25,306
(4)	Water Supply ...	...	„ 6,493

151. The total expenditure of the year including the above items, but excluding permanent establishment charges, may be also similarly detailed as follows :—

(1)	Building Works	...	Rs. 3,16,007
(2)	Roads and Bridges	...	„ 81,994
(3)	Water Supply and Tanks		„ 12,975
(4)	Miscellaneous Works	...	„ 28,397

152. The cantonment town and buildings made substantial progress during the year and a number of buildings were completed.

Cantonment.

153. The Minister's Office building also made good progress and was approaching completion about the close of the year.

Central Office Building.

154. Among the road works of the year may be mentioned

Roads.

(1) The Mogra Diversion Road.

(2) The widening of the Bishalgarh Road.

(3) The Kamalpur Kulai Haor Road.

155. In pursuance of a policy inaugurated, as a measure for giving a permanent shape to *kacha* works, a number of public buildings were supplied with C. I. Roofing while some godowns and other large buildings with similar roofing and iron posts were constructed. The total number of such works was 18.

C. I. Roofing.

7

Water supply.

156. A number of tanks were excavated during the year in the interior, and some tube wells—both at *Ṣadar* and *Mofussil* sunk for drinking purposes. An experiment to sink *pucca* wells at a moderate cost having proved successful, the question of supplying such wells on an extensive scale in the *Mofussil* is under consideration of the Department.

CHAPTER V—REVENUE AND FINANCES.

I. Revenue.

157. The total collections in the year were Rs. 18,78,321 against Rs. 19,46,421 in the previous year. The details of income under different heads with all variations are given in the statement below :—

Serial number.	Heads of Revenue.	1339 T.E.	1338 T.E.	As compared with 1338 T.E.		Remarks.
				Increase.	Decrease.	
1.	Land Revenue	6,43,315	6,08,942	34,373	—	
2.	Rents of markets	7,662	7,813	—	151	
3.	Family Tax in the hills	58,761	65,221	—	6,460	
4.	Toll on forest produce	4,83,868	5,97,080	—	1,13,212	
5.	Do. Do. on the Feni River	38,406	35,382	3,024	—	
6.	Elephant & buffalo grazing Mehal	7,427	8,530	—	1,103	
7.	Thatching grass Mehal	7,960	7,990	—	30	
8.	Reserved *Sal* trees	2,351	4,173	—	1,822	
9.	Tax on cotton and oil-seeds ...	1,47,055	1,50,241	—	3,186	
10.	Royalty on elephants caught ...	17,114	16,682	432	—	
11.	Adda Mehal	24,259	24,163	96	—	
12.	Excise	96,479	92,718	3,761	—	
13.	Stamps and Court-fees	1,06,120	89,692	16,428	—	
14.	Law and Justice (Fines)... ...	4,227	4,459	—	232	
15.	Process fees	17,897	15,089	2,808	—	
16.	Registration	14,865	15,202	—	337	
17.	Jail	1,683	3,664	—	1,981	
18.	Cattle pounds	6,187	5,980	207	—	
19.	Nazars	60,824	44,064	16,760	—	
20.	Agriculture	—	—	—	—	
21.	Education...	16,909	8,518	8,391	—	
22.	Tea Export duty	9,636	17,107	—	7,471	
23.	Jute Export duty	31,123	30,857	266		
24.	Recovery of personal advances	6,996	6,546	450	—	
25.	Recovery of personal loans ...	4,053	2,365	1,688	—	
26.	Interest on bank deposits... ..	2,447	18,733	—	16,286	
27.	Miscellaneous	60,697	65,210	—	4,513	
	Total	18,78,321	19,46,421	88,684	1,56,784	Net decrease—Rs. 68,100.

Net Decrease.

158. It will be seen that there was an increase in respect of 13 heads of income aggregating Rs. 88,684 against a decrease in 13 heads amounting to Rs. 1,56,784, which resulted in a net decrease of Rs. 68,100.

Forest Revenue.

159. The principal item contributing to the decrease was "Toll on Forest Produce" which alone accounted for Rs. 1,13,212. As already explained in the connected chapter, the fall-off was solely due to the all-round trade depression and

failure of demand owing to the prevailing distress among the border British subjects.

Tea Duty.

160. The decline under "Tea Duty" was due to insufficient prices obtained inspite of larger exports, the duty being levied on sale-proceeds, as also to a large amount assessed having fallen in arrear.

Increase.

161. Land Revenue shows a satisfactory increase of Rs. 34,373, while under Stamps and Courtfees, *Nazars*, and Education, increases amounting to Rs. 16,428, Rs. 16,760 and Rs. 8,391 reepectively, are noticeable.

162. The increase under Land Revenue may rather be ascribed to increased demand than to better collection, though special steps for realisation of arrears under the head, undertaken during the year, no doubt contributed substantially to it. The increase under *Nazars* was due to a more extensive programme of resettlement work having been gone through. That under Stamps and Courtfees was mainly due to the introduction of the new Stamp and Courtfees Act, and the consequent increase in the rates of courtfees in some cases. The increase under Education is apparent only, being the result of a change of policy and the inclusion of the income from school fees in the general receipts of the year and the abolition of "the School Fund" system under which it used to be controlled by the school authorities separately.

II. Finances.

163. A consolidated statement showing the financial transactions of the State and the attached Zemindaries, as compared with those of the previous year is given below :—

Receipts.

164. It will be seen that the total receipts from all sources including deposits, loans, as well as law charges and advances recovered, amounted to Rs. 34,37,701 against Rs. 33,05,772. With the opening balance of Rs. 9,60,673, the total sum available for expenditure was Rs. 43,98,374 as against Rs. 43,29,437 in the preceding year. The actual income of the State and Zemindaries, including deposits and loans, was however Rs. 30,09,502 against Rs. 31,02,911, showing a decrease of Rs. 93,409.

Expenditure.

165. The total expenditure during the year amounted to Rs. 34,23,952 against Rs. 33,68,764 in the previous year, showing an increase of Rs. 55,188 which was mainly attributable to larger expenditure on improvement works under P. W. D. budget. The closing balance at the end of the year under review was Rs. 9,74,422 against Rs. 9,60,673. Of this balance, Rs. 2,07,708 was in cash in the treasuries, Rs. 1,36,222 in the banks and Rs. 6,30,492 in loans and advances.

Receipts.	1338 T. E.	1339 T. E.
1. Opening balance :–		
(1) State	6,94,785	6,56,488
(2) Zemindaries ...	3,28,880	3,04,185
Total ...	10,23,665	9,60,673
2. Income :—		
(1) State	19,46,421	18,78,321
(2) Zemindaries ...	10,99,010	10,21,483
Total ...	30,45,431	28,99,804
3. Law charges recovered :—		
(1) Zemindaries ...	47,947	46,302
4. Refunds and compensation for lands acquired :—		
(1) Zemindaries ...	9,533	63,396
5 Deposits :—		
(1) State	60,446	1,06,979
(2) Zemindaries ...	42,415	58,220
Total ...	1,02,861	1,65,199
6. Loans received :—		
(1) State	1,00,000	2,63,000
GRAND TOTAL ...	43,29,437	43,98,374

Expenditure.	1338 T. E.	1339 T. E.
1. General Administration charges :—		
(a) State	5,45,147	6,11,787
(b) Zemindaries :—		
1. Cost of management	1,54,961	1,54,406
2. Cost of litigation	1,09,287	1,00,610
	2,64,248	2,55,016
Total ...	8,09,395	8,66,803
2. Revenue and Taxes on account of the Zemindaries	2,70,852	2,71,413
3. Public Works—(a) State	3,55,337	4,74,652
(b) Zemindaries ...	58,064	76,651
Total ...	4,13,401	5,51,303
4. Electric Light—State	24,727	17,741
5. Municipality—State	9,915	11,234
6. Education—(a) State	1,33,106	1,41,110
(b) Zemindaries	10,992	11,356
Total ...	1,44,098	1,52,466
7. Medical and Sanitation :—		
(a) State	73,725	71,497
(b) Zemindaries	12,329	13,600
Total ...	86,054	85,097
8. Survey and Settlement—(a) State ...	19,391	21,923
(b) Zemindaries ...	1,063	1,346
Total ...	20,454	23,269
9. Agriculture, Commerce and Industries—State	4,129	11,903
10. Religious Expenses—(a) State ...	63,713	58,621
(b) Zemindaries ...	6,635	6,408
Total ...	70,348	65,029
11. Sultanat—State	55,181	56,850
12. Purchase of Land Tenures :—		
(a) State	3,500	502
(b) Zemindaries	4,270	9,504
Total ...	7,770	10,006
13. Pension and Gratuity—(a) State ...	34,636	41,051
(b) Zemindaries ...	5,091	7,120
Total ...	39,727	48,171
14. Ordinary *Sansar* charges :—		
(a) His Highness's own and the late Maharaja's family	82,300	94,772
(b) Other branches of the Raj family...	1,35,741	1,39,625
(c) Thakurs	31,887	33,918
(d) *Sansar* office establishment ...	11,037	10,551
(e) Miscellaneous	86,675	94,003
Total ...	3,47,640	3,72,869
15. Charity and Donation :—		
(a) State	63,985	48,900
(b) Zemindaries	35,481	14,701
Total ...	99,466	63,601
16. His Highness's Nij Tahabil :—		
(a) State	1,20,000	1,20,000
(b) Zemindaries	3,00,000	2,00,000
Total ...	4,20,000	3,20,000
17. His Highness's tour	54,000	73,725
18. Payment of liabilities and deposits :—		
(a) State	91,057	83,538
(b) Zemindaries	9,202	31,168
Total ...	1,00,259	1,14,706
19. Miscellaneous—(a) State	6,790	6,984
(b) Zemindaries ...	27,352	17,775
Total ...	34,142	24,759
20. Advances to employees :—		
(a) State	13,467	7,377
(b) Zemindaries...	2,481	2,911
Total ...	15,948	10,288
21. Expenditure in connection with H. H.'s Marriage, Investiture, Installation etc.—State	3,41,258	87,219
22. Investment—(a) State	—	5,500
(b) Zemindaries ...	—	1,80,000
Total ...	—	1,85,500
Total Expenditure ...	33,68,764	34,23,952
26. Closing Balance :—		
(a) State		
In Cash	1,50,161	1,17,113
At Bank	29,374	8,253
In bonds and advances	4,76,953	4,69,979
Total ...	6,56,488	5,95,345
(b) Zemindaries :—		
In Cash	72 066	90,595
At Bank	1,10,630	1,27,969
In bonds and advances	1,21,489	1,60,513
Total ...	3,04,185	3,79,077
Total of State & Zemindaries' balances ...	9,60,673	9,74,422
Total of State & Zemindari's expenditure ...	33,68,764	34,23,952
GRAND TOTAL ...	43,29,437	43,98,374

166. The noticeable variations in expenditure are explained below :—

i. Administration Charges :—

State—The main reasons for the increase were (*a*) Re-organisation of the State Military forces involving an increase of Rs. 36,618 in the running expenses; (*b*) Opening of new Departments viz., Publicity, Reclamation and Immigration; (*c*) Extra provision for a whole-time Chief Judge on a higher pay; (*d*) Kheda expenses under *khas* management; (*e*) Usual grade increments of pay allowed to officers and the ministerial staff and (*f*) Increased expenditure for the management of the jails and the training expenses of a police cadet.

i. (*b*) Cost of litigation :—

Zemindaries—The decrease was due to the decrease in the number of suits instituted.

iii. Public Works :—

State—The increase was mainly due to (1) construction of a military cantonment at Kunjaban (2) the extension of the Central Administration Office building (3) the construction of the Kamalpur and Mogra roads (4) improvement of the Bishalgarh road and (5) the acquisition of lands for improvement works in the capital.

Zemindaries—The increase was mainly due to the repairing charges of the Ballygunge Buildings and to the payment, during the year, of the previous year's contribution to Govt. for maintenance of the Goomti Embankment.

iv. Electric Light :—

The decrease was due to an indirect cause, namely the payment of a number of arrear bills in the year previous.

v. Municipality :—

State—The increase was due to the transfer of the sanitation charges to the Municipal allotment from the Medical Budget.

vi. Education :—

State—Increased expenditure in primary education owing to an increase in the number of Pathsalas, the introduction of the grade system of pay to the teaching staff, the increase in the number of boarders in the Kumar Boarding at Comilla, and the inclusion of the pay of occasional extra staff of the High English schools in the general expenditure, instead of in local school funds, as previously done, account for the increase.

vii. Medical and Sanitation :—

State—The decrease has been explained in (v) above.

viii Survey and Settlement :—

State—The increase was attributable to a larger programme of survey operations during the year.

ix Agriculture Commerce and industries :—

State—The increase was due to the formation of the new Department of Commerce and Industries.

x. Religious Expenditure :—

State—The decrease was due to economies effected in certain religious rites.

xii. PURCHASE OF LAND TENURES :—

STATE—Land acquisition charges were incorporated in the expenditure on the connected improvement works, and hence the decrease, as compared with the previous year.

ZEMINDARIES—The increase was due to purchase of lands at Feni, Sreemangal and other places.

xiii. PENSIONS AND GRATUITIES :—

STATE—The increase was partly due to new pensions and gratuities sanctioned during the year under review and partly to the transfer to this head of certain old pensions which had previously been paid from the Sansar allotment.

xiv. ORDINARY SANSAR CHARGES :—

(*a*) His Highness's own and the late Maharaja's family :—

The increase was mainly due to new provision made for Her Highness the Maharanee Saheba.

(*b*) and (*c*) Other branches of Raj family and Thakurs :—

The increase was due to the monthly allowances being enhanced in some cases.

(*d*) Miscellaneous :—

The increase was mainly due to the medical treatment of the late Fifth Maharanee and to the extra expenses incurred in connection with Her Highness the Dowager Maharanee's journey to Bombay and other places.

xv. CHARITY AND DONATION :—

The decline both in the State and the Zemindaries was due to the following unusual payments in the previous year which did not occur in the year under review :—

(i) Payment of contribution to the Chamber of Princes from the State.

(ii) Payment of Charities on the occasion of H. H's visit to Comilla during the Punyaha Ceremony.

(iii) Contribution towards improvement of the Comilla Hospital and the repairing charges of Prince J. M. Deb Barman Bahadur's house.

xviii. PAYMENT OF LIABILITIES AND DEPOSITS :—

The expenditure during the year under review mostly represents repayment of deposits.

The marked variation in the figures of the Zemindaries as compared with the previous year was due to the withdrawal of the Raj Central Bank and *Devatter* deposits.

xix. MISCELLANEOUS :—

Extra expenditure had to be incurred on account of His Highness's visit to Comilla on the occasion of the *Punyaha* in the preceding year, which accounted for the decrease in the year under review.

xxii. INVESTMENT :—

Rs. 5,500 was invested in tea shares from the General Revenue of the State and Rs. 1,80,000 was paid as loan from the surplus cash of the Zemindary for the State improvement works.

167. Two statements comparing the receipts and expenditure of the State and of the Zemindaries showing the respective revised estimates are given in the appendices XXVI and XXVII.

168. In the State the actual receipts fell short of the original Budget Estimate and the revised estimate by Rs. 1,66,700 and Rs. 60,700 respectively. This shortage was mainly confined to export duties and due partly to the slump in the jute and cotton markets and partly to the general unfavourable economic condition all round. The Budget allotment of expenditure had thus to be curtailed which, in the end brought in a saving of Rs. 1,17,702, just leaving a cash balance of Rs. 1, 25,366.

169. In the Zemindaries, there was, as compared with the Revised Estimates, an increase of Rs. 2,057 under the receipts and a saving of Rs. 71,362 under expenditure. These variations resulted in an increase in the closing cash balance.

170. Babu J. C. Maulik, Naib Dewan, continued to be in charge of the Accounts and Treasury Departments as before.

CHAPTER VI—MEDICAL.

171. With the addition of two new dispensaries during the year under review, the State maintained 20 dispensaries—the V. M. Hospital at the capital included.

172. The total number of new patients treated in the above hospitals and dispensaries together with their daily average, as compared with the previous year, is shewn in the following table :—

PATIENTS.	1338 T. E.			1339 T. E		
	Outdoor.	Indoor.	Total.	Outdoor.	Indoor.	Total.
	1,01,111	423	1,01,534	1,06,839	478	1,07,317
Daily average	277·01	1·15	278·16	291·90	1·30	293·20

Out-door attendance.

173. The out-patients (new and old) totalled 1,90,190 as against 1,78,833 of the year before, the daily average being 519·64 against 489·87.

In-door attendance.

174. With the last year's balance of 17, the in-patients numbered 478 as against 423 in the preceding year. Of them 313 were cured, 133 were relieved or otherwise discharged, 17 died and 15 remained under treatment at the close of the year.

Surgical operations.

175. The total number of operations performed was 1217 with 23 major cases. The previous year's figures were 1,259 and 19 respectively.

Police Cases.

176. Altogether 165 cases were admitted during the year as against 173 in the year before of which post-mortem cases numbered 13 against 15.

177. The number of new patients seeking out-door relief in the V. M. Hospital totalled 14,972 against 13,857, the daily average (new and old) being 85·00 against 68·57. This shows an increase on the figures for the previous year. Similarly the number of in-patients rose from 393 in the preceding year to 453 in the year under report with the daily average of 17·92 against 17·11. Of them 293 were cured, 128 were relieved or otherwise discharged, 17 died and 15 remained under treatment at the end of the year. The total expenditure in the V. M. Hospital stood at Rs. 10,296 against Rs. 9,495 in the year previous.

V. M. Hospital.

178. The post of a single Kabiraj was continued in this Department during the year under review. 44 patients were treated by him against 38 in the previous year. Rs. 2,680-2-9 was spent on account of his salary and the cost of medicines as against Rs. 2,676-10-6 in the year before.

Ayurvedic Department.

179. As before the staff in this Department consisted of one State Homœopath, Dr. Hira Lall Banerjee, H. M. B. and his two assistants. 13003 new patients were treated by them during the year as against 15096 in the preceding year, the daily average (new and old) being 60·84 against 94·28. The total expenditure in this Department amounted to Rs. 6,065 against Rs. 5,638 of the previous year.

Homœopathic Department.

180. Altogether 7,695 persons were successfully vaccinated out of 9,710, as against 7,551 and 9,221 respectively of the previous year. As before, the inspecting staff consisted of 2 permanent small-pox doctors and 2 temporary inspectors while 30 licensed and 1 paid vaccinators were employed during the year. The total expenditure amounted to Rs. 1,567-10-3 as against Rs. 1,414 in the preceding year.

Vaccination.

181. During the year under review 177 patients came under treatment at the Capital and in the moffussil dispensaries, as against 128 in the preceding year. Of them 87 were cured, 3 died and the remainder left during the course of treatment.

Kala-azar.

182. Cholera visited some parts of the State in a rather virulent form, especially in Dharmanagar and Amarpur Divisions, and reaped a more or less heavy toll amongst the inhabitants before vaccination could be resorted to. So far as reported, 152 deaths took place out of 283 attacks. Small-pox also broke out in some parts of the State with 165 seizures and 12 deaths, as against 283 and 65 respectively in the previous year. Out of the above, the 2 small-pox doctors treated 47 with 4 deaths. The total cost on this head amounted to Rs. 574-9-3 as against Rs. 275-8-6 of the previous year.

Public Health.

183. Dr. M. M. Majumdar, L. M. S., was the Chief Medical Officer with Dr. S. K. Datta, L. M. S., and Dr. A. Sen Gupta, M. B., as his assistants. Besides, a staff of subordinate medical men, 2 mid-wives worked during the year. The lady doctor was away on leave for most part of the year before her retirement.

Staff.

184. Dr. M. M. Majumdar inspected 7 dispensaries during the year and was out for 24 days in all.

Tour.

185. The total expenditure incurred for the Medical Department in the year under report stood at Rs: 71,497 as against 73,725 of the previous year. The decrease is attributable to the transfer of the expenses on sanitation to the Municipal Department.

Total expenditure.

CHAPTER VII—PUBLIC INSTRUCTION.

186. Mr. S. C. Deb Barman M. A. (Harvard), Senior Naib Dewan, continued to be in charge of the Education Department.

Charge.

187. The total number of schools during the year under report was 170 against 168 in the previous year, and the total numerical strength 7,401 against 7,345, excluding 241 pupils reading in private institutions numbering 11, as against 52 students in 2 institutions.

Number of Schools.

188. There were 5 H. E. Schools as before and one Branch H. E. School in the State, *viz:*—the Umakanta Academy at Agartala, the Radhakishore Institution at Kailashahar, the Brajendrakishore Institution at Bilonia, the Birbikram Institution at Dharmanagar, the Navadwipchandra Institution at Sonamura, and the Branch H. E. School at Udaipur. All the H. E. Schools (except the Branch H. E. School) are affiliated to the Calcutta University. The total number of pupils in all these institutions was 1,738 against 1,589 in the previous year, and the average daily attendance stood at 1,333·48 against 1,182·54.

H. E. Schools.

189. Agartala, the capital of the State, continued to be a centre for the Matriculation Examination for the year 1930. Only the State H. E. Schools were allowed to send up candidates to this centre. The Examination was conducted under the direct control and supervision of the Dewan. The Department looked after the convenience of the candidates coming from mofussil, in respect of accommodation and other necessary matters.

Matriculation centre.

190. Altogether 62 candidates were sent up for the Matriculation Examination against 77 in the previous year. One of the candidates sat for the examination on the first two days only but was not in a position to appear on the subsequent days owing to illness. The details of the result are noted below :—

	No. sent up.	Passed.	1st Division.	2nd Division.	3rd Division.
1. U. K. Academy	17	8	4	4	0
2. R. K. Institution	11	8	4	2	2
3. B. K. Institution	16	10	2	6	2
4. B. B. Institution	8	6	1	5	0
5. N. Ch. Institution	10	5	2	3	0
Total ...	62	37	13	20	4

191. Two boys—one of the Dharmanagar B. B. Institution and the other of the Sonamura N. C. Institution—got 'letters' in Mathematics (compulsory) and another boy of the Bilonia B. K. Institution in Sanskrit (compulsory). The results on the whole, were not satisfactory.

M. E. Schools for boys.

192. In the year under review, there were 7 Middle English Schools for boys with 841 pupils on the rolls, against 8 Schools with 990 pupils in the previous year. The average daily attendance was 685·36 against 760·78.

M. E. Schools for girls.

193. There was one M. E. School for girls at Agartala, namely, the Maharani Tulsibati Girls' School, the numerical strength of which was 56 as against 66 in the previous year and the average daily attendance 39·56 against 48·30. The statistical figures from 1336 T. E. disclose a gradual decrease in the number on the rolls of this school. By special permission of this Department, some girls were allowed to continue higher studies in this school under the tuition of the Head Mistress, who is a graduate of the Calcutta University. A motor bus was maintained by the Department as before, for the conveyance of the girls.

H. V. Schools.

194. There was only one Higher Vernacular School for boys as in the previous year, with 71 students on the roll as against 77, while the average daily attendance was 64·67 against 53·51.

L. V. Schools.

195. The total number of Lower Vernacular Schools for boys was 23 against 22 in the previous year. The total numerical strength was 1,384 against 1,239 and the average daily attendance 996·88 against 893·87 in the previous year. In some of these schools boys and girls read together.

Pathshalas for boys.

196. There were 113 Pathshalas for boys against 112 in the previous year. The total number of boys was 2,773 against 2,830 and the average daily attendance 2,106·45 against 2,311·36. In some of these schools, boys and girls read together. Under special orders of the Education Department some boys in some of these institutions were allowed to read the Lower Vernacular standard.

Pathshalas for girls.

197. There were 10 Pathshalas for girls in the year under review against the same number in the previous year. The total numerical strength was 302 as against 319 and the average daily attendance 217·25 against 223·10 in the previous year. In some of these schools, some girls were allowed, under special order, to read the Lower Vernacular standard.

Scholarship Examinations.

198. Altogether 605 candidates appeared at the different scholarship examinations of this State against 478 in the preceding year. Of these, 446 including 42 girls came out successful. The result on the whole, particularly that of the Khowai M. E. School, was found to be satisfactory as in the previous year. 35 students including 6 girls passed the M. E. Examination and 4 including 1 girl passed the H. V. Examination. In the L. V. Examination the number of successful candidates was 112 including 9 girls, and in the Pathsala Examination the number was 295 including

26 girls. On the results of the examinations, 17 boys and 5 girls were awarded monthly scholarships varying from Rs. 2 to Rs. 5 tenable for two to four years.

199. In the year under review, there were, as before, 9 schools for special training, consisting of 3 Sanskrit 'Tols, 5 Madrassas and Moktabs, and 1 Artisan school. The Sanskrit 'Tols' had 31 students on the rolls against 34 in the previous year and the average daily attendance was 24·62 against 27·42. The *Rajakiya Sanskrit Vidyalaya* at Agartala sent up 4 candidates for the Government Sanskrit Intermediate and Preliminary Examinations against 1 in the previous year, and 3 candidates for different sanskrit examinations—Title and Preliminary—of the Saraswat Samaj, against 2 in the previous year. The Madrassas and Moktabs had 186 students on the rolls as against 183 in the previous year and the average daily attendance was 118·56 against 104·37. The Woodburn Artisan School had 19 boys on the roll against 18 and the average daily attendance was 9·58 against 6·25 in the previous year. Under orders of His Highness, the control of the Woodburn Artisan School was transferred from the Education Department just before the close of the year under report and placed with the Chief Secretary in the new Department of Commerce and Industries. His Highness was graciously pleased to award special stipends from the Sansar Department to 4 students, who attended the smithy class of the school.

Schools for special Training.

200. The comparative statement below will show the number of non-Bengalee students receiving education in the several schools of the State :—

Non-Bengalee students.

Serial number.	Nationality.	Number of students.		Remarks.
		Past year.	Present year.	
1.	Rajkumars	9	7	
2.	Thakurs	176	324	
3.	Manipuris	660	574	
4.	Tripuras	753	671	
5.	Reangs	42	14	
6.	Kukis	18	2	
7.	Chakmas	0	0	
8.	Lushais	0	5	
9.	Others...	88	63	
	Total	1,746	1,660	

201. The policy of holding reward examinations for hill boys was continued and 199 boys appeared at the examination against 209 in the previous year.

Reward Examination.

202. Placed under the charge of a graduate teacher, the two Maharajkumars continued their studies in the Rajkumar College at Raipur in the Central Provinces as before. Under orders of His Highness, however, arrangement for the education of the elder Maharajkumar was made at Agartala in the middle of the year and consequently he did not go back to Raipur after the Puja holidays. The progress and health of the Maharajkumars were satisfactory. The Maharajkumaris received their education as before under a graduate lady teacher and a pundit.

Education of Princes & Princesses.

Education of other Kumars.

203. Kumar Bepin Behari Deb Barman and Kumar Bankim Behari Deb Barman continued their studies in the Ashutosh College, Calcutta.

Kumar Boarding House at Comilla.

204. The Kumar Boarding House had 15 inmates, of whom 13 were from the different branches of the Ruling family and the remaining two were Rana Bahadurs related to the Raj family. 11 of the inmates were reading in the Zilla School, Comilla. Their results at the annual examination of the school were satisfactory. The Kumars were under the charge of a Superintending Tutor, who, in addition to his tutorial work, looked after the management of the boarding. Two other private tutors including a pundit, were engaged for coaching some of the Kumars in the morning and evening.

The Day School for the young Kumars.

205. Some young Kumars having been admitted into the Kumar Boarding House at Comilla, it was found unnecessary to retain a regular establishment for the Day School at Agartala. There was only one Kumar receiving instruction at the school against 3 in the previous year, and one tutor was engaged for coaching him. The number however increased to 4 towards the close of the year.

Education of Thakur Boys.

206. 12 Thakur boys were awarded stipends from the Education Department, the respective courses of studies taken up are noted below against their names.

1. Surendra Chandra Deb Barman—I. A. Class, Comilla Victoria College.
2. Promode Ranjan Deb Barman—I. Sc. Class, Comilla Victoria College.
3. Harisankar Deb Barman—I. A. Class, Comilla Victoria College.
4. Hiran Kumar Deb Barman—B. A. Class, Comilla Victoria College.
5. Binode Behari Deb Barman—B. A. Class, Comilla Victoria College.
6. Suresh Chandra Deb Barman—Government School of Art, Calcutta.
7. Ajit Bandhu Deb Barman—I. A. Class, Ripon College, Calcutta.
8. Brajendra Chandra Deb Barman—I. A. Class, Ripon College, Calcutta.
9. Sushil Krishna Deb Barman—I. Sc. Class, Ripon College, Calcutta.
10. Harendra Chandra Deb Barman—Bengal Forest School, Kurseong. (completed the course successfully).
11. Amaredra Chandra Deb Barman—Martin's Ry. Workshop, Howrah. (for 2 months only).
12. Niranjan Chandra Deb Barman—Carmichael Medical College. (For 3 months only). (Passed the Final M. B. Examination from the Calcutta University).

Thakur Boarding House at Agartala.

207. During the early part of the year under report, the number of boarders in the Thakur Boarding House was 35, which became 29 in the latter part, against 34 in the previous year. 10 boarders only were successful in the last annual examinations of the U. K. Academy. 3 boarders

appeared at the last Matriculation Examination, 1930, of whom 2 came out successful—both passing in the 1st. Division. They secured the first and the 2nd place among the successful candidates of the U. K. Academy. The staff consisted of one Guardian Superintendent, one graduate Resident Tutor, one Assistant Tutor, and one Manager and Tutor. The average daily attendance of the boarders was 23·50 against 27·40 in the previous year.

Tripura Boarding House at Agartala.

208. There were altogether 18 boarders in the Tripura Boarding House against 14 in the previous year. Out of these 18 boarders, 10 received free boarding and lodging, 4 were partially helped with their boarding expenses for 8 months, and the remaining 4 received no allowance for messing. A Superintending Tutor looked after the boys as well as the boarding management as before.

Tripura Boarding House at Khowai.

209. There were 14 boarders in the Tripura Boarding House at Khowai against the same number in the previous year, all receiving free boarding and lodging. Two tutors were appointed to coach the boys both in the morning and in the evening, and one of the tutors was engaged to look after the boarding management.

Schools for convicts and for Soldiers.

210. Under the order of His Highness, Lower Primary Schools were opened in the Agartala Central Jail and in the soldiers' barracks—thus affording illiterate convicts and soldiers opportunities for study. The Primary School of the Central Jail reported that some candidates were expected to appear at the next scholarship examination.

Night School at Agartala.

211. To popularise adult education, a night school was opened by the local Students' Association, where traders and labouring classes received instruction in the evening. This institution received a suitable monthly grant from the Department.

Special Stipends.

212. 31 boys were awarded special stipends in the year under review, of whom some boys read in different schools of this State and some others, whose names are given below, continued their studies elsewhere in different colleges and technical institutions :—

1. Chandrahas Singha—3rd. Year B. L. Class, Dacca.
2. Babuchand Singha—2nd. Year " " "
3. Kuleswar Singha—I. A. Class (2nd. Year), M. C. College, Sylhet.
4. Mahendra Kumar Roy—3rd. Year B. L. Class, Dacca.
5. Swadesh Ranjan Sen—Ahsanullah Engineering School, Dacca.
6. Sonachand Singha—I. A. Class (1st Year), Comilla Victoria College.
7. Manoranjan Banerjee—I. A, Class (1st. Year), B. M. College, Barisal.
8. Mafizer Rahman—I. A. Class (2nd. Year), Feni College.

Inspection Work.

213. Mr. S. C. Deb Barman, M. A. (Harvard), Senior Naib-Dewan of the Education Department, inspected the Rajkumar Boarding at Comilla twice in the year under report and inspected also the schools at Bilonia, Kailashahar and Sadar Divisions—the tour, on the whole, comprising 21 days.

214. The Sub-Inspectors of Schools visited all the schools within their respective jurisdictions. Their inspection work was satisfactory.

215. Maharajkumar Narottamkishore Deb Barman continued to be the Librarian of the Birchandra Library at Agartala which was maintained in two separate sections as before, viz :—(1) The English section, located at the Ujjayanta Palace, and (2) the vernacular section in the building, situated near the local H. E. School. The latter section was open to the public. The number of English books (including foreign literature) was 5,025 against 4,974 in the previous year, and the number of Bengali and Sanskrit books was 2008 against 1,981. There were 5 daily newspapers against 4 in the previous year, 3 weeklies against the same number, and 9 monthly magazines against 9. In the year under report, the average daily attendance in the public section of the library was 14·2 against 14·5 in the previous year, but the total number of books issued to the public was 3,925 against 2,707.

Library.

216. The total expenditure incurred in the Education Department, in the year under report, amounted to Rs. 1,41,110 against Rs. 1,33,106. Some of the more important details of expenditure are noted below :—

Expenditure.

1.	Primary Education	Rs.	25,331
2.	Secondary Education	,,	50,458
3.	Schools for Special Training	,,	3,388
4.	Boarding Institutions for Thakur Boys ...	,,	9,828
5.	Education of Kumars & Kumaris	,,	26,481
6.	Scholarships and Stipends	,,	9,382
7.	Library	,,	2,894
8.	Tripura Boarding	,,	1,348
9.	Miacellaneous	,,	9,648
		Rs.	1,38,758
10.	Grain Allowance	,,	2,352
		Rs.	1,41,110

217. In modification of the previous policy of payment of only a fixed contribution to the State from the funds of school fees realised, the balance of which was controlled by the schools, it was settled that all such receipts would be paid into the State Treasury, and all expenditure met previously from School Funds, would be met from the Education Budget.

Income.

CHAPTER VIII—ZEMINDARIES.

Chakla Roshnabad Estates.

218. The management of His Highness's Zemindaries in British India remained with Rai J. C. Sen Bahadur, B. A., B. C. S., upto the 15th Jaistha, 1339 T. E. and thereafter with Dewan Bahadur B. K. Sen, M. A., B. L. who relieved him.

Management.

219. A new post of Deputy Manager was created at Comilla and the Assistant Manager of the Central Division was placed under him. The other three Divisions continued to be in charge of Assistant Managers.

Administrative changes.

220. The year began under the shadow of various adverse circumstances, specially heavy and untimely floods, which caused extensive breaches in the Gumti embankment inundating a vast area of the Zemindaries, with the result that the tenants in general were in serious distress, while the slump in the jute market added to the pinch of the situation. Relief operations were organised in co-operation with the Government authorities and occasionally with other public bodies, and a portion of the sum of Rupees one lac, placed by His Highness promptly at the disposal of the Dewan Shashan and Manager, was utilised in the Zemindaries. The total amount debited in this head in the Zemindaries during the year amounted to Rs. 36,000, paid to the affected tenants in loans and gratuitous relief. Loans were also issued from the Tippera Raj Central Co-operative Bank in the affected areas to the extent of Rs. 54,000.

221. A most important event of the year was the visit of His Excellency the Governor of Bengal to Comilla on the 22nd July 1929 during which Sir Stanley and Lady Jackson very kindly occupied the Dharmasagar House.

The Governor's visit.

222. The gross revenue demand of the year was Rs. 10,14,623 against Rs. 10,07,985 in the previous year.

Demand.

223. The total receipts amounted to Rs. 11,89,401 (including Rs. 35,777 on account of the Tripura Raj Central Co-operative Bank and Rs. 1,188 on account of *Devottar Mahals*) against Rs. 11,98,905 in the previous year. The decline in collection was mainly due to the prevailing distress among tenants.

Receipts.

224. The total expenditure in the year under review was 11,14,509 including adjustment of old advances, and loans issued to the Improvement Fund in the State, against Rs. 12,23,600 in the previous year. Of this Rs. 2,71,413 was on account of Land Revenue and Cesses. The total administration charges of the Zemindaries, including Public Works and Law Charges, amounted to Rs. 3,67,912. The following other items of expenditure aggregating Rs. 4,75,184 are noticeable :—

Expenditure.

1.	Loans & advances	Rs.	2,911
2.	Donation	,,	14,701
3.	Medical Charges	,,	13,600
4.	Education Charges	,,	11,356
5.	Religious ceremonies	,,	6,408
6.	Sansar stipends...	,,	15,540
7.	Repayment of old deposits ...	,,	30,668
7.	Contribution & Loan to the State ...	,,	3,80,000
		Rs.	4,75,184

225. The result of the year's settlement operations will appear from the figures noted below :—

Settlement.

Kinds of Settlement.	Addition to Rental.		Nazar.	
1. Ry. relinquished land ...	Rs.	8	Rs.	48
2. Kaiemi & Taksisi Taluk in the Comilla Town ...	,,	76	,,	6350
3. Ordinary Town Settlement	,,	52	,,	2090
4. *Khas Patit* ,, ...	,,	1282	,,	8167
5. Enhancement of rent ...	,,	1742	,,	19803
6. Resettlement of auction purchased land ...	,,	121	,,	7652
7. Settlement of rent free holdings ...	,,	340		—
8. Taksisi Taluk in the moffisil ...	,,	76	,,	1801
9. *Ijara* settlement ...	,,	646		—
		4343		45911

226. The year's operations thus improved the rent roll by Rs. 4343 and brought in a *nazarana* of Rs. 45,911, against Rs. 2929 and Rs. 45997 respectively, in the previous year.

CHAPTER IX—MISCELLANEOUS.

227. The printing of the third part of the Rajmala (Chronicles of the State) continued during the year. Some difficulty was experienced in connection with the matter owing to the abolition of the Rajmala Press and the amalgamation of all printing work in the State Press. A machine press was indented during the year and it is hoped that when the arrangements are complete there will be a speedier issue of the publication. The expenditure for the Rajmala amounted to Rs. 5,984 against Rs. 6,790 of the previous year.

Rajmala.

228. Dewan B. K. Sen Bahadur, Dewan Shashan, was in camp for 85 days during the year, both in and outside State. This includes three visits to Calcutta on urgent business in two of which he accompanied His Highness.

Tours of high officers.

229. Manyabara Rana Bodhjung Bahadur, Chief Secretary, accompanied His Highness in all his tours and visited, besides, the Kailashahar Division for 13 days in connection with immigration work.

230. The late Babu Brajendra Kumar Chatterjee M. A., B. L., Officer-in-charge, Revenue Department, was on tour for 4 days early in the year, before his death, and his successors under the new arrangement, Mr. S. C. Dev Barman, M. A. (Harvard), Senior Naib Dewan, and Thakur Kamini Kumar Singha, Naib Dewan, were out for 10 days and 21 days respectively.

Departmental Heads.

231. Tours of other officers of the status have already been noted in the connected sections.

232. Among Divisional Officers, Thakur Rebati Mohan Deb Barman, Sadar Magistrte and Collector, toured for 36 days in his capacity of Sadar Collector, and his assistants, Thakur Jyotilal Dev Barman, B. L., and Kumar Narsingh Chandra Dev Barman, for 42 days and 58 days respectively.

Divisional Officers.

233. Babu Sasanka Bhushan Roy, M. A., Divisional Officer, Kailashahar, was out for 87 days and Babu Surendra Chandra Guha, B. A., Second Officer of the Division for 62 days.

234. In the Sonamura Division there was a transfer of officers and the two successive Divisional Officers, Thakur Kamini Kumar Singha and Thakur Lalit Mohan Dev Barman, M. A., B. L., toured for 59 days between them, while Babu Jyotirmay Ghosh, M. A., Second Officer of the place was out for 27 days.

235. In Dharmanagar, Babu Akhil Chandra Majumdar, M. A. B. L., Divisional Officer, camped for 27 days and his assistant, Babu Jogendra Lal Ganguli, B. L., for 39 days.

236. Babu Kunja Bihari Chakravarty, M. A., B. L., Divisional Officer, Udaipur, toured for 48 days. Thakur Jaysingh Dev Barman, B. L., Assistant Collector, posted under the Udaipur Officer at Amarpur was out for 21 days.

237. Babu Suresh Chandra Chakravarty, B. L., Divisional Officer, Khowai, was out for 46 days; and Thakur Gokul Chandra Dev Barman, Divisional Officer, Sabroom, for 53 days.

238. Babu Bisweswar Guha, B. A., Divisional Officer, Bilonia camped for 22 days and his assistants, Babu Sarada Charan Sarkar, B. L., and Thakur Jogesh Chandra Dev Barman, B. Com. had 7 days tour between them.

239. In the Zemindaries Babu P. R. Bhattacherjee, B. A., Deputy Manager, was in camp, in and outside his charge, for 61 days, 13 days representing tour within jurisdiction.

Zemindari Officers

240. Babu J. C. Majumdar M. A., B. L., Assistant Manager, Feni, was out for 106 days and Babu T. M. Gupta, Assistant Manager, Mogra for 72 days.

241. In the Sreemangal Division there were transfers, and the three successive Assistant Managers, Babu N. K. Chakravarty, B. L., Babu M. R. Chaudhuri, B. L., and Babu Sailesh Chandra Kar, B. L., toured for 49 days in the aggregate.

242. Though the touring of the year was, on the whole, better than that of the previous year, there is yet, in respect of some cases at least, ample room for improvement.

DATED, AGARTALA,
The 14th August, 1930.

B. K. Sen
Dewan, Shashan.

APPENDIX.

List of the principal Laws and Regulations in force in the Tripura State during 1339 T.E.

Description.	Whether adapted from British Indian Acts.	Whether introduce during the year under report.
CRIMINAL.		
1. Regulation No. III. of 1280 T. E.		
2. Regulation No. I. of 1283 T. E.		
3. Jail Regulation, 1283 T. E.		
4. Regulation No. IV. of 1283 T. E. (Cattle trespass and pound).		
5. Regulation No. III. of 1296 T. E. (Police Regulation).		
6. Act No. IV. of 1321 T. E.–Penal Laws (an amending Act)		
CIVIL.		
1. Civil Law of 1284 T. E.		
2. Rules regarding *chit* suits (small causes) 1287 and 1300 T. E.		
3. Act No. II. of 1313 T. E.—an Act for the regulation of interest on debts.		
4. Act No. II. of 1314 T. E.—Limitation Act	Partly adapted.	
5. Succession Act II of 1339 T. E.		
REVENUE.		
1. Act No. I. of 1290 T. E.—Sale Law		
2. Act No. I. of 1296 T. E.—Tenancy Act.		
3. Act No. II. of 1296 T. E.—*Abkari*		
4. Act No. II. of 1297 T. E.—Reserved forests.		
5. Act No. I. of 1304 T. E.—Duties on *til* and cotton.		
6. Act No. I. of 1306 T. E.—Registration	Do.	
7. Survey and Settlement Act, 1309 T.E.	Do.	
8. *Tuccavi* Regulation, 1310 T. E.		
9. Act No. I. of 1313 T. E.—Forests.		
10. Act No. I. of 1314 T. E.—(amending the above)		
11. A Law imposing export duty on jute and mustard-seed, 1317 T. E.		
12. Act No. II. of 1321 T.E. Ghasuri Act		
13. P. W. & Road Cess Act IV of 1339 T. E.		
MISCELLANEOUS.		
1. An Act promulgating certain rules as Law, 1283 T. E.		
2. Regulation for the record of judicial decisions &c., 1284 T. E.		
3. Municipal Regulation, 1284 T. E.		
4. Legal Practitioners' Regulation.		
5. Act No. I. of 1297 T. E.—an Act for the regulation of commissions for the examination of witnesses.		
6. Regulation against cow slaughter		
7. Rules of evidence		
8. Act I. of 1318 T. E.—Constitution of Courts—(an amending Act).		
9. Leave and allowance Rules	Do.	
10. Act No. I. of 1321 T. E.—Arms Act	Do.	
11. Act No. III. of 1321 T.E.—Constitution of Courts (an amending Act)		

Description.	Whether adapted from British Indian Acts.	Whether introduced during the year under report.
12. Municipal Act No. I of 1322 T. E.		
13. Revenue Sale Amendment Act—1323 T.E.		
14. An Act for the destruction of old records—1323 T. E.		
15. Act I of 1326 T. E.—Regulation regarding Privy Council Appeals.		
16. Act II of 1326 T. E.—Registration of Births and Deaths	Partly adapted.	
17. Act III of 1326 T. E.—Vaccination Act	Do.	
18. Act IV of 1326 T. E.—Public Demands Recovery Act	Do.	
19. Act V of 1326 T. E.—Excise Amendment Act		
20. Act I of 1327 T. E.—Settlement of lands for tea cultivation		
21. Rules of Import and Sale of Opium—1327 T. E.		
22. Regulation No. 1 of 1328 T. E.—regarding Registration of Coolies		
23. Regulation No. 2 of 1328 T. E.—regarding Export of Tea		
24. Act I of 1329 T. E.—(Absconding sepoys Act)		
25. Act II of 1329 T. E.—(Control of prices of food stuff)		
26. Act III of 1329 T. E. (Elephants and Buffaloes grazing Act)		
27. Act IV of 1329 T. E. (House tax on Hill tribes)	Do	
28. Act V of 1329 T. E.- (Legal practitioners, Act)		
29. Act I of 1332 T. E.—Encumbered Estates Act.		
30. Act III of 1332 T. E.—The Opium and Intoxicating Drugs Act.		
31. Rules and Regulations under the Opium and Intoxicating Drugs Act III of 1332 T. E.		
32. Act I of 1336 T. E.—(Hackney Carriages)		
33. Act II of 1336 T. E.—(Amending Act I of 1327)		
34. Act III of 1336 T. E.—(Amending the Survey & Settlement Regulation)		
35. Act IV of 1336 T. E.—(Prevention of gambling)		
36. Act I of 1337 T. E.—(Amending the State Tenancy Act I of 1296 T. E.)		
37. Land Acquisition Rules under Act I of 1337 T. E.		
38. State Motor Vehicles Act I of 1338 T. E.		
39. Act II of 1338 T. E. for prevention of smuggling of elephant tusks.		
40. State Stamp Act III of 1338 T. E.		
41. Tripura State Bank Act I of 1339 T. E.		
42. Census Act III of 1339 T. E.		

II

Statement showing the strength, cost and other particulars of the Military Force in Tripura State for 1339 T. E.

Arm of service.	NUMBER OF FIGHTING OFFICERS AND MEN.						DETAILS OF FORCE AT THE END OF THE CURRENT YEAR.						Buglers.	Total cost on account of pay and allowances of the force, including followers.	REMARKS.
	At the end of last year.	Recruited this year.	Casualties.			At the end of the current year.	Number of regiments, battalions, or Batteries.	Number of guns.	Number of men.						
									Commisioned Officers.		Non-commissioned officers.	Fighting men.			
			Died.	Invalided.	Discharged, deserted, &c.				European	Indian.					
1	2	3	4	5	6	7	8	9	10	11	12	13	14	15	16
Infantry ...	344	207	3	—	165	383	1	329 and one small cannon.	—	19	34	321	9	Rs. 1,29,297	* Including 4 officers of superior rank.
Band Party	21	—	—	—	1	20	—	—	—	—	1 Band master.	19 Band men.	—		
Total ...	365	207	3	—	166	403	1	329 and one small cannon.	—	19	35	340	9	Rs. 1,29,297	

III.

Statement showing the strength, cost, discipline, and education of the Police for the year 1339 T. E.

Description of office.	Number.	Grade of pay.	Total cost.	Punishments.			Rewards.		Education.		Remarks.
				Dismissed.	Fined, degraded or suspended departmentally.	Punished judicially.	By promotion.	By money.	Number able to read and write.	Number under instruction.	
1	2	3	4	5	6	7	8	9	10	11	12
		Rs.									
Superintendent of Police	1	200-10-300	Rs 81,399	—	—	—	—	—	1	—	
Asst. Superintendent „	1	75-5-100		—	—	—	—	—	1	—	
Inspectors	3	55 to 90		—	—	—	—	—	3	—	
Darogas	23	25-2-45		—	2	—	—	1	23	—	
Naib Darogas	14	15-1-25		—	—	—	—	1	14	—	
Writer Constables	13	15-0-0		—	2	—	—	—	13	—	
Subedar	1	25-2-45		—	—	—	—	—	1	—	
Jamadar	6	15-1-25		—	—	—	—	1	6	—	
Constables	221	10 to 13		3	22	1	—	4	221	—	
Chaukidars	175	5-0-0		—	—	—	—	—	—	—	
Spy	3	15 to 20		—	—	—	—	—	—	—	
Armed Jamadar	1	20-1-30		—	—	—	—	—	1	—	
„ Havildar	2	19-1-25		—	—	—	—	—	2	—	
„ Amaldar (Naik)	4	15-1-20		—	1	—	—	—	4	—	
„ Writer Constable	1	15-0-0		—	—	—	—	—	1	—	
„ Lance Naik	2	14-1-15		—	1	—	—	—	2	—	
„ Constables	25	14-1-15		—	1	2	—	2	22	—	
Total ...	496			3	29	3		9	315		

IV.

Statement showing the working of the Police in the Tripura State during the year 1339 T. E.

State.	Number of offences.		Number of accused arrested.		Number of accused sent up for trial.		Number of accused convicted.		Number of accused acquitted or discharged.		Percentage convicted of accused arrested.		Percentage convicted of accused sent up for trial.		REMARKS.
	Past year.	Present year.	Past year.	Present year.	Past year.	Present year.	Past year.	Present year.	Past year.	Present year.	Past year.	Present year.	Past year.	Present year.	
1	2	3	4	5	6	7	8	9	10	11	12	13	14	15	16
Tripura State	1,336	1,295	964	772	821	718	169	133	252	223	17·53	17·22	20·58	18·52	

V.

Statement showing the value of property stolen and amount of recoveries in the Tripura State during the year 1339 T. E.

State.	Amount stolen.		Amount recovered.		Percentage of recoveries of property stolen.		REMARKS.
	Past year.	Present year.	Past year.	Present year.	Past year.	Present year.	
1	2	3	4	5	6	7	8
Tripura State	Rs 16,199-3-9	Rs 15,149-14-3	Rs 3,540-10-9	Rs 2,991-13-6	21·23	19·74.	

VI.

Statement showing the number of crimes committed, number of cases disposed of, and cases awaiting trial in the Tripura State during the year 1339 T. E.

Description of offences.		Number of offences.			Number of cases disposed of during the past year.	Number of cases disposed of during the present year.	Number of cases awaiting trial.	Number of persons apprehended.	Number of persons convicted.	Number of persons sentenced.								Number of persons acquitted or discharged.	Number of persons confined being insane.	Number of persons died during or before trial.	Term of imprisonment.											Persons awaiting trial.	Remarks.
		Balance from past year.	Committed during the present year.	Total.						Imprisonment. Simple.	Imprisonment. Rigorous.	Imprisonment and fine. Simple.	Imprisonment and fine. Rigorous.	Fine only.	Whipping.	Capital punishment.	Total.				Under one month.	From 1 to below 2 months.	From 2 to below 3 months.	From 3 to below 6 months.	From 6 to below 12 months.	From 1 to below 2 years.	From 2 to below 3 years.	From 3 to below 5 years.	5 years and above.	Transportation.	Capital punishment.		
1		2	3	4	5	6	7	8	9	10	11	12	13	14	15	16	17	18	19	20	21	22	23	24	25	26	27	28	29	30	31	32	33
Class I. Offences against the State, public tranquility, safety and justice &c.	cognizable ...	14	38	52	23	34	18	70	26	0	4	1	2	19	0	0	26	14	0	1	3	1	0	0	2	0	0	1	0	0	0	29	*a.* Four persons have been warned for the future.
	non-cognizable	18	41	59	70	52	7	8	*a*4	0	0	0	0	0	0	0	0	1	0	0	0	0	0	0	0	0	0	0	0	0	0	3	*b.* Nineteen persons transferred.
Class II. Offences against person.	cognizable ...	103	279	382	244	274	108	*b*683	74	0	24	0	17	32	0	1	74	356	0	4	5	7	7	5	7	1	1	2	1	5	1	230	*c.* One person has been warned for the future.
	non-cognizable	65	283	348	302	298	50	350	*c*30	1	1	0	0	27	0	0	29	273	0	0	2	0	0	0	0	0	0	0	0	0	0	47	
Class III. Offences against property.	cognizable ...	317	889	1206	801	854	352	*d* 1762	*d*292	1	63	3	16	206	0	0	289	949	0	4	29	12	8	15	10	4	3	2	0	0	0	515	*d.* One person transferred, one person escaped, one person released on bail and two persons have been warned for the future.
	non-cognizable	41	218	259	175	200	59	287	20	0	5	0	0	15	0	0	20	185	0	0	5	0	0	0	0	0	0	0	0	0	0	82	
Class IV. Other offences.	cognizable ...	76	110	186	123	137	49	220	45	0	13	0	2	30	0	0	45	108	0	3	1	8	5	1	0	0	0	0	0	0	0	64	
	non-cognizable	72	237	309	251	223	86	172	10	0	3	0	0	7	0	0	10	104	0	2	0	0	3	0	0	0	0	0	0	0	0	56	
Total cognizable ...	...	510	1316	1826	1191	1299	527	2735	437	1	104	4	37	287	0	1	434	1427	0	12	38	28	20	21	19	5	4	5	1	5	1	838	
Total non-cognizable ...	...	196	779	975	798	773	202	817	64	1	9	0	0	49	0	0	59	563	0	2	7	6	3	0	0	0	0	0	0	0	0	188	
GRAND TOTAL ...	...	706	2095	2801	1989	2072	729	3552	501	2	113	4	37	336	0	1	493	1990	0	14	45	28	23	21	19	5	4	5	1	5	1	1026	

VII.

Statement showing the number of offences reported and dealt with by the various Courts in the Tripura State during the year 1339 T.E.

Name of Court.	Number of offences reported during.		Number of persons dealt with.								Persons disposed of.					Persons remaining at the end of the year.	Remarks
			Remaining at the end of last year.	Brought to trial during present year.					Total.								
	Last year.	Present year.		Arrested by Police.	Upon warrant.	On summons.	Voluntary.	Arrested in presence of the Magistrate.	Last year.	Present year.	Discharged without trial.	Acquitted.	Convicted.	Committed or referred.	Died, escaped, or transferred &c.		
1	2	3	4	5	6	7	8	9	10	11	12	13	14	15	16	17	18
Sadar Magistracy	184	605	389	195	101	242	42	18	985	988	304	276	105	17	2	284	
Sonamura „ ...	239	268	79	41	53	203	48	2	489	426	148	98	62	9	0	109	
Bilonia „ ...	234	235	86	117	17	41	146	8	402	415	108	127	90	0	10	80	
Kailashahar „ ...	218	272	108	181	124	126	22	3	396	564	148	115	75	13	14	199	
Khowai „ ...	128	152	53	8	21	52	33	0	164	167	56	36	16	3	1	55	
Dharmanagar „ ...	327	206	196	43	78	158	30	0	460	505	211	39	53	2	6	194	
Udaipur „ ...	302	315	34	57	106	198	27	6	565	428	175	92	67	1	2	91	
Sabrum „ ...	44	42	9	8	1	15	8	0	100	41	0	23	13	2	0	3	
TOTAL ...	2,076	2,095	954	651	501	1,035	356	37	3,561	3,534 a	1,150	806	481	47 b	35	1,015	

a. Excluding 18 persons pending before the Court of Sessions at the close of the previous year.

b. Including 18 persons pending from last year, the total number of persons for trial before the Court of Sessions was 65; of these 20 were convicted, 34 acquitted and 11 remained under trial at the close of the year.

VIII.

Statement of Criminal cases in which British Subjects were concerned for 1339 T. E.

DESCRIPTION OF OFFENCES.		Cases pending since the previous year.	Cases instituted during the year.	Total number of cases.	Cases in which complainants were British subjects.	Cases in which both parties were British subjects.	CASES IN WHICH DEFENDANTS WERE BRITISH SUBJECTS.													REMARKS.
							Cases pending since the previous year	Cases instituted during the year.	Total number of cases.	Cases disposed of.		Cases pending at the close of the year.	Persons under trial at the close of the previous year.	Persons brought to trial during the year.	Total number of persons under trial.	Convicted.	Acquitted or discharged.	Died or escaped &c.	Under trial at the close of the year.	
										Rejected, compromised or dismissed without enquiry.	Tried.									
Class I. Offences against the State &c.	cognizable ...	2	7	9	0	0	2	7	9	0	7	2	1	18	19	14	2	1	2	Of this number 134 were discharged without trial, the cases being dismissed, compromised or struck off on default. Excluding 3 died, and 161 pending, the actual number of persons tried was 296, of whom 178 or 60·13 were convicted as against 55·27 of the previous year.
	non-cognizable ...	1	0	1	0	0	1	0	1	1	0	0	0	0	0	0	0	0	0	
Class II. Offences against person.	cognizable ...	8	30	38	12	7	8	18	26	8	8	10	7	36	43	18	12	1	12	
	non-cognizable ...	6	17	23	5	9	6	12	18	12	5	1	8	9	17	0	15	0	2	
Class III. Offences against property.	cognizable ...	76	216	292	29	47	68	195	263	55	122	86	75	312	387	139	137	1	110	
	non-cognizable ...	2	83	85	2	56	2	81	83	69	4	10	2	79	81	1	64	0	16	
Class IV. Other offences.	cognizable ...	14	8	22	1	4	14	7	21	6	8	7	24	14	38	4	16	0	18	
	non-cognizable ...	6	14	20	2	10	6	12	18	8	5	5	3	6	9	2	6	0	1	
Total cognizable ...		100	261	361	42	58	92	227	319	69	145	105	107	380	487	175	167	3	142	
Total non-cognizable ...		15	114	129	9	75	15	105	120	90	14	16	13	94	107	3	85	0	19	
GRAND TOTAL ...		115	375	490	51	133	107	332	439	159	159	121	120	474	594*	178	252	3	161	

IX.

Statement of Extradition Cases for the year 1339 T. E.

Names of Courts.	Nature of cases.	NUMBER BORNE ON THE REGISTER.				NUMBER BROUGHT TO TRIAL.			RESULT.		Number at large at the close of the year.	Number of persons awaiting trial (after arrest) at the close of the year.	REMARKS.
		Number of persons at large at the close of the previous year.	Number of persons awaiting trial at the close of the previous year.	Number of persons against whom warrants were applied for during the year.	Total.	Number of persons arrested and surrendered within the year.	Number of persons who appeared of their own accord or were subsequently arrested in the State within the year.	Total (Columns 4+7+8).	Convicted.	Acquitted or discharged.			
Sadar Magistracy	Theft	2	0	1	3	1	1	2	0	0	(a)	2	* One previously arrested was released.
	Criminal breach of trust	2	0	0	2	0	0	0	0	0	(b)	0	
	Theft and receiving stolen property	2 *	0	0	2	1	0	1	0	1	1	0	
	Rescuing offenders from lawful custody	0	4	0	4	0	0	4	0	0	0	4	
	Dishonest misappropriation of property	0	0	5	5	0	5	5	4	0	0	1	
	Cheating	0	0	2	2	0	2	2	0	2	0	0	
Bilonia " ...	Theft and escape from lawful custody	1	0	0	1	0	0	0	0	0	1	0	
	Culpable homicide not amounting to murder	3	0	0	3	1	0	1	0	0	2	1	
	Lurking house trespass (Sections 446, 456, 354)	3	0	0	3	0	0	0	0	0	(c)	0	
	Theft	0	0	3	3	3	0	3	0	3	0	0	
Sonamura " ...	Theft	22	14	13	49	10	3	27	3	6	22	18	
Kailashahar " ...	Theft	3	0	1	4	0	0	0	0	0	4	0	
	Escape from lawful custody	0	0	1	1	0	0	0	0	0	1	0	
	Mischief by maiming cattle	0	0	1	1	1	0	1	0	0	0	1	
Dharmanagar " ...	Theft	6	0	2	8	2	0	2	0	0	6	2	
	Highway robbery	1	0	0	1	0	0	0	0	0	1	0	
	Criminal trespass and assault with deadly weapons ...	12	0	0	12	0	0	0	0	0	12	0	
	Theft and wrongful confinement	2	0	0	2	1	0	1	1	0	1	0	
	Theft and receiving stolen property	0	0	3	3	1	0	1	0	1	2	0	
Khowai " ...	Theft	1	0	1	2	1	0	1	0	0	1	1	
	Dacoity	0	0	1	1	1	0	1	1	0	0	0	
Udaipur " ...	Theft and receiving stolen property	3	0	0	3	0	0	0	0	0	3	0	
	Criminal breach of trust	2	0	1	3	3	0	3	0	3	0	0	
	Criminal breach of trust by servant	0	1	0	1	0	0	1	0	1	0	0	
Sabroom " ...	Theft	2	2	0	4	0	2	4	1	1	0	2	
	Escape from lawful custody	0	1	0	1	0	0	1	1	0	0	0	
	Total	67	22	35	124	26	13	61	11	18	57	32	

(a) Pending arrest of the accused one case struck off. (b) Cases struck off pending arrest of the accused.
(c) Facts disclosing non-extraditable offence, case transferred to a British Court under arrangement.

X.

Statement showing the results of appeals against decisions passed by the Criminal Courts in the Tripura State during the year 1339 T. E.

Tribunals.	Number of applications	Number of persons and cases.																Remarks.
		Applications rejected.		Sentences.						Proceedings quashed.		Referred.		Furher enquiry &c, ordered.		Pending.		
				Confirmed.		Modified.		Reversed.										
		Persons.	Cases.	Persons.	Cases.	Persons.	Cases.	Persons.	Cases.	Persons.	Cases.	Persons.	Cases.	Persons	Cases.	Persons.	Cases.	
Khas Adalat ...	207	40	39	60	45	61	24	26	13	—	—	—	—	19	15	97	71	

XI.

Civil Work—Nature and value of original suits filed and disposed of during the year 1339 T. E.

Tribunal.	Opening balance.		Filed during the year, received by transfer or on remand.		Total.		Disposed of during the year.		Closing balance.		Suits filed during present year.										Suits disposed of during present year.						Suits not estimable in money.	Remarks.
	Past year	Present year.	Past year.	Present year.	Past year.	Present year.	Past year.	Present year.	Past year.	Present year.	Value.	Suits *re* landed property.	Suits for money transaction.	Suits for other rights.	Number of suits under Rs. 100.	Number of suits above Rs. 100 and under Rs. 500.	Number of suits above Rs. 500 and under Rs. 1,000.	Number of suits above Rs. 1,000 and under Rs. 5,000.	Number of suits above Rs. 5,000.	*Exparte.*	Admitted and compromised.	Struck off the file.	Otherwise disposed of.	Value.	Average duration.		
											Rs. a. p.													*Rs a. p*	*Y.m.d.*		
Khash Adalat Original side	50	48	25	50	75	98	27	39	48	59	75,295-11-9	27	3	20	0	0	0	33	2	1	18	9	11	99,111-2-3	0-4-7	15	
Sadar Dewani Adalat	402	390	648	686	1,050	1,076	660	698	390	378	55,549-13-6	267	216	203	286	189	99	0	0	430	94	33	141	48,376-2-3	0-11-26	112	
Sonamura „	73	80	208	234	281	314	201	205	80	109	8,820-11-0	73	130	31	144	63	2	0	0	90	25	46	44	9,155-11-9	0-1-27	25	
Bilonia „	30	53	146	173	176	226	123	168	53	58	13,269-9-3	68	72	33	106	40	1	0	0	77	9	39	43	12,078-13-9	0-3-6	26	
Kailashahar „	218	284	348	326	566	610	282	369	284	241	21,656-11-3	70	231	25	221	47	2	0	0	139	42	55	133	22,968-15-6	0-4-8	56	
Khowai „	58	54	136	213	194	237	140	219	54	48	13,603-14-6	27	184	2	188	20	3	0	0	88	89	24	18	12,676-4-9	0-0-1	2	
Dharmanagar „	143	141	192	204	335	345	194	227	141	118	13,543-7-3	19	59	126	142	28	1	0	0	60	25	54	88	18,999-6-6	0-1-1	33	
Udaipur „	99	128	491	590	590	718	462	559	128	159	55,960-1-3	11	546	33	378	162	11	0	0	285	105	63	106	48,135-13-9	0-2-23	39	
Sabrum „	5	4	22	19	27	23	23	15	4	8	3,316-1-0	6	12	1	7	11	1	0	0	8	3	2	2	1,025-5-6	0-2-18	0	
Total ...	1,078	1,182	2,216	2,495	3,294	3,677	2,112	2,499	1,182	1,178	2,61,046-0-9	568	1453	474	1472	560	120	33	2	1178	410	325	586	2,71,927-12-0	0-3-16	308	

XII.

Civil Work.—Results of applications for Execution of Decrees, 1339 T.E.

Tribunal.	Opening balance.		Value of opening balance for present year.	Applications brought to the Register.			Total.			Disposed of.			Closing balance.			Nature of applications pending disposal at the close of the year.			Remarks.
	Past year.	Present year.		Past year.	Present year.	Value for present year.	Past year.	Present year.	Value for present year.	Past year.	Present year.	Value for present year.	Past year.	Present year.	Value for present year.	Below 6 months.	Below 12 months.	Above 12 months.	
			Rs. a. p.			Rs. a. p.			Rs. a. p.			Rs. a. p.			Rs. a. p.				
Khas Adalat (Original side)	24	15	43,555-10-3	2	11	10,490-5-3	26	26	54,045-15-6	11	1	802-12-0	15	25	53,243-3-6	4	7	14	
Sadar Dewani Adalat ...	162	211	32,568-5-3	291	213	22,322-8-9	453	424	54,890-14-0	242	217	26,878-3-9	211	207	28,012-10-3	110	23	74	
Sonamura Ditto ...	34	28	4,690-2-9	65	63	8,820-10-0	99	91	13,510-12-9	71	64	9,155-8-9	28	27	4,355-4-0	22	4	1	
Bilonia Ditto ...	6	12	875-12-6	43	46	4,073-11-3	49	58	4,949-7-9	37	44	3,572-6-0	12	14	1,377-1-9	8	5	1	
Kailashahar Ditto ...	107	93	19,147-3-9	109	121	14,496-1-9	216	214	33,643-5-6	123	83	10,706-14-6	93	131	22,936-7-0	50	31	50	
Khowai Ditto ...	18	23	2,753-8-3	45	86	9,782-10-3	63	109	12,536-2-6	40	63	7,902-7-3	23	46	4,633-11-3	40	3	3	
Dharmanagar Ditto ...	29	36	4,635-5-0	55	43	6,559-12-9	84	79	11,195-1-9	48	55	4,702-12-0	36	24	6,492-5-9	12	6	6	
Udaipur Ditto ...	46	118	16,590-9-6	231	274	38,971-14-3	277	392	55,562-7-9	159	233	28,576-6-3	118	159	26,986-1-6	124	21	14	
Sabrum Ditto ...	1	2	375-12-6	7	4	502-11-9	8	6	878-8-3	6	6	878-8-3	2	0	0-0-0	0	0	0	
Total ...	427	538	1,25,192-5-9	848	861	1,16,020-0-0	1,275	1,399	2,41,212-11-9	737	766	93,175-14-9	538	633	1,48,036-13-0	370	100	163	

XIII.

Civil Work—Number and results of appeals in civil suits, 1339 T. E.

Tribunal.	Opening balance.		Filed during.		Total.		Disposed of during.		Closing balance.		Value of appeales filed during.		How disposed of.										Average duration.	
													Decisions confirmed.		Decisions reversed.		Decisions amended.		Cases remanded for retrial.		Cases compromised and otherwise disposed of.			
	Past year.	Present year.	Past year.	Present year.	Past year.	Present year.	Past year.	Present year.	Past year.	Present year.	Past year.	Present year.	Past year.	Present year.	Past year.	Present year.	Past year.	Present year.	Past year.	Present year.	Past year.	Present year.	Past year.	Present year.
											Rs. a. p.	*Rs. a. p.*											*Y.m.d.*	*Y.m.d.*
Khas Adalat	90	122	179	146	269	268	147	130	122	138	37,248-9-9	61,737-15-0	50	66	7	19	29	6	37	25	24	14	0-2-4	0-2-6

XIV.

Statement showing the number of persons confined in the jails and lock-ups in the Tripura State during the year 1339 T. E.

Stations.	Number of prisons.	Number of prisoners.				Daily average.		Number of prisoners remaining at the end of the year.	Cost of jails and prisoners.	Average period in days of stay of accused under-trial.	Remarks showing mortality among convicts in jail.
		Remaining from last year.	Admitted during the year.	Total.							
				Past year.	Present year.	Past year.	Present year.				
Agartala	1	100	252	352	352	77·54	88·49	84	17,388	44	6 convicts died during the year 1339 T. E.—
Sonamura	1	12	70	119	82	5·9	·22	1	784	13·77	Dysentery—3. Apoplexy—1.
Bilonia	1	4	64	52	68	·13	2·86	3	482	12·56	Enlarged Spleen and extreme Anæmia—1.
Kailashahar	1	8	106	66	114	4·49	9·23	12	1,237	34·48	Grievous hurt by another convict—1.
Dharmanagar	1	2	93	53	95	2·91	6·63	3	818	22·83	
Udaipur...	1	3	54	91	57	5·87	2·56	—	490	2·36	
Sabrum	1	5	16	23	21	1·16	·05	1	387	20	
Khowai	1	6	47	54	53	3·60	4·24	1	573	34·16	
TOTAL. ...	8	140	702	810	842	101·60	114·28	105	22,159	23·02	

XV

Registration of documents in the Tripura State during the year 1339 T.E.

Name of State.	Documents presented for registration including pending from the last year.		Nature of documents presented.										Documents registered.		Value of documents registered.		Documents of which registration has been refused.		Documents remaining unregistered at the end of the year.		Remarks.
			Mortgages.		Sale deeds.		Wills.		Money bonds.		Miscellaneous.										
	Past year.	Present year.	Past year.	Present year.	Past year.	Present year.	Past year.	Present year.	Past year.	Present year.	Past year.	Present year.	Past year.	Present year.	Past year.	Present year.	Past year.	Present year.	Past year.	Present year.	
1	2	3	4	5	6	7	8	9	10	11	12	13	14	15	16	17	18	19	20	21	22
															Rs.	Rs.					
Tripura State	12,362	12,089	3,143	3,121	5,297	4,981	10	5	334	907	3,082	2,820	11,948	11,590	20,48,167	19,95,905	159	122	255	377	

XVI.

Statement showing the receipts and expenditure on account of Registration during the year 1339 T.E.

Description.	Past Year.			Present Year.			Remarks.
	Number of deeds.	Value of property.	Fees realised.	Number of deeds.	Value of property.	Fees realised.	
		Rs.	Rs.		Rs.	Rs.	
Mortgages	3,143	4,47,374	3,286	3,121	6,05,540	3,502	
Sale deeds	5,297	11,25,971	7,696	4,981	9,15,647	6,889	
Will	10	1,450	57	5	1,000	25	
Money bonds	334	42,716	322	907	93,533	765	
Miscellaneous	3,082	5,02,724	3,841	2,820	4,07,486	3,684	
Total ...	11,866	21,20,235	15,202	11,834	20,23,206	14,865	
Total Expenditure ...	—	—	5,007	—	—	5,002	
Net Income ...	—	—	10,195	—	—	9,863	

XVII.

Receipts and expenditure of the Municipalities in the Tripura State during the year 1339 T.E.

NAME.	Opening balance.	RECEIPTS DURING THE YEAR.					Total in the current year.	EXPENDITURE DURING THE YEAR.		Balance at the close of the year.	REMARKS.
		Past.	Present.								
			State grant.	Tax.	Miscellaneous.	Total.		Past.	Present.		
1	2	3	4	5	6	7	8	9	10	11	12
	Rs. A.P.	Rs. A.P.	Rs. A.P.	Rs. A.P.	Rs. A.P.	Rs. A.P.	Rs. A.P.	Rs. A.P.	Rs. A.P.	Rs. A.P.	
Agartala Municipality. ...	16,628-8-0	33,426-12-3	11,234 *	3,920-2-9	8,188-2-9 *a*	23,342-5-6	39,970-13-6	16,798-4-3	17,975-9-0 *b*	21,995-4-6 *c*	*a.* Including Rs. 6,670-11-9 as income from the Bazar and Rs. 380 as deposits and advances recovered. *b.* Including Rs. 967-8-9 as expenditure on the Bazar improvement and Rs. 50 as deposits and advances paid. *c.* Including Rs. 21,810-12-6 of the Bazar improvement fund and Rs. 184-8 as balance at the close of the year.

*Including Sanitation.

XVIII.

Statement of rainfall in the Tripura State during the year 1339 T. E.

STATE.	Baisak.	Jaisth.	Asar.	Sravan.	Bhadra.	Asvin.	Kartik.	Agrahayan.	Pous.	Magh.	Falgoon.	Chait.	Total.	Total of past year.	Average of past 5 years.	REMARKS.
Tripura State ...	20·61	26·5	8·92	9·58	14·75	8·51	1·09	—	·73	·95	2·01	4·65	98·30	87·67	98·13	

1. Maximum in Kailashahar—153·90. 2. Minimum in Sonamura—78·33.

XIX.

Statement as to the prices of staple food-grains for the year 1339 T. E.

Articles.	Price per maund during Chait, 1338 T. E.			Price per maund during chait, 1339 T. E.			REMARKS.
	Rs.	*a.*	*p.*	*Rs.*	*a.*	*p.*	
(1) RICE							
Maximum	7	4	0	8	0	0	
Minimum	4	0	0	4	8	0	
(2) PADDY							
Maximum	4	8	0	4	0	0	
Minimum	2	0	0	1	8	0	

XX.

Expenditure on Public Works during the year 1339 T.E.

Description of work.	State Funds.			Local Funds.			Total.	Remarks.
	Original.	Repairs.	Total.	Original.	Repairs.	Total.		
	Rs.	*Rs.*	*Rs.*	*Rs.*	*Rs.*	*Rs.*	*Rs.*	
Buildings	2,19,149	95,749	3,14,898	929	180	1,109	3,16,007	
Roads and Bridges ...	56,818	25,176	81,994	—	—	—	81,994	
Tanks	10,082	2,893	12,975	—	—	—	12,975	
Miscellaneous works ...	25,425	2,972	28,397	—	—	—	28,397	
Total ...	3,11,474	1,26,790	4,38,264	929	180	1,109	4,39,373	
Minor works at the Rajbari (*Karkhana*)	—	3,957	3,957	—	—	—	3,957	
Establishment charges ..	—	—	24,211	—	—	—	24,211	
Grand Total ...	3,11,474	1,30,747	4,66,432*	929	180	1,109	4,67,541	

*Out of this amount Rs. 2,71,692 have been spent for improvement works under the following heads :—

Original works—

(1) Buildings	... Rs.	1,83,559.
(2) Roads and Bridges	... ,,	56,334.
(3) Misc. works	... ,,	25,306.
(4) Water works	... ,,	6,493.
Total	... Rs.	2,71,692.

XXI.

Statement showing the excise shops and excise revenue of the Tripura State during the year 1339 T. E.

Name of State.	Country spirit.		Country spirit, Opium and Ganja.		Opium and Ganja.		Tari.		Total.		Remarks.
	Number of shops.	Revenue. demand.	Number of shops.	Revenue demand.	Number of shops.	Revenue. demand.	Number. of shops.	Revenue. demand.	Number of shops.	Revenue realised.	
		Rs.		*Rs.*						*Rs.*	
Tripura State	1	15	31	96,129	—	—	—	—	32	96,479	

XXII.

Statement of Medical Relief afforded in the Tripura State during the year 1339 T.E.*

Dispensary.	Number of patients treated. (new)		Results of in-door patients. (new)				Expenditure.	Daily average. (old + new)			No. of surgical operations performed.			No. of persons vaccinated during the year.		
	Outdoor.	Indoor.	Dis-charged cured.	Relieved or dis-charged otherwise.	Died.	Remain-ing under treatment.		Outdoor.	Indoor.	Total.	Major.	Minor.	Total.	Success-fully.	Unsuc-cessfully.	Total.
							Rs.									
1. Victoria Memorial Hospital at Agartala and the Charitable Dispensary attached to it ...	14,972	453	293	128	17	15	10,296	85·00	17·92	102·92	11	224	235	801	473	1,274
2. Palace Dispensary	9,634	0	0	0	0	0	7,968	61·05	0	61.05	0	0	0	0	0	0
3. Homœopathic	13,003	0	0	0	0	0	6,065	60·84	0	60·84	0	0	0	0	0	0
4. Dhaleswar	5,767	0	0	0	0	0	1,476	30·50	0	30·50	0	22	22	0	0	0
5. Kunjaban †	997	0	0	0	0	0	1,416	27·59	0	27·59	0	0	0	0	0	0
6. Old Agartala	4,068	0	0	0	0	0	1,319	23·37	0	23·37	1	39	40	509	72	581
7. Bishalgar	5,146	0	0	0	0	0	1,412	19·43	0	19·43	0	59	59	576	6	582
8. Mohanpur	4,320	0	0	0	0	0	1,048	16·57	0	16·57	0	75	75	349	23	372
9. Sonamura	6,182	6	2	4	0	0	1,704	26·79	·20	26·99	0	100	100	437	75	512
10. Udaipur	6,111	0	0	0	0	0	1,437	23·51	0	23·51	0	56	56	194	31	225
11. Amarpur	915	0	0	0	0	0	1,025	4·51	0	4·51	0	12	12	273	29	302
12. Sabroom	1,848	0	0	0	0	0	974	9·80	0	9.80	0	32	32	1,071	250	1,321
13. Bilonia	5,160	3	3	0	0	0	1,611	29·72	·10	29·82	7	111	118	654	62	716
14. Loongthung	2,880	0	0	0	0	0	793	14·15	0	14·15	1	28	29	555	102	657
15. Khowai	6,551	0	0	0	0	0	1,227	21·46	0	21·46	0	81	81	1,393	242	1,635
16. Kailashahar	7,075	0	0	0	0	0	1,900	28·62	0	28·62	0	166	166	141	184	325
17. Fatikroy	2,391	0	0	0	0	0	1,013	10·19	0	10·19	0	25	25	96	186	282
18 Kamalpur	4,921	0	0	0	0	0	1,415	17·16	0	17·16	0	92	92	317	204	521
19. Kulai Howar ‡	675	0	0	0	0	0	299	13·32	0	13·32	0	3	3	0	0	0
20. Dharmanagar	4,223	16	15	1	0	0	1,676	19·39	·58	19·97	3	69	72	329	76	405
Total	¶1,06,839	478	313	133	17	15	46,074	542·97	18·80	561·77	23	1,194	1,217	7,695	2,015	9,710

Remarks.

* This Statement excludes figures regarding Kaviraji treatment.

† The work of the Kunjaban Dispensary was begun from 23rd Bhadra, 1339 T. E.

‡ The work of the Kulai Howar Dispensary was began from the 21st Magh, 1339 T. E.

¶ This figure shows the actual number of outdoor patients treated, the total outdoor attendance during the year being 1,90,190 against 1,78,833 in the previous year.

XXIII.

Vital statistics of the Tripura State for the year 1339 T.E.

State.	Population.	Births.				Deaths.				Ratio per 1,000 of population.				Remarks.
										Births.		Deaths.		
		Past year.	Present year.	Increase.	Decrease.	Past year.	Present year.	Increase.	Decrease.	Past year.	Present year.	Past year.	Present year.	
Tripura State ...	3,02,421	2,244	2,368	124	—	2,394	2,658	264	—	7·42	7·83	7·93	8·78	

XXIV.

Education Return (A)—Particulars as to the schools maintained during the year 1339 T.E.

Number of Schools.		Class of Schools.	Number of Pupils on the Rolls on the Last Day of Chait.		Average Daily Attendance.		Remarks.
Past year.	Present year.		Past year.	Present year.	Past year.	Present year.	
5	6	High English Schools ... ... (including one Branch H. E. School).	1,589	1,738	1,182'54	1,333'48	
8	7	Middle English Schools for boys ...	990	841	760'78	685'36	
1	1	Middle English School for girls ...	66	56	48'30	39'56	
1	1	Higher Vernacular School for boys	77	71	53'51	64'67	* In some of these schools boys and girls read together.
22	23	* Lower Vernacular Schools for boys	1,239	1,384	893'87	996'88	
112	113	* Pathsalas for boys	2,830	2,773	2,311'36	2,106'45	
10	10	Do for girls	319	302	223'10	217'25	
		Special Schools :—					
5	5	Madrassas and Muktabs	183	186	104'37	118'56	
3	3	Sanskrit *Tols*	34	31	27'42	24'62	
1	1	Woodburn Artisan School... ...	18	19	6'25	9'58	
TOTAL 168	170		7,345	7,401	5,611'50	5.596'41	

XXV.

Education Return (B) Race of Students, 1339 T. E.

Names of Divisions.	No. of Schools.			No. of Students.			Race.												Average daily attendance.		Remarks.
							Hindus.														
	For boys.	For girls.	Total.	Boys.	Girls.	Total.	Rajkumars.	Thakurs.	Manipuris.	Tripuras.	Bengalees.	Others.	Reangs.	Chakmas.	Kukis.	Lusais.	Musalmans.	Christians.	Boys.	Girls.	
1. Sadar Division ...	55	3	58	2,146	100	2,246	7	131	108	278	1,194	18	0	0	0	0	508	2	1,600·10	72·94	
2. Kailashahar "	25	3	28	1,098	155	1,253	0	2	350	32	614	0	2	0	2	0	251	0	762·36	128·13	
3. Sonamura "	24	1	25	1,199	38	1,237	0	0	1	112	255	0	0	0	0	0	869	0	906·93	28·45	
4. Bilonia "	12	1	13	892	19	911	0	0	0	26	608	4	12	0	0	0	261	0	757·49	13·89	
5. Khowai "	11	1	12	304	14	318	0	191	43	0	54	17	0	0	0	0	13	0	229·21	9·35	
6. Dharmanagar "	14	1	15	654	17	671	0	0	72	4	424	0	0	0	0	5	166	0	479·74	13·98	
7. Udaipur "	10	1	11	482	15	497	0	0	0	128	135	0	0	0	0	0	234	0	361·51	13·43	
8. Sabrum "	6	0	6	237	0	237	0	0	c	91	118	0	0	0	0	0	28	0	196·58	0	
9. Amarpur Sub-division ...	2	0	2	32	0	32	0	0	0	0	8	24	0	0	0	0	0	0	22·32	0	
TOTAL ...	159	11	170	7,044	358	7,402	7	324	574	671	3,410	63	14	0	2	5	2,330	2	5,316·24	280·17	

APPENDIX XXVI. (A)

Statement of Audited Receipts for the year 1339 T. E.

State.

Heads of Revenue.	1338 T. E.		1339 T. E.		REMARKS.
	Revised Estimate.	Actuals.	Revised Estimate.	Actuals.	
1. Land Revenue ...	6,10,000	6,06,942	6,35,000	6,43,315	
2. Rents of markets ..	8,000	7,813	8,000	7,662	
3. Family tax in the hills	62,000	65,221	65,000	58,761	
4. Toll on Forest Produce	5,92,000	5,97,080	5,20,000	4,83,868	
5. Do on the Feni River	36,000	35,382	36,000	38,406	
6. Elephant and Buffalo grazing mehals ...	8,000	8,530	8,000	7,427	
7. Thatching grass mehals	8,000	7,990	8,000	7,960	
8. Reserved *Sal* trees ...	6,000	4,173	8,000	2,351	
9. Tax on cotton and Oil seeds ...	1,26,000	1,50,241	1,75,000	1,47,055	
10. Royalty on elephants caught ...	20,000	16,682	25,000	17,114	
11. Adda mehal ...	22,000	24,163	23,000	24,259	
12. Excise ...	90,000	92,718	94,000	96,479	
13. Stamps and Court fees	90,000	89,692	1,10,000	1,06,120	
14 Law and Justice (fines)	4,000	4,459	4,000	4,227	
15. Process Fees ...	15,000	15,089	16,000	17,897	
16. Registration ...	16,000	15,202	16,000	14,865	
17. Jail ...	4,000	3,664	4,000	1,683	
18. Cattle pounds ...	6,000	5,980	6,000	6,187	
19. *Nazars* ...	48,000	44,064	50,000	60,824	
20. School Fees ...	8,000	8,518	16,000	16,909	
21. Duty on Tea ...	20,000	17,107	20,000	9,636	
22. Duty on jute ...	35,000	30,857	20,000	31,123	
23. Personal Howlats recovered	7,000	6,546	6,000	6,996	
24. Personal Loans recovered ...	3,000	2,365	4,000	4,053	
25. Interest on Bank deposit ...	18,000	18,733	2,000	2,447	
26. Miscellaneous ...	54,000	65,210	55,000	60,697	
Total ...	19,16,000	19,46,421	19,34,000	18,78,321	
27. Deposits ...	94,000	60,446	75,000	1,06,979	
28. Contribution from Chakla ...	2,00,000	2,00,000	—	—	
29. Loans ...	1,00,000	1,00,000	3,00,000	2,63,000	
Total ...	23,10,000	23,06,867	23,09,000	22,48,300	
Opening Balance :—					
Cash ...	3,98,748	3,98,748	1,79,535	1,79,535	
Advances ...	2,10,816	2,10,816	1,86,542	1,85,542	
Loans ...	90,221	90,221	2,91,411	2,91,411	
Total ...	6,99,785	6,99,785	6,56,488	6,56,488	
Grand Total ...	30,09,785	30,06,652	29,65,488	29,04,788	

APPENDIX XXVI. (B)

Statement of Audited Expenditure for the year 1339 T. E.

State.

Heads of Expenditure.	1338 T. E.		1339 T. E.		REMARKS.
	Revised estimate.	Actuals.	Revised Estimate.	Actuals.	
1. Controlling Charges	91,035	89,813	94,130	92,184	
2. Revenue General ...	84,227	82,834	85,400	83,605	
3. Survey & Settlement	19,629	19,391	22,500	21,923	
4. Tahasil ...	55,903	54,397	56,120	53,816	
5. Registration ...	5,245	5,007	5,190	5,002	
6. Police ...	79,720	77,145	83,170	81,399	
7. Judicial ...	31,676	31,144	35,500	34,376	
8. Jail ...	19,006	18,536	22,430	22,159	
9. Forest ...	64,682	60,251	70,200	65,213	
10. Medical ...	70,734	69,346	73,100	71,497	
11. Sanitation ...	5,000	4,379	} 12,000	11,234	
12. Municipality ...	10,000	9,915			
13. Education General ...	1,11,595	1,08,404	1,20,700	1,14,629	
14. Education of Rajkumars ...	26,235	24,702	26,800	26,481	
15. (*a*) Public Works ...	1,73,771	1,70,563	1,95,000	1,94,740	
(*b*) Improvement ...	1,85,000	1,78,099	2,76,000	2,71,692	
16. Electric Light ...	25,744	21,727	18,760	17,741	
17. Small Donations ...	1,300	1,108	200	188	
18. Relief to distressed subjects ...	700	—	30,000	25,254	
19. Purchase of Landed Property ...	3,500	3,500	1,000	502	
20. Repayment of Deposits ...	80,000	75,597	77,500	76,207	
21. Interest on Deposits	12,000	11,070	12,000	7,331	
22. Unforeseen charges ...	2,300	1,774	4,300	4,270	
23. Advances to employees ...	7,000	6,467	8,000	7,377	
24. Loans to employees ...	7,000	7,000	—	—	
25. Pension ...	26,000	25,890	35,900	33,579	
26. Advisory Council ...	3,960	3,960	3,960	3,960	
27. Chief Secretary's Office & H. H.'s Tour	67,318	67,204	1,08,500	1,06,177	
28. Palace Sultanat ...	27,248	26,841	28,860	27,634	
29. Zoo ...	6,700	6,675	8,970	8,220	
30. Agriculture, Commerce and Industries	5,746	4,129	13,020	11,903	
31. Publicity, Reclamation and Immigration	—	—	25,000	9,953	
32. H. H.'s Private Secretary's Office ...	14,552	14,421	12,600	11,576	
33. Rajmala Office ...	6,826	6,790	6,558	5,984	
34. Military Secretary's Office ...	3,000	3,000	2,510	2,460	
35. Military ...	94,620	89,661	1,51,767	1,29,297	
36. Nijtahabil ...	1,20,000	1,20,000	1,20,000	1,20,000	
37. Expenditure in connection with H. H.'s Installation, Investiture & Marriage etc.	3,49,000	3,41,258	88,000	87,219	
38. Investment	—	—	5,500	5,500	
39. Chamber of Princes...	25,000	25,000	—	—	
40. Adjustment of irrecoverable advances ...	—	—	22,000	—	
41. Sansar Charges ...	4,86,599	4,80,166	4,04,000	4,57,161	
Total ...	24,09,571	23,50,164	24,27,145	23,09,443	
Closing balance :—					
Cash ...	1,30,214	1,79,535	1,06,343	* 1,25,366	
Advances ...	1,80,000	1,85,542	1,41,000	1,77,241	* Cash ... 8,253
Loans issued ...	2,90,000	2,91,411	2,91,000	2,92,738	In Bank ... 1,17,113
Total ...	6,00,214	6,56,488	5,38,343	5,95,345	1,25,366
Grand Total ...	30,09,785	30,06,652	29,65,488	29,04,788	

APPENDIX XXVII. (A)

Statement of Audited Receipts for the year 1339 T. E.

Chakla Roshnabad Estates.

Heads of Receipts.	1338 T. E.		1339 T. E.		REMARKS.
	Revised Estimate.	Actuals.	Revised Estimate.	Actuals.	
1. Rent and Cess ...	11,05,800	10,84,526	10,50,000	10,13,997	
2. Cess for Rent free holdings ...	11,200	14,484	8,100	7,486	
3. Law charges recovered	60,200	47,947	52,000	46,302	
4. Misc. receipts including deposits ...	13,000	51,948	77,244	1,17,002	
5. Refund of loans and advances ...	—	—	—	4,614	
Total	11,90,200	11,98,905	11,87,344	11,89,401	
Opening Balance :—					
Cash ...	1,03,986	1,03,746	72,066	72,066	
Advance ...	1,22,537	1,09,608	1,13,663	1,11,147	
Loans issued ...	12,000	10,474	10,342	10,342	
Bank deposits ...	1,05,052	1,05,052	1,10,630	1,10,630	
Total ...	3,43,575	3,28,880	3,06,701	3,04,185	
Grand Total ...	15,33,775	15,27,785	14,94,045	14,93,586	

APPENDIX XXVII. (B)

Statement of Audited Expenditure for the year 1339 T. E.

Chakla Roshnabad Estates.

Heads of Expenditure.	1338 T. E.		1339 T. E.		REMARKS.
	Revised Estimate.	Actuals.	Revised Estimate.	Actuals.	
i. 1. Revenue and Cess ...	2,72,351	2,70,852	2,73,556	2,71,413	
2. Establishment ...	1,56,554	1,54,339	1,53,849	1,53,828	
3. Settlement ...	1,424	1,063	1,274	1,346	
4. Legal Expenses ...	1,15,000	1,09,287	1,10,000	1,00,610	
5. Education ...	11,248	10,992	11,606	11,356	
6. Medical ...	12,597	12,329	13,921	13,600	
7. Public Works ...	63,060	58,064	88,028	76,651	
8. Religious Expenses	7,151	6,685	6,675	6,408	
9. Purchase of property	4,700	4,270	7,325	9,504	
10. Miscellaneous ...	28,000	26,454	19,645	11,309	
11. Loans and Advances	2,500	2,481	3,000	2,911	
12. Pension and Gratuity	5,500	5,091	6,700	7,120	
13. Forest ...	650	622	650	578	
14. Unforeseen ...	1,000	898	6,700	6,466	
ii. Sansar ...	15,540	15,540	15,540	15,540	
iii. Donation ...	35,500	35,481	32,900	14,701	
iv. Repayment of debts	—	—	500	500	
iv. (a) Repayment of deposits ...	12,000	9,202	34,000	30,668	
v. Nijtahabil Contribution ...	3,00,000	3,00,000	2,00,000	2,00,000	
vi. Marriage Contribution ...	2,00,000	2,00,000	—	—	
vii. Loans to the State ...	—	—	2,00,000	1,80,000	
Total ...	12,44,775	12,23,600	11,85,871	11,14,509	
Closing Balance :—					
Cash ...	57,033	72,066	49,575	90,595	
Advances ...	1,09,537	1,11,147	90,662	1,11,620	
Loans issued ...	11,800	10,342	40,000	48,884	
Bank deposits ...	1,10,630	1,10,630	1,27,936	1,27,969	
Total ...	2,89,000	3,04,185	3,08,174	3,79,077	
Grand Total ...	15,33,775	15,27,785	14,94,045	14,93,586	

To

His Highness The Bisama-Samara-Bijayee Mahamahodaya
Pancha-Srijukta Maharaja Manikya
BIR BIKRAM KISHORE DEV BARMAN BAHADUR,
Maharaja of Tripura.

Dated, Agartala, the 9th October, 1932.

MAY IT PLEASE YOUR HIGHNESS,

I have the honour to submit the accompanying Report on the General Administration of the State and the attached Zemindaries for the year 1341 T. E., corresponding to the period extending from the 14th April, 1931 to the 13th April, 1932.

The charge of the Administration as well as of the Zemindaries was with Dewan B. K. Sen Bahadur, M. A., B. L., Dewan–Shashan and Manager, Chakla Roshnabad Estates, during the year under report. He went on leave from the 28th August, 1932 and I have been appointed to act as Dewan–Shashan and Manager, Chakla Roshnabad Estates, in his place.

I have the honour to be,
Your Highness's most obedient servant,
Rana Bodhjung,
DEWAN–SHASHAN.

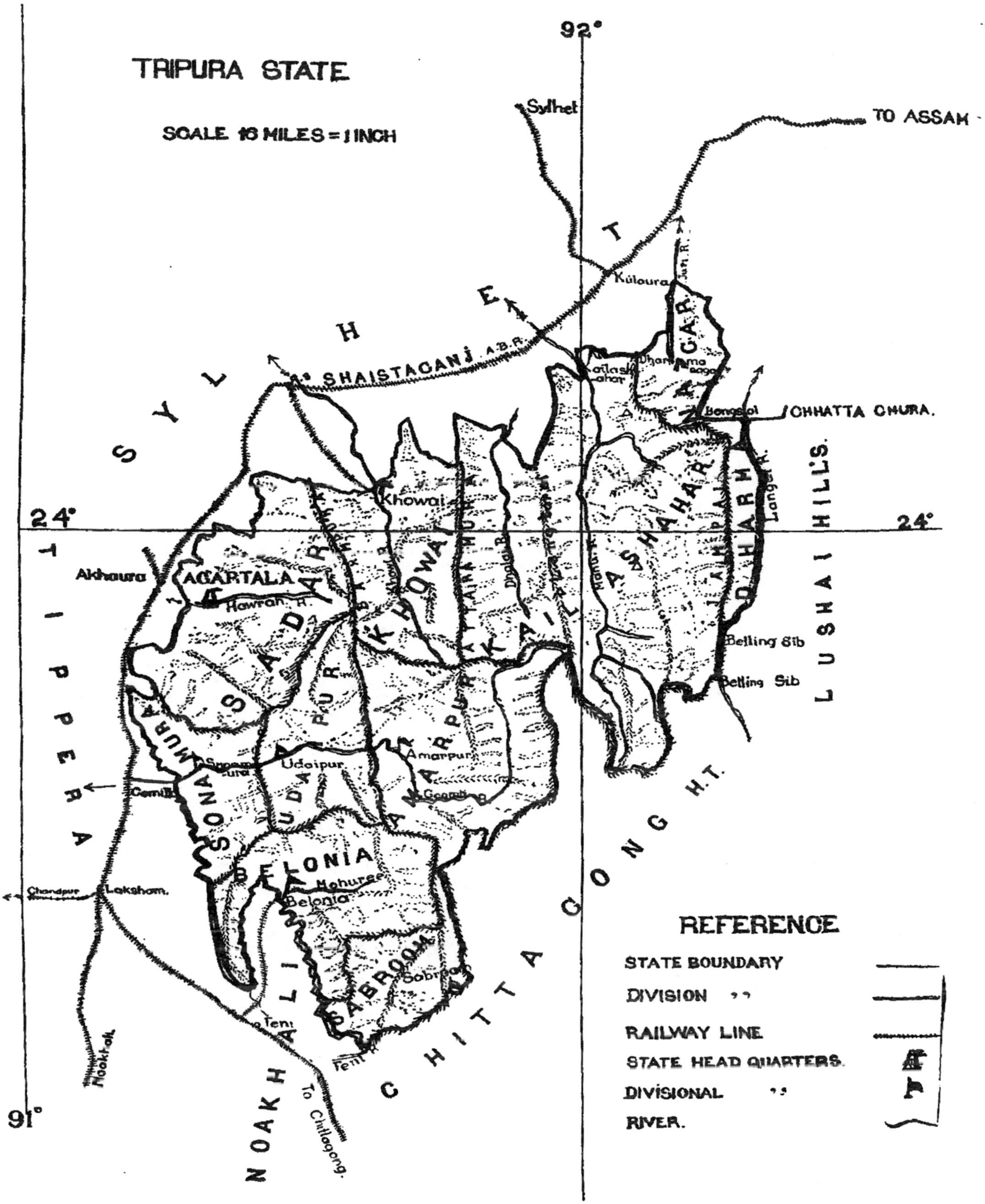
TRIPURA STATE
SCALE 16 MILES = 1 INCH
92°
24°
24°
91°
Sylhet
TO ASSAM
SYLHET
SHAISTAGANJ A.B.R.
Kuloura
CHHATTA CHURA.
LUSHAI HILLS.
TIPPERA
Akhaura
AGARTALA
Hawrah R.
SADAR
KHOWAI
Khowai
KAILASHAHAR
DHARMANAGAR
Belling Sib
UDAIPUR
Udaipur
AMARPUR
Amarpur
SONAMURA
BELONIA
Belonia
SABROOM
Sabroom
Comilla
Chandpur
Laksham.
Tent
NOAKHALI
To Chittagong.
CHITTAGONG H.T.
REFERENCE
STATE BOUNDARY
DIVISION ,,
RAILWAY LINE
STATE HEAD QUARTERS.
DIVISIONAL ,,
RIVER.

Book Twenty-three
Report on the General Administration of the Tripura State for the year 1341 T. E. (1931-1932 A.D.)

REPORT ON THE ADMINISTRATION

OF

THE TRIPURA STATE

FOR

1341 T. E. (1931-32.)

CHAPTER I—GENERAL AND POLITICAL.

Area of the State—4,116 sq. miles.
Population—3,82,450.
Gross Revenue (based on the average of the previous five years):—

(*a*) State	... ...	Rs. 21,21,349.
(*b*) Zemindaries	... .	Rs. 10,95,984.

Tribute—Nil.
Ruler of the State—His Highness The Bisama-Samara-Bijayee Mahamahodaya Pancha-Srijukta Maharaja Manikya Bir Bikramkishore Dev Barman Bahadur. *Age*—24 years. (Born—19th August, 1908). *Caste*—*Kshatriya* (of the Lunar race).

I.

The year and the people.

1. Tripura in 1341 T. E. was not free from the disturbances due to world's economic depression as in the previous year. The acute scarcity of money among the people, the low prices of indigenous commodities, the extremely gloomy trade conditions and their concomitants, showed no signs of improvement whatsoever in the year under review. With a further drop in the prices of paddy, rice and other food grains and jute being no more a paying crop, the agriculturists forming the majority of the population, found themselves in a most deplorable condition, dependent as they always are, on the sale of their produce for ready money to buy their necessaries and meet other monetary obligations. For the same reason, the demand for forest produces did not improve resulting in a further fall of revenue in the year under report. The condition of the Tea Industry had become worse in the year under review inspite of an increased outturn, which was due perhaps to a desperate attempt made by the garden authorities to cope with the low price in the market.

2. Fortunately the rice crop was generally a good one and there was no scarcity of food. The general situation was nevertheless aggravated by the appearance of a flood which, though never assumed dangerous proportions, affected some of the Divisions of the State and also some parts of the Zemindaries. Measures had to be taken by the State Department concerned, to give direct relief to the subjects affected. A sum of Rs 4,000, including the price of paddy distributed and *taccavi* loan amounting to Rs. 1,000, was spent in the shape of distress loan

and gratuitous relief. Besides this, a sum of Rs. 3,000 was placed at the disposal of the Goverment of Bengal from the State and Rs. 5,000 out of the Lottery Fund at the joint disposal of the Collector of Tippera and Manager, Chakla Roshnabad Estates. In the Zemindaries there was a general remission of interest on the arrear land revenue and a good number of tenants were allowed to execute bonds in lieu of payment in cash of their dues about to be time-barred. In some cases demands were allowed to be time-barred on parole promise of payment, the step having proved successful in the past.

3. The already low rates of wages of the skilled and unskilled labours showed a downward tendency. The condition of the middle class continued almost static.

Finances of the year.

4. The opening balance for the year was Rs. 9,72,666 against Rs. 9,74,422 in the year before and fell short of the estimate by Rs. 1,756. The total collections from the permanent sources were Rs. 20,84,512 against Rs. 22,40,999. Gross receipts including those from deposits, loans as well as law charges recovered, stood at Rs. 25,93,182 against Rs. 27,69,492. The total amount available for expenditure was thus Rs. 35,65,848 against Rs. 37,43,914. The closing balance stood at Rs. 10,65,150 which comprised Rs. 1,85,650 in actual cash in the treasuries and Rs. 8,79,500 in the banks and in loans and advances.

II.

His Highness's marriage.

5. The year was marked by a most happy event, the union of two historic Ruling Houses of Tripura and Panna by the solemnization of the marriage of His Highness the Maharaja Manikya Bahadur with the first Maharajkumari Saheba of Panna—daughter of His Highness Capt. Mahendra Maharaja Sir Jadavendra Singhji Saheb Bahadur, K. C. I. E., K. C. S. I., Maharaja of Panna, on the 14th Jaistha, 1341 T. E. (28th may, 1931) with great pomp and eclat.

Tilak Ceremony.

6. The Tilak Ceremony was performed with great eclat at the Ujjayanta Palace on the 2nd Baishak, 1341 T. E.

The bridal party and their reception.

7. The bridal party consisting of the leading members of the ruling family, nobles, high officials, relatives and other distinguished guests. His Highness the Maharaja Manikya Bahadur left the Capital on the 11th Jaistha, 1341 T. E. (*i. e.* 25th May, 1931). All along the route to the railway station His Highness was accorded great ovation by the public and the Special left amidst loud cheers from a huge concourse of people assembled to see Highness off.

8. His Highness arrived at the Satna Station on the 13th Jaistha, 1341 T. E. (*i. e.* 27th May, 1931) and motored to Panna. On the way a reception was arranged where His Highness the Maharaja of Panna and all other distinguished Ruling Princes invited, were present to meet

His Highness. The bridal party was introduced to the guests and Guard of Honour was furnished.

9. The bridal party was accommodated at the Mahendra Bhavan Palace and other buildings near by.

Return to Agartala.

10. The return of Highness to the Capital was the occasion of an enthusiasm still greater in its demonstration. Akhaura—the railway station of the Capital where distinguished personages, officials of both the State and Zemindaries were present, accorded welcome to Their Highnesses in which the general public also took part. His Highness the Maharaja Manikya Bahadur with Her Highness the Maharanee Saheba arrived at the Capital in procession. His Highness was carried in Chaudal and Her Highness the Maharanee Saheba in decorated motor car in the procession.

11. The ceremony marked by a number of subsequent festivities at the Capital was enjoyed by the people with a full and free heart.

Movement of their Highnesses

12. His Highness the Maharaja Manikya Bahadur paid a short visit to Shillong with Her Highness on the 21st Ashar, 1341 T. E, for three weeks and returned to Agartala on the 24th Sravan, 1341 T. E. (9th August, 1931). His Highness was also pleased to accept the kind invitation of H. H. the Mahendra Maharaja Saheb of Panna, to a shooting excursion and left for Panna on 3rd Agrahayan (19th November, 1931) with Her Highness. Leaving Panna His Highness came down to Calcutta on 8th December and stayed there during the Christmas, where His Highness had interviews with H. E. the Viceroy on the 30th December, 1931 and with H. E. the Governor of Bengal on the 19th December and again on the 10th January, 1932. Her Highness the Maharanee Saheba had a private interview with Hon'ble Lady Jackson on the 1st January, 1932. On the 3rd January His Highness proceeded to Dehra-dun to see Maharajkumari Basantaprabha on the eve of her departure for Switzerland for the benefit of her health, on medical advice and remained there from the 5th to the 7th January, 1932. His Highness returned to the Capital on the 12th January via Calcutta.

13. His Highness the Maharaja Manikya Bahadur left Agartala on the 8th Chaitra, 1341, for Delhi to attend the Session of the Chamber of Princes (Narendra Mandal). From the 24th March to the 2nd April His Highness attended all the formal and informal meetings and various other functions of the 1932 Session of the Chamber. His Highness had, besides, important discussion with the Right Hon'ble J. C. C. Davidson, Chairman, Indian States Enquiry Committee, in connection with the State's Memorandum to the Committee. From Delhi His Highness went to Mussooree by Motor on the 3rd and stayed there till the end of the year.

Demise of Dowager Bara Iswari Ratnamanjuri Mahadevya.

14. A sad event of the year was the death on the 7th Ashar, 1341 T. E. at the Palace, of Her Highness the Dowager Bara Iswari Ratnamanjuri Mahadevya, grand-mother of His Highness the Maharaja Manikya Bahadur. The deceased Iswari, a near relation of His Highness the Maharaja Saheb of Manipur, endeared herself to all of her circle and was held in high esteem. Offices and institutions were closed for 3 days.

15. Another calamity that overtook the Ruling family and the State was the demise of Mahamanyabara Maharajkumar Navadwip Chandra Dev Varma Bahadur, son of His late Highness Maharaja Ishan Chandra Manikya Bahadur, at His Highness's Calcutta residence, at the ripe old age of over 80, on the 29th Bhadra 1341 T. E. (5th September, 1931). The Maharajkumar had a very successful public career. He began his public life as a Chairman of the Comilla Municipality and Vice-President of the District Board, Comilla. He was also an Honorary Magistrate there for many years. In November, 1909, he was appointed Minister of the State which office he continued to hold till 28th Falgun, 1323 T. E. (12th March, 1914) during the reign of His late Highness Maharaja Birendra Kishore Manikya Bahadur. By virtue of his position as the senior member of the Ruling family and his administrative experience, he was selected, during the minority of His Highness, President of the Council of Administration. The distinction of Mahamanyabara was conferred on him by His Highness after the Installation Ceremony in 1928.

Death of Maharajkumar Navadwip Chandra.

16. A born administrator and perfect gentleman with many qualities of head and heart the Maharajkumar was held in high esteem throughout the territory and its neighbourhood. His goodness, his affability and above all his high moral standard of life are sacred memory to all. In his death the Ruling family has lost a loving guardian and the State, a sound Counsellor. Offices and institutions were closed for 3 days.

17. Yet another sad event of the year deserving mention was the premature death of Kumar Surendra Chandra Deb Barman Bahadur. He was a son of Rajkumar Debendra Chandra, a brother of Maharaja Radhakishore Manikya Bahadur. The late Kumar was a member of the State Civil Service and rose to occupy the position of a puisne judge and was widely respected.

Another death.

III.

18. The fall in the revenue which began in 1339 T. E. continued still in the year under review the collections from the permanent sources stood at Rs. 20,84,512 as against Rs. 31,02,911 in 1338 T. E. The heavy deficits in previous years had to be met by retrenchment almost in every direction but in the year under report the budget could not be balanced without also touching the salaries of the employees as well as the maintenance allowances met from the *Sansar* budget. And therefore an all-round reduction affecting salaries and maintenances of over Rs. 10, varying from 10 to 20 P. C., was resorted to.

Retrenchment.

19. The No. 12 Survey party, Government of India, continued their operations in the course of which a boundary dispute known as Gourangala Boundary dispute came up for local inspection under arrangement and the representatives submitted their recommendation.

Topographical Survey

20. The population of the State as provisionally given in the preceding year's Report was 3,82,219 but the tables as finally published showed the population to be 3,82,450. The difference however is insignificant.

Census.

21. An allotment of Rs. 3,150 was announced in favour of the State for improvement projects of arterial roads. The scheme of improvement did not, however, come for final approval.

Indian Road Development Board and apportionment of petrol duty.

22. Political Agent Mr. C. G. B. Stevens was shot in his Bungalow on the 14th December, 1931. The Durbar was deeply grieved at his tragic end and expressed its strong abhorrence of the dastardly and cowardly crime committed. Offices and institutions were closed for 3 days.

Political Agent Mr. C. G. B. Stevens shot dead.

CHAPTER II—LAND ADMINISTRATION.

23. Mr. S. C. Deb Barman, M. A., Harvard), Senior Naib Dewan and Thakur Kamini Kumar Singh, Naib Dewan remained in charge of this Department in addition to other duties assigned to them. During the absence of the Senior Naib Dewan from headquarters, while in Switzerland as the guardian of a Maharajkumari, the Naib Dewan held sole charge of this Department till his return.

Charge.

24. As shown in the subjoined statement, the total area held under settlement and borne on the *toujis* at the close of the year was 643 sq. miles as against 639 sq. miles in the previous year.

Area held under Settlement.

Kinds of settlement.	Area in square miles.		Increase.	Decrease.	REMARKS.
	1341 T.E.	1340 T.E.			
Jotes ...	325	321	4	—	
Taluks ...	318	318	—	—	
Total ...	643	639	4	—	

25. There was no settlement of *Khas* land for tea cultivation during the year under report.

Tea Settlement.

26. The average of *jama* per *kani* of *jote* lands in *khas mehals* (exclusive of cesses) stood at 15 annas and 2 pies against 15 annas and 1 pie in the previous year. The maximum rate for *jote* was Rs. 45 per *kani* while the minimum was 4 annas and those for *taluks* Re. 1 and annas 3 respectively. The maximum *jote* rate was a special one in respect of a small piece of bazar land of a very advantageous position.

Rates of *Jama*.

27. The different sources of land revenue demand with the collection under each head are detailed below:—

Sources of land Revenue.

Sources.	Current demand.		Arrear demand up to the end of		Realization up to the end of		REMARKS.
	1341 T.E.	1340 T.E.	1340 T.E.	1339 T.E.	1341 T.E.	1340 T.E.	
Taluks ...	1,66,695	1,62,403	2,89,995	2,44,925	1,10,008	1,28,964	
Khas Mehal joles	5,07,298	4,86,571	10,55,715	8,36,606	2,57,455	2.74.427	
Bazars ...	7,244	7.755	2,438	1,403	5,742	6,717	
Cesses ...	42,504	40,940	92,939	75.093	22,229	24,275	
Total ...	7,23,741	6,97,669	14,41,087	11,58,027	3,95.434	4.34,383	

28. The above statement shows that the current demand under all heads was Rs. 7,23,741 and with the arrear demand of Rs. 14,41,087 the total demand of the year was Rs. 21,64,828 against Rs. 18,55,696 in the previous year.

Demand.

29. The total collection under all heads during the year amounted to Rs. 3,95,434 being Rs. 1,79,983 under current and Rs. 2,15,451 under arrears; as against Rs. 4,34,383 in the previous year. The percentage of current collection was 24·86 against 33·04 and that of the arrears 14·95 against 17·6. In the *Khas mehal* the percentage of current collection was 12·94 against 20·78 and in *Taluki mehal* the percentage was 60·03 against 68·41 in the previous year.

Collection.

30. Altogether 4,652 certificate cases, covering a demand of Rs. 2,26,778 were instituted during the year. With 3,262 cases valued at Rs. 4,45,558 pending from the previous year, the total number of cases awaiting final orders on disposal of preliminary notices issued on debtors, was 7,914 covering a total demand of Rs. 6,72,336. Of these, 22 cases with a demand of Rs. 1,829 were rejected or struck off and Rs. 12,155 in 450 cases was realised before decree, while 4,171 cases with a total value of Rs. 4,94,340 remained pending.

Coercive measures—Certificates.

31. Orders under provisions of the State Certificate Act were passed during the year in 3,271 cases with a total value of Rs. 1,64,013 making the demands absolute.

Execution.

32. With 6,516 cases to the value of Rs. 4,76,427 pending in execution from the previous year, the total number of cases dealt with was 9,787 covering a demand of Rs. 6,40,440. Out of the total demand, Rs. 6,298 was remitted or written off and of the remainder, Rs. 95,199 was actually realised leaving a balance of Rs. 5,38,943. Of the amount realised Rs. 75,529 represents land revenue and Rs. 19,670 miscellaneous demands.

33. The number of defaulting *taluks* brought under the operation of the Sunset law (including 42 pending from the previous year) was 175. Of these, 118 were released on payment of dues with penalty while 4 was sold in auction and 53 remained undisposed of at the close of the year.

Operation of the Sunset Law.

34. The results of the survey (including resurvey) operations are given in the statement below. It will be seen that an area of 3,533 *drones*, comprising 1,367 *drones* of *taluk* and 2,166 *drones* of *Khas mehal* was surveyed as against a total of 9,345 *drones* in the previous year. The sanctioned programme for survey for the year was for 3,139 *drones* in *Khash Mehal* and 2,270 *drones* in *taluks*. The total expenditure incurred in the survey operations in *Khas Mehal* was Rs. 2,922.

Survey.

Names of Divisions.	Quantity of land in *drones* surveyed in 1341 T. E.			Quantity of land in *drones* surveyed in 1340 T. E.			REMARKS.
	Taluki land.	*Khas mehal* land.	Total.	*Taluki* land.	*Khas mehal* land.	Total.	
1. Sadar Division ...	1,305	1,286	2,591	611	4,733	5,344	
2. Kailashahar " ...	62	122	184	42	307	349	
3. Sonamura " ...	—	—	—	—	1,277	1,277	
4. Bilonia " ...	—	71	71	—	1,258	1,258	
5. Khowai " ...	—	10	10	—	75	75	
6. Dharmanagar " ...	—	385	385	—	636	636	
7. Udaipur " ...	—	78	78	10	363	373	
8. Sabroom " ...	—	201	201	—	33	33	
9. Amarpur Sub " ...	—	13	13	—	—	—	
TOTAL ...	1,367	2,166	3,533	663	8,682	9,345	

35. The total area of the capital town as surveyed, was found to be 218 *drones* (2·15 sq miles) of land. The settlement work was in rapid progress. After finishing the distribution of *parchas*, the attestation work was taken up and finished during the year The expenditure incurred was Rs. 967 only.

Town Survey.

36. This work continued under the direction of Babu Kamini Kumar Kar, Superintendent of Surveys. Compilation of *Mouzmil* maps of the Divisions on a scale of one inch to the mile from the survey maps of villages and *Taluks* was in progress. Maps of 483 villages and *Taluks* were reduced to one inch scale; of these, 450 maps were compiled during the year, the remaining 33 maps having been found to necessitate local enquiry to fit them in with maps of neighbouring surveyed areas. In addition, 119 maps of villages, reduced last year, were compiled, out of 165 reduced maps remaining uncompiled in the previous year.

Map Compilation.

37. 6 case maps in connection with some disputes about boundary between *Taluk* and *Khas* land within the State, and also along the British border line were prepared and three copies of each case map traced.

38. 11 maps of boundary award, 4 maps of *Taluk*, 27 maps of Divisional *Mouzmil* and 30 maps of different Thanas were traced and the area of 13 maps checked with Planimeter by the same staff. The total expenditure incurred was Rs. 972-12 only.

Settlement.

39. It will be seen that no *Taskhichi Taluk* land came under the settlement operations in the year under report as against an area of 1,398 *drones* coming under the operations in the year previous. Settlement operations were fully carried out in respect of 4,562 *drones* of *jote* land against 4,075 *drones* in the preceding year.

Nature of Settlement.	1341 T. E.		1340 T. E.		REMARKS.
	Area in *drones.*	*Jama* in whole rupees.	Area in *drones.*	*Jama* in whole rupees.	
1. Permanent *taluki* settlement of cultivated land ...	—	—	—	—	
2. Permanent *taluki* settlement of waste land	—	—	—	—	
3. * *Taskhichi taluki* settlement of cultivated land ...	—	—	—	—	
4. *Taskhichi taluki* settlement of waste land	—	—	1,398	3,106	
5. *Jotedari* re-settlement of cultivated land	4,363	61,891	3,704	63,926,	
6. *Jotedari* settlement of waste land	199	2,416	371	3,497	
TOTAL. ...	4,562	63,307	5,473	70,529	

* A *Tashkhichi Taluk* of 3 *kanis* of land was granted in Sadar Division with a *Jama* of Rs. 30.

Taluki Settlement.

40. One *Taskhichi Taluk* for the site of a rice mill in Sadar Division comprising 3 *Kanis* of land was settled during the year under review. Rs. 605 wes realised as *Nazar*.

Resettlement of *jote* lands.

41. A net increase of Rs. 15,841 in *jama* was secured by resettlement of *abadi jote* land, the *nazarana* being Rs. 55,894. The average *jama* per *kani* was 14 annas 2 pies against 12 annas in the previous year.

Jotedari Settlement of waste land.

42. During the year an area of 199 *drones* of waste land was settled for a prospective rental of Rs. 2,416 the average *jama* per *kani* obtained being 12 annas 1 pie against 9 annas 5 pies in the previous year. The maximum rates were Rs. 2 and annas 4 respectively. The *nazarana* realised was Rs. 3,315, the rent-free period allowed ranging from 1 to 3 years.

Settlement work.

43. No wholetime Settlement Officer was employed in any Division in the State except in Sadar and Sonamura Divisions. Other Divisional Officers were entrusted with the settlement work within their respective jurisdictions. The total expenditure incurred in the settlement operations was Rs. 3,636

44. It will be seen that the *nazarana* obtained and obtainable by settlement and resettlement of *abadi jote* land and settlement of waste land as *jotes* amounted to Rs. 69,053 and (Rs. 55,894 + Rs. 13,159).

Private Estates under State Management.

45. As detailed below there were altogether 12 private estates under State management during the year under report.

Class.	Name of Estates.	Area.	Revenue.
Encumbered	1. Kakrabon Estate	283 *drones*	1,871
	2. Jogendranagar Trust Estate	64 ,,	163
	3. Kamalnagar and Mahendranagar Estate	51 ,,	255
	4. Gouranga Tripura's Estate	13 ,,	57
	5. Maharam Ali Chaudhuri Khanje Khan Bahadur's Estate—*Taluk*	236 ,,	450
	Jote	6 ,,	149
	6. Thakur Nalini Mohan Deb Barma's Estate	68 ,,	170
	7. Brajendra Kumar Das's Estate	408 ,,	1,936
	8. Brajapur Estate (Kamala Kanta Deb Barman and others)	246 ,,	982
Unencumbered	9. Prabhu Goswamis' Estate	31 ,,	61
	10. Late Brajakumar Thakur's Estate	47 ,,	297
	11. Naba Kumar Chakrabarty's Estate—*Taluk*	32 ,,	225
	Jote	5 ,,	19
Endowment	12. Taranagar Estate	140 ,,	52

46. The subjoined table shows the demands and collections of the estates during the year. Compared with the year previous, collections improved in 7 cases and fell in 2 cases. Estates Nos. 8 & 11 came under State management during the latter part of the year and no realisation could be made therein.

Estate No.	Demand			Collection			P. C. of collection
	Current	Arrear	Total	Current	Arrear	Total	
1.	7,118	34,464	41,582	2,041	4,267	6,308	12·77
2.	1,234	5,543	6,777	83	444	527	7·79
3.	1,274	2,145	3,419	147	948	1,095	32·03
4.	220	74	294	37	74	111	37·75
5.	3,365	12,644	16,009	254	1,621	1,875	11·71
6.	1,163	2,794	3,957	64	243	307	7·76
7.	4,000	2,000	6,000	100	2,330	2,430	40·50
8.	—	—	—	—	—	—	—
9.	912	2,797	3,709	91	347	438	11·80
10.	1,590	2,328	3,918	240	776	1,016	25·93
11.	—	—	—	—	—	—	—
12.	3,100	8,598	11,698	228	13,21	1,540	13·35

CHAPTER III—PROTECTION.

I. Legislation.

47. No legislation was introduced during the year and there was no sitting of the Legislative Council.

CIRCULARS.

48. The following important circulars were issued :—

(1) Circular No. 19—Disallowing leave charge allowance for a period below one month except under special order of the Dewan-Shashan.

(2) Circular No. 20—Enjoining previous sanction of the Revenue Department—imperative on the part of *Talukdars* in the matter of starting bazars on *taluki* land.

(3) Circular No. 24—Directing printing of the *Dakhila* forms of *Khash Mehal* on both sides of paper.

(4) Circular No. 25—Directing the Thana Officers to report the cases of excise smuggling to the Collector concerned and to Superintendent of Police; as also prescribing a form for register of such cases.

II. Military.

49. Major Kumar Dina Mohan Deb Barman Bahadur continued to be in charge of the Military Forces.
Charge.

50. The total strength of the forces at the end of the year was 412 against 432 of the preceding year.
Strength.

51. The First Tripura Bir Company was supplied during the year with H. V. Rifles (·303 bore) replacing the former E. Y. Rifles which was transferred to the Second Tripura Bikram Company in anticipation of this Company being recognised as Indian States Forces.
Armament.

52. During the year His Highness the Maharaja Manikya Bahadur inspected the Third Jangi Company in April and the First Tripura Bir Company in March.
Inspection.

53. Military Adviser, Central India States Forces, arranged for the training at Shillong and accordingly Subader Jogendra Chandra Deb Barman and Jamader Bimal Chandra Deb Barman, one N. C. O. and 5 Sepoys were sent there. The result was satisfactory. Individual training in summer and collective training in winter was done in accordance with the programme.
Training.

54. Some improvements and petty repairs of the barracks were done during the year, special attention was given to gardening.
Cantonment.

55. As in the previous year, the health of the forces was generally good.
Health.

56. The total expenditure for the year excluding that for the repair works amounted to Rs. 1,05,730 against Rs. 1,13,897.
Expenditure.

57. Besides the ordinary sentry and escort duties the force had to do some patrolling work. For the suppression of crimes in the locality it was thought necessary to send a military force to patrol in the Bisalgarh Road and accordingly
Extra Duties.

on the 27th April, 1931, 3 platoons marched to Bisalgarh and Hatileta and encamped there for a fortnight. This had a very good effect.

58. The military was called upon to patrol the town at night after the committal of an armed dacoity in the night of 5th April, 1932, and a Platoon was detailed for the duty for sometime.

Camping and Marching

59. On the 26th October, all the available military forces of the State, undertook camping march for 10 days. His Highness the Maharaja Manikya Bahadur as Commender-in-Chief of the force accompanied by the Chief Secretary, the Private Secretary, and A. D. C. and the State Engineer, headed the party. From the cantonment the force started in the morning against torrent of rains and reached Bisalgarh a distance of 14 miles in the afternoon and camped there for the night. The march was resumed in the morning after strainously negotiating a hilly tract of 20 miles, in rains, and crossing the Goomti river, was reached Radhakishorepur (Udaipur) at 6 P. M.. There the party stopped for 4 days. On the 31st October the march was again resumed and the force proceeded towards Sonamura. On the way camped for a night at Kakrabon and the next day they arrived at Sonamura, where there was a halt for 2 days. Another short march brought them to Comilla. There His Highness the Maharaja Manikya Bahadur and the troops received a grand reception. The force travelled next day, the 4th November, by special train from Comilla to Akhaura, from where they marched back to their cantonments.

60. With a view to have training in tactics and manoeuvres, the troops after doing tactical training for a month with their respective Company Commanders were engaged for 4 days in tactical practice from the 29th January to 2nd February. (31st January being a holiday) under the supervision of His Highness the Maharaja Manikya Bahadur and did satisfactory work.

III. Police.

Charge.

61. Honorary Lieutenant J. C. Datta, B. A., continued as Superintendent of Police during the year. Babu Naresh Kumar Bhattacherjee, B. Sc., joined office on 3rd Jaistha, 1341 T. E. as a Probationery Assistant Superintendent of Police on the completion of his training in the Police Training College at Sardah.

Strength.

62. The total numerical strength of the Police force during the year was 493 against 532 in the previous year. As the duty of guarding some of the *moffassil* treasuries hitherto performed by the police was taken up by the Military a reduction in the force was made.

Rural Police.

63. The total number of village chaukidars was 175.

Inspecting Staff.

64 There were 4 Inspectors of Police. The main duty of the Inspectors was to supervise important cases and control the staff placed under them.

Investigating and Prosecuting Staff.

65. During the year, there were 25 Sub-Inspectors and 20 Naib Darogas as against 25 and 17 respectively in the previous year. 3 posts were sanctioned tantatively.

C. I. D. and Intelligence Staff.

66. As in the previous year, only one Sub-Inspector worked in the C. I. D., besides 4 Naib Darogas and 5 Constables as against 1 Naib Daroga and 4 Constables in the previous year.

Crime.

67. The total number of cases reported during the year under review was 1,300 against 1,377 in the previous year.

68. The result of the cases investigated will be seen from the following table :—

Number of cases reported
1,300

Enquiry refused	Number investigated	Number pending
71	1,107	122

Number investigated (1,107):

Maliciously false	True	Doubtful etc.
4	744	329

True (744):

Charge-sheet	Finally reported
437	337

Result of Prosecution.

69. Altogether 925 persons were arrested in connection with various offences and 835 persons sent up for trial by Police against 802 and 801 respectively in the previous year. Of the number 835 sent up, 284 were convicted and 217 acquitted (including 64 on compromise, 24 on withdrawal of cases), while 1 died and 333 awaited trial (including absconding accused). The percentage of conviction was 30·97 against 27·80 of the previous year.

70. Of 336 awaiting trial at the end of the previous year, 93 were convicted, 170 acquitted (including 26 on compromise and 16 on withdrawal of cases) and 73 were awaiting trial.

Badlivelihood cases.

71. 6 bad livelihood cases with 14 persons as accused were instituted during the year. 1 person was convicted, 4 discharged and 9 persons were pending trial at the end of the year.

Arms Act Cases

72. 26 Arms Act cases with 25 persons as accused were instituted. 10 persons were convicted, 6 discharged and 9 were awaiting trial (including 4 absconding) as the year closed.

Recovery of Stolen Property.

73. Total value of the property stolen during the year amounted to Rs. 20,558-9-9 against Rs. 21,276-14-6 of the previous year. Of this amount, Rs. 4,600-6 was recovered as against Rs. 4,859-9-0 of the previous year. The percentage of recoveries was 22·38 against 22·83 of the previous year and 19·74 of 1339 T. E.

74. There were 32 cases of dacoity reported during the year against 26 in the year preceding. 41 persons were sent up in charge-sheet in connection with 9 cases, of whom 1 was convicted and 40 were awaiting trial at the close of the year.

Dacoities.

75. There were altogether 62 cases of unnatural deaths. Regular enquiries were held by the police into all these cases and no foul play was detected.

Unnatural deaths.

76. 1 Inspector, 6 Sub-Inspectors, 1 Naib Daroga, 6 constables received money rewards; while 2 Naib Darogas, 1 Jamader (civil), 1 Havilder, 2 Naiks, 2 Lance Naiks, 7 constables (Armed), 31 constables (civil) and 2 choukidars were fined, suspended or degraded.

Rewards & punishments.

77. The Superintendent of Police was out on tour for 57 days against 92 days in the previous year and the Assistant Superintendent of Police for 30 days.

Tours.

78. The relation with the neighbouring districts in British India continued to be satisfactory.

Co-operation.

79. The expenditure amounted to Rs. 83,334 against Rs. 85,471 in the previous year.

Expenditure.

IV. Justice.

80. There were 14 courts of justice in the State during the year under report exercising both civil and criminal jurisdiction, viz :—the Khas Adalat or the High Court with its original and appellate sides and 13 courts of Magistrate-Munsiffs exercising original jurisdiction only.

Courts.

81. Babu Jnanendra Mohan Das, B. L., continued as Chief Judge and Babu Ramani Mohan Goswami, M. A., B. L., as Civil and Sessions Judge in the original side during the year. Kumar S. C. Deb Barman, who was Puisne Judge, died on the 26th Agrahayan, 1341 T. E. On his death Uzir Bahadur B. K. Deb Barman, the retired Judge, was recalled. The late Kumar served in the Khas Adalat for nearly 10 years and was greatly esteemed by everybody he came in contact with, for his independence and sound common sense.

Khas Adalat.

82. Altogether 1,949 criminal cases were instituted during the year under report as against 1,879 of the previous year. With the balance of 451 pending from the last year, the total number of cases for disposal before the several subordinate original courts was 2,400 against 2,608 of the previous year as detailed below ; and out of these 2,400 cases,

Number of original criminal cases.

1,883 were disposed of as against 2,157 of the last year, leaving 517 cases pending at the close of the year. Thus in the year under report, the number of cases for disposal decreased from that of the last year by 208, and there was also a decrease in disposal by 274.

DESCRIPTION OF OFFENCES.	1340 T.S.	1341 T.S.
Offences against the State and public tranquillity	84	58
Offences against person	580	631
Offences against property	1,324	1,206
Other offences	610	505
TOTAL	2,608	2,400

Extradition from British India.

83. Extradition of 96 persons was asked for during the year. With 92 persons pending surrender at the close of the previous year, the total number of offenders involved in the requisitions was 188, of whom 51 persons were arrested and surrendered by the British Indian Police and 20 persons appeared of their own accord or were subsequently arrested within the State.

Persons brought to trial.

84. The total number of persons awaiting trial in the year under report, inclusive of the number pending from the preceding year was 3,056 against 3,760 of the previous year. The number brought to trial within the year was 2,384. Of these, 817 persons were arrested by the police, 569 were produced on warrant, 692 appeared on summons, 301 appeared voluntarily and 5 persons were arrested in presence of the Magistrates.

Results of cases.

85. Out of 3,056 persons before the courts including the Sessions, 919 were discharged without trial, 672 were acquitted, 673 were convicted, 7 died, 10 escaped and 775 remained under trial at the close of the year. Of the persons convicted, 246 were sentenced to various terms of imprisonment extending from below 1 month to below 5 years, 2 persons were imprisoned for life and 378 were sentenced to fine only, 13 persons were bound down and 34 persons were warned for the future. The number of persons actually tried was 1,345 as against 1,723 of the previous year and the percentage of conviction was thus 50·04 against 40·51 of the preceding year.

Cases concerning British subjects.

86. Of 2,400 cases for disposal as stated above, the number of cases concerning British subjects was 448 as against 389 of the previous year. Out of these cases, 354 were cognizable cases and 94 non-cognizable cases. In 49 cases, British subjects were complainants and in 399 cases they were the accused. In 113 cases both the parties were British subjects. In these cases, 606 persons were actually under trial during the year under report against 633 of the previous year. Of the persons involved, 316 persons were convicted, 192 acquitted or discharged, 1 died and 97 remained under trial at the close of the year.

87. The following statement will show the number of original criminal cases instituted during the last two years.

Comparative Statement.

DESCRIPTION OF OFFENCES.	1340 T. E.	1341 T. E.	Increase.	Decrease.
Offences against the State and public tranquillity ...	59	46	0	13
Offences against person	432	535	103	0
Offences against property	913	977	64	0
Other offences	475	391	0	84
TOTAL	1,879	1,949	167	97

Increased by 70.

88. 30 cases were committed to the Sessions during the year under report and 4 cases were pending from the previous year. Out of these 34 cases, 25 were disposed of during the year as detailed in the following table. The number of persons involved in these cases was 124, of whom 31 persons were convicted, 63 acquitted and 30 remained under trial at the close of the year.

Sessions cases.

Description of cases.	Number of cases.	Disposed of.	Pending.	REMARKS.
Murder	9	7	2	
Culpable homicide not amounting to murder	5	4	1	
Dacoity	8	5	3	
Robbery	3	2	1	
Arson	1	0	1	
Grievous hurt	2	2	0	
Rape	2	2	0	
Forgery	1	1	0	
Using counterfeit coin	1	1	0	
Criminal trespass	1	1	0	
Causing hurt with unlicensed gun ...	1	0	1	
Total	34	25	9	

89. There were altogether 308 criminal appeals as against 304 of the previous year. These appeals were disposed of as shown below :—

Criminal appeals.

Rejected	19
Judgment affirmed	148
Modified	46
Reversed	19
Further enquiry ordered	14
	246
Pending	62
Total	308

90. The percentage of judgments affirmed and modified was 85·46 as against 80·86 of the previous year.

91. The number of original civil suits instituted during the year under report was 1,919 as against 2,161 of the previous year. With the balance of 788 suits from the preceding year, the total number of suits for disposal was 2,707

Original Civil suits.

against 3,339 of the previous year. They were disposed of as shown below :—

Exparte	964
Admitted and compromised	199
Dismissed for want of prosecution ...	102
Disposed of on contest	709
	1,974
Pending	733
Total	2,707

Duration of suits.

92. The average duration of suits before the civil courts was 2 months and 28 days as against 4 months and 5 days in 1340 T. E.

Nature and value of suits.

93. The total value of civil suits instituted during the year was Rs. 2,18,100-15-6 as against Rs. 2,63,613-12-6 of the previous year, which gives an average of Rs. 113-10-6 per case. Out of 1,919 suits instituted during the year under report, 435 related to land, 1,238 to money transactions and 246 to other transactions. 1,155 suits were of the value of Rs. 100 and under ; 422 suits were of value above Rs. 100 and below Rs. 500 ; 41 suits of value above Rs. 500 and below Rs. 1,000 ; 21 suits of value above Rs. 1,000 and below Rs. 5,000 ; and 280 were not estimable in money value.

Execution of decrees.

94. The number of applications for the execution of decrees filed during the year was 898 and there were 559 pending from the previous year. The total number for disposal was thus 1,457 as against 1,506 of the preceding year. The aggregate value of the new applications was Rs. 1,35,207-2-0, and that of the pending applications was Rs. 1,39,398-7-6. The value thus amounted to Rs. 2,74,605-9-6. The number of applications disposed of was 845, the value thereof being Rs. 1,23,161-4-9. The number of execution cases pending at the close of the year was 612, the value of which was Rs. 1,51,444-4-9.

Civil appeals.

95. There were 203 civil appeals filed during the year as against 214 of the previous year. With the balance of 164 from the last year, the total number of civil appeals for disposal was 367 against 352 of the preceding year. Out of these, 200 were disposed of during the year under review as against 188 of the previous year, leaving a balance of 167 cases at the close of the year.

Results of appeals.

96. The following figures indicate the results of appeals :—

Decisions confirmed	85
" reversed	22
" modified	29
Remanded	21
Compromised and otherwise disposed of ...	43
	200

97. The percentage of judgments wholly or partly upheld, excluding those in the cases compromised, was 72·61 as against 61·49 of the preceding year.

Percentage.

98. The total value of appeals filed during the year under review was Rs. 20,242-2-9 and the average duration of each appeal was 4 months and 5 days against 2 months and 16 days of the previous year.

Value and duration of appeals.

99. 28 civil suits were instituted in the Khas Adalat original side in 1341 T. E. as against 35 of the previous year. With the balance of 67 suits from 1340 T. E. the total for disposal was thus 95 against 94 of the preceding year. Of these, 31 suits were disposed of against 27, leaving 64 suits pending at the close of the year. There were 51 execution cases during the year under report, including 32 cases pending from the previous year. Of these, 15 were disposed of and 36 remained pending at the close of the year There were 23 applications filed for the grant of succession and other certificates during the year. With the balance of 28 from the previous year the total number of cases was 51, out of which, 35 were disposed of as shown below and 16 remained pending at the close of the year.

Cases of the original side.

Description of cases.	Total.	Disposed of.	Pending.
Probate case	6	1	5
Succession certificate	22	17	5
Guardianship	23	17	6
Total	51	35	16

100. The total number of civil and criminal appeals, inclusive of the number pending from 1340 T. E., was 675 as against 656 of the previous year. Out of these, 446 were disposed of as against 417. In comparison with the previous year, the total for disposal increased by 19 and there was also a corresponding increase in disposal by 29.

Total number of appeals.

Description of appeals.	Number of appeals.		Disposed of.	
	Past year.	Present year.	Past year.	Present year.
Civil	352	367	188	200
Criminal	304	308	229	246
Total	656	675	417	446

V. Prisons.

101. There were 8 jails in the State during the year under report one at each of the Divisions and Sub-Divisions including the Central Jail at the Capital. Dr. M. M. Majumdar continued to be the Superintendent of the Central Jail.

Number of Jails.

102. The total jail population during the year was 1,332 as against 997 in the previous year with the daily average of 161·55 against 103·59. Of them, 592 were convicts, 734 under-trials and 6 civil prisoners.

Jail population.

103. The following table shows details about the offence and sentence of the 78 prisoners who were under more than 2 years' imprisonment against 51 of the previous year :—

Long-term prisoners.

Class of offence.	Number of prisoners.	Occupation.	REMARKS.
Murder	15	They are employed in brick manufacture, oilmills, wheat grinding, *soorki* pounding, *khoa* breaking, bamboo and cane work, gardening, weaving, tailoring, paddy husking, rice manufacturing &c.	55 had sentences of 2 to 5 years, 12 of 5 to 10 years, 11 for life *i. e.* 20 years.
Culpable homicide not amounting to murder... ...	11		
Grievous hurt	10		
Theft	6		
Rape	1		
Dacoity	11		
Forgery	6		
Robbery	3		
Unlawful assembly	10		
Kidnapping	1		
Counterfeiting coin	3		
Sec. 110 (Security for good behaviour for habitual offenders)	1		
Total	78		

104. The health of the jail was on the whole good. Only 3 convicts and 1 under-trial died during the year. One of T. B. infection, one of pneumonia and one each of Kalazar and chronic malaria with complications.

Jail health.

105. One convict from the Central Jail and one under-trial from the Sabrum Jail escaped during the year under review. None of them could be re-arrested.

Escape.

106. 20 convicts underwent training in the Reformatory School inside the Central Jail at the hands of a paid tutor. 3 of them appeared at the Pathshala Scholarship Examination of the State of whom 2 came out successful one being placed in the first Division and the other in the 2nd Division. Religious instructions were also given to Hindu and Muhammadan inmates of the Jail by honorary instructors once a week.

Education.

107. 3 senior warders and 26 warders were kept employed during the year under review. Of them, 2 having left their services of their own accord and 4 being discharged, the posts had to be filled in.

Warders.

108. The total income from the Central Jail only amounted to Rs. 2,254 as against Rs. 1,308 in the preceding year. This income excludes Rs. 1,840–14–3 as being unrealised at the end of the year.

Income.

109. The total expenditure during the year under report was Rs. 17,995 as against Rs. 17,568 in the year before.

Expenditure.

VI. Registration.

110. The charge of the Department continued with Thakur K. K. Singh, Naib Dewan.

Charge.

111. The number of registration offices continued to be 9 as in the previous year, there being one at the headquarters station of each of the Divisions or Sub-Divisions. In the mofussil the Divisional and the Sub-Divisional Officers and in certain Divisions the Second Officers acted as Registrars. For the Sadar Division there was a separate Registrar at Agartala.

Registration Offices.

112. The total number of documents presented for registration during the year including 217 documents pending at the end of the previous year was 6,302 against 9,382. Of this number, 71 deeds were refused registration on different grounds and 1,036 remained pending at the end of the year against 217 pending at the end of the previous year. This huge accumulation of work is anything but satisfactory. Considerable reduction in the number of these cases have however been effected since the close of the year.

Registration and Disposal.

113. The total value covered by the documents presented amounted to Rs. 8,85,085 as compared with Rs. 17,55,137 while the total value covered by the documents actually registered was Rs. 7,09,868 as against Rs. 15,17,763 in the year before. It will be seen that the value covered by the deeds presented has considerably gone down, the figure for 1339 being Rs. 20,23,206. It is due to the world-wide economic depression and scarcity of money among all classes of people.

Value of deeds presented and registered.

114. The number of suits filed in the Registration Department in respect of the documents, the registration of which had been refused in the Registration offices, was 20 against 33 suits and 4 appeals in the previous year. There were 26 suits pending from the previous year, making a total of 46 suits. Out of these, 15 suits were disposed of during the year leaving 31 suits pending at the end of the year. No appeal was pending at the end of the previous year nor any appeal was filed during the year under review.

Suits and Appeals.

115. The total income of the Department from fees and fines amounted to Rs. 6,897 against Rs. 11,045 and the expenditure to Rs. 3,840 against Rs. 4726 in the previous year. The net income thus amounted to Rs. 3,057 against Rs. 6,319 in the previous year.

Income and expenditure.

116. The fall of income in 1340 T. E. was Rs. 3,820 in comparison with previous year (1339 T. E.). In the year under review it further went down and the fall amounted to Rs. 8,000 and odd in comparison with 1339 T. E. and to Rs. 5,000 and odd in comparison with 1340 T. E.

VII. Municipality and Sanitation.

117. As before, the State had the only Municipal Institution in the capital town of Agartala during the year under report with a population of about 10,000 according to the last census.

Municipality.

118. On the expiry of the term of the previous committee a new committee with nine members—all nominated—including an official chairman and a non-official vice-chairman was formed towards the end of the year. Thakur Hriday Ranjan Deb Barman was nominated Chariman of the new committee and Babu Haridas Bhattacharjee was elected Vice-Chairman by the unanimous vote of the committee. Altogether 9 sittings of the committee (new & old) were held during the year, the average attendance of members being 5·3 as against 5·0 of the year before.

Municipal Committee.

119. The realization on account of Municipal and Latrine taxes was Rs. 3,509-10-3 as against Rs. 3,094-2-3 of the previous year, the total demand inclusive of arrears being Rs. 8,639-6-0. against Rs. 8,616-7-9. The miscellaneous income from all sources including deposits and advances recovered amounted to Rs. 908-4-3 as against Rs. 642-13-0 of the year before. The State grant for the year was Rs. 9,000 against Rs. 10,000 in the preceding year. Thus the total income of the municipality came up to Rs. 13,417-14-6 as against Rs. 13,737 of the previous year. The above figure excludes the income derived from the municipal market.

Income.

120. The total expenditure of the municipality excluding the amount spent on the Bazar improvement amounted to Rs. 14,178-9-0 as against Rs. 13,110-11-6 in the previous year.

Expenditure.

121. The control and management of the Bazar continued to be in the hands of the municipal Committee. The total collection came up to Rs. 6,144-7-6 as against Rs. 6,310-6-6 in the preceding year. The fall is due to the reduced rent payable by the *Izaradar* to the extent of Rs. 500 on account of general economic depression. The total demand including arrears was Rs. 12,272-9-0. After necessary expenditure of Rs. 464-7-0, the Bazar improvement fund stood at Rs. 33,234-12-3 at the close of the year. As before, the Bazar income is earmarked for the Bazar improvement only.

Ishanganja Bazar.

122. Within the municipal area the general health of the public was on the whole satisfactory. Kala-azar and cholera cases went down. There were no cases of small-pox and othes contagious disease.

Public health.

123. Dr. M. M. Mazumdar, Chief Medical Officer of the State, continued to be in charge of the Municipal and Sanitation Department during the year under report. Under his direct supervision some minor sanitary works were carried out in the town at a cost of Rs. 309.

Sanitation.

CHAPTER IV—PRODUCTION AND DISTRIBUTION.

I. Weather and Crops—Agriculture.

124. As in the previous year, the charge of the Department remained with Manyabara Rana Bodhjung Bahadur, Chief Secretary to His Highness the Maharaja Manikya Bahadur, who was assisted by Mr. J. C. Chaudhury, Superintendent of Agriculture.

The Charge of the Department.

125. The average rainfall during the year was 82·74″ against 92·58″ in the previous year. The quinquennial average was 87·93″. The maximum fall was reported from Bilonia Division as 108·67″ and minimum from Amarpur Sub-Division as 64·56″. Distribution was fairly even.

Rainfall.

126. The highest rise of temperature was noted on the 26th Chait as 97°, and the lowest on the 14th Pous as 52°. Spring season lasted for 5 to 6 weeks.

Temperature.

127. The principle crops in the State are paddy, cotton, *til*, mustard, jute and sugarcane. Potatoes, tobacco, chillies of various types are also grown to a considerable extent.

Crops

128. There was heavy flood in different parts of the State and relief was given in the shape of gratuitous relief and loans except in Sabroom Division and about Rs. 4000 was distributed for the purpose which also comprises cost of 640 and 410 mds. of paddy distributed as relief loans in Sonamura and Kailashahar Divisions respectively. Rs. 847 was realised against loans for relief measures.

Floods.

129, The outturn and export of tea increased during the year under review. There was some extension of old plantations in spite of slump in the tea market. Though the revenue payable by the gardens has fallen in arrear heavily, they are being very leniently dealt with. The export duty also fell in spite of a marked increase in the export and this is due to low prices as also to a large amount of duty assessed having fallen in arrear. The arrear land revenue of tea garden settlements amounted to more than 2 lacs, there was no improvement in the tottering condition of tea industry in the State as elsewhere.

Tea Industry.

130. The people were seriously affected by the all-round economic depression which led to a slump in the market for indigenous commodities such as cotton, jute and oil-seeds.

Condition of the people.

131. Wages for field labour including those for jooming were 4 to 8 annas per day, those of masons 8 to 12 annas per day, of carpenters 8 annas to Re. 1, thatchers 6 to 10 annas and for labour for earth work 8 to 10 annas per day.

Labour and Wages.

132. One fieldman was employed for the northern Divisions with his headquarters at Kailashahar with a view to promote cultivation of various agricultural crops and another fieldman was placed at Udaipur for the southern Divisions for pushing on Eri-culture and propaganda.

Activities of the Department.

133. The Kashipur farm continued to be a seed-producing farm.

Kashipur Farm.

134. Taccavi of Rs. 1,000 was issued in Sadar Division.

Taccavi.

135. The condition of cattle was not good on the whole. Rinderpest was reported from Sabroom and Khowai Divisions. All possible veterinary aid was given.

Cattle.

II. Immigration and Emigration.

136. The charge of the Department continued to be, with Manyabara Rana Bodhjung Bahadur, F. R. G. S., Chief Secretary to His Highness the Maharaja Manikya Bahadur, who was assisted by Mr. B. C. Dev Varman, Assistant.

137. During the year under review, 1,222 families immigrated into and 1,239 families emigrated out of the State as against 1,869 and 1,270 in the previous year.

138. The settlement and reclamation work in Kulaihaor made a fair progress during the year under report. Some of the new settlers managed to live in their respective *Jotes* and reclaimed their own lands under the Jooming system. The Department was able to secure a good number of candidates from outside for settlement, of whom 100 were granted settlement of lands.

139. The Department up to date spent an amount of Rs. 21,000/- (twentyone thousand) on the whole towards construction of a new road extending over 32 miles, in the immigration area in Kulaihaor to facilitate the transport etc. in the interior. Unfortunately some portion of the newly constructed road was badly damaged immediately after construction by heavy flood The repair work was, however, immediately undertaken.

140. Arrangement for good drinking water, establishment of primary school and other necessary improvements in the immigration area are under contemplation.

141. 11,000 *drones* of land in Khowai Division has been reserved only for Hill people and the survey and settlement works in the reserved area made a considerable progress.

III. Forests.

142. Babu Jatindra Nath Mitra, Naib Dewan, continued to be in charge of the Department. With the exception of a few *Mahals* which were let out in *Ijara*, all the forests were under *Khas* management as before.

Charge and management.

143. The Department employed a staff of 1 Station Officer, 3 Forest Circle Inspectors, 15 Foresters, 22 Assistant Foresters and Rangers, 9 Mohurers, 21 Head Guards and 191 Literate Guards and Guards. Besides these, there were 129 Commission Agents for the sale of forest permits for the shoulder-borne export of minor forest produce not coming under any definite *Mahal*. There were 54 forest stations for collection of duty and prevention of forest offences against 55 in the year preivous.

Staff.

144. The reserved *Sal* forests of the Sonamura Division continued to be worked under the system of coppice with standards and those of the Udaipur Division under the Improvement Method, while the open unclassed forests were worked under the State Forest Rules of 1323 T. E. For the Feni River *Mahal* the working rules of the Bengal Forest Department were followed.

Working.

145. Out of the four coupes selected and marked in the Sonamura Division, operations were undertaken in one. No work was undertaken in the remaining three as they could not be sold for want of purchasers. The two *Sal* blocks selected and marked in the Udaipur Division could not be sold for want of purchasers.

146. The following table shows the results of the collection of forest revenue.

Sources of Forest Revenue.

Heads of Revenue.	1341 T.E.	1340 T.E.	Increase.	Decrease.	REMARKS.
I. Unclassed open forests :—					
(a) Toll on forest produce exported by the river mehals	2,55,805	2,88,797	—	32,992	
(b) Toll on forest produce exported by land route under permit	60,692	71,233	—	10,541	
(c) Toll collection (share) of the Feni river mehal ...	27,850	30,524	—	2,674	
(d) Grazing mehal ...	5,690	6,024	—	334	
(e) Thatching grass mehal	4,008	5,789	—	1,781	
II. Reserved Forests :—					
Sale of *Sal* and *Garjan* trees ...	1,470	5,500	—	4,030	
III. Elephant Kheddas	—	4,099	—	4,099	
TOTAL ...	3,55,515	4,11,966	—	56,451	

147. The total forest revenue of the year under report was
Receipts. Rs. 3,55,515 against Rs. 4,11,966 in the previous year, showing a decrease of Rs. 56,451. This fall of revenue is noticeable under each head and is due to the general dullness of trade in all kinds of forest produce.

148. In the year under report no *Kheda* operations were under-
***Kheda* Operations.** taken for want of bidders. This accounts for the fall of revenue under "Elephant *Kheda*."

149. The Toll Station at Amlighat continued to be under the
Feni River *Mahal*. management of the State Forest Department. The total revenue collected at the station in the year under review was Rs. 39,850 against Rs. 44,524 in the previous year. As before a doctor of the Sub-Assistant Surgeon class was appointed temporarily for four months from December last for giving medical relief to the wood-cutters at Amlighat Toll Station as well as to the station staff.

150. As in the previous year, the forest produce from Lot No. 98
Fee Simple Lots. as well as from the other Fee Simple Lots was exported under passes granted by the Collector of Chittagong.

151. In the year under review there were 271 forest cases against
Forest Offences. 491 persons including 69 cases against 131 persons pending from the previous year. The offences were mainly for illicit export of forest produce without payment of duty.

152. Altogether 207 cases against 398 persons were tried, of
Results. whom one was sentenced to imprisonment and to pay fine, 6 were sentenced to imprisonment 289 were punished with fine and 102 were acquitted. 26 cases against 32 persons were compounded and 38 cases against 61 persons remained pending at the close of the year.

153. One guard was rewarded for clever detection of a case
Rewards and Punishments. of smuggling of forest produce. One Head Guard was dismissed for misconduct and one guard was suspended.

154. The health of the staff in general was good except that two
Health of the Staff. guards died of fever.

155. The patrol staff consisting of one Forester, two Head Guards
Patrol Staff. and 14 guards went out on patrol duty in the Sadar, Sonamura, Bilonia and Sabroom Divisions, where they detected and arrested men accused of smuggling forest produces who were mostly convicted. This had a salutary effect on the exporters of forest produce.

156. It may be noted here that a factory for the manufacture of
General, matches was started near Agartala during the year. If the factory is properly worked, it is expected to yield a handsome revenue to the State.

157. The Naib Dewan was out on tour for 35 days in the year
Tour. under report, against 79 days in the year before.

IV. Trade and Manufacture.

158. The principal exports were timber, forest produce of various kinds, cotton, oil-seeds (*til* and mustard seed), paddy, jute, tea, rice and *Gur* (molasses). Some homespun cotton fabrics manufactured by the hill-people, especially the Manipuries, were also exported. The principal exports for the year under review and of the previous year are shewn below.

	1340 T. E.	1341 T. E.
Cotton	54,785 mds.	56,034 mds.
Til	29,617 ,,	14,761 ,,
Mustard seeds	33,270 ,,	25,936 ,,
Jute	74,512 ,,	30,454 ,,

159. Altogether 14,02,725 lbs, 12,18,161 lbs and 15,21,534 lbs of tea were exported in 1339 T. E., 1340 T. E. and 1341 T. E. respectively. In the previous year's report the export of tea was incorrectly stated as 9,51,564 lbs in place of 12,18,161 lbs.

V. Public Works.

160. Charge. Hony. Lieutenant J. N. Bhaduri, B. A., B. E., continued as State Engineer during the year. The Dewan-Shashan was personally in charge of the Public Works Department as before.

161. Expenditure. Statement XX in the appendix gives details of the works executed during the year, the total expenditure being Rs. 81,397 as detailed below against Rs. 2,38,724 in the previous year.

(1)	Buildings	Rs. 41,615
(2)	Roads and Bridges	,, 6,234
(3)	Tanks and Tube wells ...	,, 3,225
(4)	Miscellaneous works	,, 9,490
(5)	Minor works at Rajbari (*Karkhana*)	,, 1,959
(6)	Establishment charges ...	,, 18,874

162. Improvement. Out of the total, Rs. 8,604 was spent for improvement works under the following heads :—

(1)	Buildings	Rs. —
(2)	Roads and Bridges	,, 849
(3)	Water supply	,, 1,084
(4)	Miscellaneous works	,, 6,671

163. Considerable progress was made in the construction of the west wing of the Minister's Office Building and towards the close of the year under report it was nearing completion. Construction of type quarters for State officials also proceeded. Construction of the Sabroom Office building was also started in the year and some progress was made.

Buildings.

164. The following public buildings were reconstructed with corrugated iron roofing in Sadar and Mofussil.

1. Cook-shed for Hindu prisoners in Sadar Jail.
2. Radhakishorepur Tahasill Office.
3. Radhakishorepur Barrack.
4. Radhakishorepur Police Station.
5. Srinagar Range Office.
6. Sabroom Tahasil Office.

165. The following new roads were completed in the year under report.

Roads and Bridges.

(1) Extension of the Thana road up to South Gangail.

(2) Part of the Agartala town Gangail road lying to the west of the Hospital road.

(3) Road connecting the main road of His Highness's Domain with the proposed Palace Avenue road.

(4) Road from Her Highness the Dowager Maharani Saheba's garden to the Domain Office Tilla.

166. The decking of one of the bridges of the Agartala town was reconstructed with re-inforced cement concrete.

167. The work of excavation of a big tank at Agartala was completed in the year under report. Four tube-wells were sunk at Agartala, one at the Kunjaban Cantonment and one at Sabroom.

Water Supply.

168. Construction of the parade ground at Kunjaban Cantonment was completed in the year. The work of diversion of the course of the Gomati river at Amarpur and that of the Dhalai river at Abhanga was also completed.

Miscellaneous Works.

169. The total expenditure in connection with Electric Supply was Rs. 17,700.

Electric Supply.

170. The seriousness of the financial situation caused by the all-round economic depression necessitated the introduction of a very cautious policy with regard to Public Works and it was due to this economic depression that no local funds were available for Public Works in the year under report.

Economic Depression.

CHAPTER V—REVENUE AND FINANCES.

I. Revenue.

171. The total collection in the year was Rs. 12,37,252 against Rs. 13,92,709 in the previous year.

172. The details of income under different heads with all variations are given in the statement below :—

Serial number.	Heads of Revenue.	1341 T.E.	1340 T.E.	As compared with 1340 T.E.		Remarks.
				Increase.	Decrease.	
1.	Land Revenue	3,97,658	4,40,180	—	42,522	
2.	Rents of markets	5,485	6,668	—	1,183	
3.	Family Tax in the hills	42,685	37,204	5,481	—	
4.	Toll on forest produce	3,16,497	3,60,030	—	43,533	
5.	Do. Do. on the Feni River	27,850	30,524	—	2,674	
6.	Elephant & buffalo grazing Mehal	5,690	6,024	—	334	
7.	Thatching grass Mehal	4,008	5,789	—	1,781	
8.	Reserved *Sal* trees	1,470	5,500	—	4,030	
9.	Tax on cotton and oil-seeds ...	1,12,868	1,07,281	5,587	—	
10.	Royalty on elephants caught ...	—	4,099	—	4,099	
11.	Adda Mehal	23,333	19,769	3,564	—	
12.	Excise	50,086	92,302	—	42,216	
13.	Stamps and Court-fees	67,070	82,738	—	15,668	
14.	Law and Justice (Fines)... ...	4,813	4,865	—	52	
15.	Process fees	12,563	14,830	—	2,267	
16.	Registration	6,897	11,045	—	4,148	
17.	Jail	2,254	1,400	854	—	
18.	Cattle pounds	4,566	5,219	—	653	
19.	Nazars	27,390	37,733	—	10,343	
20.	Education...	14,502	16,581	—	2,079	
21.	Tea Export duty	8,033	12,742	—	4,109	
22.	Jute Export duty	11,463	27,978	—	16,515	
23.	Recovery of personal advances	3,746	5,062	—	1,316	
24.	Depreciation Contribution ...	42,110	—	42,110	—	
25.	Interest on bank deposits... ..	—	1,549	—	1,549	
26.	Miscellaneous	43,615	55,597	—	11,882	
	Total	12,37,252	13,92,709	57,596	2,12,953	Net decrease— Rs. 1,55,457.

173. It will be seen that there was an increase in respect of 5 heads of income. Amongst them the increase under the head Depreciation Contribution is not in comparison with the last year as this head of income came to being in the year under review.

174. The increase in respect of other 4 heads of income amounted to Rs. 15,486 and they are due to good *jhum* harvest and strenuous efforts of collection.

175. There was a decrease in respect of 21 heads of revenue amounting to Rs. 2,12,953.

176. The fall under the head Land Revenue is heavier than in 1340 T. E. and is attributable to world-wide economic depression and scarcity of money among the people. There was a fall of revenue to the extent of Rs. 10,000 from tea gardens, compared with the previous year.

177. There was a decrease of a very considerable amount in Excise revenue owing to diminished buying capacity of the consumers, Reduction of *jama* in many cases was inevitable.

II. Finances.

178. A consolidated abstract account of the financial transactions of the State and the attached Zemindaries as compared with those of the year previous is given below :—

Receipts.	1340 T. E.	1341 T. E.
1. Opening balance :—		
(1) State ...	5,95,345	6,01,671
Zemindaries ...	3,79,077	3,70,995
Total ...	9,74,422	9,72,666
2. Income :—		
(1) State ...	13,92,709	12,37,252
(2) Zemindaries ...	7,90,161	7,88,230
Total ...	21,82,870	20,25,482
3. Law charges recovered :—		
(1) Zemindaries ...	50,422	52,581
4. Refunds and compensation for lands acquired :—		
(1) Zemindaries ...	7,707	6,449
5. Deposits :—		
(1) State ...	1,83,735	2,26,312
(2) Zemindaries ...	32,357	23,769
Total ...	2,16,092	2,50,081
6. Loans received :—		
(1) State ...	1,73,992	1,60,222
(2) Zemindaries ...	1,38,409	—
Total ...	3,12,401	1,60,222
7. Provident fund :—		
(1) State ...	—	21,472
(2) Zemindaries ...	—	1,895
Total ...	—	23,367
8. Marriage Contribution from Nijtahabil :—		
(1) State ...	—	75,000
GRAND TOTAL ...	37,43,914	35,65,848

Expenditure.	1340 T. E.	1341 T. E.
1. General Administration charges :—		
(a) State	5,79,206	5,45,910
(b) Zemindaries :—		
1. Cost of management	1,59,382	1,55,532
2. Cost of litigation	1,16,279	96,967
	2,75,661	2,52,499
Total ...	8,54,867	7,98,409
2. Revenue and Taxes on account of the Zemindaries	2,64,523	2,65,974
3. Public Works—(a) State	2,45,067	87,231
(b) Zemindaries ...	75,789	50,651
Total ...	3,20,856	1,37,882
4. Electric Light—State	14,821	17,700
5. Municipality—State	10,000	9,000
6. Education—(a) State	1,34,669	1,27,620
(b) Zemindaries	12,171	13,546
Total ...	1,46,840	1,41,166
7. Medical and Sanitation :—		
(a) State	70,663	65,360
(b) Zemindaries	13,662	14,035
Total ...	84,325	79,395
8. Survey and Settlement—(a) State ...	26,374	10,237
(b) Zemindaries ...	1,511	440
Total ...	27,885	10,677
9. Agriculture, Commerce and Industries—State	10,461	8,811
10. Religious Expenses—(a) State ...	43,385	45,696
(b) Zemindaries ...	6,840	6,337
Total ...	50,225	52,033
11. Sultanat—State	45,690	36,256
12. Purchase of Land Tenures :—		
(a) State	344	510
(b) Zemindaries	7,774	8,110
Total ...	8,118	8,620
13. Pension and Gratuity—(a) State ...	36,808	41,478
(b) Zemindaries ...	5,906	7.191
Total ...	42,714	48,669
14. Ordinary *Sansar* charges :—		
(a) His Highness's own and the late Maharaja's family	78,422	79,995
(b) Other branches of the Raj family...	1,40,062	1,31,181
(c) Thakurs	33,272	33,791
(d) *Sansar* office establishment ...	10,936	11,446
(e) Miscellaneous	28,589	39,507
Total ...	2,91,281	2,95,920
15. Charity and Donation :—(a) State ...	19,915	18,950
(b) Zemindaries ...	2,472	5,740
Total ...	22,387	24,690
16. His Highness's Nij Tahabil :—		
(a) State	1,12,469	1,09,000
(b) Zemindaries	1.18,181	50,000
Total ...	2,30,650	1,59,000
17. His Highness's tour	18,930	19,358
18. Payment of liabilities and deposits :—		
(a) State	65,885	* 57,604
(b). Zemindaries	69,939	36,598
Total ...	1,35,824	94,202
19. Miscellaneous—(a) State	4,920	2,440
(b) Zemindaries ...	8,852	6,646
Total ...	13,772	9,086
20. Advances to employees :—(a) State ...	5,020	175
(b) Zemindaries ...	2,795	995
Total ...	7,815	1,170
21. Expenditure in connection with H. H.'s Marriage, Investiture, Installation etc.—State	13,166	55,112
22. Investment—(a) State	—	—
(b) Zemindaries ...	1,45,522	30,000
Total ...	1,45,522	30,000
23. Write off of irrecoverable advances ...	10,576	18,710
24. Repayment of old debts—State ...	—	1,78,858
Total Expenditure ...	27,71,248	25,00,698
25. Closing Balance :—		
(a) State		
In Cash	1,01,794	93,623
At Bank	2,799	20,627
In bonds and advances	4,97,078	5,36,765
Total ...	6,01,671	6,51,015
(b) Zemindaries :—		
In Cash	76 632	92,027
At Bank	1,30,127	1,36,188
In bonds and advances	1,64,236	1,85,920
Total ...	3,70,995	4,14,135
Total of State & Zemindaries' balances ...	9,72,666	10,65,150
Total of State & Zemindaries' expenditure ...	27,71,248	25,00,698
GRAND TOTAL ...	37,43,914	35,65,848

* Deposits only.

179. The year opened with a balance of Rs. 9,72,666 against Rs. 9,74,422 in the year before. During the year under report, the total receipts from all sources including deposits, loans and law charges recovered, amounted to Rs. 25,93,182 against Rs. 27,69,492 in the previous year. Thus the total sum available for expenditure, including the opening balance, was Rs. 35,65,848 against Rs. 37,43,914. The actual income including receipts under debt-heads amounted to Rs. 20,84,512 against Rs. 22,40,999 showing a decrease of Rs. 1,56,487. This fall in revenue was due to the general trade depression both in the State and the neighbouring British districts.

Receipts.

180. The total expenditure incurred during the year amounted to Rs. 25,00,698 against Rs. 27,71,248 in the year before, showing a reduction of Rs. 2,70,550. The year, however, closed with a balance of Rs. 10,65,150 of which Rs. 1,85,650 represented actual cash in the treasuries, while the balance of Rs. 8,79,500 was in the banks and in loans and advances.

Expenditure.

181. The noticeable variations in expenditure are explained below :—

i. ADMINISTRATION CHARGES :—

STATE—The decrease was really Rs. 33,296. The reason of this decrease was due to the general curtailment of expenditure and to the with-holding of certain bills.

ZEMINDARIES—The decrease was Rs. 23,162. The reason for this decrease was due greatly to the curtailment of expenditure under the law charges and partly under the establishment charges.

ii. REVENUE AND TAXES :—

ZEMINDARIES—The increase was Rs. 1,451. This was due to payment of arrears of 1340. T. E.

iii. PUBLIC WORKS :—

STATE AND ZEMINDARIES—The stoppage of costly Public Works as well as non-payment of some bills both in the State as well as in the Zemindariis were the main causes for the heavy decrease under this head.

iv. ELECTRIC LIGHT ;—

STATE—The increase was due to payment of arrear bills.

v. MUNICIPALITY :—

The decrease was due to general curtailment of expenditure.

vi. EDUCATION :—The decrease was due to reduced Budget provision in the year under report.

vii. MEDICAL AND SANITATION :—

STATE—The decrease was due to non-payment of some bills.

ZEMINDARIES—There was little increase in expenditure due to payment of arrear bills.

viii. SURVEY AND SETTLEMENT :—

STATE—There was heavy decrease as no operations in a larger scale were undertaken during the year under report.

ZEMINDARIES—No extra staff was engaged this year as was done the year before. This accounted for the decrease under this head.

ix. AGRICULTURE, COMMERCE AND INDUSTRIES :—

STATE—The decrease was due to curtailment of general expenditure.

x. RELIGIOUS EXPENDITURE :—

STATE—The increase was due to payment of arrear bills.

ZEMINDARIES – There was only little decrease in the general expenditure.

xi. SULTANAT :—

STATE—The decrease was due to the reduced budget provision of the year under report.

xii. PURCHASE OF LAND TENURES :—

STATE—The increase was due to purchase of lands generally under rent-sale.

ZEMINDARIES—The increase was due to purchase of Mission House at Comilla.

xiii. PENSION AND GRATUITY :—

The increase was due to retirement of officers both in the State and the Zemindaries.

xiv. ORDINARY SANSAR CHARGES :—

The increase was due to payment of arrear bills..

xv. CHARITY AND DONATION :—

The increase was due to payment of arrear dues in the Zemindaries.

xvi. HIS HIGHNESS'S TOUR AND NIJTAHABIL :—

The decrease was due to curtailment of Nijtahabil contribution during the year.

xvii. PAYMENT OF LIABILITIES AND DEPOSITS :—

The decrease was due to non-payment of bills both in the State as well as in the Zemindaries.

xviii. MISCELLANEOUS :—

The decrease was due to curtailment of general expenditure both in the State and in the Zemindaries.

182. Two Statements comparing the receipts and expenditure of the State and the Zemindaries with the respective revised estimates are given in appendices XXVI and XXVII.

183. In the State, the actual receipts fell short of the Original and Revised Budget Estimates by Rs. 3,93,742 and Rs. 2,04,742 respectively. This deficit was due to the general unfavourable economic conditions which in consequence seriously affected the financial position of the State.

184. In the Zemindaries, the actual receipts fell short of the original Budget estimate by Rs. 1,83,372, but as compared with the Revised Budget estimate there was an increase of Rs. 30,253 under receipts and a saving of Rs. 31,983 under expenditure. Thus the anticipated surplus rose from Rs. 3,51,899 to Rs. 4,14,135.

185. The Accounts and the Treasury Departments suffered a great loss in the most lamentable and untimely death of their able and experienced Naib Dewan Babu Jatindra Chandra Moulik which melancholy event took place on the 19th January, 1932, up to which he held the charge of the Department. He was succeeded by Babu Jatindra Nath Mitra, Naib Dewan, who remained in charge till the end of the year.

CHAPTER VI—MEDICAL.

186. As before, the year under review opened and closed with 20 dispensaries—the Victoria Memorial Hospital at the Capital included.

New patients.

187. The following comparative statement for the two consecutive years shows the total number of new patients treated in the above hospital and dispensaries together with their daily average.

	1340 T. E.			1341 T. E		
	Outdoor.	Indoor.	Total.	Outdoor.	Indoor.	Total.
PATIENTS.	1,19,477	396	1,20,173	1,27,550	793	1,28,343
Daily average	327·33	1·90	329·23	348·49	2·16	350·65

Outdoor attendance.

188. 2,30,381 patients (new+old) sought outdoor relief as against 2,15,914 in the year previous, so the daily average rose from 590·61 in 1340 T. E. to 629·68 in 1341 T. E.

Indoor attendance.

189. Inclusive of the last year's balance of 23, the total in-patients numbered 793 as against 696 in the preceding year. Of them, 580 were discharged cured, 165 were relieved or other wise discharged, 28 died and 20 remained under treatment at the close of the year.

Surgical Operations.

190. Altogether 1360 operations including 8 major cases were performed as against 1247 and 17 respectively of the year before.

Police case.

191. 162 police cases were attended to during the year including 14 post mortem cases, as against 157 and 22 respectively of the previous year.

V. M. Hospital.

192. The total number of new out-patients treated was 15,888 as against 15,574 in the preceding year—the daily average (new+old) being 83·65 against 84·95. The in-patients totalled 458 as against 453 in the year before, the daily

average (new+old) being 18·60 against 16·99. Of these patients, 295 were discharged cured, 119 were relieved or discharged otherwise, 27 died and 17 remained under treatment at the end of the year. The total expenditure in this institution stood at Rs. 9,192-5-3 as against Rs. 8,184 of the previous year.

Ayurvedic Department.

193. As before, Kaviraj Surendra Chandra Bhattacharya, Baidyaratna, continued in this department and treated 42 patients during the year under report as against 48 in the previous year. The expenditure due to his salary and the price of medicines came up to Rs. 2,404-11-6 as against Rs. 2,904-6-0.

Homoeopathic Department.

194. The post of the State Homœopath remained vacant during the year under review. Two Assistants under Dr. M. M. Mazumdar, Chief Medical Officer, treated 13,894 patients as against 12,531 the daily average (new+old) being 64·26 against 61·78 in the preceding year. Rs. 2,226-8-3 was spent for this Department as against Rs. 3,757 in the year before.

Vaccination.

195. In the whole State both hills and plains, 4,503 vaccine operations were successful out of 5,845 performed as against 7,474 and 9,037 respectively of the previous year. The decrease in the number is attributed to the non-appearance of small-pox epidemically in different parts of the State. Inspection work in the interior was done by the two permanent Small-pox Doctors assisted by two Inspectors. The total cost on this account was Rs. 1,554-6 as against Rs. 1,484-6 of the preceding year.

Kala-azar.

196. 322 patients were treated at the capital during the year under report as against 197. Of them, 209 were cured, 31 relieved or discharged otherwise, 21 left treatment, 3 died and 58 remained under treatment at the end of the year.

Public Health.

197. During the year under report cholera appeared with virulence in some parts of the State and made a frightful toll especially in Khowai and Dharmanagar Divisions. There were 329 seizures with 270 deaths so far as the figures could be collected. Had it not been for the intensive and extensive measures taken to check it by vaccine inoculation, the toll would have been far greater. 2,552 persons were inoculated. 14 persons were attacked with small-pox in the Sadar Division of which only 2 died.

Staff.

198. Dr. M. M. Mazumdar, L. M. S., Chief Medical Officer, remained in charge of the Medical Department with Dr. S. K. Dutt, L. M. S. and Dr. A. Sen Gupta, M. B. as his assistants. Besides, Dr. Niranjan Deb Barma, M. B. was appointed during the year under report. As in the previous year, a staff of subordinate medical officers and 4 midwives and nurses was kept employed throughout the year. One Lady Doctor was appointed during the year under review but she left service on better prospects elsewhere 5 months after. Since then the post has remained vacant.

199. Dr. A. Sen Gupta, M. B., was out for 9 days and inspected 3 dispensaries.

Inspection.

200. The expenditure in the Medical Department totalled Rs. 65,360 as against Rs. 70,663 in the year before. The decrease is due to some unadjusted bills at the end of the year.

Expenditure.

CHAPTER VII—PUBLIC INSTRUCTION.

201. Mr. S. C. Deb Barman, M. A. (Harvard), Senior Naib Dewan continued to be in charge of the Education Department. During his absence on a visit to Switzerland as guardian to a Maharajkumari, Mr. K. K. Singh, Naib Dewan, remained in charge from Poush till some days in the year following.

Charge.

202. The total number of schools (including the private schools) during the year under review was 213 against 220 in the previous year and the total numerical strength 9,230 against 8,928 including 1,008 pupils reading in private institutions numbering 34 as against 43 in the preceding year.

Number of Schools.

203. There were 5 H. E. Schools as before and one Branch H. E. School in the State, *viz*:—the Umakanta Academy at Agartala, the Radhakishore Institution at Kailashahar, the Brojendrakishore Institution at Bilonia, the Bir Bikram Institution at Dharmanagar, the Navadwip Chandra Institution at Sonamura and the Branch H. E. School at Udaipur. All the H. E. Schools are permanently affiliated to the Calcutta University. Class IX was opened in the previous year provisionally in the Branch H. E. School at Udaipur, on condition that the public would agree to bear the additional cost of maintaining extra staff. The total number of pupils in all these institutions was 1,450 as against 1,646 in the previous year and the average daily attendance stood at 1209·5 against 1289·0.

H. E. Schools.

204. Agartala, the capital of the State, continued to be a centre for the Matriculation Examination for the year 1932. The State H. E. Schools were generally allowed to send up candidates to this centre. One private student and one candidate from Debagram H. E. School in Tippera District sat for the examination in this centre this year.

Matriculation Examination.

205. The Examination was conducted under the direct control and supervision of the Dewan Shasan, Tripura State. The Department looked after the convenience of the candidates coming from *Mofussil* in respect of accommodation and other necessary matters.

206. Altogether 71 candidates were sent up for the Matriculation Examination against 69 in the previous year, from the State H. E. Schools The result of the Examination is given below :—

Results of the Matriculation Examination.

		No. sent up.	Passed.	1st Division.	2nd Division.	3rd Division.
1.	U. K. Academy	24	19	13	5	1
2.	R. K. Institution	14	13	7	5	1
3.	B. K. Institution	19	11	4	3	4
4.	B. B. Institution	6	6	4	1	1
5.	N. Ch. Institution	8	5	2	2	1
	Total ...	71	54	30	16	8

207. One boy of the Dharmanagar B. B. Institution got a star. The result on the whole was satisfactory, percentage of successful candidates being 76·05.

208. The three successful candidates topping the list so for as the State was concerned were awarded scholarships of Rs. 15, Rs. 9 and Rs. 9 per month in order of merit.

209. In the year under review, there were 8 Middle English Schools for boys with 950 pupils on the rolls, against 7 schools with 857 pupils in the previous year. The average daily attendance was 717·34 against 649·79 in the previous year.

M. E. Schools for boys.

210. There was one M. E. School for girls at Agartala, namely, the Maharani Tulsibati Girls' School, the numerical strength of which was 85 as against 87 in the previous year and the average daily attendance was 51·95 against 50·97. By special permission of this Department, some girls were allowed to continne higher studies in this school under the tution of the Head Mistress, who is a graduate of the Calcutta University. For the conveyance of the girls, the State motor bus service was continued till after the Puja holidays but in order to ensure regularity in the service, a contract was made with a private party from the middle of Agrahayan.

M. E. Schools for girls.

211. There was only one Higher Vernacular School for boys as in the previous year, with 80 students on the roll as against 72, while average daily attendance was 58·76 against 55·92 in the year previous.

H. V. Schools

212. The total number of Lower Vernacular Schools for boys was 25 against 24 in the previous year. The total numerical strength was 1,502 against 1,352 and the average daily attendance 1,110·30 against 1,041·20 in the previous year. In some of these schools boys and girls read together.

L. V. Schools.

213. There were 150 Pathshalas for boys against 160 in the previous year. The total number of boys was 4,545 against 4,337 and the average daily attendance 2,990·27 against 2,434·76. In some of these schools, boys and girls read together. Under special orders of the Education Department, some boys of some of these institutions were allowed to read the Lower Vernacular Standard.

Pathshalas for boys.

214. There were 10 Pathshalas for girls in the year under review against the same number in the previous year. The total numerical strength was 291 as against 290 and the average daily attendance 232·38 against 222·97 in the year preceding.

Pathshalas for girls.

In some of these schools, some girls were allowed, under special order, to read the Lower Vernacular Standard.

Scholarship Examination.

215. Altogether 788 candidates appeared at the different Scholarship Examinations of this State against 625 in the previous year. Of these 555 boys including 59 girls came out successful. The result on the whole, particularly that of the Khowai and Kamalpur M. E. Schools, was found to be satisfactory as in the previous year. 47 students including 6 girls passed the M. E. Examination, and 3 girls passed the H. V. Examination.

216. In the L. V. Examination, the number of successful candidates was 116 including 16 girls, and in the Pathshala Examination the number was 389 including 34 girls. On the results of the examination, 13 boys and 6 girls were awarded monthly scholarships varying from Rs. 2 to Rs. 5 tenable for two to four years.

Schools for special training.

217. In the year under review, there were, as before 12 schools for special training, consisting of 4 Sanskrit Tols, 7 Madrassas and Muktabs and one Silpasram (Artisan School). The Sanskrit Tols had 43 students on the rolls against 48 in the previous year and the average daily attendance was 30.25 against 35.04. The ***Rajakiya Sanskrit Vidyalaya*** at Agartala sent up 4 candidates for the Government Sanskrit Intermediate and Preliminary Examinations against 7 in the preceding year, and 1 candidate for Sanskrit Title Examinations in *Smriti* of the *Saraswat Samaj*, against 5 in the previous year. Only the *Sama Veda Adya* candidate came out successful in Government Examination. Result of the *Saraswat* Examination is not yet out.

218. The Madrassas and Muktabs had 238 students on the rolls as against 217 in the previous year and the average daily attendance was 160·51 against 155·61.

Non-Bengalee students.

219. The comparative statement below will show the number of non-Bengalee students receiving education in the several schools of the State.

Serial number.	Nationality.	Number of students.		Remarks.
		Past year.	Present year.	
1.	Rajkumars	8	14	
2.	Thakurs	122	163	
3.	Manipuris	837	744	
4.	Tripuras	1214	1300	
5.	Reangs	10	31	
6.	Kukis	0	41	
7.	Chakmas	0	1	
8.	Lushais	4	5	
9.	Others...	152	41	
10.	Christians	3	0	
	Total	2,350	2,340	

Reward Examination.

220. Reward Examination for hill-boys was not held during the year for want of funds.

Education of Princes and Princesses.

221. Maharajkumar Durjoy Kishore Deb Barman Bahadur left Raipur Raj Kumar College and joined Mayo College after the summer vacation. He was placed under the special care of Mr. V. A. S. Stow, M. A., I. E. S., V. D., the Principal of the college, and continued his studies

under a graduate B. T. teacher deputed from the State. The progress and health of the Maharajkumar were satisfactory. The Department takes the opportunity to express its appreciation of the kind care taken by the Principal in the general welfare of the Maharajkumar.

222. The Maharajkumaries received their education as before under a graduate lady teacher and a Pandit. Special arrangement has been made for the education of Maharajkumar Karna Kishore Deb Barman Bahadur as before at Agartala.

Education of other Kumars.

223. Kumar Anilendra Chandra Deb Barman continued his studies in the Comilla Victoria College.

Kumar Bording House at Comilla.

224. The Rajkumar boarding house at Comilla had 15 inmates of whom 12 were from the different branches of the Ruling family and the remaining 3 were Rana Bahadurs, related to the Raj family. 12 of the inmates were reading in the Comilla Zilla school and 2 were reading in the 1st year I. Sc. class in Victoria College, Comilla.

225. The results of the examinations in school were satisfactory. One Kumar Bahadur appeared at the last Matriculation Examination and passed in the 1st Division. The boarders were placed under the charge of a Superintending Tutor, who, in addition to his tutorial work, looked after the management of the Boarding House. Three other private tutors including a Pandit, were engaged to coach the Kumars in the morning and evening.

Day School for the young Kumars.

226. Some young Kumars having been admitted into the Kumar Boarding House at Comilla, it was found unnecessary to retain a regular establishment at Agartala for the Day School. There were only 5 Kumars receiving instruction at the school against 4 in the previous year and one tutor was engaged to coach them.

Education of Thakur boys.

227. Some Thakur boys were awarded stipends from the Education Department to receive higher education.

Thakur Boarding House at Agartala.

228. During the early part of the year under report, the number of boarders in the Thakur Boarding House was 29 which came down to 28 in the latter part of the year, against 32 in the previous year. The staff consisted of one Guardian Superintendent, one graduate Resident Tutor, one Assistant Tutor and one Manager and Tutor. The average daily attendance of the boarders was 26·11 against 20·20 in the previous year.

Tripura Boarding House.

229. There were altogether 17 boarders in the Tripura Boarding House against 18 in the previous year. Out of these 17 boarders 13 were allowed free boarding and lodging. A Superintending Tutor looked after the boys as well as the boarding management as before. One Tripura boy belonging to this institution was sent up for the Matriculation Examination this year and he passed in the 2nd Division.

Tripura Boarding House at Khowai.

230. There were 41 boarders in the Tripura Boarding House at Khowai against 32 in the previous year, some receiving free boarding. Two tutors were appointed for coaching the boys both in the morning and

evening, and one of the tutors was engaged to look after the boarding management.

School for Convicts.

231. There were 20 convicts reading in the Primary School of the Central Jail, out of which 3 appeared in the Scholarship Examination of the year under report and 2 came out successful.

Woodburn Artisan School & Silpasram.

232. The Woodburn Artisan School and Silpasram had on the roll at the end of Chaitra, 26 students against 22 in the preceding year. In the year under review the average daily attendance was 11·43 against 10·91 in the previous year. There were 16, 5 and 5 students in the Carpentry, Black & Brass-smith Sections respectively. The sub-joined statement will show the number of students, their classes (castes) and their average attendance in the year under review.

Name of School	Number of Students	Thakurs	Tripura	Laskar	Manipuri	Bengali Hindu	Mahomedan	Average attendance
Woodburn Artisan School and Silpasram ...	26	5	2	0	2	14	3	11·43

4 left school.

Night School at Agartala.

233. During the year, 16 students from the trading and labouring classes received instruction in the Night School at Agartala under the auspices of the local Students Association. The institution received a monthly grant from the State.

Special Stipends.

234. 33 students were awarded special stipends in the year under review of whom 23 read in different schools of the State and 10 others prosecuted their studies elsewhere in different schools, colleges and technical institutions.

Inspection Work.

235. Mr. S. C. Deb Barman, M. A., (Harvard), Senior Naib Dewan, inspected, in the year under report, the schools at Khowai and Kamalpur. The tour comprised 11 days.

236. Thakur K. K. Singh, Naib Dewan, inspected Dharmanagar, Bilonia, Udaipur and Sonamura H. E. schools and girl schools. The tour comprised 20 days.

237. The Sub-Inspectors of schools inspected all the schools within their respective jurisdictions in Sadar, Khowai, Kailashahar, and Dharmanagar Divisions. Their inspection work was satisfactory. Revenue and Forest Inspectors visited and inspected the schools in the southern Divisions.

Library.

238. Maharajkumar Narottamkishore Deb Barman continued to be the Librarian of the Birchandra Library at Agartala which was maintained in two separate sections as before, *viz* :—(1) The English section, located at the Ujjayanta Palace, and (2) the Vernacular section in the building

10

near the local H. E. School. The latter section was open to the public. The number of English books (including foreign literature) was 5,025 against the same number in the previous year, and the number of Bengali and Sanskrit books was 2,207 against the same number. In the year under report there were 4 Daily newspapers against 5 in the previous year, 1 Weekly and 4 Monthlies against 4 and 6 respectively in the previous year. The average daily attendance in the public section of the Library was 13 against 15·6 in the previous year, but the total number of books issued to the public was 3,765 against 5,213.

Expenditure

239. The total expenditure on public instruction in the year under report, amounted to Rs. 1,34,669 against Rs. 1,27,620. Some of the more important details of expenditure are noted below :—

1.	Primary Education	Rs.	27,391
2.	Secondary Education	„	50,164
3.	Schools for Special Training	„	2,063
4.	Boarding Institutions for Thakur boys ...	„	7,855
5.	Education of Kumars & Kumaris	„	24,123
6.	Scholarships and Stipends	„	7,115
7.	Library	„	1,683
8.	Tripura Boarding	„	1,977
9.	Miscellaneous	„	5,249
		Rs.	1,27,620

Income.

240. The total receipts from the schools amounted to Rs. 14,502 against Rs. 16,581 in the previous year.

CHAPTER VIII—ZEMINDARIES.

Chakla Roshnabad Estates.

Management.

241. The management of His Highness's Zemindaries in British India was conducted during the year by Dewan Bahadur B. K. Sen, M. A., B. L., who was assisted by a Deputy Manager at Comilla in charge of the Central Division and three Assistant Managers in charge of the three other divisions.

The year and the tenantry.

242. The year under review was far from being satisfactory in comparison with the year preceding. The all round economic depression had its adverse effects both on the Raj and the tenants, the low prices of jute and paddy being the most deciding factors. Continued economic depression for years told heavily both upon the general condition of the tenants and of the Raj treasury.

243. As in the previous year this year also a generous and bold policy was adopted to relieve the tenantry by way of demands having been allowed to be time barred either on execution of bonds or on parole promise of payment. Occasional help was also rendered to the

tenants in the shape of general remission of interests etc. during particular periods of the year.

244. The gross revenue demand of the year was Rs. 10,22,914 against Rs. 10,17,557 in the previous year.

Demand.

245. The total receipts amounted to Rs. 8,72,924 (including Rs. 11,674 on account of the Tripura Raj Central Co-operative Bank Ltd., and Rs. 446 on account of *Debottar Mohals*) against Rs. 10,19,056 in the previous year. The abnormal fall in collection was mainly due to low prices of jute, paddy and other commodities and the general economic depression and unrest.

Receipts.

246. The total expenditure in the year under review was Rs. 8,29,784 including adjustment of all advances and loans issued to the Improvement Fund in the State together with the contributions to the State and also to His Highness's Nijtahabil, against Rs. 10,27,138 in the previous year. Of this Rs. 2,65,974 was on account of Land Revenue, taxes and cesses. The total administration charges of the Zemindaries including Public works and Law charges amounted to Rs. 3,17,427 against Rs. 3,75,493 in the previous year. The following other items of expenditure aggregating Rs. 2,46,383 are noticeable :—

Expenditure.

1.	Loans and advances	Rs.	995
2.	Donation	,,	5,740
3.	Medical charges	,,	14,035
4.	Education charges	,,	13,546
5.	Religious ceremonies	,,	6,337
6.	*Sansar* stipends	,,	11,022
7.	Repayment of old deposits ...	,,	26,101
8.	Contribution and loan to the State including contribution to His Highness's Nijtahabil ...	,,	1,50,000
9.	Repayment of old debts	,,	10,497
10.	Purchase of property	,,	8,110
		Rs.	2,46,383

247. The result of the year's settlement operations will appear from the figures noted below :—

	Kinds of settlement.	Addition to rental.	Nazar.
1.	Ry. relinquished land	—	—
2.	*Kaimi* and *Takshishi* settlement in the Comilla Town ...	Rs. 176	Rs. 30,905
3.	Ordinary Town Settlement ...	,, 49	,, 290
4.	*Khas Patit*	,, 563	,, 3,520
5.	Enhancement of rent ...	,, 164	,, 3,173
6.	Resettlement of auction purchased holdings ...	,, 36	,, 4,220
7.	Settlement of rent free holdings	,, 27	,, —
8.	*Takshishi Taluks* in the Moffusil	,, 23	,, 43
		Rs. 1,038	Rs. 42,151

248. The settlement operations of this year improved the rent roll by Rs. 1,038 and brought in a *nazarana* of Rs. 42,151 against Rs. 3,606 and Rs. 25,479 respectively in the previous year.

CHAPTER IX—MISCELLANEOUS.

Rajmala.

249. The printing of the third part of the *Rajmala* (State Chronicle) was finished during the year but its publication was delayed owing to the necessary sketches and maps not being printed in time. The fourth part is in the press and the connected maps and sketches are being collected. The total expenditure incurred during the year Rs. 2,018 against Rs. 3,064 in the year before.

Tours of high officials—Dewan-Shashan.

250. Dewan B. K. Sen Bahadur, Dewan-Shashan, was in camp for 78 days during the year under review, both in and outside the State. This includes two visits to Calcutta on urgent business.

Chief Secretary to His Highness.

251. Manyabara Rana Bodhjung Bahadur, F. R. G. S, Chief Secretary, was out with His Highness the Maharaja Manikya Bahadur in all his tours during the year and also visited Khowai and Kalyanpur for seven days in connection with the settlement of Kalyanpur reserved area. Dewan Saheb K. Dutt, M. A., B. L., M. R. A. S. etc. who was in charge of Chief Secretary's Departments for some time went out for four days and visited the Kalyanpur reserved area.

252. Tours of Senior Naib Dewan and Naib Dewan have been noted below :—

Mr. S. C. Deb Barman, M. A., (Harvard), Senior Naib Dewan, and Thakur Kamini Kumar Singha, Naib Dewan, were out for 11 days and 20 days respectively. The touring can by no means be said to be satisfactory.

253. The tours of the Divisional Officers and their Assistants are noted below :—

State.

1.	Sadar—			
	Sadar Collector—	Thakur Rebati Mohan Deb Barman	...	17 days.
	Asst. ,,	Babu Jogendra Lal Ganguly, B. L.	...	81 ,,
	,, ,,	Kumar Narsingha Chandra Deb Barman Bahadur	...	33 ,,
2.	Kailashahar—			
	Divisional Officer—	Babu Sasanka Bhusan Roy, M. A.	...	45 ,,
	Second ,,	,, Surendra Chandra Guha, B. A.	...	26 ,,
3.	Sonamura—			
	Divisional Officer—	Thakur Lalit Mohan Deb Barman, M. A., B. L.	...	42 ,,
	Second ,,	Babu Jyotirmoy Ghosh, M. A.	...	12 ,,
4.	Belonia—			
	Divisional Officer—	Babu Bisweswar Guha, B. A.	...	15 ,,
	Second ,,	Kumar Bhupendra Chandra Deb Barman	...	37 ,,
5.	Khowai—			
	Divisional Officer—	Babu Suresh Chandra Chakravarty, B. L.	...	45 ,,

6. Dharmanagar—
Divisional Officer—Babu Akhil Chandra Majumdar, M. A., B. L. ... 10 days.
Second ,, Thakur Jyoti Lal Deb Barman, B. L. ... 2 ,,

7. Udaipur—
Divisional Officer—Babu Kunja Behari Chakravarty, M. A., B. L. ... 28 ,,
Second ,, Thakur Joysingh Deb Barman, B. A. ... 84 ,,

8. Sabroom—
Divisional Officer—Thakur Gokul Chandra Deb Barman ... 29 ,,

Zemindaries.

1. Babu P. R. Bhattacharjee, B. A., Deputy Manager, Chakla Roshnabad Estates, Comilla ... 70 days.
2. Babu N. K. Chakravarty, B. L., Assistant Manager, Central Division ... —
3. Babu J. C. Majumdar M. A., B. L., Assistant Manager, Feni ... 100 ,,
4. Babu T. M. Gupta, Assistant Manager, Mogra ... ... 67 ,,
5. Babu S. N. Bose, B. L., Assistant Manager, Srimangal ... ... 46 ,,

DATED, AGARTALA,
The 9th October, 1932.

Rana Bodhjung.
Dewan-Shashan.

APPENDIX.

List of the principal Laws and Regulations in force in the Tripura State during 1341 T.E.

Description.	Whether adapted from British Indian Acts.	Whether introduced during the year under report.
CRIMINAL.		
1. Regulation No. III. of 1280 T. E.		
2. Regulation No. I. of 1283 T. E.		
3. Jail Regulation, 1283 T. E.		
4. Regulation No. IV. of 1283 T. E. (Cattle trespass and pound).		
5. Regulation No. III. of 1296 T. E. (Police Regulation).		
6. Act No. IV. of 1321 T. E.–Penal Laws (an amending Act)		
CIVIL.		
1. Civil Law of 1284 T. E.		
2. Rules regarding *chit* suits (small causes) 1287 and 1300 T. E.		
3. Act No. II. of 1313 T. E.—an Act for the regulation of interest on debts.		
4. Act No. II. of 1314 T. E.—Limitation Act	Partly adapted.	
5. Succession Act II of 1339 T. E.		
REVENUE.		
1. Act No. I. of 1290 T. E.—Sale Law		
2. Act No. I. of 1296 T. E.—Tenancy Act.		
3. Act No. II. of 1296 T. E.—*Abkari*		
4. Act No. II. of 1297 T. E.—Reserved forests.		
5. Act No. I. of 1304 T. E.—Duties on *til* and cotton.		
6. Act No. I. of 1306 T. E.—Registration	Do.	
7. Survey and Settlement Act, 1309 T.E.	Do.	
8. *Tuccavi* Regulation, 1310 T. E.		
9. Act No. I. of 1313 T. E.—Forests.		
10. Act No. I. of 1314 T. E.—(amending the above)		
11. A Law imposing export duty on jute and mustard-seed, 1317 T. E.		
12. Act No. II. of 1321 T.E. Ghasuri Act		
13. P. W. & Road Cess Act IV of 1339 T. E.		
MISCELLANEOUS.		
1. An Act promulgating certain rules as Law, 1283 T. E.		
2. Regulation for the record of judicial decisions &c., 1284 T. E.		
3 Municipal Regulation, 1284 T. E.		
4. Legal Practitioners' Regulation.		
5. Act No. I. of 1297 T. E.—an Act for the regulation of commissions for the examination of witnesses.		
6. Regulation against cow slaughter		
7. Rules of evidence		
8. Act I. of 1318 T. E.—Constitution of Courts—(an amending Act).		
9. Leave and allowance Rules	Do.	
10. Act No. I. of 1321 T. E.—Arms Act	Do.	
11. Act No. III. of 1321 T. E.—Constitution of Courts (an amending Act)		

Description.	Whether adapted from British Indian Acts.	Whether introduced during the year under report.
12. Municipal Act No. I of 1322 T. E.		
13. Revenue Sale Amendment Act—1323 T.E.		
14. An Act for the destruction of old records—1323 T. E.		
15. Act I of 1326 T. E.—Regulation regarding Privy Council Appeals.		
16. Act II of 1326 T. E.—Registration of Births and Deaths	Partly adapted.	
17. Act III of 1326 T. E.—Vaccination Act	Do.	
18. Act IV of 1326 T. E.—Public Demands Recovery Act	Do.	
19. Act V of 1326 T. E.—Excise Amendment Act		
20. Act I of 1327 T. E.—Settlement of lands for tea cultivation		
21. Rules of Import and Sale of Opium—1327 T. E.		
22. Regulation No. 1 of 1328 T. E.—regarding Registration of Coolies		
23. Regulation No. 2 of 1328 T. E.—regarding Export of Tea		
24. Act I of 1329 T. E.—(Absconding sepoys Act)		
25. Act II of 1329 T. E.—(Control of prices of food stuff)		
26. Act III of 1329 T. E. (Elephants and buffaloes grazing Act)		
27. Act IV of 1329 T. E. –(House tax on Hill tribes)	Do	
28. Act V of 1329 T. E. - (Legal practitioners, Act)		
29. Act I of 1332 T. E.—Encumbered Estates Act.		
30. Act III of 1332 T. E.—The Opium and Intoxicating Drugs Act.		
31. Rules and Regulations under the Opium and Intoxicating Drugs Act III of 1332 T. E.		
32. Act I of 1336 T. E.—(Hackney Carriages)		
33. Act II of 1336 T. E.—(Amending Act I of 1327)		
34. Act III of 1336 T. E.—(Amending the Survey & Settlement Regulation)		
35. Act IV of 1336 T. E.—(Prevention of gambling)		
36. Act I of 1337 T. E.—(Amending the State Tenancy Act I of 1296 T. E.)		
37. Land Acquisition Rules under Act I of 1337 T. E.		
38. State Motor Vehicles Act I of 1338 T. E.		
39. Act II of 1338 T. E. for prevention of smuggling of elephant tusks.		
40. State Stamp Act III of 1338 T. E.		
41. Tripura State Bank Act I of 1339 T. E.		
42. Census Act III of 1339 T. E.		

II

Statement showing the strength, cost and other particulars of the Military Force in Tripura State for 1341 T. E.

Arm of service.	Number of fighting officers and men.						Details of force at the end of the current year.									Remarks.
			Casualties.						*Number of men.*							
									Commisioned Officers.							
	At the end of last year	Recruited this year.	Died.	Invalided.	Discharged, deserted, &c.	At the end of the current year.	Number of regiments, battalions, or Batteries.	Number of guns.	European.	Indian.	Non-commissioned officers.	Fighting men.	Buglers.	Total cost on account of pay and allowances of the force, including followers.	
1	2	3	4	5	6	7	8	9	10	11	12	13	14	15	16
Infantry ...	411	201	—	218	3	391	1	644	—	† 19	44	319	9	Rs. 1,02,072	
Band Party	21	—	—	—	—	21	—	—	—	—	3	18	—	Rs. 3,658	† Including 5 officers of superior rank.
Total ...	432	201	—	218	3.	412	1	644	—	† 19	47	337	9	Rs. 1,05,730	

III.

Statement showing the strength, cost, discipline, and education of the Police for the year 1341 T. E.

Description of office.	Number.	Grade of pay.	Total cost.	Punishments.					Rewards.		Education.		Remarks.
				Dismissed.	Fined, degraded or suspended departmentally.			Punished judicially.	By promotion.	By money.	Number able to read and write.	Number under instruction.	
1	2	3	4	5	6			7	8	9	10	11	12
		Rs.			*F.*	*D.*	*S.*						
Superintendent of Police	1	210-10-300		—		—		—	—	—	1	—	F. = Fined. D. = Degraded. S. = Suspended.
Asst. Superintendent " (Probationer)	1	75-0-0		—		—		—	—	—	1	—	
Inspectors	4 { 3 1	55-2-65 65 5-90	Rs 83,334	—		—		—	—	1	4	—	
Sub-Inspectors	25	25-2-45		—		—		—	—	6	25	—	
Naib Darogas	20	15-1-25		—	1	1	0	—	—	1	20	—	3 were taken in tantatively at the end of the year.
Writer Constables	10	15-0-0		—		—		—	—	—	10	—	
Subedar	1	25-2-45		—		—		—	—	—	1	—	
Sergeant	1	40-0-0		—		—		—	—	—	1	—	
Jamadar (civil)	6	15-1-25		—	1	0	0	—	—	—	6	—	
Jamadar (Armed)	1	20-1-30		—		—		—	—	—	1	—	
Havildars	2	20-1-25		—	0	1	0	—	—	—	2	—	
Naik	4	18-1-20		—	1	0	1	—	—	—	4	—	
Lance Naik	2	15-0-0		—	1	0	1	—	—	—	2	—	
Constables (Armed)	25	14 to 15		1	1	1	1	—	—	—	10	—	
Constables (Civil)	212	10 to 13		1	25	1	5	—	—	6	95	—	
Chaukidars	175	5-0-0		1	1	0	1	—	—	—	—	—	
Spy	3	15 to 20		—		—		—	—	—	3	—	
Total ...	493			3	31	4	9	—	—	14	186	—	

IV.

Statement showing the working of the Police in the Tripura State during the year 1341 T. E.

State.	Number of offences.		Number of accused arrested.		Number of accused sent up for trial.		Number of accused convicted.		Number of accused acquitted or discharged.		Percentage convicted of accused arrested.		Percentage convicted of accused sent up for trial.		REMARKS.
	Past year.	Present year.	Past year.	Present year.	Past year.	Present year	Past year.	Present year.	Past year.	Present year.	Past year.	Present year.	Past year.	Present year.	
1	2	3	4	5	6	7	8	9	10	11	12	13	14	15	16
Tripura State	1,377	1,300	802	917	801	835	224	284	124	129	27·80	30·97	67·14	* 65·71	* Excluding Pending trial— 329 Withdrawal— 64 Compromise— 24 Dead— 1 418

V.

Statement showing the value of property stolen and amount of recoveries in the Tripura State during the year 1341 T. E.

State.	Amount stolen.		Amount recovered.		Percentage of recoveries of property stolen.		REMARKS.
	Past year.	Present year.	Past year.	Present year.	Past year.	Present year.	
1	2	3	4	5	6	7	8
Tripura State	Rs 21,276-14-6	Rs 20,558-9-9	Rs 4,859-9-0	Rs 4,600-6-0	22·83	22·38	

VI.

Statement showing the number of crimes committed, number of cases disposed of, and cases awaiting trial in the Tripura State during the year 1341 T. E.

Description of offences.		Number of offences. Balance from past year.	Number of offences. Committed during the present year.	Number of offences. Total.	Number of cases disposed of during the past year.	Number of cases disposed of during the present year.	Number of cases awaiting trial.	Number of persons apprehended.	Number of persons convicted.	Number of persons sentenced. Imprisonment. Simple.	Number of persons sentenced. Imprisonment. Rigorous.	Number of persons sentenced. Imprisonment and fine. Simple.	Number of persons sentenced. Imprisonment and fine. Rigorous.	Number of persons sentenced. Fine only.	Number of persons sentenced. Whipping.	Number of persons sentenced. Capital punishment.	Number of persons sentenced. Total.	Number of persons acquitted or discharged.	Number of persons confined being insane.	Number of persons died during or before trial.	Term of imprisonment. Under one month.	From 1 to below 2 months.	From 2 to below 3 months.	From 3 to below 6 months.	From 6 to below 12 months.	From 1 to below 2 years.	From 2 to below 3 years.	From 3 to below 5 years.	5 years and above.	Transportation.	Capital punishment.	Persons awaiting trial.	Remarks.
1		2	3	4	5	6	7	8	9	10	11	12	13	14	15	16	17	18	19	20	21	22	23	24	25	26	27	28	29	30	31	32	33
Class I. Offences against the State, public tranquility, safety and justice &c.	cognizable ...	3	15	18	32	9	9	48	11	0	0	0	4	7	0	0	11	9	0	0	1	2	1	0	0	0	0	0	0	0	0	28	
	non-cognizable	9	31	40	40	33	7	80	3	0	2	0	1	0	0	0	3	48	0	0	1	0	0	0	2	0	0	0	0	0	0	29	*a.* 4 persons have been warned for the future.
Class II. Offences against person.	cognizable ...	58	280	338	249	250	88	606	67	3	31	0	7	26	0	0	67	394	2	2	12	2	2	9	5	5	2	2	0	2	0	141	*b.* 30 persons have been warned for the future and 9 persons bound down under security.
	non-cognizable	38	255	293	245	252	41	185	*a* 21	3		0	1	9	0	0	17	120	0	0	6	0	1	1	0	0	0	0	0	0	0	44	
Class III. Offences against property.	cognizable ...	202	790	992	911	772	220	1524	*b* 454	9	119	0	24	263	0	0	415	698	0	3	79	17	10	12	19	4	5	6	0	0	0	369	*c.* 4 persons have been bound down under security.
	non-cognizable	27	187	214	184	176	38	189	11	3	1	0	0	7	0	0	11	142	0	0	3	0	0	1	0	0	0	0	0	0	0	36	
Class IV. Other offences.	cognizable ...	48	199	247	168	190	57	228	75	3	21	0	11	40	0	0	75	79	0	1	10	9	2	2	1	1	8	2	0	0	0	73	
	non-cognizable	66	192	258	328	201	57	196	*c* 31	0	1	0	0	26	0	0	27	116	0	1	1	0	0	0	0	0	0	0	0	0	0	48	
Total cognizable		311	1284	1595	1360	1221	374	2406	607	15	171	0	46	336	0	0	568	1180	2	6	102	30	15	23	25	10	15	10	0	2	0	611	
Total non-cognizable		140	665	805	797	662	143	650	66	6	8	0	2	42	0	0	58	426	0	1	11	0	1	2	2	0	0	0	0	0	0	157	
GRAND TOTAL		451	1949	2400	2157	1883	517	3056	673	21	179	0	48	378	0	0	626	1606	2	7	113	30	16	25	27	10	15	10	0	2	0	768	

VII.

Statement showing the number of offences reported and dealt with by the various Courts in the Tripura State during the year 1341 T.E.

Name of Court.	Number of offences reported during.		Number of persons dealt with.								Persons disposed of.						Persons remaining at the end of the year.	Remarks
			Remaining at the end of last year.	Brought to trial during present year.					Total.									
	Last year.	Present year.		Arrested by Police.	Upon warrant.	On summons.	Voluntary.	Arrested in presence of the Magistrate.	Last year.	Present year.	Discharged without trial.	Acquitted.	Convicted.	Committed or referred.	Died, escaped, or transferred &c.			
1	2	3	4	5	6	7	8	9	10	11	12	13	14	15	16	17	18
Sadar Magistracy	519	538	86	201	127	186	17	0	703	617	139	147	140	46	0	145	
Sonamura „ ...	209	231	92	75	39	97	9	0	337	312	101	48	54	22	0	87	
Bilonia „ ...	236	243	63	157	40	89	73	4	456	426	131	76	171	5	0	43	
Kailashahar „ ...	261	273	125	187	185	65	5	0	576	567	177	91	110	4	10	175	
Khowai „ ...	122	113	47	41	13	48	2	0	165	151	31	41	14	2	0	63	
Dharmanagar „ ...	235	255	148	89	99	110	159	0	889	605	253	117	26	16	6	187	
Udaipur „ ...	261	238	86	35	58	76	28	0	570	283	77	73	91	9	0	33	
Sabrum „ ...	45	58	6	32	8	21	8	1	34	76	10	16	36	1	1	12	
TOTAL ...	1,879	1,949	653	817	569	692	301	5	3,749	3,037 a	919	609	642	105 b	17	745	

a. Excluding 19 persons pending before the Court of Sessions at the close of the previous year.

b. The total number of persons for trial before the Court of Sessions, including 19 persons pending from the last year was 124, of whom 31 were convicted 63 acquitted and 30 remained under trial at the close of the year.

VIII.

Statement of Criminal cases in which British Subjects were concerned for 1341 T. E.

Description of Offences.		Cases pending since the previous year.	Cases instituted during the year.	Total number of cases.	Cases in which complainants were British subjects.	Cases in which both parties were British subjects.	Cases in which defendants were British Subjects.													Remarks
							Cases pending since the previous year	Cases instituted during the year.	Total number of cases.	Cases disposed of.		Cases pending at the close of the year.	Persons under trial at the close of the previous year.	Persons brought to trial during the year.	Total number of persons under trial.	Convicted.	Acquitted or discharged.	Died or escaped &c.	Under trial at the close of the year.	
										Rejected, compromised or dismissed without enquiry.	Tried.										
Class I. Offences against the State &c.	cognizable	2	3	5	1	0	2	2	4	2	1	1	3	5	8	0	8	0	0	
	non-cognizable	0	2	2	0	0	0	2	2	2	0	0	0	0	0	0	0	0	0	
Class II. Offences against person.	cognizable	6	34	40	9	7	6	25	31	6	17	8	12	48	60	14	31	0	15	
	non-cognizable	0	20	20	5	6	0	15	15	12	0	3	0	6	6	0	5	0	0	
Class III. Offences against property.	cognizable	53	222	275	22	50	41	212	253	37	170	46	55	387	442	288	112	1	41	
	non-cognizable	3	40	43	7	30	3	33	36	24	7	5	5	14	19	2	6	0	11	
Class IV. Other offences	cognizable	4	30	34	4	5	4	26	30	9	7	14	10	37	47	6	17	0	24	
	non-cognizable	2	27	29	1	15	2	26	28	22	5	1	0	24	24	6	12	0	6	
Total cognizable		65	289	354	36	62	53	265	318	54	195	69	80	477	557	308	168	1	80	
Total non-cognizable		5	89	94	13	51	5	76	81	60	12	9	5	44	49	8	24	0	17	
Grand Total		70	378	448	49	113	58	341	399	114	207	78	85	521	606*	316	192	1	97	

* Of this number, 57 persons were discharged without trial, on compromise or on account of being struck off on default etc. Excluding 1 dead and 97 pending trial, the actual number of persons tried was 451, of whom 316 were convicted, the percentage of conviction being 70·07 against 44·17 of the previous year.

IX.

Statement of Extradition Cases for the year 1341 T. E.

Names of Courts.	Nature of cases.	Number Borne on the Register.				Number Brought to Trial.			Result.		Number at large at the close of the year.	Number of persons awaiting trial (after arrest) at the close of the year.	Remarks.
		Number of persons at large at the close of the previous year.	Number of persons awaiting trial at the close of the previous year.	Number of persons against whom warrants were applied for during the year.	Total.	Number of persons arrested and surrendered within the year.	Number of persons who appeared of their own accord or were subsequently arrested in the State within the year.	Total (Columns 4+7+8).	Convicted.	Acquitted or discharged.			
Sadar Magistracy	Dacoity and criminal trespass	0	0	1	1	1	0	1	1	0	0	0	
	Theft and receiving stolen property	2	0	0	2	0	0	0	0	0	2	0	
	Causing mischief	2	0	0	2	0	0	0	0	0	2	0	
	Kidnapping	0	0	8	8	4	0	4	2	2	4	0	
	Theft	0	0	1	1	1	0	1	0	0	0	1	
	Rescuing offenders from lawful custody	0	0	5	5	4	0	4	0	0	1	4	
Bilonia ,, ...	Theft and escape from lawful custody	1	0	0	1	0	0	0	0	0	1	0	
	Culpable homicide not amounting to murder	2	1	0	3	0	0	1	0	0	2	1	
	Theft	0	1	19	20	5	1	7	2	5	13	0	
Sonamura ,, ...	Theft	23	1	26	50	17	0	18	1	13	32	4	
	Murder	2	3	4	9	0	0	3	0	0	6	3	
	Dacoity and mischief...	0	2	5	7	3	0	5	0	0	2	5	
	Escape from lawful custody	1	0	0	1	0	0	0	0	0	1	0	
Kailashahar ,, ...	Theft	10	0	3	13	3	0	3	0	1	10	2	
Dharmanagar ,, ...	Theft	1	1	1	3	1	0	2	0	1	1	1	
	Highway robbery	1	0	0	1	0	0	0	0	0	1	0	
	Theft and wrongful confinement	2	0	0	2	0	0	0	0	0	2	0	
	Criminal trespass and assault with deadly weapons ...	11	0	0	11	0	0	0	0	0	11	0	
	Arson	9	0	0	9	0	0	0	0	0	9	0	
	Criminal trespass and theft	14	0	1	15	0	9	9	0	9	6	0	
	Escape from lawful custody	1	0	0	1	1	0	1	1	0	0	0	
	Murder...	0	0	1	1	1	0	1	0	1	0	0	
Khowai ,, ...	Wrongful confinement	0	0	1	1	1	0	1	0	0	0	1	
	Cheating	1	0	0	1	0	1	1	1	0	0	0	
	Kidnapping	0	2	1	3	0	1	3	0	3	0	0	
Udaipur ,, ...	Theft and receiving stolen property	3	0	2	5	2	0	2	2	0	3	0	
	Criminal breach of trust	0	0	1	1	1	0	1	1	0	0	0	
	Murder...	0	0	2	2	1	0	1	0	0	1	0	
Sabroom ,, ...	Theft	3	0	6	9	2	1	3	2	0	6	1	
	Escape from lawful custody	2	0	1	3	2	0	2	2	0	1	0	
	Criminal breach of trust by servant	1	0	0	1	1	0	1	0	1	0	0	
	Resistance or obstruction to lawful apprehension of another person (Sec. 224)	0	0	7	7	0	7	7	0	0	0	7	* Committed to Sessions.
	Total	92	11	96	199	51	20	82	15	36	117	30	

X.

Statement showing the results of appeals against decisions passed by the Criminal Courts in the Tripura State during the year 1341 T. E.

Tribunals.	Number of applications.	Number of persons and cases.																Remarks.
		Applications rejected.		*Sentences.*						Proceedings quashed.		Referred.		Further enquiry &c, ordered.		Pending.		
				Confirmed.		Modified.		Reversed.										
		Persons.	Cases.	Persons.	Cases.	Persons.	Cases.	Persons.	Cases.	Persons.	Cases.	Persons.	Cases.	Persons.	Cases.	Persons.	Cases.	
Khas Adalat ...	308	21	19	175	148	98	46	41	19	—	—	—	—	16	14	98	62	

XI.

Civil Work—Nature and value of original suits filed and disposed of during the year 1341 T. E.

Tribunal.	Opening balance.		Filed during the year, received by transfer or on remand.		Total.		Disposed of during the year.		Closing balance.		Suits filed during present year.									Suits disposed of during present year.						Suits not estimable in money.	Remarks.
	Past year.	Present year.	Past year.	Present year.	Past year.	Present year.	Past year.	Present year.	Past year.	Present year.	Value.	Suits re landed property.	Suits for money transaction.	Suits for other rights.	Number of suits under Rs. 100.	Number of suits above Rs. 100 and under Rs. 500.	Number of suits above Rs. 500 and under Rs. 1,000.	Number of suits above Rs. 1,000 and under Rs. 5,000.	Number of suits above Rs. 5,000.	Exparte.	Admitted and compromised.	Struck off the file.	Otherwise disposed of.	Value.	Average duration.		
											Rs. a. p.													Rs a. p.	Y. m. d.		
Khas Adalat Original side	59	67	35	28	94	95	27	31	67	64	43,562-8-0	9	9	10	0	0	0	21	0	6	2	9	14	37,209-2-6	0-4-13	7	
Sadar Dewani Adalat	378	230	629	660	1,007	890	777	708	230	182	66,522-10-6	238	396	31	306	145	19	0	0	440	17	0	242	44,870-6-0	0-0-21	100	
Sonamura „	109	56	223	193	332	249	276	188	56	61	9,635-11-0	59	107	27	118	48	0	0	0	71	37	23	57	7,575-12-9	0-1-17	27	
Bilonia „	58	40	143	98	201	138	161	120	40	18	8,987-4-0	41	37	20	66	17	0	0	0	63	11	4	42	9,301-14-9	0-5-27	15	
Kailashahar „	241	188	312	280	553	463	364	291	189	177	30,487-5-0	8	207	63	154	51	13	0	0	114	35	5	137	29,721-12-9	0-4-7	62	
Khowai „	48	47	120	82	168	129	121	80	47	40	6,844-10-3	23	49	10	47	30	1	0	0	23	17	9	40	5,992-3-9	0-4-1	4	
Dharmanagar „	118	58	236	177	354	235	296	158	58	77	16,201-8-9	38	89	62	111	34	4	0	0	43	19	16	80	12,471-3-0	0-1-14	28	
Udaipur „	159	90	428	385	587	475	497	365	90	110	33,747-6-9	36	328	21	253	91	4	0	0	184	54	33	94	32,185-14-0	0-1-17	37	
Sabrum „	8	12	35	16	43	28	31	24	12	4	2,111-14-6	0	16	0	10	6	0	0	0	11	7	3	3	3,089-7-9	0-2-12	0	
Total ...	1,178	788	2,161	1,919	3,339	2,707	2,550	1,974	789	733	2,18,100-15-6	435	1238	246	1155	422	41	21	0	964	199	102	709	1,82,417-13-3	0-2-28	280	

XII.

Civil Work.—Results of applications for Execution of Decrees, 1341 T.E.

Tribunal.	Opening balance.		Value of opening balance for present year.	Applications brought to the Register.			Total.			Disposed of.			Closing balance.			Nature of applications pending disposal at the close of the year.			Remarks.
	Past year.	Present year.		Past year.	Present year.	Value for present year.	Past year.	Present year.	Value for present year.	Past year.	Present year.	Value for present year.	Past yaer.	Present year.	Value for present year.	Below 6 months.	Below 12 months.	Above 12 months.	
			Rs. a. p.			*Rs. a. p.*			*Rs. a. p.*			*Rs. a. p.*			*Rs. a. p*				
Khas Adalat (Original side)	25	32	48,920-2-6	15	19	9,918-15-9	40	51	58,839-2-3	8	15	5,730-8-6	32	36	53,108-9-9	5	14	17	
Sadar Dewani Adalat ...	207	164	30,025-12-0	229	230	35,729-8-9	436	394	65,755-4-9	272	208	31,876-3-3	164	186	33,879-1-6	104	33	49	
Sonamura Ditto ...	27	21	3,946-4-3	58	67	9,476-13-9	85	88	13,423-2-0	64	61	8,746-6-9	21	27	4,676-11-3	19	8	0	
Bilonia Ditto ...	14	14	1,865-12-0	52	73	7,757-5-3	66	87	9,623-1-3	52	63	7,069-1-3	14	24	2,554-0-0	16	5	3	
Kailashahar Ditto ...	131	87	15,253-15-3	118	111	17,492-13-0	249	198	32,746-12-3	162	95	12,229-9-6	87	103	20,517-2-9	36	31	36	
Khowai Ditto ...	46	50	4,862-6-9	71	44	2,040-2-0	117	94	6,902-8-9	67	65	5,004-6-0	50	29	1,898-2-9	23	5	1	
Dharmanagar Ditto ...	24	22	6,265-13-6	55	59	7,395-2-9	79	81	13,661-0-3	57	50	8,076-13-6	22	31	5,584-2-9	26	3	2	
Udaipur Ditto ...	159	165	27,440-7-0	267	284	43,707-6-9	426	449	71,147-13-9	261	283	43,357-12-9	165	166	27,790-1-0	137	8	21	
Sabrum Ditto ...	0	4	817-14-3	8	11	1,688-14-0	8	15	2,506-12-3	4	5	1,070-7-3	4	10	1,436-5-0	4	4	2	
Total ...	633	559	1,39,398-7-6	873	898	1,35,207-2-0	1,506	1,457	2,74,605-9-6	947	845	1,23,161-4-9	559	612	1,51,444-4-9	370	111	131	

XIII.

Civil Work—Number and results of appeals in civil suits, 1341 T. E.

Tribunal.	Opening balance.		Filed during.		Total.		Disposed of during.		Closing balance.		Value of appeales filed during.		How disposed of.										Average duration.	
													Decisions confirmed.		Decisions reversed.		Decisions amended.		Cases remanded for retrial.		Cases compromised and otherwise disposed of.			
	Past year.	Present year.	Past year.	Present year.	Past year.	Present year.	Past year.	Present year.	Past year.	Present year.	Past year.	Present year.	Past year.	Present year.	Past year.	Present year.	Past year.	Present year.	Past year.	Present year.	Past year.	Present year.	Past year.	Present year.
											Rs. a. p.	*Rs. a. p.*											*Y. m. d.*	*Y. m. d.*
Khas Adalat	138	164	214	203	352	367	188	200	164	167	33,418-9-0	20,242-2-9	80	85	28	22	18	29	35	21	27	43	0-2-16	0-4-5

XIV.

Statement showing the number of persons confined in the jails and lock-ups in the Tripura State during the year 1341 T. E.

Stations.	Number of prisons.	NUMBER OF PRISONERS.				DAILY AVERAGE.		Number of prisoners remaining at the end of the year.	Cost of jails and prisoners.	Average period in days of stay of accused under-trial.	Remarks showing mortality among convicts in jail.
		Remaining from last year.	Admitted during the year.	Total.							
				Past year.	Present year.	Past year.	Present year.				
									Rs.		
Agartala	1	116	395	400	511	80·5	121·5	175	13,826	60.6	
Sonamura	1	15	97	92	112	·23	·3	2	732	34·66	
Bilonia	1	2	179	67	181	1·35	4·17	4	538	7·28	3 convicts and 1 undertrial prisoner died during the year 1341 T. E.—
Kailashahar	1	8	185	127	193	6·65	13·79	14	863	30·8	Kala-azar—1. T. B. infection—1. Malaria—1. } Convicts.
Dharmanagar	1	5	125	142	130	6·07	10 14	11	850	28·66	Pneumonia—1. under-trial.
Udaipur...	1	12	111	104	123	5·89	7·96	2	543	7·83	
Sabrum	1	—	36	24	36	·06	·09	2	265	19·88	
Khowai	1	2	44	41	46	2·84	3·60	2	378	34·15	
TOTAL. ...	8	160	1172	997	1332	103·59	161·55	212	17,995	27·98	

XV.

Registration of documents in the Tripura State during the year 1341 T.E.

Name of State.	Documents presented for registration including pending from the last year.		Nature of documents presented.										Documents registered.		Value of documents registered.		Documents of which registration has been refused.		Documents remaining unregistered at the end of the year.		Remarks.
			Mortgages.		Sale deeds.		Wills.		Money bonds.		Miscellaneous.										
	Past year.	Present year.	Past year.	Present year.	Past year.	Present year.	Past year.	Present year.	Past year.	Present year.	Past year.	Present year.	Past year.	Present year.	Past year.	Present year.	Past year.	Present year.	Past year.	Present year.	
1	2	3	4	5	6	7	8	9	10	11	12	13	14	15	16	17	18	19	20	21	22
															Rs.	*Rs.*					
Tripura State	9,382	6,302	2,484	1,530	3,554	3,002	2	2	481	137	2,484	1,414	9,051	5,195	15,17,763	7,09,868	114	71	217	1,036	

XVI.

Statement showing the receipts and expenditure on account of Registration during the year 1341 T.E.

Description.	Past year.			Present year.			Remarks.
	Number of deeds.	Value of property.	Fees realised.	Number of deeds.	Value of property.	Fees realised.	
		Rs.	Rs.		Rs.	Rs.	
Mortgages	2,484	5,98,605	2,803	1,530	2,31,712	1,572	
Sale deeds	3,554	7,07,507	4,418	3,002	4,38,801	3,326	
Wills	2		11	2	—	12	
Money bonds	481	53,957	456	137	11,659	126	
Miscellaneous	2,484	3,95,068	3,357	1,414	2,02,913	1,861	
Total ...	9.005	17,55,137	11,045	6,085	8,85,085	6,897	
Total Expenditure ...	—	—	4,726	—	—	3,840	
Net Income ...	—	—	6,319	—	—	3,057	

XVII.

Receipts and expenditure of the Municipalities in the Tripura State during the year 1341 T.E.

NAME.	Opening balance.	RECEIPTS DURING THE YEAR.				Total Receipt		EXPENDITURE DURING THE YEAR.		Balance at the close of the year.	REMARKS.
		State grant.	Tax.	Miscel-laneous.	Total.	Past. year.	Present year	Past.	Present.		
1	2	3	4	5	6	7	8	9	10	11	12
	Rs. A.P.	Rs. A.P.	Rs. A.P	Rs. A.P.	Rs. A.P.	Rs. A.P.	Rs. A.P	Rs. A.P.	Rs. A.P.	Rs. A.P.	
Agartala Municipality. ...	28,365-8-3	9,000	3,509-10-3	7,052-11-9 a	19,562-6-0	42,042-11-0	47,927-14-3	13,677-2-9	14,643-0-0 b	33,284-14-3 c	a. Including Rs. 6,144-7-6 as income from the Bazar and Rs. 203-10-0 as deposits and advances recovered. b. Including Rs. 464-7-0 as expenditure on the Bazar improvement. c. Including Rs. 33,234-12-3 of the Bazar improvement fund and Rs. 50-2-0 as income from the municipality.

XVIII.

Statement of rainfall in the Tripura State during the year 1341 T. E.

State.	Baisak.	Jaisth.	Asar.	Sravan.	Bhadra.	Asvin.	Kartik.	Agrahayan.	Pous.	Magh.	Falgoon.	Chait.	Total.	Total of past year.	Average of past 5 years.	Remarks.
Tripura State ...	14·13	11·19	16·16	16·40	8·42	5·62	6·39	—	—	·58	·28	3·57	82·74	92·58	87·93	

Maximum in Bilonia—108·67″ Minimum in Amarpur—64·66″

XIX.

Statement as to the prices of staple food-grains for the year 1341 T. E.

Articles.	Price per maund during Chait, 1340 T. E.			Price per maund during chait, 1341 T. E.			REMARKS.
	Rs.	a.	p.	Rs.	a.	p.	
(1) RICE							
Maximum	8	0	0	4	0	0	
Minimum	3	0	0	2	0	0	
(2) PADDY							
Maximum	3	8	0	2	0	0	
Minimum	1	8	0	0	12	0	

XX.

Expenditure on Public Works during the year 1341 T.E.

Description of work.	State Funds.			Local Funds.			Total.	Remarks.
	Original.	Repairs.	Total.	Original.	Repairs.	Total.		
	Rs.	*Rs.*	*Rs.*	*Rs.*	*Rs.*	*Rs.*	*Rs.*	
Buildings	7,391	34,224	41,615	—	—	—	41,615	* Out of this amount Rs. 8,604 was spent for improvement works under the following heads :— (1) Buildings ... — (2) Roads and Bridges ... Rs. 849 (3) Water supply ... " 1,084 (4) Miscellaneous ... " 6,671 Total ... Rs. 8,604
Roads and Bridges ...	2,012	4,222	6,234	—	—	—	6,234	
Tanks and Tubewells ...	2,110	1,115	3,225	—	—	—	3,225	
Miscellaneous works ...	7,566	1,924	9,490	—	—	—	9,490	
Total ...	19,079	41,485	60,564	—	—	—	60,564	
Minor works at the Rajbari (*Karkhana*)	—	1,959	1,959	—	—	—	1,959	
Establishment charges ..	—	—	18,874	—	—	—	18,874	
Grand Total ...	—	—	81,397*	—	—	—	81,397	

XXI.

Statement showing the number of excise shops and excise revenue of the Tripura State during the year 1341 T. E.

Name of State.	Country spirit.		Country spirit, Opium and Ganja.		Opium and Ganja.		Tari.		Total.		Remarks.
	Number of shops.	Revenue demand.	Number of shops.	Revenue demand.	Number of shops.	Revenue demand.	Number of shops.	Revenue demand.	Number of shops.	Revenue realised.	
		Rs.		*Rs.*						*Rs.*	
Tripura State	1	15	30	63,421	—	—	—	—	31	50,086	

XXII.

Statement of Medical Relief afforded in the Tripura State during the year 1341 T.E.*

Dispensary.	Number of patients treated. (new) Outdoor.	Indoor.	Results of in-door patients. (new) Dis-charged cured.	Relieved or dis-charged otherwise.	Died.	Remain-ing under treatment.	Expenditure.	Daily average. (old + new) Outdoor.	Indoor.	Total.	No. of surgical operations performed. Major.	Minor.	Total.	No. of persons vaccinated during the year. Success-fully.	Unsuc-cessfully.	Total.	Remarks.
1. Victoria Memorial Hospital at Agartala and the Charitable Dispensary attached to it ...	15,888	458	295	119	27	17	Rs. 8,075	83·65	18·60	102·25	6	283	289	712	415	1,127	
2. Palace Dispensary	11,284	0	0	0	0	0	7,753	63·60	0	63·60	0	0	0	0	0	0	
3. Homœopathic	13,894	0	0	0	0	0	2,197	64·26	0	64·26	0	0	0	0	0	0	* This Statement excludes figures regarding Kaviraji treatment.
4. Dhaleswar	7,005	0	0	0	0	0	1,211	32·27	0	32·27	0	46	46	0	0	0	
5. Kunjaban	2,882	306	269	33	1	3	1,826	29·56	9·66	39·22	0	11	11	0	0	0	
6. Old Agartala	3,974	0	0	0	0	0	1,263	36·97	0	36·97	0	44	44	442	111	553	† This figure shows the actual number of outdoor patients treated, the total outdoor attendance during the year being 2,30,381 against 2,15,914 in the previous year.
7. Bishalgar	7,654	0	0	0	0	0	1,111	38·01	0	38·01	0	45	45	594	45	639	
8. Mohanpur	4,747	0	0	0	0	0	9,78	17·32	0	17·32	0	75	75	172	7	179	
9. Sonamura	7,371	12	5	7	0	0	1,838	36·22	·03	36·25	0	132	132	482	22	504	
10. Udaipur	8,854	0	0	0	0	0	1,454	37·24	0	37·24	0	58	58	372	188	560	
11. Amarpur	3,350	0	0	0	0	0	1,079	15·96	0	15·96	0	23	23	53	11	64	
12. Sabroom	1,992	3	3	0	0	0	1,267	11·38	·07	11.45	0	56	56	44	29	73	
13. Bilonia	6,365	2	2	0	0	0	1,810	35·36	·07	35·43	0	140	140	160	4	164	
14. Loongthung	3,002	0	0	0	0	0	1,082	15·95	0	15·95	0	56	56	166	18	184	
15. Khowai	8,480	0	0	0	0	0	1,694	27·59	0	27·59	0	93	93	519	55	574	
16. Kailashahar	6,091	0	0	0	0	0	1,910	25·60	0	25·60	0	132	132	207	47	254	
17. Fatikroy	2,383	0	0	0	0	0	868	9·80	0	9·80	0	22	22	127	57	184	
18. Kamalpur	4,473	0	0	0	0	0	1,516	15·70	0	15·70	0	69	69	283	317	600	
19. Kulai Howar	1,671	0	0	0	0	0	819	6·34	0	6·34	0	9	9	0	0	0	
20. Dharmanagar	6,190	12	6	6	0	0	1,804	26·90	·04	26·94	2	58	60	170	25	195	
Total	†1,27,550	793	580	165	28	20	41,505	629·68	28·47	658·15	8	1,352	1,360	4,503	1,351	5,854	

XXIII.

Vital statistics of the Tripura State for the year 1341 T.E.

STATE.	Population.	BIRTHS.				DEATHS.				RATIO PER 1,000 OF POPULATION.				REMARKS.
										BIRTHS.		DEATHS.		
		Past year.	Present year.	Increase.	Decrease.	Past year.	Present year.	Increase.	Decrease.	Past year.	Present year.	Past year.	Present year.	
Tripura State ...	3,82,163	2,510	2,689	179	—	2,412	2,976	564	—	6·56	7·03	6·31	7·78	The figures are far from being correct—although attempt was made to collect accurate figures.

XXIV.

Education Return (A)—Particulars as to the schools maintained during the year 1341 T.E.

Number of Schools.		Class of Schools.	Number of pupils on the rolls on the last day of Chait.		Average daily attendance.		Remarks.
Past year.	Present year.		Past year.	Present year.	Past year.	Present year.	
6	6	High English Schools ... ... (including one Branch H. E. School).	1,646	1,450	1,289'04	1,209'25	
7	8	Middle English Schools for boys ...	857	950	649'79	717'34	* In some of these schools boys and girls read together.
1	1	Middle English School for girls ...	87	85	50'97	51'95	† Private schools have been included.
1	1	Higher Vernacular School for boys	72	80	55'92	58'76	
24	25	* Lower Vernacular Schools for boys	1,352	1,502	1,041'20	1,110'30	
160	150	*Pathsalas for boys	4,337	4,545	2,434'76	2,990'27	
10	10	Do for girls	290	291	222'97	232'38	
		Special Schools :—					
6	7	Madrassas and Muktabs	217	238	155'61	160'51	
4	4	Sanskrit *Tols*	48	43	35'04	30'25	
1	1	Artisan School & Silpasram ...	22	26	10'91	11'43	
—	1	Jail Reformatory School	—	20	—	19'45	
TOTAL 220	214†		8,928	9,230	5,946'21	6,591'99	

XXV.

Education Return (B) Race of Students, 1341 T. E.

Names of Divisions.	No. of Schools.				No. of Students.					Race.												Average daily attendance.		REMARKS.
										Hindus.														
	For boys.	For girls.	Total.	Private schools.	Boys.	Girls.	Total.	Students of private schools.	Total	Rajkumars.	Thakurs.	Manipuris.	Tripuras.	Bengalees.	Others.	Reangs.	Chakmas.	Kukis.	Lusais.	Musalmans.	Christians.	Boys.	Girls.	
1. Sadar Division ...	62	3	65	13	2,696	124	2,820	400	3,220	4	149	133	750	979	17	1	1	36	0	750	0	2,185·53	81·46	
2. Kailashahar "	25	3	28	4	1,180	212	1,392	80	1,472	0	3	345	49	715	10	0	0	5	0	265	0	914·73	139·28	
3. Sonamura "	25	1	26	4	1,233	87	1,320	138	1,458	0	9	0	177	267	0	0	0	0	0	867	0	928·34	71·01	
4. Bilonia "	11	1	12	3	758	32	790	87	877	0	0	1	28	468	13	30	0	0	0	250	0	610·37	23·61	
5. Khowai "	11	1	12	1	327	12	339	25	364	0	0	52	193	79	0	0	0	0	0	15	0	265·13	11·16	
6. Dharmanagar "	16	1	17	6	763	71	834	203	1,037	0	1	141	0	456	9	0	0	0	5	222	0	478·61	62·94	
7. Udaipur "	9	1	16	1	412	23	435	29	464	0	1	72	0	162	0	0	0	0	0	200	0	223·88	19·58	
8. Sabrum "	8	0	8	1	255	26	381	23	304	0	0	0	104	120	2	0	0	0	0	55	0	226·47	16·58	
9. Amarpur Sub-division ...	1	0	1	1	9	2	11	23	34	0	0	0	1	10	0	0	0	0	0	0	0	7·55	1·94	
TOTAL ...	168	11	179	34	7,633	589	8,222	1,008	9,230	4	163	744	1,302	3,256	51	31	1	41	5	2,624	0	5,840·01	427·56	

N. B.—In the Sub-columns under "Race" the number of students of private schools is not included.

APPENDIX XXVI. (A)

Statement of Audited Receipts for the year 1341 T. E.

State.

Heads of Revenue.	1340 T. E. Revised Estimate.	1340 T. E. Actuals.	1341 T. E. Revised Estimate.	1341 T. E. Actuals.	Remarks.
1. Land Revenue ...	5,50,000	4,40,180	5,10,000	3,97,658	
2. Rents of markets ..	7,000	6,668	7,000	5,485	
3. Family tax in the hills	50,000	37,204	50,000	42,685	
4. Toll on Forest Produce	4,00,000	3,60,080	3,75,000	3,16,497	
5. Do on the Feni River	35,000	30,524	28,000	27,850	
6. Elephant and Buffalo grazing mehals ...	7,000	6,024	7,000	5,690	
7. Thatching grass mehals	5,000	5,789	5,000	4,008	
8. Reserved *Sal* trees ...	6,000	5,500	3,000	1,470	
9. Tax on cotton and Oil seeds ...	1,00,000	1,07,281	1,25,000	1,12,868	
10. Royalty on elephants caught ..	10,000	4,099	4,000	—	
11. *Adda* mehal ...	23,000	19,769	20,000	23,333	
12. Excise ...	90,000	92,302	75,000	50,086	
13. Stamps and Court fees	1,00,000	82,738	85,000	67,070	
14 Law and Justice (fines)	4,000	4,865	4,000	4,813	
15. Process Fees ...	17,000	14,830	14,000	12,563	
16. Registration ...	14,000	11,045	12,000	6,897	
17. Jail ...	3,000	1,400	2,000	2,254	
18. Cattle pounds ...	6,000	5,219	5,000	4,566	
19. *Nazars* ...	50,000	37,733	40,000	27,390	
20. School Fees ...	17,000	16,581	17,000	14,502	
21. Duty on Tea ...	9,000	12,742	10,000	8,633	
22. Duty on jute ...	24,000	27,978	15,000	11,463	
23. Personal *Howlats* recovered	4,000	5,062	2,000	3,746	
24. Interest on Bank deposit ...	1,000	1,549	—	—	
25. Miscellaneous ...	55,000	55,597	55,000	43,615	
26. Depreciation Contribution ...	—	—	50,000	42,110	
Total ...	15,87,000	13,92,709	15,20,000	12,37,252	
27. Deposits ...	75,000	1,83,785	80,000	2,26,312	
28. Loans from Chakla ...	1,50,000	1,61,642	30,000	30,000	
29. Contribution from Chakla ...	—	—	70,000	70,000	
30. Marriage Contribution	—	—	75,000	75,000	
31. Provident fund ...	—	—	20,000	21,472	
32. Loans from Nijtahabil	—	—	2,00,000	1,00,000	
33. Other loans ...	2,48,287	12,350	—	30,222	
Total ...	20,60,287	17,50,436	19,95,000	17,90,258	
Opening Balance :—					
Cash ...	1,25,000	1,25,366	1,03,000	* 1,04,593	* In Cash ... 1,01,794
Advances ...	1,77,000	1,77,241	1,98,000	2,02,653	In Bank ... 2,799
Loans ...	2,93,000	2,92,788	2,93,000	2,94,425	1,04,593
Total ...	5,95,000	5,95,345	5,94,000	6,01,671	
Grand Total ...	26,55,287	23,45,781	25,89,000	23,91,929	

APPENDIX XXVI. (B)

Statement of Audited Expenditure for the year 1341 T. E.

State.

Heads of Expenditure.	1340 T. E.		1341 T. E.		REMARKS.
	Revised estimate.	Actuals.	Revised Estimate.	Actuals.	
1. Controlling Charges	1,01,150	90,050	82,207	79,157	
2. Revenue General ...	92,640	87,510	88,802	84,858	
3. Survey & Settlement	29,430	26,374	11,930	10,237	
4. Tahasil ...	57,160	55,138	54,033	52,224	
5. Registration ...	5,440	4,726	4,806	3,840	
6. Police ...	93,130	85,471	84,250	83,334	
7. Judicial ...	37,710	36,838	33,142	33,078	
8. Jail ...	21,900	17,568	20,142	17,995	
9. Forest ...	64,750	55,707	55,039	54,009	
10. Medical ...	77,490	70,063	71,566	65,360	
11. Municipality and Sanitation ...	10,000	10,000	9,000	9,000	
12. Education General ...	1,42,700	1,34,669	1,32,162	1,27,620	
13. (*a*) Public Works ...	1,50,000	1,15,736	1,46,740	72,793	
(*b*) Improvement ...	1,86,000	1,21,288	30,000	8,604	
14. Electric Light ...	19,000	14,821	18,579	17,700	
15. Small Donations ...	500	384	320	239	
16. Relief to distressed subjects ...	500	076	300	107	
17. Purchase of Landed Property ...	1,000	344	1,000	510	
18. Repayment of Deposits ...	65,000	61,510	64,000	49,923	
19. Interest on Deposits	18,000	4,375	20,000	7,672	
20. Unforeseen charges ...	3,500	859	2,500	2,136	
21. Advances to employees ...	7,000	5,020	200	175	
22. Pension ...	33,000	29,997	37,000	34,646	
23. Advisory Council ...	4,552	4,525	2,280	2,440	
24. Chief Secretary's Office & H. H.'s Tour	72,582	55,913	57,197	53,896	
25. Palace Sultanat ...	26,074	23,237	21,614	16,858	
26. Zoo ...	8,750	8,043	6,135	5,834	
27. Agriculture, Commerce and Industries	12,744	10,461	10,043	8,811	
28. Publicity, Reclamation and Immigration	2,100	1,414	1,379	1,177	
29. H. H.'s Private Secretary's Office ...	9,200	8,637	8,856	8,372	
30. Rajmala Office ...	5,058	3,064	4,842	2,018	
31. Military Secretary's Office ...	2,640	2,630	2,760	2,750	
32. Military ...	1,37,767	1,13,897	1,29,976	1,05,730	
33. Nijtahabil ...	1,20,000	1,12,469	1,20,000	1,09,000	
34. Expenditure in connection with H. H.'s Installation, Investiture & Marriage etc.	50,000	13,166	75,000	55,112	
35. Adjustment of irrecoverable advances ...	20,000	10,576	10,000	8,865	
36. Census ...	1,200	997	2,000	422	
37. Repayment of old Debts ...	—	—	2,00,000	1,78,858	
38. Sansar Charges ...	4,19,620	3,45,655	3,98,200	3,67,559	
Total ...	21,09,287	17,44,110	20,18,000	17,40,914	
Closing balance :—					
Cash ...	1,00,000	1,01,593	1,10,000	* 1,14,250	* In Cash ... 93,623
Advances ...	1,53,000	2,02,653	1,88,000	2,61,681	In Bank ... 20,627
Loans issued ...	2,93,000	2,94,425	2,73,000	2,75,084	1,14,250
Total ...	5,46,000	6,01,671	5,71,000	6,51,015	
Grand Total ...	26,55,287	23,45,781	25,89,000	23,91,929	

APPENDIX XXVII. (A)

Statement of Audited Receipts for the year 1341 T. E.

Chakla Roshnabad Estates.

Heads of Receipts.	1340 T. E.		1341 T. E.		REMARKS.
	Revised Estimate.	Actuals.	Revised Estimate.	Actuals.	
1. Rent and Cess ...	8,58,031	7,28,451	7,54,671	7,11,458	
2. Cess for Rent free holdings ...	5,500	8,570	7,000	8,159	
3. Law charges recovered	54,000	50,422	51,000	52,581	
4. Misc. receipts including deposits ...	27,000	90,523	27,000	98,324	
5. Refund of loans and advances ...	3,000	2,681	3,000	2,402	
6. Loans received ...	1,00,000	1,38,409	—	—	
Total ...	10,47,531	10,19,056	8,42,671	8,72,924	
Opening Balance :—					
Cash ...	90,595	90,595	76,632	76,632	
Advance ...	1,11,629	1,11,629	94,405	94,405	
Loans issued ...	48,884	48,884	69,831	69,831	
Bank deposits ...	1,27,969	1,27,969	1,30,127	1,30,127	
Total ...	3,79,077	3,79,077	3,70,995	3,70,995	
Grand Total ...	14,26,608	13,98,133	12,13,666	12,43,919	

APPENDIX XXVII. (B)

Statement of Audited Expenditure for the year 1341 T. E.

Chakla Roshnabad Estates.

Heads of Expenditure.	1340 T. E. Revised Estimate.	1340 T. E. Actuals.	1341 T. E. Revised Estimate.	1341 T. E. Actuals.	Remarks.
i. 1. Revenue and Cess ...	2,73,584	2,64,523	2,67,033	2,65,974	
2. Establishment ...	1,58,623	1,58,762	1,60 000	1,55,008	
3. Settlement ...	1,254	1,511	1,000	440	
4. Legal Expenses ...	1,30,000	1,16,279	99,500	96,967	
5. Education ...	12,638	12,171	13,994	13,546	
6. Medical ...	13,603	13,662	14,300	14,035	
7. Public Works ...	97,132	75,789	68,800	50,651	
8. Religious Expenses	6,970	6,840	6,866	6,337	
9. Miscellaneous ...	10,920	7,590	6,500	5,581	
10. Loans and Advances	3,000	2,795	2,000	995	
11. Pension and Gratuity	7,398	5,906	7,500	7,191	
12. Forest ...	647	620	602	524	
13. Purchase of property	9,000	7,774	8,150	8,110	
14. Unforeseen ...	3,000	1,262	2,000	1,065	
ii. Sansar ...	15,540	15,540	11,022	11,022	
iii. Donation ...	5,275	2,472	5,800	5,740	
iv. Nijtahabil Contribution ...	1,20,000	1,18,181	50,000	50,000	
v. Contribution and Loans to the State ...	1,50,000	1,45,522	* 1,00,000	* 1,00,000	* Contribution ... Rs. 70,000 Loans ... ,, 30,000 1,00,000
vi. Repayment of debts	10,700	10,700	10,700	10,497	
vii. Repayment of old deposits ...	58,000	59,239	26,000	26,100	
Total ...	10,87,484	10,27,138	8,61,767	8,29,784	
Closing Balance :—					
Cash ...	77,051	76,632	7,536	92,027	
Advances ...	81,629	94,405	88,405	1,12,301	
Loans issued ...	48,000	69,831	69,770	73,619	
Bank deposits ...	1,32,444	1,30,127	1,36,188	1,36,188	
Total ...	3,39,124	3,70,995	3,51,899	4,14,135	
Grand Total ...	14,26,608	13,98,133	12,13,666	12,43,919	

ADDENDUM

Some important letters on the reorganisation of State troops : Appendix No. 1-5.

Appendix No.1

No. 457/Camp

Agartala

12th September '21.

My dear Mr. Gupta,

I send you herewith, as promised, the draft of my letter to the Political Secretary, regarding the Reorganisation of Tippera State Troops. If there is anything in it which you consider misleading or as contrary to the views or intentions of His Highness, I hope you will let me know.

In any case will you please indicate your concurrence with, or remarks on, the draft as early as convenient. I shall be at Imphal Manipur until 18th September. Thereafter it would be better to address me at Simla.

Yours sincerely,

Sd. Harry D. Watson

To

Rai P. K. Das Gupta Bahadur,

Minister, Tippera State.

(Major General H.D. Watson's Draft Letter as mentioned in Appendix No.1)

From

The Inspector-General,

Imperial Service Troops,

To

The Political Secretary to the Government of India,

Foreign and Political Department

Simla.

Dated the September, 1921.

Sir,

I have the honour to report for your information that Lieut-Colonel Thompson and I arrived at Agartala, Tripura State, on the 10th instant, for the purpose of discussing the question of the reorganisation of the Tripura State Troops.

2. His Highness the Maharaja, who has extended the utmost hospitality to us, will furnish Government later on with his detailed proposals in the matter.

3. His Highness is most anxious to do all in his power to assist the Imperial Government not only with troops but with all the resources of his State, in time of grave emergency, and is in full accord with all the main principles of the Scheme for Reorganization of Indian State Forces. At present His Highness maintains a force of Infantry amounting to some 276 all told. He is now anxious to maintain a small battalion of Infantry consisting of 1 Head Quarter Company and two Companies on Indian Army Establishment and organization – the Military Budget of the State not permitting of the maintenance of greater numbers. This small battalion will be primarily maintained for Internal Security of the Tripura State, but on grave emergency if other arrangements can be made for Internal Security duties, this unit may possibly be offered to Government for service outside the State.

4. Lieut-Colonel Thompson and I, having discussed details with His Highness's Minister and Council are fully in accord with His Highness' proposal.

5. We consider that this small battalion will be able to suitably maintain the Internal Security of the Tripura State, and should normally be earmarked for that alone and that the finances of the State do not at present permit of the maintenance of larger numbers, to include the maintenance of a complete unit for loan to Government on emergency, together with the necessary maintenance and Internal Security troops, in addition.

6. His Highness' Minister informs me that the troops will be adequately paid and kept contented and loyal to their Ruler - and that His Highness will, for the efficient training of these troops probably apply for the services of a "lent" officer to act as Military Adviser.

My Committee recommend the issue of modern rifles to the above preferably the Long H. V. .303 Rifle.

7. His Highness afforded us every opportunity of inspecting his troops and his police, The personnel of the former is good, the men are well turned out, handle their arms well, and march very well.

8. The question of armed police cropped up during the discussions. The present armed police are armed with "gas pipes" totaly useless and unserviceable, and we are strongly in sympathy with the Durbar's request for the early supply of better weapons to the Police.

I have the honour to be,

Sir,

Your most obedient servant,

Major-General,

Inspector-General,
Imperial Service Troops.

Appendix No.2

Agartala

D.O.No. 112.

The 19th September, 1921.

Dear General Watson,

Thank you for your kind note of the 12th September (D. O. No. 457 Camp) and its enclosure.

The draft of your letter to the Political Secretary to the Government of India correctly embodies all that we agreed to in the conference and I have hardly anything to add. As, however, His Highness was ill during the conference and we were denied the benefit of direct consultation with him, I have placed the proceedings of the conference for His Highness's consideration and final orders. Rana Bodhjung Bahadur, Private Secretary to His Highness informed me yesterday that His Highness seemed inclined to favour the alternative suggested by you to appoint an Assistant Military Adviser for Tripura and Manipur, stationed at a central place. With such an arrangement it may not be necessary to lend an officer to the Durbar.

The Durbar appreciate your remarks about the arming of the police and trust that an adequate number of good guns will be available almost immediately I may be permitted to remind you that we have been in correspondence with the Local Government on the subject for a long time now.

Yours sincerely,

Sd. P. K. Das Gupta

Minister, Tripura State.

Major-General Sir H. D. Watson,

Camp Imphal (Manipur State).

Appendix No.3

Minister's Office
Tripura State
Agartala.

No. 911/I-2

From

Rai P. K. Das Gupta Bahadur,
Minister, Tripura State

To

The Political Agent,

Dated, Agartala, the 24th July, 1922.

Sir,

I have the honour to invite reference to the correspondence resting with your letter No. 646/8-4 P. of the 16th/17th May on the subject of the reorganisation of the Tripura State Troops and to submit under the direction of His Highness the Maharaja of Tripura, the proposals embodied in the following paragraphs.

2. As I informed you in my D. O. letter No. 115 of the 15th September, 1921, His Highness has accepted most of the recommendations of the Government of India and the Military Committee presided over by Major General Sir H. D. Watson. The Durbar gratefully acknowldges the efforts of the Government of India to improve the Military Strength of the Indian States and records its appreciation of the opportunity given to this small State to participate in the scheme of reorganisation of the Imperial Defence of India.

3. His Highness is always anxious to do his bit in the Imperial Defence and the Durbar will gladly do for the Defence of India all that the financial capacity of the State allows. His Highness appreciates the fact that the scheme has been put on a voluntary basis.

4. The present Military strength of the State consists of 212 men and 64 officers, making a total of 276. The Durbar proposes to increase the strength to half a Battalion.

5. The Force will for the present be employed in maintaining internal security in the State.

6. His Highness would immediately ask for the services of an officer of the Indian Army of the rank of Subedar Major to give a start to the work with the present force, also for assisting in recruiting work and a separate letter on the

subject will be addressed to you shortly.

7. The question of the pay and allowances of the men and the officers should be left to the discretion of the Durbar it being however understood that if the State Forces are ever called upon to be on active service outside the State, they should be entitled to the standard pay of the Indian Army.

8. The views of the Durbar regarding the special proposals contained in the Government of India letter No. 43-IB dated the 5th January, 1921, and the questions framed thereon are noted below : –

(i) The Durbar recognises the impossibility of referring to the State authorities and waiting for their orders about promotion in the Field: so they agree that promotions while on active service should rest with the Field Commanding Officer, subject to subsequent confirmation by the Durbar concerned.

(ii) The Durbar agrees that the State Forces should be so organised and improved that they might deal with internal security themselves. The Durbar would however make it clear that when the State Forces find themselves unable to cope with a serious internal trouble, the Imp erial Government should render effective assistance.

(iii). The advantage of having the same or similar disciplinary rules is recognised.

(iv) When the Rank and Titles are based on the strength of the Units in accordance with the standard of the Indian Army, the honours and privileges accorded to the Officers of the Indian Army should be extended to the officers of the State Force either in time of war or in time of peace and they should wear the same badge and Uniform for a particular Rank with the name of the State impressed somewhere on them.

(v) The advantages of a training college are recognised.

(vi) The Durbar would readily avail itself of the opportunity of having the ~~the~~ State Forces trained by attaching them to regular Units for some time or placing them occasionally under a British Officer, if necessary.

(vii) The advantage of joining some army school or class is recognised.

(viii) An officer might be lent if the Durbar wanted it or the system of Military Advisers continued. There might be one Military Adviser with Head Quarters at a Central place – say Sylhet, for this State and Coochbehar.

(ix) The Durbar would welcome the expert assistance of the Military Adviser whenever needed.

(x) It is recognised that a complete army list of Indian State Forces would be of advantage.

(xi) The Durbar might correspond direct with the Military Adviser or the Political Department of the Government of India in all Military matters.

9. State Forces should be supplied with standard arms and ammunitions from the Government arsenals on payment, if required. The Military Committee thought that arms might perhaps be supplied by the Imperial Government free of cost.

10. The Durbar wish to make it clear that the present proposals should be regarded as entirely voluntary and subject to reconsideration by the Durbar at any future time, the Durbar being at liberty to add to or reduce the Military strength according to its financial capacity and the exigencies of the time.

11. During war time or service outside the State, the entire cost of mobilisation, maintenance and equipment should be charged to Imperial Revenues, unless the Durbar offers to bear the cost in particular cases.

12. The Durbar think that the full number of commissioned and non-commissioned officers entertained in the Indian army Units need not be employed here immediately.

13. The Durbar would ask for the immediate supply of at least Two hundred Standard Rifles for the existing force.

14. The Durbar trusts that these proposals, though very modest, will be acceptable to the Government of India as representing the loyal co-operation of the Durbar with the scheme of Imperial defence and regarded as quite in proportion to the resources of the State.

I have the honour to be,

Sir,

Your most obedient servant,

Sd. P. K. Das Gupta,

Minister, Tripura State.

APPROVED.

(Signed) B. K. M.

9. 4. 32.

Submitted to His Highness for approval.
Sd. P. K. Das Gupta
Minister
24. 7. 22.

Appendix No.4

NO. 2181
I-2

From

Rai P. K. Das Gupta Bahadur,
Minister, Tripura.

To

The Political Agent, Tripura,
Comilla.

Dated, Agartala, the 10th January, 1923.

Sir,

With reference to your Memo. No. 38-P of the 8th January last forwarding copy of letter No. 48-P of the 4th January from the Chief Secretary to the Government of Bengal on the subject of the re-organisation of the Tripura State troops, I have the honour to state that "Half battalion" will consist of one headquarter company and two companies of the Indian Army unit, with 481 men and 9 commissioned officers and 9 non-comissioned officers.

2. Referring to para 2 of the Government letter, I beg leave to point out that the question of the system of command in war has been referred to in clauses 1, 3 and 4 of para 8 of this office letter No. 911 of the 24th July, 1922, in which it was stated that the Durbar recognised the impossibility of referring to the State authorities and waiting for their orders about promotion in the field, the Durbar agreeing that promotion while on active service should rest with the field commanding officer subject to subsequent confirmation by the Durbar concerned. The Durbar agreed as to the advantage of having the same or similar disciplinary rules as governing the Indian Army for the State troops. They also agreed that the rank and titles should be based on the strength of the units in accordance with the standard of the Indian Army and suggested that the honours and privileges accorded to the officers of the Indian Army should be extended to the officers of the State Force - either in time of war or

in time of peace, and they should wear the same badge and uniform for a particular rank with the name of the State impressed somewhere on them. Thus the Durbar accepted practically all the recommendations contained in appendices A, B, C & D to your letter No. 319 P dated the 24th February, 1921.

I have the honour to be,

Sir,

Your most obedient servant,

(Sd.) P.K. Das Gupta,

Minister, Tripura.

Appendix No.5

No. 812 Fl / III-3

From

J. D. Vere Hodge, Esq., I. C. S.,

Political Agent, Tripura State

To

The Minister, Tripura, Agartala.

Dated, Comilla, the 22nd / 25th May, 1923.

Sir,

With reference to the correspondence resting with your letter No. 2181 / I-8 of the 10th January last on the subject of the Re-organisation of the Indian State Force, I have the honour to say that the proposals contained in that letter and in your letter No. 911/I-2 of the 24th July last were duly submitted to the Government of India, and to communicate their orders :-

2. The Durbar propose to increase the present State Forces of 276 Infantry and to maintain a half Battalion consisting of a Headquarters Company and two Companies on Indian Army establishments. The force is intended for the internal security of the State for which the Durbar are prepared to undertake responsibility. The Government of India prefer that Durbars should maintain their troops so as to ensure internal security rather than that they should endeavour to provide a fractional unit for loan to Government which would be difficult to utilise and which would reduce the number of troops for internal security at the time when they would be of most value. The maintenance of units ear-marked for internal security would enable the Military authorities to withdraw regular troops for active service should the necessity arise. At the same time should a Durbar be unable to cope with serious internal disorder arising out of a general disturbance in India, Government would be prepared to render assistance to the State. In the circumstances the Government of India approve of the Tripura Durbar's Re-organisation Scheme.

3. Para 10 of your letter No. 911/I-2 of 24. 7. 22, referred to above, the Durbar stipulate that they should be at liberty to add to or reduce the military strength of the State if this is necessary on financial and other grounds. The Government of India consider however that any material change in

the strength of the military forces should be submitted for the approval of Government since this is necessary on military grounds.

4. With regard to the Durbar's request made in para 13 of your aforesaid letter and your letter No. 722/IV-1 dated 20th/25th June, 1921, to be supplied on payment with at least 200 rifles for the existing force I am to say that the Government of Indian cannot agree to the issue of arms, which would be given on loan, until the reorganization has been carried out and the troops are reported by the Military Adviser-in-Chief, Indian State Forces, to be efficient, and until the State has provided the necessary bells of arms and magazine for the storage of the arms and ammunition. It is also necessary that the Tripura State Forces should be commanded by a suitable Indian Officer before sanction can be accorded to the issue of rifles.

5. In regard to the question of incidence of cost of troops when employed on active service, vide para 11 of your letter No. 911, I enclose copy of Government of India, Foreign ~~and~~ Department Resolution No. 3712-I.B., dated the 29th September, 1897 for the information of the Durbar.

6. The question of the appointment of an Assistant Military Adviser to supervise the training of the Tripura State Forces (para 8(ix) of your letter quoted above) is under the consideration of the Government of India.

I have etc. etc.,

Sd. J. D. V. Hodge,

Political Agent

25. 5.